WELCOME TO

LITERACY PLACE

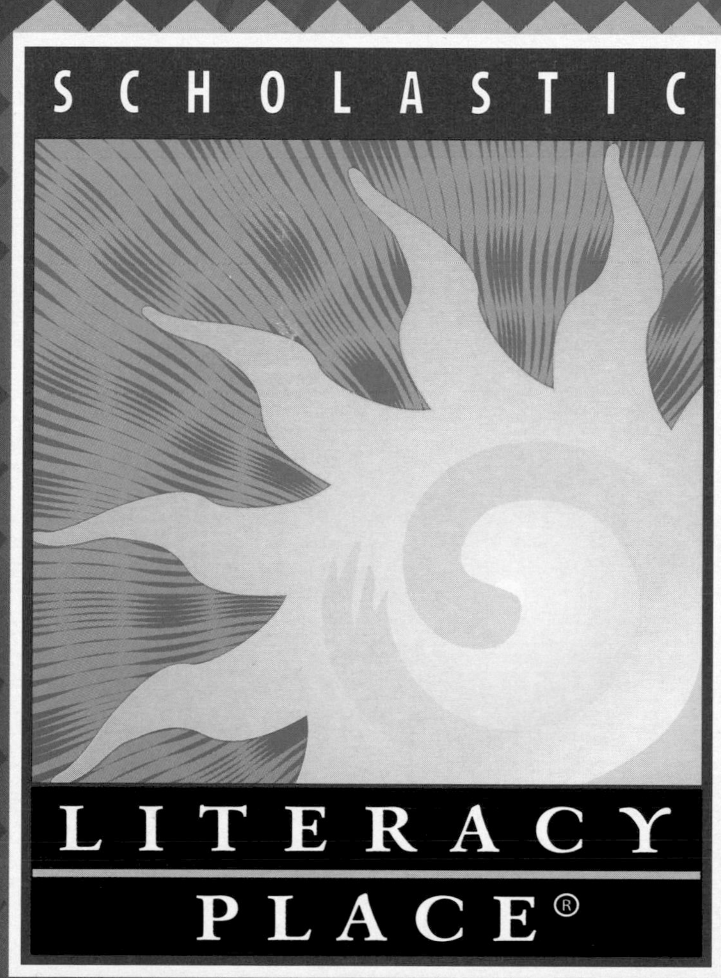

A NEW CORE, K-6 READING AND LANGUAGE ARTS PROGRAM FROM SCHOLASTIC

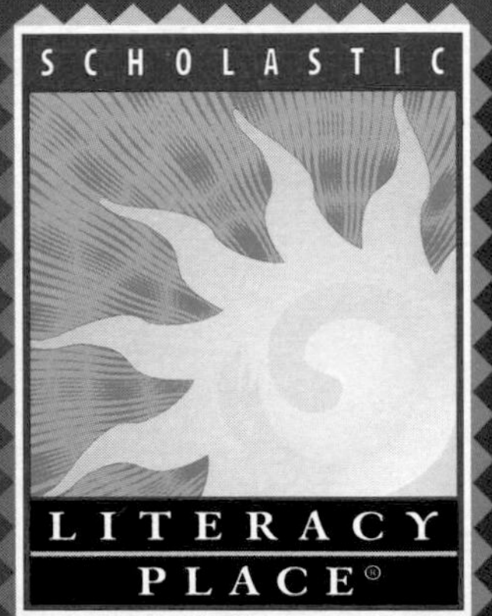

Our Commitment...

Giving children the gift of reading is empowering them for success.

As a company committed to children, Scholastic shares the concerns expressed by educators, parents, and national leaders that many of our children are not learning to read. Like you, we believe that the right to read is every child's birthright. Reading successfully is essential to living productively in today's world and in the 21st Century. We believe we must — and can — do better for our children.

Teachers trust Scholastic for our ability to work well and easily with them and have come to rely on us for materials that reach and motivate children.

We developed Literacy Place because we believe teachers and children need and deserve more support — a coherent plan of skills development (including phonics), better assessment, and of course, the best children's literature. We also recognized that ensuring each child's right to read would require a new approach to staff development along with a plan to marshal support from families and communities.

Literacy Place began with a single goal: Every child will be a fluent reader by the end of third grade and possess the reading skills to succeed in *all* subject areas thereafter. Every component, every test, every lesson in the program was designed to achieve that goal.

Scholastic starts with certain strengths: great literature, proven technology, and a heritage of engaging parents and supporting teachers. As we worked with nationally known reading experts to develop Literacy Place, we brought all these elements together in a systematic, skills-intensive program.

In short, we developed the tools you asked for to help give children the gift of reading and empower them for success. We believe that in the hands of committed educators, Literacy Place will be a part of the solution for all children and all teachers.

Richard Robinson

Richard Robinson

Chairman & CEO
Scholastic Inc.

What You'll Find Up Front...

Lesson Plans for this unit begin on page **T1**.

TABLE OF CONTENTS

It all begins with a comprehensive **Blueprint** *for Literacy.*

The Literacy Place Matrix is a blueprint for learning based on a carefully articulated developmental sequence of how children learn to read and write. It ensures that children will develop the literacy skills required for a productive life in the 21st Century—managing information, solving problems, and working effectively in teams.

The experts agree! Children acquire literacy within the Personal, Social, and Intellectual contexts of their lives. All three are represented here.

Grade	Personal Literacy: Personal Voice (Unit 1) — We communicate in our unique voices as we grow and learn.	Intellectual Literacy: Problem Solving (Unit 2) — People have the power to solve problems.	Social Literacy: Teamwork (Unit 3) — Successful teams depend on the collaboration of individuals.
K	**Stories About Us** — We listen to, tell, and create stories.	**See It, Solve It** — We see problems and find solutions.	**All Together Now!** — We share and help each other.
1	**Hello!** — We share what we like.	**Problem Patrol** — There are many kinds of problems.	**Team Spirit** — It's fun to do things together.
2	**Snapshots** — Our actions tell about us.	**Super Solvers** — There may be more than one way to solve a problem.	**Lights! Camera! Action!** — Creative teams produce great performances.
3	**What's New?** — We learn about our world through new experiences.	**Big Plans** — Making and using plans can help us solve problems.	**On the Job** — Teams work best when they use each member's strengths to get the job done.
4	**Chapter by Chapter** — We are always adding to our life story.	**What an Idea!** — People solve problems by inventing new things.	**Discovery Teams** — When we work as a team, we learn new things about our world.
5	**Making a Difference** — Each of us is inspired by the lives of others.	**It's a Mystery** — We can solve mysteries using reason, logic, and intuition.	**Voyagers** — We depend on a network of people when we explore.
6	**Self-Portraits** — Individuals are a composite of their experiences.	**Meet the Challenge** — Problem solving is a survival skill.	**Open for Business** — Teamwork can make a business successful.

MATRIX

Literacy Place is divided into six strands; each representing about six weeks of instruction. Strands are thematically organized.

PERSONAL LITERACY CREATIVE EXPRESSION UNIT 4 People express themselves in many creative ways.	INTELLECTUAL LITERACY MANAGING INFORMATION UNIT 5 Finding and using information helps us live in our world.	SOCIAL LITERACY COMMUNITY INVOLVEMENT UNIT 6 Communities are built on the contributions of the people who live there.
Express Yourself We express ourselves through songs, sounds, stories, dance, and art.	**I Spy!** Information is all around us.	**Join In!** We help our community.
Imagine That! Imagination lets us look at things in new ways.	**Information Finders** Information comes from many sources.	**Hometowns** We are all members of a community.
Story Studio People express themselves through stories and pictures.	**Animal World** We use information to understand the interdependence of people and animals.	**Lend a Hand** People can make a difference in their communities.
Hit Series A creative idea can grow into a series.	**Time Detectives** Finding information in stories and artifacts brings the past to life.	**Community Quilt** In a community, some things continue and some things change.
The Funny Side Sometimes humor is the best way to communicate.	**Nature Guides** Gathering and using information helps us understand and describe the natural world.	**It Takes a Leader** In every community there are people who inspire others to take action.
In the Spotlight We use our creativity to reach an audience.	**America's Journal** Considering different points of view gives us a fuller understanding of history.	**Cityscapes** Cities depend on the strengths and skills of the people who live and work there.
Worlds of Wonder We use imagination to explore and explain the world.	**In the News** An informed person analyzes the facts and opinions found in the media.	**Voices for Democracy** Literacy empowers us to be part of the democratic process.

Developmentally appropriate unit themes help students build the literacy skills they will need for the rest of their lives.

"Over the years, I've used all the major reading programs. But I've never seen anything like the Literacy Place Matrix. *With so much to cover every year, it really helps me keep focused on the important things–the literacies that are going to make a difference for my kids."*

Amy Gordon,
Third Grade Teacher

Each unit is built on skills development, writing, spelling, school-to-work literacies, mentors, workshops, and projects. **Read on to find out more!**

A Grade *at a Glance*

There are six units per year, each with its own student anthology and Teacher's SourceBook.

UNIT 1 **Personal Voice**

UNIT 2 **Problem Solving**

UNIT 3 **Teamwork**

UNIT 4 **Creative Expression**

At Grades 2-6, *the student anthologies are also available in two-volume editions.*

UNIT 5 **Managing Information**

UNIT 6 **Community Involvement**

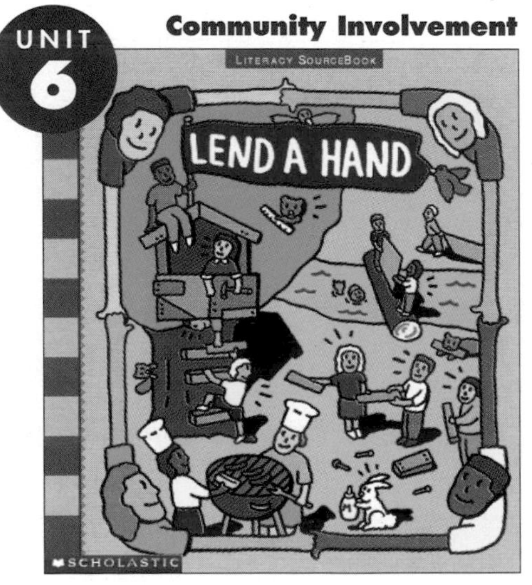

There are six plans per unit, each representing about one week of instruction.

UNIT 2

LITERACY SOURCEBOOK

SUPER SOLVERS

Week 1

Week 2

Week 3

Week 4

Week 5

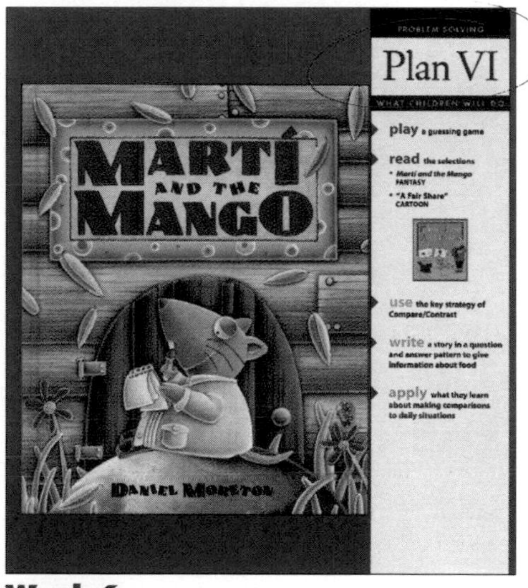

Week 6

For detailed information on literature, tested skills, and assessment for the grade you teach, ask your Scholastic representative for a copy of Grade at a Glance. Or call 1 800 SCHOLASTIC.

For a complete list of **components,** *please see page 36.*

A lesson plan that's as easy as a,b,c!

EVERY LESSON in *Literacy Place* follows the same pattern: **a** *Read* a selection from the student anthology using key strategies, including phonics; **b** integrate the language arts by providing instruction in *writing*, grammar, usage and mechanics, and spelling, using the literature as a model; **c** focus on systematic and intentional *skills* instruction, including phonics, using the literature as a model.

You'll find an easy-to-use organizer at the beginning of every lesson plan.

SOURCEBOOK

The Night Sky

PLAN IV ORGANIZER

The Night Sky

	Instructional Path	Supporting All Learners	Resources and Technology
a READING THE SOURCES pp. T178–197	**Build Background** ✔ **Develop Vocabulary** • *twinkle • bright • stars • planets • comets • when • many* **Reading Selection** *The Night Sky* Launch the Key Strategy: Categorize Information ✔ **Assess Reading**	EXTRA HELP pp. T179, T195 ESL pp. T175, T179, T182, T187 CHALLENGE p. T190 MINI-LESSON Picture Clues, p. T185; Nonfiction, p. T195 **Idea File:** p. T197 **Cultural Connections:** p. T197	**Transparency** Build Background, 4 **Literacy-at-Work Book** Vocabulary, p. 38; Comprehension Check, p. 39 **WiggleWorks™ Plus,** pp. T178, T180, T196
b INTEGRATING LANGUAGE ARTS pp. T198–203	✔ **Writing:** Nonfiction: List of Tips, p. T199 ✔ **Grammar:** Action Words **Mechanics:** Capitalizing Names ✔ **Spelling:** Words With Blends • *tree • trunk • track • bright • blaze • plane • many • when*	EXTRA HELP p. T199 ESL pp. T199, T203 **Activity File:** p. T202 Write About the Day Sky; Write a Postcard; Make a Mobile; Write Directions MINI-LESSON Address Envelopes, p. T202	**Literacy-at-Work Book** Writing, p. 40 **Grammar, Usage, and Mechanics Practice:** pp. 37–38 **Spelling Practice:** p. 19 **Handwriting Practice:** p. 19 **WiggleWorks™ Plus,** pp. T198, T203, T209
c BUILDING SKILLS AND STRATEGIES pp. T204–211	Quickcheck ✔ Key Strategy: Categorize Information Quickcheck ✔ Phonics: *r*-Blends Quickcheck ✔ Phonics: *l*-Blends	EXTRA HELP p. T205 ESL pp. T205, T207 CHALLENGE pp. T205, T209 ACCESS p. T207	**Literacy-at-Work Book** Categorize Information, pp. 41–42; Phonics, pp. 44–47 **WiggleWorks™ Plus,** pp. T207

✔ = Assessed

LAN IV T1

The A,B,Cs of Phonics Instruction

a *While reading, mini-lessons provide direct instruction of phonics elements featured in the lesson.*

b *While writing and spelling, phonics elements are reinforced and reviewed.*

c *Explicit and sequential phonics lessons are supported by practice pages and lots of reading practice.*

Here's an example of how one first-grade teacher organized *her* week...

Weekly Planner (A Week at Literacy Place)

	Monday	Tuesday	Wednesday	Thursday	Friday
a Read	• Model reading with Big Book • Build Background for selection	• Develop Vocabulary* • Guided reading	• Finish guided reading • Revisit • Check comprehension*	• Repeat reading • Revisit • Check comprehension*	• Read independently*
Write *b*	• Write interactively in response to Big Book	• Journal writing • Set purpose and generate ideas	• Connect writing to literature • Prewrite*	• Draft • Write interactively or independently	• Revise • Share, publish
Grammar, Usage & Mechanics	• Daily Language Practice *Worksheets if I need them.	• Daily Language Practice	• Daily Language Practice • Teach grammar lesson* • Connect to Writing	• Daily Language Practice • Teach usage/ mechanics* • Connect to Writing	• Daily Language Practice • Apply grammar, usage and mechanics to writing
Spelling	• Spelling pretest	• Teach words • Practice*	• Apply to Writing	• Use Spelling Practice*	• Give spelling test
c Skills & Strategies	• Mini skill lesson (in Creating a Community of Learners)	• Introduce the key strategy	• Teach the first skill lesson* • Track key strategy through guided reading*	• Teach the second skill lesson*	• Transfer skills to Literacy-at-Work Book*
Phonics	• Develop phonemic awareness	• Teach the phonics element • Connect to lit.	• Teach the first phonics skills lesson*	• Teach the second phonics skills lesson*	• Transfer phonics skills to "My Book"*
Assess	• Implement plan for flexible grouping	• Observe as children read	• Observe as children read • Quickcheck for first skills lesson	• Observe as children read • Assess reading with conference • Quickcheck for second skills lesson	• Use Writing Benchmarks • Assess independent reading

We're here to help!

When your school adopts Literacy Place, *your first inservice will help you develop six weeks of lesson plans. You'll receive this easy-to-use planner during the first session.*

A closer look at a One-Week Plan...

READING THE SOURCES

At Literacy Place, students read a rich variety of literature and expository text that only Scholastic could offer. Children develop the skills and vocabulary necessary to be fluent readers. Skills and strategies, including an emphasis on phonics, are taught in the context of what is read. Because reading and writing are reciprocal processes, the literature students read is also the model for all writing. Grammar, usage and mechanics, and spelling instruction also come directly from the reading and writing lessons.

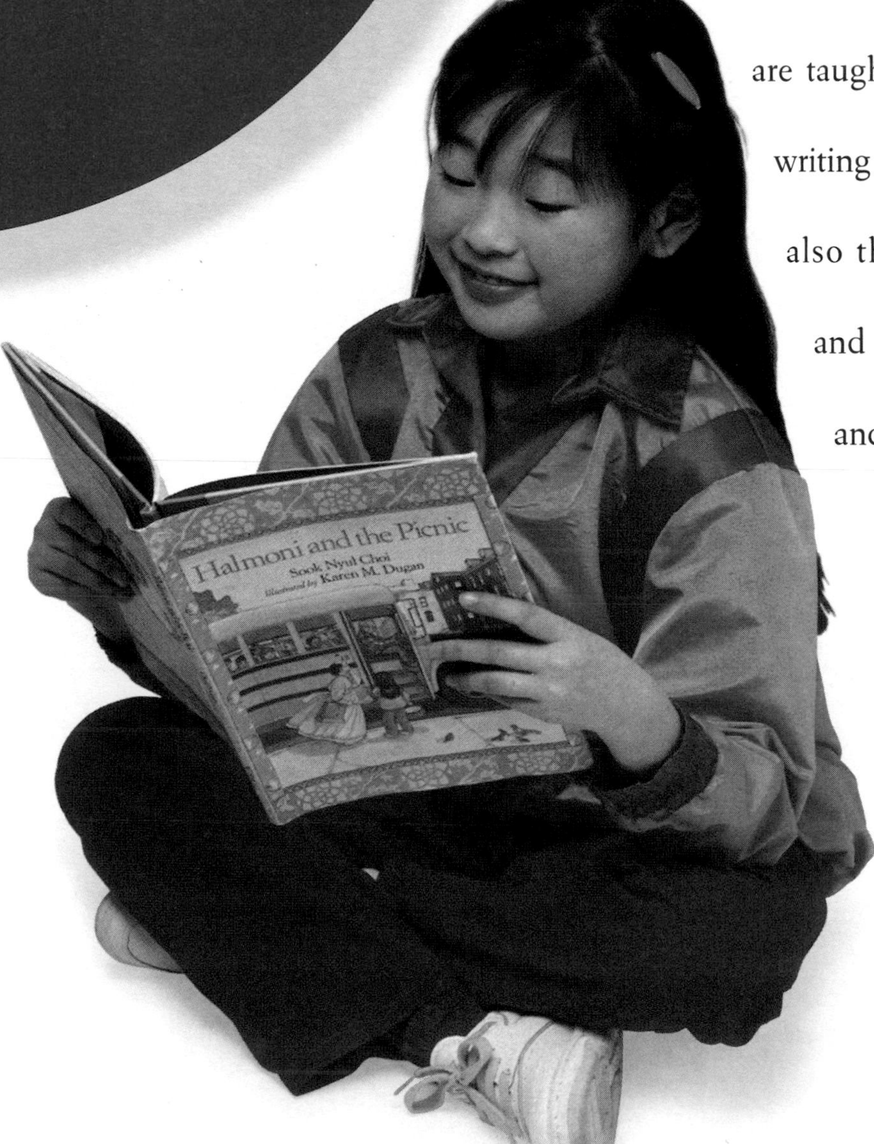

Before READING...

Planning is easy at Literacy Place! Before reading, you'll always find the information you need to get started:

- ✓ Clearly stated objectives are real time-savers for developing written lesson plans.
- ✓ Materials, time, and suggested groupings help you get organized quickly.
- ✓ Technology Options offer another way to prepare students for reading.

At Literacy Place, selections are often strategically paired to enhance comprehension. Students transfer their skills from one selection to another as they move from circular story to traditional folk song, for example, or from repetitive story to poetry.

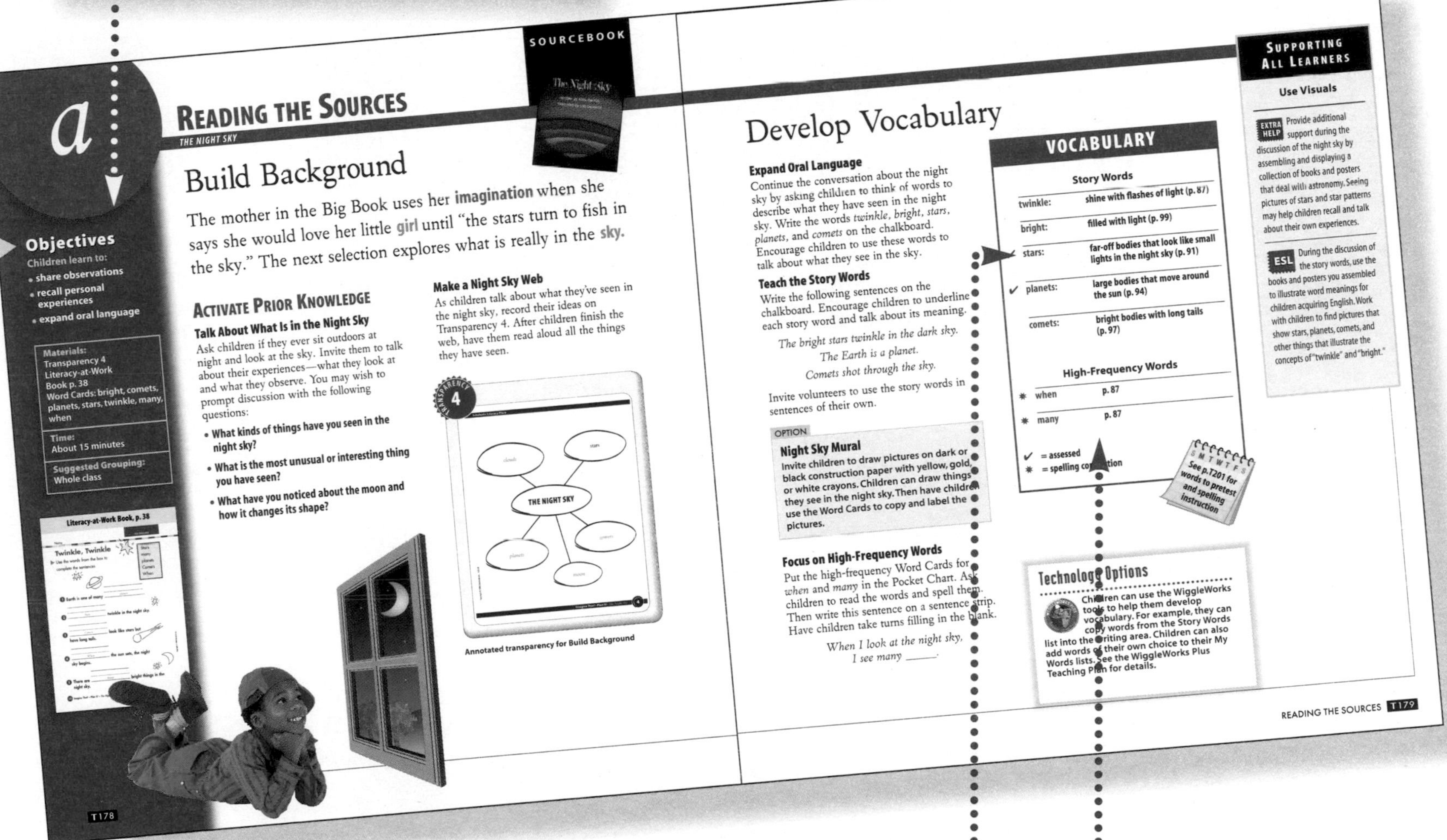

SOURCEBOOK

The Night Sky

a

READING THE SOURCES

THE NIGHT SKY

Build Background

The mother in the Big Book uses her **imagination** when she says she would love her little **girl** until "the stars turn to fish in the sky." The next selection explores what is really in the **sky**.

Objectives

Children learn to:

- share observations
- recall personal experiences
- expand oral language

Materials: Transparency 4; Literacy-at-Work Book p. 38; Word Cards: bright, comets, planets, stars, twinkle, many, when

Time: About 15 minutes

Suggested Grouping: Whole class

Literacy-at-Work Book, p. 38

Twinkle, Twinkle

ACTIVATE PRIOR KNOWLEDGE

Talk About What Is in the Night Sky

Ask children if they ever sit outdoors at night and look at the sky. Invite them to talk about their experiences—what they look at and what they observe. You may wish to prompt discussion with the following questions:

- **What kinds of things have you seen in the night sky?**
- **What is the most unusual or interesting thing you have seen?**
- **What have you noticed about the moon and how it changes its shape?**

Make a Night Sky Web

As children talk about what they've seen in the night sky, record their ideas on Transparency 4. After children finish the web, have them read aloud all the things they have seen.

THE NIGHT SKY

Annotated transparency for Build Background

T178

Develop Vocabulary

Expand Oral Language

Continue the conversation about the night sky by asking children to think of words to describe what they have seen in the night sky. Write the words *twinkle, bright, stars, planets,* and *comets* on the chalkboard. Encourage children to use these words to talk about what they see in the sky.

Teach the Story Words

Write the following sentences on the chalkboard. Encourage children to underline each story word and talk about its meaning.

The bright stars twinkle in the dark sky.
The Earth is a planet.
Comets shot through the sky.

Invite volunteers to use the story words in sentences of their own.

OPTION

Night Sky Mural

Invite children to draw pictures on dark or black construction paper with yellow, gold, or white crayons. Children can draw things they see in the night sky. Then have children use the Word Cards to copy and label the pictures.

Focus on High-Frequency Words

Put the high-frequency Word Cards for *when* and *many* in the Pocket Chart. As children to read the words and spell them. Then write this sentence on a sentence strip. Have children take turns filling in the blank.

When I look at the night sky, I see many ____.

VOCABULARY

Story Words

	twinkle:	shine with flashes of light (p. 87)
	bright:	filled with light (p. 99)
	stars:	far-off bodies that look like small lights in the night sky (p. 91)
✓	planets:	large bodies that move around the sun (p. 94)
	comets:	bright bodies with long tails (p. 97)

High-Frequency Words

*	when	p. 87
*	many	p. 87

✓ = assessed
* = spelling connection

See p. T201 for words to pretest and spelling instruction

SUPPORTING ALL LEARNERS

Use Visuals

EXTRA HELP Provide additional support during the discussion of the night sky by assembling and displaying a collection of books and posters that deal with astronomy. Seeing pictures of stars and star patterns may help children recall and talk about their own experiences.

ESL During the discussion of the story words, use the books and posters you assembled to illustrate word meanings for children acquiring English. Work with children to find pictures that show stars, planets, comets, and other things that illustrate the concepts of "twinkle" and "bright."

Technology Options

Children can use the WiggleWorks tools to help them develop vocabulary. For example, they can copy words from the Story Words list into the Writing area. Children can also add words of their own choice to their My Words lists. See the WiggleWorks Plus Teaching Plan for details.

READING THE SOURCES T179

There are multiple options to Develop Vocabulary, focusing on story words organized around a concept. Tested words are highlighted and practice pages are reproduced for your convenience. One or more vocabulary words are always used as the exemplar for the upcoming spelling lesson.

Children learn high-frequency words to develop fluency.

During READING...

Guided Reading questions are strategically placed to help students move through the text with understanding. Opportunities to reread the selection for a specific purpose are highlighted in the Revisit section.

Skills are introduced in the context of the literature.
All literature in the program systematically supports the scope and sequence of skills.

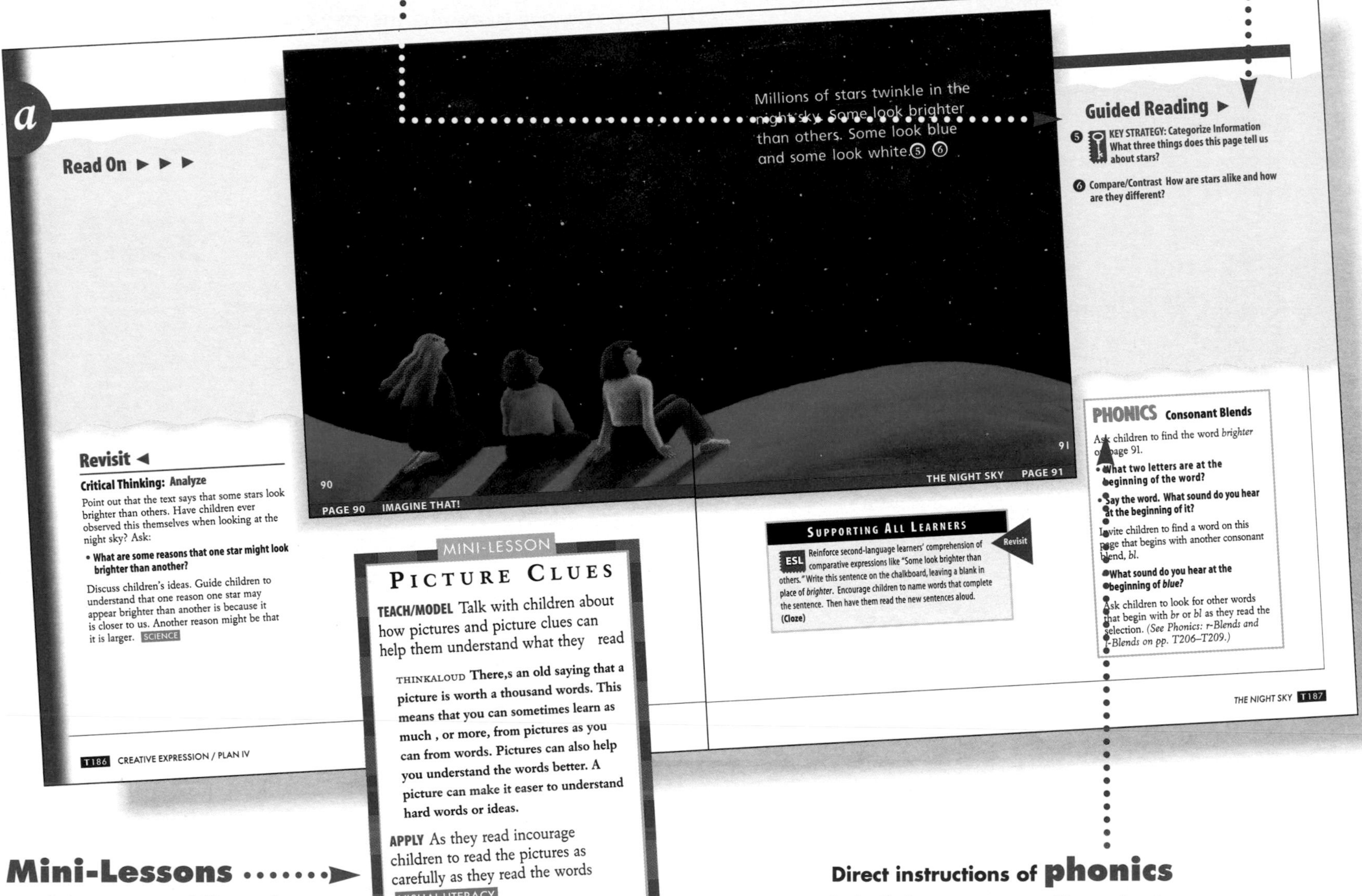

a

Read On ▶ ▶ ▶

Millions of stars twinkle in the night sky. Some look brighter than others. Some look blue and some look white. 5 6

90 PAGE 90 IMAGINE THAT!

91 THE NIGHT SKY PAGE 91

Guided Reading ▶

5 KEY STRATEGY: Categorize Information What three things does this page tell us about stars?

6 Compare/Contrast How are stars alike and how are they different?

Revisit ◀

Critical Thinking: Analyze

Point out that the text says that some stars look brighter than others. Have children ever observed this themselves when looking at the night sky? Ask:

- **What are some reasons that one star might look brighter than another?**

Discuss children's ideas. Guide children to understand that one reason one star may appear brighter than another is because it is closer to us. Another reason might be that it is larger. SCIENCE

SUPPORTING ALL LEARNERS

ESL Reinforce second-language learners' comprehension of comparative expressions like "Some look brighter than others." Write this sentence on the chalkboard, leaving a blank in place of *brighter*. Encourage children to name words that complete the sentence. Then have them read the new sentences aloud. **(Cloze)**

Revisit

PHONICS Consonant Blends

Ask children to find the word *brighter* on page 91.

- **What two letters are at the beginning of the word?**
- **Say the word. What sound do you hear at the beginning of it?**

Invite children to find a word on this page that begins with another consonant blend, *bl*.

- **What sound do you hear at the beginning of *blue*?**

Ask children to look for other words that begin with *br* or *bl* as they read the selection. *(See Phonics: r-Blends and l-Blends on pp. T206–T209.)*

T186 CREATIVE EXPRESSION / PLAN IV

THE NIGHT SKY T187

MINI-LESSON

PICTURE CLUES

TEACH/MODEL Talk with children about how pictures and picture clues can help them understand what they read

THINKALOUD **There,s an old saying that a picture is worth a thousand words. This means that you can sometimes learn as much , or more, from pictures as you can from words. Pictures can also help you understand the words better. A picture can make it easer to understand hard words or ideas.**

APPLY As they read incourage children to read the pictures as carefully as they read the words

VISUAL LITERACY

Mini-Lessons ·······▶
teach important skills and strategies and appear throughout the guided reading.

Direct instructions of **phonics** is built into every reading selection.

After READING...

Assess reading for students' aesthetic response, understanding of information, and critical analysis.

Ideas for **conferencing** follow every selection. Reading rubrics for assessment are available in the Assessment Handbook.

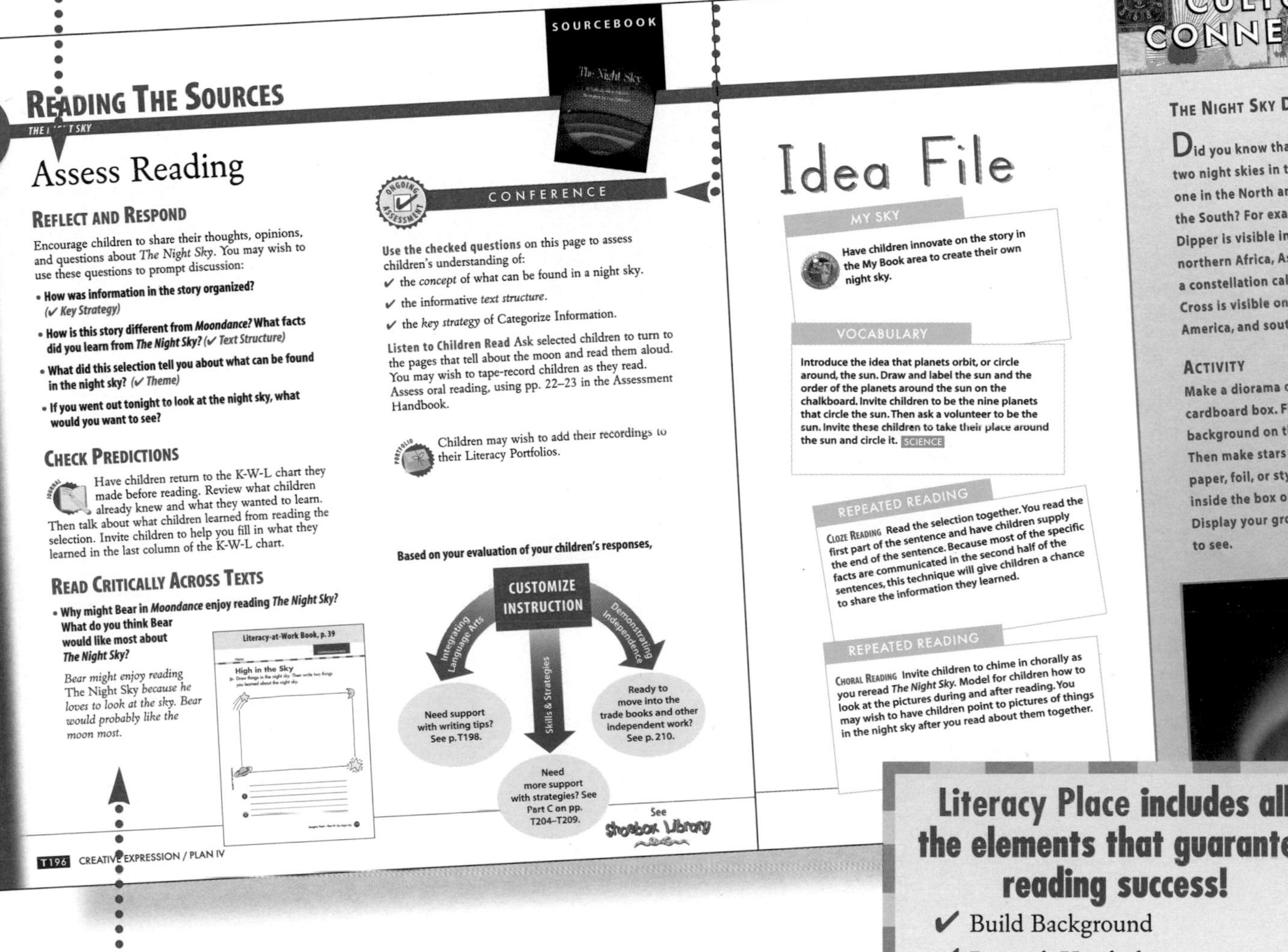

SOURCEBOOK

The Night Sky

READING THE SOURCES

a

THE NIGHT SKY

Assess Reading

REFLECT AND RESPOND

Encourage children to share their thoughts, opinions, and questions about *The Night Sky.* You may wish to use these questions to prompt discussion:

- **How was information in the story organized?** *(✔ Key Strategy)*
- **How is this story different from *Moondance*? What facts did you learn from *The Night Sky*?** *(✔ Text Structure)*
- **What did this selection tell you about what can be found in the night sky?** *(✔ Theme)*
- **If you went out tonight to look at the night sky, what would you want to see?**

CHECK PREDICTIONS

JOURNAL Have children return to the K-W-L chart they made before reading. Review what children already knew and what they wanted to learn. Then talk about what children learned from reading the selection. Invite children to help you fill in what they learned in the last column of the K-W-L chart.

READ CRITICALLY ACROSS TEXTS

- **Why might Bear in *Moondance* enjoy reading *The Night Sky*? What do you think Bear would like most about *The Night Sky*?**

Bear might enjoy reading The Night Sky *because he loves to look at the sky. Bear would probably like the moon most.*

Literacy-at-Work Book, p. 39

High in the Sky

ONGOING ASSESSMENT

CONFERENCE

Use the checked questions on this page to assess children's understanding of:

✔ the *concept* of what can be found in a night sky.

✔ the informative *text structure.*

✔ the *key strategy* of Categorize Information.

Listen to Children Read Ask selected children to turn to the pages that tell about the moon and read them aloud. You may wish to tape-record children as they read. Assess oral reading, using pp. 22–23 in the Assessment Handbook.

PORTFOLIO Children may wish to add their recordings to their Literacy Portfolios.

Based on your evaluation of your children's responses,

CUSTOMIZE INSTRUCTION

Integrating Language Arts — Need support with writing tips? See p. T198.

Skills & Strategies — Need more support with strategies? See Part C on pp. T204–T209.

Demonstrating Independence — Ready to move into the trade books and other independent work? See p. 210.

See Shoebox Library

T196 CREATIVE EXPRESSION / PLAN IV

Idea File

MY SKY

Have children innovate on the story in the My Book area to create their own night sky.

VOCABULARY

Introduce the idea that planets orbit, or circle around, the sun. Draw and label the sun and the order of the planets around the sun on the chalkboard. Invite children to be the nine planets that circle the sun. Then ask a volunteer to be the sun. Invite these children to take their place around the sun and circle it. SCIENCE

REPEATED READING

CLOZE READING Read the selection together. You read the first part of the sentence and have children supply the end of the sentence. Because most of the specific facts are communicated in the second half of the sentences, this technique will give children a chance to share the information they learned.

REPEATED READING

CHORAL READING Invite children to chime in chorally as you reread *The Night Sky.* Model for children how to look at the pictures during and after reading. You may wish to have children point to pictures of things in the night sky after you read about them together.

CULTURAL CONNECTIONS

THE NIGHT SKY DIORAMA

Did you know that there are two night skies in the world—one in the North and one in the South? For example, the Big Dipper is visible in North America, northern Africa, Asia, and Europe, while a constellation called the Southern Cross is visible only in Australia, South America, and southern Africa.

Constellation of Southern Cross

ACTIVITY

Make a diorama of night sky scenes in a cardboard box. First, paint a night background on the inside of the box. Then make stars and a moon out of paper, foil, or styrofoam and hang them inside the box on black thread or string. Display your group's scene for others to see.

T197

Extend critical-thinking skills.

Assess reading with questions that allow you to determine your students' understanding of what they have read.

Literacy Place includes all the elements that guarantee reading success!

- ✔ Build Background
- ✔ Preteach Vocabulary
- ✔ Offer Flexible Grouping Strategies
- ✔ Phonics and Word Study
- ✔ Preview Text Structure
- ✔ Provide Revisit Opportunities
- ✔ Track Key Strategy
- ✔ Guided Reading
- ✔ Teach Mini-Lessons
- ✔ Check Comprehension

INTEGRATING LANGUAGE ARTS

At Literacy Place you also get four language arts programs: 1) writing, 2) grammar, usage and mechanics, 3) spelling, and 4) handwriting (through grade 3).

What makes a good writing assignment?

- ✔ Set Purpose and Audience
- ✔ Model
- ✔ Connection to Literature
- ✔ Opportunities to learn Grammar, Usage and Mechanics
- ✔ Ideas for Sharing
- ✔ Rubrics for Evaluation

b

INTEGRATING LANGUAGE ARTS

THE NIGHT SKY

SOURCEBOOK MODEL

WRITE A LIST OF TIPS

WRITING

The Night Sky ends with a list of tips. Children will write their own **list of tips** for doing something they know how to do.

Objectives
Children learn to:
- write nonfiction in the form of a list (pp. T198–199)
- identify verbs (p. T200)
- capitalize proper nouns (p. T200)
- spell words with blends (p. T201)

Materials:
SourceBook pp. 86–99
Literacy-at-Work Book p. 33
Strips of paper
Crayons or markers

Suggested Grouping:
Whole class and cooperative groups

Literacy-at-Work Book, p. 40

THINK ABOUT WRITING

At the end of *The Night Sky*, there is a list of tips to help someone looking at the sky at night. Help children see that tips are written:

- to help someone do something.
- to explain something new.

Put It in Context
Invite children to turn to page 98 to review "Tips for Watching the Night Sky." Ask them:

- **If you wanted to know how to look at the night sky, why would you read these tips?**
- **Who do you think wrote these tips? Why do you think the person wrote them?**

Help children conclude that someone who knew about watching the night sky wrote the tips to help people who might know less.

INTRODUCE THE WRITING EVENT

Invite children to write a list of tips for doing something they know how to do well. They will be writing this list for someone who has never done the activity before.

PREWRITE

COOPERATIVE GROUPS Invite children to use the prewriting organizer in the Literacy-at-Work Book to list things they know how to do well. Then ask volunteers to tell you what they do well. Write their ideas on chart paper. Place children in cooperative groups.

- Ask each group to choose one thing everyone in the group knows about. For example, they could choose riding a bike.
- Have them think about what they would tell someone to help that person do the activity. For riding a bike, they could start with, "First, raise your training wheels. . ." For baking cookies, they could begin, "First, buy everything you need."

CREATE A CLASS LIST OF TIPS

- Model how to write a tip. Have each group of children write or dictate tips for the thing they do well on strips of paper.
- Then give children time to draw pictures to go with their tips.
- Create a class list of tips by helping each group number their tips and paste them onto paper. Attach the lists to make a class book, or post on a bulletin board.

T198

PERFORMANCE

Children's Self-Assessment The following questions will help children assess their work:
- ✔ Will our tips help someone do the thing we can do well?
- ✔ Are our tips written in a list?

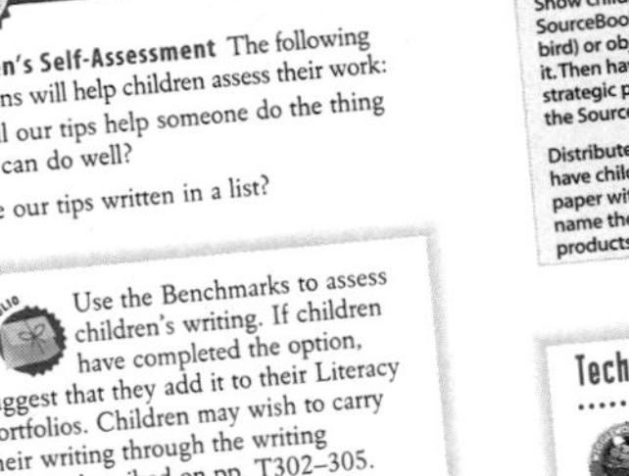

Use the Benchmarks to assess children's writing. If children have completed the option, suggest that they add it to their Literacy Portfolios. Children may wish to carry their writing through the writing process described on pp. T302–305.

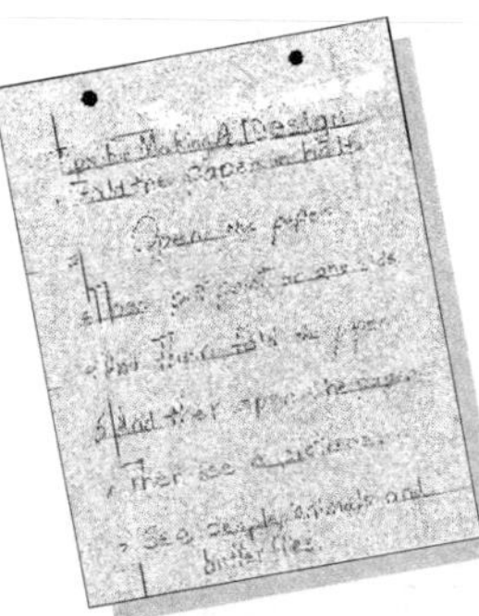

Proficient sample: Tips show how to do something and are numbered.

Show children the Big and Little ... SourceBook. Ask children to think of an animal (cat, bird) or object (house, toy) and draw the outline of it. Then have them draw stars over the outline at strategic points to look like the constellations in the SourceBook.

Distribute pieces of black construction paper and have children transfer their constellations onto the paper with white crayons. Then have children name their constellation. Display the finished products on a "Milky Way" bulletin board.

Technology Options

Using the computer, children can record and play back ideas for their tips. Children can then use the writing area to write or record their tips, adding their own illustrations using the Paint Tools. Help children print their tips to combine into a class book.

For more writing ideas, see the WiggleWorks Plus Teaching Plan.

help deciding what to write about by encouraging them to think about things they especially enjoy doing or look forward to doing. Help them realize that the things they enjoy doing are usually the things they do well.

ESL Help children acquiring English understand that a tip can be a way of teaching something to someone else. During Prewrite, encourage them to think of something they think they do well and could teach someone else. Help children focus on one part of what they would teach and suggest that they use that as their tip.

CHILDREN'S WRITING BENCHMARKS		
Novice: The tips do not show how to do something well. They are not written in a numbered list.	**Apprentice:** The tips may not show how to do something. The list may not be numbered.	**Proficient:** The tips show how to do something. The tips are written in a numbered list.

INTEGRATING LANGUAGE ARTS T199

1

Children have opportunities to write every day. **Children start writing with some assistance and then with increasing independence as they write for a variety of purposes. Children will experience writing letters, words and sentences while mastering the conventions of grammar and punctuation.**

Grammar and usage and mechanics instruction is explicit and intentional.

All lessons are supported with reproducible practice pages.

At grades K-3, Literacy Place provides a full Handwriting program (licensed from Zaner-Bloser) that ties to spelling.

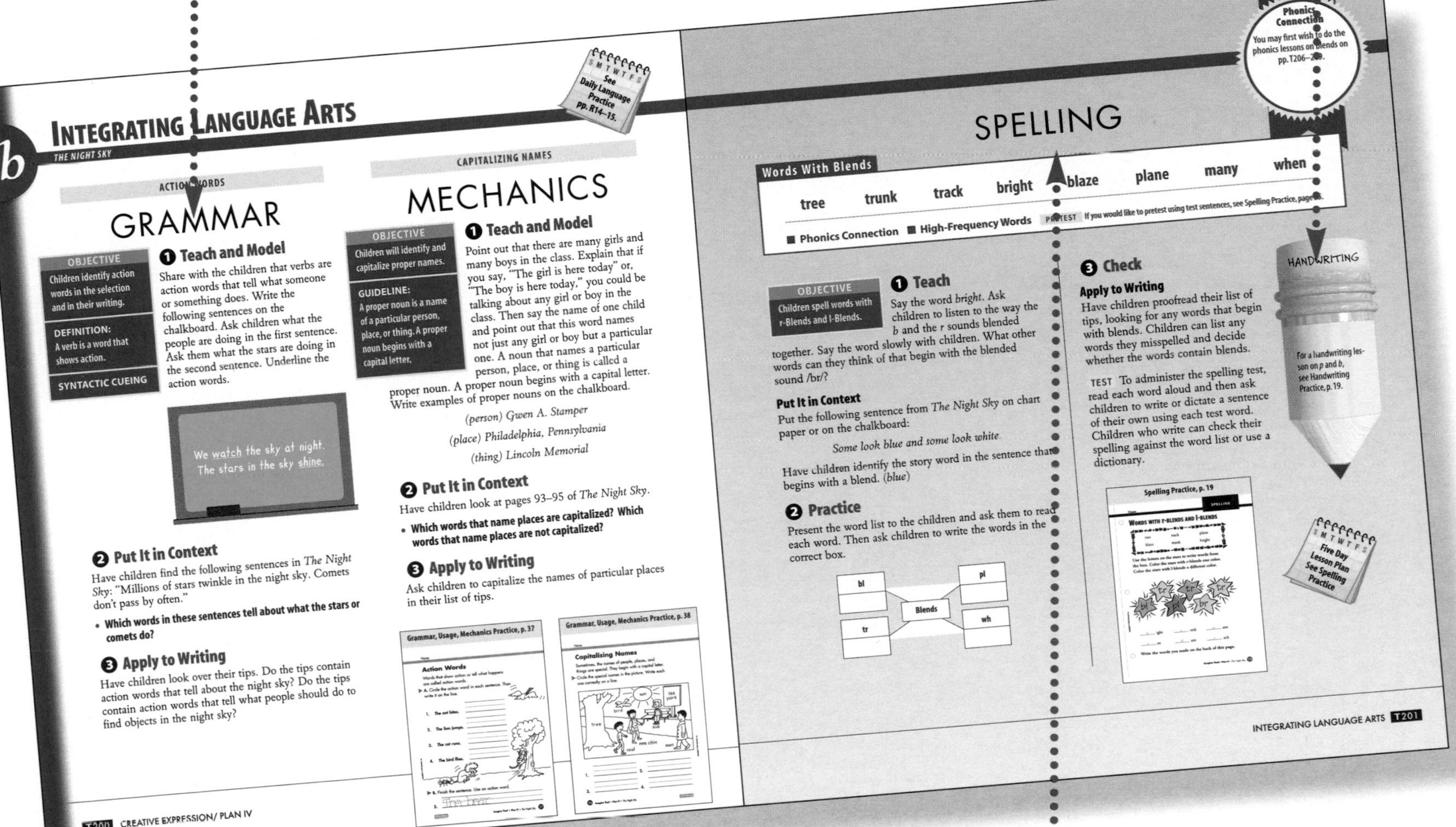

INTEGRATING LANGUAGE ARTS

THE NIGHT SKY

See Daily Language Practice pp. R14–15.

ACTION WORDS

GRAMMAR

OBJECTIVE
Children identify action words in the selection and in their writing.

DEFINITION:
A verb is a word that shows action.

SYNTACTIC CUEING

❶ Teach and Model

Share with the children that verbs are action words that tell what someone or something does. Write the following sentences on the chalkboard. Ask children what the people are doing in the first sentence. Ask them what the stars are doing in the second sentence. Underline the action words.

We watch the sky at night.
The stars in the sky shine.

❷ Put It in Context

Have children find the following sentences in *The Night Sky*: "Millions of stars twinkle in the night sky. Comets don't pass by often."

- **Which words in these sentences tell about what the stars or comets do?**

❸ Apply to Writing

Have children look over their tips. Do the tips contain action words that tell about the night sky? Do the tips contain action words that tell what people should do to find objects in the night sky?

CAPITALIZING NAMES

MECHANICS

OBJECTIVE
Children will identify and capitalize proper names.

GUIDELINE:
A proper noun is a name of a particular person, place, or thing. A proper noun begins with a capital letter.

❶ Teach and Model

Point out that there are many girls and many boys in the class. Explain that if you say, "The girl is here today" or, "The boy is here today," you could be talking about any girl or boy in the class. Then say the name of one child and point out that this word names not just any girl or boy but a particular one. A noun that names a particular person, place, or thing is called a proper noun. A proper noun begins with a capital letter. Write examples of proper nouns on the chalkboard.

(person) Gwen A. Stamper
(place) Philadelphia, Pennsylvania
(thing) Lincoln Memorial

❷ Put It in Context

Have children look at pages 93–95 of *The Night Sky*.

- **Which words that name places are capitalized? Which words that name places are not capitalized?**

❸ Apply to Writing

Ask children to capitalize the names of particular places in their list of tips.

Grammar, Usage, Mechanics Practice, p. 37

Grammar, Usage, Mechanics Practice, p. 38

T200 CREATIVE EXPRESSION/ PLAN IV

Phonics Connection
You may first wish to do the phonics lessons on blends on pp. T206–209.

SPELLING

Words With Blends

tree trunk track bright blaze plane many when

■ Phonics Connection ■ High-Frequency Words PRETEST If you would like to pretest using test sentences, see Spelling Practice, page 20.

OBJECTIVE
Children spell words with r-Blends and l-Blends.

❶ Teach

Say the word *bright*. Ask children to listen to the way the *b* and the *r* sounds blended together. Say the word slowly with children. What other words can they think of that begin with the blended sound /br/?

Put It in Context

Put the following sentence from *The Night Sky* on chart paper or on the chalkboard:

Some look blue and some look white.

Have children identify the story word in the sentence that begins with a blend. (*blue*)

❷ Practice

Present the word list to the children and ask them to read each word. Then ask children to write the words in the correct box.

bl | pl | Blends | tr | wh

❸ Check

Apply to Writing

Have children proofread their list of tips, looking for any words that begin with blends. Children can list any words they misspelled and decide whether the words contain blends.

TEST To administer the spelling test, read each word aloud and then ask children to write or dictate a sentence of their own using each test word. Children who write can check their spelling against the word list or use a dictionary.

HANDWRITING

For a handwriting lesson on *p* and *b*, see Handwriting Practice, p. 19.

Spelling Practice, p. 19

Five Day Lesson Plan See Spelling Practice

INTEGRATING LANGUAGE ARTS T201

Best of all, everything is taught in context and pulled together *for* you:

- ✔ What students read is the model for what they write
- ✔ What students read and write is the basis for all grammar, usage, and mechanics instruction
- ✔ Spelling words are connected to the phonics skills and high-frequency words being taught
- ✔ Students apply what they have learned about grammar, usage, and mechanics to their own writing

Only at Literacy Place will you find a complete spelling program that reinforces phonics through grade six, including a word list, a five day lesson plan, and a test every week. New spelling skills are taught in plans I-V of every unit. The lesson in plan VI is always a review lesson. Spelling lessons are taught in the context of the literature and have three easy steps: teach, practice, check.

BUILDING

SKILLS AND STRATEGIES

At the heart of Literacy Place is intentional, systematic skills instruction, with an emphasis on *phonics.*

Save time! Quickcheck helps you see how much instruction your students really need and customize instruction based on what you find out.

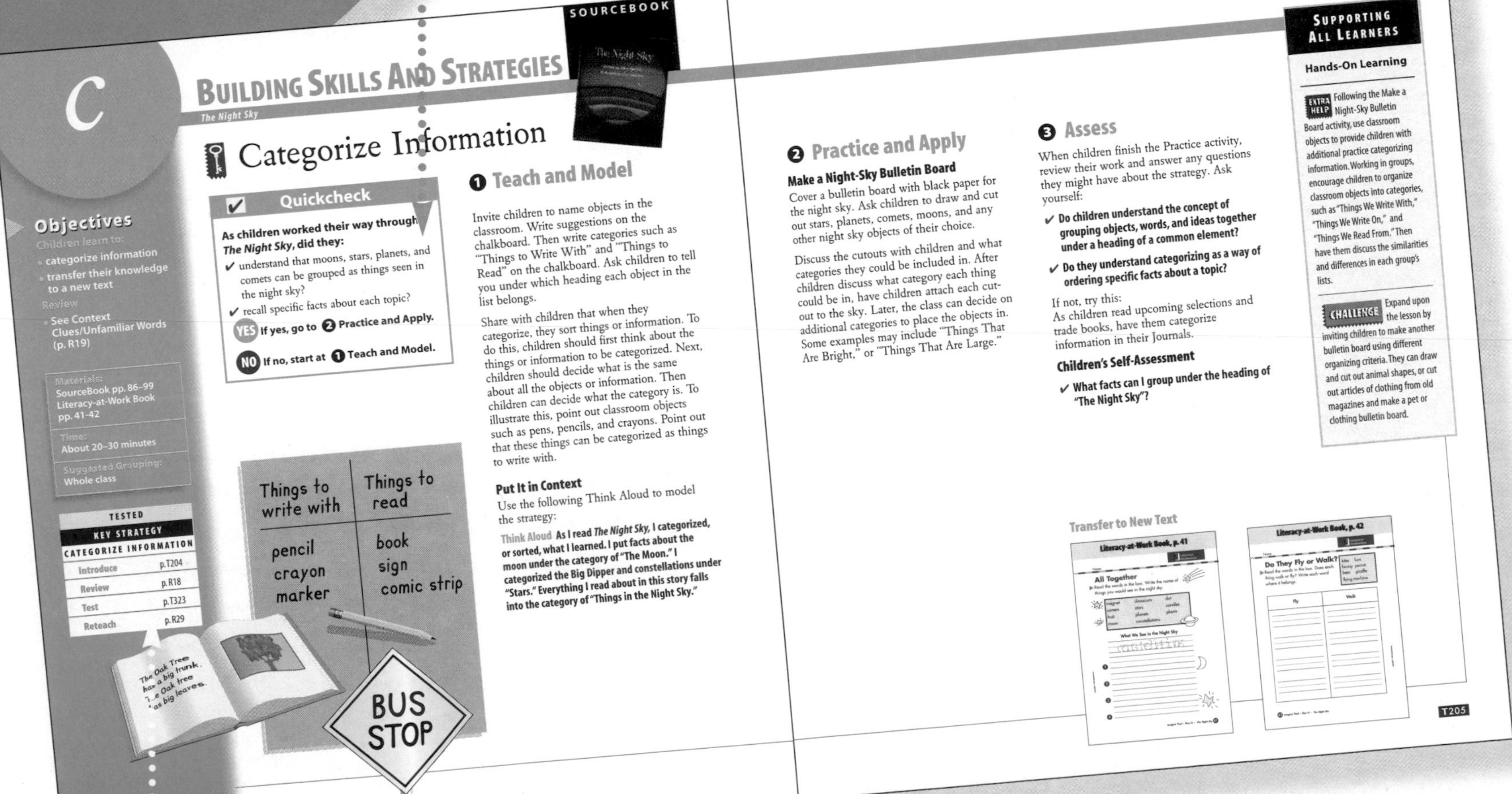

SOURCEBOOK

C

BUILDING SKILLS AND STRATEGIES

The Night Sky

Categorize Information

Objectives

Children learn to:

- categorize information
- transfer their knowledge to a new text

Review

- See Context Clues/Unfamiliar Words (p. R19)

Materials: SourceBook pp. 86–99, Literacy-at-Work Book pp. 41–42

Time: About 20–30 minutes

Suggested Grouping: Whole class

TESTED	
KEY STRATEGY	
CATEGORIZE INFORMATION	
Introduce	p. T204
Review	p. R18
Test	p. T323
Reteach	p. R29

Quickcheck

As children worked their way through *The Night Sky*, did they:

✔ understand that moons, stars, planets, and comets can be grouped as things seen in the night sky?

✔ recall specific facts about each topic?

YES If yes, go to ❷ Practice and Apply.

NO If no, start at ❶ Teach and Model.

❶ Teach and Model

Invite children to name objects in the classroom. Write suggestions on the chalkboard. Then write categories such as "Things to Write With" and "Things to Read" on the chalkboard. Ask children to tell you under which heading each object in the list belongs.

Share with children that when they categorize, they sort things or information. To do this, children should first think about the things or information to be categorized. Next, children should decide what is the same about all the objects or information. Then children can decide what the category is. To illustrate this, point out classroom objects such as pens, pencils, and crayons. Point out that these things can be categorized as things to write with.

Put It in Context

Use the following Think Aloud to model the strategy:

Think Aloud **As I read *The Night Sky*, I categorized, or sorted, what I learned. I put facts about the moon under the category of "The Moon." I categorized the Big Dipper and constellations under "Stars." Everything I read about in this story falls into the category of "Things in the Night Sky."**

T204

❷ Practice and Apply

Make a Night-Sky Bulletin Board

Cover a bulletin board with black paper for the night sky. Ask children to draw and cut out stars, planets, comets, moons, and any other night sky objects of their choice.

Discuss the cutouts with children and what categories they could be included in. After children discuss what category each thing could be in, have children attach each cut-out to the sky. Later, the class can decide on additional categories to place the objects in. Some examples may include "Things That Are Bright," or "Things That Are Large."

❸ Assess

When children finish the Practice activity, review their work and answer any questions they might have about the strategy. Ask yourself:

✔ **Do children understand the concept of grouping objects, words, and ideas together under a heading of a common element?**

✔ **Do they understand categorizing as a way of ordering specific facts about a topic?**

If not, try this:

As children read upcoming selections and trade books, have them categorize information in their Journals.

Children's Self-Assessment

✔ **What facts can I group under the heading of "The Night Sky"?**

SUPPORTING ALL LEARNERS

Hands-On Learning

EXTRA HELP Following the Make a Night-Sky Bulletin Board activity, use classroom objects to provide children with additional practice categorizing information. Working in groups, encourage children to organize classroom objects into categories, such as "Things We Write With," "Things We Write On," and "Things We Read From." Then have them discuss the similarities and differences in each group's lists.

CHALLENGE Expand upon the lesson by inviting children to make another bulletin board using different organizing criteria. They can draw and cut out animal shapes, or cut out articles of clothing from old magazines and make a pet or clothing bulletin board.

Transfer to New Text

Literacy-at-Work Book, p. 41

Literacy-at-Work Book, p. 42

T205

The skills trace helps ensure systematic skill development. Every tested reading skill is introduced reviewed, tested and retaught if needed.

Every lesson begins with activities to develop **phonemic awareness.**

Use **sound/symbol** correspondence to build and read words.

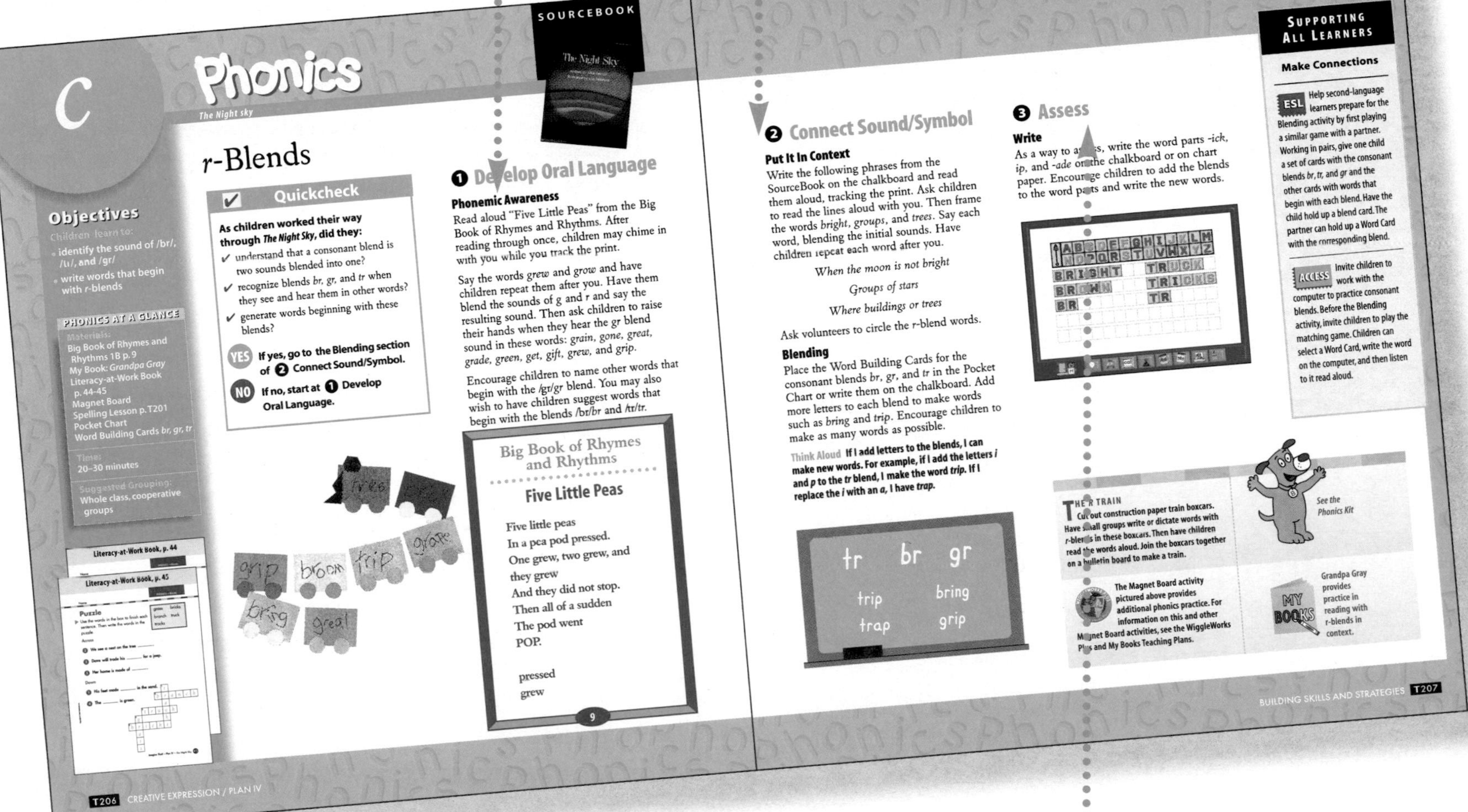
C

Phonics

The Night Sky

SOURCEBOOK

The Night Sky

Objectives

Children learn to:

- identify the sound of /br/, /tr/, and /gr/
- write words that begin with r-blends

PHONICS AT A GLANCE

Materials:
Big Book of Rhymes and Rhythms 1B p. 9
My Book: *Grandpa Gray*
Literacy-at-Work Book p. 44-45
Magnet Board
Spelling Lesson p. T201
Pocket Chart
Word Building Cards *br, gr, tr*

Time:
20–30 minutes

Suggested Grouping:
Whole class, cooperative groups

r-Blends

Quickcheck

As children worked their way through *The Night Sky*, did they:

✓ understand that a consonant blend is two sounds blended into one?

✓ recognize blends *br, gr,* and *tr* when they see and hear them in other words?

✓ generate words beginning with these blends?

YES **If yes, go to the Blending section of ❷ Connect Sound/Symbol.**

NO **If no, start at ❶ Develop Oral Language.**

❶ Develop Oral Language

Phonemic Awareness

Read aloud "Five Little Peas" from the Big Book of Rhymes and Rhythms. After reading through once, children may chime in with you while you track the print.

Say the words *grew* and *grow* and have children repeat them after you. Have them blend the sounds of *g* and *r* and say the resulting sound. Then ask children to raise their hands when they hear the *gr* blend sound in these words: *grain, gone, great, grade, green, get, gift, grew,* and *grip.*

Encourage children to name other words that begin with the /gr/gr blend. You may also wish to have children suggest words that begin with the blends /br/br and /tr/tr.

Big Book of Rhymes and Rhythms

Five Little Peas

Five little peas
In a pea pod pressed.
One grew, two grew, and they grew
And they did not stop.
Then all of a sudden
The pod went
POP.

pressed
grew

9

❷ Connect Sound/Symbol

Put It In Context

Write the following phrases from the SourceBook on the chalkboard and read them aloud, tracking the print. Ask children to read the lines aloud with you. Then frame the words *bright, groups,* and *trees.* Say each word, blending the initial sounds. Have children repeat each word after you.

When the moon is not bright

Groups of stars

Where buildings or trees

Ask volunteers to circle the *r*-blend words.

Blending

Place the Word Building Cards for the consonant blends *br, gr,* and *tr* in the Pocket Chart or write them on the chalkboard. Add more letters to each blend to make words such as *bring* and *trip.* Encourage children to make as many words as possible.

Think Aloud **If I add letters to the blends, I can make new words. For example, if I add the letters *i* and *p* to the *tr* blend, I make the word *trip.* If I replace the *i* with an *a,* I have *trap.***

❸ Assess

Write

As a way to assess, write the word parts *-ick, -ip,* and *-ade* on the chalkboard or on chart paper. Encourage children to add the blends to the word parts and write the new words.

SUPPORTING ALL LEARNERS

Make Connections

ESL Help second-language learners prepare for the Blending activity by first playing a similar game with a partner. Working in pairs, give one child a set of cards with the consonant blends *br, tr,* and *gr* and the other cards with words that begin with each blend. Have the child hold up a blend card. The partner can hold up a Word Card with the corresponding blend.

ACCESS Invite children to work with the computer to practice consonant blends. Before the Blending activity, invite children to play the matching game. Children can select a Word Card, write the word on the computer, and then listen to it read aloud.

THE TRAIN Cut out construction paper train boxcars. Have small groups write or dictate words with *r*-blends in these boxcars. Then have children read the words aloud. Join the boxcars together on a bulletin board to make a train.

The Magnet Board activity pictured above provides additional phonics practice. For information on this and other Magnet Board activities, see the WiggleWorks Plus and My Books Teaching Plans.

See the Phonics Kit

Grandpa Gray provides practice in reading with r-blends in context.

T206 CREATIVE EXPRESSION / PLAN IV

BUILDING SKILLS AND STRATEGIES T207

Use dictation and writing to assess students' mastery of **phonics skills.**

Literacy Place provides explicit and intentional instruction in phonics.

Every lesson...

- ✓ Provides systematic instruction
- ✓ Develops phonemic awareness
- ✓ Follows a developmental continuum
- ✓ Connects sound to symbol in context of reading
- ✓ Provides instruction in blending
- ✓ Connects phonics to spelling lessons
- ✓ Includes writing in every lesson

Each year there are **hundreds of opportunities to practice and apply skills.** *You'll find them in mini-lessons, review lessons, the reteaching section, the Literacy-at-Work Book, My Books and WiggleWorks Plus.*

Informal assessment at point-of-use helps you make sound instructional decisions, day in and day out.

Assessment *that truly informs instruction*

Teachers told us they needed tools to *inform instruction* on a daily basis as well as formal assessment to gauge student progress, *assign grades,* and *prepare for standardized tests.* At *Literacy Place,* you'll find the best of both worlds: Highly practical *informal* assessment as well as *formal* tests designed and validated by the most respected name in standardized testing: ETS.

OBSERVATION

As children read the selection, notice how they:

- ✔ make connections with the theme of imagination.
- ✔ understand the literary element of Setting.
- ✔ use the key strategy of Make Inferences.

Begin With Observation Observe students as they read.

CONFERENCE

Use the checked questions on the opposite page to assess children's understanding of:

- ✔ the theme of using imagination.
- ✔ the literary element of Setting.
- ✔ the key strategy of Make Inferences.

Assess children's reading skills and understanding quickly with an informal conference after reading. Reading rubrics and suggested next steps are in the assessment kit.

Children's Self-Assessment The following questions will help children assess their work:

- ✔ How is our story like the story *In the Attic?* How is it different?
- ✔ How did we make our object come to life?

Have students participate in their ongoing assessment through Portfolio opportunities.

STUDENTS' WRITING BENCHMARKS		
Novice: The student has difficulty adopting an animal's point of view. The student uses little or no factual information.	**Apprentice:** The student can maintain the animal's point of view but has difficulty integrating facts and emotions into the story.	**Proficient:** The student successfully presents the animal's life and writes from its point of view. The story includes factual information as well as emotions.

Evaluate writing with student writing benchmarks.

✔ QUICKCHECK

As children worked their way through *In the Attic,* did they:

- ✔ understand the use of pictures and words as story clues?
- ✔ use story clues to make guesses about nonstated information?
- ✔ use personal experience and prior knowledge to make guesses about nonstated information?

 If yes, go to ❷ Practice and Apply.

 If no, start at ❶ Teach and Model.

Meet Individual Needs. Quickcheck helps you determine students' grasp of each plan's skills and strategies and offers clear instructional paths to meet individual needs.

The comprehensive Assessment Kit includes formal tests developed and validated by ETS.

Placement Tools include a collection of leveled Benchmark Books for Diagnosis (with guides) for each grade as well as formal Placement Tests and an Early Reading and Writing Assessment at Grade One.

Unit Tests come in two forms: A & B. **Mid-Year** and **End-of-Year Tests.**

The unique **Assessment Handbook** provides guidance on what, when, and how to assess.

Only at Literacy Place...

All programs give you tools designed to report student progress. Only Literacy Place helps you decide what to do next. This support provides great training for new teachers and is a welcome time-saver for experienced teachers.

To develop and validate formal assessment, we turned to the experts — the Educational Testing Service (ETS), developer of the National Assessment of Educational Progress (NAEP) tests, as well as the SATs.

Literacy Place guarantees **success for *all* learners.**

FROM THE VERY BEGINNING,

Literacy Place was developed with a clear *goal* in mind: *To ensure that all children learn to read and write.* Borrowing from architecture, the program was built on the concept of *"universal design"*, providing access for all.

Strategies for supporting all learners are embedded at point-of-use throughout the Teacher's SourceBook.

SUPPORTING ALL LEARNERS

Hands-on Lear

EXTRA HELP Following the M Night Sky Bullet activity, use classroom ob provide children with adc practice categorizing info Working in groups, encou children to organize class objects into categories, su "Things We Write With,"" We Write On," and "Thing Read From." Then have th discuss the similarities an differences in each group

CHALLENGE Expan the le inviting children to make bulletin board using diffe organizing criteria. They c and cut out animal shape out articles of clothing fro magazines and make a p clothing bulletin board.

SUPPORTING ALL LEARNERS

Hands-on Learning

ESL During the Expand Oral Language activity, give children acquiring English, who may not have the vocabulary needed to express their ideas, the option of drawing pictures to show what they think might be found in an attic or what they do when they are bored.

ACCESS Children who have difficulty expressing themselves orally can use drawing as an alternative way to share their ideas and experiences. Activate prior knowledge by asking them to draw pictures of the places they go when they use their imagination.

Woven throughout the Teacher's SourceBook edition, you'll find classroom tested strategies for addressing the needs of all the children in your class:

EXTRA HELP **Children who require extra help.**

Children who are acquiring English.

CHALLENGE **Children who require extra challenge.**

Children with physical disabilities.

These tips are always presented at point of use — you'll never have to flip around or search in a separate book while you're trying to teach.

In every lesson begin with ···············► end with

CREATING A COMMUNITY OF LEARNERS

Each lesson begins with an activtity designed to include every child regardless of language or ability level.

DEMONSTRATING INDEPENDENCE

Leveled trade books provide an opportunity for all children to demonstrate independence at the end of each lesson.

Additional components offer activities designed to support all learners.

Projects and Workshops provide hands-on learning in every lesson. All children are invited to bring *their* real-world knowledge into the classroom.

Audiocassettes help children connect the written and spoken word.

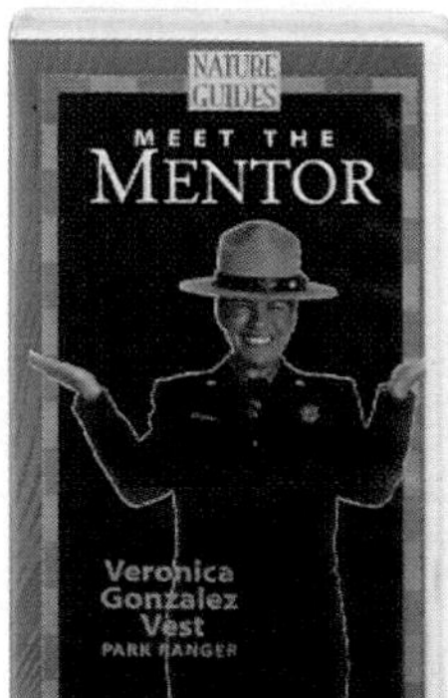

Videos are a great way to include all the children in your classroom. You'll find one in each unit.

Practice, Practice, Practice! *Hundreds of practice opportunities ensure* ***all*** *children will get the practice they need.*

Flexible grouping strategies for *every* lesson support *every* learner

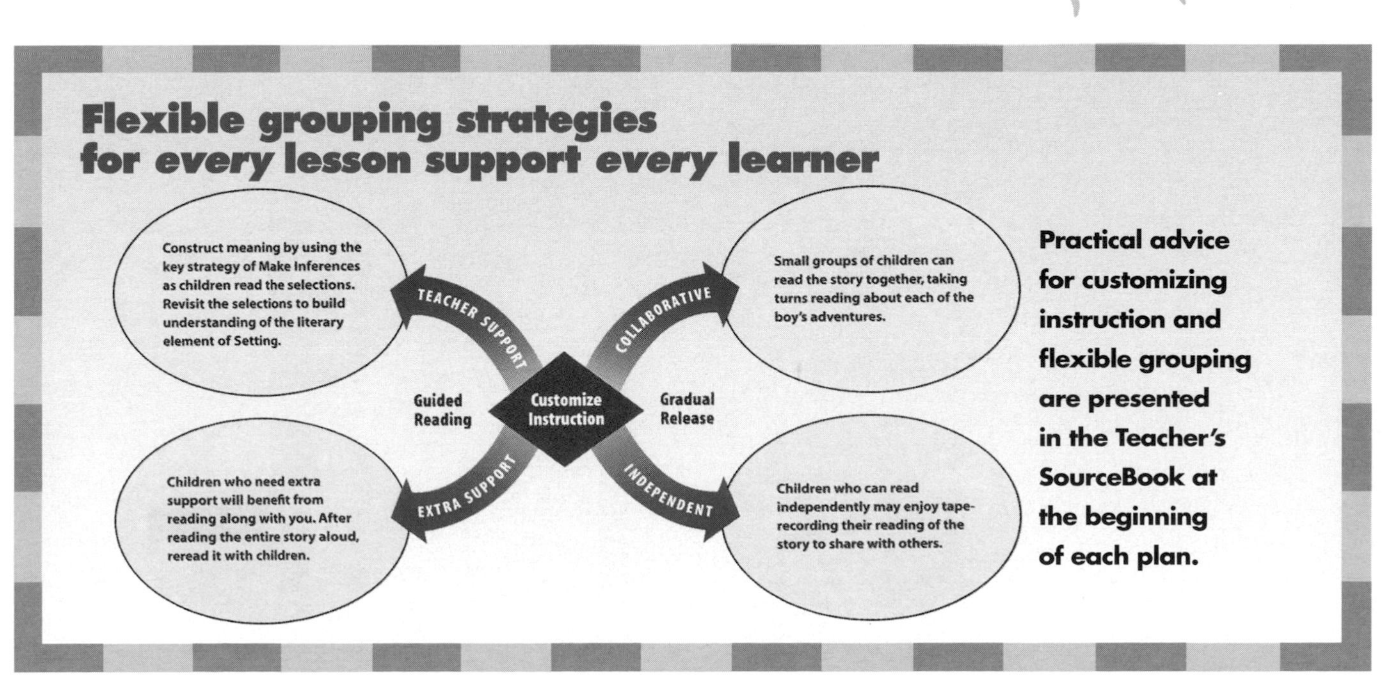

Practical advice for customizing instruction and flexible grouping are presented in the Teacher's SourceBook at the beginning of each plan.

Multiple resources ensure **success** for language development.

Language learners need oral language development, access to the literature, and support in their primary language.

By its very nature, *Literacy Place* is a program that welcomes and is accessible to all students. There is an ESL teaching plan and resources in every lesson that foster language development and competence for *Literacy Place*. Strategies for supporting all learners are also included throughout the teacher's edition at point-of-use. Several *additional* components offer second language support.

There are over 100 languages spoken in California schools. **The Multiple Languages Kit** *empowers teachers to meet the individual language needs of their students (including those who speak Spanish, Cambodian, Vietnamese, Cantonese, Hmong, Korean and Tagalog). It provides your school or district with a license to translate selected components to the languages represented in your school, information on how to access translators, and a video on how to tailor the program to your own needs.*

Language Development Kits include story cards to provide access to the literature and picture cards to develop oral language.

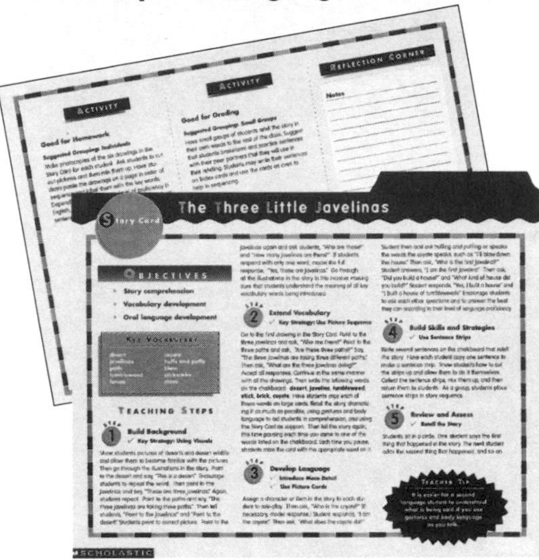

Literacy Place technology, described in detail on the following pages, provides excellent teacher-directed and self-paced support and reinforcement for second-language learners. WiggleWorks Plus is also accompanied by a comprehensive ESL handbook.

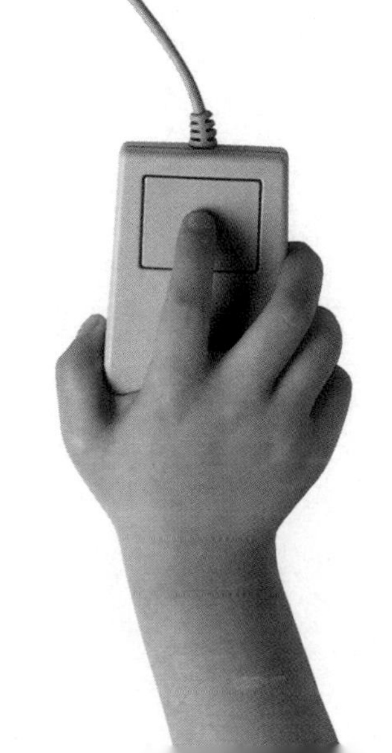

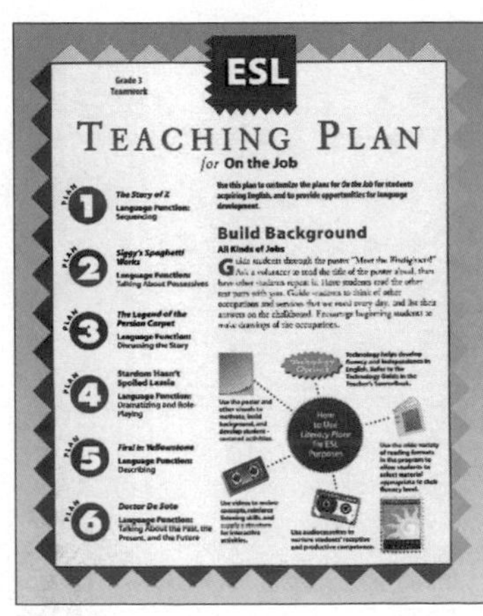

Literacy Place includes **ESL Plans** to support every selection in every unit.

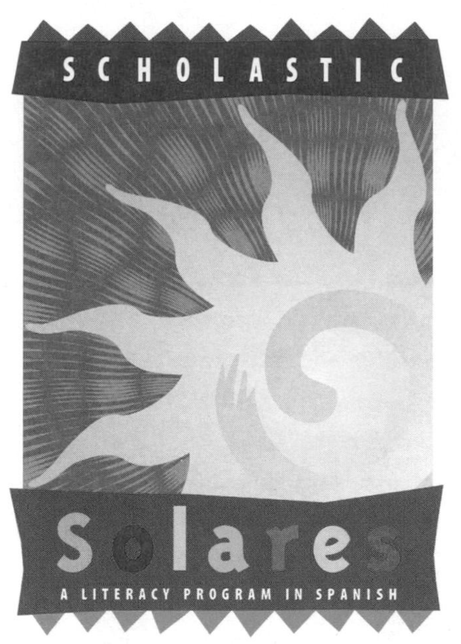

Introducing Solares™

A K-6 integrated reading and language arts program that develops reading and writing skills in Spanish while helping students add English.

At grades K-3...Your students will read on level in Spanish.

Solares is a complete literacy program in Spanish that builds on children's language, culture, and experiences to ensure that they read at grade level by the end of grade three.

In grades 4-6, there are two options that provide solid reading and language arts instruction for all students.

El Taller Intensivo de Español is an intervention program for students with a wide range of literacy skills, from little or no previous schooling to reading just below grade level. This intensive, hands-on workshop draws on the students' real-world experience and oral language abilities to promote accelerated learning.

La Biblioteca Solares is a collection of trade books, teaching guides, and student activity cards for students who are reading on grade level in Spanish and who may already be participating in *Literacy Place.*

To learn more about Solares,
call 1-800 SCHOLASTIC
or your local Scholastic representative.

EL BOSQUE TROPICAL

HELEN COWCHER

SCHOLASTIC

LANGUAGE DEVELOPMENT

Proven **technology** *gets results for every child.*

CD-ROM technology helps every child read with power and purpose.

Two full selections per unit are available as fully interactive electronic books. Designed to be used by children independently, in pairs, or small groups, these books are proven to build fluency quickly. Reading, writing, speaking, and listening activities are tied to each unit's instruction.

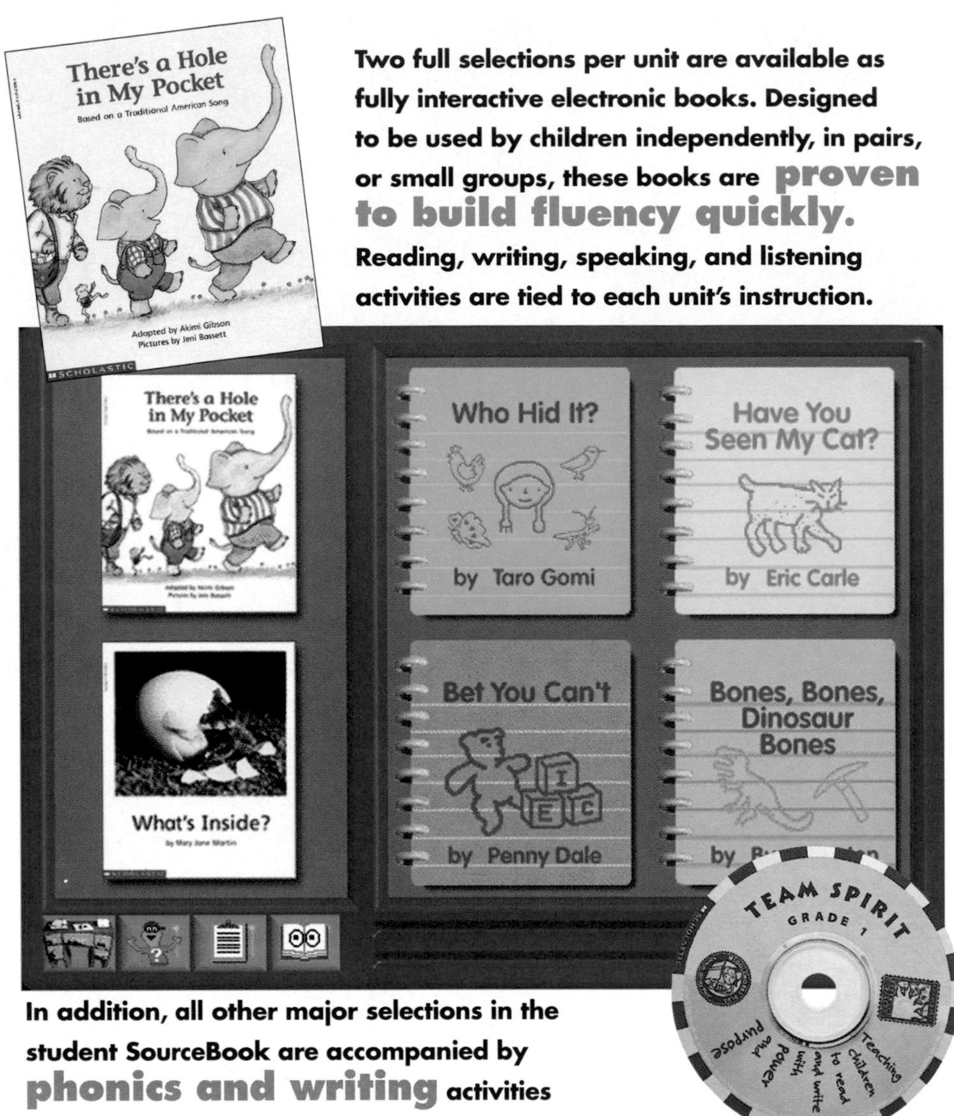

In addition, all other major selections in the student SourceBook are accompanied by phonics and writing activities tied to that selection.

THE HEART of our primary technology is *WiggleWorks Plus*, a collection of fully *interactive* books on CD-ROM. This technology is an enhanced version of the highly successful WiggleWorks Beginning Literacy System, which was recently proven to *raise reading scores*. Developed in conjunction with the Center for Applied Special Technologies (CAST) at Harvard, WiggleWorks Plus is a wonderful tool for early reading and writing.

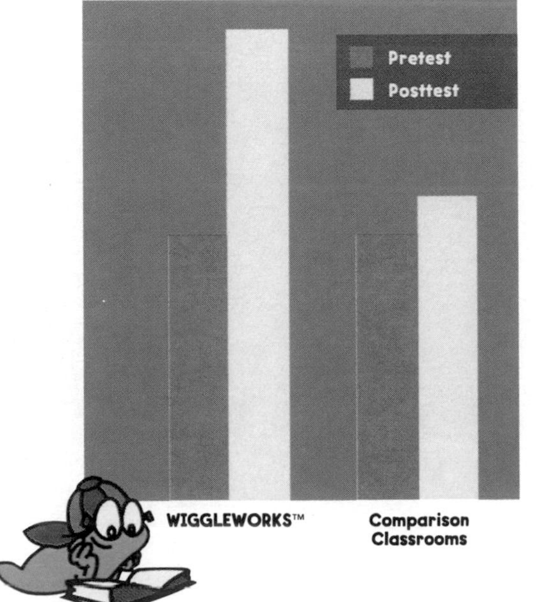

WiggleWorks works! A recent study by a Harvard researcher confirms that WiggleWorks raises scores on four measures of the IOWA Test of Basic Skills. Most important, scores went up among *all* children, from the most challenged to those who need challenge.

Audio, video, and on-line access deliver literacy in multiple technologies.

Audiocassettes enforce the connection between the spoken and written word. Selections from the student anthology as well as every Big Book in grades K-2 are available on audiocassette.

42 Meet the Mentor **Videos** (one per unit) give all students an opportunity to visit adult role models in the workplace and experience literacy at work firsthand.

Scholastic Network
Every student can participate in the larger community that extends beyond the walls of your school with the Scholastic Network. This on-line service gives your students unprecedented access to people like Rosa Parks and U.S. Presidents as well as other children from across the country.

Throughout the Teacher's SourceBook you'll find activities for integrating technology into the lesson.

Mae Jemison, Astronaut. Mentor, Grade 4, Unit 3.

Literacy Place technology *is packed with teacher support, all designed to mirror the way teachers really teach!*

TECHNOLOGY

Phonics Readers and My Books provide opportunities for controlled reading.

Match **every child** *to text.*

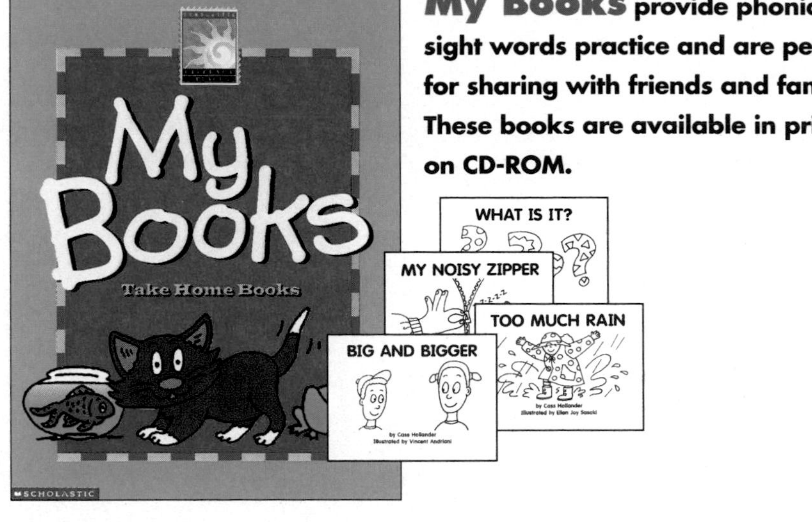

My Books provide phonics and sight words practice and are perfect for sharing with friends and family. These books are available in print or on CD-ROM.

Literacy Place ensures success by providing teachers with the *resources* and *instructional strategies* to match children to text. That's why *Literacy Place* provides *more reading* material than any other program, including controlled Phonics Readers, leveled libraries, and authentic literature. There is something for every child to *read fluently every day*.

Phonics Readers. These 36 little readers provide systematic and sequential introduction of phonics skills, using the Literacy Place matrix. The teaching plan gives practical guidance on how to develop phonemic awareness, introduce high-frequency words, connect sound to symbol, read the story, and take dictation and write.

Authentic literature fosters a love of reading while building skills.

Every unit is accompanied by **related trade books,** each with its own teaching guide. These can be used for direct instruction or independent reading.

The Shoebox Leveled Library helps students reinforce and practice early reading skills, such as phonics, reading strategies and concepts of print. It contains 96 books, grouped in stages. A teaching guide includes lessons for guided reading, leveling of books and a bibliography of familiar titles found in most schools.

The Fluency Library offers colorful, fun, thematically connected selections that reinforce unit skills and provide plenty of additional practice.

With hundreds of selections at Grade 1, *children will find more to read at* Literacy Place *than any other program!*

Mentors inspire movitating, purposeful projects and model 21st century literacies.

Bringing Literacy to **Life**

Mentors **are real life professionals who model the literacy skills required for a successful and productive career. Students are introduced to a mentor in every unit, through video, CD-ROM and in the student SourceBook.**

Meet the Mentor Video

SCHOLASTIC

NATURE GUIDES GRADE 4

At Literacy Place, students meet mentors, people who model real-life literacies and inspire motivating purposeful projects. Only here will you find so many ways to show every student the role of literacy in a successful and productive life.

Emergency Worker César Rivera, Mentor, Grade 6

Literacy Place is unique. *It uses the language arts to help students build the critical workplace competencies now included in many districts' standards.*

Students prepare for the workplace and demonstrate skills by tackling real world situations.

Students **apply literacy skills** to real world situations through workshops and projects. (In grades 1 and 2, workshops and projects are on doublesided, laminated cards. In grades 3 - 6, workshops and projects appear in the student SourceBook.)

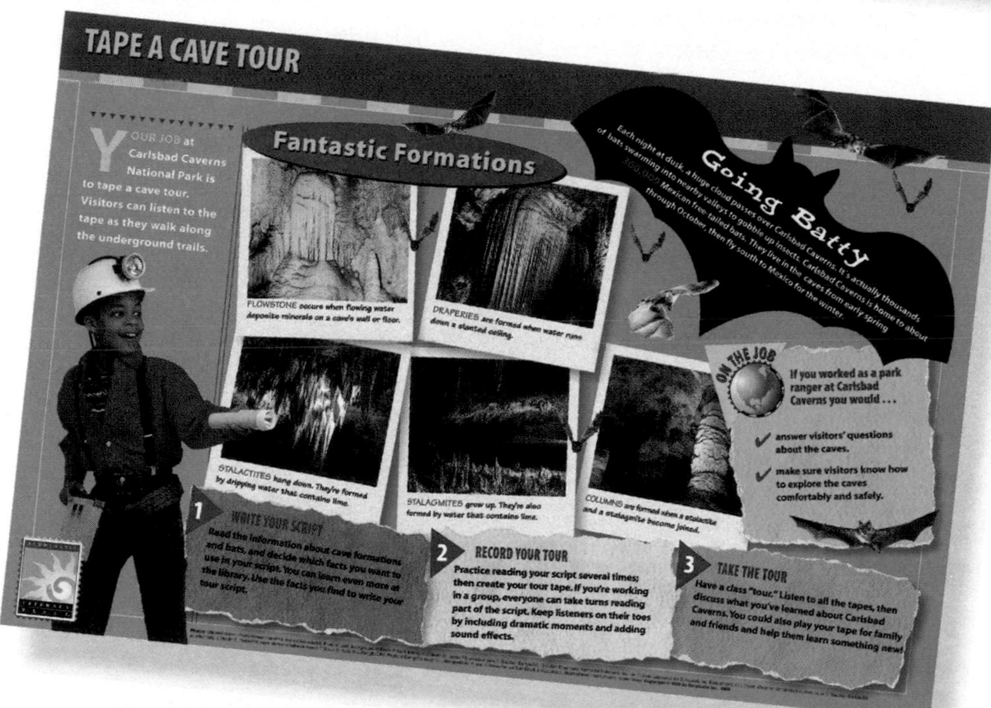

From Grade 4, Nature Guides

Place Cards take students on in-class field trips to real life places. Only Literacy Place gives students an opportunity to **apprentice with the mentor** and practice newly acquired skills. You'll find four Place Cards per unit.

Real world connections help students develop 21st century skills:

- ✓ Managing information
- ✓ Working in teams
- ✓ Using technology
- ✓ Problem solving

Support *for teachers, families and community members*

EDUCATORS around the country have recognized that *families* and *communities* play a critical role in literacy development. And that *teachers* need and deserve ongoing training. That's why *Literacy Place* is full of components to *support* teachers, families, and the community at large.

Literacy Place supports the people who support our children: families, teachers, and members of the community.

Various components encourage family members to become active participants in literacy development.

- ✔ Family Guide to Literacy at Home
- ✔ Audiocassettes of the Literacy Place Family Guides
- ✔ Home Letters
- ✔ Home and School Partnership Letters
- ✔ Take-Me-Home Books
- ✔ Take Home Book Bag
- ✔ Parent Bookshelf — collection of titles devoted to raising good readers.
- ✔ "Giving the Gift of Reading," a video for parents.

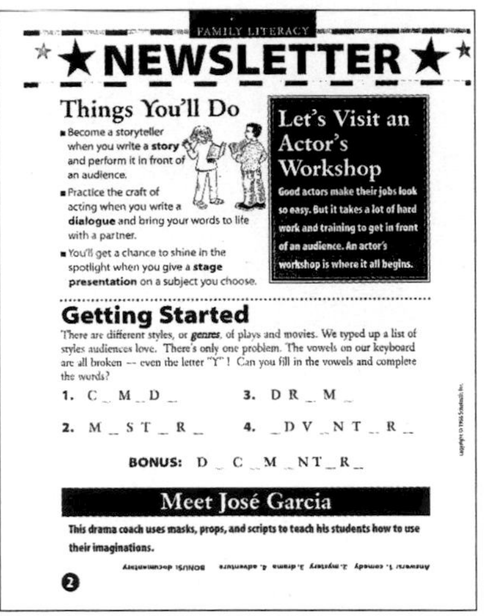

FAMILY LITERACY

★ NEWSLETTER ★

Things You'll Do

- Become a storyteller when you write a **story** and perform it in front of an audience.
- Practice the craft of acting when you write a **dialogue** and bring your words to life with a partner.
- You'll get a chance to shine in the spotlight when you give a **stage presentation** on a subject you choose.

Let's Visit an Actor's Workshop

Good actors make their jobs look so easy. But it takes a lot of hard work and training to get in front of an audience. An actor's workshop is where it all begins.

Getting Started

There are different styles, or *genres*, of plays and movies. We typed up a list of styles audiences love. There's only one problem. The vowels on our keyboard are all broken -- even the letter "Y"! Can you fill in the vowels and complete the words?

1. C _ M _ D _
2. M _ S T _ R _
3. D R _ M _
4. _ D V _ N T _ R _

BONUS: D _ C _ M _ NT _ R _

Meet José Garcia

This drama coach uses masks, props, and scripts to teach his students how to use their imaginations.

Answers: 1. comedy 2. mystery 3. drama 4. adventure BONUS: documentary

2

Communicating with parents is easy with **Family Literacy Newsletters.** These two page, reproducible "newspapers" are a great way to preview the unit with students and parents. You'll find one per unit in the Literacy-at-Work Book.

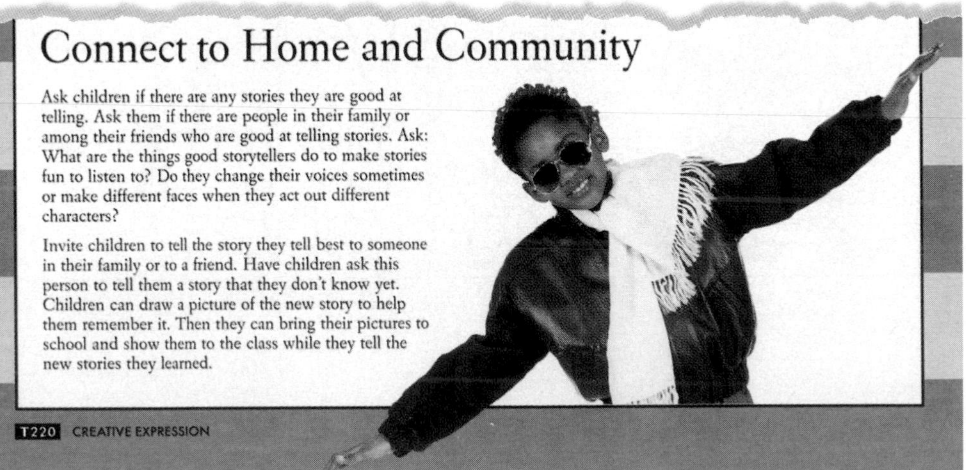

Connect to Home and Community

Ask children if there are any stories they are good at telling. Ask them if there are people in their family or among their friends who are good at telling stories. Ask: What are the things good storytellers do to make stories fun to listen to? Do they change their voices sometimes or make different faces when they act out different characters?

Invite children to tell the story they tell best to someone in their family or to a friend. Have children ask this person to tell them a story that they don't know yet. Children can draw a picture of the new story to help them remember it. Then they can bring their pictures to school and show them to the class while they tell the new stories they learned.

T220 CREATIVE EXPRESSION

The first activity in every unit encourages students to draw upon **knowledge of their community** and its members. Closing each unit are suggestions for hosting "Family Literacy Night,"an event in which students present their work and family members are invited to participate in activities tied to the unit's theme.

Professional development materials create a supportive environment for teachers to grow.

The Scholastic Network is the first and only on-line service exclusively for teachers and students. Available only from Scholastic, the Network gives you unprecedented access to editors, authors, and other teachers across the country.

- ✓ **Get answers fast when you post your questions on the Literacy Place bulletin board. Also, see how others have addressed similar situations.**
- ✓ **Chat with Authors. Live, interactive chats with Literacy Place authors are scheduled monthly.**
- ✓ **Attend Special Events. Each month new activities highlight lesson plans and professional development materials.**

Stay current!
The Literacy Place professional library helps you keep current on all the latest research on literacy development.

These unique workshops cover topics of concern to educators, including Early Literacy Development, Assessment, Learning for the 21st Century, and the Home-School Connection. Depending on the needs of your school, Scholastic University can come to your school through on-site visits, video, or teleconferencing.

The Teacher's Desk Reference is a professional manual filled with resources to support literacy development.

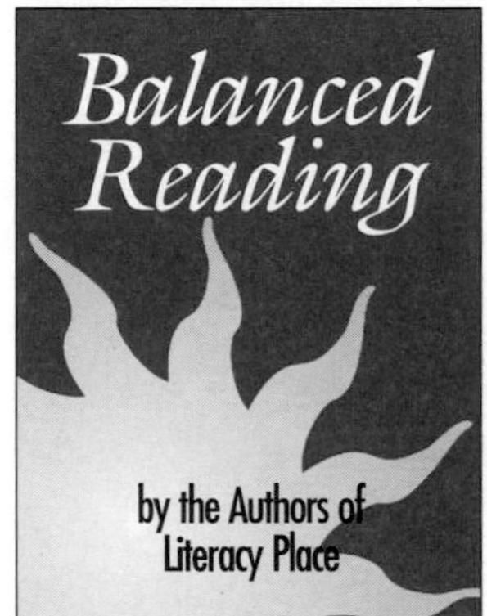

Balanced Reading is a compilation of writings by Literacy Place authors.

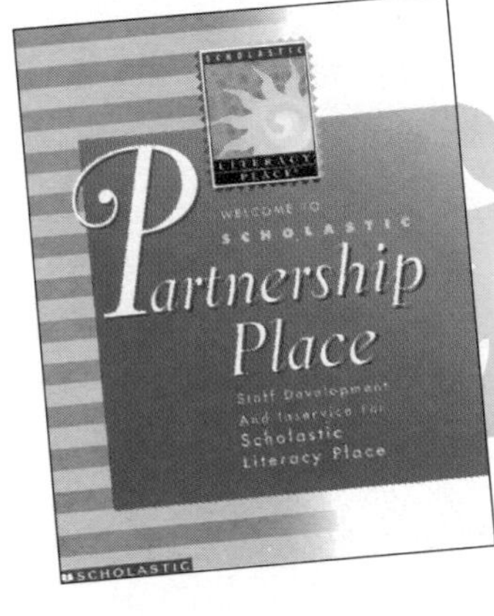

For a copy of our inservice and staff development proposal, ask your Scholastic representative for a copy of **Partnership Place**.

Founded on ten concepts drawn from the **very best research**

1. LITERACY IS DEVELOPED WITHIN THE PERSONAL, SOCIAL, AND INTELLECTUAL CONTEXTS OF THE LEARNER.
2. A LITERACY PROGRAM SHOULD PROVIDE DEVELOPMENTAL CONTINUITY.
3. THE SUCCESSFUL LEARNER IS MOTIVATED, STRATEGIC, KNOWLEDGEABLE, AND INTERACTIVE.
4. CHILDREN LEARN BEST WHEN THEY HAVE REAL PURPOSES AND CAN MAKE CONNECTIONS TO REAL LIFE.
5. EFFECTIVE LEARNING IS A COMBINATION OF STUDENT EXPLORATION AND TEACHER AND MENTOR MODELING.

How was Literacy Place developed?

1990

- **Teacher demand for a new kind of reading program** — one that emphasizes both literature and skills — prompts Scholastic to form the Instructional Publishing Group.
- Experienced **editors from top basal companies** come on board.
- Howard **Gardner**, Dorothy Strickland, Adele Brodkin, Gay Su **Pinnell**, James **Comer**, Ramon **Cortines** and Ernest **Boyer** are consulted.

1991

- **Thousands of teachers are surveyed** to identify "what works" in reading instruction.
- Editors gather and **analyze state and district frameworks** for reading curricula.
- Editors visit nationally recognized programs to observe best practices — **Reading Recovery, Success for All and Running Start.**
- **Authorship team** is established, drawing respected thinkers and daily practitioners from leading universities.

1992

- **Developmental model is created.**
- **Authorship team** is formed.
- **Partnership with Center for Applied Special Technologies** (CAST) is formed to create a platform for supporting all learners.
- SCANs report advisor **Arnold Packer** updates editors on literacies needed in tomorrow's workplace.
- Teachers, students, parents, policy makers, and business leaders contribute examples of **real-world literacies and 21st century skills.**

6 ASSESSMENT IS AN ONGOING AND MULTIDIMENSIONAL PROCESS THAT IS AN INTEGRAL PART OF INSTRUCTION.

7 MAKING READING AND WRITING CONNECTIONS ACROSS MULTIPLE SOURCES AND CURRICULA FACILITATES MEANING.

8 LITERACY FOR THE FUTURE MEANS LITERACY IN MULTIPLE TECHNOLOGIES.

9 EDUCATION MUST RESPOND TO SOCIETY'S DIVERSE POPULATION AND MUST SERVE ALL CHILDREN.

10 INTERACTIONS AMONG STUDENTS, TEACHERS, PARENTS, AND COMMUNITY FORM THE NETWORK THAT SUPPORTS LEARNING.

1993

- **Educational Testing Service** (ETS), begins to design formal assessment for Literacy Place.
- Scholastic introduces **WiggleWorks** Beginning Literacy System and SmartBooks — technology supported literacy programs.
- Scholastic **National Hispanic Advisory Board** convenes to create bilingual edition.
- **The Thursday Group**, 20 classroom teachers from the New York area, reviews the "teachability" of the program page by page.
- **Student review teams** review all selections.

1994

- **42 Mentors** from all walks of life (among them Donald Crews, Mae Jemison, Ben and Jerry, Tomie dePaola, Joanna Cole and Bruce Degen) agree to model real-life literacies.
- Harvard researcher confirms that **WiggleWorks significantly raises reading scores** among young children. WiggleWorks is adopted as the platform for primary technology.
- Authors and Teacher Advisors undertake **rigorous classroom testing** of Literacy Place.
- **Solares**, a program for reading and writing in Spanish is announced by Scholastic.

1995

- **800 editors, artists, illustrators** and photographers work with authors to complete program components.
- **Literacy Place adopted** in Oklahoma, South Carolina, Florida, and many major districts across the country.
- **California Literacy Leadership Retreat** conducted for supervisors and classroom teachers.
- Literacy Place **validation study** gets underway.

1996

- **Make *Your* School a Literacy Place!**

Authors

Linda Gambrell
Associate Dean for Faculty Development, College of Education; Professor and Principal Investigator, National Reading Research Center, University of Maryland.

Virginia Hamilton
The recipient of every major award and honor in her field, Virginia Hamilton is one of today's most distinguished writers for children and young adults.

Douglas K. Hartman
Associate Professor of Language and Literacy, University of Pittsburgh; Editorial Board of *The Reading Teacher* and the National Reading Conference's Yearbook.

Adria F. Klein
Professor of Reading and Teacher Education at California State University; Editor of Literacy Teaching and Learning; President-elect of the California Reading Association.

Kate Kirby-Linton
Instruction Coordinator, Student Assessment, Gwinnett County Public Schools, Georgia.

Hilda Medrano
Associate Professor, University of Texas — Pan American; Language Arts Consultant; Coordinator: Language, Literacy, and Culture —Accelerated Master's Degree Program for Today's Teachers.

Arlene Harris Mitchell
Dean for Academic Affairs; Head of the Division of Teacher Education at the University of Cincinnati.

Gay Su Pinnell
Professor, Department of Educational Theory and Practice, Ohio State University; Co-Director of the Ohio State Early Literacy Project.

D. Ray Reutzel
Recipient of the Karl G. Maeser Research Professorship and Department Chair of Elementary Education, Brigham Young University; Board of Directors, College Reading Association.

David Rose
Founder and Executive Director of the Center for Applied Special Technology (CAST); Educator and Clinical Psychologist; Lecturer, Harvard University Graduate School of Education.

Alfredo Schifini
Professor, Curriculum and Instruction, California State University, Los Angeles. National Curriculum Consultant for Guatemalan Ministry of Education.

Delores Stubblefield Seamster
Principal, N.W. Harley Elementary School, Dallas, TX; Recipient of the Dallas Independent School District Academic Excellence Award for Outstanding Student Achievement.

Quality Quinn Sharp
Author, Teacher-Educator; Launched Ready-Set-Go Program in the State of California; Author of ASSESSMENT: Charts and Checklists to Inform Instruction.

John Shefelbine
Associate Professor, Reading Education, California State University, Sacramento; Nationally recognized speaker on phonics and skill instruction.

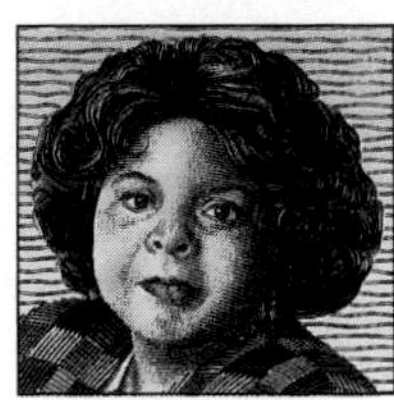

Gwendolyn Y. Turner
Associate Professor of Literacy Education, University of Missouri —St. Louis; Editorial Board, Reading Research and Instruction.

Wilma M. Wells
Assistant to the Superintendent for the University City School District, Missouri; Nationally recognized consultant on early childhood and family support programs.

Consultants

James Bauman
Skills, Strategies, Instruction
Professor, University of Georgia,
Athens, Georgia

James Cummins
Bilingual Education
Professor, Ontario Institute for Studies in Education
Ontario, Canada

Adele Fiderer
Assessment/Writing
Consultant and Educational Writer
Scarsdale, New York

Steve Graham
Handwriting
Professor, University of Maryland
College Park, Maryland

Shelley Harwayne
Writing
Director Manhattan New School
New York, New York

Richard E. Hodges
Spelling
Professor, University of Puget Sound
Tacoma, Washington

Jacqueline Kiraithe-Cordova
ESL/Foreign language Preparation
Professor, California State University
Fullerton, California

Priscilla Lynch
Literacy Author
Consultant,
Brick Township, New Jersey

Rae E. McKee
Instruction
1991 National Teacher of the Year
New York, New York

William E. Nagy
Vocabulary
Asst. Professor, University of Illinois
Champagne-Urbana, Illinois

Kim Quan Nguyen-Lam
Training Specialist Asian Languages
California State University
Long Beach, California

Robert Parker
ESL
Consultant,Brown University
Providence, Rhode Island

Cao Anh Quan
Second language Acquisition
ESOL Program Specialist
Tallahassee, Florida

Ronald Rohac
Sheltered Content Specialist
Training Specialist, California State University
Long Beach, California

Yvonne S. Runyan
Integrated language Arts
Associate Professor, University of Northern Colorado
Boulder, Colorado

Diane Snowball
Emergent Literacy
Consultant
New York, New York

Michael Strickland
Writing
Author, Consultant
Orange, New Jersey

Phyllis I. Ziegler
ESL/Bilingual
Consultant
New York, New York

Teacher Reviewers

Kim Andrews
Fourth Grade Teacher
Baltimore, Maryland

Shirley Beard
Fourth Grade Teacher
El Paso, Texas

Barbara Bloom
Fifth Grade Teacher
Wall Lake, Iowa

Arnette Bolden
Sixth Grade Teacher
Memphis, Tennessee

Martha Carter
Reading Curriculum Specialist
Milwaukee, Wisconsin

Marianne Chorba
Fourth Grade Teacher
Baltimore, Maryland

Peggy Colley
Third Grade Teacher
Rocky Face, Georgia

Mary Cool
Fifth Grade Teacher
Deltona, Florida

Carol Curry
Third Grade Teacher
Tallahassee, Florida

Claire Dale
First Grade Teacher
National City, California

Renee Dale
First Grade Teacher
Santa Clarita, California

Mildred DeStefano
First Grade Teacher
Brooklyn, New York

Diana Doyle
Sixth Grade Teacher
North Haven, Connecticut

Ethel Durham
Third Grade Teacher
Grand Rapids, Michigan

Oneaster Drummer
First Grade Teacher
Cincinnati, Ohio

Meryl R. Egers
Fifth Grade Teacher
New York, New York

Maxine Erlanger
K–3 Teacher
Nanuet, New York

Patty Ernst
Second Grade Teacher
Naples, New York

Alzada Fowler
First Grade Teacher
Lake Helen, Florida

Carmen Fulford
Fifth & Sixth Grade Teacher
Brooklyn, New York

Peggy Gilbert
Third Grade Teacher
Dallas, Texas

Jane Ginn
First Grade Teacher
Rohnert Park, California

Kathleen Code Gomez
Principal
Milwaukee, Wisconsin

Amy Gordon
Third Grade Teacher
New City, New York

Janet Gray
Fourth Grade Teacher
Lake Helen, Florida

Velma Gunn
Second Grade Teacher
New Rochelle, New York

Dalia Hale
Sixth Grade Teacher
Wichita, Kansas

Annie Ruth Harris
Third Grade Teacher
Decatur, Alabama

Barbara Ann Hawkins
Second Grade Teacher
Hamer, South Carolina

Deborah Hayes
Sixth Grade Teacher
Ripon, California

Lois Henderson
Pre K–3 Teacher
New York, New York

Anna Higley
Fifth Grade Teacher
Bostic, North Carolina

Amy Hom
Second Grade Teacher
New York, New York

Min Hong
First Grade Teacher
Brooklyn, New York

Susan Howe
Third Grade Teacher
Ellicott City, Maryland

Barbara Jansz
First Grade Teacher
Naperville, Illinois

Michele Jessen
First Grade Teacher
El Paso, Texas

Ellen W. Johnson
Second Grade Teacher
Chalfont, Pennsylvania

Vera Johnson
First Grade Teacher
Uniondale, New York

Carol Kaiser
Third Grade Teacher
Los Angeles, California

Judy Keyak
Second Grade Teacher
St. Petersburg, Florida

Karen Kolsky
Third Grade Teacher
Philadelphia, Pennsylvania

Jacqueline Krass
Second Grade Teacher
Gulfport, Mississippi

Linda Le Fever
Fifth Grade Teacher
Roanoke, Virginia

Warren Livesley
Fourth Grade Teacher
New York, New York

Dora I. Magana
Fourth Grade Teacher
El Paso, Texas

Tim Mason
Second Grade Teacher
Willington, Florida

Terri McBride
Sixth Grade Teacher
Laurel, Mississippi

Jacqi McGarry
Second Grade Teacher
Brooklyn, New York

Carol Mercer
Fourth Grade Teacher
National City, California

Rebecca Mills
Sixth Grade Teacher
Spotsylvania, Virginia

Martha Niederhauser
Fifth Grade Teacher
Salt Lake City, Utah

Carol Ochs
Fifth Grade Teacher
Noble, Oklahoma

Cynthia Orange
Second Grade Teacher
Bronx, New York

Sue Panek
Fourth Grade Teacher
Hawthorne, New Jersey

Arturo Perez
Second Grade Teacher
Ventura, California

Barbara Pinto
First Grade Teacher
New York, New York

Jeanette Reber
First Grade Teacher
Rock Hill, South Carolina

Charlene Richardson
Fourth Grade Teacher
Everett, Washington

Daria Rigney
Fifth Grade Teacher
Brooklyn, New York

Linda Roberts
Multi-Grade Teacher
Tulsa, Oklahoma

Andrea Ruff
First Grade Teacher
Brooklyn, New York

Andrea Sherman
Fourth Grade Teacher
Scarsdale, New York

Barbara Solomon
Second Grade Teacher
Hempstead, New York

Elaine Steinberg
Third Grade Teacher
Fresh Meadows, New York

Bobby Stern
Third Grade Teacher
Winston-Salem, North Carolina

Laura Stewart
First Grade Teacher
Logan, Utah

Kate Taylor
Fifth Grade Teacher
Baltimore, Maryland

Marisa Terry
Kindergarten Teacher
Freehold, New Jersey

Patricia Terry
Language Arts Consultant
Cincinnati, Ohio

Vasilika Terss
Second Grade Teacher
St. Louis, Missouri

Arthur Thau
Sixth Grade Teacher
Brooklyn, New York

Linda Thorn
Fifth Grade Teacher
Cranford, New Jersey

Jerry Trotter
Fifth Grade Teacher
Chicago, Illinois

Julia Tucker
First Grade Teacher
Hampton, Virginia

Patricia Viales
First Grade Teacher
Salinas, California

Janielle Wagstaff
Second Grade Teacher
Salt Lake City, Utah

Gail Weber
Fourth Grade Teacher
Sherman Oaks, California

Elizabeth White
First Grade Teacher
Bronx, New York

Robin Williams
Resource Teacher
Roosevelt Island, New York

The components that make *your* school a Literacy Place!

For information about **Solares,** *a program for reading and language arts in Spanish, ask your Scholastic Representative.*

PERSONAL VOICE	PROBLEM SOLVING	TEAMWORK	CREATIVE EXPRESSION	MANAGING INFORMATION	COMMUNITY INVOLVEMENT

	Snapshots	Super Solvers	Lights! Camera! Action!	Story Studio	Animal World	Lend a Hand
Suggested Core Components						
Literacy SourceBook Unit Anthology	●	●	●	●	●	●
Two-Volume SourceBook (Option)	▬	▬	▬	▬	▬	▬
Teacher Edition SourceBook	●	●	●	●	●	●
Literacy-at-Work Book	●	●	●	●	●	●
Meet-the-Mentor Video	●	●	●	●	●	●
Trade Books	● ● ●	● ● ●	● ● ●	● ● ●	● ● ●	● ● ●
Big Books	●	●	●	●	●	●
Read Alouds	● ●	● ●	● ●	● ●	● ●	● ●
Workshop Cards	● ●	● ●	● ●	● ●	● ●	● ●
Project Cards	●	●	●	●	●	●
Vocabulary Cards	▬	▬	▬	▬	▬	▬
Big Book of Rhymes and Rhythms	▬	▬	▬	▬	▬	▬
Big Books Sentence Strip Set	▬	▬	▬	▬	▬	▬
Trade Book Guides	● ● ●	● ● ●	● ● ●	● ● ●	● ● ●	● ● ●
Support Materials						
Integrated Language Arts Practice Books:						
Spelling	▬	▬	▬	▬	▬	▬
Grammar, Usage, & Mechanics	▬	▬	▬	▬	▬	▬
Handwriting	▬	▬	▬	▬	▬	▬
Literacy-at-Work Book ATE	●	●	●	●	●	●
Assessment Kit:						
Assessment Handbook	▬	▬	▬	▬	▬	▬
End-of-Unit/End-of-Year Tests	●	●	●	●	●	●
Benchmark Books	▬	▬	▬	▬	▬	▬
Teacher's Test Manual	▬	▬	▬	▬	▬	▬
Management System on CD-ROM	▬	▬	▬	▬	▬	▬
Teacher Resource Kit Practice Masters on Disk	▬	▬	▬	▬	▬	▬
Transparency Set	●	●	●	●	●	●
Charts Set	▬	▬	▬	▬	▬	▬
Multiple Language Translation Kit	▬	▬	▬	▬	▬	▬
Technology for Students						
WiggleWorks™ Plus CD-ROMs	●	●	●	●	●	●
Meet-the-Mentor Video	●	●	●	●	●	●
Listening Center Audiocassettes	● ●	● ●	● ●	● ●	● ●	● ●
Big Book Audiocassette	●	●	●	●	●	●
Trade Book Audiocassette	●	●	●	●	●	●
Support for Beginning Readers						
ShoeBox Leveled Libraries	▬	▬	▬	▬	▬	▬
Big Books and Little Books	●	●	●	●	●	●
Fluency Library	▬	▬	▬	▬	▬	▬
Phonics Readers	▬	▬	▬	▬	▬	▬
Phonics kit						
My ABC Chart	▬	▬	▬	▬	▬	▬
ABC Cards	▬	▬	▬	▬	▬	▬
Sounds of Phonics Audiocassette	●	●	●	●	●	●
High-Frequency Word Cards	▬	▬	▬	▬	▬	▬
Word Frame	▬	▬	▬	▬	▬	▬
My Books	▬	▬	▬	▬	▬	▬
Word Building Kit:						
Pocket Alphabet Cards	▬	▬	▬	▬	▬	▬
Sound Cards	▬	▬	▬	▬	▬	▬
Phonogram Cards	▬	▬	▬	▬	▬	▬
Magnetic Letters	▬	▬	▬	▬	▬	▬
Pocket Chart	▬	▬	▬	▬	▬	▬

Each ● represents the number of components in each unit. Each ▬ represents one component for multiple units.
*Developed for Literacy Place by Educational Testing Service (ETS), creators of the National Assessment of Educational Progress (NAEP)

SNAPSHOTS

Our actions tell about us.

Teacher's SourceBook

Literacy Place Authors

Linda Gambrell
Associate Dean for Faculty Development, College of Education; Professor and Principal Investigator, National Reading Research Center, University of Maryland

Virginia Hamilton
Children's Author, Winner of the Newbery Medal, the Coretta Scott King Award, and the Laura Ingalls Wilder Lifetime Achievement Award

Douglas K. Hartman
Associate Professor of Language and Literacy, University of Pittsburgh; Editorial Board of the *Reading Teacher* and the National Reading Conference's Yearbook

Kate Kirby-Linton
Instruction Coordinator, Student Assessment, Gwinnett County Public Schools, Georgia

Adria Klein
Professor of Reading and Teacher Education at California State University; Editor of *Literacy Teaching and Learning;* President-elect of the California Reading Association

Hilda Medrano
Associate Professor, University of Texas—Pan American; Language Arts Consultant; Coordinator: Language, Literacy, and Culture—Accelerated Master's Degree Program for Today's Teachers

Arlene Harris Mitchell
Associate Professor of Literacy and English Education; Head of the Division of Teacher Education at the University of Cincinnati

Gay Su Pinnell
Professor, Department of Educational Theory and Practice, Ohio State University; Co-Director of the Ohio State Early Literacy Project

D. Ray Reutzel
Recipient of the Karl G. Maeser Research Professorship and Department Chair of Elementary Education, Brigham Young University; Board of Directors, College Reading Association

David Rose
Founder and Executive Director of the Center for Applied Special Technology (CAST); Educator and Clinical Psychologist; Lecturer, Harvard University Graduate School of Education

Alfredo Schifini
Associate Professor, School of Education, Division of Curriculum Instruction, California State University, Los Angeles

Delores Stubblefield Seamster
Principal, Phyllis Wheatley Elementary School, Texas; Recipient of the Dallas Independent School District Academic Excellence Award for Outstanding Student Achievement

Quality Quinn Sharp
Author, Teacher-Educator; Launched Ready-Set-Go Program in the State of California; Author of *Assessment: Charts and Checklists to Inform Instruction*

John Shefelbine
Associate Professor, Reading Education, California State University, Sacramento

Gwendolyn Y. Turner
Associate Professor of Literacy Education, University of Missouri, St. Louis; Editorial Board, *Reading Research and Instruction*

Wilma M. Wells
Assistant to the Superintendent for the University City School District, Missouri; Nationally Recognized Consultant on Early Childhood and Family Support Programs

 Published by Scholastic Inc. Printed in the U.S.A.

ISBN 0-590-90646-1

2 3 4 5 6 7 8 9 10 14 03 02 01 00 99 98 97 96

TABLE OF CONTENTS

PERSONAL VOICE

SNAPSHOTS

What's in Front?

TRADE BOOKS

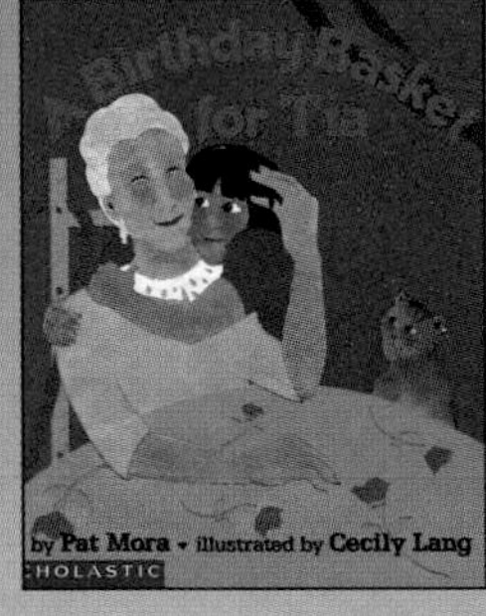

What's Behind the Tab?

1 SECTION

CLOSE-UPS

Subconcept: *We find out what we like to do.*

2

SECTION

TALENT SHOW

Subconcept: *We find out what we can do well.*

3

SECTION

MAKE YOUR MARK

Subconcept: *When we try our best, we find out how much we can do.*

UNIT AT A GLANCE

UNIT TRADE BOOKS
- *Chester's Way*
- *A Birthday Basket for Tía*
- *Frog and Toad Are Frier*

UNIT CONCEPT: Our actions tell about us.

	READING	WRITING AND LANGUAGE ARTS		
	Reading Experiences	Writing	Listening, Speaking, and Presenting	Viewing
SUBCONCEPT 1: CLOSE-UPS: We find out what we like to do.				
PLAN I 3-5 Days • **Meet the Mentor Video: Photographer Bruce Thorson** • **"Top Ten"** (pp.T16–21) • ***"A, My Name Is Alice"*** (pp.T22–23)	• Survey • Street Rhyme	✔**WRITING EVENT:** ✱ Write a Survey (Informative) **Writing:** Create Game Directions	• **Speaking/Listening:** Play a Memory Game • **Street Rhyme** MINI-LESSON • **Reading/Speaking/Listening:** Share a Biography	• **Meet the Mentor Video:** Photographer Bruce Thorson • **Set a Purpose for Viewing** MINI-LESSON
PLAN II 3-5 Days • **Big Book:** ***Max Found Two Sticks*** • ***Ronald Morgan Goes to Bat*** (pp.T50–73) • **"Baseball Greats"** (pp.T74–75)	• Realistic Fiction • Realistic Fiction • Baseball Cards	**Writing:** ✱ Create a Sports Poster ✔**WRITING EVENT:** Write ✱ a Trading Card (Informative)	• **Listening/Speaking/Viewing:** Listen to a Sports Broadcast **Speaking/Listening:** Be a Sports Announcer • **Reading:** Dramatize the Story • **Active Listening** MINI-LESSON • **Oral Expression** MINI-LESSON • **Listening Center:** *Max Found Two Sticks*	
WORKSHOP 1: 1 Day How to Make a Trading Card (pp.T93–97)	• Trading Cards	**Trading Cards** ✱		
SUBCONCEPT 2: TALENT SHOW: We find out what we can do well.				
PLAN III 3-5 Days • **Read Aloud:** ***Stellaluna*** • ***Ruby the Copycat*** ✱ (pp.T110–137) • **"I Can" from *Pass It On*** (pp.T138–139)	• Fantasy • Humorous Fiction/ WiggleWorks Plus: Interactive Reading • Poem	• **Write Directions** MINI-LESSON ✔**WRITING EVENT:** ✱ Write a Poem (Descriptive)	• **Speaking/Listening:** Contribute to Angela's Journal • **Listening/Reading/Speaking:** Perform a Puppet Play • **Reading/Writing/Listening:** Create a Dance ✱ • **Listening Center:** *Ruby the Copycat*	• **Visualize** MINI-LESSON • **Writing/Viewing/Vocabulary:** Draw Describing Words • **Illustrator's Craft:** Humor VISUAL LITERACY
PLAN IV 3-5 Days • ***Louanne Pig in Making the Team*** (pp.T166–183) • **MENTOR: Photographer Bruce Thorson** (pp.T184–187)	• Fantasy • Article	✔**WRITING EVENT:** ✱ Write a Real-Life Story (Narrative) • **Writing:** Write a Friendly Letter • **Friendly Letter** MINI-LESSON	• **Reading/Speaking:** Role-Playing Good Friends • **Reading/Writing/Speaking:** Ask the Pros ✱ • **Listening/Speaking:** Create Cheers • **Listen Critically** MINI-LESSON • **Rhythm and Rhyme** MINI-LESSON	
WORKSHOP 2: 1 Day How to Make a Graph (pp.T205–209)	• Graph	• **Graph** ✱		
SUBCONCEPT 3: MAKE YOUR MARK: When we try our best, we find out how much we can do.				
PLAN V 3-5 Days • **Big Book:** ***Max Found Two Sticks*** • ***George Ancona: Then & Now*** ✱ (pp.T222–237)	• Realistic Fiction • Nonfiction/ WiggleWorks Plus: Interactive Reading	• **Writing/Viewing:** Be a Photographer • **Captions** MINI-LESSON ✔**WRITING EVENT:** Write a ✱ Photo Essay (Narrative) • **Writing/Viewing:** Picture This!	• **Reading/Writing/Speaking:** ✱ Talk About Good Times • **Speaking/Listening:** Life Stories Game • **Listening Center:** *George Ancona: Then & Now*	• **Recognize Feelings** MINI-LESSON
PLAN VI 3-5 Days • **Read Aloud:** ***Thunder Cake*** • ***Amazing Grace*** (pp.T264–283) • **"An Amazing Peter Pan"** (pp.T284–285)	• Historic Fiction • Realistic Fiction • Article	• **Writing/Speaking:** Write a Book Report • **Book Titles** MINI-LESSON ✔**WRITING PROCESS WORKSHOP:** ✱ Write About a Story Character (Descriptive) ✔ Unit Test	• **Writing/Speaking:** ✱ Write and Perform a Script • **Oral Expression** MINI-LESSON	• **Picture Clues** MINI-LESSON • **Writing:** Make a Play Poster or Program VISUAL LITERACY • **Listening/Viewing:** Watch a Video of *Peter Pan*
PROJECT: 1-3 Days How to Make an Exhibit (pp.T303–309)	• Exhibit	• **Descriptive Labels** ✱	• **Presentation Skill:** Show and Tell	

✔ = Assessed = Key Strategy = ✱ = WiggleWorks Plus™

UNIT FLUENCY READERS

•Monkey See, Monkey Do *•Two Crazy Pigs*
•The Bunny Hop

Snapshots

SKILLS AND STRATEGIES				INTEGRATING LEARNING	
Comprehension/ Thinking and Literary Elements	**Phonics, Spelling, and Word Skills**	**Grammar, Usage, and Mechanics**	**Study Skills**	**Integrated Curriculum**	**Strand Focus: Personal Voice**
✔ **Summarize** ✔Unit Test • **Nonfiction** MINI-LESSON • **Survey** MINI-LESSON	✔**Spelling:** Words With *r*-Blends ✔**Phonics:** ✱ Vowel /e/*e* ✔**Phonics:** ✱ *r*-Blends	✔**Grammar:** Question Sentences ✔Unit Test • **Mechanics:** Question Marks • **Nouns** MINI-LESSON	• **Viewing/ Writing:** Use a Map	• **MATH:** Class Favorites • **SCIENCE:** Have a Ball • **SOCIAL STUDIES:** Choose Your Favorite Place • **THE ARTS:** Illustrate Numbers	• **MATH/SOCIAL STUDIES:** Survey Another Class
✔ **Character** ✔Unit Test • **Sports Jargon** MINI-LESSON • **Evaluate Author's Purpose** MINI-LESSON • **Baseball Card** MINI-LESSON	✔**Spelling:** Words with *s*-Blends ✔**Phonics:** ✱ Vowels /a/*a*, /i/*i* ✔**Phonics:** ✱ *s*-Blends	✔**Grammar:** Naming Places ✔Unit Test ✔**Mechanics:** Commas ✔Unit Test • **Action Verbs** MINI-LESSON		• **MATH:** Chart a Relay Race • **SCIENCE:** Explore Motion • **SOCIAL STUDIES:** Make a Sports Scrapbook • **THE ARTS:** Show the Path of a Ball	• **MATH:** Tickets, Hot Dogs, and Popcorn
			✔**Lists** ✔Unit Test		
✔ **Make Predictions** ✔Unit Test • **Problem/Solution** MINI-LESSON • **Humorous Fiction** MINI-LESSON • **Poem:** Varying Text Size MINI-LESSON • **Character** MINI-LESSON	✔**Spelling:** Words With *ch, th,* and *sh* ✔**Phonics:** ✱ Vowels /o/*o*, /u/*u* ✔**Phonics:** ✱ Digraphs	✔**Grammar:** Action Words ✔Unit Test • **Mechanics** Capitalizing Pronoun *I*		• **MATH:** Copy Ruby the Copycat • **SCIENCE:** Copycats in Nature • **SOCIAL STUDIES:** Choose a Role Model • **THE ARTS:** Copycat Art	• **THE ARTS:** Copy This!
✔ **Plot** ✔Unit Test • **Compare/Contrast** MINI-LESSON • **Fantasy** MINI-LESSON	✔**Spelling:** Words With Long *a, i* ✔**Phonics:** ✱ 3-Letter Blends ✔**Phonics:** Final *e* ✱ • **Word Study:** Idioms	• **Grammar:** Simple Sentences • **Mechanics:** Capitalizing First Word	✔**Article** MINI-LESSON	• **MATH:** Keep Score • **SCIENCE:** Measure Your Heartbeat • **SOCIAL STUDIES:** Teamwork • **THE ARTS:** Create a Pennant	• **SOCIAL STUDIES:** I'd Like to Be a…
			✔**Graphs** ✔Unit Test		
Main Idea/Details • **Autobiography** MINI-LESSON	✔**Spelling:** Words With Soft *c, g* ✔**Context Clues:** Specialized Vocabulary ✔Unit Test ✔**Phonics:** ✱ Soft /s/*c*, /j/*g*	✔**Grammar:** Action Words: Past Time ✔Unit Test • **Mechanics:** Capitalizing Place Names		• **MATH:** Measure a Group Photo • **SCIENCE:** Make Sun Prints • **SOCIAL STUDIES:** Create a Travel Brochure • **THE ARTS:** Make Prints From Rubbings	
Theme • **Setting** MINI-LESSON • **Visualize** MINI-LESSON • **Theater Program** MINI-LESSON	✔**Spelling:** Words With Final *e* • **Phonics:** ✱ *l*-Blends	✔**Grammar:** Describing Words ✔Unit Test • **Mechanics:** Periods		• **MATH:** Estimate Space for a Play • **SCIENCE:** How Does Peter Pan Fly? • **SOCIAL STUDIES:** Outfit a Character • **THE ARTS:** Create a Set Design	

SETTING UP THE PLACE

Why a Sports Arena?

"I try to find the moment that best shows what the person or activity is about."

Unit Mentor: Bruce Thorson

CREATE A WORKPLACE MODEL

Your children can explore the world of sports through cooperative, hands-on activities. The picture demonstrates how a simple setup can transform a corner of your classroom into a Sports Arena. A workplace learning center is an ideal framework for introducing and reinforcing communication skills, because it offers a variety of options for individual and group activities.

◀ Have children take turns creating a bulletin board display with pictures and words about their favorite game or sport.

▼ Fill a box with paper and other materials for making tickets or programs. If possible, include seating charts, floor plans, or souvenir programs from real sports arenas.

Also for use with this plan

Literacy at Home — **Connect families to the school.**

◀ Start a sports facts file. Write an interesting fact about a sport or an athlete on an index card and illustrate it. Provide a pile of old magazines that can be cut up for pictures to prompt children to make their own fact cards to add to the file.

◀ Old sports magazines, equipment catalogs, and sports sections from the local newspaper can be the basis for a Sports Arena archive. Children can read files that you begin or start their own folders with information on topics that interest them.

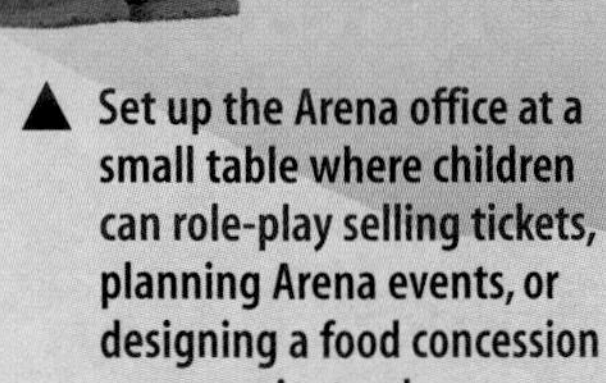

▲ Set up the Arena office at a small table where children can role-play selling tickets, planning Arena events, or designing a food concession or souvenir stand.

▼ Help children take the initiative in organizing their learning center by posting a list of simple communication tasks; for instance: "Make a sign that shows when the ticket office is open."

▼ Inspire children to voice their opinions about the SourceBook readings and to follow their interests by posting thought-provoking questions or challenging tasks.

▼ Encourage children to use a calendar to schedule use of the learning center and to highlight special events or announce big games.

◀ Use PlaceMaker to make banners, calendars, and posters to organize the Sports Arena.

◀ *Catch, ball, goal...* Write down words children use when they talk about sports and post a list they can add to and use in their individual writing projects.

▼ Library books about sports, athletes, and games can form the core for a Sports Arena library. If possible, include copies of sports magazines. Encourage children to add their own handmade books to the shelf.

SPORTS EQUIPMENT

◀ Have children decorate a cardboard box in which they can store sports equipment appropriate to a classroom, such as sponge balls, small weights, and a stopwatch.

Training Area

◀ Children can meet in the training area to time their heartbeats or teach each other exercises. It can also be a place for cooperative groups to gather and listen to one another's plans and projects.

BEGINNING THE UNIT

BASELINE ASSESSMENT

The Baseline Assessment helps you determine the conceptual level at which each child starts the unit. By repeating the assessment task at the end of the unit, you and the children can better understand the progress they have made in grasping and applying the concept that each of us has a unique set of inner resources.

Have children bring pictures of themselves to class. In small groups (three or four children), have them show their photos to each other and explain what they are doing in the photo. Have them write about what they are doing in the photo and save these descriptions to use for comparison at the end of the unit.

K-W-L

Start a K-W-L chart that you will return to at the end of the unit. Ask children the following questions to help them better understand what they know and what they want to know.

- **What are you doing in the photo?**
- **What would you like to have a picture of yourself doing? Why?**

What Do We Know?	What Do We Want to Know?	What Did We Learn?

INTRODUCE THE SOURCEBOOK

While children are looking at the title page of the SourceBook, ask: What information about a book can you find on its title page?

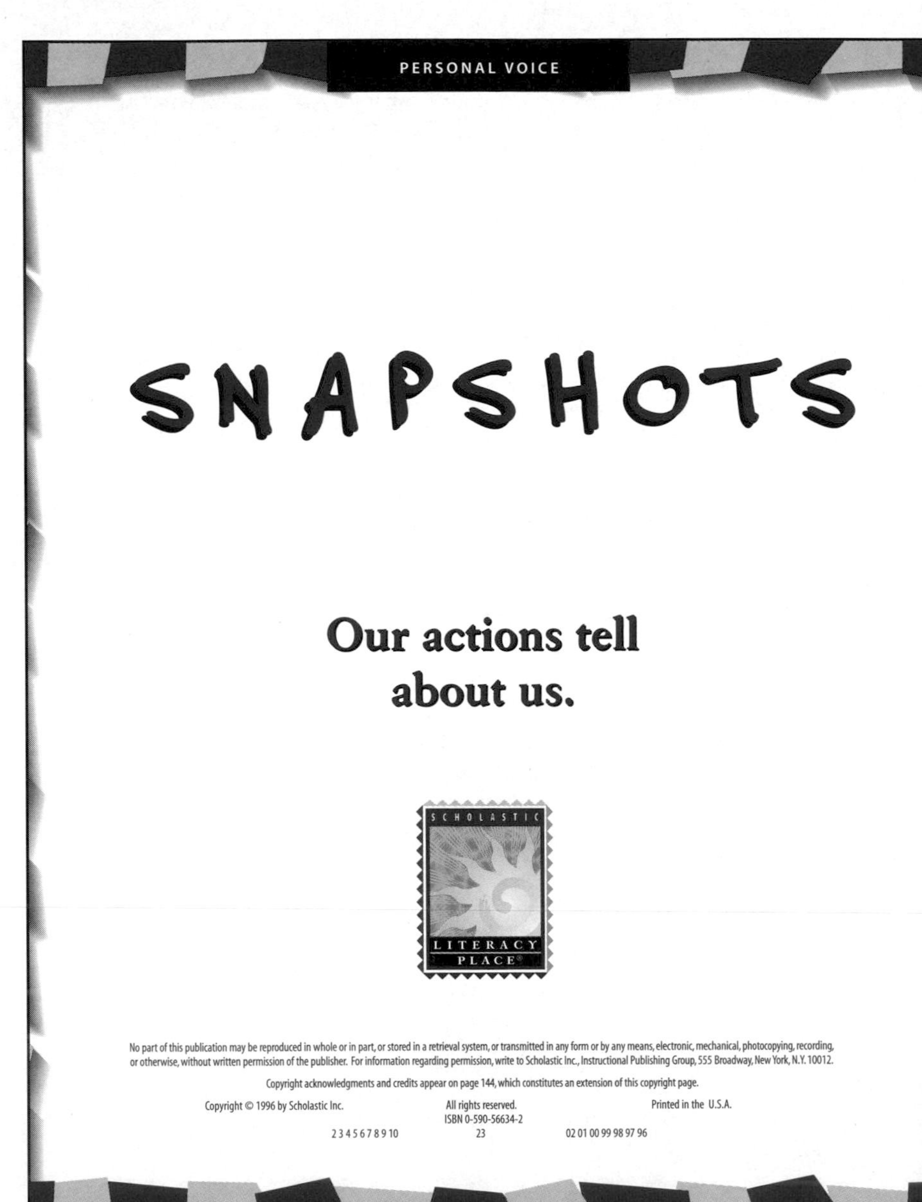
PERSONAL VOICE

SNAPSHOTS

Our actions tell about us.

Copyright acknowledgments and credits appear on page 144, which constitutes an extension of this copyright page.

Printed in the U.S.A.
ISBN 0-590-56634-2
2 3 4 5 6 7 8 9 10 23 02 01 00 99 98 97 96

▼ Children will visit a sports arena in this unit. Do they know how sports photographers choose what to take a picture of and when to take it? What would children like to learn about the process? You can add their response to the K-W-L chart.

▲ Ask a volunteer to read the Unit Concept aloud. Ask children to discuss some of their favorite activities and what their choices say about them. What might they learn about understanding themselves and others?

SourceBook Table of Contents

Preview

Ask children to preview the Table of Contents on these pages. Can they predict what "Top Ten" will be about? What are some of their favorite extracurricular activities?

TABLE OF CONTENTS

SECTION 1

Close-ups

We find out what we like to do.

SECTION 2

Talent Show

We find out what we can do well.

▲ "Top Ten" informs children about their peers' ten favorite extracurricular activities and teaches about opinion polls at the same time.

▲ In *Ruby the Copycat*, Ruby and readers learn that being oneself is not a compromise but a contribution.

▲ Meet Mentor Bruce Thorson. He's a photographer for a newspaper in Oregon. What can we learn about him from the pictures he has taken?

▼ *Frog and Toad Are Friends* is a story of two amphibians who couldn't be closer friends yet couldn't be more distinct in personality, likes, and dislikes.

SECTION 3

Make Your Mark

When we try our best, we find out how much we can do.

Trade Books

The following books accompany this *Snapshots* SourceBook.

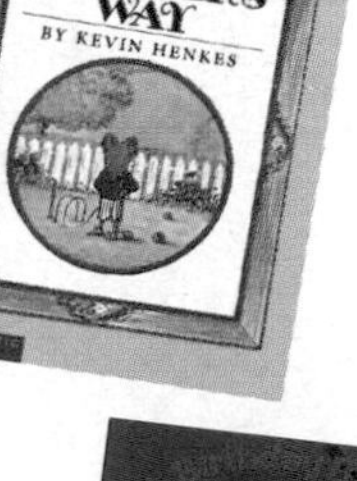

Fantasy
Chester's Way
by Kevin Henkes

Fantasy
Frog and Toad Are Friends Caldecott Honor
by Arnold Lobel

Realistic Fiction
A Birthday Basket for Tía
by Pat Mora
illustrated by Cecily Lang

Big Book

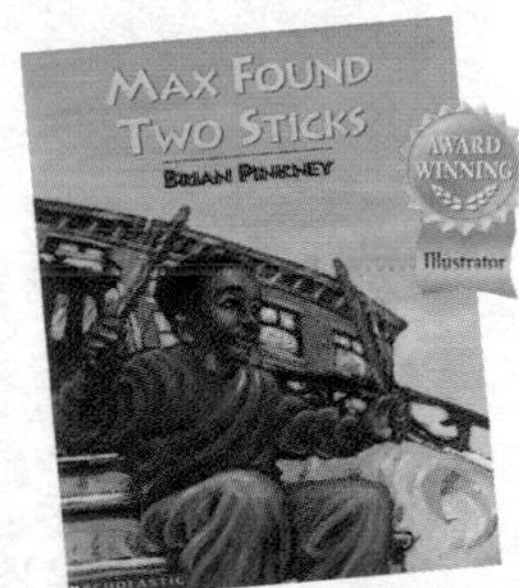

Realistic Fiction
Max Found Two Sticks
by Brian Pinkney

▲ In *Amazing Grace* a young girl finds out that she can be anything she wants when she plays the part of Peter Pan in a school play, even though her friends think she can't.

▲ *A Birthday Basket for Tía* is a story of a young girl who, by gathering personally meaningful possessions to give her aunt, gives herself as a birthday present.

1 SECTION

We find out what we like to do.

Close-Ups

Find out what other kids like to do.

•

Read about a boy who loves baseball.

•

Then meet two real-life baseball players.

BLUE

WHAT'S IN THIS SECTION?

Plan I

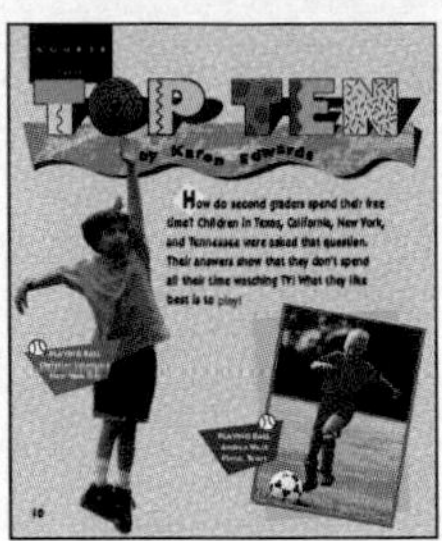

▲ "Top Ten"
by Karen Edwards
Survey

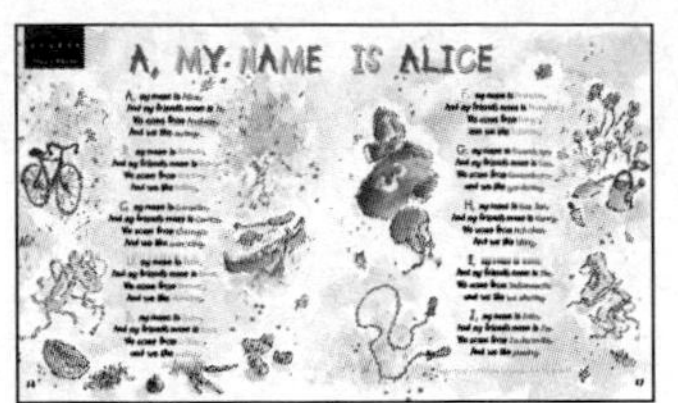

▲ "A, My Name Is Alice"
Street Rhyme

Plan II

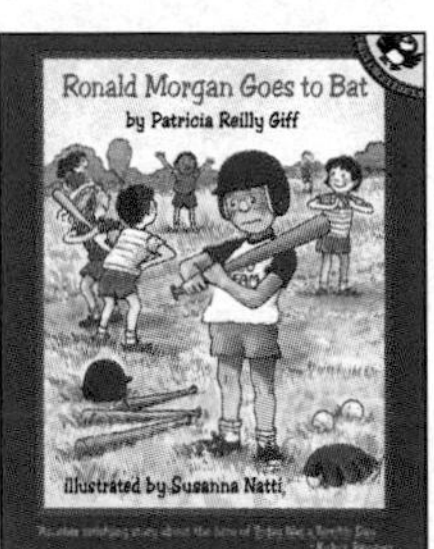

▲ *Ronald Morgan Goes to Bat*
by Patricia Reilly Giff
Realistic Fiction

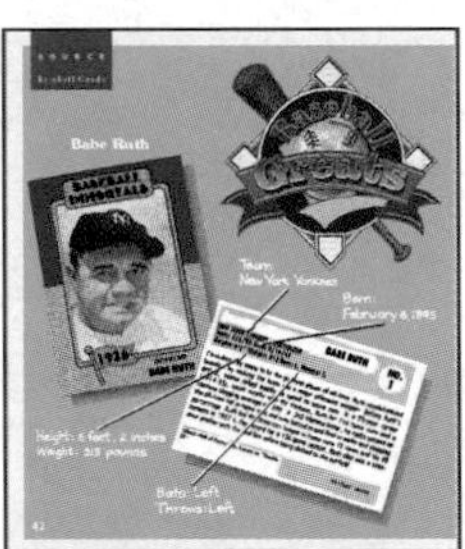

▲ "Baseball Greats"
Baseball Cards

Workshop 1

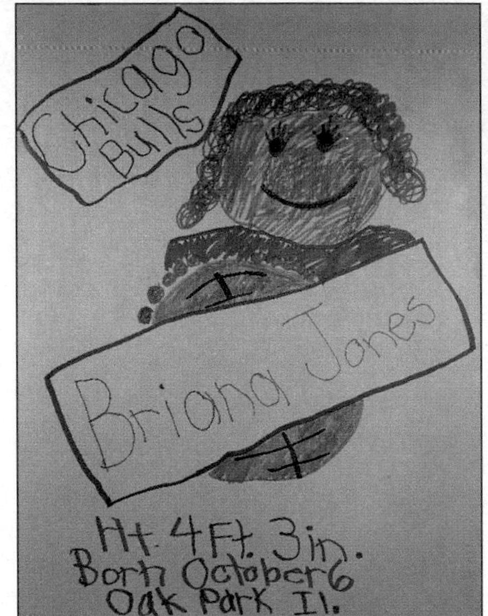

How to Make a Trading Card

Children will make trading cards featuring themselves that are loosely based on the examples in "Baseball Greats."

Connect to Home and Community

Ask children if they can think of anything that they like to do now but didn't think they'd enjoy before they tried it. Why didn't they expect to like it? What made them change their minds?

Invite children to ask a person in their family or neighborhood about an experience they had trying something that they at first thought they would not like. Suggest that children write down what they are told. Encourage them to try something new, like a new game, book, sport, or food. Ask them to write down their reactions to the new thing they tried. Have them share their reactions and the information they obtained from their family member or neighbor with the class.

PERSONAL VOICE

Plan I

WHAT CHILDREN WILL DO

view a video about photographer Bruce Thorson

read the selections

- "Top Ten" SURVEY
- "A, My Name Is Alice" STREET RHYME

use the key strategy of Summarize

blend words with /e/*e* and *r*-blends

write questions, survey classmates, and record results

apply what they learn about surveys to their own experiences

SOURCE

Survey

by Karen Edwards

How do second graders spend their free time? Children in Texas, California, New York, and Tennessee were asked that question. Their answers show that they don't spend all their time watching TV! What they like best is to play!

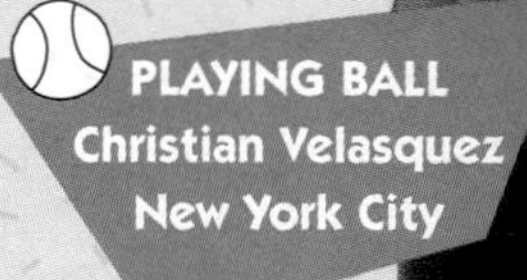

PLAYING BALL
Christian Velasquez
New York City

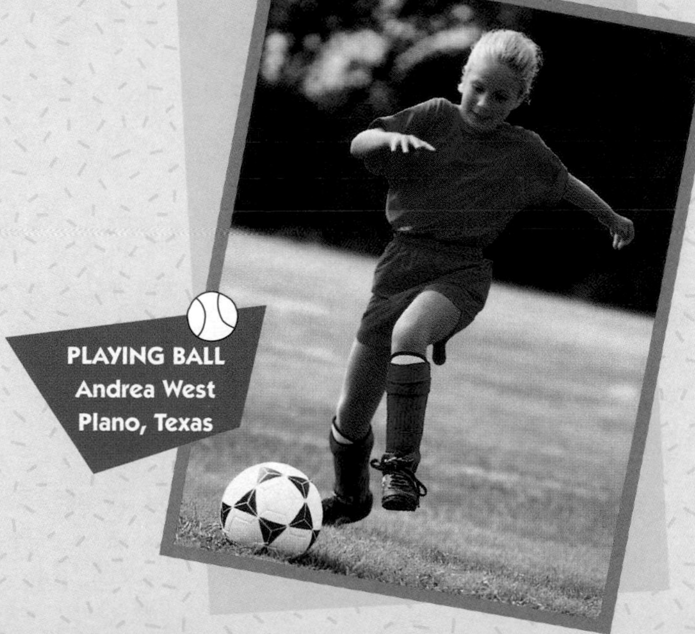

PLAYING BALL
Andrea West
Plano, Texas

Assessing Your Students

ASSESSMENT	TEACHER'S SOURCEBOOK	ASSESSMENT KIT
Vocabulary Test	T13	Assessment Handbook
Observation	T14	Assessment Handbook
Assess Reading	T24	Classroom Management Forms
Conference	T24	Assessment Handbook
Performance-Based	T27	Assessment Handbook
Writing Benchmarks	T27	Assessment Handbook
Spelling Tests	T13, T29	Assessment Handbook
Quickcheck	T32, T34 ,T36	Assessment Handbook
Formal Tests	T311	Unit/Year Tests

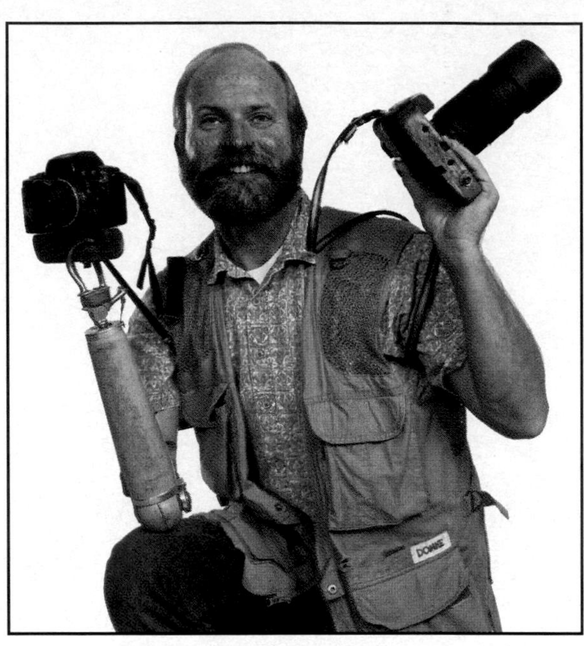

Creating a Community of Learners

Meet the Mentor: Bruce Thorson pp. T10–11

- Appreciate people's different interests
- Share ideas
- Pantomime actions
- Set a Purpose for Viewing MINI-LESSON

Demonstrating Independence

Using the Trade Books: pp. T38–39

- *Monkey See, Monkey Do* by Marc Gave
- *Chester's Way* by Kevin Henkes

Integrating Learning: p. T40

- Activity: Survey Another Class

Focus on Phonics

Phonics Lessons

- Vowel /e/*e*
- *r*-Blends

Phonics Kit

Literacy-at-Work Book

- Vowel /e/*e*, pp. 9–10
- *r*=Blends, pp. 11–12

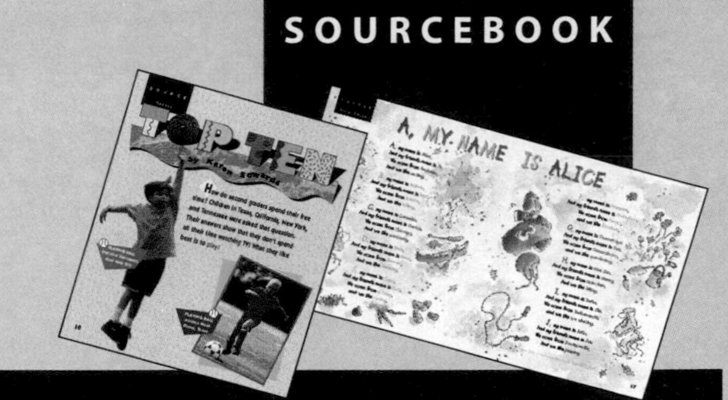

PLAN I ORGANIZER

"Top Ten" / "A, My Name Is Alice"

	Instructional Path	Supporting All Learners	Resources and Technology
a READING THE SOURCES pp. T12–25	**Build Background** ✔ **Develop Vocabulary** *• basketball • soccer • baseball • computer • crafts • activities* **Reading Selections** "Top Ten" "A, My Name Is Alice" 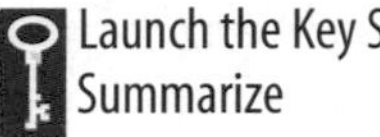 Launch the Key Strategy: Summarize ✔ **Assess Reading**	 EXTRA HELP p. T13 ESL pp. T13, T16, T22 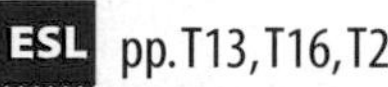 CHALLENGE p. T21  ACCESS p. T13 MINI-LESSON Nonfiction, p. T17 Survey, p. T20 Street Rhyme, p. T23 **Idea File:** p. T25 **Cultural Connections:** pp. T22, T25	**Transparency** Build Background, 1 **Literacy-at-Work Book** Vocabulary, p. 3 Comprehension Check, p. 4  **WiggleWorks™ Plus,** pp. T17, T19, T21  **Scholastic Network** p. T12 **Additional Technology:** p. T24
b INTEGRATING LANGUAGE ARTS pp. T26–31	✔ **Writing:** Write a Survey Daily Language Practice ✔ **Grammar:** Question Sentences **Mechanics:** Question Marks ✔ **Spelling:** Words With *r*-Blends *• grass • graph • grab • bring • brick • truck • trip • trick*	ESL pp. T27, T30  CHALLENGE p. T27  ACCESS p. T27 **Activity File:** pp. T30–31 Use a Map Play a Memory Game Share a Bibliography Create Game Directions MINI-LESSON Nouns, p. T30	**Literacy-at-Work Book** Writing, p. 5 **Grammar, Usage, and Mechanics Practice:** pp. 1–2 **Spelling Practice:** p. 1 **Handwriting Practice:** p. 1  **WiggleWorks™ Plus,** p. T27
 **c BUILDING SKILLS AND STRATEGIES** pp. T32–37	✔ Quickcheck ✔  Key Strategy: Summarize ✔ Quickcheck Phonics: Vowel /e/*e* ✔ Quickcheck Phonics: *r*-Blends	 EXTRA HELP pp. T33, T35 ESL p. T33  CHALLENGE pp. T35, T37  ACCESS p. T37	**Transparency** Key Strategy, 2 **Literacy-at-Work Book** Summarize, pp. 6–8 Phonics, pp. 9–12  **WiggleWorks™ Plus,** pp. T35, T37

✔ = **Assessed**

CREATING A COMMUNITY OF LEARNERS

MEET THE MENTOR

Objectives

Children learn to:

- appreciate people's different interests
- share ideas
- set a purpose for viewing
- pantomime actions

Meet the Mentor Video: *Photographer: Bruce Thorson* Video running time: 5:43 minutes
Time: About 30 minutes
Suggested Grouping: Whole class

Technology Options

Use the SourceBook Activities writing area to help children work through the mini-lesson. Children can write the steps on the computer, then add their own illustrations that show or give examples of the steps.

Photographer: Bruce Thorson

Get children involved in the **work** of **sports photographer** Bruce Thorson. The **video** will give children a close-up look at what a sports photographer does.

INTRODUCE THE VIDEO

Invite children to join Bruce Thorson for a close-up look at what a sports photographer's work is like. Show them the cover of the video and read the title. Encourage children who know something about what a sports photographer does to briefly share information.

- **A lot happens before a photograph appears on the sports page of a newspaper. What steps do you think a sports photographer follows to do his or her job?**

Set a Purpose for Viewing

Ask children to watch and listen for what they can learn about Bruce Thorson's job. Encourage them to jot down facts about what a sports photographer does as they watch the video. MINI-LESSON

VIEW THE VIDEO

Once you begin the video, you may wish to pause to ask questions such as these:

- **What have you learned about Bruce Thorson's job?**
- **What steps has he followed so far?**

Have children continue viewing, pausing at one or two more discussion points if you wish.

ESL Use the pause button, if you have one, to foster discussion of actions or events in the video. With the sound turned off, replay the video and ask volunteers to retell *Bruce Thorson*'s story. **(Video)**

Think About the Video

Engage children in a discussion about Bruce Thorson:

- **How would you describe Bruce Thorson to a friend?**
- **What do you like or not like about Bruce Thorson's work?**
- **What do you suppose Mr. Thorson means when he calls himself "an athlete with a camera"?**

Activity: Pantomime

Children can take turns pantomiming sports for volunteer sports photographers to catch the action. Other children can guess the sport. To get children started, pantomime a game or sport you enjoy. THE ARTS

Make Connections

To Children's Lives

Bruce Thorson is interested in sports and photography. Have children take a moment to think about their interests in sports or photography. They may want to share photos, such as team pictures or pictures of themselves engaged in other activities, for a display.

MINI-LESSON

Set a Purpose for Viewing

TEACH/MODEL Help children set a purpose for viewing the video.

THINK ALOUD This video shows and tells what Bruce Thorson does from the time he gets an assignment to when one of his photographs appears in the newspaper. As I watch the video, I'll keep track of his steps so I'll have a better idea of what his work is like.

APPLY Write on sentence strips the steps a sports photographer follows (talk, prepare camera, photograph, develop, choose, write, see in newspaper) and read them aloud. After children watch the video, invite them to explain each step and to put them in order. VISUAL LITERACY

READING THE SOURCES

TOP TEN / A, MY NAME IS ALICE

Build Background

In the video children learned about the special **activities** of a sports **photographer.** "Top Ten" describes special **interests** of **second graders** from various parts of the United States.

Objectives

Children learn to:

- relate personal experiences
- create a graph
- analyze information
- access prior knowledge to develop vocabulary
- expand oral language

Materials:
Transparency 1
Literacy-at-Work Book p. 3
Word Cards 1–6

Time:
About 30 minutes

Suggested Grouping:
Whole class

Literacy-at-Work Book, p. 3

Name VOCABULARY

What Do You Like to Do?

▶ Finish each sentence with a word from the box.

activities
baseball
basketball
computer
crafts
soccer

1. The new computer came in a box with a keyboard and a mouse.
2. To play basketball, you need a hoop.
3. There are scissors, yarn, and crayons in the crafts kit.
4. When you play baseball, don't forget your ball, bat, and glove.
5. The soccer coach showed us how to kick a goal.
6. After school there are lots of activities to choose from.

▶ Write one of the words from the box in a sentence of your own.

Unit 1 • Snapshots • Plan I • Top Ten 3

ACTIVATE PRIOR KNOWLEDGE

Discuss Free-Time Interests

Have children share experiences about games or sports they like to play and other activities they enjoy doing after school in their spare time. Make a list on the chalkboard of activities children mention. Encourage all children to express their preferences. Then have each child select a favorite activity. Tally each child's selection on the chalkboard next to the name of the activity. Use the following questions to help children analyze the information on the list.

- **How many different activities did we list?**
- **Which activities were chosen by more than one person? How can you tell?**
- **Find the name of your favorite activity. How many people chose the same favorite activity?**

Create a Bar Graph

Help children make a graph showing the activities from their list. Use the graph shown on Transparency 1 as a model. Each child can place a name card next to his or her favorite activity. Children can count the name cards or compare the lengths of the rows to interpret the information shown. Discuss the children's graph. MATH

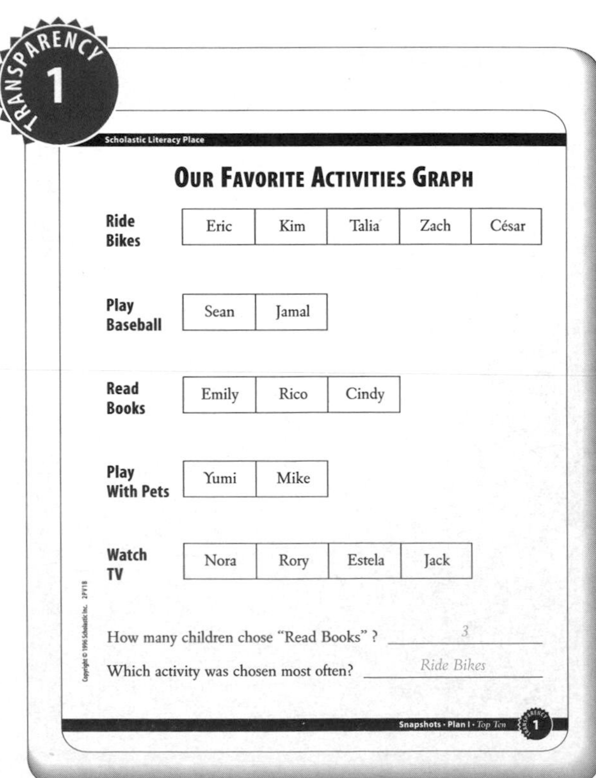

TRANSPARENCY 1

Scholastic Literacy Place

OUR FAVORITE ACTIVITIES GRAPH

Ride Bikes	Eric	Kim	Talia	Zach	César
Play Baseball	Sean	Jamal			
Read Books	Emily	Rico	Cindy		
Play With Pets	Yumi	Mike			
Watch TV	Nora	Rory	Estela	Jack	

How many children chose "Read Books"? 3

Which activity was chosen most often? Ride Bikes

Snapshots • Plan I • Top Ten 1

Annotated transparency for building background

Develop Vocabulary

Teach the Concept Words

Strategy: Semantic Categories Have children use what they know about sports and other activities to match the concept words to the following word groups. Write the concept words on cards or use Word Cards 1–6. As you say each group of words, have volunteers select the card that names the category. Discuss why each concept word fits the category.

- **basket, shoot, team**
- **kick, field, ball**
- **string, beads, paper**
- **ball, bat, mitt**
- **screen, key, games**

OPTION

Begin a Word Wall
Have children use markers to write the new words on chart paper or on a roll of shelf paper taped on a classroom wall. Words can be saved for children to refer to easily.

Support Words As children read "Top Ten," you may want to point out other interesting words in the article:

answers: replies to things written or said
catcher: a person who catches something
favorite: something or someone that is liked the most
graph: a picture that shows amounts
second: next after the first

Personal Word List Children can generate their own lists of new and interesting vocabulary they encounter during reading.

VOCABULARY

ORGANIZING CONCEPT: ACTIVITY WORDS

Concept Words

	basketball:	a game played by two teams trying to throw a large ball through a high hoop (p. 11)
✔	soccer:	a game played by two teams with a big ball that can be moved with every part of the body except the hands (p. 11)
	baseball:	a game played by two teams with a bat and a ball (p. 11)
✔	computer:	a machine that does many kinds of work very quickly (p. 12)
	crafts:	things that are handmade (p. 13)
✔	activities:	things that you do (p. 15)

✔ = assessed

See p. T29 for words to pretest and spelling instruction

Technology Options

Invite children to use the Scholastic Network to help build background on this topic. Suggest that they go on-line to conduct a poll in which they ask second graders from around the country about their special interests.

Supporting All Learners

Use Word Cards

EXTRA HELP During the Teach the Concept Words activity, provide visual support to children who need practice using the new vocabulary. Have them make one word card and one picture card for each new word. Then they can mix up the cards and place them face down. Children take turns turning over two cards to make a match.

ESL Following the Develop Vocabulary activities, second-language learners can practice the new vocabulary by using the word cards to play Go Fish. Deal out all cards and have children take turns asking another player for a specific card that matches one they hold in their hand. The child then surrenders the matching card requested or tells the other player to Go Fish.

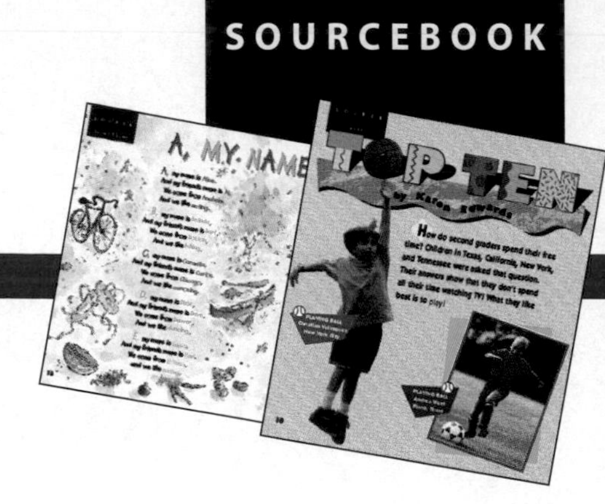

READING THE SOURCES

TOP TEN / A, MY NAME IS ALICE

Prepare to Teach

OBSERVATION

As children read "Top Ten," notice how they:

- ✔ make connections with the *theme* of children having different favorite activities and interests.
- ✔ use the *key strategy* of Summarize.
- ✔ understand a *text structure* in which information from a survey is presented in a picture/bar graph.

Use the Individual and Class Plan Checklists in the Classroom Management Forms, pp. 4 and 10.

KEY STRATEGY:

SUMMARIZE

The headings in "Top Ten" help to organize and draw children's attention to the most important information about a survey of children's favorite activities. The picture/bar graph displays the results of the survey. Children will build confidence in their own abilities as they use the headings and information from the graph to apply the skill of summarizing.

Customize Instruction

FLEXIBLE GROUPING

Teacher Support

Construct meaning by using the key strategy of Summarize as children read the selections. Revisit the selection survey to build understanding of a text in which survey information is presented in a graph.

Collaborative

Partners can alternate reading paragraphs of "Top Ten" and verses of "A, My Name Is Alice". They can record themselves reading the rhyme.

Extra Support

Read aloud the survey and then reread, leaving out key words and encouraging children to supply them. After reading aloud the entire rhyme, reread and invite children to join in for the repetitive phrases.

Independent

Let children read the survey silently without interruption. Use the questions on page T24 to encourage discussion and to check comprehension.

Meet the Author

Karen Edwards

Karen Edwards decided she wanted to become a writer when she was just 12 years old. Since then, she has written articles for many magazines, but she also loves to write poetry. While researching "Top Ten," Ms. Edwards discovered that where children live may affect the kinds of activities they enjoy. She was surprised—and pleased—to learn that what children like most are simple things, such as throwing a ball or running. Karen Edwards grew up in Connecticut and Minnesota but now lives in New York City. Swimming, ice-skating, and reading are among her top ten favorite activities, but her favorite activity is spending time with her daughter.

More Books About Favorite Things

- ***Going to My Gymnastics Class***
  by Susan Kuklin
  In this photo essay, Gasper tells about his experiences going to gymnastics lessons.
- ***It's About Time***
  by Lee Bennett Hopkins
  Children will easily identify with poems that talk about common daily activities, such as eating sloshy spaghetti or refusing to go to bed.
- ***Roxaboxen***
  by Alice McLerran
  illustrated by Barbara Cooney
  Enter this cherished imaginary town created by children from just rocks and boxes.

Books for Word Study

- ***Emma's Pet***
  by David McPhail
  Emma searches for the perfect pet. (**vowel /e/*e***)
- ***The Princess & the Beggar***
  by Anne Sibley O'Brien
  In this Korean folk tale, the princess surprisingly marries poor Pabo Ondal and makes a great discovery. (***r*-blends**)
- ***The Three Hundred Twenty-Ninth Friend***
  by Marjorie Sharmat
  Emery Raccoon finds he's his own best friend—but only after he's invited everyone in the forest to lunch. (**vowel /e/*e*; *r*-blends**)

SOURCE Survey

TOP TEN by Karen Edwards

How do second graders spend their free time? Children in Texas, California, New York, and Tennessee were asked that question. Their answers show that they don't spend all their time watching TV! What they like best is to play!

PLAYING BALL Christian Velasquez New York City

PLAYING BALL Andrea West Plano, Texas

10

◀ SourceBook pp. 10–15

A, MY NAME IS ALICE

SourceBook pp. 16–17 ▶

a READING THE SOURCES

Preview and Predict

READER TO READER

"Before writing "Top Ten," the author questioned second graders from all over the United States. Read "Top Ten" to find out what children from different places like to do in their free time."

Have children read the title "Top Ten" and point out the author's name. Tell children this selection is a survey that gives children's opinions about how they like to spend their free time. Invite children to look over the photographs and predict what the top ten responses might be.

To help children focus on reading for specific information, you may want to use the questions and the KWL chart below.

- **What do you expect to find out in "Top Ten"?**
- **What do you think the top ten favorite free-time activities might be?**

JOURNAL Have children think of what the favorite activity of children their age might be and draw a picture in their Journals.

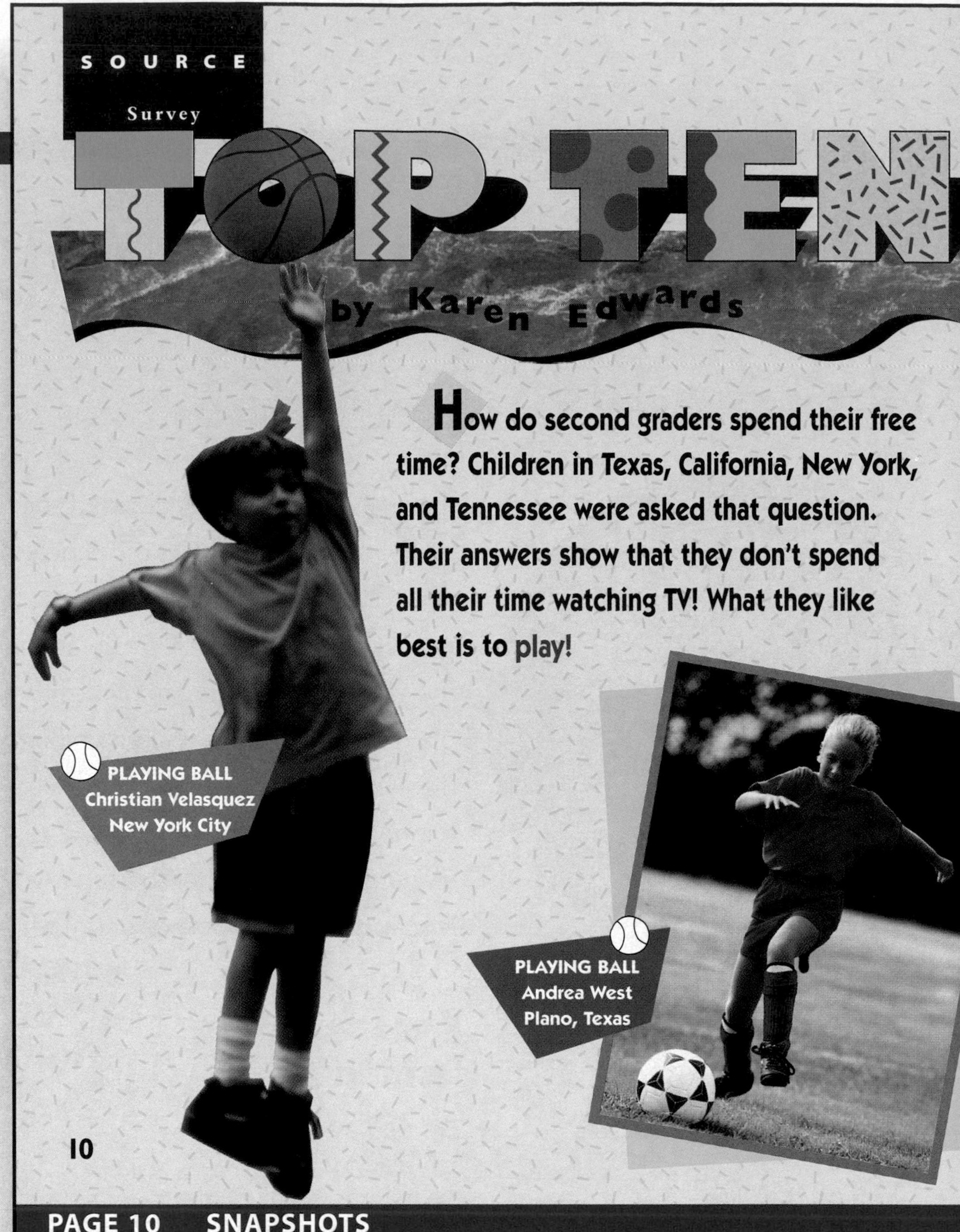

SUPPORTING ALL LEARNERS

Preview **ESL** Preview the reading with second-language learners by choosing volunteers to pantomime the activities named in the survey. Children can take turns pantomiming other activities they enjoy. **(Pantomime)**

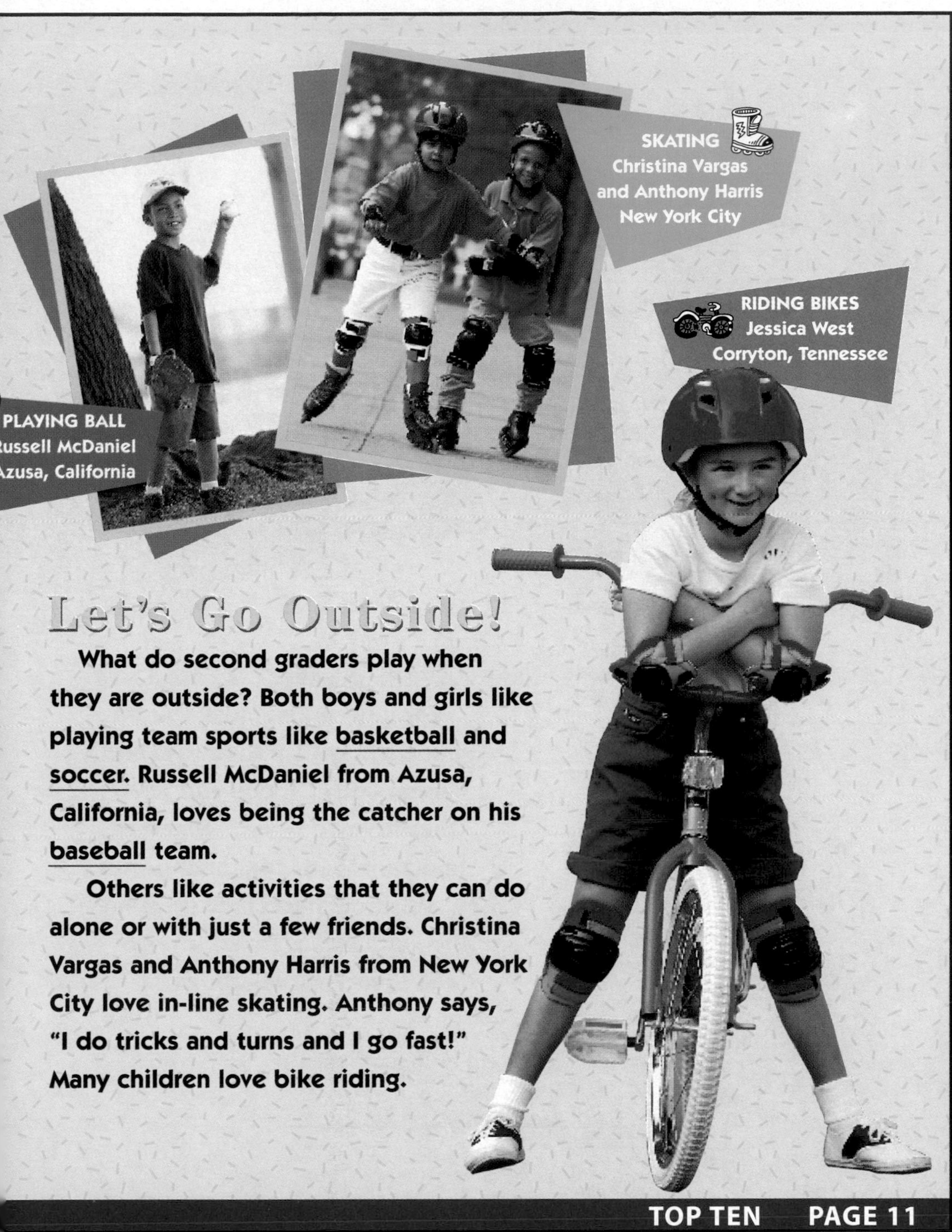

Let's Go Outside!

What do second graders play when they are outside? Both boys and girls like playing team sports like basketball and soccer. Russell McDaniel from Azusa, California, loves being the catcher on his baseball team.

Others like activities that they can do alone or with just a few friends. Christina Vargas and Anthony Harris from New York City love in-line skating. Anthony says, "I do tricks and turns and I go fast!" Many children love bike riding.

TOP TEN PAGE 11

▶ INTEGRATED CURRICULUM **SCIENCE** *(See p. R2.)*

Children test various balls and discover their different properties.

Guided Reading ▶

LAUNCH THE KEY STRATEGY:

SUMMARIZE

THINK ALOUD When I look at the survey, I notice headings and photographs on the pages. I know that each heading and photograph tells me about that part of the selection. After I read that part, I'm going to stop and think about what I just read. Then I'll summarize by retelling the most important ideas in what I've just read.

I might summarize the first page this way: Second graders in different parts of the United States like to spend their free time playing. When I finish reading, I'll summarize the whole selection in one or two sentences to help me remember what I've read.

PHONICS **Vowel /e/e**

Have children find the word *when,* point to the letter *e,* and say the word aloud.

- **What other words do you know that have the same vowel sound as *when*?**

(See Phonics: Vowel /e/e on pp. T34–35.)

See the WiggleWorks Plus Teaching Plan for more phonics activities.

a

Guided Reading ▶

❶ **Main Idea/Details What did you find out about the survey so far? Did anything you learned surprise you? If so, what was it?**

❷ **Nonfiction How can you tell this selection is nonfiction? How can you tell that the places, the people, and the things that they do are real?** MINI-LESSON

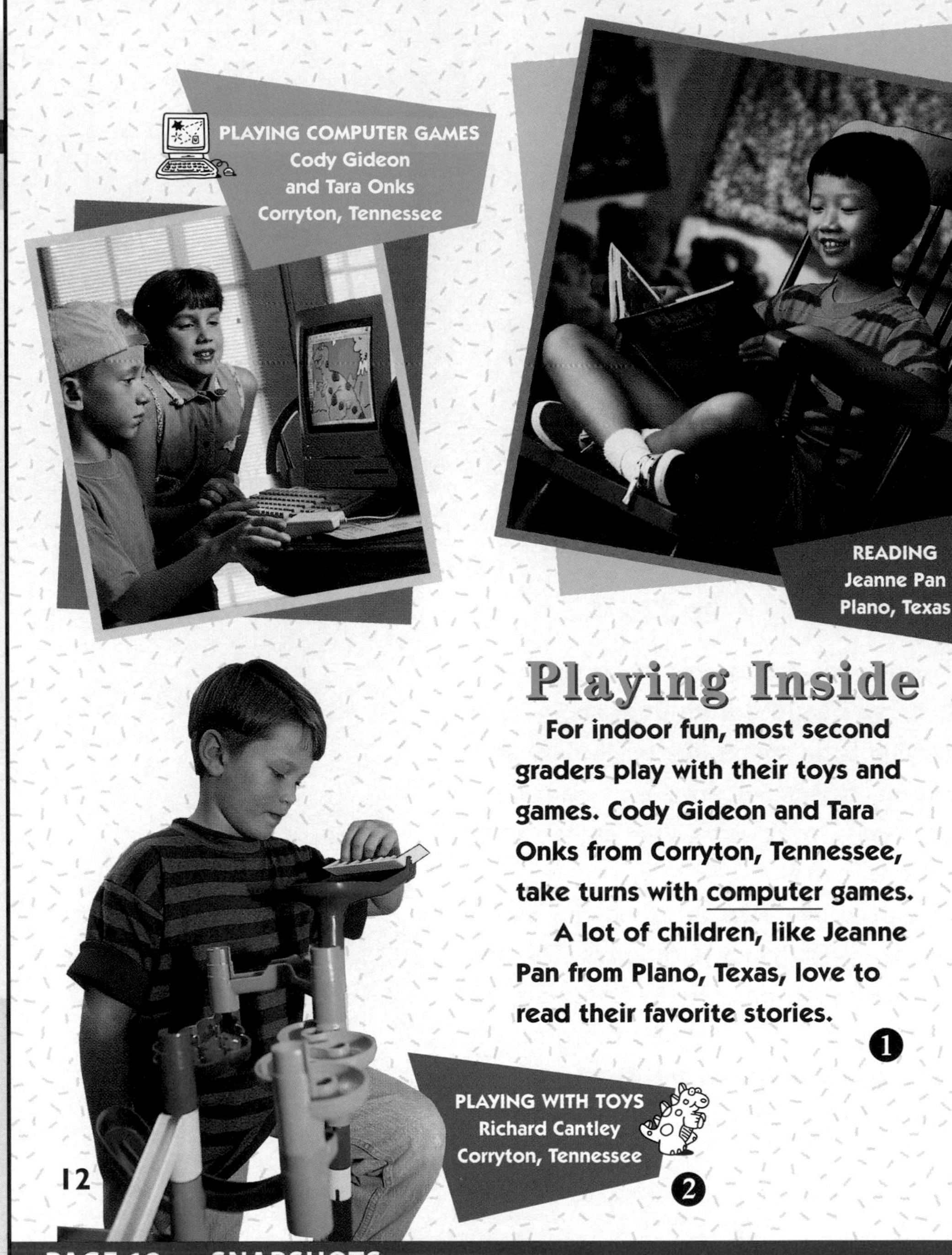

Playing Inside

For indoor fun, most second graders play with their toys and games. Cody Gideon and Tara Onks from Corryton, Tennessee, take turns with computer games.

A lot of children, like Jeanne Pan from Plano, Texas, love to read their favorite stories. ❶

❷

12

PAGE 12 SNAPSHOTS

MINI-LESSON

NONFICTION

TEACH/MODEL Ask children if they think "Top Ten" tells a story or gives information. Discuss that a selection that gives information is called nonfiction.

THINK ALOUD After reading the first few sentences, I can tell that "Top Ten" is about something that really happened. It gives information about real people and the photographs are of real people. These are clues that the selection may be nonfiction.

APPLY Have children read pages 10–13 to find clues that the selection is nonfiction. You may want to read from different selections and have children decide if you are reading from a fiction or a nonfiction selection.

▶ INTEGRATED CURRICULUM MATH *(See p. R2.)*

Children conduct a class survey about favorite fruits and make a graph like the one shown in "Top Ten."

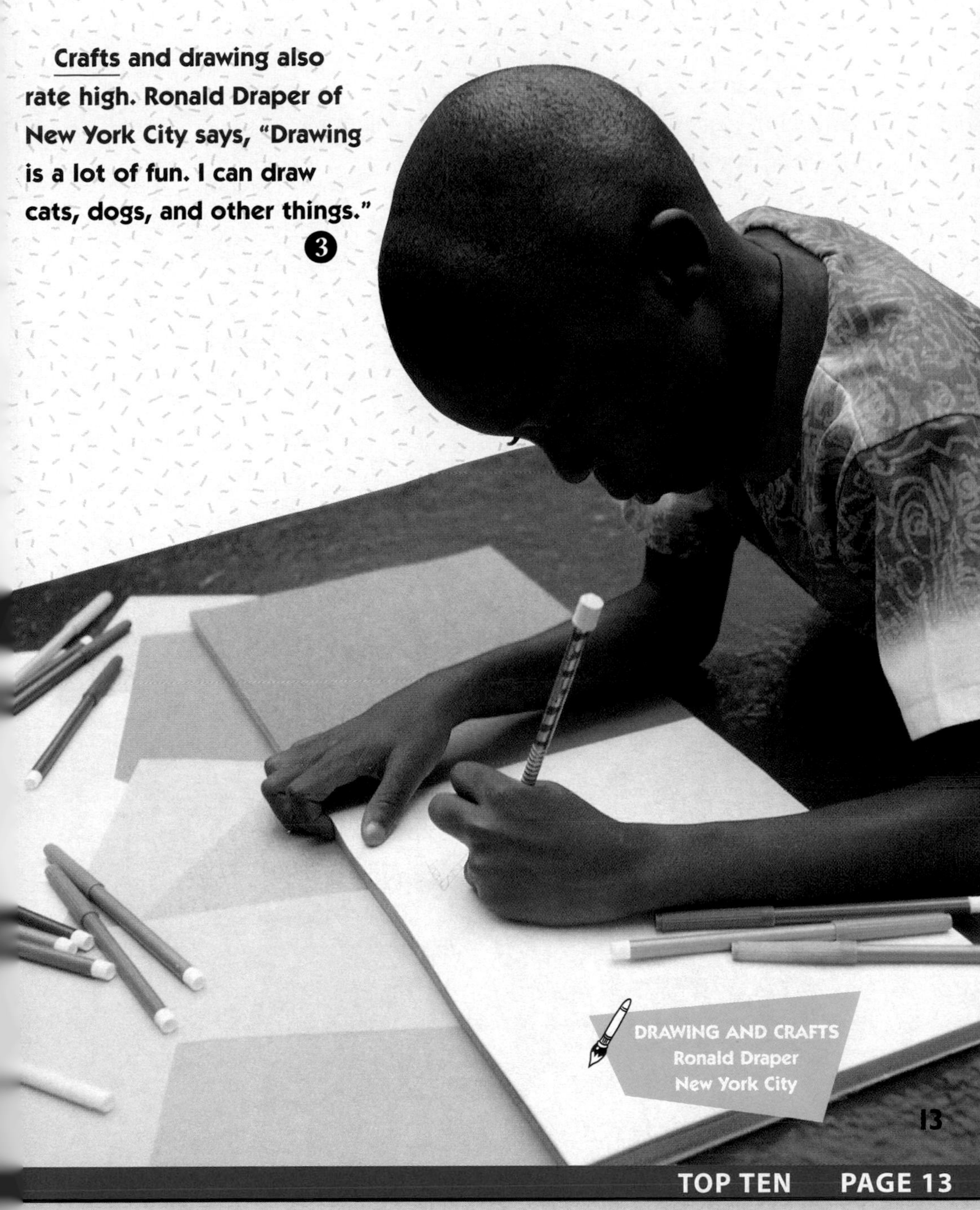

Guided Reading ►

3 KEY STRATEGY: Summarize **This is a good place to stop and summarize what we've read. To do this, we can focus on picture clues and important words, such as *outside* and *inside*. Now let's make up a sentence or two to summarize the "Let's Go Outside" page and the pages for "Playing Inside." Try to summarize each page by retelling it in one or two sentences.**

Encourage children to use the SourceBook Activities writing area to write or record their summaries.

PHONICS r-Blends

Have children find the word *crafts,* point to the letters *cr,* and read the word aloud. Ask children what other words they know that begin with the same sounds. Repeat the activity with the word *drawing* and the letters *dr.* *(See Phonics: r-Blends on pages T36–37.)*

Critical Thinking: Analyze

What do children think might affect whether they play indoors or outdoors?

► INTEGRATED CURRICULUM **SOCIAL STUDIES** *(See p. R3.)*
Children list the top three places they'd like to visit and make a graph.

► INTEGRATED CURRICULUM **THE ARTS** *(See p. R3.)*
Children illustrate the numerals for the favorite activities in the "Top Ten" graph.

a

Guided Reading ▶

❹ **Word Attack** **Follow along as I read: *Whether they play inside or out . . .* Wait, is *inside* correct? It makes sense in the sentence, but the word on the page has the letter *d* after the letter *n*. Let's look at the word on the page again. I see the words *in* and *doors* in the word *indoors*. I know that *indoors* means almost the same as *inside* so the word must be *indoors.* Let's read the sentence again with the new word to be sure it makes sense.**

❺ **Survey** **The author asked second graders how they spend their free time. What did you learn?** MINI-LESSON

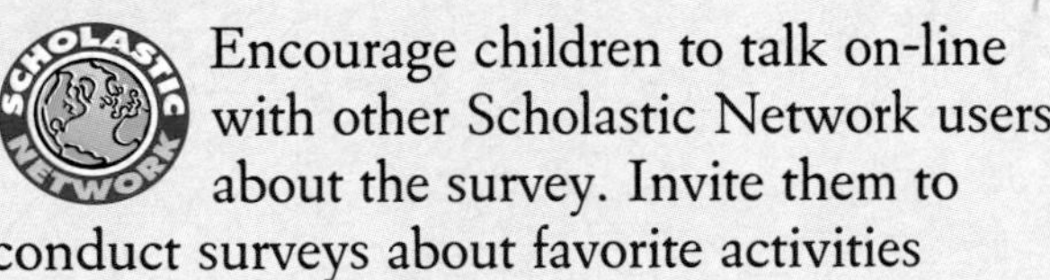

Encourage children to talk on-line with other Scholastic Network users about the survey. Invite them to conduct surveys about favorite activities

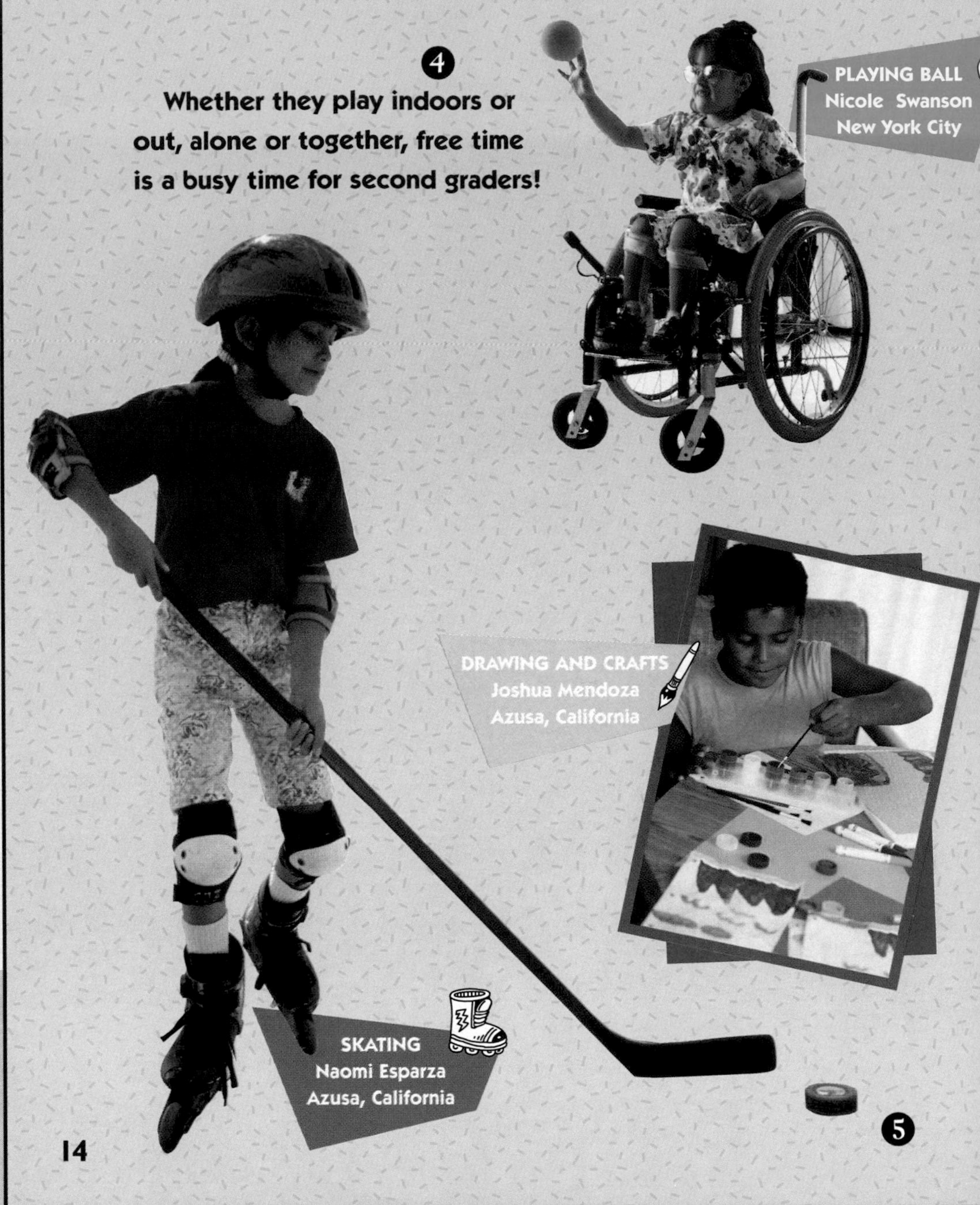

▶ INTEGRATING LANGUAGE ARTS **VIEWING/WRITING** *(See p. T30.)*

MINI-LESSON

SURVEY

TEACH/MODEL Remind children that a survey or a poll is a collection of information. The information can be organized and recorded in different ways.

THINK ALOUD I know from reading "Top Ten" that information can be shown in a graph. Another way to show the information is with a tally. When I make a tally, I put a mark next to the activity that a person votes for. Then I count up the number of marks.

APPLY Children might like to tally the information in the graph on page 15. You may want to have groups of eight to ten children tally their answers to a survey question like: "What is your favorite sandwich?" MATH

What is your favorite sandwich?

cheese	X X X
tuna	X X X X X
turkey	X X
peanut butter and jelly	X X X X

The Vote Is In!

Here is a graph that shows the top ten activities for all the second graders questioned. Is your favorite activity on the graph? ❻

15

TOP TEN PAGE 15

Guided Reading ▶

❻ **KEY STRATEGY: Summarize I see the graph as a summary of the selection. According to the graph, what is the favorite activity of all the second graders questioned?** VISUAL LITERACY

INTERVENTION STRATEGY

Graphic Aids

Children may not understand how to interpret the information on the graph. Explain that a graph is like a picture. The title tells what this graph is about. In this graph, the words along the side name activities; the numbers tell how many people chose this activity. Playing ball is the favorite activity because it has the most boxes filled in. Ask what else can be learned from this graph. MATH

SUPPORTING ALL LEARNERS

Revisit

CHALLENGE Invite children to brainstorm about different ways they can present the survey information, including tallies, bar graphs, and pie graphs. Working in cooperative groups, challenge them to present the survey results using one of these methods. **(Work in Groups)**

- Children can also use the PlaceMaker to present the survey results.

PHONICS /ā/ay

Have children find the word *playing* on page 15, point to the letters *ay*, and read the work aloud. Ask them what other words they know in which /ā/ is spelled *ay*.

a READING THE SOURCES

Preview and Predict

READER TO READER

The pattern in this rhyme gives you a pretty good idea about what will come next. You can think ahead to continue the rhyme.

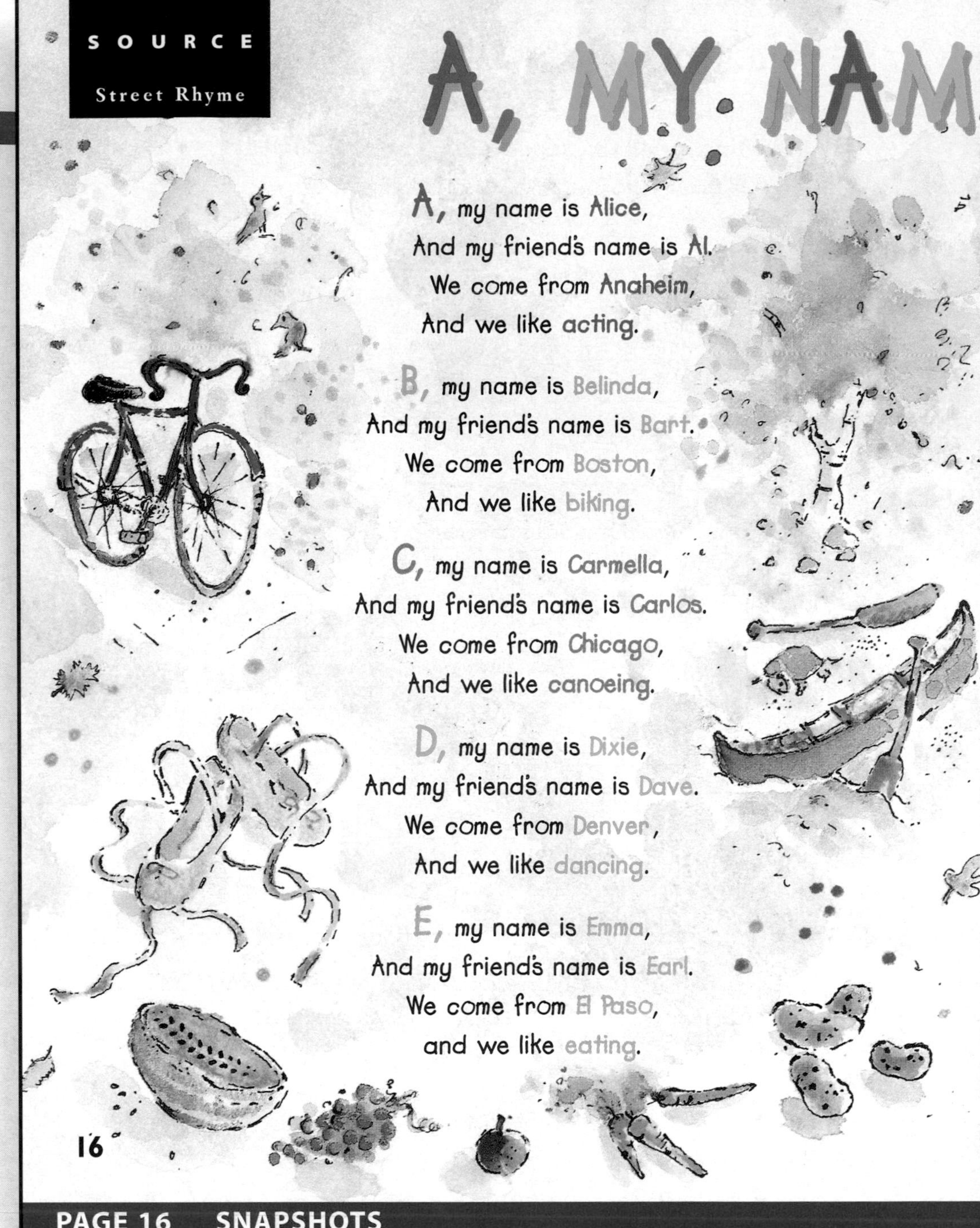

PAGE 16 SNAPSHOTS

Read the title, "A, My Name Is Alice." As children read through the rhyme, help them discover the repetitive text structure and the verse-by-verse arrangement of the letters of the alphabet.

- **Look at the end of the rhyme. What letter do you think the next verse will begin with? Tell why you think so.**

JOURNAL When they finish reading, you may wish to have children write a verse that will continue the rhyme in their Journals.

PHONICS Vowel /i/y

Invite children to find the word *my* each time it appears on page 16, point to the letter *y*, and read the word aloud. Ask children what other words they know in which /i/ is spelled *y*.

SUPPORTING ALL LEARNERS

Preview ESL Preview the selection with second-language learners to help them identify the pattern of the rhyme. Focus children's attention on the alphabet words that change from verse to verse by clapping each time you read one. Encourage children to join in the clapping. **(Follow Patterns)**

Guided Reading ►

❶ **Repetitive Text** **After reading three verses, I am beginning to see a pattern. I see that the first line of each verse always names a girl and the second line always names a boy. What does the third line always name? What about the fourth line?**

❷ **Street Rhyme** **How can we continue the rhyme?**
MINI-LESSON

► INTEGRATING LANGUAGE ARTS **SPEAKING/LISTENING** *(See p. T30.)*

► INTEGRATING LANGUAGE ARTS **WRITING** *(See p. T31.)*

MINI-LESSON

STREET RHYME

TEACH/MODEL Point out how the repeated words of the rhyme help readers to predict text.

APPLY As you read several verses, encourage children to raise their hands each time you say a word that changes from verse to verse. Then invite them to tap or clap the rhythm as you continue to read aloud. You may wish to have children suggest street rhymes they know for others to clap the rhythm.

a

Reading The Sources

TOP TEN / A, MY NAME IS ALICE

Assess Reading

Reflect and Respond

Encourage children to share their thoughts, opinions, and questions about "Top Ten" and "A, My Name Is Alice." You can prompt discussion with these questions:

- **Which activity on the "Top Ten" graph do you like best? Why do you like it? *(✔ Theme)***
- **How does the title "Top Ten" help us when we think about summarizing this survey? *(✔ Key Strategy)***
- **How did you feel about reading the survey results in the form of a graph? Did any of the survey results surprise you? *(✔ Text Structure)***

Check Predictions

What did children learn from the survey? Have them return to the KWL chart they made before reading and fill in the L part of the chart, "What Did We Learn?"

Read Critically Across Texts

- **Why would the children in the survey enjoy meeting sports photographer Bruce Thorson? What advice might he give them about pursuing their interests?**
  Bruce Thorson loves sports and he is highly inspiring. He would probably tell children to stick with their interests.
  How is "A, My Name Is Alice" like "Top Ten"? How are the two selections different?
- *Both selections are about things children like to do. One is nonfiction; the other is a street rhyme.*

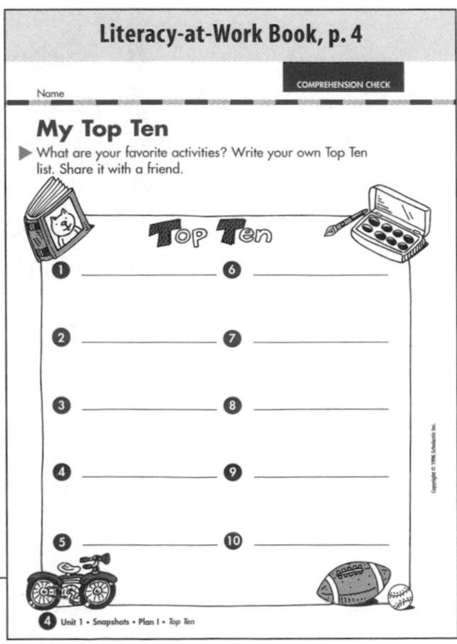

Literacy-at-Work Book, p. 4

Name

COMPREHENSION CHECK

My Top Ten

▶ What are your favorite activities? Write your own Top Ten list. Share it with a friend.

Top Ten

1 ____ 6 ____
2 ____ 7 ____
3 ____ 8 ____
4 ____ 9 ____
5 ____ 10 ____

4 Unit 1 • Snapshots • Plan I • Top Ten

CONFERENCE

Use the checked questions on this page to assess children's understanding of:

✔ the *theme* of children's different interests.

✔ the *key strategy* of Summarize.

✔ the *text structure* of Survey results presented in a graph.

Listen to Children Read Ask selected children to choose one of the favorite activities mentioned in "Top Ten" and read aloud the passage that describes it. You may wish to tape-record children as they read aloud. Assess oral reading using pages 22–23 in the Assessment Handbook.

Children may wish to add their recordings to their Literacy Portfolios.

Based on your evaluation of your children's responses,

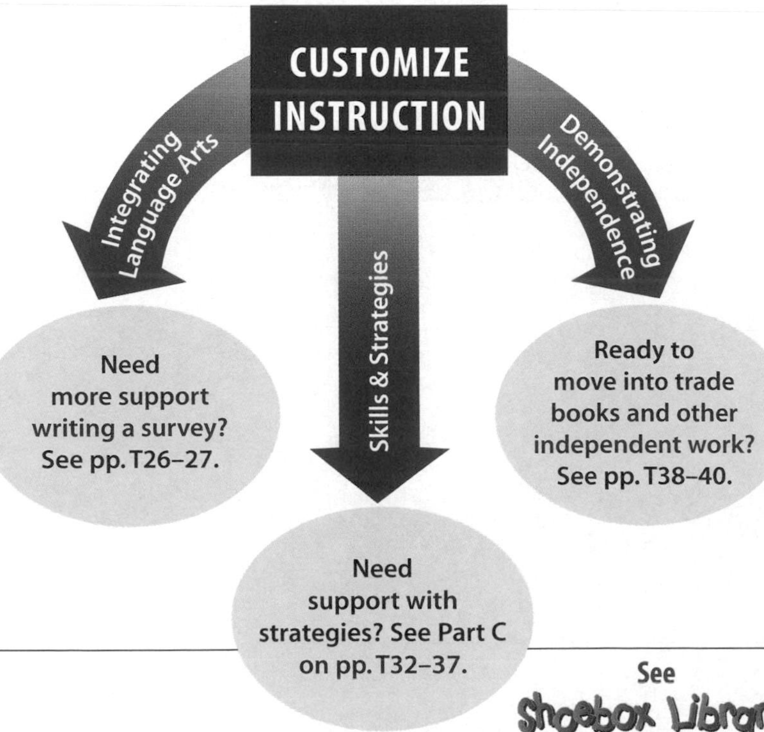

See Shoebox Library

Idea File

REPEATED READING

ROUND-ROBIN READING To help children read expressively and fluently, invite them to sit in a circle to reread "Top Ten." Go around the circle and have each child in turn read one or more sentences. Have everyone chime in to read the favorite activities graph.

VOCABULARY

JOURNAL

Is there something children would like to ask Karen Edwards about "Top Ten"? If they could question the children in the survey, what would they ask? Encourage children to write questions in their Journals using vocabulary from the selection or words for other activities of interest.

REPEATED READING

Technology Options **INDEPENDENT READING** To help foster reading fluency and self-confidence, invite children to read aloud and record on an audiocassette a reading of both selections.

PERSONAL PROFILE

HOMEWORK

Have children bring to class a photograph or a picture they drew of themselves enjoying a game, a sport, or a crafts activity. They can write a few sentences telling what they are doing in the picture and why they like the activity. After the pictures and sentences are shared, display them on a bulletin board. VISUAL LITERACY

CULTURAL CONNECTIONS

BALL GAMES AROUND THE WORLD

Most of the world's team sports are ball games, including baseball, basketball, soccer, and a game called baggataway, played by native North Americans long ago and known today as lacrosse.

ACTIVITY

Have children brainstorm a list of other ball games. Maybe there are children in the class who know about different kinds of ball games played in other countries. Make a class list of games. Children can illustrate the list with drawings of the equipment and people playing the game.

b

INTEGRATING LANGUAGE ARTS

TOP TEN

WRITE A SURVEY

WRITING

"Top Ten" presents survey results showing the interests of second graders across the United States. Children will write **survey questions,** record **results,** and present them in an informative **summary.**

Objectives

Children learn to:

- write survey questions, record results, and summarize (pp. T26-27)
- write question sentences (p. T28)
- use question marks (p. T28)
- spell words with *r*-blends (p. T29)

Materials:
SourceBook pp. 10–15
Literacy-at-Work Book p. 5
Pencils or markers

Suggested Grouping:
Whole class and cooperative groups

Literacy-at-Work Book, p. 5

Name WRITING

Get Ready to Write

▶ What questions would help you find out what your classmates like? Write some on the lines below.

Survey Questions

1. ______
2. ______
3. ______
4. ______
5. ______

To the Teacher: This is the prewriting organizer referenced in the lesson on writing a survey.

Unit 1 • Snapshots • Plan 1 • Top Ten 5

THINK ABOUT WRITING

Often people conduct surveys to find out what people like or think. The answers are recorded, organized, and then summarized. The recording can be done in different ways. Help children discover that in surveys:

- questions and answers are used to obtain information about what people like or think.
- results are recorded.
- information is presented and results are summarized.

Put It in Context

As children browse through the article "Top Ten," remind them that the author presents the results of a survey. Have children note that the article:

- opens with the survey question.
- gives details about children's responses to questions about what they like to play.
- presents the information in chart form.
- summarizes the information.

INTRODUCE THE WRITING EVENT

Explain to children that they are going to write questions and conduct their own survey to find out what their classmates like. They will record the results on a chart, and then write a short summary.

Prewrite

Invite children to use the prewriting organizer in the Literacy-at-Work Book to brainstorm questions for their surveys. Have them choose their survey questions and make a list of the classmates they will survey.

Draft

Children will now write their questions and conduct their survey. Invite them to record their results on a chart. They can then write a brief summary.

Favorite T.V. Programs	Yes	No
1. Do you like funny programs?	18	0
2 Do you like cartoon programs?	15	3
3 Do you like scary programs?	15	3
4 Do you like Nickalodian?	17	1
5 Do you like mystery programs?	17	1
6 Do you watch America's Funniest Home Vidoes?	13	5
7 Do you watch Rug Rats?	16	2

Summary: 18 people like funny programs, 17 people Nickalodian and mystery programs and only 13 people like America's Funniest Home Vidoes.

Proficient sample: Questions are clear, results charted, summary informative.

Revise

Encourage children to reread their writing to check for any changes they wish to make. It may help them to ask:

- **Does my summary tell what I found out from my survey?**
- **Did I include all the important information on my chart?**

SHARING TIPS Place children from groups together to share their results. Children can give each other feedback about what was most surprising about each other's survey results.

ONGOING ASSESSMENT

PERFORMANCE-BASED

Children's Self-Assessment The following questions may help children assess their work:

✔ Are my questions clear?

✔ Did I record the results of my survey clearly enough to su mmarize them?

✔ Does my summary explain the results of my survey?

Children may wish to carry this piece through the writing process described in Plan VI pp. T288–291.

PORTFOLIO

Use the Benchmarks to assess children's writing. Suggest that children include their drafts and peer comments in their Literacy Portfolios.

Technology Options

Invite children to use the SourceBook Activities writing area for this activity. They can begin by recording their questions using the Record Tool. When they've decided on a final question, children can also record the answers to their question, then write their summaries on the computer. See the WiggleWorks Plus Teaching Plan for more writing activities.

SUPPORTING ALL LEARNERS

Record

ESL Working in pairs, encourage second-language learners to prepare for the Draft activity by first expressing the survey results orally to each other. Then they can record their ideas in their Journals and use them to support their writing.

ACCESS Following the Prewrite activity, children with physical disabilities can use the computer recording tool to write their interpretation of the survey results.

CHALLENGE To expand upon the Writing Event, have children record a number of prospective survey questions. Then challenge them to select one question and conduct the survey among their classmates. They can use the computer to record their results.

CHILDREN'S WRITING BENCHMARKS

Novice:	Apprentice:	Proficient:
The questions are not clear. Results are not presented in chart form. The summary results may not relate to the question or be informative.	The questions are clear. Results are recorded in chart form. The summary paragraph relates to the question but may not be informative.	The questions are clear. Results are recorded in chart form. The summary presents the results of the survey in a few informative sentences.

INTEGRATING LANGUAGE ARTS

S M T W T F S
See Daily Language Practice pp. R14–R15.

(✔ *Unit Test*)

QUESTION SENTENCES

GRAMMAR

OBJECTIVE

Children will identify examples of question sentences in the story and in their writing.

DEFINITION: A question sentence is a sentence that asks a question.

SYNTACTIC CUEING

❶ Teach and Model

Invite children to ask you one or more questions. Write their questions on the chalkboard. Explain that a question sentence asks a question. Remind children that question sentences often begin with the words *who, what, when, where, why,* or *how,* and always end with question marks. Read a question aloud to model intonation of your voice at the end of the sentence and have children repeat it. Put the sentences below on the chalkboard and read them aloud.

What sports do you like?
Do you have a pet?
Who is your best friend?

❷ Put It in Context

Have children find the three questions asked in "Top Ten" and read each question aloud, modeling how to read the questions expressively.

❸ Apply to Writing

Call on volunteers to read aloud the survey questions they just wrote. Have children identify the question word, such as *what* or *who,* that begins each question. Ask children to check for question marks.

QUESTION MARKS

MECHANICS

OBJECTIVE

Children will identify question marks in the story and in their writing.

GUIDELINE: A question sentence ends with a question mark.

❶ Teach and Model

Explain to children that a sentence that asks a question begins with a capital letter and ends with a question mark. Point out that question sentences often begin with the words *who, what, why, where, when,* or *how.* However, some question sentences may begin with words such as *is, will,* and *can.*

❷ Put It in Context

Have children find the question mark on the last page of "Top Ten" as they read the question "Is your favorite activity on the graph?" Write the question on the chalkboard and have children read it aloud. Call on a volunteer to point to the punctuation mark at the end and identify it. Write the other questions from the selection without question marks. Have children read the questions and add question marks.

❸ Apply to Writing

Invite children to write their survey questions on sentence strips and display them. Children can check for question marks at the end of the questions and add them if they've been left out. Children should also check to see that their question sentences begin with capital letters.

Grammar, Usage, Mechanics Practice, p. 1

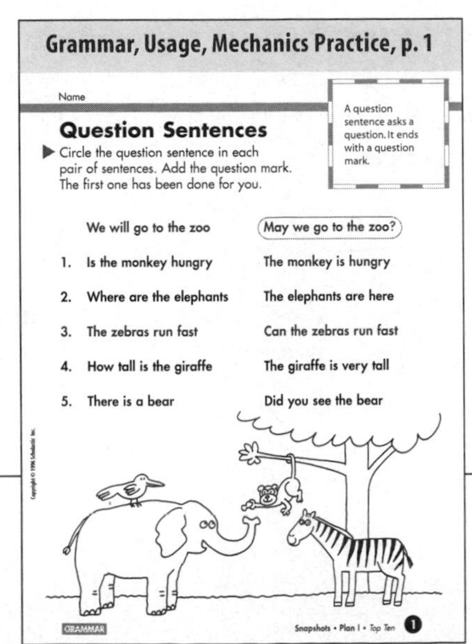

Name

Question Sentences

▶ Circle the question sentence in each pair of sentences. Add the question mark. The first one has been done for you.

A question sentence asks a question. It ends with a question mark.

	We will go to the zoo	May we go to the zoo?
1.	Is the monkey hungry	The monkey is hungry
2.	Where are the elephants	The elephants are here
3.	The zebras run fast	Can the zebras run fast
4.	How tall is the giraffe	The giraffe is very tall
5.	There is a bear	Did you see the bear

GRAMMAR

Snapshots • Plan I • *Top Ten* ❶

Grammar, Usage, Mechanics Practice, p. 2

Name

Question Marks

▶ Write each question sentence correctly. The first one has been done for you.

Begin a question sentence with a capital letter. End it with a question mark (?).

will it rain today
Will it rain today?

1. do you want to splash in the puddles
2. do you have an umbrella
3. what makes rain fall
4. did you bring a raincoat
5. do you like rainy days

▶ Write your own question sentence about the rain.

❷ Snapshots • Plan I • *Top Ten*

MECHANICS

Phonics Connection

You may first wish to do the phonics lesson on *r*-blends on pp. T36–37.

SPELLING

Words With *r*-Blends

grass **graph** **grab** **bring** **brick** **truck** **trip** **trick**

✷ **Selection Vocabulary**

PRETEST If you would like to pretest using test sentences, see Spelling Practice, p. 37.

OBJECTIVE

Children spell words with *r*-blends.

1 Teach

On the chalkboard write the blends *tr* and *gr*. Then write the phonogram *-ip*. Ask children to make words by combining the *r*-blends with the phonogram. Repeat with the blends *br* and *tr* and the phonogram *-ick*. Have children read the words and listen for the two sounds at the beginning of each one.

Put It in Context

Write the following sentence from "Top Ten" on the chalkboard. Have children read the sentence and identify the word that begins with a blend.

"I do tricks and turns and I go fast!"

2 Practice

Have children copy and complete the following chart with list words. Point out that hearing the two letters in the blend can help spell these words.

Words Beginning With		
gr	tr	br

3 Check

Apply to Writing

Have children use their spelling words to write three sentences about things they think children their age like to do.

OPTION

Spell Teaser

Have children work in cooperative groups. Give children some simple words that begin with *gr, tr,* or *br* blends, for example, *train*. Have them supply a rhyming word that begins with one of the other blends—for example, *brain* or *grain*.

TEST To administer the spelling test, read each word aloud and ask children to write a sentence of their own using each test word. Children can check their spelling against the word list or use a dictionary.

Spelling Practice, p. 1

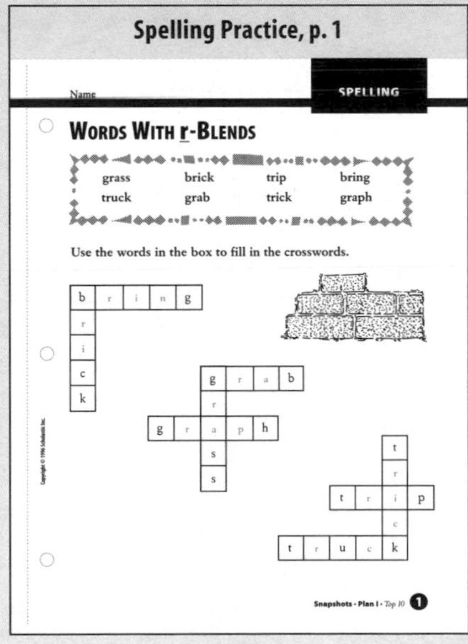
Name

SPELLING

WORDS WITH r-BLENDS

grass	brick	trip	bring
truck	grab	trick	graph

Use the words in the box to fill in the crosswords.

Snapshots • Plan I • Top 10 1

HANDWRITING

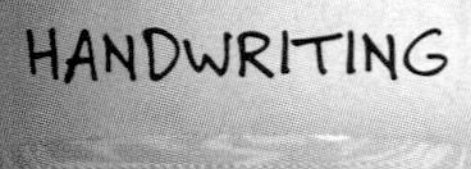

See Handwriting Practice, p. 1, for practice writing manuscript letters *l, i, t, o, c, s,* and *e*.

VIEWING/WRITING

Use a Map

GOOD FOR HOMEWORK

Materials:
U.S. map
Construction paper
Scissors
Thumbtacks

Time:
About 20 minutes

Suggested Grouping:
Cooperative groups

Point out that the children surveyed in "Top Ten" were from different places in the United States. Invite children to compile a list of cities and states where they have lived or visited or where relatives or friends live. Photographs or picture postcards of any of these locations can help to bring them to life.

Display a map of the United States. Help cooperative groups locate the places mentioned in "Top Ten." Children can tack triangular markers cut from paper to the map to mark those places, as well as the places on their lists. SOCIAL STUDIES

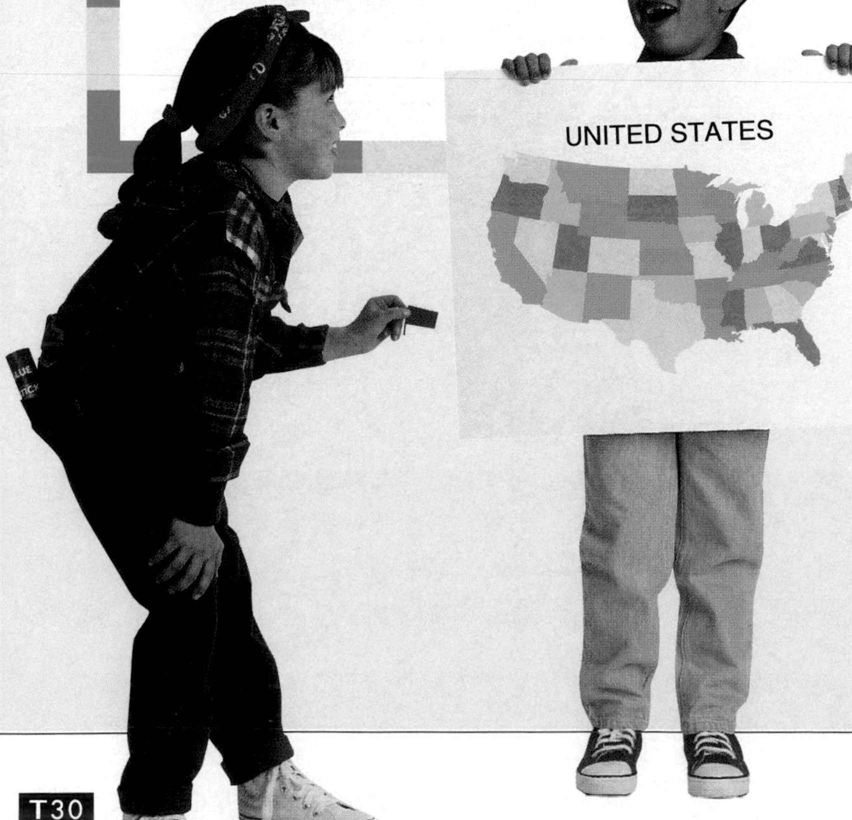

SPEAKING/LISTENING

ESL Play a Memory Game

Materials:
None

Time:
About 20 minutes

Suggested Grouping:
Whole class

Play a memory and alphabetical-order game. Have children sit in a circle. Begin by saying, "Abby likes acrobatics" (or "art" or another word for an activity that begins with the letter *a*). In turn, each player repeats the first sentence and adds another sentence with a name and an activity—in alphabetical order. For example, the next sentence might be "Brian likes biking." MINI-LESSON

Encourage creativity. If children need help, suggest that they think of board games or sports. If someone is unable to repeat the sequence, let the next child help out.

MINI-LESSON

NOUNS

TEACH/MODEL Remind children that nouns name people, places, and things. Read aloud some of the concept words, as well as the names of children and places from "Top Ten," and write them on a chart. Talk about the difference between proper nouns and common nouns. Have children note that proper nouns begin with capital letters.

APPLY As they play the memory game, have children stick up a thumb when they hear a proper noun.

ACTIVITY FILE

READING/SPEAKING/LISTENING

Share a Biography

Materials:
Library books
Audiocassette player and tape

Time:
Variable

Suggested Grouping:
Individuals

Children can go to the library to look for a book about a sports star, a musician, or an author to use in preparation for an oral report. Allow time for them to look over the book or read it and then share a favorite part by recording a short summary. Children may be able to add to their research by looking in newspapers and magazines. Perhaps they can find photographs of their subjects to make the summaries more interesting.

Set up a listening center for others to enjoy the recorded information.

Pick up sticks

1. Hold sticks in your hand on the floor.
2. Let go.
3. Carefully pick up each stick so no other sticks move.
4. If a stick moves you lose your turn.
5. The player who picks up the most sticks wins!

WRITING

Create Game Directions

GOOD FOR GRADING

Materials:
Pencil
Paper
Game directions

Time:
About 15 minutes

Suggested Grouping:
Partners

Invite children to work with a partner to write directions for a game they like to play. Ask them to imagine that another child has never heard of this game.

Display actual directions for a board game for children to refer to as they work. Have children write numbered step-by-step directions for others to follow.

Provide free time for children to read the directions and play the games.

How to Grade When grading, look for numbered steps that are written in logical order.

Children might want to include their directions in their Portfolios.

BUILDING SKILLS AND STRATEGIES

TOP TEN

Summarize (✔ Unit Test)

Objectives

Children learn to:

- summarize a selection
- transfer their learning to a new text

Materials:
SourceBook pp. 10–15
Transparency 2
Literacy-at-Work Book pp. 6–8

Time:
About 30 minutes

Suggested Grouping:
Whole class and partners

TESTED	
KEY STRATEGY	
SUMMARIZE	
Introduce	p. T32
Review	p. R17
Test	p. T311
Reteach	p. R24

Literacy-at-Work Book, p. 6

Name

SUMMARIZE

Sum It Up!

▶ Think about the important parts of "Top Ten." Write a summary of "Top Ten" for a school newspaper.

SCHOOL NEWS

6 Unit 1 • Snapshots • Plan 1 • Top Ten

✔ Quickcheck

As children worked their way through "Top Ten," did they:

✔ retell a part of the selection? retell the whole selection?

✔ use photographs and headings to retell what was discussed in the text?

✔ understand that a graph is a way to summarize the results of a survey?

YES **If yes, go to ❷ Practice and Apply.**

NO **If no, start at ❶ Teach and Model.**

TRANSPARENCY 2

Scholastic Literacy Place

SUMMARY CHART

What Second Graders Like to Do

Outdoor Activities	Indoor Activities
1. play team sports	1. play with toys and games
2. in-line skating	2. play computer games
3. bike riding	3. read
	4. draw
	5. crafts

Top Ten Activities

According to the graph, the favorite activity is *playing ball*.

Snapshots • Plan 1 • Top Ten

Annotated transparency for teaching Summarize

❶ Teach and Model

Have children think about a story that they have heard during story time. Ask volunteers to summarize the story by telling just the important things that happened. When they finish, explain that when they summarize, they should give only the most important points.

Put It in Context

Have children turn to the beginning of "Top Ten." Discuss how looking at the main points in the first part of the selection can help them to summarize what they read.

Think Aloud **When I finished reading the first two pages, I wanted to summarize so I could remember the main points. To do this, I looked at the title, the introduction, the heading "Let's Go Outside!" and the photographs. The title and the introduction told me that "Top Ten" is about the top ten ways second graders across the country spend their free time. The heading "Let's Go Outside!" reminded me that this section is about things second graders like to do outside. Looking at the photographs reminded me that children like to ride bikes, play ball, and skate. I summarized this section in my own words with one or two sentences. My summary was: According to this part of the survey, second graders like to spend their free time playing outdoors, either doing team sports, playing alone, or playing with a few friends.**

Display Transparency 2 and list the main points of this part of the selection.

❷ Practice and Apply

Make a Summary Chart

PARTNERS Ask pairs of children to summarize the main points in the next part of the selection. When they finish, list the points in the appropriate column on the summary chart.

Point out that to summarize the entire selection, children can use these main points along with main points from the first part.

Call attention to the graph on page 15 of the selection. Discuss that the graph summarizes the results of the survey question asked of the second graders. Explain that the graph shows the activities that second graders liked and the number of children who voted for each activity. Ask questions such as the following to help children interpret and summarize the information:

- **What are the top ten favorite activities shown?**
- **Which activities got the same number of votes?**
- **How many children voted for jumping rope?**

OPTION

TV Summary

Encourage children to summarize in one or two sentences a TV show that they saw. Children may want to share their summaries with each other.

❸ Assess

Were children able to summarize "Top Ten" based on text clues, picture clues, and information in a graph?

- ✔ **Can children retell a part of the selection? retell the whole selection?**
- ✔ **Can children summarize using the headings and photographs as clues?**
- ✔ **Can children summarize the information shown in the graph?**

If not, try this:
Use the Review lesson on Summarize with Plan V. Have children continue to write summaries in their Journals.

Children's Self-Assessment

- ✔ **How did I use text clues and picture clues to help me summarize?**

Transfer to New Text

Literacy-at-Work Book, p. 7

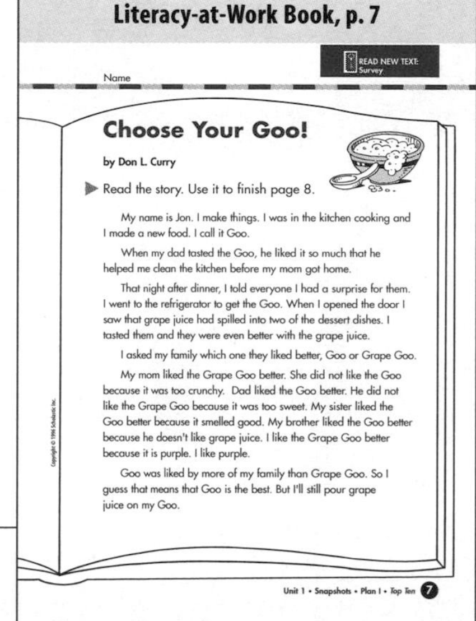

READ NEW TEXT: Survey

Name

Choose Your Goo!

by Don L. Curry

▶ Read the story. Use it to finish page 8.

My name is Jon. I make things. I was in the kitchen cooking and I made a new food. I call it Goo.

When my dad tasted the Goo, he liked it so much that he helped me clean the kitchen before my mom got home.

That night after dinner, I told everyone I had a surprise for them. I went to the refrigerator to get the Goo. When I opened the door I saw that grape juice had spilled into two of the dessert dishes. I tasted them and they were even better with the grape juice.

I asked my family which one they liked better, Goo or Grape Goo.

My mom liked the Grape Goo better. She did not like the Goo because it was too crunchy. Dad liked the Goo better. He did not like the Grape Goo because it was too sweet. My sister liked the Goo better because it smelled good. My brother liked the Goo better because he doesn't like grape juice. I like the Grape Goo better because it is purple. I like purple.

Goo was liked by more of my family than Grape Goo. So I guess that means that Goo is the best. But I'll still pour grape juice on my Goo.

Unit 1 • Snapshots • Plan I • *Top Ten* 7

Literacy-at-Work Book, p. 8

SUMMARIZE

Name

What's It All About?

▶ Write the important details from "Choose Your Goo!" on the chart. Then fill in the main idea of the story.

	Who Voted for It	Why People Voted for It
Goo	*dad*	*The Grape Goo was too sweet.*
	sister	*The Goo smelled good.*
	brother	*He doesn't like grape juice.*
Grape Goo	*mom*	*Goo was too crunchy.*
	Jon	*He likes the color purple.*

Results of the Survey:

The family likes Goo better than Grape Goo.

8 Unit 1 • Snapshots • Plan I • Top Ten

SUPPORTING ALL LEARNERS

Peer Partner

EXTRA HELP During the Practice and Apply activity, guide children who need extra help selecting appropriate details from "Top Ten" for their summary. Help them record the main points they select in the correct columns on their chart. Then they can use these points to complete the summary.

ESL After the Practice and Apply activity, support second-language learners' use of the key strategy by pairing them with experienced English speakers. Have each pair choose a photograph from "Top Ten." Then encourage them to take turns summarizing orally what is happening in the picture.

C

TOP TEN

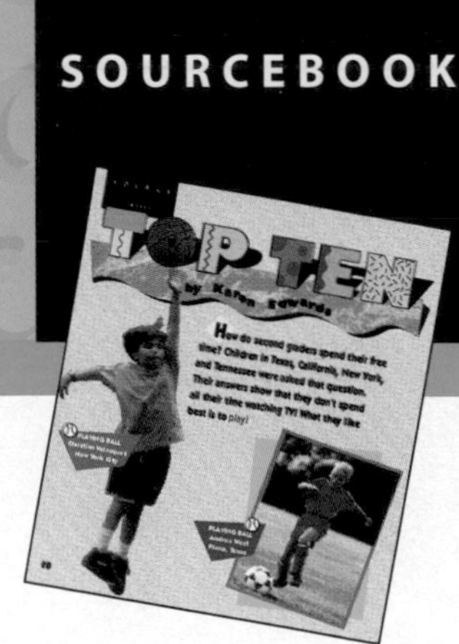

Vowel /e/*e*

Objectives

Children learn to:

- identify the sound of the short vowel *e*
- build words that contain /e/*e*
- write words with /e/*e*

PHONICS AT A GLANCE

Materials:
Sourcebook pp. 10–15
Big Book of Rhymes and Rhythms 2A, p. 3
Tracking Device (optional)
Literacy-at-Work Book p. 9–10
Magnet Board

Time:
About 15–30 minutes

Suggested Grouping:
Whole class or cooperative groups

Literacy-at-Work Book, p. 9

Name

PHONICS: Vowel /e/e

Literacy-at-Work Book, p. 10

Name

PHONICS: Vowel /e/e

Pictures and Words

▶ Read each sentence. Draw a picture of what the sentence tells.

The nest has ten red eggs.	Ned's pen is next to the letter on the desk.

▶ Write six words from above with the short *e* sound as in *get*.

1 ________ 2 ________
3 ________ 4 ________
5 ________ 6 ________

10 Unit 1 • Snapshots • Plan 1 • Top Ten

✔ Quickcheck

As children worked their way through "Top Ten," did they:

✔ recognize the letter *e* in print?

✔ identify the sound of the letter *e* as in *ten*?

YES **If yes, go to the Blending section of ❷ Connect Sound/Symbol.**

NO **If no, start at ❶ Develop Oral Language.**

❶ Develop Oral Language

Phonemic Awareness

As you read aloud "Mary Wore a Red Dress" from the Big Book of Rhymes and Rhythms, emphasize the words *red* and *dress*. On repeated readings, encourage children to join in. You may want to track the print as you read.

Have children say the words *red* and *dress*. Ask what sound they hear in the middle of each word. Have children decide if the vowel /e/*e* is in their names, such as in *Ben, Hector, Betty,* or *Jenny*.

Then ask children to name other words with the vowel /e/*e* in the middle or at the beginning, as in *get, bed, hen, egg,* and *elephant*.

Big Book of Rhymes and Rhythms

Mary Wore a Red Dress

Mary wore a red dress,
Red dress,
Red dress,
Mary wore a red dress,
All day long.

red

3

❷ Connect Sound/Symbol

Put It In Context

Write sentences from "Top Ten" on the chalkboard:

How do second graders
spend their free time?

What they like best
is to play!

After children read these with you, ask which words have the same vowel sound as *ten* and underline them. Have children listen to /e/ as you blend the sounds and run your hand under the letters in *spend* and *best*.

Blending

On the chalkboard or on chart paper, write words such as those in the left column.

Think Aloud **I can change *mat* to *met* by changing the *a* in the middle of the word to an *e*. Let's say the word slowly as I run my hand under it. Now, who can change the vowel in the next word to an *e* to make a new word?**

Invite children to substitute *e* and write new words. Ask them to read the new words.

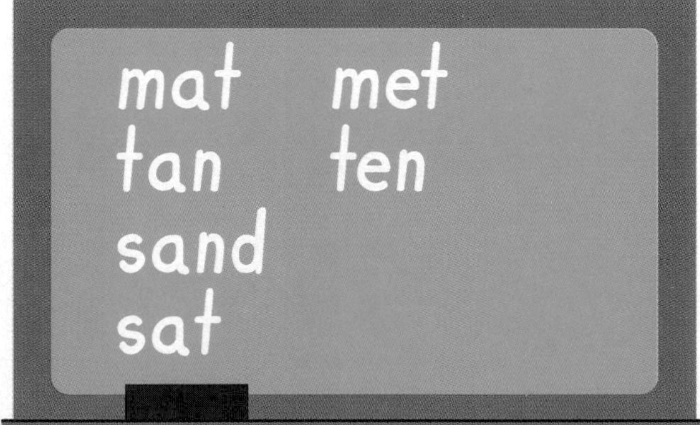

❸ Assess

Write

As a way of assessing children's understanding of /e/e, ask them to write the word *bed* on a piece of paper. Have them change one letter to write a new word. Then see if they can change one letter in the new word to write another word.

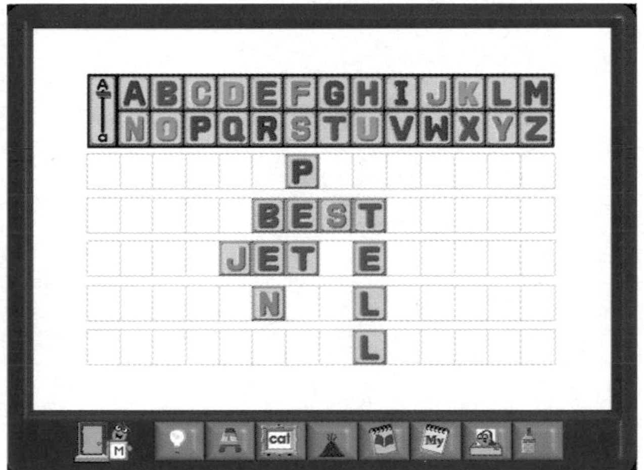

SUPPORTING ALL LEARNERS

Use Picture Cards

EXTRA HELP Following the Phonemic Awareness activity, ask children to collect pictures that depict words with short vowel sounds and use them to make picture cards. Hold up the cards as you say the words. Have children listen to the vowel sounds and raise their hands each time you say an /e/ word. As children progress, have them take turns saying the words for the picture names to their classmates.

CHALLENGE Stimulate children's creativity by having them select a picture card that depicts an /e/ word. Challenge them to change the first letter to make a word that rhymes with it and then make up a two-line rhyme using both words.

TOP TEN ELEPHANT WORDS

Draw a large outline of an elephant on paper. Children can list their ten favorite words that begin with or contain /e/e, including words from "Top Ten." They can use their lists to create a top ten /e/e words list on the elephant.

See the Phonics Kit

The Magnet Board activity pictured above provides additional phonics practice. For information on this and other Magnet Board activities, see the WiggleWorks Plus Teaching Plan.

SOURCEBOOK

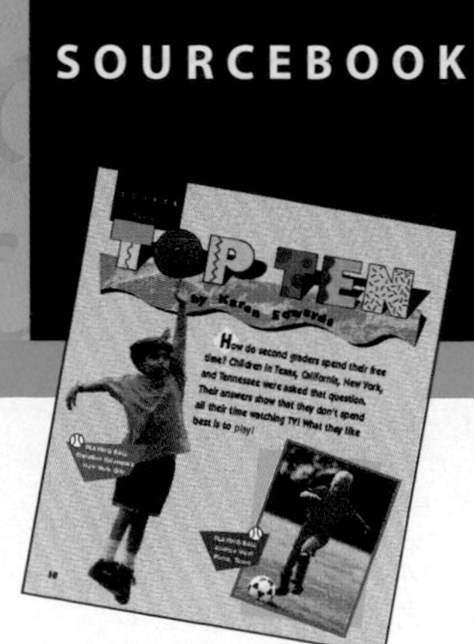

r-Blends

Objectives

Children learn to:

- identify the sounds of consonant blends with *r*
- build words that contain *r*-blends
- write words with *r*-blends

PHONICS AT A GLANCE

Materials:
SourceBook pp. 10–15
Big Book of Rhymes and Rhythms 2A, pp. 4–5
Word Building Cards for *r*-Blends
Literacy-at-Work Book pp. 11–12
Magnet Board
Spelling Lesson p. T29

Time:
About 15–30 minutes

Suggested Grouping:
Whole class or

Literacy-at-Work Book, p. 11

Literacy-at-Work Book, p. 12

Name

PHONICS: *r*-Blends

The *r* Puzzle

▶ Pick a word from the box to finish each sentence. Write the word in the puzzle.

trick	grade
drip	free
trip	

Down

1 Did the water ______ into the drain?
3 We got the small toy for ______.

Across

2 He played a funny ______ on me.
4 We took a ______ to the park on Friday.
5 Fred got the best ______ on the test.

12 Unit 1 • Snapshots • Plan 1 • Top Ten

✔ Quickcheck

As children worked their way through "Top Ten," did they:

✔ recognize the printed forms of *r*-blends?

✔ discriminate which words begin with a particular *r*-blend?

✔ think of words that begin with the letters *gr, fr, dr,* or *tr*?

YES **If yes, go to the Blending section of 2 Connect Sound/Symbol.**

NO **If no, start at 1 Develop Oral Language.**

1 Develop Oral Language

Phonemic Awareness

Read aloud "Where the Green Grass Grows" from the Big Book of Rhymes and Rhythms. As you read, have children clap each time you say a word that begins with an *r*-blend. Invite children to join in on repeated readings of the poem.

Focus on the sounds of /gr/*gr*. Have children say the words *green, grass,* slowly, and *grows* emphasizing the beginning sounds. Ask which sounds they hear at the beginning of these words. If any children have names beginning with the letters *gr*, point that out. Follow a similar procedure with *fr* words such as *Franky*, and *tr* words such as *tries*.

Big Book of Rhymes and Rhythms

Where the Green Grass Grows

Down in the valley,
Where the green grass grows,
Franky's counting to eleven,
On his tiny, tiny toes.
He counts up to ten,
Then tries and tries again.
Pretty soon we smile,
'Cause everybody knows,
You can't find eleven,
On your tiny, tiny toes.

grass
Franky
tries
pretty

4–5

❷ Connect Sound/Symbol

Put It in Context

On chart paper, write these sentences from "Top Ten."

How do second graders spend their free time?

I do tricks!

Crafts and drawing also rate high.

Underline *gr* in graders and ask children to listen to the sounds as you point to the letters and blend the sounds. Repeat for *fr* in *free, tr* in *tricks, cr* in *crafts*, and *dr* in drawing.

Invite children to offer more words that begin with *r*-blends, and add them to the chart. Have volunteers underline the first two letters and blend the sounds as they read the words.

Blending

Place *r*-blend cards for *gr, fr, dr,* and *tr* on the chalk tray. Write *made* and read it aloud. Ask a volunteer to choose a card and cover the *m* in *made* to make a new word, such as *grade*. Have children read it. Repeat with *rain*, challenging children to make more than one new word.

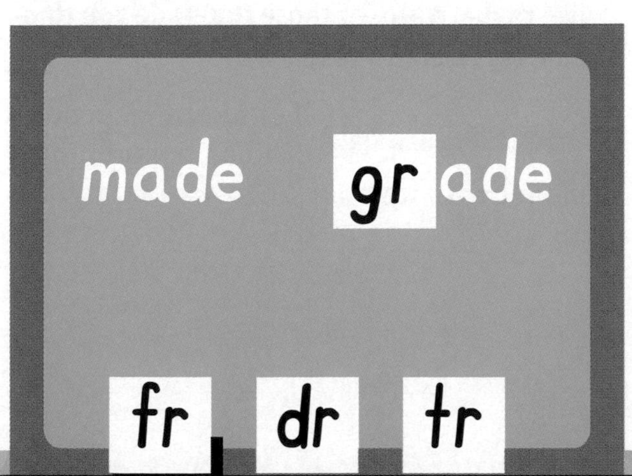

❸ Assess

Write

As a way of assessing children's understanding of *r*-blends, invite them to write the word *dip* on a piece of paper. Have them write another word by substituting an *r*-blend for the initial consonant. They can share the new words by writing a list on chart paper.

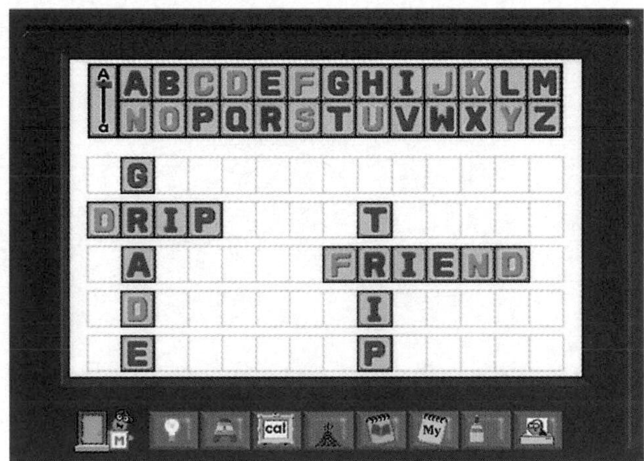

MAKE A COLLAGE OF *r*-BLEND WORDS Divide a large roll of paper into five sections. Put a word and corresponding picture with each *r*-blend in a section. Have children cut and paste pictures from old magazines for objects that begin with the same blends.

See Phonics and Word Building Kit for additional suggestions.

The Magnet Board activity pictured above provides additional phonics practice. For information on this and other Magnet Board activities, see the WiggleWorks Plus Teaching Plan.

SUPPORTING ALL LEARNERS

Peer Partners

ACCESS During the Make a Collage activity, have children with physical disabilities work with a buddy who can help them page through the magazines while they identify pictures beginning with these blends. Buddies can cut out the pictures and paste them on the collage according to the other's instructions.

CHALLENGE Challenge children to expand upon the Blending activity by working with a buddy to create a list of words for familiar objects that begin with *gr, fr, dr,* or *tr*. Encourage them to use the electronic Magnet Board to write down the words.

Building Fluency

Objectives

Children read *Monkey See, Monkey Do* for fluency.

Technology Options

Encourage children to listen to the audiocassette recording of *Monkey See, Monkey Do.*

Monkey See, Monkey Do

Written by Marc Gave

Illustrated by Jacqueline Rogers

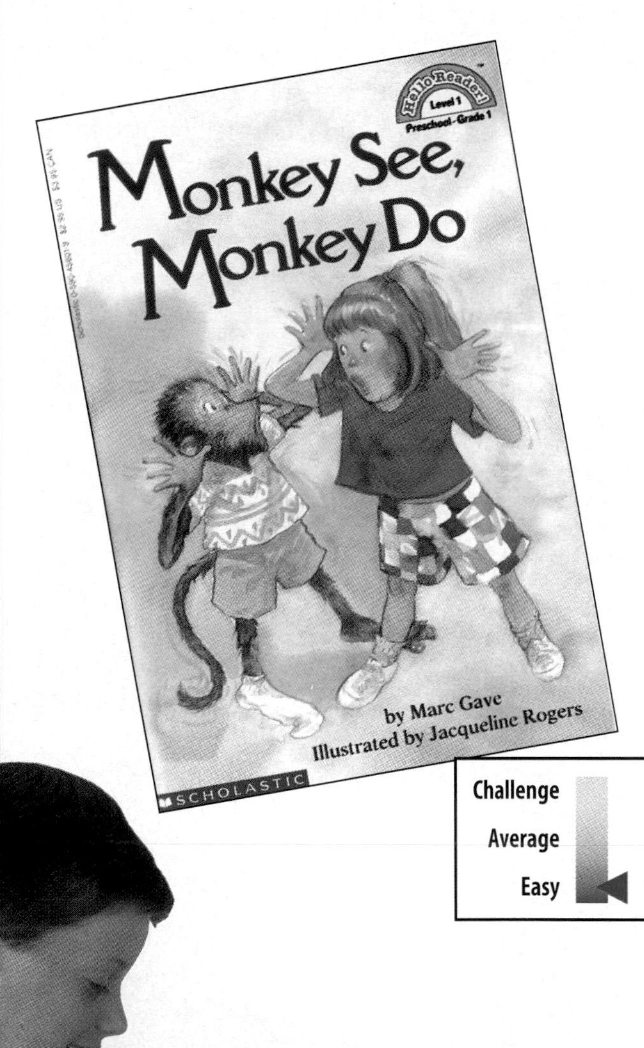

Challenge
Average
Easy

Preview and Read

Have children read the title and help them read the author's and illustrator's names. Let them flip through the book to look at the pictures. Before children begin reading, allow them to discover the repetitive text structure of every sentence beginning with the word *monkey* or *monkeys.*

- **Do you think the book is going to be fun? Why do you think that?**
- **What do you notice about some of the words in the story?**

Response Ideas

After children have read the book, they can meet with you or with a partner to discuss the story. Questions such as these will help the discussion:

- **What rhyming words can you find in the story?**
- **What words have opposite meanings?**

Read Across Texts

- **Think about what the children in "Top Ten" like to do. Which of those things do you think monkeys would like to do?**

Shoebox Library For more independent reading opportunities, choose books from the Shoebox Library.

USING THE TRADE BOOKS

Chester's Way

by Kevin Henkes

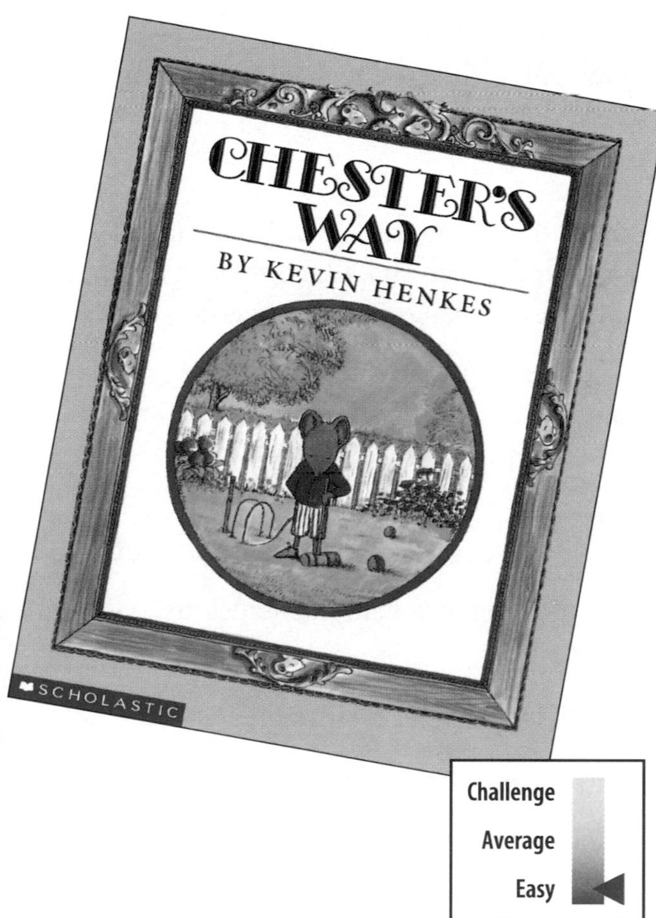

Challenge
Average
Easy

USING THE TRADE BOOK GUIDE

For in-depth teaching ideas, refer to the individual Trade Book Guide for *Chester's Way* by Kevin Henkes.

MAKE THEME CONNECTIONS:

WE HAVE DIFFERENT INTERESTS

Talk About It

Show the cover of *Chester's Way* and the first page of "Top Ten." Discuss that *Chester's Way* is fiction and "Top Ten" is nonfiction. Help children discover that both selections show how people can be different and still be friends. After reading *Chester's Way,* children can answer questions such as these.

- **How are Chester and Wilson alike?**
- **How are Chester and Wilson different from Lilly?**
- **What did Lilly do so that the boys accepted her?**

Write About It

After reading *Chester's Way,* invite children to write about their favorite part of the book.

Read Across Texts

After reading *Chester's Way,* encourage children to relate it to "Top Ten" and explore such questions as:

- **If Chester and Wilson were part of the "Top Ten" survey, which activities do you think they would have liked the best? What makes you think this?**
- **Do you think Chester, Wilson, and Lilly would prefer playing outside or inside? Why?**

Show what the graph in "Top Ten" would look like after Chester, Wilson, and Lilly vote for their favorite activity.

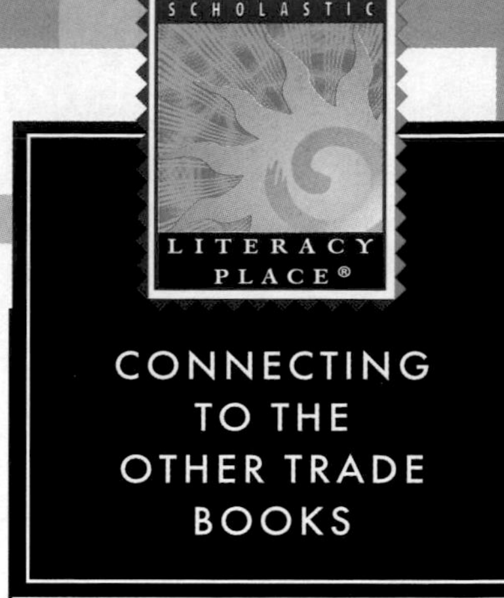

CONNECTING TO THE OTHER TRADE BOOKS

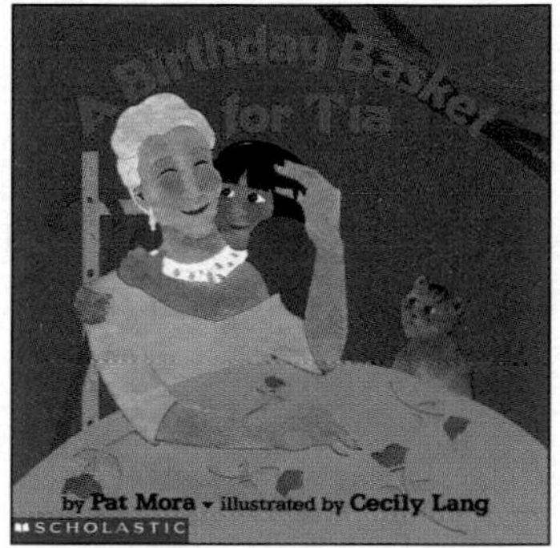

Ask children to summarize *A Birthday Basket for Tía.* Each child should pick up the story where the previous child left off.

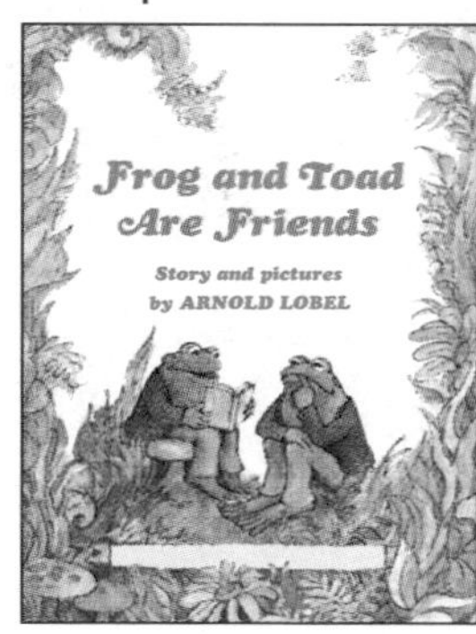

"Top Ten" is nonfiction while *Frog and Toad Are Friends* is fiction. Ask children which sentences in each suggest friendship.

Also for use with this plan

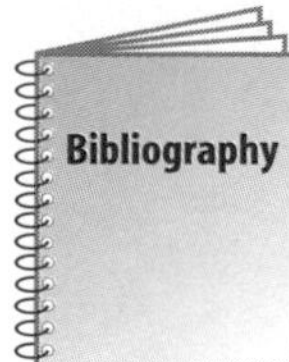

Use Your Sports Arena

Survey Another Class

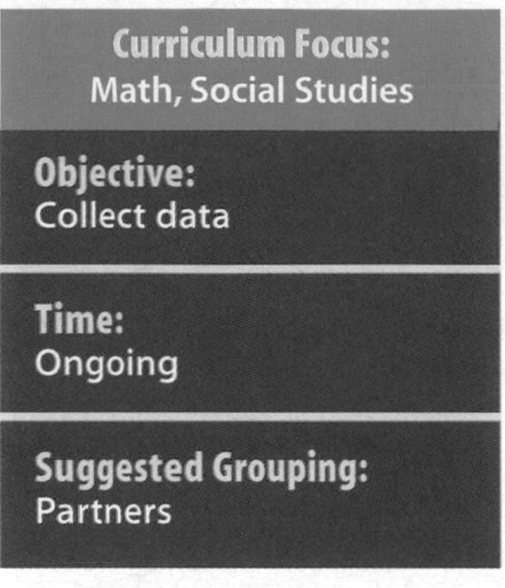

ACTIVITY Children survey students from other classrooms about their favorite sports.

Connect to the SourceBook Have children review the favorite activities of the children in the SourceBook selection.

Make New Discoveries

- In the Integrated Curriculum option on page R2, children will survey their own class and graph their results. Once they've done that, they're ready to take a bigger survey outside the class.
- Each pair questions two children from other classes during recess or lunch hour about their three favorite sports activities. The pair should note the grade level of each respondent.
- In the Sports Arena, post a sheet of chart paper for each grade level in your school. Children can write respondents' favorite sports activities on the appropriate grade level chart.
- Once all pairs have entered their results, ask children if they can draw any conclusions about favorite sports of different age groups.
- Some children might want to continue on with this activity, surveying many other people.

✔ **How to Assess** Were children able to collect and organize their data?

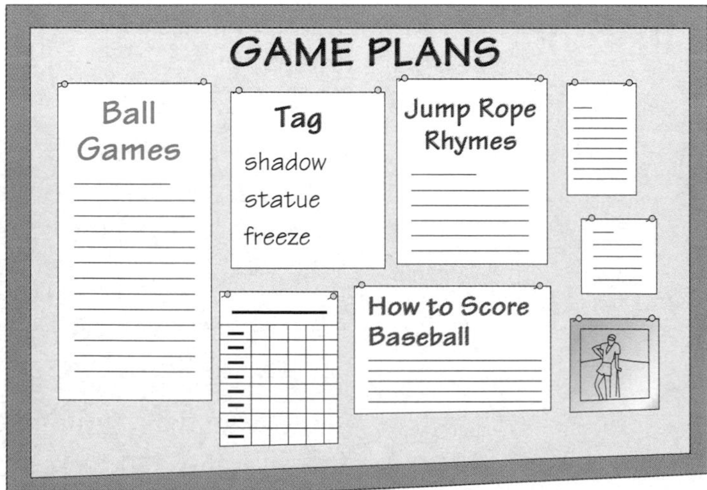

Curriculum Areas

Math

Children conduct a class survey about favorite fruits and make a graph like the one shown in "Top Ten." *See page R2.*

Science

Children test various balls and discover their different properties. *See page R2.*

Social Studies

Children list the top three locations they'd like to visit and make a graph. *See page R3.*

The Arts

Children illustrate the numerals for the favorite activities in the "Top Ten" graph. *See page R3.*

PERSONAL VOICE

Plan II

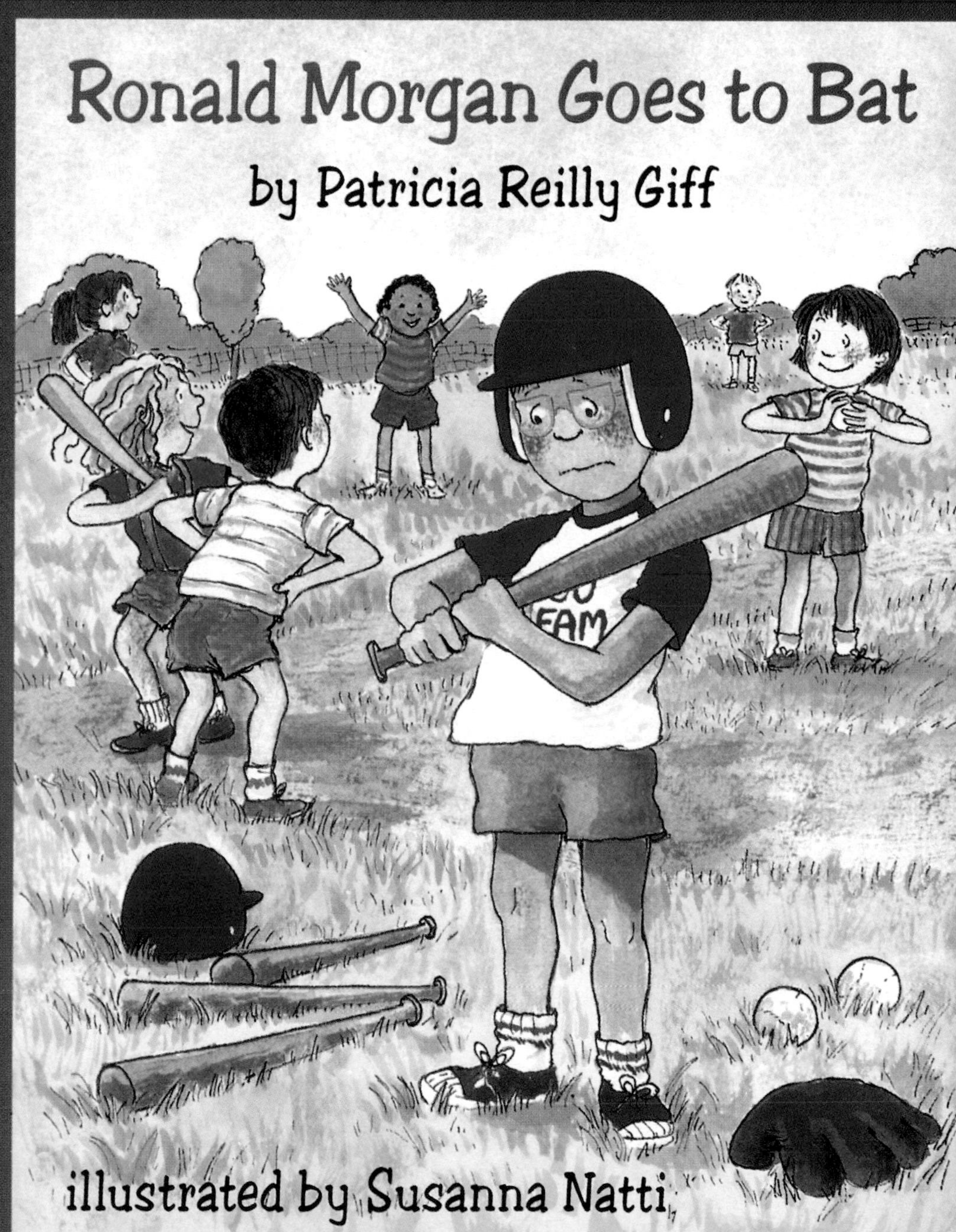

"Another satisfying story about the hero of Today Was a Terrible Day"
–Kirkus Reviews

WHAT CHILDREN WILL DO

share the Big Book *Max Found Two Sticks*

read the two selections

- *Ronald Morgan Goes to Bat* REALISTIC FICTION
- "Baseball Greats" BASEBALL CARDS

use the key strategy of Character

blend words with /a/*a*, /i/*i*, and *s*-blends

write details for a trading card about a sports or entertainment hero

apply what they learn about team spirit to activities they participate in

Assessing Your Students

ASSESSMENT	TEACHER'S SOURCEBOOK	ASSESSMENT KIT
Vocabulary Test	T47	Assessment Handbook
Observation	T48	Assessment Handbook
Assess Reading	T76	Classroom Management Forms
Conference	T76	Assessment Handbook
Performance-Based	T79	Assessment Handbook
Writing Benchmarks	T79	Assessment Handbook
Spelling Tests	T47, T81	Assessment Handbook
Quickcheck	T84, T86, T88	Assessment Handbook
Formal Tests	T311	Unit/Year Tests

Creating a Community of Learners

Max Found Two Sticks: pp. T44–45

- Express personal ideas
- Make predictions
- Active Listening MINI-LESSON

Demonstrating Independence

Using the Trade Books: pp. T90–91

- *The Bunny Hop* by Teddy Slater
- *Frog and Toad Are Friends* by Arnold Lobel

Integrating Learning: p. T92

- Activity: Tickets, Hot Dogs, and Popcorn

Focus on Phonics

Phonics Lessons

- Vowels /a/*a*, /i/*i*
- *s*-Blends

Phonics Kit

Literacy-at-Work Book

- Vowels /a/*a*, /i/*i*, pp. 19–20
- *s*-Blends, pp. 21–22

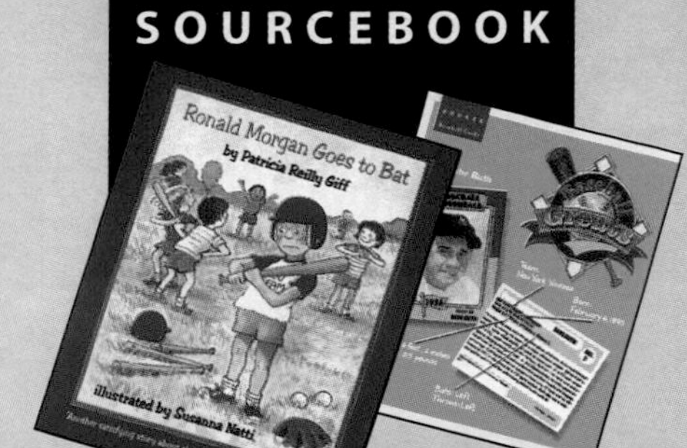

PLAN II ORGANIZER

Ronald Morgan Goes to Bat / "Baseball Greats"

	Instructional Path	Supporting All Learners	Resources and Technology
a READING THE SOURCES pp. T46–47	**Build Background** ✔ **Develop Vocabulary** *• practice • clutched • helmet • sneaker* **Reading Selections** *Ronald Morgan Goes to Bat* "Baseball Greats" Launch the Key Strategy: Character ✔ **Assess Reading**	EXTRA HELP p. T67 ESL pp. T47, T50, T74 CHALLENGE pp. T47, T56 MINI-LESSON Sports Jargon, p. T60; Evaluate Author's Purpose, p. T71; Baseball Card, p. T75 **Idea File:** p. T77 **Cultural Connections:** pp. T59, T77	**Transparency** Vocabulary, 3 **Literacy-at-Work Book** Vocabulary, p. 13; Comprehension Check, p. 14 **WiggleWorks™ Plus,** pp. T56, T58, T68, T77 **Scholastic Network** pp. T46
b INTEGRATING LANGUAGE ARTS pp. T78–83	✔ **Writing:** Write a Trading Card; Daily Language Practice ✔ **Grammar:** Naming Places ✔ **Mechanics:** Commas ✔ **Spelling:** Words with *s*-Blends *• snap • snack • slide • sled • swim • swing • step • stage*	ESL pp. T79, T83 ACCESS p. T79 **Activity File:** pp. T82–83 Listen to a Sports Broadcast; Be a Sports Announcer; Dramatize the Story; Create a Sports Poster MINI-LESSON Action Verbs, p. T82; Oral Expression, p. T83	**Literacy-at-Work Book** Writing, p. 15 **Grammar, Usage, and Mechanics Practice:** pp. 3–4 **Spelling Practice:** p. 2 **Handwriting Practice:** p. 2 **WiggleWorks™ Plus,** pp. T79, T83 **Additional Technology** p. T82
 **c BUILDING SKILLS AND STRATEGIES** pp. T84–89	✔ Quickcheck Launch the Key Strategy: Character ✔ Quickcheck PHONICS: Vowels /a/ *a*, /i/ *i* ✔ Quickcheck PHONICS: *s*-Blends	EXTRA HELP pp. T85, T89 ESL pp. T85, T87 CHALLENGE pp. T85, T87, T89	**Transparency** Key Strategy, 4 **Literacy-at-Work Book** Character, pp. 16–18; Phonics, pp. 19–22  **WiggleWorks™ Plus,** pp. T87, T89

✔ = **Assessed**

Share the Big Book

Objectives

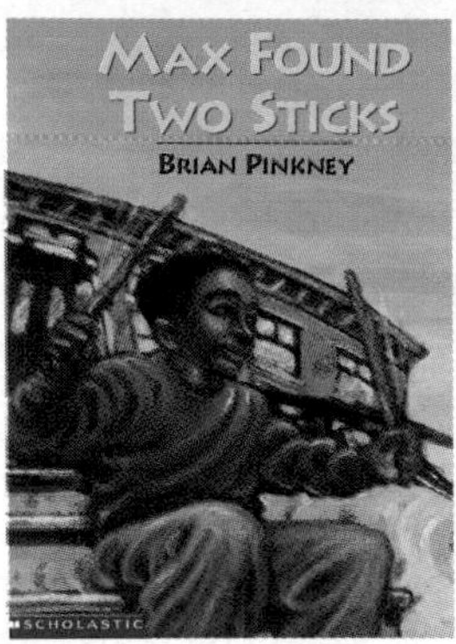

Children learn to:
- **express ideas**
- **make predictions as they read**
- **listen actively**

Materials: Big Book: *Max Found Two Sticks*
Time: About 20–40 minutes
Suggested Grouping: Whole class

Technology Options

Children may enjoy listening to *Max Found Two Sticks* on audiocassette.

Max Found Two Sticks

Children will share a Big Book about a boy who experiences the joys of **making music** before they read *Ronald Morgan Goes to Bat,* the story of a boy who experiences his first successes playing **baseball**.

Introduce the Big Book

Spark children's interest in the Big Book by asking the question, "What could you do with two sticks?" Write the question on chart paper.

Ask children to think about the question. Then invite volunteers to tell their answers to the question. Record their ideas on the chart. Next, explain to children that the story they are going to read is about a boy who finds some interesting things to do with two sticks he finds.

Read the Big Book

Read the Big Book aloud, pausing as children comment or make predictions. You might ask questions such as the following at strategic breaks in the reading.

When the two twigs fall to the ground, ask:

- **What do you think Max might do with the two sticks?**

When the children show up with sodas, ask:

- **What do you think Max will play with next?**

When Max taps on the garbage cans, ask:

- **What sound do the sticks make when Max hits them on the cans? Try to imitate the sound with your voices.**

THE ARTS

THINK ABOUT THE BIG BOOK

After you have read the book, invite children to share their thoughts and opinions. Ask questions such as:

- **Did you like the story? Why or why not?**
- **What was your favorite part?**
- **Do you like the illustrations? What do you like about them?**

Look again at the chart with children's ideas about what they would do if they found two sticks. Encourage children to compare their ideas with what Max does.

Activity: Discover Sounds

Invite children to discover different sounds they can make by tapping on objects. Encourage volunteers, one at a time, to choose an object in the classroom and tap on it with pencils or drumsticks as the rest of the class listens closely. Ask children to describe each sound and compare it to sounds other children have made.

- **Why do you think different objects make different sounds?** SCIENCE

MAKE CONNECTIONS

To Children's Lives

Some people say that everything has a rhythm of its own. Encourage children to listen to the rhythm of sounds in and around your classroom. Have children close their eyes and name the sounds they hear. If needed, point out sounds such as:

- the clock ticking
- the rhythm of footsteps in the hall
- birds chirping
- car motors rumbling

Write the sounds on the chalkboard. Invite children to describe each sound, then tap to its rhythm with their fingers.

MINI-LESSON

ACTIVE LISTENING

TEACH/MODEL Invite children to listen for the sounds Max makes in the story, and to hear the sounds in their imaginations. Read to the place in the story when Max taps his thighs.

> **THINK ALOUD When I hear the words *pat...pat-tat*, I can imagine Max rhythmically tapping the sticks on his thighs. The words *pat...pat-tat* suggest the sounds Max makes.**

APPLY Reread the story and ask children to listen for the sounds Max makes. Each time you read the sound words, invite children to try to imagine the sound.

a

READING THE SOURCES

RONALD MORGAN GOES TO BAT / BASEBALL GREATS

Build Background

In the Big Book, children read about Max's **special interest** in **drumming.** Now they will read in *Ronald Morgan Goes to Bat* and "Baseball Greats" about another special interest—**baseball.**

Objectives

Children learn to:

- brainstorm ideas
- expand oral language
- develop context for vocabulary

Materials:
Transparency 3
Literacy-at-Work Book p. 13
Word Cards 7–10

Time:
About 20 minutes

Suggested Grouping:
Whole class or cooperative groups

Literacy-at-Work Book, p. 13

Name | VOCABULARY

Play Ball!

▶ Fill in the blanks. Use the words from the box.

clutched
helmet
practice
sneaker

I want to be a good hitter so I *practice* a lot. When I bat, I always wear a *helmet* to protect my head. When the pitch came, I *clutched* the bat tightly and hit the ball hard! As I ran from home plate, I heard everyone laughing. I looked down at my feet and saw I was missing a *sneaker*. I laughed, too!

Unit 1 • Snapshots • Plan II • *Ronald Morgan Goes to Bat* 13

ACTIVATE PRIOR KNOWLEDGE

Discuss Learning New Skills

Engage children in a discussion about a time they worked hard to learn a new skill, such as tying shoelaces, riding a two-wheeler, or playing a game.

- **What was the hardest part of learning the new skill? What was the easiest part?**
- **Once you learned the skill, what did you do to get better at it?**
- **Who helped you?**
- **If you were going to teach a friend this new skill, what would you tell your friend is the most important thing to do?**

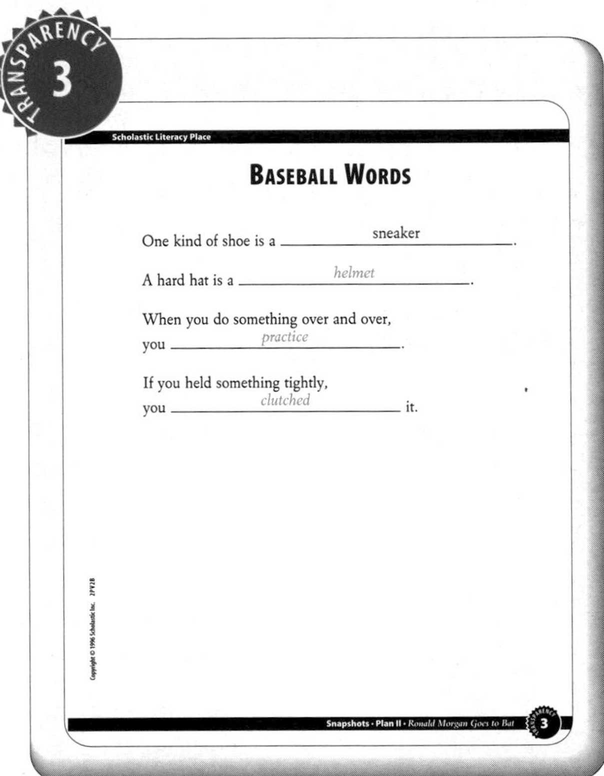

TRANSPARENCY 3

Scholastic Literacy Place

BASEBALL WORDS

One kind of shoe is a *sneaker*.

A hard hat is a *helmet*.

When you do something over and over, you *practice*.

If you held something tightly, you *clutched* it.

Snapshots • Plan II • *Ronald Morgan Goes to Bat* 3

Annotated transparency for teaching concept words

Develop Vocabulary

TEACH THE CONCEPT WORDS

Strategy: Prior Knowledge For each of the concept words, create simple riddles for children to solve, such as those that follow:

- **You wear this on your head when you ride a bicycle or play hockey. What is it?**
- **This is something you do to learn a new skill, like playing the piano. You also do it to get better at the skill. What is it?**
- **You wear this on your feet when you walk in a gym or play outside. What is it?**
- **This is an action you may have done with your hands to hold something tight. What did you do?**

OPTION

Have children complete the sentences on Transparency 3 and read them aloud to determine if their answers make sense. You may want to create more sentences on the transparency, using the concept words.

Support Words As children read, point out other new words in the story.

afraid: frightened
deserve: be worthy of something
raisins: sweet, dried grapes
spirit: a feeling; enthusiasm or liveliness
terrific: wonderful; excellent
whispered: spoke quietly

Personal Word List As they read, children may look for other sports-related words and add these to their personal word lists.

VOCABULARY

ORGANIZING CONCEPT: BASEBALL WORDS

Concept Words

✔	**practice:**	**to do something again and again (p. 21)**
	clutched:	**held tightly (p. 22)**
✔	**helmet:**	**a hard hat that protects the head (p. 22)**
✔	**sneaker:**	**a soft shoe with a flat rubber bottom (p. 31)**

✔ = assessed

See p. T81 for words to pretest and spelling instruction

Technology Options

To help build background about learning new skills, invite children to initiate an on-line chat over the Scholastic Network. Encourage them to discuss with other users new skills they've recently acquired and how they would help others learn those skills. Children might enjoy chatting about new computer skills they are learning.

SUPPORTING ALL LEARNERS

Work in Groups

ESL Children acquiring English may not be familiar with the new language presented in the word riddles. Support them in the riddles activity by grouping them with children who can explain or act out difficult words and expressions for them.

CHALLENGE After reviewing the support words, challenge children to work together in cooperative groups to make up their own word riddles to describe them.

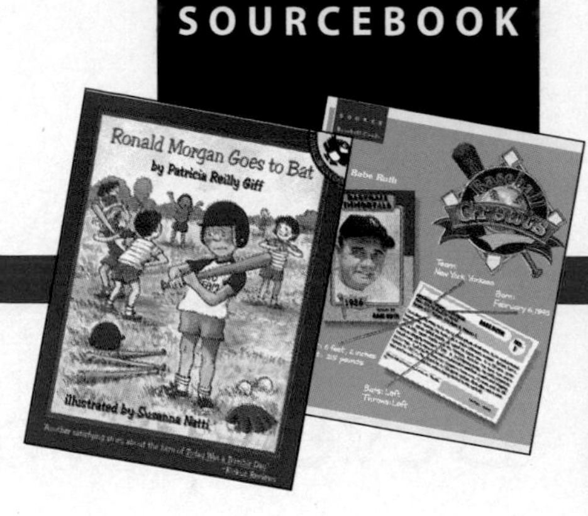

a

READING THE SOURCES

RONALD MORGAN GOES TO BAT/BASEBALL GREATS

Prepare to Teach

OBSERVATION

As children read Ronald Morgan Goes to Bat, notice how they:

- ✔ make connections with the *theme* that all people have special talents to offer others.
- ✔ use the *key strategy* of Character.
- ✔ recognize the *literary elements* of Realistic Fiction.

Use the Individual and Class Plan Assessment Checklists in the Classroom Management Forms, pp. 5 and 11.

KEY STRATEGY:

CHARACTER

Ronald Morgan Goes to Bat provides tremendous opportunities for children to identify character traits and feelings. They can do this through what Ronald Morgan says and does, what other characters say about him, what inferences children make about him, and what story events takes place.

Customize Instruction

FLEXIBLE GROUPING

Teacher Support

Construct meaning by using the key strategy of Character as children read the selection. Revisit the selection to build understanding of the literary elements of Realistic Fiction.

Collaborative

Since the text on each page of the story is equivalent in length, this is a good opportunity for buddy reading. Children can take turns reading consecutive pages aloud.

Extra Support

Reread the story as Readers Theater. Read the part of Ronald Morgan. Invite children to read the parts of other characters. Develop oral language as you discuss what is happening in the illustrations.

Independent

After children read silently without interruption, use the questions on page T76. Children may also want to respond in their Journals.

Meet the Author

Patricia Reilly Giff

Patricia Reilly Giff has always loved books and, in fact, became interested in writing by reading. As a child, Ms. Giff spent hours in the library and at one point had actually read every book in the children's section! Today this celebrated children's author writes several popular series for younger readers, including the Polk Street School and the Polka Dot Private Eye, as well as the award-winning Ronald Morgan series. *Ronald Morgan Goes to Bat* was an IRA Children's Choice Winner. Children may read about this author on pages 142–143 of the SourceBook.

◀ **SourceBook pp. 18–41**

More by Patricia Reilly Giff

- ***The Beast in Ms. Rooney's Room***
  A sympathetic teacher gives Richard "The Beast" Best the confidence to enter a reading contest.
- ***Today Was a Terrible Day***
  An unexpected occurrence finally changes poor Ronald's luck.
- ***Watch Out, Ronald Morgan!***
  The world is seen through a new perspective after a teacher advises Ronald to get fitted for glasses.

Books for Word Study

- ***Inch by Inch***
  by Leo Lionni
  A clever inchworm outwits a hungry bird. **(vowel /i/*i*)**
- ***Millions of Cats***
  by Wanda Gag
  This classic tale is about a couple who want one cat but wind up with millions instead. **(vowels /a/*a*, /i/*i*)**
- ***Slither, Swoop, Swing***
  by Alex Ayliff
  An exuberant, easy-to-read book, it describes different ways to move. **(*s*-blends)**

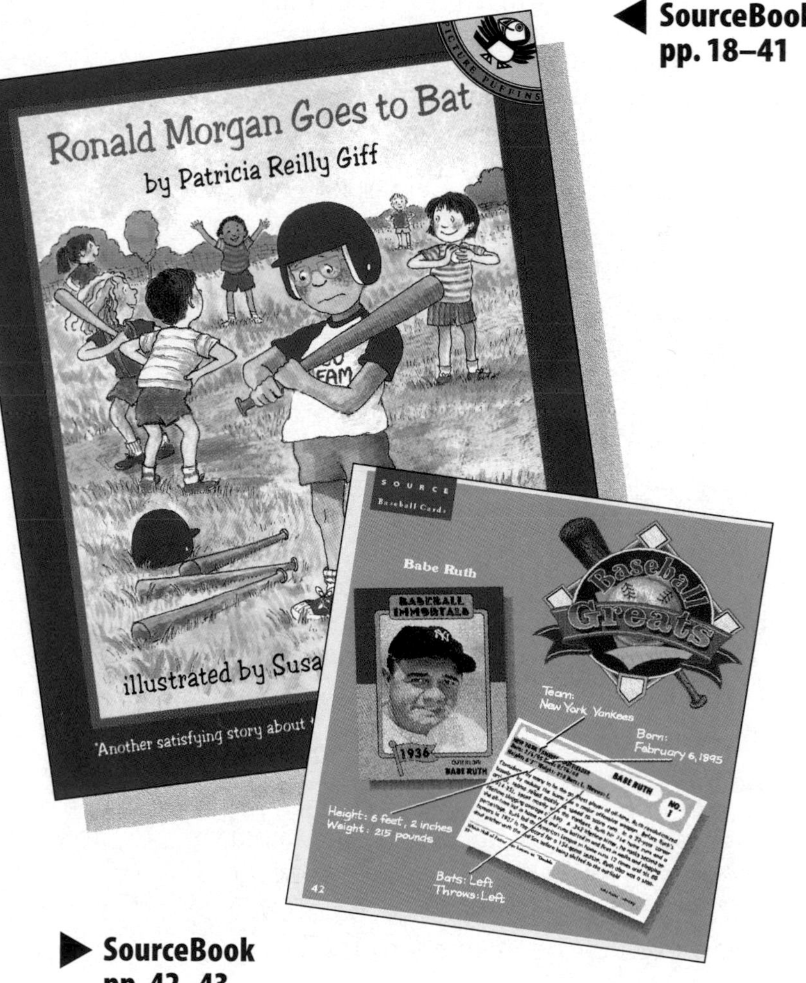

▶ **SourceBook pp. 42–43**

a

Reading the Sources

Preview and Predict

Reader to Reader

As soon as I saw the cover of *Ronald Morgan Goes to Bat,* I wanted to read the story because baseball is such a popular sport. And Patricia Reilly Giff is a popular author.

Read the title and the author's and the illustrator's names to children. Ask questions to help children note Ronald Morgan's facial expression and why he might look unhappy. As children study the pictures, help them identify the words printed on Ronald's shirt and what clue that may give about him.

After children look through the story, have them wonder aloud about what will happen. List their questions on a chart.

Have children glance at the baseball cards. Ask what they think they will learn about the ballplayers from the information given.

We Wonder. . .

- What will happen to Ronald Morgan when he tries to play baseball?
- Will Ronald become a good player?

Have children record what they wonder about *Ronald Morgan Goes to Bat*. They can predict the answers to their questions.

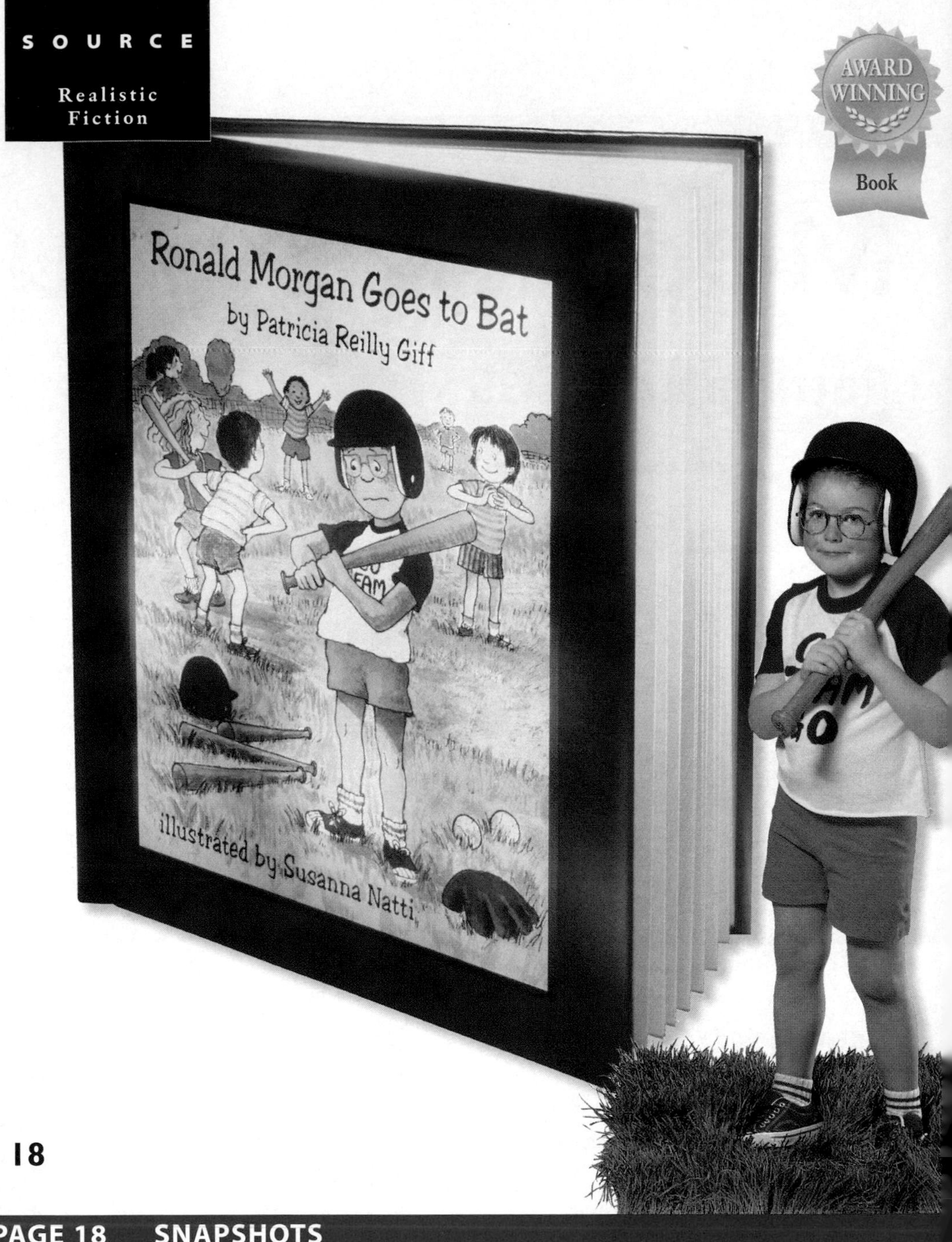

PAGE 18 SNAPSHOTS

Supporting All Learners

Preview ESL Ronald Morgan's changing facial expressions parallel the turns the story takes. As children preview the pictures, draw a simple time line on the chalkboard. Encourage them to help you mark when Ronald Morgan's expression changes and indicate why they think it does. **(Graphic Device)** VISUAL LITERACY

Baseball started today.
Mr. Spano said everyone could play.
"Even me?" I asked.
And Tom said,
"You're letting Ronald Morgan play?
He can't hit, he can't catch.
He can't do anything."
Mr. Spano looked at me.
"Everyone," he said.
"Yahoo!" I yelled.

19

RONALD MORGAN GOES TO BAT PAGE 19

Guided Reading ▶

LAUNCH THE KEY STRATEGY:

CHARACTER

THINK ALOUD The more I know about a character, the better I understand and appreciate the story. I look for clues in the pictures. When I look at the picture on the cover, Ronald seems worried, but on the first page of the story he seems happy.

I also look for clues in the words. An author chooses words carefully to describe a character. On the first page, another character describes Ronald as a player who's not very good. Ronald himself seems surprised when the coach says everyone can play because he asks "Even me?" I know he's happy because he says "Yahoo!" These clues help me figure out what the character is like.

a

Read On ► ► ►

I pulled on my red and white shirt,
the one that says GO TEAM GO,
and ran outside to the field.
"Two things," Mr. Spano told us.
"Try hard, and keep your eye on the ball."

20

PAGE 20 SNAPSHOTS

Revisit ◄

Print Awareness: Exclamation Marks

Provide a model of fluent reading. Read aloud the first two pages, and ask children to imitate, or echo, what they hear.

Explain that punctuation marks at the ends of sentences are clues that the author gives to help us read with expression. Point out that the exclamation mark after *Yahoo* on page 19 means that Ronald shouted that word.

Remind children that an exclamation mark at the end of a sentence tells us to read that sentence with excitement.

Encourage children to look for other exclamation marks as they read the story.

Then it was time to practice.
Michael was up first.
He smacked the ball with the bat.
The ball flew across the field.
"Good," said Mr. Spano.
"Great, Slugger!" I yelled.
"We'll win every game."

❶

21

RONALD MORGAN GOES TO BAT PAGE 21

Guided Reading ▶

❶ **KEY STRATEGY: Character Look at Ronald in the picture on this page. He looks happy and excited when Michael hits the ball, and he cheers for him. What does this tell you about Ronald? Ronald seems to be a good sport, doesn't he?** VISUAL LITERACY

Revisit ◀

Author's Craft: First-Person Narrative

After reading the first few pages, children should realize that Ronald Morgan is the narrator of the story.

- **Who is telling this story?**
- **How do you know?**

Point out the use of pronouns such as *I*, *me*, and *my*. You may wish to tell children that when a story is told from a character's point of view, it is written in the first person.

▶ INTEGRATED CURRICULUM **SCIENCE** *(See p. R4)*

Children diagram the movement of a ball rebounding against a wall.

a

Read On ▶ ▶ ▶

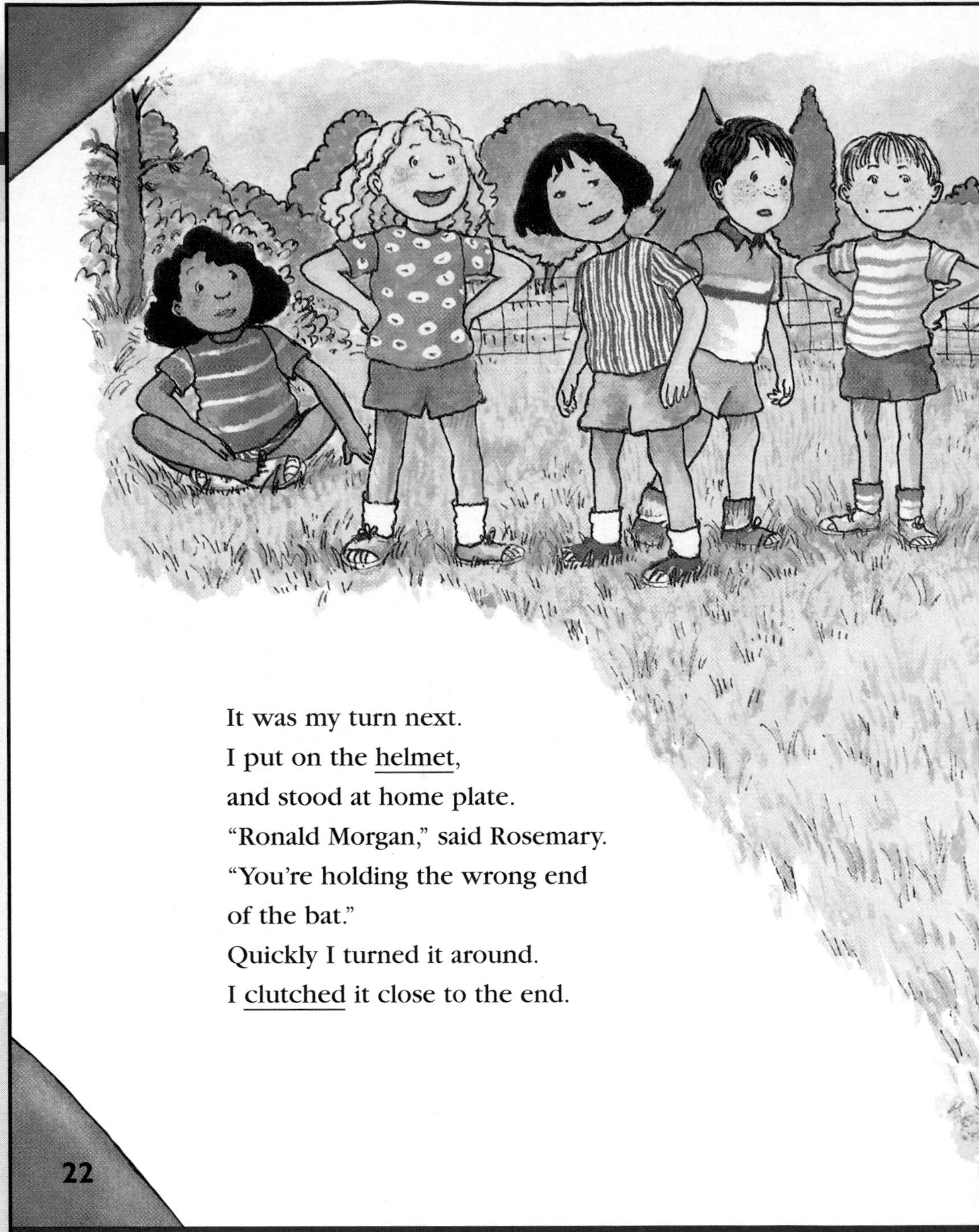

Revisit ◀

Context Clues: Unfamiliar Words

Point out that Ronald says he clutched the bat close to the end. Ask children how they could figure out what *clutched* means by looking for clues on the page. Help children recognize that Rosemary tells Ronald that he's holding the wrong end of the bat. After they determine that *clutched* means "held," substitute *held* for *clutched* in the sentence to see if the meaning is correct.

Summarize how to use the strategy:

- **Read the sentence carefully.**
- **Think about what the word may mean in that sentence.**
- **Substitute another word with a similar meaning to see if the word you chose is correct.**

Guided Reading ►

❷ **Make Predictions** **Look at the picture on this page. What is Ronald doing wrong? What does this tell you about Ronald and how he will be at hitting the ball?** VISUAL LITERACY

a

Guided Reading ▶

3 Make Judgments **Tom says that Ronald Morgan is the worst. That's not a very nice thing to say about someone. Tom probably thinks that Ronald Morgan will be bad for the team. What do you think? Should Ronald Morgan be allowed to play on the team or not?**

4 Word Attack **Let's read the fourth sentence together: *It hit me in the....* How can we figure out the word after *the*? I see that the word begins with *k*. Is it *kitten*: *It hit me in the kitten*? That doesn't make sense. Now look at the picture. Ronald looks upset and is holding his knee. *It hit me in the knee.* Yes, *knee* has a silent *k* at the beginning and it makes sense in the sentence and with the picture.** VISUAL LITERACY

Whoosh went the first ball.
Whoosh went the second one.
Wham went the third.
4 It hit me in the knee.
"Are you all right?" asked Michael.
But I heard Tom say,
"I knew it.
3 Ronald Morgan's the worst."

24

PAGE 24 SNAPSHOTS

Revisit ◀

Figurative Language: Onomatopoeia

Reread the three lines on page 24 that contain the words *whoosh* and *wham*. Remind children that writers sometimes use words to stand for sounds. Sometimes writers make up a word to stand for a sound. You may want to mention that a word describing a sound is called onomatopoeia.

Explain that when you say the word *whoosh*, you can hear the sound the ball makes as it goes right past Ronald Morgan. Have children listen as you say the word *wham* and tell what they think the ball did. Help them recognize that this is the sound the ball makes when it hits Ronald.

Supporting All Learners

Revisit

CHALLENGE Challenge children to brainstorm their own list of words that imitate sounds, and encourage them to make up sentences using onomatopoeia. Then they can share these sentences with classmates. **(Brainstorm)**

- Invite children to write or record their sentences on the computer.

At snack time,
we told Miss Tyler about the team.
"I don't hit very well," I said.
And Rosemary said,
"The ball hits him instead."
Everybody laughed, even me.
I shook my head.
"I hope it doesn't happen again."
Miss Tyler gave me some raisins.
"You have to hit the ball
before it hits you," she said.

Read On ► ► ►

a

Guided Reading ▶

5 **Personal Response Ronald hasn't gotten hit by the ball again, but from what Rosemary says, I know that he hasn't hit it yet either. What do you think the problem is? What advice would you give him?**

Encourage children to write their advice in the form of a letter on the computer.

We played every day.
I tried hard, but the ball came fast.
I closed my eyes and swung.
5 "If only he could hit the ball once,"
Rosemary said.
And Billy shook his head.
I couldn't tell them I was afraid
of the ball.
"Go team go," I whispered.

26

PAGE 26 SNAPSHOTS

PHONICS Vowels /a/*a*, /i/*i*

Have children find the word *fast* on page 26, point to the letter *a*, and read the word aloud.

- **What other words in the story have the same vowel sound? What other words do you know that have this vowel sound?**

Then have children find the word *hit* on the same page, point to the letter *i*, and read the word aloud.

- **Do you see other words on this page that have the same vowel sound? What other words do you know that have the same vowel sound?**

*(See Phonics: Vowels /a/*a*, /i/*i* on p. T86–87.)*

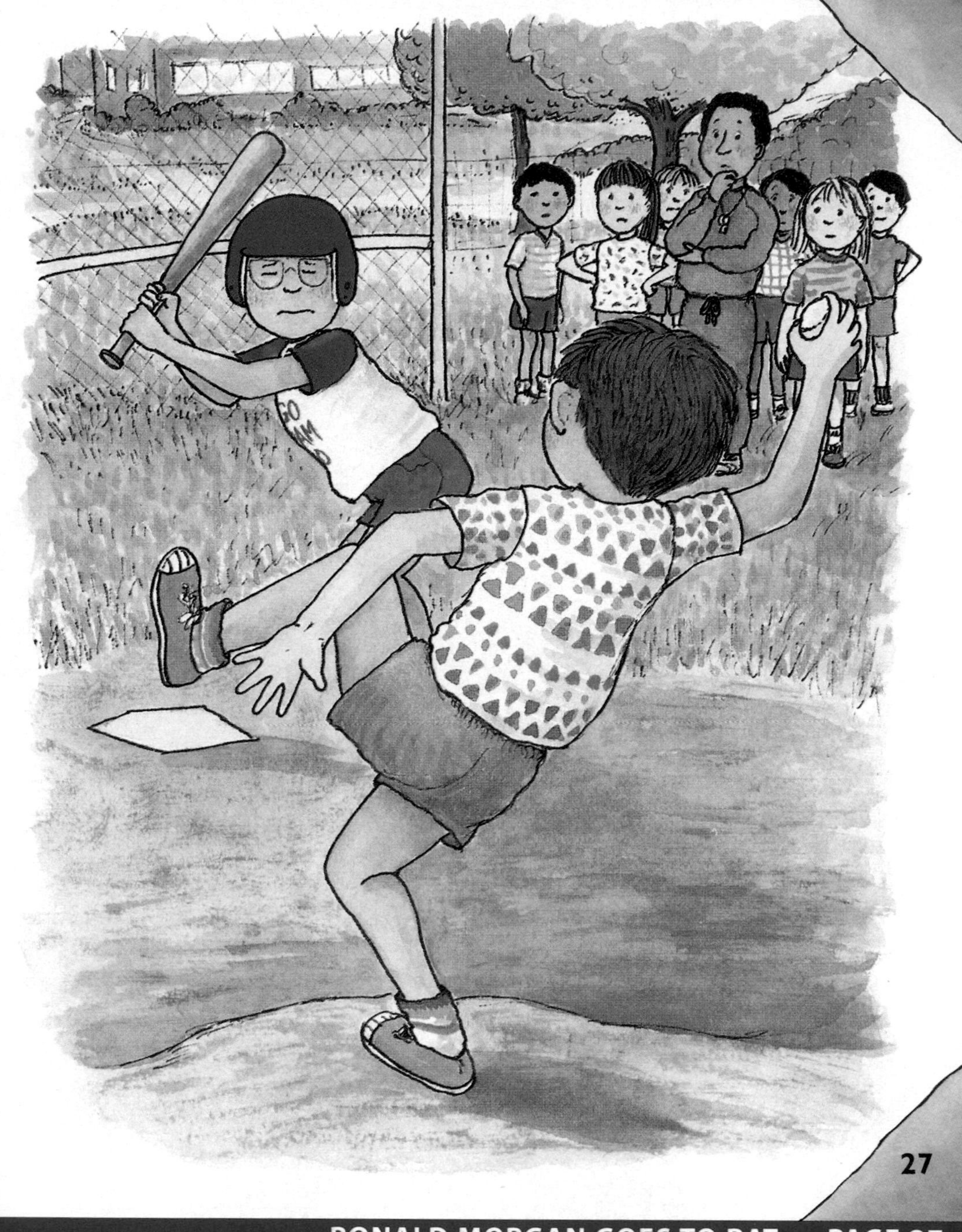

Read On ► ► ►

CULTURAL CONNECTIONS

Baseball is the national sport of the United States. It is also very popular in the Dominican Republic, a country in the Caribbean. You might be surprised to hear that a number of today's major league players all come from the same small Dominican Republic town of San Pedro de Macoris. In what other countries is baseball a popular sport?

a

Guided Reading ►

6 Sports Jargon Ronald says the third-grade team is big, strong, and good. What makes the third-grade team so good? Why is a baseball team good if it "hits a home run" or "tags a man out"? These words have special meaning when they're used to describe an action in baseball. MINI-LESSON

One day, the team sat on the grass.
We watched the third grade play.
They were big, they were strong,
6 they were good.
Johnny hit a home run,
and Joy tagged a man out.

28

PAGE 28 SNAPSHOTS

MINI-LESSON

SPORTS JARGON

TEACH/MODEL Explain to children that certain words have different meanings when used in connection with sports. Food is served on a plate, but on page 22 Ronald is standing at home plate. Home plate is where the batters stand in baseball. Read the last sentence on page 28.

THINK ALOUD I know what *home* means. I know what *run* means. But together the words *home* and *run* have a new meaning. In baseball, a batter hits a home run when he or she runs around all the bases and reaches home plate before the ball does.

APPLY Have volunteers explain what *tagged a man out* means. Invite children to identify other baseball terms they know, such as *diamond.*

SUPPORTING ALL LEARNERS

ESL Baseball expressions like *hit a home run* and *tagged a man out* offer a good opportunity to introduce and practice sports jargon. Reread the text on page 28 aloud, placing emphasis on these phrases. Then choose volunteers to act out these and other sports expressions to ensure children's comprehension. **(Pantomime)**

Revisit

"We'll never hit like that," said Tom.
And Rosemary said,
"We'll never catch like that either." 8
But I said,
"Our team is the best."
Mr. Spano nodded.
"That's the spirit, Ronald." 7

29

RONALD MORGAN GOES TO BAT PAGE 29

Guided Reading ►

7 **KEY STRATEGY: Character** **We're learning about Ronald from what he says and from what others say about him. When Ronald says their team is best, Mr. Spano tells Ronald, "That's the spirit." What does this comment tell us about the kind of person Ronald is?**

8 **Make Judgments** **Do you agree with Tom and Rosemary, who say that their team will never be as good as the third-grade team, or with Ronald, who says their team is the best? Explain why you think so.**

► INTEGRATED CURRICULUM **SOCIAL STUDIES** *(See p. R5)*
Children make a scrapbook of a team sport showing players encouraging each other.

► INTEGRATING LANGUAGE ARTS **SPEAKING/LISTENING** *(See p. T82)*

a

Read On ► ► ►

Mr. Spano told us,
"Now we'll run the bases.
Rosemary, you can go first."
Rosemary went fast.
She raced for first base.
"Terrific, Speedy!" I yelled.

30

PAGE 30 SNAPSHOTS

► INTEGRATED CURRICULUM **MATH** *(See p. R4)*

Children chart the results of a fast-walking relay race to see how practice helped Ronald in the story.

"Let me go next," I said.
"I can do that, too."
But the field was muddy.
My sneaker came off.
Jimmy said, "That kid's running
bases the wrong way."
And Tom yelled, "Ronald Morgan.
You're heading for third base."

31

RONALD MORGAN GOES TO BAT PAGE 31

Guided Reading ▶

❾ Compare/Contrast **Look at the children in the pictures on pages 30 and 31. Why do their expressions change?** VISUAL LITERACY

SUPPORTING ALL LEARNERS

Read

ACCESS Before asking Read 9, guide children in making the connection between the characters' facial expressions and what they are feeling by drawing on personal experience. Choose volunteers to take turns making different facial expressions. Help children guess what their classmates are feeling.
(Make Connections)

PHONICS Vowel /e/*e*

Have children find the words *next* and *yelled* on page 31 and read the words aloud. Ask how these two words are alike, and have children point to the letter *e* in each word.

- **What other words in the story have the same vowel sound? What other words do you know that have this vowel sound?**

a

Read On ►►►

Revisit ◄

Relate to Experience

Discuss with children the problems that Ronald has had playing ball so far.

- **Has anything like this ever happened to you? Tell us about it.**
- **Thinking about experiences you've had that are similar to those in a story can help you understand what you read.**

The next day, we worked on catching.
I was out in left field.
While I waited, I found a stick,
and started to scratch out the mud.
I wrote G for go.
I wrote G for great.
Our team is the best, I thought.
Then I wrote H for hit.
H for home run.
If only I could do that.

32

PAGE 32 SNAPSHOTS

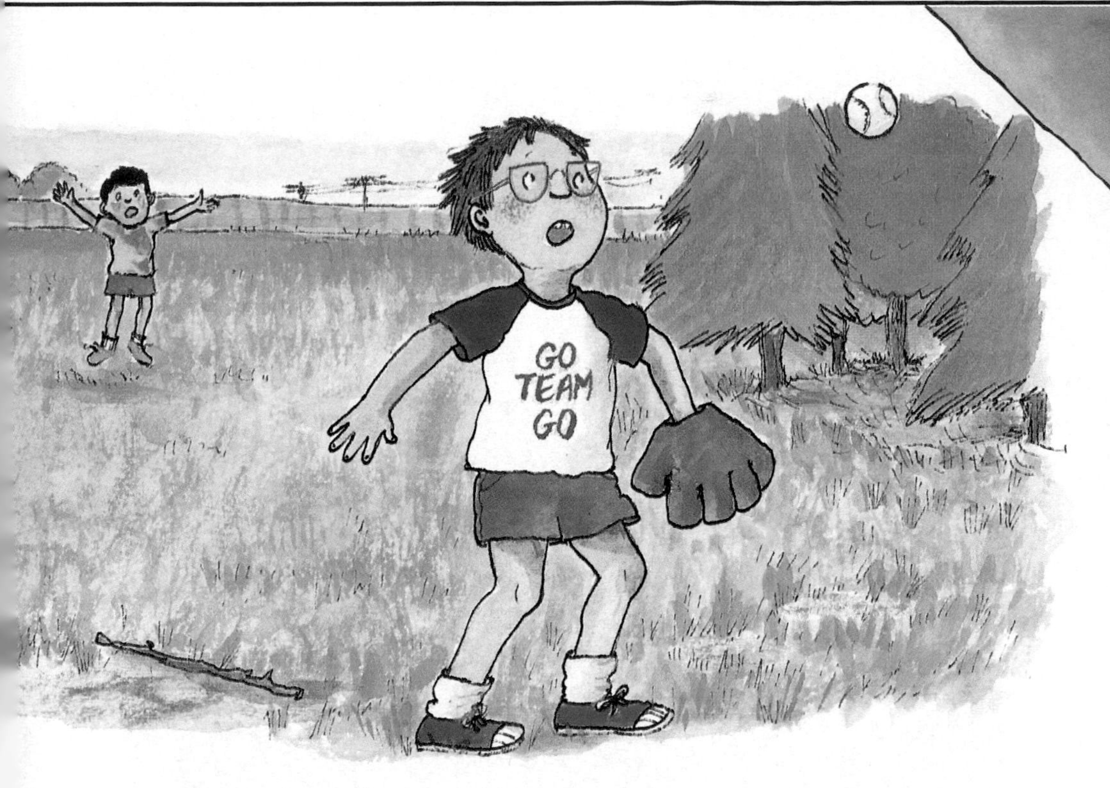

Just then I heard yelling.
Someone had hit the ball.
"Catch it, Ronald!" Tom shouted.
10 I put down the stick.
I put up my mitt.
Too late.
The ball sailed into the trees.

33

RONALD MORGAN GOES TO BAT PAGE 33

Guided Reading ►

10 Draw Conclusions Poor Ronald! He's not very good at hitting the ball or running. Why isn't he good at catching the ball either?

PHONICS *r*-Blends

Have children find the word *trees* on page 33, point to the letters *tr,* and read the word aloud. Mention that the two consonant letters at the beginning of the word are blended together when they say *trees*.

- **What other words do you know that start with the same sounds as trees?**

Encourage children to look for other words in the story that begin with *r*-blends, including *trying, practice, grade, grass,* and *grabbed.*

a

Read On ▶ ▶ ▶

Mr. Spano took us for ice cream.
"You deserve it for trying," he said.
"Our team is really good."
I had a chocolate cone.
Michael's a slugger, I thought.
And Rosemary can really run.
But I'm still afraid of the ball.

34

PAGE 34 SNAPSHOTS

On the way home,
we saw some kids playing ball.
"Want to hit a few?" Michael asked.
I shook my head.
"Maybe I won't play ball anymore."
Michael said, "We need you. 
You have spirit.
You help the team feel good." 
"But how can we win?" I asked.
"I can't even hit the ball."

35

RONALD MORGAN GOES TO BAT PAGE 35

Guided Reading ►

11 CRITICAL THINKING: Synthesize What does Michael mean when he tells Ronald that the team needs him because he has spirit? What is spirit? Why is it important?

12 KEY STRATEGY: Character What has Ronald done in the story that shows he has spirit?

INTERVENTION STRATEGY

Quotation Marks

Speaker changes may be confusing. Point out Michael's first speech on page 35 and the speaker tag. Read the next two lines where there is no new speaker tag when Ronald says, "Maybe I won't play ball anymore." Help children figure out that Ronald is speaking now.

Supporting All Learners

Read

EXTRA HELP Some children will benefit from role-playing what each speaker says. After introducing quotation marks, select two children to play the roles of Michael and Ronald. You may want to write the spoken sentences on the chalkboard, have different pairs read the lines labeling which character says each sentence. **(Role-Play)**

a

Guided Reading ►

13 **KEY STRATEGY: Character How do you think Ronald feels about himself? What makes you think so?**

I saw my father and ran to catch up.
"See you, Michael," I said.
My father asked, "How's the champ?"
13 "I'm the worst," I said.
"I was the worst, too," said my father.
"But then..."
"What?"
My father laughed. "I stopped closing my eyes when I swung."
"Maybe that's what I do."

36

PAGE 36 SNAPSHOTS

PHONICS s-Blends

Have children find the word *stopped* on page 36, point to the letters *st,* and read the word aloud.

- **What other words do you know that start with the same sounds?**

Repeat for the word *swung* and the letters *sw*. Then challenge children to find other words with *s*-blends in the story, such as those on pages 21, 25, 29, 34, and 40. *(See Phonics:* s-*Blends on pp. T88–89.)*

See the WiggleWorks Plus Teaching Plan for more phonics activities.

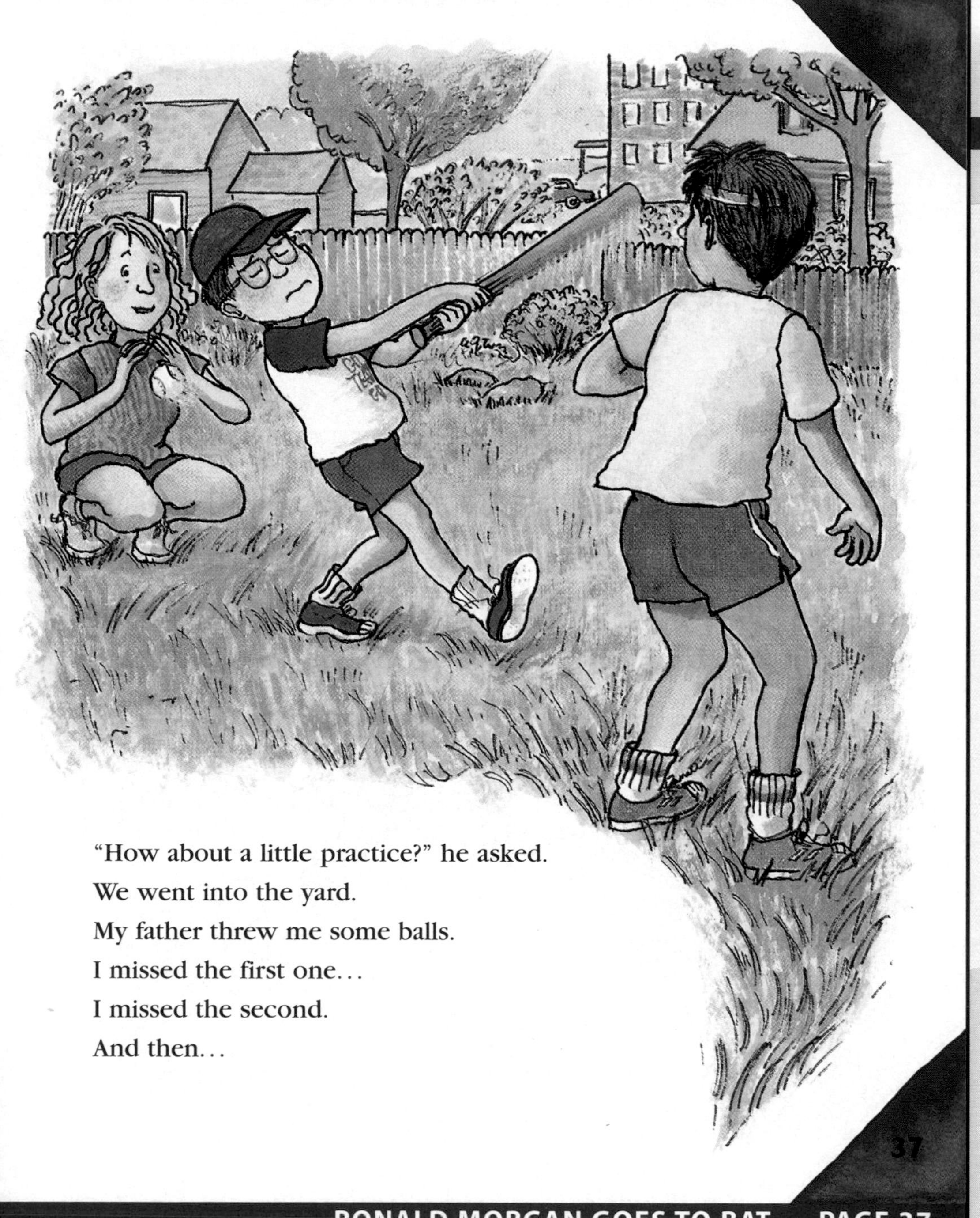

"How about a little practice?" he asked.
We went into the yard.
My father threw me some balls.
I missed the first one...
I missed the second.
And then...

37

RONALD MORGAN GOES TO BAT PAGE 37

Read On ► ► ►

a

Guided Reading ►

⓮ Problem/Solution Like Ronald, his father had trouble hitting a ball when he was young. How does his experience finally help Ronald learn to hit the ball?

⓯ Compare/Contrast Ronald Morgan missed the first ball his father threw. He missed the second ball. What happened when Ronald swung at the third ball? What did he do differently this time that helped him succeed?

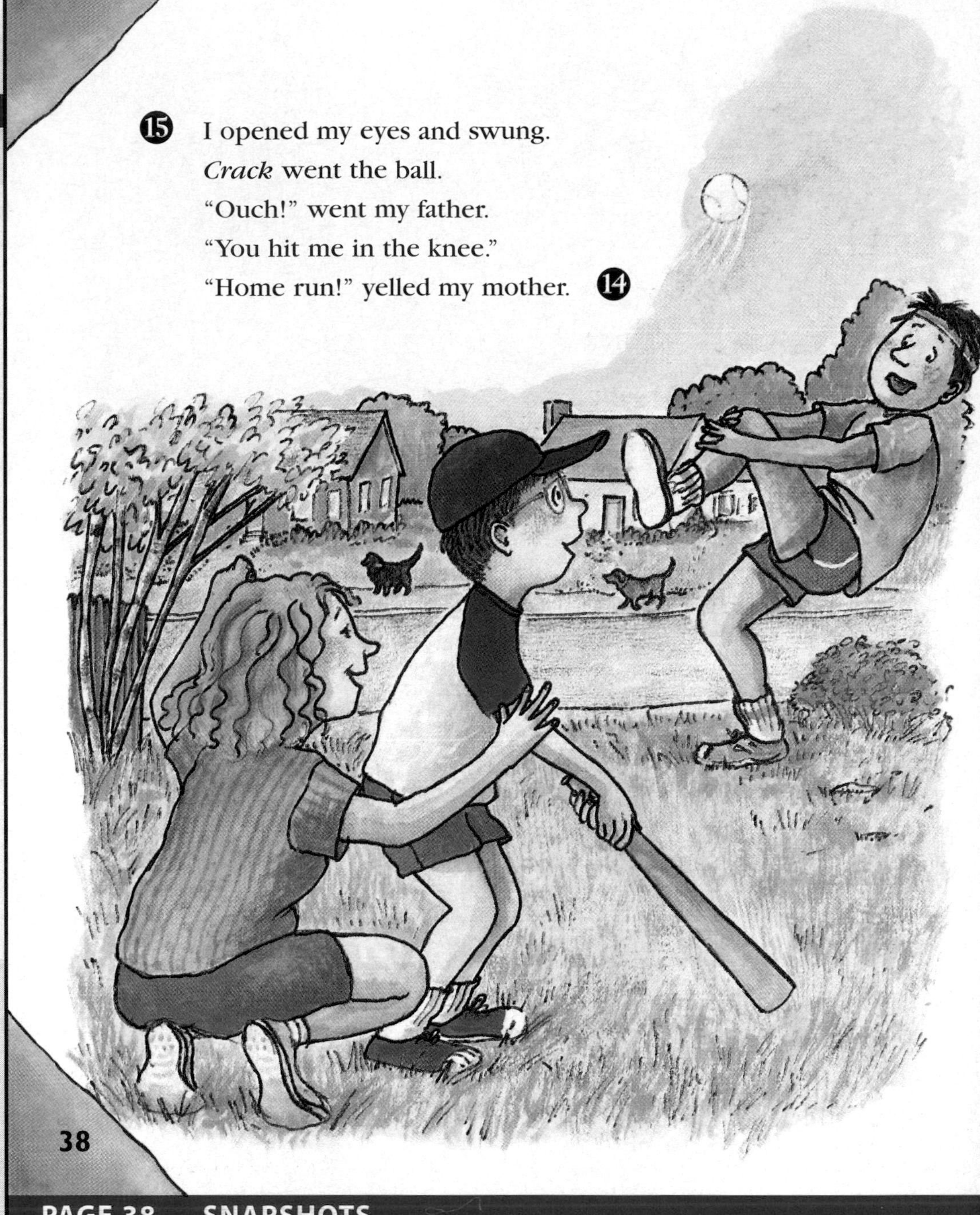

PAGE 38 SNAPSHOTS

► INTEGRATED CURRICULUM **THE ARTS** *(See p. R85)*
Children make a simple flipbook to show the path of a moving ball.

"Sorry," I said.
"Hey, I did it!"
My father rubbed his knee.
"You certainly did," he said. 

Guided Reading ►

16 Evaluate Author's Purpose So far I find the story funny, even though many children learning a new game or sport have probably felt like Ronald did. Why do you think the author wrote this story?
MINI-LESSON

MINI-LESSON

Evaluate Author's Purpose

TEACH/MODEL Tell children that every writer writes for at least one purpose: to entertain, to give information, to explain, to teach how to do something, or to persuade.

THINK ALOUD When I think about why the author wrote the story, I ask myself: Does the author tell how to play baseball? Is she giving information about the game? Is she persuading me what a great game baseball is? Did she write this story to entertain? I'm enjoying reading about Ronald Morgan. This tells me that the author's purpose is to entertain.

APPLY Ask children what the author's purpose was in writing *Max Found Two Sticks.* How can they tell?

a

Guided Reading ►

17 **KEY STRATEGY: Character** **From what I know about people, hitting the ball made Ronald Morgan feel better about himself. How did Ronald Morgan answer at first when Michael invited him to play ball? What has Ronald decided to do now? What can you tell about Ronald from this?**

18 **Realistic Fiction** **Is this a story that could happen in real life or one that could never happen? What clues in the story help you to make this decision?**

18

I ran to pick up the ball.
"See you later," I said.
My father smiled.
"Where are you going?"
I grabbed the bat.
"Some kids are playing ball.
17 I think I'll hit a few."

40

PAGE 40 SNAPSHOTS

Revisit ◄

Genre: Realistic Fiction

Discuss with children the elements of this story that make it realistic fiction. Point out such clues as these:

- **All the characters look, act, and speak as real people do.**
- **Everything that takes place in the story could happen in real life.**

I looked back.

"And you know what else?

I guess I'll stay on the team.

I have spirit...

19 and sometimes I can hit the ball.

Mike was right.

I think they need me."

41

RONALD MORGAN GOES TO BAT PAGE 41

Guided Reading ►

19 **CRITICAL THINKING: Evaluate What has Ronald Morgan learned about himself since he first tried to play baseball?**

Encourage children to initiate an on-line chat with other Scholastic Network users about the information and ideas they have explored in this selection.

Revisit ◄

Teacher Tip: Partners

Because this realistic story is one that many children can relate to, they might enjoy rereading it with a partner.

Supporting All Learners

Read

ESL Children acquiring English can refer to the time line they made in the Preview activity to guide them in retelling the story. One by one, point out Ronald Morgan's facial expressions and encourage children to fill in details about what happened to make him feel that way. **(Graphic Device)**

a Reading the Sources

Preview and Predict

Reader to Reader

I know lots of people who collect baseball cards. Do you?

Help children read the title of the selection. Ask them to look at the pages and tell what they show. Have children discuss what they know about baseball cards.

- **What is on the front of a baseball card?**
- **What is on the back?**

If necessary, explain that a photograph of the player appears on the front and information about the player is on the back. Help children notice that the information on the back of these two cards is similar even though it looks different. What do children expect to learn about the players from reading the cards?

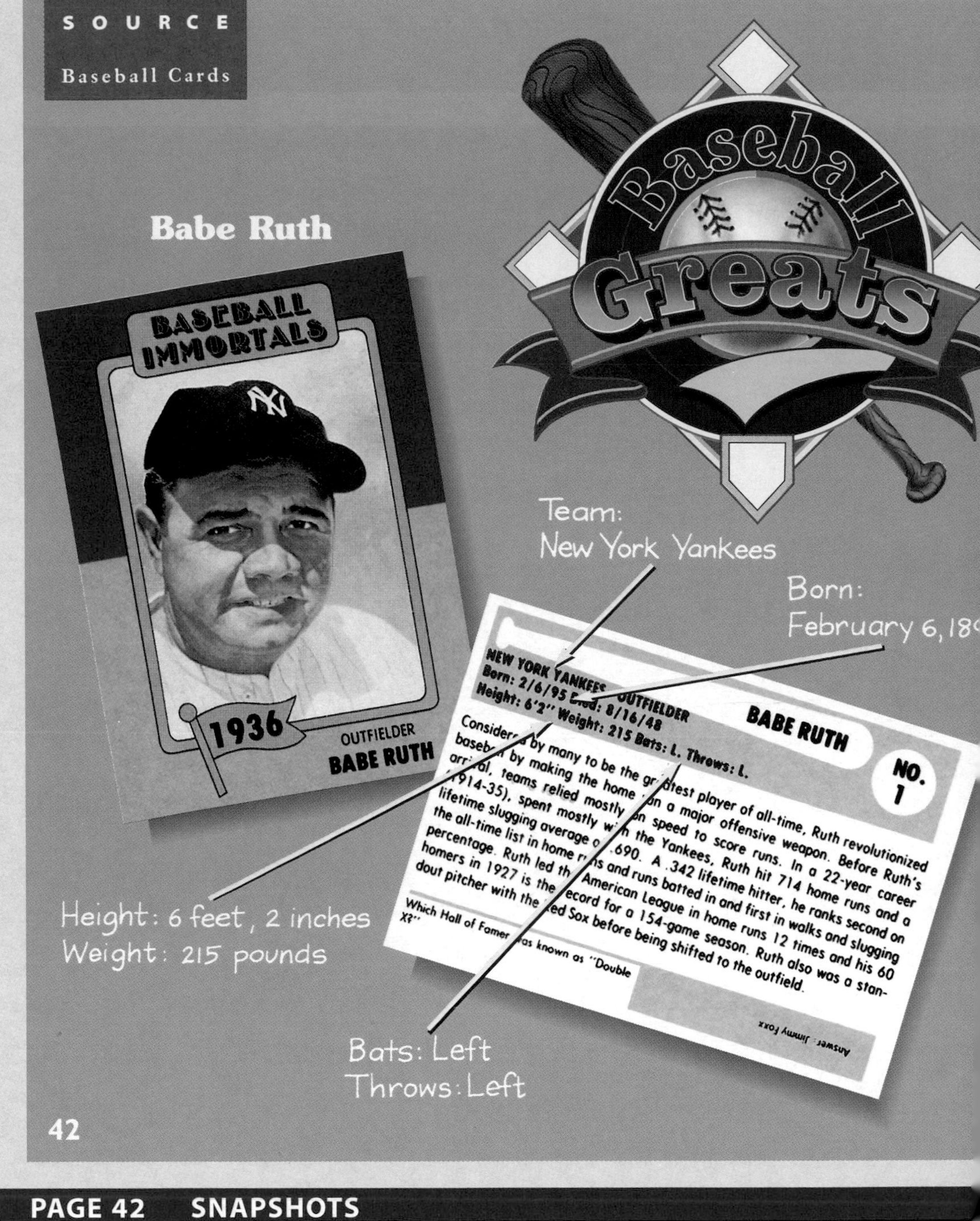

PAGE 42 SNAPSHOTS

Have children write in their Journals what they know about either Babe Ruth or Juan Gonzalez. After reading they can confirm or add to what they wrote.

Supporting All Learners

Preview **ESL** Some children may not be familiar with baseball cards. Pair them with children who collect cards. Encourage the baseball-card owners to introduce the players and tell their partner something about each one. **(Peer Partners)**

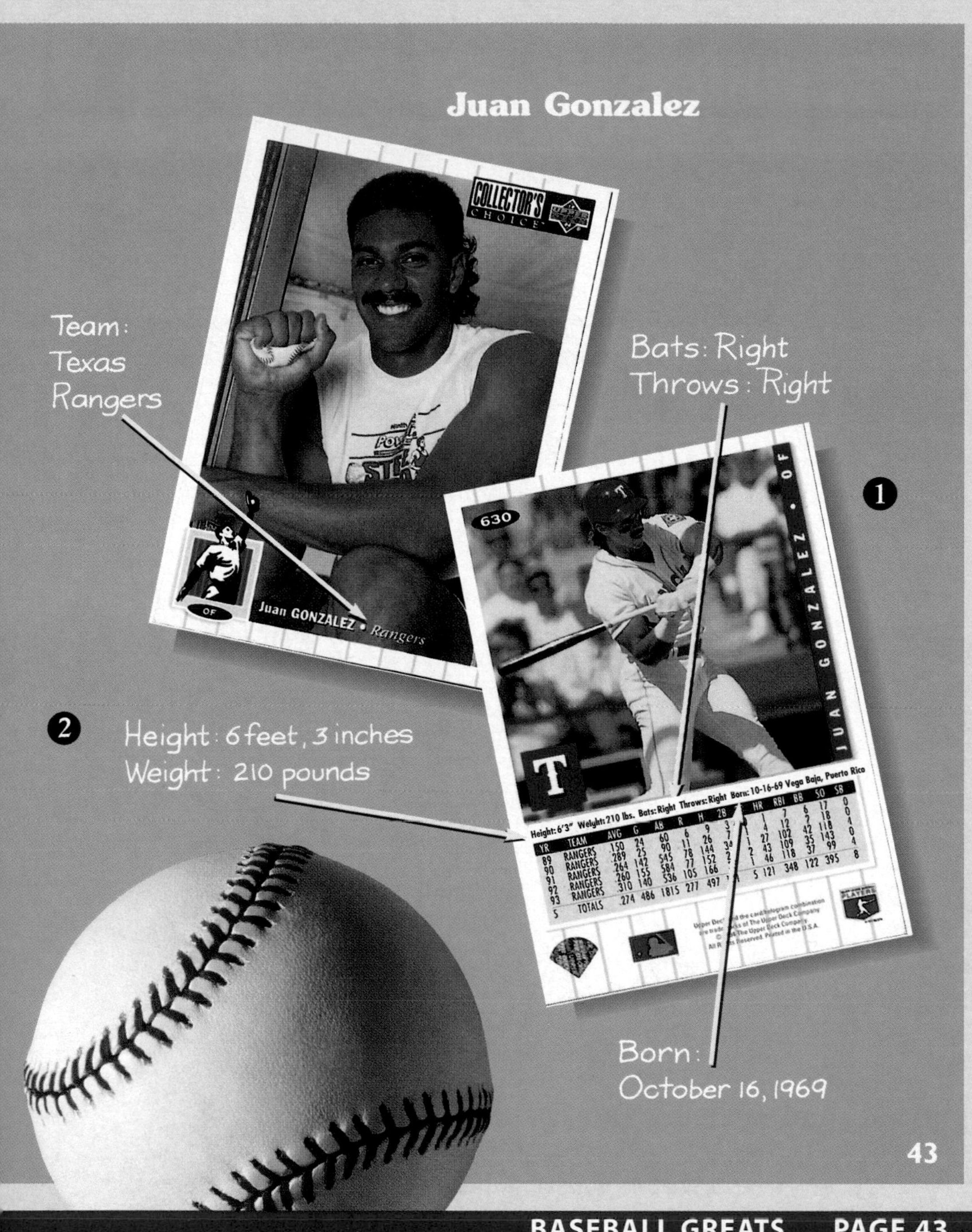

▶ INTEGRATING LANGUAGE ARTS **WRITING** *(See p. T83)*

Guided Reading ▶

❶ **Baseball Card What can you learn about these players from reading the baseball cards? Does the information on the cards give real facts or did a writer make these up? How do you know?**
MINI-LESSON

❷ **Compare/Contrast How is the information on these two cards the same? different? In what ways are these two players alike and different?**
MATH

MINI-LESSON

BASEBALL CARD

TEACH/MODEL As children read the baseball cards, point out that they may answer the questions *who, what, where, when, why,* and *how*. Write these words on the chalkboard.

> **THINK ALOUD When I look at the first card, I notice that many questions are answered. *Who?* The information is about Babe Ruth. *What?* He was a baseball player for the New York Yankees. Other questions answered include: When was he born, how big he was, and what arm did he bat and throw with?**

APPLY Ask similar questions about Juan Gonzalez for children to answer.

a READING THE SOURCES

RONALD MORGAN GOES TO BAT

Assess Reading

REFLECT AND RESPOND

Invite children to share their thoughts, opinions, and questions about *Ronald Morgan Goes to Bat* and "Baseball Greats." You may wish to prompt discussion with the following questions:

- **Do you think this story could really happen? Why or why not? *(✔ Literary Element)***
- **As Ronald worked harder at learning how to play baseball, what did he learn about himself? *(✔ Key Strategy)***
- **Why would Ronald Morgan be a good person to have in your class or on your team? *(✔ Theme)***

CHECK PREDICTIONS

Have children return to what they wondered about Ronald Morgan. Ask them to write responses in their Journals.

READ CRITICALLY ACROSS TEXTS

- **In *Max Found Two Sticks* and *Ronald Morgan Goes to Bat*, Max and Ronald gave us a picture of themselves. How are they alike? different? What are each of their talents?**

  Both boys have special interests. Max is creative and makes rhythms with two sticks. Ronald is spirited and plays on a baseball team with classmates.

- **If he could, what do you think Ronald might ask Babe Ruth or Juan Gonzalez?**

  He might ask for advice on how to be a better player.

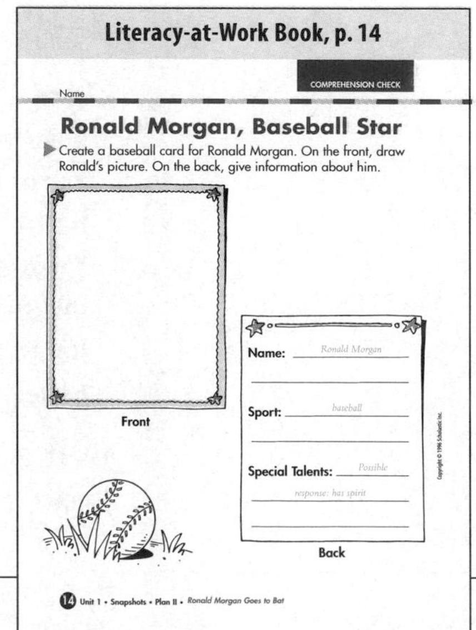

Literacy-at-Work Book, p. 14

Name ______ COMPREHENSION CHECK

Ronald Morgan, Baseball Star

▶ Create a baseball card for Ronald Morgan. On the front, draw Ronald's picture. On the back, give information about him.

Front

Name: *Ronald Morgan*

Sport: *baseball*

Special Talents: *Possible response: has spirit*

Back

14 Unit 1 • Snapshots • Plan II • Ronald Morgan Goes to Bat

CONFERENCE

Use the checked questions on this page to assess children's understanding of:

✔ the *literary elements* of Realistic Fiction.

✔ the *key strategy* of Character.

✔ the *theme* that we have special talents to offer other people.

Listen to Children Read Ask selected children to find the part in the story where Ronald's father helps him. You may wish to record children as they read aloud. Assess oral reading, using the pp. 22–23 in the Assessment Handbook.

Children may wish to add their recordings to their Literacy Portfolios.

Based on your evaluation of your children's responses,

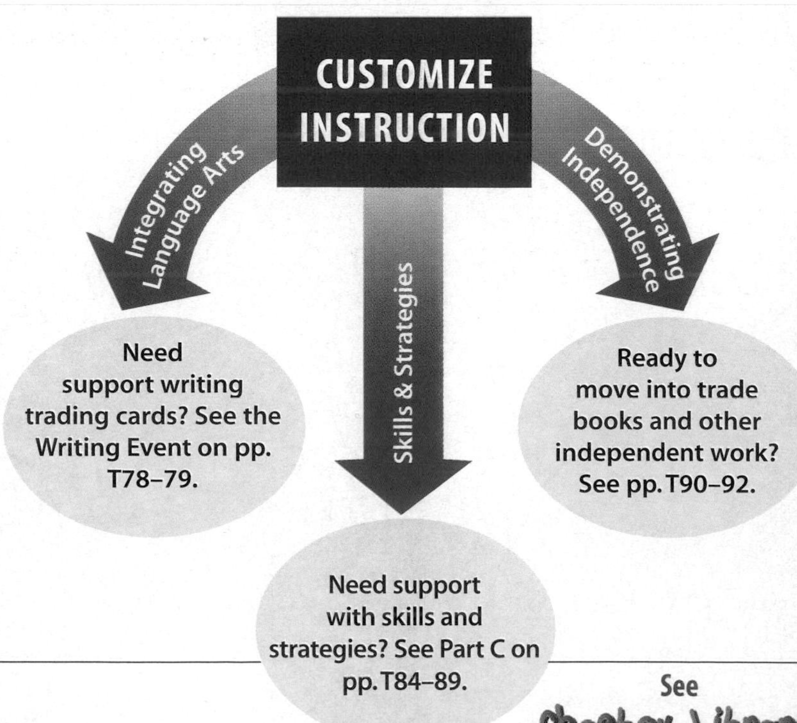

See Shoebox Library

Idea File

VOCABULARY

HOMEWORK Invite children to brainstorm a list of baseball players or sports words. Suggest that they write a short story about Ronald Morgan, using some of the words.

ADVICE COLUMN

Have children share advice that they have gotten from their family, teachers, or friends. They can draw a picture of each person who gave advice and write what that person said in a speech balloon. Children can draw their pictures and speech balloons in the SourceBook Activities writing area.

REPEATED READING

Choral Reading To enhance reading fluency, invite children to chime in chorally as you reread the story. Model for children how their tone of voice should change when they are reading an exclamation, a question, or a statement.

REPEATED READING

Independent Reading Provide opportunities for sustained silent reading to foster reading fluency. You might also encourage children to read the story aloud and record their reading on an audiocassette so they can listen to themselves.

CULTURAL CONNECTIONS

The Origins of Sports

Baseball, the game Ronald Morgan learned to play, was first played in the United States in the 1800s. Today it is popular around the world. Another sport with an interesting history is tennis. In France during the 1200s, players used their hands instead of racquets. Wrestling is actually one of the oldest forms of sport known.

Activity

Encourage children to choose a sport they like as participants or spectators and learn about its history. Where and when was it first played? What interesting facts can children uncover? Have groups prepare a short presentation for the class, including some of the equipment used, if possible.

b

SOURCEBOOK MODEL

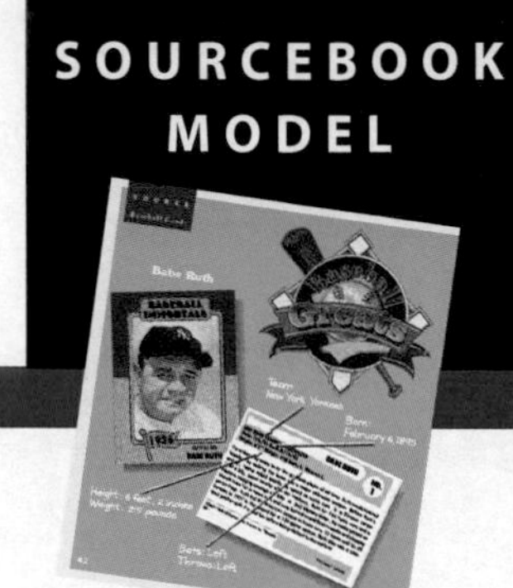

INTEGRATING LANGUAGE ARTS

BASEBALL GREATS

Objectives

Children learn to:

- write a trading card (p. T78–79)
- recognize naming places (p. T80)
- use commas to separate city, state, and country (p. T80)
- spell words with s-blends (p. T81)

Materials:
SourceBook pp. 42–43
Literacy-at-Work Book p. 15

Suggested Grouping:
Whole class, individuals, and cooperative groups

Literacy-at-Work Book, p. 15

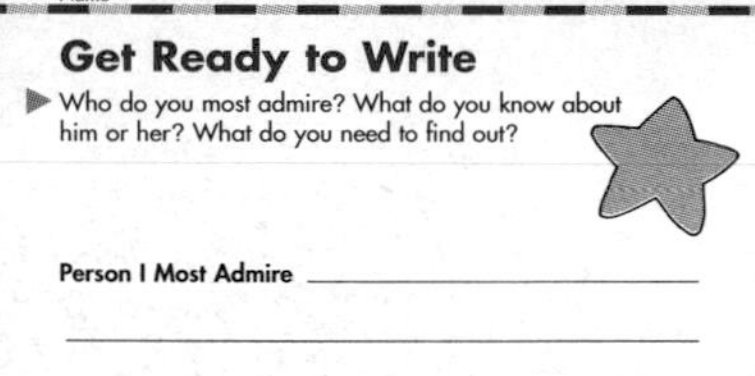

Name ______ WRITING

Get Ready to Write

▶ Who do you most admire? What do you know about him or her? What do you need to find out?

Person I Most Admire ______

Things I Need to Know About Him or Her ______

Things I Need to Find Out ______

To the Teacher: This is the prewriting organizer referenced in the lesson on writing a trading card.

Unit 1 • Snapshots • Plan II • *Ronald Morgan Goes to Bat* 15

WRITE A TRADING CARD

WRITING

Using "Baseball Greats" as a model, children will create an **informative card** about a figure they admire.

THINK ABOUT WRITING

Discuss the uses of cards such as baseball cards. Why might children like to collect them? What information do they contain? Help children understand that a card has:

- a picture of the person.
- information about the person that answers *Who? What? Where? When? Why?* and *How?*
- information that is easy to find.

Put It in Context

Have children look back at "Baseball Greats." Write the following questions on the chalkboard and invite children to find the answers as they look at the card:

- **Who is the card about?**
- **What does (did) he do?**
- **Where did he play?**
- **When was he born?**
- **How tall was he and how much did he weigh?**
- **Why is he great?**

Discuss why the information was so easy to find.

INTRODUCE THE WRITING EVENT

Invite children to create a card about a person they admire. Is it a famous sports person or a favorite author? Suggest that they think about who might like to collect the cards they create.

Prewrite

Children may wish to use their prewriting organizer in the Literacy-at-Work Book to gather information for their cards.

Brainstorm with children a list of people they admire.

- Invite children to choose a favorite person for their card. What do they know about the person? They might want to look through books, magazines, and newspapers for more facts about their person. They can write down any information they wish to include on their cards.
- Discuss with children whether they have enough information for their card.
- Have children decide if they are going to draw a picture of their person or find one in a newspaper or magazine.

Draft

Have children write answers for questions such as those on the chalkboard and cut out or draw a picture of their person. This question may help children:

- **Does my card have all the information about my person that is important?**

Revise

In revising, children might ask:

- **Have I answered all the questions?**
- **Is the information easy to find?**

SHARING TIPS Suggest that groups share or trade their cards. Encourage children to tell what they like most about each card.

PERFORMANCE-BASED

Children's Self-Assessment

✔ Does my card have all the important information about my person?

✔ Can a reader easily find the information?

Children may wish to continue working on their trading cards and take this piece through the writing process described in Plan VI, pp. T288–291.

Use the Benchmarks to assess children's writing. Suggest that children add their drafts and revisions to their Literacy Portfolios.

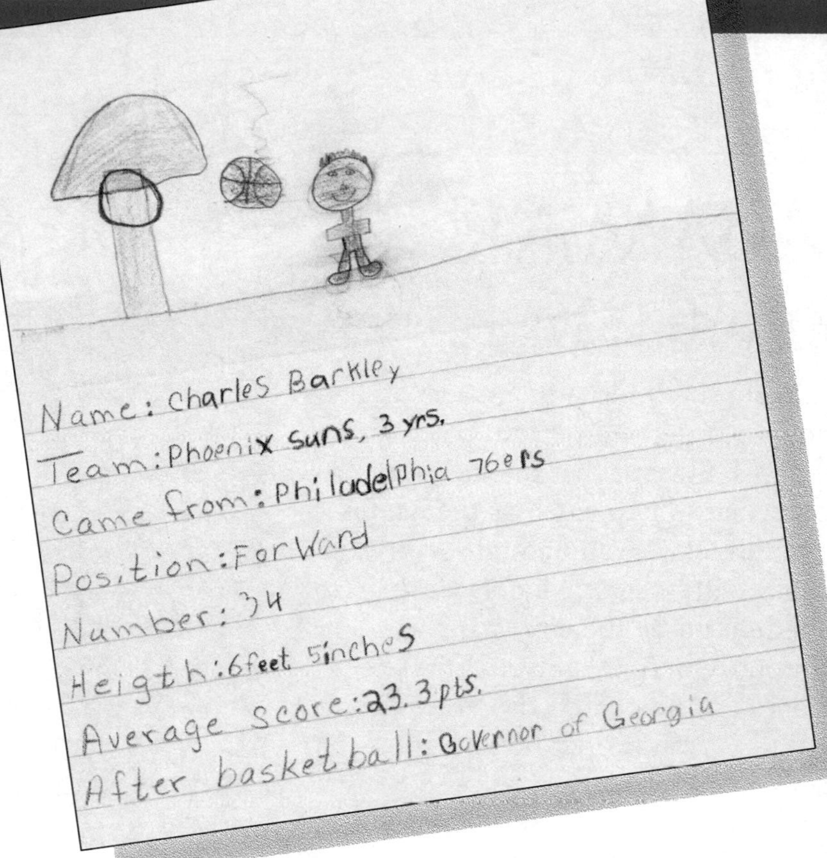

This second-grader's work shows informational details of a sports figure for a trading card.

Technology Options

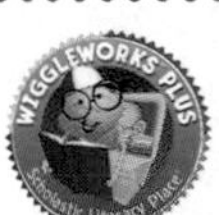

Invite children to create their trading cards on the computer, using either the SourceBook Activities writing area or the PlaceMaker. They can use the Record Tools to record ideas for their cards. For more information and other writing activities, see the WiggleWorks Plus Teaching Plan.

SUPPORTING ALL LEARNERS

Wait Time

ESL Second-language learners may require some extra time to verbalize their ideas. Before exchanging ideas for Sharing Tips, provide children with a few moments of quiet so they can think about how to express their ideas.

ACCESS Facilitate children's participation in the brainstorming activity by providing them with a few moments of silence in which to formulate their ideas. Children are more likely to participate when they have time to prepare their answers.

CHILDREN'S WRITING BENCHMARKS

Novice:	Apprentice:	Proficient:
Only one or two questions may be answered. A picture of the person does not appear on the card. It is difficult to find information.	Some questions (who, what, where, when, how, why) are answered. A picture of the person may not appear on the card. The information may not be easy to find.	All questions (who, what, where, when, how, why) are answered. A picture of the person appears on the card. The information is easy to find.

b INTEGRATING LANGUAGE ARTS

BASEBALL GREATS

S M T W T F S
See Daily Language Practice pp. R14-15.

(✔ Unit Test)

NAMING PLACES

GRAMMAR

OBJECTIVE

Children will identify word that name places in the story and in their writing.

DEFINITION: The name of a city, state, or country is a proper noun.

SYNTACTIC CUEING

❶ Teach and Model

Explain to children that a proper noun can name a person, place, or thing. Point out that the names of particular places, such as the names of cities, states, and countries, always begin with a capital letter. Have children name the city, state, and country where they live. Write the words on the chalkboard and point out that each proper noun begins with a capital letter.

Newton, Massachusetts
Los Angeles, California
Kansas City, Missouri
Nome, Alaska, United States

❷ Put It in Context

Have children look back at the trading cards. Direct attention to the name of the place where each person was born. Ask children to notice the first letter in each place name. Make sure children are aware that the name of each place begins with a capital letter.

❸ Apply to Writing

Call on volunteers to point to the names of places on the cards they created. Have children check to make sure that each place-name begins with a capital letter.

(✔ Unit Test)

COMMAS

USAGE

OBJECTIVE

Children will identify commas that separate the name of a city from the name of its state or country.

GUIDELINE: A comma is a punctuation mark used to separate names of cities, states, and countries.

❶ Teach and Model

Write the name of your city, state, and country on the chalkboard and read them aloud to the children. Explain that a comma is used to separate the name of a city from a state, and a state from a country. Reread to model how you pause between the words. Then rewrite the names and have a volunteer put commas in the correct places.

❷ Put It in Context

Have children look again at "Baseball Greats." Direct their attention to place names on the baseball cards. Ask children what punctuation mark they notice between the name of the city and the state and between the name of the state and the country.

❸ Apply to Writing

Have children find the names of cities, states, or countries they have included on the cards they created and read them aloud. Invite children to point out the commas between place names and to add commas if they've been left out.

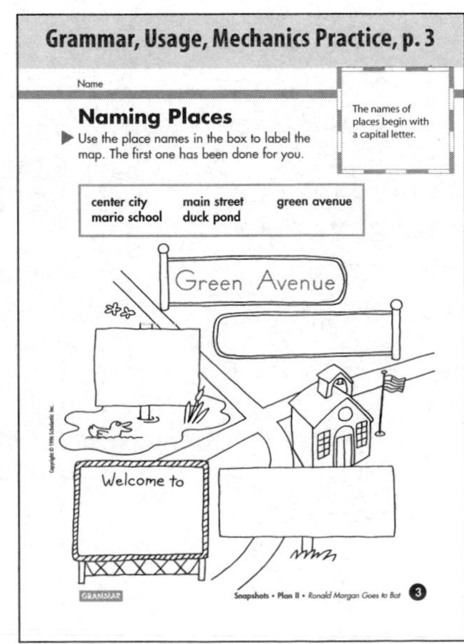

Grammar, Usage, Mechanics Practice, p. 3

Name

Naming Places

▶ Use the place names in the box to label the map. The first one has been done for you.

The names of places begin with a capital letter.

center city · main street · green avenue · mario school · duck pond

Green Avenue

Welcome to

GRAMMAR

Snapshots • Plan II • *Ronald Morgan Goes to Bat* 3

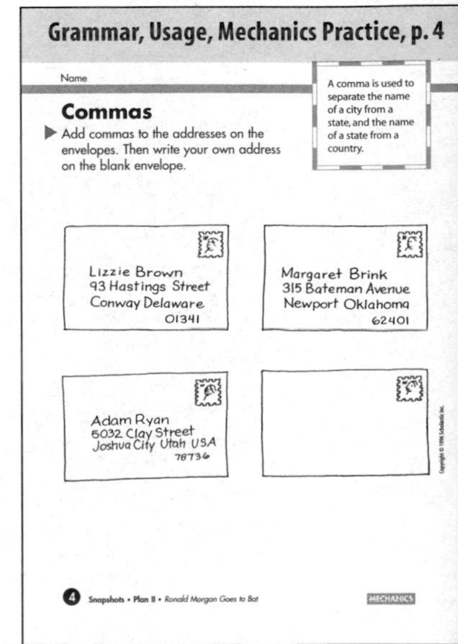

Grammar, Usage, Mechanics Practice, p. 4

Name

Commas

▶ Add commas to the addresses on the envelopes. Then write your own address on the blank envelope.

A comma is used to separate the name of a city from a state, and the name of a state from a country.

Lizzie Brown
93 Hastings Street
Conway Delaware
01341

Margaret Brink
315 Bateman Avenue
Newport Oklahoma
62401

Adam Ryan
5032 Clay Street
Joshua City Utah USA
78736

4 Snapshots • Plan II • *Ronald Morgan Goes to Bat*

MECHANICS

Phonics Connection

You may first wish to do the phonics lesson on *s*-blends on pp. T88–89.

SPELLING

Words With *s*-Blends

snap **snack** **slide** **sled** **swim** **swing** **step** **stage**

✷ **Selection Vocabulary**

PRETEST If you would like to pretest using test sentences, see Spelling Practice, p. 37.

OBJECTIVE

Children spell words with *s*-blend.

❶ Teach

Write these puzzles on the chalkboard:

S__OW *S__AY*

Ask children to suggest letters that complete each word. (*snow, slow, stow; stay, sway*) Point out that each answer begins with an *s*-blend: *sl, sn, st,* or *sw*.

Put It in Context

Have children look through *Ronald Morgan Goes to Bat* to find examples of words that begin with *s*-blends. Have children read the examples as you write them on the chalkboard. Say each word, and then spell out one letter at a time. Then have volunteers underline the *s*-blend in each word.

❷ Practice

Have children write spelling list words in each circle.

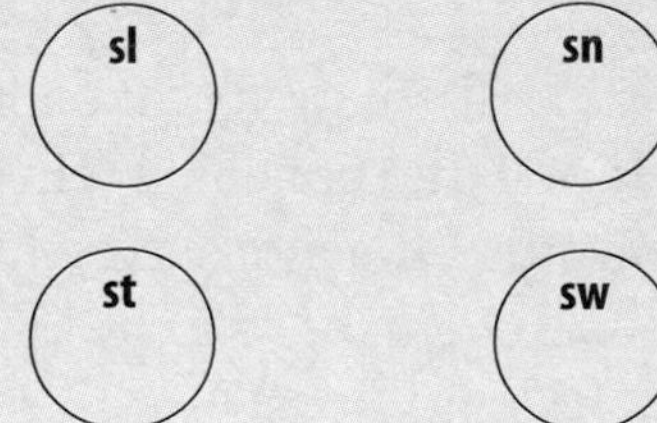

❸ Check

Apply to Writing

Have children use their spelling words to write three sentences about things that they do outside on nonschool days.

OPTION

Spell Teaser

Have children create tongue twisters that contain words with *s*-blends. Encourage children to challenge others to say their trickiest sentences quickly. For example, "Slide the sled to the swing."

TEST To administer the spelling test, read each word aloud, then read it in a sentence, then say the word again. Have children write the word. Spelling partners can work together to check each other's papers.

Spelling Practice, p. 2

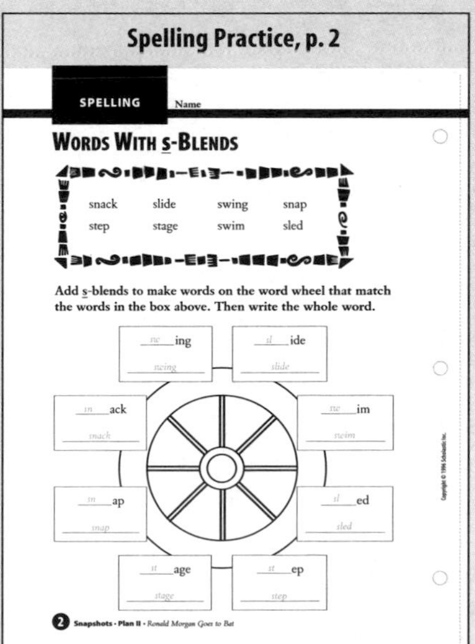

SPELLING Name

WORDS WITH S-BLENDS

snack slide swing snap
step stage swim sled

Add s-blends to make words on the word wheel that match the words in the box above. Then write the whole word.

___ing swing
___ide slide
___ack snack
___im swim
___ap snap
___ed sled
___age stage
___ep step

2 Snapshots · Plan 8 · Ronald Morgan Goes to Bat

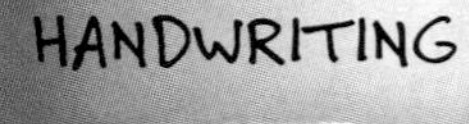

See Handwriting, p. 2, for practice writing the manuscript letters *r, m, n, h, f, b, p, u, s,* and *j*.

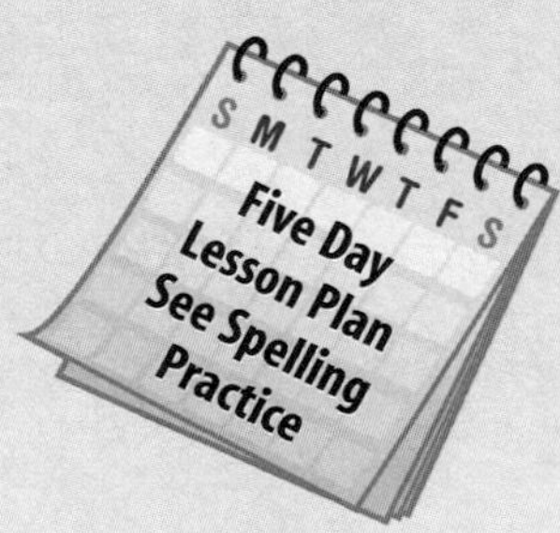

LISTENING/SPEAKING/VIEWING

Listen to a Sports Broadcast

GOOD FOR HOMEWORK

Materials: Television or radio

Time: About 15 minutes

Suggested Grouping: Individuals

Suggest that children view a few minutes of a sporting event on television or listen to a radio broadcast. Remind them to listen for important information the announcer provides.

Invite children to summarize what they saw and heard in class. Children should try to include answers to questions that ask who, what, when, where, and why.

SPEAKING/LISTENING

Be a Sports Announcer

GOOD FOR GRADING

Materials: Audiocassette recorder; Blank audiocassette tape

Time: About 20 minutes

Suggested Grouping: Partners

Technology Options **Invite** children to pretend to be the sports announcers for Ronald Morgan's team. Let children listen to part of a sports broadcast. They can focus on how the announcer's voice changes during the course of the game.

Partners might first decide what will happen during the game. Then they can plan a play-by-play broadcast.

Suggest that children record their broadcasts and play back their tapes to share with fans.

How to Grade When grading, look for use of description, sequence, and expressive language.

MINI-LESSON

ACTION VERBS

TEACH/MODEL Tell children that sports announcers use words that describe actions. Help children realize that verbs are words for actions. Read aloud page 21 of *Ronald Morgan Goes to Bat,* pointing out the action verbs *smacked* and *flew*.

APPLY Have children find other action verbs in the story. Encourage volunteers to act out some of these verbs. Ask children to offer other action verbs that a sports announcer might use.

ACTIVITY FILE

READING

ESL Dramatize the Story

Materials:
SourceBook pp. 18–41

Time:
About 30 minutes

Suggested Grouping:
Cooperative groups

Invite cooperative groups of children to read *Ronald Morgan Goes to Bat* aloud, with different children reading the parts of the narrator and other story characters.

Encourage each group to read aloud a different part of the story. Allow time for children to practice. Provide props, such as a baseball bat and catcher's mitt, and have each group present its part of the story as a Readers Theater performance. THE ARTS

MINI-LESSON

Oral Expression

TEACH/MODEL Help children develop reading fluency and expression, using *Ronald Morgan Goes to Bat*. Model rate, intonation, and volume variations as you read aloud selected passages.

APPLY Suggest that children practice their oral reading in cooperative groups. Encourage them to explore different rates, intonations, and volumes as they read. Group members may make positive suggestions to improve one another's reading.

WRITING

Create a Sports Poster

Materials:
SourceBook pp. 42–43
Posterboard
Markers

Time:
About 30 minutes

Suggested Grouping:
Individuals or cooperative groups

Ask children to imagine that they are sports stars. They can create posters with information about their achievements, which can be based on their own interests. Review the kind of information on the baseball cards in the SourceBook, including details that answer who, what, when, and where.

Encourage children to plan their posters by selecting a sport, listing the information to include, and then organizing that information in order of importance. Children can illustrate their posters using markers. VISUAL LITERACY

Invite children to create their posters using the computer PlaceMaker.

C

SOURCEBOOK

BUILDING SKILLS AND STRATEGIES

RONALD MORGAN GOES TO BAT

Ronald Morgan Goes to Bat by Patricia Reilly Giff

Illustrated by Susanna Natti

 Character (✔ Unit Test)

Objectives

Children learn to:

- identify character traits and feelings
- transfer their learning to a new text

Materials:
SourceBook pp. 18–41
Transparency 4
Literacy-at-Work Book pp. 16–18

Time:
About 30 minutes

Suggested Grouping:
Whole class and partners

TESTED	
KEY STRATEGY	
CHARACTER	
Introduce	p. T84
Review	p. R16
Test	p. T311
Reteach	p. R24

Literacy-at-Work Book, p. 16

CHARACTER

Name

What About Ronald?

▶ Write how you found out each of these things about Ronald Morgan.

I learned this from looking at the pictures.
I learned this from reading the words.
I learned this from looking at the pictures and reading the words.

1. Ronald couldn't hold a bat. *I learned this from looking at the pictures and reading the words.*
2. He smiled a lot. *I learned this from looking at the pictures.*
3. He had spirit. *I learned this from looking at the pictures and reading the words.*
4. Ronald ran the wrong way. *I learned this from reading the words.*

16 Unit 1 • Snapshots • Plan II • Ronald Morgan Goes to Bat

✔ Quickcheck

As children worked their way through *Ronald Morgan Goes to Bat,* did they:

✔ use words and picture clues to identify character's feelings?

✔ make inferences to figure out the character's traits and feelings?

YES If yes, go to  ❷ Practice and Apply.

NO If no, start at ❶ Teach and Model.

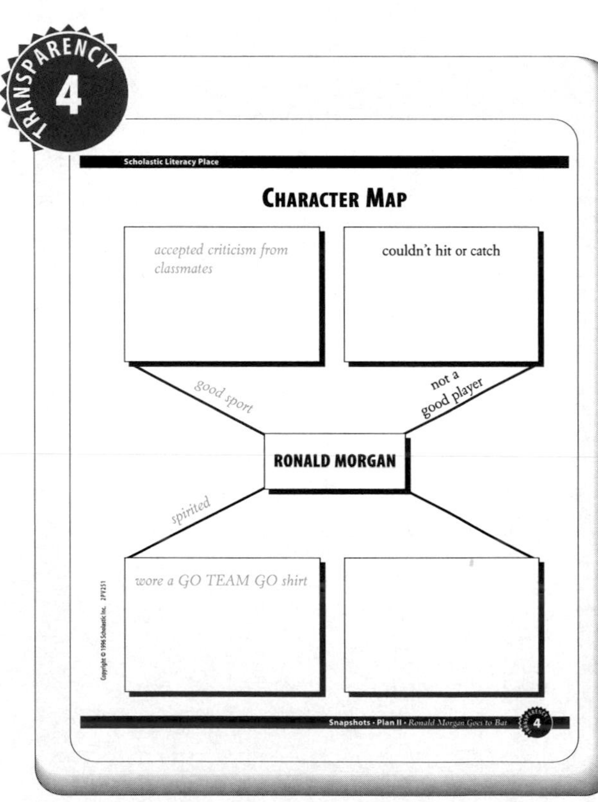

Annotated transparency for teaching Character

❶ Teach and Model

Invite children to think about a special person they know. What would they tell the class about this person? What makes the person special? What words would they use to describe him or her? After children share their ideas, explain that the qualities they have just described told the class a lot about the person.

Put It in Context

Discuss how to use the pictures, what Ronald Morgan says, and what others say about him to learn more about Ronald.

Think Aloud **I learned a lot about Ronald Morgan at the beginning of the story. I learned that he was eager to play baseball even though he wasn't a very good player. I figured this out from what the other kids said about him and from what Ronald himself said. For example, when the coach said everyone could play, Ronald asked, "Even me?" He seemed surprised and yelled "Yahoo!" That told me he was very excited to be playing. I could also tell from the pictures that Ronald was happy about playing baseball because he had a big smile.**

Ask children what other clues at the beginning of the story tell what Ronald Morgan was like and how he felt. Questions such as the following may be used to prompt children:

- **How would you describe Ronald's expression on page 19? How do you think he feels?**
- **On page 20 Ronald puts on a shirt that says "GO TEAM GO." What does this say about him?**

Use Transparency 4 to help children keep track of what they learn about Ronald Morgan.

❷ Practice and Apply

Make a Character Map

PARTNERS Have pairs of children work together to look through the rest of the story to find more clues about Ronald Morgan. What words would describe Ronald? What clues in the story would support their ideas? To help children, remind them to think about picture clues, what Ronald says, and what others say about him. A character map like the one on Transparency 4 may be distributed to help children keep track of their answers.

OPTION

Guess Who?

Ask children to describe someone in the classroom by telling about things this person does and says. Have classmates try to guess who is being described.

❸ Assess

Were children able to describe Ronald Morgan's character?

- ✔ **Can children use words and picture clues to tell about Ronald's feelings?**
- ✔ **Can children use what they know about people to make inferences about Ronald's character traits and feelings?**

If not, try this:
Use the Review lesson on Character with Plan IV. Have children continue to identify character in their Journals.

Children's Self-Assessment

- ✔ **How did I use word and picture clues to figure out what Ronald Morgan was like?**

SUPPORTING ALL LEARNERS

Graphic Device

EXTRA HELP Help children identify information they can use to create a Character Map by turning to a page in the story and pointing out which picture clues tell something about character traits. Then model how to search the story for words that illustrate these traits.

ESL Support second-language learners in the Character Map activity by using a page in the story to model how they can find clues about character traits in the text and pictures. Then select another page and choose a volunteer to practice pointing out text and picture clues.

CHALLENGE To build independence invite children to select another character from the story. Challenge them to search the story for character clues and use them to create another Character Map.

Transfer to New Text

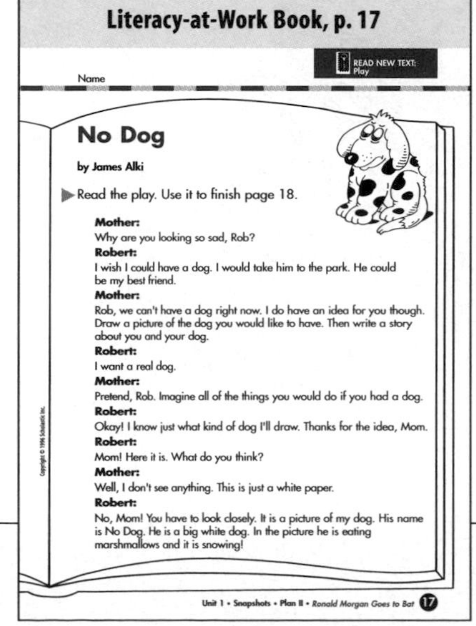

Literacy-at-Work Book, p. 17

Name

READ NEW TEXT: Play

No Dog

by James Alki

▶ Read the play. Use it to finish page 18.

Mother:
Why are you looking so sad, Rob?
Robert:
I wish I could have a dog. I would take him to the park. He could be my best friend.
Mother:
Rob, we can't have a dog right now. I do have an idea for you though. Draw a picture of the dog you would like to have. Then write a story about you and your dog.
Robert:
I want a real dog.
Mother:
Pretend, Rob. Imagine all of the things you would do if you had a dog.
Robert:
Okay! I know just what kind of dog I'll draw. Thanks for the idea, Mom.
Robert:
Mom! Here it is. What do you think?
Mother:
Well, I don't see anything. This is just a white paper.
Robert:
No, Mom! You have to look closely. It is a picture of my dog. His name is No Dog. He is a big white dog. In the picture he is eating marshmallows and it is snowing!

Unit 1 • Snapshots • Plan II • *Ronald Morgan Goes to Bat* 17

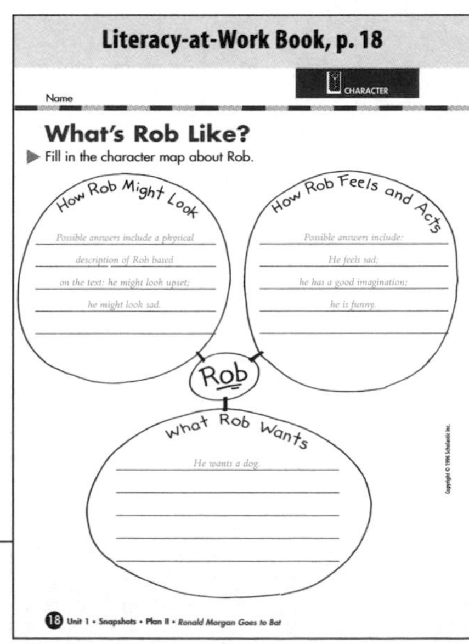

Literacy-at-Work Book, p. 18

Name

CHARACTER

What's Rob Like?

▶ Fill in the character map about Rob.

How Rob Might Look
Possible answers include a physical description of Rob based on the text: he might look upset; he might look sad.

How Rob Feels and Acts
Possible answers include: He feels sad; he has a good imagination; he is funny.

Rob

What Rob Wants
He wants a dog.

18 Unit 1 • Snapshots • Plan II • *Ronald Morgan Goes to Bat*

C

RONALD MORGAN GOES TO BAT

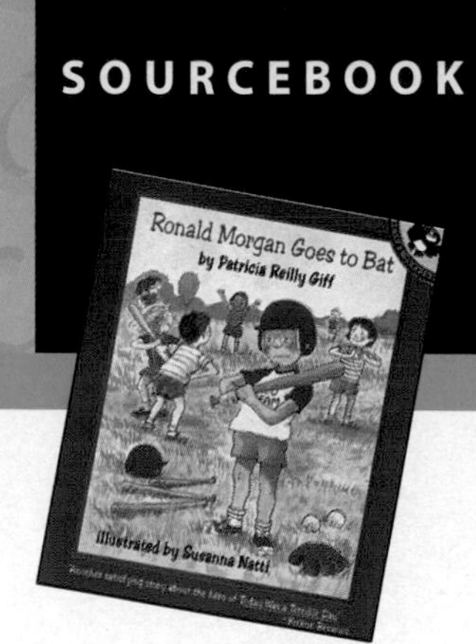

Vowels /a/*a*, /i/*i*

Objectives

Children learn to:

- identify the sound of the short vowels /a/*a* and /i/*i*
- build words that contain /a/*a* and /i/*i*
- write /a/*a* and /i/*i* words

PHONICS AT A GLANCE

Materials:
SourceBook pp. 18–41
Big Book of Rhymes 2A, and Rhythms p. 6
Magnet Board
Literacy-at Work Book p.19-20

Time:
About 15–30 minutes

Suggested Grouping:
Whole class or cooperative groups

Literacy-at-Work Book, p. 19

Name | PHONICS: Vowels /a/*a*, /i/*i*

Literacy-at-Work Book, p. 20

Name | PHONICS: Vowels/a/*a*, /i/*i*

Another Magic Square

▶ Use your Magic Square with these words. Write a sentence for one of the words you made.

i

tr ☐ p — l ☐ st

trip, trap — list, last

dr ☐ nk — sw ☐ m

drink, drank — swim, swam

20 Unit 1 • Snapshots • Plan II • *Ronald Morgan Goes to Bat*

✔ Quickcheck

As children worked their way through *Ronald Morgan Goes to Bat*, did they:

✔ identify the sound of the letter *a*? *i*?

✔ discriminate which words contain or begin with /a/*a* or /i/*i* when they hear a list of words?

✔ think of a word that contains or begins with /a/*a* or /i/*i*?

YES **If yes, go to the Blending section of ❷ Connect Sound/Symbol.**

NO **If no, start at ❶ Develop Oral Language.**

❶ Develop Oral Language

Phonemic Awareness

Read aloud "Jack Be Nimble" from the Big Book of Rhymes and Rhythms. On the second or third reading, ask children to join in and read the poem chorally. After a few readings, you may notice that children can recite the rhyme easily on their own.

Ask children what other word in the poem has the same vowel sound they hear in *Jack*. Encourage them to name other words with that vowel sound, such as *bat, cap,* and *sad*.

Read the rhyme again, omitting the words *nimble, quick,* and *candlestick*. Ask children to finish each line with other words that have the vowel sound they hear in *quick*, such as *hit*.

Big Book of Rhymes and Rhythms

Jack Be Nimble

Jack be nimble,
Jack be quick,
Jack jump over
The candlestick.

Jack
quick

6

❷ Connect Sound to Symbol

Put It in Context

On the chalkboard, write these sentences from *Ronald Morgan Goes to Bat*:

He smacked the ball with the bat.

"We'll win every game."

Underline the letter *a* in *smacked* and *bat*, and ask children to listen for the vowel sound in these words as you blend the sounds and point to each letter. Write some /a/*a* words children offered earlier or other /a/*a* words from the story. Follow a similar procedure for /i/*i* using the other sentence.

Blending

Draw a ladder on the chalkboard and write the word *bat* on the top rung.

Think Aloud **I can use *bat* to make another word. If I change the *b* to *c*, I have *cat*. Let's say the new word together. Now who would like to change the first or last letter to make another new word?**

Have volunteers write other words with the same vowel letter on the ladder. Then continue with an /i/*i* ladder and the word *hit*.

❸ Assess

Write

PARTNERS To assess children's understanding of /a/*a* and /i/*i*, have them write sentences using at least one of the /a/*a* and /i/*i* words from the ladders. They can work independently or with partners. Encourage children to share their sentences by reading them aloud. They may enjoy rereading their sentences at home.

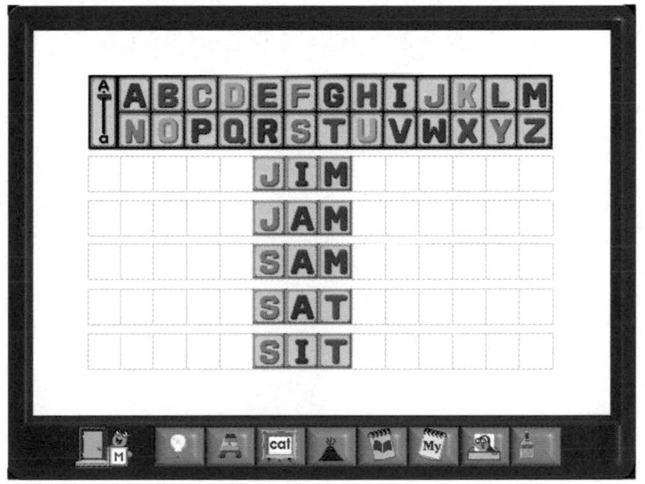

WHAT A DIFFERENCE ONE LETTER MAKES Have children make up word families for /a/*a* and /i/*i*, such as *fan, pan, tan*. Encourage them to write at least three words using the same phonogram and to illustrate each word.

See Phonics and Word Building Kit for additional suggestions.

The Magnet Board activity pictured above provides additional phonics practice. For more information on this and other Magnet Board activities, see the WiggleWorks Plus Teaching Plan.

SUPPORTING ALL LEARNERS

Hands-On Learning

ESL In preparation for the Blending activity, have second-language learners write the words *bat* and *hit* in two columns on the Magnet Board. Encourage them to create a list of /a/*a* words under *bat* and /i/*i* words under *hit*. By clicking on each word, they can listen to the short vowel sounds. Then they can use these words to guide them in creating word ladders.

CHALLENGE After completing their word ladders, children can take the last /a/*a* word and the first /i/*i* word from their ladders and write them on the Magnet Board. Challenge children to create a word ladder connecting these two words by changing one letter at a time.

RONALD MORGAN GOES TO BAT

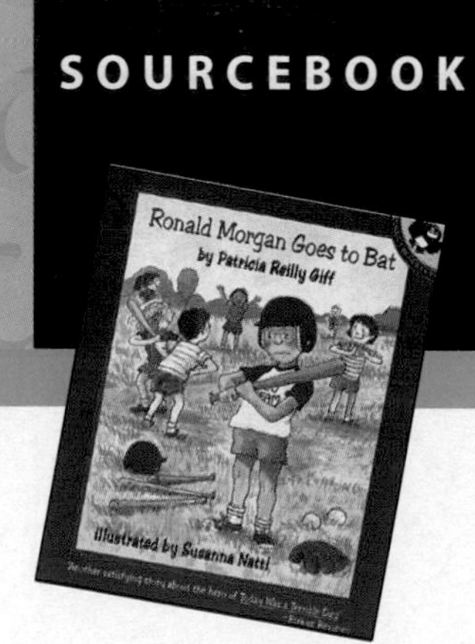

s-Blends

Objectives

Children learn to:

- identify the sounds of s-blends *sk, sl, sm, sn, sp, st*
- build words that contain /sk/, /sl/, /sm/, /sn/, /sp/, and /st/
- write words with s-blends

PHONICS AT A GLANCE

Materials:
SourceBook pp.18–41
Big Book of Rhymes and Rhythms 2A, p. 7
Literacy-at-Work Book pp. 21–22
Word Building for *s*-blend
Magnet Board
Spelling Lesson p. T81

Time:
About 15–30 minutes

Suggested Grouping:
Whole class and cooperative groups

✔ Quickcheck

Do children know s-blends and the sounds they represent? Can they:

✔ recognize the blends in print?
✔ discriminate which words begin with a particular s-blend when they hear a list of words?
✔ Can they think of words that begin with s-blends?

YES **If yes, go to the Blending section of ❷ Connect Sound/Symbol.**

NO **If no, start at ❶ Develop Oral Language.**

❶ Develop Oral Language

Phonemic Awareness

Read aloud "I'm a Little Teapot" from the Big Book of Rhymes and Rhythms. Focus on the sounds of the *s*-blends. Have children say the words *stout, steamed,* and *spout* slowly after you. Ask what sounds children hear at the beginning of each word. Have children tell which two words begin with the same *s*-blend.

On repeated readings, let children chime in on their own on every other line. Demonstrate how children can use their arms and hands for the handle and spout and how they can lean over for the last line.

Big Book of Rhymes and Rhythms

I'm a Little Teapot

I'm a little teapot,
Short and stout.
Here is my handle,
Here is my spout.
When I get all steamed up,
Hear me shout.
Tip me over and pour me out.

stout
spout

7

Literacy-at-Work Book, p. 21

Literacy-at-Work Book, p. 22

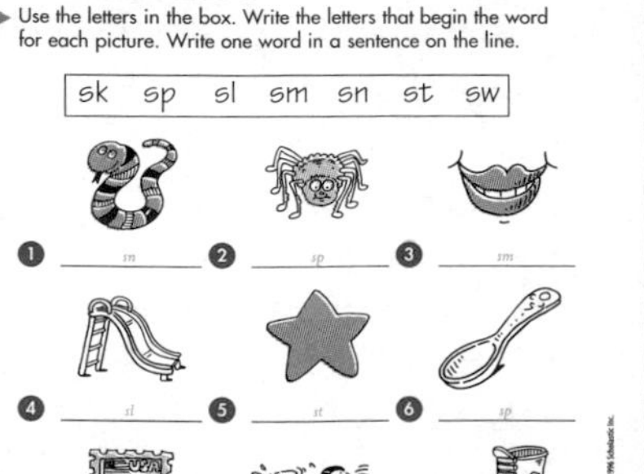

Sounds Like *s*

Use the letters in the box. Write the letters that begin the word for each picture. Write one word in a sentence on the line.

sk sp sl sm sn st sw

❷ Connect Sound Symbol

Put It in Context

On the chalkboard, write these sentences from *Ronald Morgan Goes to Bat:*

Baseball started today.

He smacked the ball with the bat.

"Great, Slugger!" I yelled.

My sneaker came off.

"Terrific, Speedy!" I yelled.

I closed my eyes and swung.

Underline the words with *s*-blends. Ask children to listen to the sounds as you point to the letters and blend the sounds. Repeat with other *s*-blend words children offer.

Blending

Place cards for *sk, sl, sm, sn, sp,* and *st* on the chalk rail. Write *tip* on the chalkboard and read it aloud. Invite a volunteer to choose a card and cover the *t* in *tip* to make a new word such as *skip, slip,* or *snip*. Repeat other words, encouraging children to make more than one new word if possible.

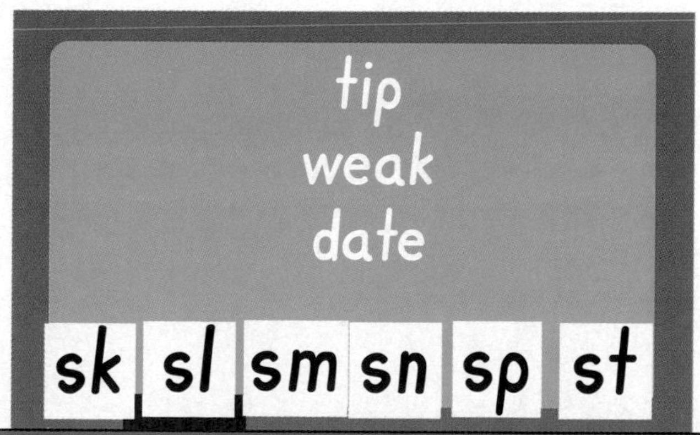

❸ Assess

Write

To assess children's understanding of *s*-blends, invite them to write the word *cap* on a piece of paper. Ask them to write another word by changing the *c* to one of the *s*-blends on the chalk rail. Have them share their new words.

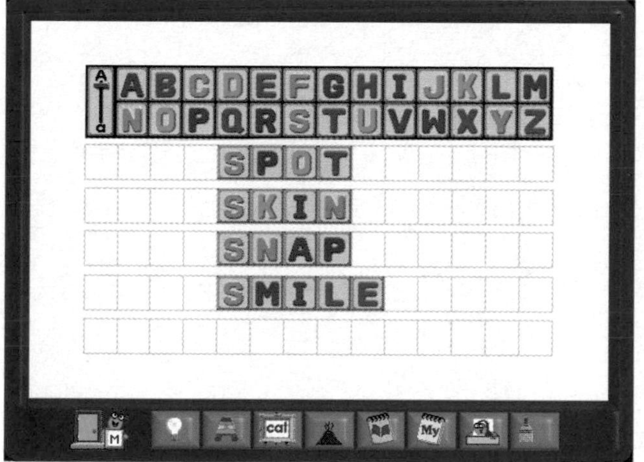

SUPPORTING ALL LEARNERS

Use Realia

EXTRA HELP For additional practice pronouncing the *s*-blend words, give children a bag and fill it with classroom objects that begin with the *s*-blend. Children can take turns drawing an object from the bag and saying its name aloud.

CHALLENGE Children can draw an object from the bag. Challenge them to make up a sentence using as many *s*-blend words as they can to describe the object.

SWINGING WORDS

Make a swing, using construction paper loops which can be stapled to a cardboard seat. Have children find story words and other words they see that begin with s-blends. They can write the words and tape them to the swing.

See Phonics and Word Building Kit for additional suggestions.

The Magnet Board activity pictured above provides additional practice. For more information on this and other Magnet Board activities, see the WiggleWorks Plus Teaching Plan.

BUILDING FLUENCY

Objectives

Children read *The Bunny Hop* for fluency.

Technology Options

Encourage children to listen to the recording of the The Bunny Hop.

The Bunny Hop

Written by Teddy Slater

Illustrated by Larry Di Fiori

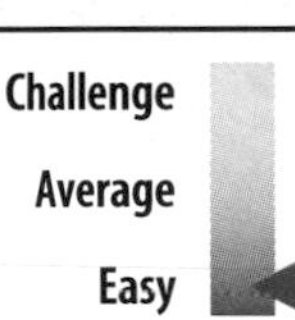

PREVIEW AND READ

Have children read the title and names of the author and the illustrator. Ask them to take note of Buddy Rabbit's feet as they flip through the book.

- **What is unusual about Buddy Rabbit's feet?**
- **What do you think the size of his feet might have to do with the story?**

RESPONSE IDEAS

After children have read *The Bunny Hop,* they can meet with you or with a partner to discuss the story. Questions such as the following can be used:

- **Why was Buddy Rabbit unhappy?**
- **How did Buddy solve his problem?**
- **How did the number words in Chapter 1 help you read the story?**

Read Across Texts

- **How are Buddy Rabbit and Ronald Morgan alike?**

Shoebox Library For more independent reading opportunities choose books from the Shoebox Library.

USING THE TRADE BOOKS

Frog and Toad Are Friends

by Arnold Lobel

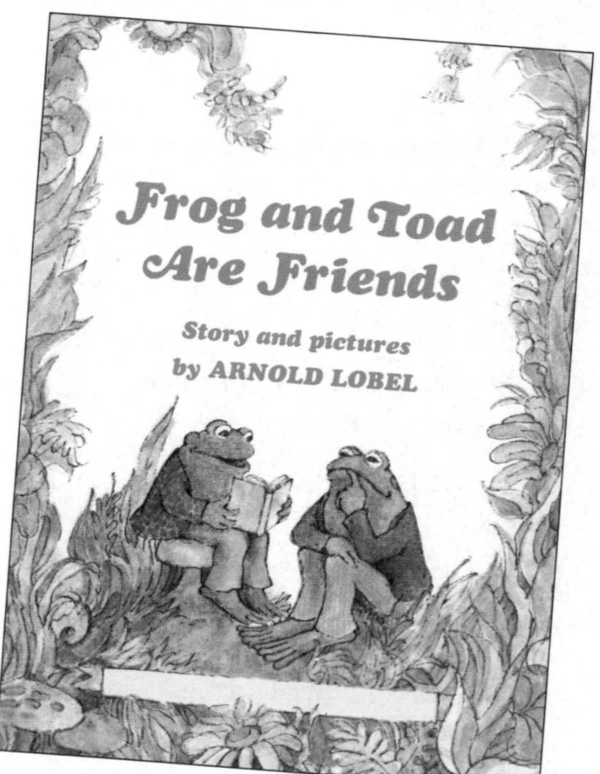

Challenge
Average
Easy

TRADE BOOK GUIDE REFERENCE

For more teaching ideas, refer to the individual Trade Book Guide for *Frog and Toad Are Friends* by Arnold Lobel.

MAKE STRATEGY CONNECTIONS:

CHARACTER

Talk About It

In the selection *Ronald Morgan Goes to Bat,* children learn what kind of a person Ronald Morgan is. Through reading *Frog and Toad Are Friends,* children learn characteristics of Frog and Toad.

- **How would you describe Frog?**
- **How would you describe Toad?**
- **Who is more like Ronald—Frog or Toad? Tell why you think so.**

Write About It

After reading *Frog and Toad Are Friends,* invite children to choose their favorite chapter in the book. Ask them to write about what the two friends did for each other in that chapter.

Read Across Texts

After children read *Frog and Toad Are Friends,* encourage them to compare this book with *Ronald Morgan Goes to Bat.* Have them explore such questions as:

- **If Frog and Toad were members of Ronald Morgan's baseball team, which one of them do you think would be a better baseball player? Which one would have team spirit?**
- **Ronald Morgan's father and his friend Michael help him in different ways. How do Frog and Toad help each other?**

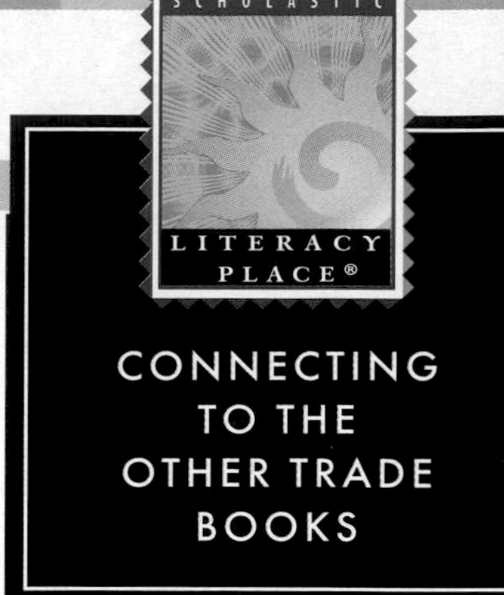

CONNECTING TO THE OTHER TRADE BOOKS

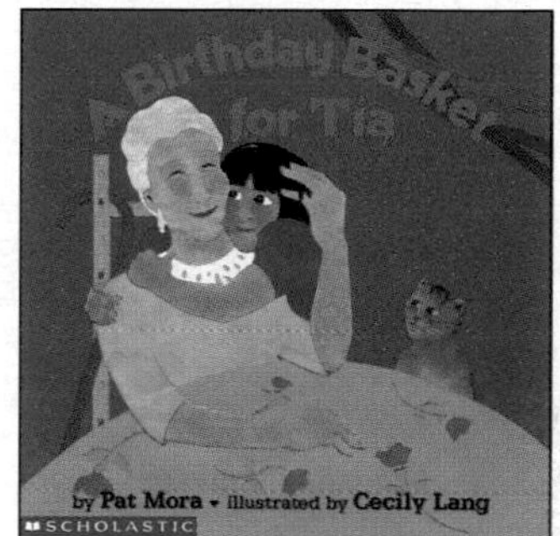

Ask children who have read *A Birthday Basket for Tía* to compare Tía with Ronald Morgan. How does each demonstrate spirit?

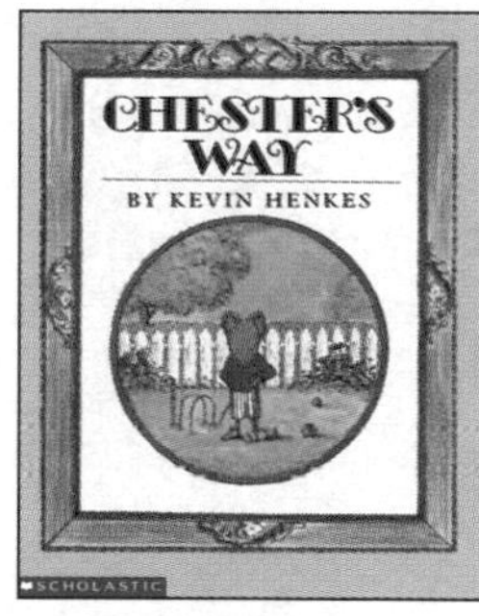

How would you compare the friendships between Chester and his friends and between Ronald Morgan and Michael?

Also for use with this plan

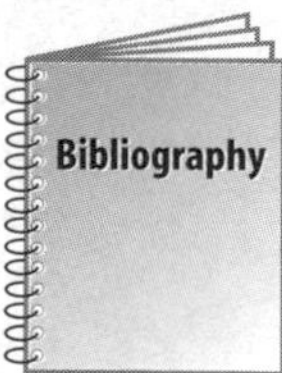

INTEGRATING LEARNING

Curriculum Areas

Math

Children chart the results of a fast-walking relay race to see how practice helped Ronald in the story.
See page R4.

Science

Children diagram the movement of a ball rebounding against a wall.
See page R4.

Social Studies

Children make a scrapbook of a team sport, showing players encouraging each other.
See page R5.

The Arts

Children make a simple flipbook to show the path of a moving ball.
See page R5.

Use Your Sports Arena

Tickets, Hot Dogs, and Popcorn

Curriculum Focus: Math

Objective: Brainstorm multiple approaches

Time: About 30 minutes

Suggested Grouping: Cooperative groups

ACTIVITY Children use addition to figure out how to keep their Sports Arena open.

Connect to the SourceBook Ask children if any of them have ever been to a real baseball stadium where they had to buy a ticket to see the game. Explain that in many stadiums, ticket sales help pay the costs of building the stadium, electric lights, security, and maintenance.

Make New Discoveries

- Tell children that in order to keep the Sports Arena open, they'll have to earn $500.00 per game.
- Have children decide on prices for adult tickets, children's tickets, hot dogs, and popcorn. Post a sign in the Sports Arena that lists the prices.
- Let cooperative groups work together to figure out different ways to earn $100.00. Encourage them to present their ideas on pictographic charts.

✔ **How to Assess** Were children able to come up with different combinations of sales?

WORKSHOP 1

Objectives

- Children think about their unique qualities and strengths.
- Children make trading cards about themselves.

Materials:
Literacy-at-Work Book pp. 23-24
Crayons or markers
Scissors
Tape or paste
Index cards
Photo or drawing of child
Examples of trading cards (optional)

Time:
About 30 minutes

Suggested Grouping:
Individuals and cooperative groups

Curriculum Connections:
Social Studies
The Arts

Technology Options

Children can use a Story Starter from the Unit Writer area to write about their trading cards. They can use the Paint Tools to first sketch out a design and then produce their actual trading cards.

How to Make a Trading Card

WHY DO THIS WORKSHOP?

Through the years, trading cards have been a colorful and engaging medium for saving facts and pictures of our many and varied cultural icons. Years ago, children began collecting, reading, sorting, and trading baseball cards, each emblazoned with a player's picture, statistics, and biographical facts. Today, children collect cards for everyone from outstanding musicians and famous authors to comic book heroes and villains. Trading cards are a great way to inspire children to read on their own and handle tables and statistics.

This Workshop allows children to recognize their individual strengths and to focus on their own unique qualities. Trading cards with classmates is an enjoyable way for children to interact and find out new and positive information about each other.

Getting Started

UNIT SKILL:

RECOGNIZE STRENGTHS

JOURNAL Review side 1 of the Workshop Card. Ask children to describe other types of illustrations or photographs they've seen on trading cards. Read aloud the written information and ask these questions:

- **What do the words and picture tell you about the person?**
- **What other information do you like to see on trading cards?**

If you have examples of trading cards, display them for the class. Have children compare these trading cards with the one on the Workshop Card. Ask children to note similarities and differences and write their responses on the chalkboard.

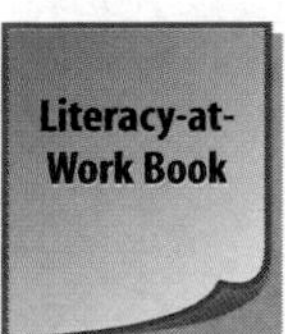

Use pages 23 and 24 of the Literacy-at-Work Book as support for the Workshop or as a separate activity to develop the Workshop.

❶ Write Your Trading Card

Encourage children to focus on what they think their strong points are and what they enjoy doing. Ask them to make a list of their ideas. Explain that lists can help them keep their ideas in order. If children have difficulty in making a list, you might want to use the Study Skill lesson plan on pages T96 and T97 of your Teacher's SourceBook.

Some children may only have small snapshots of themselves or pictures that don't show them in action. In such cases, suggest that children draw a figure doing some activity and then cut their face from a photograph and tape or paste it onto the drawing.

COOPERATIVE GROUPS Have children work in cooperative groups to make and trade their cards.

❷ Trade Your Trading Card

Make three or four photocopies of each child's trading card. Have children tape the fronts and backs together. If no copier is available, have children redraw the picture from the original and copy the information by hand. Children can exchange their cards with each member of the group to collect a whole group's set.

CONNECT TO HOME AND COMMUNITY

Have children ask friends or relatives about their trading card collections. Then ask children to report their findings to the class.

SHOP

1 Write Your Trading Card

Think of what you want to show about yourself. Put a picture of yourself on the front. Write your name and what you are doing in the picture. Write some interesting facts on the back.

2 Trade Your Trading Card

Make copies of your card to trade with your classmates. You can collect a whole set!

THINK!

Children may say that the pictures and words on the trading cards showed their classmates' favorite activities.

Tools

- crayons or markers
- scissors
- tape or paste
- index cards
- a photo or drawing of yourself

THINK

How did these cards help you find out what your classmates like to do?

Bruce Thorson
Photographer

PERFORMANCE-BASED

Review children's trading cards. Ask yourself:

✔ How did children select their information?

✔ Did children organize the written information with their visual material?

✔ Did children emphasize their strenghts?

If not, try this:

In upcoming selections, have children write or draw autobiographical sketches.

Children's Self-Assessment

✔ What favorite things do I show on my trading card?

Portfolio Opportunity

Children may want to keep their trading cards in their Portfolios. Children can review the cards for help with the Project, in which they'll produce an exhibit about themselves.

CHILDREN'S WORKSHOP BENCHMARKS		
Novice: Children may be able to plan and list personal data but can't transfer their ideas to trading cards; children may have difficulty recognizing unique things about themselves.	**Apprentice:** Children plan and list information for their trading cards but may not use their lists as guides; children may not include enough information about themselves.	**Proficient:** Children carefully plan and list what they'll include on their trading cards; children make cards that show their strengths.

WORK

STUDY SKILL

Objective

Children learn how to use lists to acquire information.

Materials:
Paper and pencils
Two or three examples of instructional lists from print materials
Handwritten examples of lists
Computer screens (or facsimiles) showing menus
Literacy-at-Work Book p.25

Time:
About 30 minutes

Suggested Grouping:
Cooperative groups

TESTED	
STUDY SKILL	
LISTS	
Introduce	p. T96
Review	p. R22
Test	p. T311
Reteach	p. R27

Use Graphic Aids: Lists

✔ QUICKCHECK

As children completed their Workshops, did they:

- ✔ use the list of steps in the text to figure out how to make their trading cards?
- ✔ identify their strong points?

YES If yes, go to ❷ Practice and Apply.

NO If no, start at ❶ Teach and Model.

Pick up sticks

1. Hold sticks in your hand on the floor.
2. Let go.
3. Carefully pick up each stick so no other sticks move.
4. If a stick moves you lose your turn.
5. The player who picks up the most sticks wins!

❶ Teach and Model

Put It in Context

Ask the class to review their Workshop for a moment. Then discuss how the list of steps on side 2 of the Workshop Card helped them make trading cards. What type of information is in each step? Where else have you seen lists used in this way? Children might mention the instructions that accompany many model toy kits.

Have children think of lists as guides. Explain how lists are used to organize ideas and sometimes put them in order. Explain that items on a list may be numbered or marked with symbols to distinguish them. Ask children how lists may be useful in their everyday lives, such as for remembering specific dates or going shopping.

SHOP

❷ Practice and Apply

Use Lists

Children can apply the skill of using lists by filling in the things they do during each school day in the chart on page 23 of the Literacy-at-Work Book. After children complete their lists, ask these questions:

- **What things do you do every day?**
- **What things do you do only once a week?**
- **How does the list help you to compare these things?**
- **What other things could you use a list for?**

Cooperative Groups Have children find the answers to the above questions. Ask a volunteer to report each group's answers.

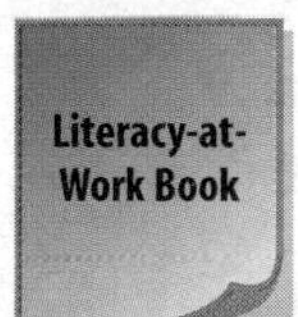

Literacy-at-Work Book

The Study Skill worksheet on p. 25 of the Literacy-at-Work Book gives children practice in making lists.

OPTION

Transfer to New Text

Ask children to bring in sample lists, such as grocery lists, schedules, or food packaging lists. Review the use of each list and ask children what type of information they get from each.

❸ Assess

After children have finished the Study Skill activity, review their work. Ask yourself:

✔ *Do children know how to make lists, as well as get information from them?*

✔ *Did children list things under the correct days?*

✔ *What strategies did children use to organize their lists?*

If children have difficulty making lists, try this:

Look for general topics in upcoming selections that would interest children. List them on the chalkboard. Ask children to choose one topic and make a list of things they'd like to learn about the topic.

Children's Self-Assessment

✔ *What are some of the things I like to do during the week?*

Supporting All Learners

Make Connections

ESL Lists can help prepare us for new experiences. As an activity during Practice and Apply, ask children what words they'd need to know if they were to visit a non-English speaking country. Secondary-language learners can take a prominent role as they share how their experiences influenced their selection. The contribution of second-language learners will provide a real-life connection.

ACCESS Have children make a list of morning preparations before going to school. How would their list change if they had a broken arm? List their responses on the chalkboard. Some children may include steps unfamiliar to their classmates as well as familiar steps.

2 SECTION

We find out what we can do well.

Talent Show

See how Ruby learns that she is special. Then read about another girl who can do anything!

•

Laugh with two friends as they try to make the team.

•

Click! Meet Bruce Thorson, a photographer.

What's in This Section?

Plan III

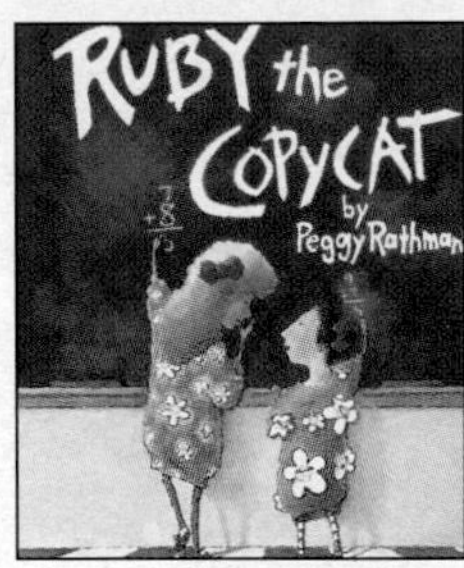

▲ *Ruby the Copycat*
by Peggy Rathmann
Humorous Fiction

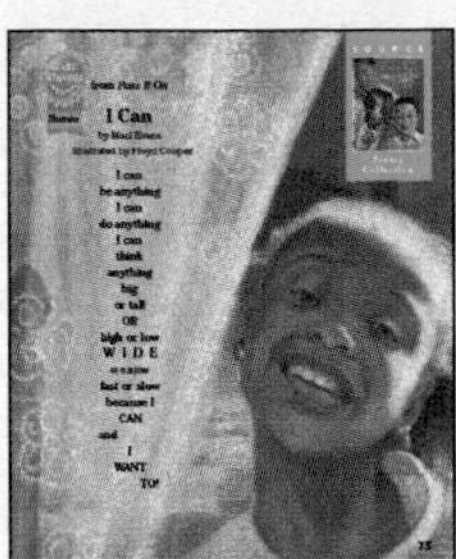

▲ "I Can"
by Mari Evans
Poem

Plan IV

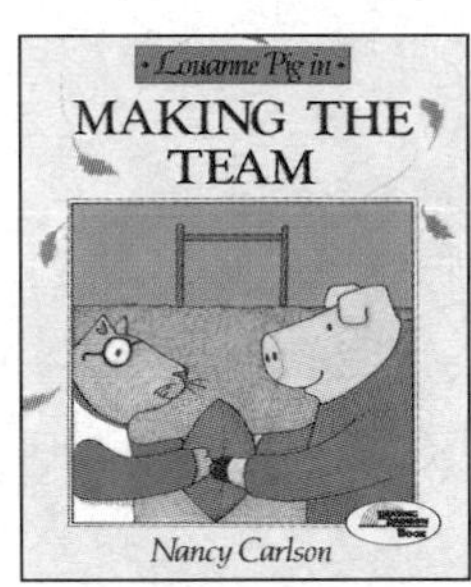

▲ *Louanne Pig in Making the Team*
by Nancy Carlson
Humorous Fantasy

▲ Photographer: Bruce Thorson
Mentor Profile

Workshop 2

How to Make a Graph
Children learn how to make and use a graph for comparing the numbers of children who have certain animals as pets.

Connect to Home and Community

Ask children if they think that everyone is good at something. Then ask them what things their families and friends do well. Invite children to ask at least five people from among their family and friends the question "What do you do best?" Remind them to make a list of the answers they are given. Have them note if any of their family members and friends said the same thing.

Have children compare the answers they got with those of their classmates. Ask them to determine how many people gave the same answer. Then they can draw pictures of their families and friends doing the things they do well. These can be put on a bulletin board entitled "Things our families and friends do well."

RUBY the COPYCAT

by Peggy Rathmann

PERSONAL VOICE

Plan III

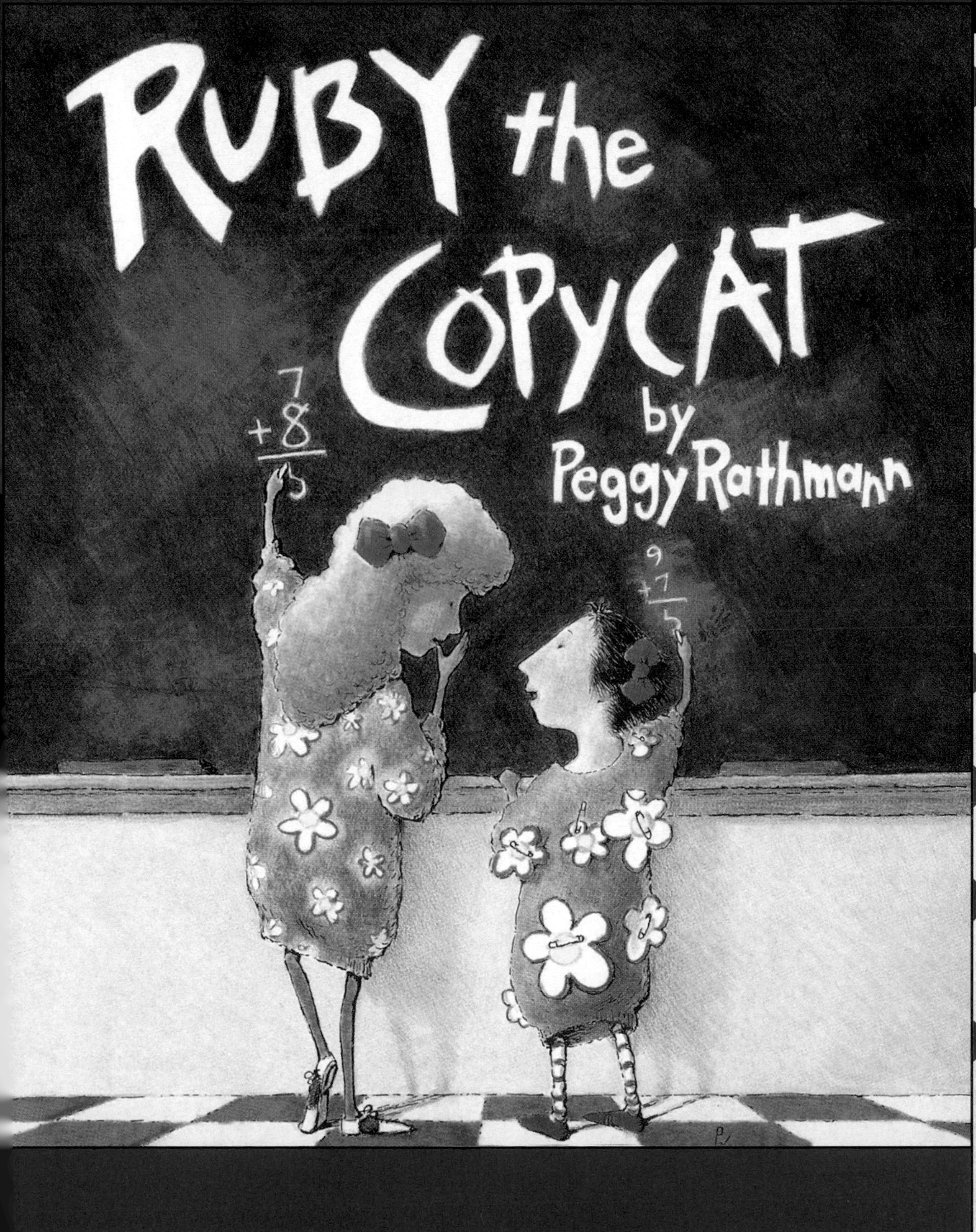

WHAT CHILDREN WILL DO

listen to the Read Aloud *Stellaluna*

read the selections

- ***Ruby the Copycat*** HUMOROUS FICTION
- **"I Can"** POETRY COLLECTION

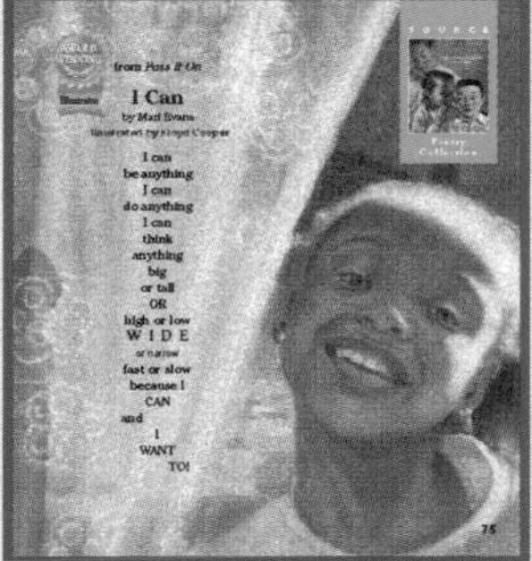

from *Pass It On*

I Can

by Mari Evans

I can
be anything
I can
do anything
I can
think
anything
big
or tall
OR
high or low
W I D E
or narrow
fast or slow
because I
CAN
and
I
WANT
TO!

75

use the key strategy of Make Predictions

blend words with /o/*o*, /u/*u*, and consonant digraphs

write a poem that uses repetition of words and sounds

apply what they read about unique abilities to their own experiences

Assessing Your Students

ASSESSMENT	TEACHER'S SOURCEBOOK	ASSESSMENT KIT
Vocabulary Test	T107	Assessment Handbook
Observation	T108	Assessment Handbook
Assess Reading	T140	Classroom Management Forms
Conference	T140	Assessment Handbook
Performance-Based	T143	Assessment Handbook
Writing Benchmarks	T143	Assessment Handbook
Spelling Tests	T107, T145	Assessment Handbook
Quickcheck	T148, T150, T152	Assessment Handbook
Formal Tests	T311	Unit / Year Tests

Creating a Community of Learners

Stellaluna: pp. T104–105

- Listen for information
- Recognize facts
- Visualize MINI-LESSON

Demonstrating Independence

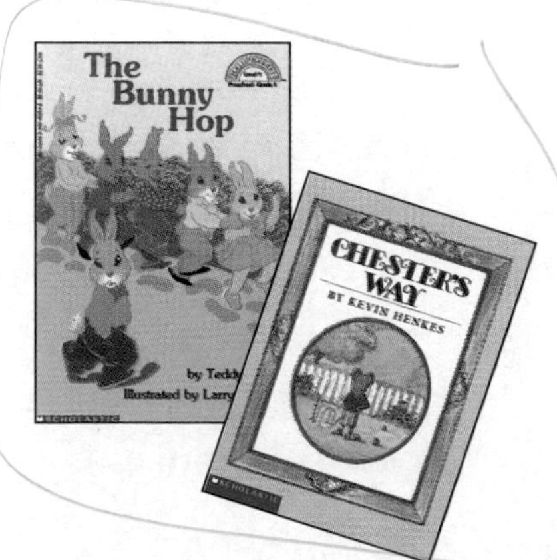

Using the Trade Books: pp. T154–155

- *The Bunny Hop* by Teddy Slater
- *Chester's Way* by Kevin Henkes

Integrating Learning: p. T156

- *Activity:* Copy This!

Focus on Phonics

Phonics Lessons

- Vowels /o/*o*, /u /*u*
- Digraphs *ch, sh, th, wh*

Phonics Kit

Literacy-at-Work Book

- Vowels /o/*o*, /u /*u*, pp. 32–33
- Digraphs *ch, sh, th, wh* pp. 34–35

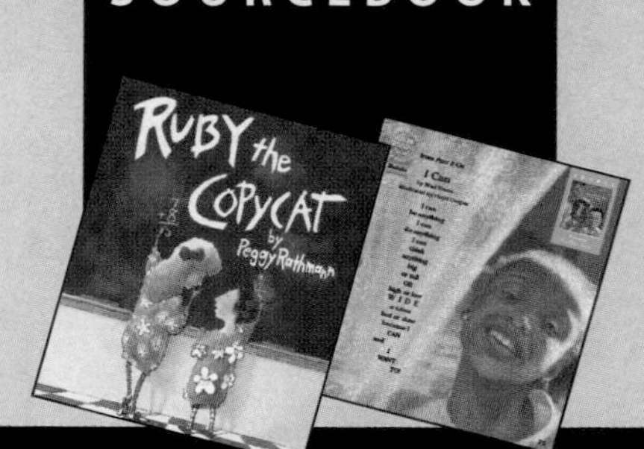

PLAN III ORGANIZER

Ruby the Copycat / "I Can"

	Instructional Path	Supporting All Learners	Resources and Technology
a READING THE SOURCES pp. T106–189	**Build Background** ✔ **Develop Vocabulary** *• announced • tiptoed • whispered • modeled • murmured • recited • scribbled* **Reading Selections** *Ruby the Copycat* "I Can" Launch the Key Strategy: Make Predictions ✔ **Assess Reading** ✔ **Develop Vocabulary**	EXTRA HELP p. T118 ESL pp. T107, T110, T115, T128, T135, T139 CHALLENGE p. T123 ACCESS pp. T107, T130 MINI-LESSON Problem/Solution, p. T128 Humorous Fiction, p. T137 Varying Text Size, p. T139 **Idea File:** p. T141 **Cultural Connections:** pp. T118, T131, T141	**Transparency** Vocabulary, 5 **Literacy-at-Work Book** Vocabulary, p. 26 Comprehension Check p. 27 **WiggleWorks™ Plus,** pp. T106, T108, T110, T114, T116, T117, T118, T119, T121, T123, T128, T132, T135, T136, T141
b INTEGRATING LANGUAGE ARTS pp. T190–195	✔ **Writing:** Write a Poem Daily Language Practice ✔ **Grammar:** Action Words **Mechanics:** Capitalizing Pronoun *I* ✔ **Spelling:** Words With *ch, th,* and *sh* *• chin • much • both • thin • bath • ship • shop • wish*	ESL pp. T143, T147 CHALLENGE p. T143 **Activity File:** pp. T146–147 Draw Describing Words Contribute to Angela's Journal Perform a Puppet Play Create a Dance MINI-LESSON Character, p. T146 Write Directions, p. T147	**Literacy-at-Work Book** Writing, p. 28 **Grammar, Usage, and Mechanics Practice:** pp. 5–6 **Spelling Practice:** p. 3 **Handwriting:** p. 3 **WiggleWorks™ Plus,** pp. T143, T147
c BUILDING SKILLS AND STRATEGIES pp. T196–201	✔ Quickcheck ✔ Key Strategy: Make Predictions ✔ Quickcheck Phonics: Vowels /o/*o*, /u/*u* ✔ Quickcheck Phonics: Digraphs *ch, sh, th, wh*	EXTRA HELP p. T149 ESL pp. T149, T151, T153 CHALLENGE pp. T151, T153	**Transparency** Key Strategy, 6 **Literacy-at-Work Book** Make Predictions, pp. 29–31 Phonics, pp. 32–35 **WiggleWorks™ Plus,** pp. T151, T153

✔ = **Assessed**

LISTEN TO THE READ ALOUD

Objectives

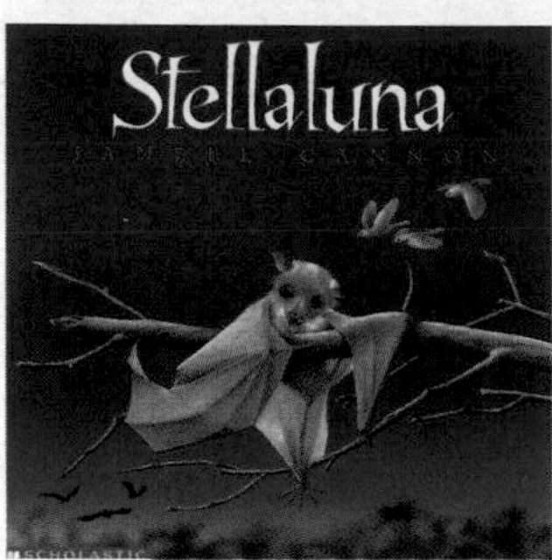

Children learn to:
- listen for information
- recognize facts
- visualize

Materials: Read Aloud Book: *Stellaluna*
Time: About 20 minutes
Suggested Grouping: Whole class and cooperative groups

Technology Options

Invite children to gather facts about bats in an on-line or electronic reference source, such as National Geographic's *A World of Animals*.

Stellaluna

First children **listen** to a **Read Aloud** about a bat who tries to **imitate** his bird friends, and then they read *Ruby the Copycat,* a selection about a girl who **copies** other people.

INTRODUCE THE READ ALOUD

Spark children's interest in the Read Aloud by asking the question, "What do you know about bats?" Write the question on chart paper.

Ask children to think about the question for a moment. Then invite volunteers to tell what they know about bats as you record their responses below the question. Next, explain to children that the story they are going to listen to is about a baby bat who is raised by birds.

ESL To improve comprehension of *Stellaluna,* help children focus on pictures that show ways in which bats and birds are alike and different. **(Use Visuals)** VISUAL LITERACY

SHARE THE READ ALOUD

Show children the cover of the book, and read aloud the title and the author/illustrator's name. Then read the first four pages of text. Pause and discuss these questions:

- **What happened so far?**
- **Why couldn't Stellaluna go home?**
- **What do you think will happen next?**
- **What have you learned about bats so far?**
- **Try to picture the night sky with Mother Bat, Stellaluna, the owl, and the birds in it. How does this help you understand the story?** MINI-LESSON

As you read the rest of the story, ask children to listen for more facts about the habits of bats and to think about how bats and birds are alike and different.

Think About the Read Aloud

Give children the opportunity to share their thoughts about the story. Use discussion questions such as:

- **Did you like the story? What did you like about it?**
- **What new information did you learn from the story?**
- **In what ways are bats and birds alike? different?**
- **What is the message in the story about friendship?**

Take a moment to examine the chart on which children listed what they know about bats. Encourage them to revise or delete any facts that are incorrect and to add new facts that they learned.

Activity: Dramatization

Cooperative Groups Have children work in cooperative groups to dramatize a part of the story they enjoyed. Once they decide on the scene and assign parts, let them role-play for a few minutes. Suggest that they improvise dialogue and move as their animal characters would.

Make Connections

To Children's Lives

Discuss the fact that although it was difficult for Stellaluna to learn to land on her feet, she was good at doing other things, such as hanging by her feet and seeing in the dark. Invite children to talk about things that they are good at, as well as what they have trouble doing or learning. Lead children to see that it's alright not to be able to do everything, and that everyone is good at something.

MINI-LESSON

Visualize

TEACH/MODEL Help children focus on a listening task. Reread the first two pages of the story to children.

> **THINK ALOUD When I listen to these pages, I picture in my mind the mother bat flying through the dark night sky with her baby. At first the scene I picture is peaceful. Then it becomes a little scary as the owl strikes the mother bat and the baby is knocked into the air and falls down.**

APPLY As children listen to you read, have them take turns telling what pictures they see in their minds.

READING THE SOURCES

RUBY THE COPYCAT / I CAN

Build Background

In the **Read Aloud,** children heard about a bat who was good at some things and who **learned** to do new things. *Ruby the Copycat* is about a girl who learns to **recognize** and **appreciate** what she is good at.

Objectives

Children learn to:

- relate personal experiences
- play a pantomime game
- expand oral language
- develop context for vocabulary

Materials:
Transparency 5
Literacy-at-Work Book p. 26
Word Cards 11–17

Time:
About 15 minutes

Suggested Grouping:
Whole class and cooperative groups

Literacy-at-Work Book, p. 26

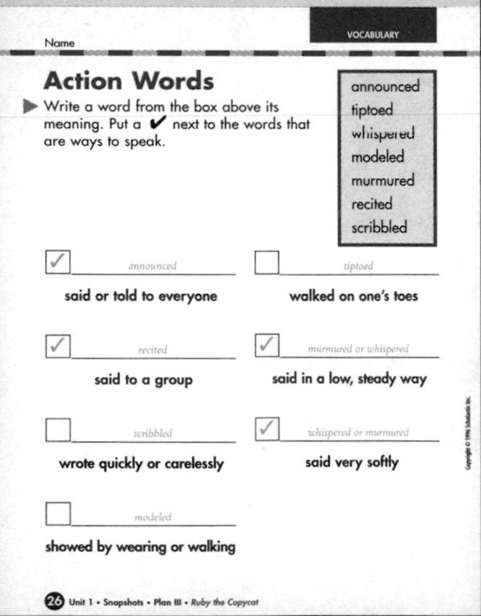

Name VOCABULARY

Action Words

Write a word from the box above its meaning. Put a ✔ next to the words that are ways to speak.

announced
tiptoed
whispered
modeled
murmured
recited
scribbled

☑ announced — said or told to everyone
☐ tiptoed — walked on one's toes
☑ recited — said to a group
☑ murmured or whispered — said in a low, steady way
☐ scribbled — wrote quickly or carelessly
☑ whispered or murmured — said very softly
☐ modeled — showed by wearing or walking

26 Unit 1 • Snapshots • Plan III • *Ruby the Copycat*

ACTIVATE PRIOR KNOWLEDGE

Discuss Copying Someone

Remind children that Stellaluna was good at doing things bats do, but she learned to be like the birds when she lived among them. Ask children how they think Stellaluna learned bird ways of doing things. Have them discuss that she watched the birds and did what they did. In other words, she copied them!

- **Have you ever copied someone else? Has someone else ever copied you? Tell about it.**
- **Do you have younger brothers, sisters, or cousins who have tried to copy you? How did you feel when this happened?**
- **What do you call someone who copies someone else?**

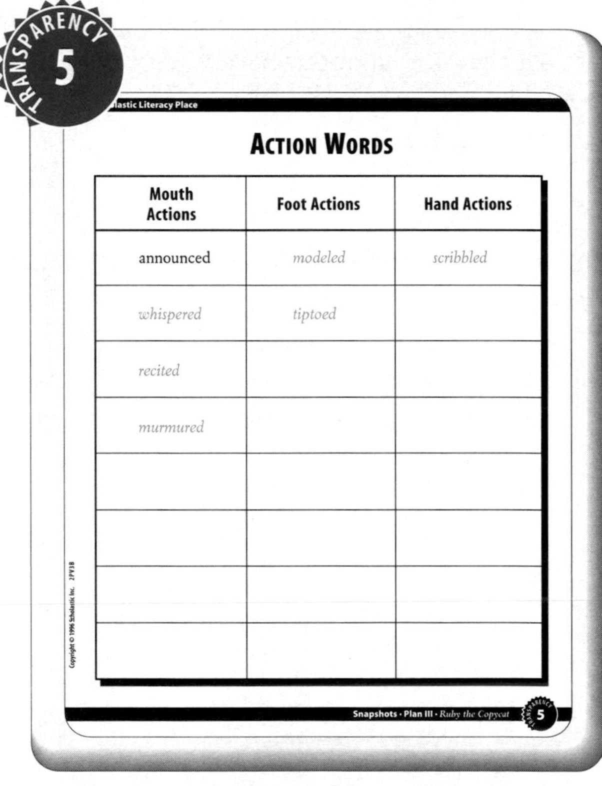

TRANSPARENCY 5

Scholastic Literacy Place

ACTION WORDS

Mouth Actions	Foot Actions	Hand Actions
announced	*modeled*	*scribbled*
whispered	*tiptoed*	
recited		
murmured		

Snapshots • Plan III • *Ruby the Copycat* 5

Annotated transparency for teaching concept words

Develop Vocabulary

Teach the Concept Words

Strategy: Categorize Distribute Word Cards 11–17 to individual children and have them stand in a row. Help children determine how the concept words are alike. Use Transparency 5 to suggest categories, or accept children's suggestions for ways to group these words. The card holders can move into groups as the words are categorized. Challenge children to think of other categories and have them regroup.

Support Words As children read *Ruby the Copycat*, you may want to point out other unusual words in the story.

opera: a play that is sung

serious: not joking; important

OPTION

Play a Pantomime Game

- Display Word Cards 11–17 on the chalk rail and read them aloud.
- Invite a child to act out one of the words.
- Children can copy the action, then guess which word was performed. Have a volunteer select the word card that corresponds to the action.

Personal Word List Children can generate their own lists of new and interesting vocabulary. They may wish to write the days as Ruby progresses through the week.

VOCABULARY

ORGANIZING CONCEPT: ACTION WORDS

Concept Words

✔	announced:	said or told (p. 47)
	tiptoed:	walked on the toes (p. 47)
✔	whispered:	spoke very softly (p. 51)
	modeled:	showed (p. 55)
✔	recited:	said out loud in front of a group (p. 60)
	murmured:	spoke in a low, soft voice (p. 61)
	scribbled:	wrote quickly or without care (p. 63)

✔ = assessed

S M T W T F S
See p. T145 for words to pretest and spelling instruction

Technology Options

Children reading the WiggleWorks selection can collect new words into their My Words lists to use in their own writing. They might also use the Paint Tools and stamp art to create picture definitions of the concept words for a computer vocabulary bulletin board. For more information, see the WiggleWorks Plus Teaching Plan.

Supporting All Learners

Make Connections

ESL Help second-language learners assimilate new vocabulary by inviting them to practice it in real-life context. After they play the pantomime game, encourage children to select one of the concept words and use it in a sentence that describes his or her personal experience.

ACCESS Children with physical disabilities may be hesitant to act out certain action words, such as *hop* or *tiptoe*. Encourage their participation by asking them to act out the words in an alternate manner. They can indicate hopping or tiptoeing with hand movements.

a READING THE SOURCES

RUBY THE COPYCAT / I CAN

Prepare to Teach

OBSERVATION

As children read *Ruby the Copycat,* notice how they:

- ✔ make connections with the *theme* of Ruby learning the value of her special talents.
- ✔ use the *key strategy* of Make Predictions.
- ✔ recognize the *literary element* of Humor.

Use the Individual and Class Plan Checklists in the Classroom Management Forms, pages 6 and 12.

KEY STRATEGY:

MAKE PREDICTIONS

Ruby the Copycat provides many opportunities to build children's confidence in making predictions. The story's use of repetitive dialogue, days of the week, and copycat theme help to make it a predictable story.

Children can use the WiggleWorks Plus tools to help launch the key strategy. For example, as they read they can record and then check their predictions.

Customize Instruction

Teacher Support

Construct meaning by using the key strategy of Make Predictions as children read the selection. Revisit the selection to build understanding of the literary element of Humor.

Collaborative

The use of dialogue in *Ruby the Copycat* provides a structure for children to read in groups of up to four.

Have groups role-play the characters using the Record and Playback tools.

Extra Support

Have children listen to the selection on audiocassette as they follow along in their texts. The story's repetition and illustrations provide support for readers.

Independent

Let children read silently without interruption. Use the questions on page T140.

Meet the Author/Illustrator

Peggy Rathmann

Peggy Rathmann began her career in children's books as an illustrator. *Ruby the Copycat* is the first book for which she both wrote the story and drew the pictures. She received the IRA/CBC Children's Choice Award in 1992 and the American Bookseller Pick of the Lists Award for this humorous book. Ms. Rathmann got the idea to write humorous stories for children from entertaining her nieces. She studied art at the Otis/Parsons School of Design in Los Angeles and resides in southern California.

More Humorous School Stories

- ***Arthur's Teacher Trouble***
  by Marc Brown
  Arthur is amazed that he is a contestant in the school spellathon in this comical adventure.
- ***The Day Jimmy's Boa Ate the Wash***
  by Trinka Hakes Noble
  An ordinary class trip becomes a hilarious adventure when Jimmy brings along his unusual pet.
- ***Song Lee in Room 2B***
  by Suzy Kline
  Song Lee and her classmate Horrible Harry find that second grade is full of funny surprises.

Books for Word Study

- ***Scrawny, the Classroom Duck***
  by Susan Clymer
  A boy develops an attachment to a school pet. **(vowel /u/u digraph *th*)**
- ***Shy Charles***
  by Rosemary Wells
  Timid Charles heroically rescues his babysitter. **(digraph *ch*)**
- ***What's So Funny, Ketu?***
  by Verna Aardma
  In this African tale, Ketu can hear animals think. **(digraph *wh*)**

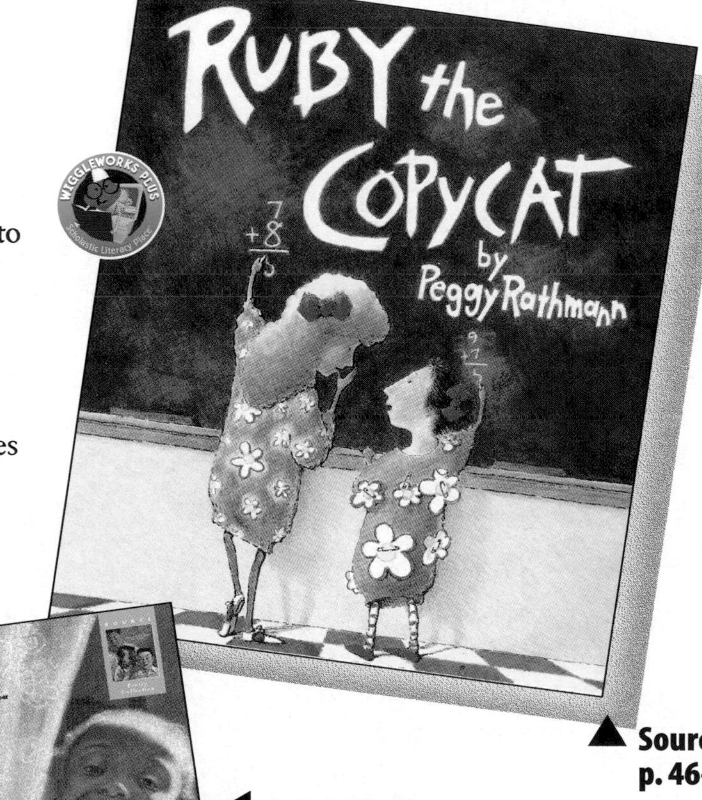

▲ SourceBook p. 46–74

◀ SourceBook p. 75

READING THE SOURCES

Preview and Predict

READER TO READER

I'm sure you have known someone who is a copycat. I know I have! That's why I enjoyed this story so much.

Show children the cover of *Ruby the Copycat*. Read aloud the title and the author/illustrator's name.

- **How are the girls on the cover alike?**
- **Which girl on the cover is probably Ruby the copycat? Why do you think so?**

Invite them to preview the pictures in the story. Encourage children to make predictions about what they think will happen.

What We Predict

- Ruby wants to make friends.
- Ruby copies people in the classroom.
- People get mad.

JOURNAL You may wish to have children write their predictions in their Journals. Suggest that, as they read, they also record their favorite funny parts of the story. Children may also want to record their predictions on the predictions chart found on R39.

SOURCE

Humorous Fiction

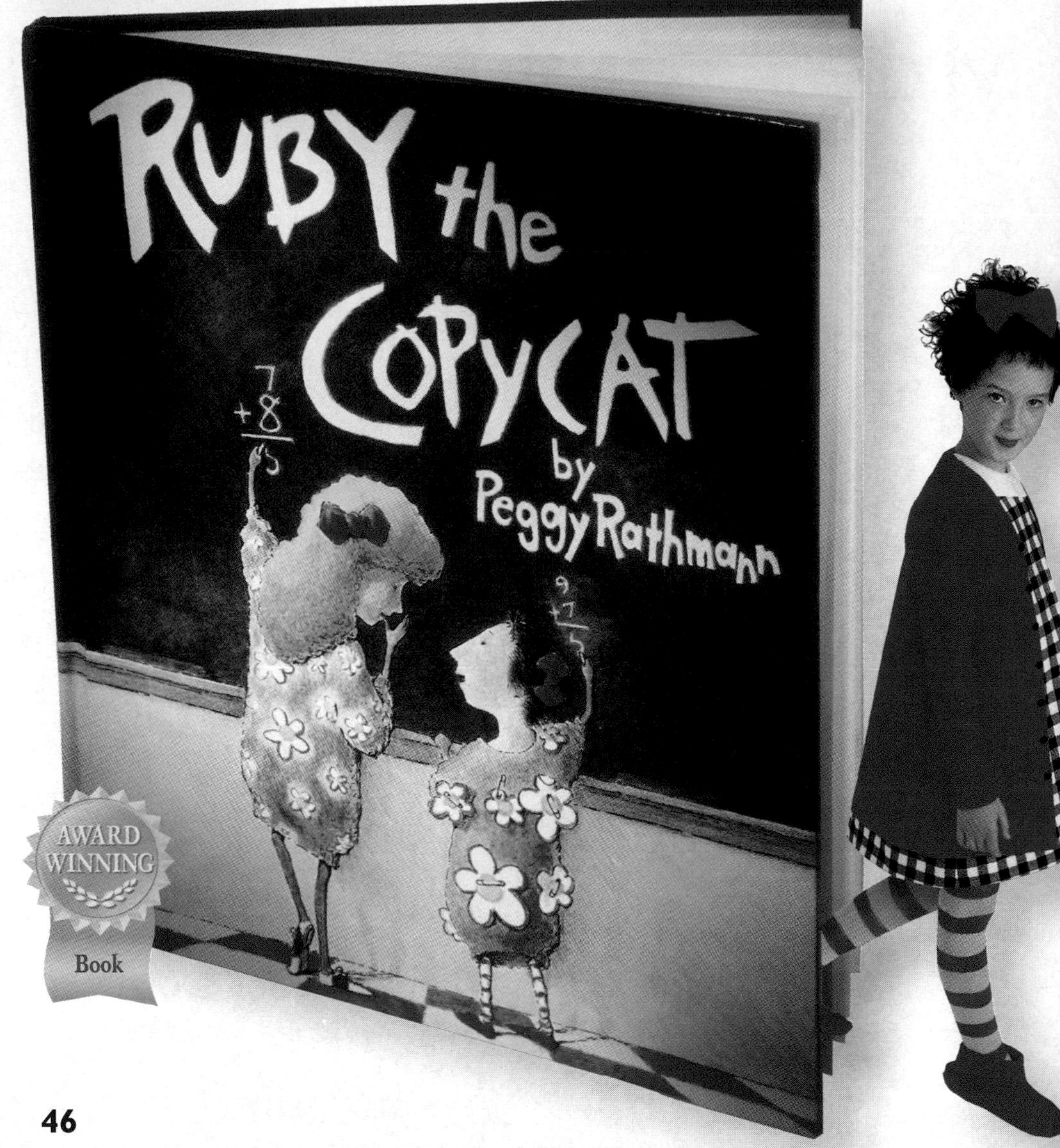

46

PAGE 46 SNAPSHOTS

SUPPORTING ALL LEARNERS

Preview **ESL** Reinforce the main story concept of being a copycat by inviting children to play a mirror game. In pairs, children stand facing each other. As one child moves, the other must imitate his or her partner. **(Hands-on Learning)**

- Encourage partners to click through the story on the computer, taking turns recording their descriptions of what they think is happening.

Monday was Ruby's first day in Miss Hart's class.

"Class, this is Ruby," announced Miss Hart. "Ruby, you may use the empty desk behind Angela. Angela is the girl with the pretty red bow in her hair."

Angela smiled at Ruby.

Ruby smiled at Angela's bow and tiptoed to her seat.

47

RUBY THE COPYCAT PAGE 47

Guided Reading ▶

LAUNCH THE KEY STRATEGY:

MAKE PREDICTIONS

THINK ALOUD I look for clues in the words and pictures to figure out what might happen in a story. I also use my own knowledge and experience to help me predict. When I first looked at the cover of the book, I saw that both girls were wearing the same sweater. From my experience I know that means it could be a coincidence that they have the same sweater, or maybe they're best friends and they like to dress alike. But I noticed that the flowers on one girl's sweater are pinned on. Since the title is *Ruby the Copycat*, I predict that the girl with the pinned-on flowers is copying the other girl.

▶ INTEGRATED CURRICULUM **MATH** *(See p. R6.)*

Children use different pairs of addends to make the same total as Ruby in *Ruby the Copycat*.

a

Guided Reading ►

❶ **Make Inferences Notice the way Ruby is looking at Angela in the picture on this page and how she says she is like Angela. How do you think Ruby feels about Angela? What makes you think that?**

VISUAL LITERACY

Revisit ◄

Conventions of Print: Quotation Marks

Point out to children that the words the characters say to each other are called dialogue. Have them point to the words Miss Hart says aloud.

- **How do you know which words Miss Hart says?**
- **Where else might we see quotation marks in the story?**

Make sure children understand that Miss Hart's words are set off from the rest of the sentence, using quotation marks. Encourage children to look for other examples of dialogue as they reread the story.

"I hope everyone had a pleasant weekend," said Miss Hart. "Does anyone have something to share?"

"I was the flower girl at my sister's wedding," said Angela.

"That's exciting," said Miss Hart.

48

PAGE 48 SNAPSHOTS

Ruby raised her hand halfway. "I was the flower girl at my sister's wedding, too."

"What a coincidence!" said Miss Hart.

Angela turned and smiled at Ruby.

Ruby smiled at the top of Angela's head.

"Class, please take out your reading books," said Miss Hart.

49

RUBY THE COPYCAT PAGE 49

Read On ► ► ►

PHONICS *s*-Blends

Have children find the word *smiled* on page 49, point to the letters *sm,* and read the word aloud. Remind them that the two consonant letters at the beginning of *smiled* are blended together when you say the word.

- **What other words do you know that start with the same sounds as *smiled?***

Encourage children to look for other words in the story that begin with *s*-blends, including *slid, sweater, sneakers, stood,* and *stayed.*

► INTEGRATING LANGUAGE ARTS **SPEAKING/LISTENING** *(See p. T146.)*

a

Read On ► ► ►

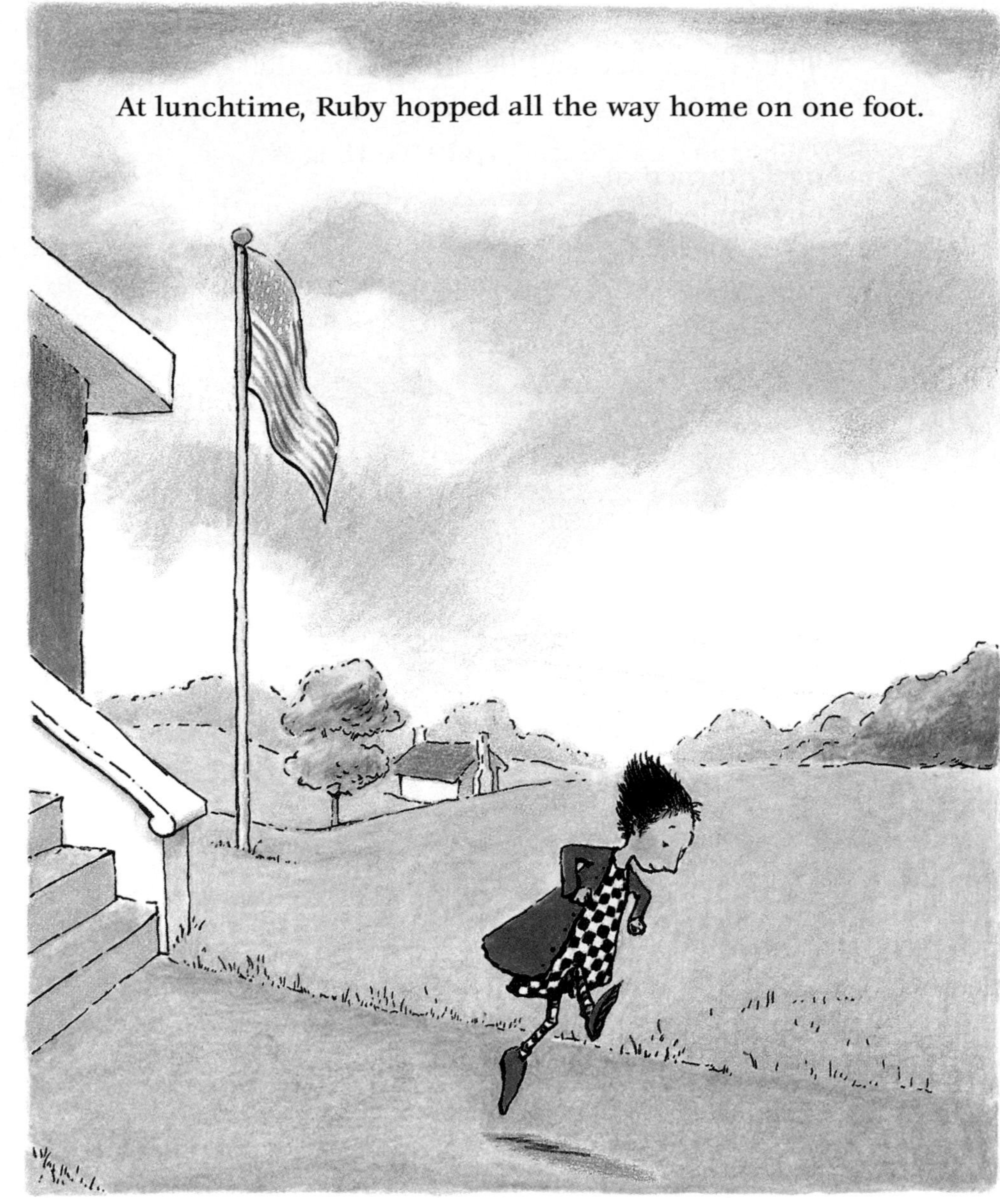

PAGE 50 SNAPSHOTS

► INTEGRATED CURRICULUM **THE ARTS** *(See p. R7.)*

Children plan methods to reproduce a painting.

PHONICS Vowels /o/*o*, /u/*u*

Have children find the word *hopped* on page 50, point to the letter *o*, and read the word aloud.

- **What other words have the same vowel sound as *hopped*? Listen for the short *o* sound in each word you name.**

Then use the same procedure for short *u* in the word *lunchtime*.
(See Phonics: Vowels /o/o, /u/u on pp. T150–151.)

For more phonics activities, see the WiggleWorks Plus Teaching Plan.

When Ruby came back to school, she was wearing a red bow in her hair. ❷ She slid into her seat behind Angela.

"I like your bow," whispered Angela. ❸

"I like yours, too," whispered Ruby.

"Class, please take out your math books," said Miss Hart.

51

RUBY THE COPYCAT PAGE 51

Guided Reading ►

❷ **Compare/Contrast** **First Ruby said she was a flower girl at her sister's wedding like Angela was. How is Ruby like Angela now?**

❸ **Make Inferences** **Why do you think Ruby put on a red bow? How do you think Angela feels about Ruby copying her bow? What makes you think that?**

Supporting All Learners

ESL Reread page 51 aloud, and invite children to review the names of the colors in English by innovating on the phrase "She was wearing a red bow in her hair." How many different colors did the group come up with? **(Follow Patterns)**

Revisit

a

Guided Reading ►

❹ **Word Attack Follow along as I read: "On Tuesday morning, Angela wore a sweater with flowers on it." Wait...is that word *flowers*? It doesn't start with *f*. It begins with the letter *d* and when I look at the flowers on Angela's sweater, they look like...daisies. Yes, *daisies* has the right sound at the beginning and it makes sense.**

❺ **KEY STRATEGY: Make Predictions Let's read this page together. What do you think Ruby will do when she returns to school after lunch? What clues from the story can you use to help you make your predictions?**

Children can use the Record Tool to record their predictions.

Revisit ◄

Literary Element: Setting

As children reread the story, have them make observations about the setting:

- The main setting is the classroom in a school.
- At lunchtime, the setting changes to outdoors.

Structural Analysis: Compound Words

Remind children that compound words are made up of two words put together.

- **What are the two compound words on page 52?**
- **Tell us other compound words you know.**

Have children look for additional compound words as they continue to read the story.

On Tuesday morning,
Angela wore a sweater with
❹ ❺ daisies on it.
At lunchtime, Ruby
hopped home sideways.

52

PAGE 52 SNAPSHOTS

When Ruby came back to school after lunch, she was wearing a sweater with daisies on it.

"I like your sweater," whispered Angela.

"I like yours, too," whispered Ruby.

53

RUBY THE COPYCAT PAGE 53

▶ INTEGRATED CURRICULUM **SCIENCE** *(See p. R6.)*

Children find out about animal mimicry and decide how it helps certain animals.

Guided Reading ▶

6 KEY STRATEGY: Make Predictions **Did Ruby do what you thought she would do? If not, how was your prediction different from what happened in the story?**

Children can use the Playback Tool to review the predictions they made.

PHONICS **Vowels /a/ *a*, /i/ *i***

Invite children to find the word *back* on page 53, point to the letter *a*, and read the word aloud.

- **What other words have the same vowel sound as *back?* Listen for the short *a* sound in each word you name.**

Then use the same procedure for the short *i* sound in the word *it*.

a

Guided Reading ▶

7 **Main Idea/Details In what ways does Ruby copy Angela in this part of the story?**

On Wednesday, Angela wore a hand-painted T-shirt with matching sneakers.

7 After lunch, Ruby hopped back to school wearing a hand-painted T-shirt with matching sneakers.

"Why are you sitting like that?" whispered Angela.

"Wet paint," said Ruby.

54

PAGE 54 SNAPSHOTS

CULTURAL CONNECTIONS

Ruby's copycatting may not be very productive, but copying can be a useful way for beginners to learn a new skill. For example, young Balinese dancers copy the steps to a new dance, just as Russian ballerinas do. Children in China begin learning to write the same way those in England do, by copying the shapes of the characters and letters. What skills have children learned by copying?

SUPPORTING ALL LEARNERS

Read EXTRA HELP Summarizing what has happened so far will reinforce children's comprehension of the text. Reread the first several pages aloud, pausing to give children a turn to summarize. Then they can use this information to respond to Read 7 **(Summarize).**

- You may wish to leave messages at appropriate points in the story, asking children to write or record their summaries.

On Thursday morning, during Sharing Time, Angela modeled the flower girl dress she wore at her sister's wedding.

Ruby modeled her flower girl dress, too, right after lunch.

Angela didn't whisper anything.

55

Guided Reading ▶

8 Make Inferences Look at the picture of Angela in her flower-girl dress. How do you think she feels? Why do you think she didn't whisper anything after Ruby modeled her dress?

PHONICS **Digraphs /sh/*sh*,/th/*th***

Have children find the words *Thursday* and *sharing*, and point to the two consonants at the beginning of each word. Pronounce each word with children, stressing the initial consonant sound. Mention that the two consonant letters at the beginning of each word stand for one sound.

- **What other words do you know that start with the same sound as *Thursday*? As *sharing*?**

(See Phonics: Digraphs on pp. T152–153.)

For more phonics activities, see the WiggleWorks Plus Teaching Plan.

Read On ► ► ►

By coincidence, on Friday morning, both girls wore red-and-lavender-striped dresses.

At lunchtime, Angela raced home.

56

PAGE 56 SNAPSHOTS

When Angela came back to school, she was wearing black. ❾

57

Guided Reading ▶

❾ **Make Inferences** **How has the story changed on this page? Why do you think Angela came back to school wearing a black dress?**

❿ **Character** **How would you feel at this point of the story if you were Angela? How would you feel if you were Ruby?**

Encourage children to write their responses in the WiggleWorks writing area.

Revisit ◀

Summarize

Ask children what they do as readers to help them remember and understand what they read. Mention that when they read, they should stop to summarize, or retell the main parts of the story in their own words. To help children summarize the story events so far, have them summarize what has happened each day.

Have children record their summaries or write them in the computer writing area.

a

Read On ► ► ►

On Friday afternoon, Miss Hart asked everyone to write a short poem.

"Who would like to read first?" asked Miss Hart.

58

PAGE 58 SNAPSHOTS

Angela raised her hand. She stood by her desk and read:

I had a cat I could not see,
Because it stayed in back of me.
It was a very loyal pet—
It's sad we never really met. 11

"That was very good!" said Miss Hart. "Now, who's next?" Miss Hart looked around the room. "Ruby?"

59

RUBY THE COPYCAT PAGE 59

Supporting All Learners

CHALLENGE Children can use Angela's poem to stimulate their own creativity. Challenge them to use the poem as a model to write their own two- or four-line poem about a cat or other pet. **(Innovate)**

Revisit

- Invite children to write their poems on the computer, using drawing tools to illustrate their work.

Guided Reading ►

11 **KEY STRATEGY: Make Predictions We've had many chances to see how Ruby copies Angela. Now Ruby writes a poem about a cat. Think about how Ruby has acted in the past. What might Ruby do when it's her turn to read her poem? How do you know?**

INTERVENTION STRATEGY

Varying Type Style

The variation in type style on page 59 may confuse some children. Point out that the words in italics are the words of the poem that Angela reads aloud. Another typeface is used so that readers will know the difference between the poem and the rest of the story. Ask children to read the poem aloud with you.

Revisit ◄

Print Awareness: Exclamation Marks

Have children point to the exclamation mark in Miss Hart's dialogue on page 59.

- **When are exclamation marks used in sentences?**
- **Think about how Miss Hart would say the words that end with the exclamation mark. Let's say those words together, just as she would say them to show she is excited or enthusiastic.**

As children continue to reread, encourage them to look for other examples of sentences that end with exclamation marks.

a

Guided Reading ▶

12  KEY STRATEGY: Make Predictions **What did you predict Ruby would do with the poem that Angela wrote? What clues from the story helped you make that prediction?**

Ruby stood and recited slowly:

I had a nice pet,
Who I never met,
Because it always stayed behind me.
And I'm sure it was a cat, too. 12

60

PAGE 60 SNAPSHOTS

Revisit ◀

Oral Reading

Point out that Angela read her poem from her paper. When Ruby said her poem aloud, she made it up at that moment to copy Angela's poem.

- **What tone might Ruby use when she recites her poem—happy, friendly, or sad?**
- **Let's read the poem together, the way Ruby might recite it. Remember to look at your audience and speak clearly and loudly enough to be heard.**

13

Ruby smiled at the back of Angela's head. Someone whispered. Ruby sat down.

"What a coincidence," murmured Miss Hart.

Guided Reading ►

13 Picture Clues **Look at the picture of Miss Hart. What clues in the picture tell you about the way Miss Hart is feeling when she murmurs the words "What a coincidence"?** VISUAL LITERACY

a

Read On ► ► ►

Angela scribbled something on a piece of paper. She passed it to Ruby.

The note said:

YOU COPIED ME!
I'M TELLING MISS HART!
P.S. I HATE YOUR HAIR THAT WAY. 14

Ruby buried her chin in the collar of her blouse. A big tear rolled down her nose and plopped onto the note.

When the bell rang, Miss Hart sent everyone home 15 except Ruby.

63

RUBY THE COPYCAT PAGE 63

Guided Reading ►

14 Make Inferences Angela uses all capital letters and exclamation marks in her note to Ruby. What does the note tell you about Angela's feelings toward Ruby now? Let's read the note together, using the same expression Angela might have used.

15 KEY STRATEGY: Make Predictions Here's where you can use your own experiences to help you make a prediction. What do you think Miss Hart will say to Ruby after everyone else goes home? Think about what teachers might say to children they ask to stay after class.

Revisit ◄

Varying Type Style

Some children may be confused by the variation in type style on page 63. Explain that the words in dark or boldface type are the words in Angela's note. The dark type is used so that:

- Readers will know the difference between the note and the rest of the story.
- Angela's feelings of anger toward Ruby are emphasized.

a

Guided Reading ▶

16 **Problem/Solution Did you predict that Miss Hart would talk to Ruby about the way that she copies Angela? That was the problem Miss Hart had in her classroom. How does Miss Hart try to solve the problem? What do you think of her solution?**

MINI-LESSON

17 **Paraphrase What very important idea is Miss Hart trying to make Ruby understand? In your own words, try to retell what Miss Hart is saying.**

Children can use the WiggleWorks Plus writing area to restate what Miss Hart is saying.

Miss Hart closed the door of the schoolroom and sat on the edge of Ruby's desk.

"Ruby, dear," she said gently, "you don't need to copy everything Angela does. You can be anything you want to be, but be Ruby first. I like Ruby."  16  17

64

PAGE 64 SNAPSHOTS

MINI-LESSON

Problem/ Solution

TEACH/MODEL Focus children on identifying the problem.

THINK ALOUD Ruby has been copying Angela, and Miss Hart knows that Angela is getting upset. Miss Hart tries to solve the problem in this part of the story by talking to Ruby. She tells Ruby that she likes her. She tells Ruby she can be anything she wants to be but to be Ruby first. I know that she is saying this to help Ruby discover that she doesn't have to copy Angela to be liked.

APPLY Story characters might have to try more than one solution to solve a problem. Ask for other solutions Miss Hart might have tried.

Supporting All Learners

Read

ESL Children must understand what Miss Hart tells Ruby in order to get the deeper meaning of the story. Read Miss Hart's words aloud and then reread, breaking them into chunks. Have second-language learners retell each chunk in their own words.

(Read Aloud)

- Guide children to use the read buttons to have text chunks read aloud to them by the computer.

Miss Hart smiled at Ruby. Ruby smiled at Miss Hart's beautiful, polished fingernails.

"Have a nice weekend," said Miss Hart.

"Have a nice weekend," said Ruby. 

Guided Reading ►

18 **KEY STRATEGY: Make Predictions** **Now let's make another prediction. Notice that Ruby says exactly what Miss Hart says and the way she looks at Miss Hart's beautiful, polished fingernails. What do you predict Ruby might do when she returns to school Monday? What makes you think so?**

a

Guided Reading ►

⓳ **KEY STRATEGY: Make Predictions Was your prediction about what Ruby would do when she returned to school correct? Ruby says she went to the opera over the weekend. Think about what's happened in the story so far. What do you think she really did?**

⓴ **CRITICAL THINKING: Evaluate Do you think Miss Hart's solution to the problem of Ruby being a copycat worked? If you were Miss Hart, what would you do now?**

Revisit ◄

Literary Element: Setting

Help children focus on the passage of time in the story.

- **Start at the beginning of the story. Look through the pages and find the names of the days of the week.**
- **Now read the last words that Ruby and Miss Hart say to each other on page 65.**
- **Look at page 66. How can you tell that a new school week has begun?**

On Monday morning, Miss Hart said, "I hope everyone had a pleasant weekend. I did! I went to the opera." Miss Hart looked around the room. "Does anyone have something to share?"

Ruby waved her hand. Glued to every finger was a pink plastic fingernail. ⓳

"I went to the opera, too!" said Ruby. 

"She did not!" whispered Angela.

66

PAGE 66 SNAPSHOTS

Miss Hart folded her hands and looked very serious.

"Ruby, dear," said Miss Hart gently, "did you do anything else this weekend?"

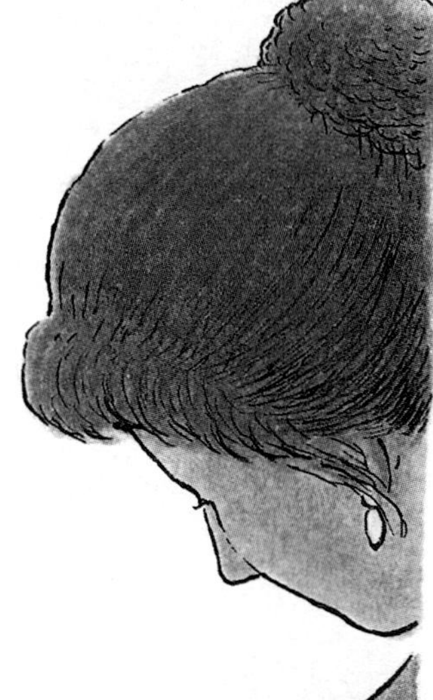

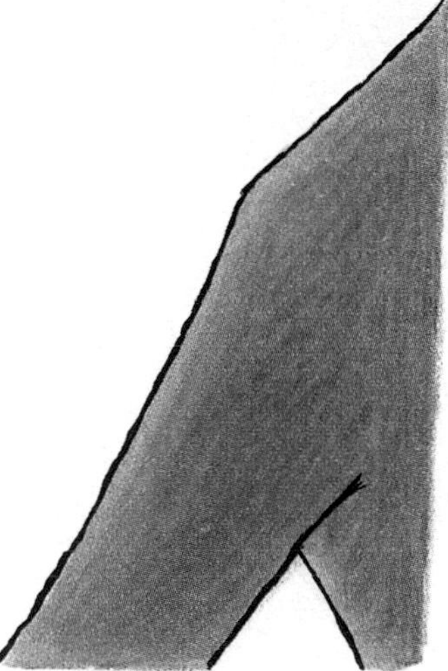

67

RUBY THE COPYCAT PAGE 67

▶ INTEGRATED CURRICULUM **SOCIAL STUDIES** *(See p. R7.)*
Children choose a person they admire and write about one feature they'd like to copy.

Read On ▶ ▶ ▶

CULTURAL CONNECTIONS

Because opera began in Italy in the 1500s, many words related to opera come from the Italian language.

- A song sung by one character in an opera is an aria.
- An aria usually describes the character's thoughts and feelings.
- The words of an opera without the music are called the libretto. It means "little book" in Italian.

THE ARTS

a

Guided Reading ►

21 KEY STRATEGY: Make Predictions **Did you predict that Ruby hopped? Tell how you made that prediction.**

Ruby peeled off a fingernail.
"I hopped," said Ruby. 21

68

PAGE 68 SNAPSHOTS

Revisit ◄

Illustrator's Craft: Humor

As children reread the story, focus their attention on the way in which the illustrations are drawn.

- **Do you like the pictures in this story? Which picture is your favorite?**
- **Do you think you would like the story better if photographs or drawings that looked more like real people were used? Why do you think so?**
- **How do the pictures help you understand the characters' feelings?** VISUAL LITERACY

Encourage children to use the My Book area to create their own versions of the illustrations.

The class giggled.

Ruby's ears turned red. 22

"But I did! I hopped around the picnic table ten times!" Ruby looked around the room. "Watch!"

69

RUBY THE COPYCAT PAGE 69

Guided Reading ►

22 **Cause/Effect** **What caused Ruby's ears to turn red?**

a

Read On ▶ ▶ ▶

Ruby sprang from her desk.

She hopped forward.

She hopped backward.

70

PAGE 70 SNAPSHOTS

THINK!

Mentor Connection

Why might Bruce Thorson like to photograph Ruby?

▶ INTEGRATING LANGUAGE ARTS READING/WRITING/LISTENING *(See p. T147)*

She hopped sideways with both eyes shut.  

71

Guided Reading ►

23 **Sequence Let's review how Ruby hops. What does she do first? What does she do next? What does she do last?**

24 **KEY STRATEGY: Make Predictions What do you think the children in the class will do after they watch Ruby hop? Make a prediction. You can use your own knowledge and experience here. What would you do?**

Revisit ◄

Vocabulary: Direction Words

Have children identify words that name directions.

- **Look at the sentences on this page. What words named the directions in which Ruby hopped?**
- **Can you name some other direction words?**

Children can add their direction words to their My Words lists.

Supporting All Learners

Revisit

ESL Encourage children to practice using the direction words by choosing volunteers to pantomime them as you point to each word on the page. Then children can take turns moving in a direction while classmates select the correct word to describe it. **(Pantomime)**

a

Read On ► ► ►

The class cheered and clapped their hands to the beat of Ruby's feet. Ruby was the best hopper they had ever seen.

72

PAGE 72 SNAPSHOTS

PHONICS **Digraph /ch/*ch***

Ask children to find the word *cheered,* point to the letters *ch,* and read the word aloud.

- **What other words do you know that begin with the same sound?**

(See Phonics: Digraphs on pp. T152–153.)

For phonics Magnet Board activities, see the WiggleWorks Plus Teaching Plan.

26

Miss Hart turned on the tape player and said, "Follow the leader! Do the Ruby Hop!" 25

So Ruby led the class around the room, while everyone copied *her*.

Guided Reading ►

25 **Make Inferences** **How do you think Ruby feels when the rest of the class copies her? How would you feel?**

26 **Humorous Fiction** **Could this story really happen? Why do you think so? How would pictures of real people change the story?** MINI-LESSON

MINI-LESSON

Humorous Fiction

TEACH/MODEL Point out the humorous aspects of the pictures in *Ruby the Copycat*.

THINK ALOUD Some stories include events that cannot happen in real life. The things that happen in *Ruby the Copycat* could really happen. The characters in the story, however, don't look like real people. The pictures make this story funny. For example, Ruby's feet don't look like real people's feet.

APPLY Invite children to look closely at the pictures. Have them tell what makes the pictures funny.

a

Guided Reading ▶

27 **Summarize** **It looks as if Ruby and Angela have finally become friends! Think about the story. In general, what has the story taught you about being a copycat?**

27

And at noon, Ruby and Angela hopped home for lunch.

74

PAGE 74 SNAPSHOTS

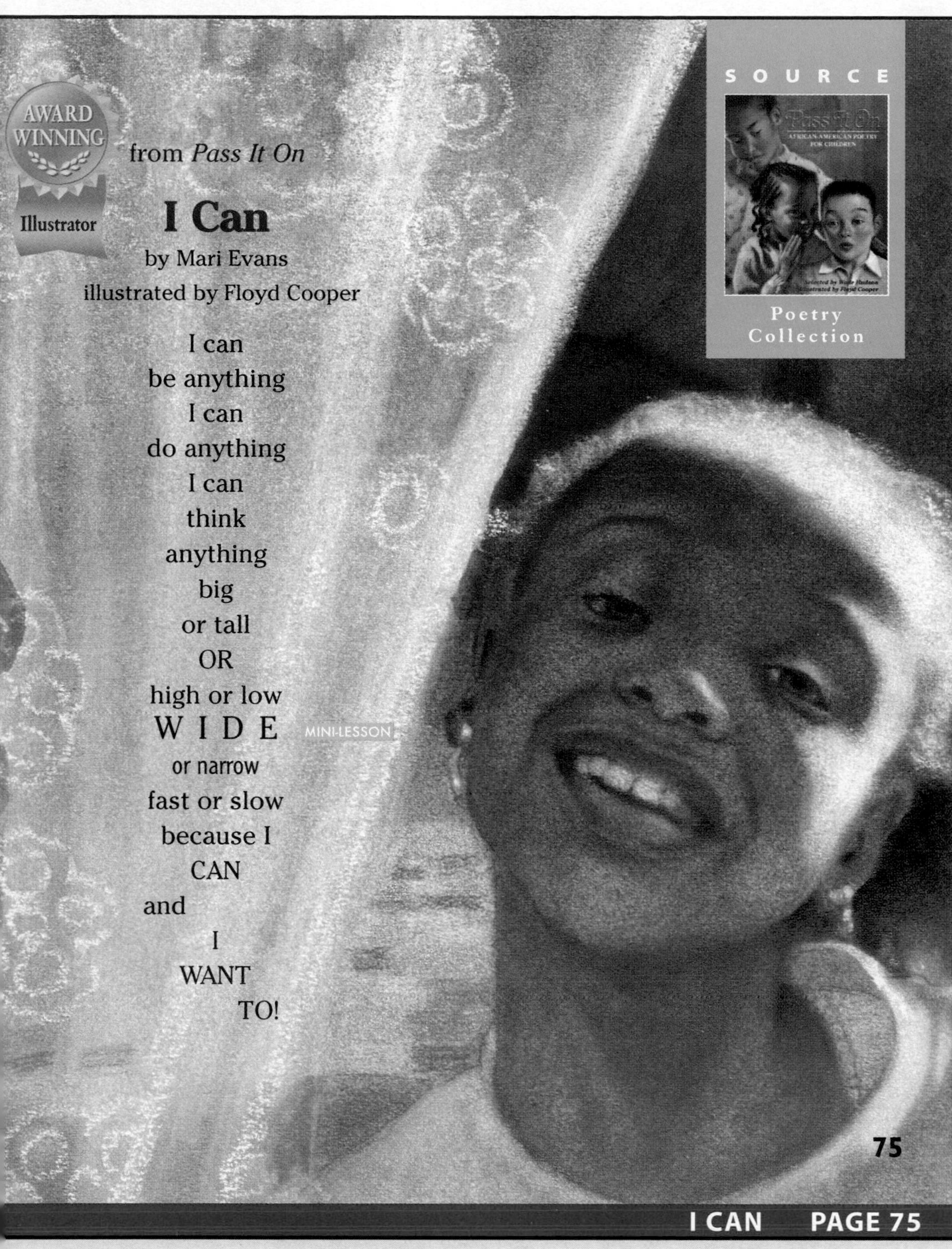
AWARD WINNING Illustrator

from *Pass It On*

I Can

by Mari Evans
illustrated by Floyd Cooper

I can
be anything
I can
do anything
I can
think
anything
big
or tall
OR
high or low
W I D E
or narrow
fast or slow
because I
CAN
and
I
WANT
TO!

SOURCE
Pass It On
African-American Poetry for Children
Poetry Collection

MINI-LESSON

75

I CAN PAGE 75

▶ INTEGRATING LANGUAGE ARTS WRITING/VIEWING/VOCABULARY (*See p. T146*)

Supporting All Learners

Preview

ESL During the preview, bring the poem closer to children by pantomiming the words and replacing the pronoun *I* with children's names. Children may want to repeat the poem and the movements after you. **(Multisensory Techniques)**

Preview and Predict

Reader to Reader

Have you ever wanted to do something but didn't think you could? The girl in this poem believes she can do whatever she tries.

Have children look at the picture on page 75. Ask what the girl might be thinking about.

Evaluate Author's Purpose How does this poem make you feel? What message do you think the poet is expressing?

MINI-LESSON

Varying Text Size

TEACH/MODEL Point out the way in which varying type size adds to the meaning of the poem.

THINK ALOUD When I look at the word *wide*, I notice that it is different from all the other words in the poem. The letters are uppercase and bigger and they are spaced out more. This makes the word *wide* look exactly like what it means! By showing the word in this way, the poet gives me a better feeling of what she is saying.

APPLY Have children point out other variations in type in the poem, such as the thin letters of *narrow* and capital letters in *or* and *I can* and *I want to* at the end of the poem. Does it help children understand the poem? How?

a

READING THE SOURCES

RUBY THE COPYCAT / I CAN

Assess Reading

REFLECT AND RESPOND

Invite children to share their thoughts, opinions, and questions about *Ruby the Copycat* and the poem "I Can." You may wish to prompt discussion with the following questions:

- **What did you find funny about *Ruby the Copycat?* Why?** ***(✔ Literary Element)***
- **Did anything in *Ruby the Copycat* surprise you? What things in the story were you able to predict? What helped you make your predictions?** ***(✔ Key Strategy)***
- **What lesson did Ruby learn about copying others? Why do you think it is important to try to be yourself?** ***(✔ Theme)***

CHECK PREDICTIONS

JOURNAL

Were children's predictions confirmed as they read? Have them return to the "What We Predict" chart that they made before reading and then revise as necessary.

READ CRITICALLY ACROSS TEXTS

- **What do you think Ruby would say about the poem "I Can"?**

  Children might say that Ruby would agree with the poem. Ruby probably felt that we can do or be anything we want.

- **How was Stellaluna like Ruby? How were they different?**

  They both copied those around them because they wanted to fit in. Stellaluna was copying the birds because she had to, and Ruby was copying Angela to be liked.

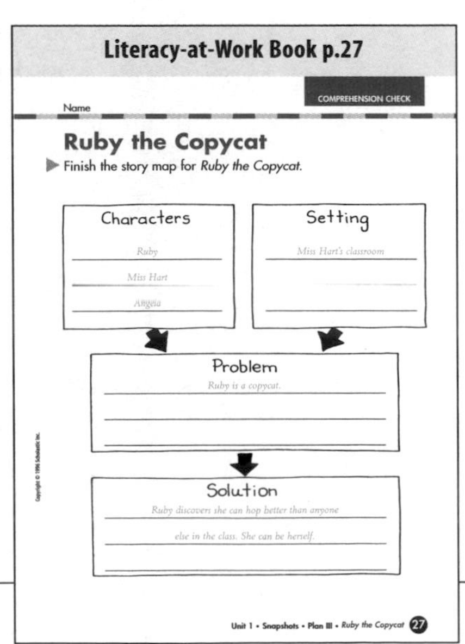

Literacy-at-Work Book p.27

COMPREHENSION CHECK

Name

Ruby the Copycat

▶ Finish the story map for *Ruby the Copycat.*

Characters	Setting
Ruby Miss Hart Angela	Miss Hart's classroom

Problem

Ruby is a copycat.

Solution

Ruby discovers she can hop better than anyone else in the class. She can be herself.

Unit 1 • Snapshots • Plan III • Ruby the Copycat 27

CONFERENCE

Use the checked questions on this page to assess children's understanding of:

✔ the *literary element* of Humor.

✔ the *key strategy* of Make Predictions.

✔ the *theme* of special talents.

Listen to Children Read Ask selected children to find the part in the story where Miss Hart talks to Ruby. Have children explain what Miss Hart said and ask them to read the passage aloud. Assess oral reading, using pages 22–23 in the Assessment Handbook.

Children may wish to add their recordings to their Literacy Portfolios.

Based on your evaluation of your children's responses,

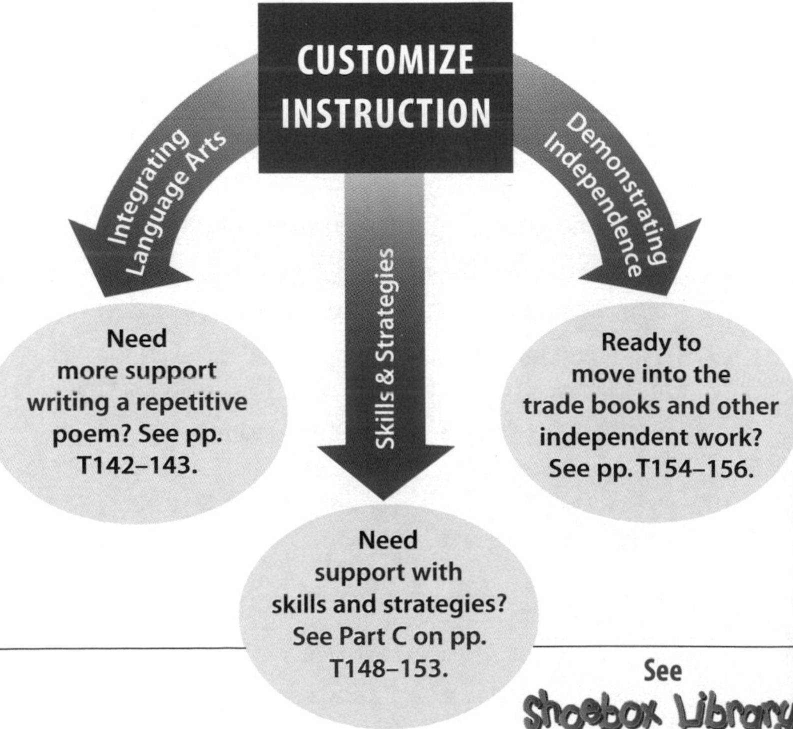

See Shoebox Library

Idea File

VOCABULARY

What would children like to ask Peggy Rathmann about *Ruby the Copycat*? Is Ruby based on someone she knows? Did anyone ever copy her? Encourage them to write questions in their Journals that include action words. Then have children categorize the verbs which might be mouth, hand, or foot actions.

STORY EXTENSION

Remind children that Ruby and Angela hopped home for lunch at the end of the story. Have children make predictions about what Ruby and Angela might do next by thinking about story clues and what they already know. Suggest that they continue the story by drawing a picture and writing a caption explaining it.

REPEATED READING

Choral Reading To help children develop fluency, invite them to join you in reading the story aloud. You may wish to divide the class into two groups and have them take turns reading a page at a time. A whole-group reading will also reinforce fluency.

REPEATED READING

Readers Theater Have children work in groups of four to stage a Readers Theater presentation. One child can be the narrator. The others can take the roles of Ruby, Angela, and Miss Hart. Have children practice their parts and then record their reading, using the computer. Invite them to use the Playback Tool to present the story to class.

CULTURAL CONNECTIONS

Make Your Own Hopping Game

Ruby's hopping would come in handy for hopscotch. Children all over the world play this very old game. It's known as potsy in Brooklyn, New York, and Hinkspiel in Germany, but the main rule is the same: Don't touch the lines.

Activity

Have children invent a new version of hopscotch or another hopping game. Encourage imagination. They can create new rules (children in southeast Asia play hopscotch in a squatting position, with their hands on their hips) and new diagrams like the ones on this page.

SOURCEBOOK MODEL

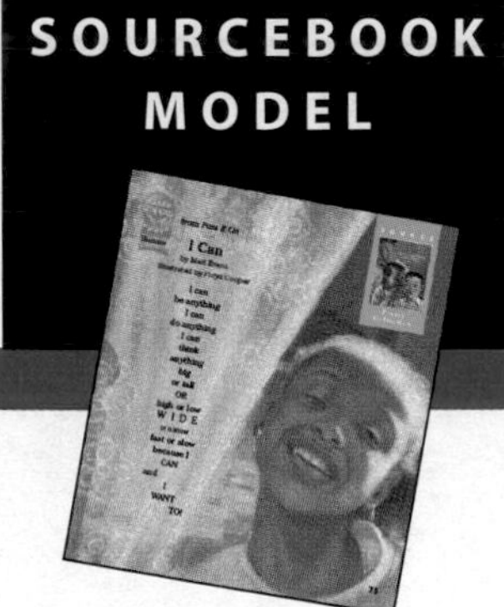

WRITE A POEM

WRITING

Using "I Can" as a model, children will write a **poem** that uses **repetition** of words or sounds and expresses a **feeling**.

Objectives

Children learn to:

- write a poem that uses repetition of words and expresses feelings (pp. T142–143)
- use action words (p.T144)
- capitalize the pronoun I (p.T144)
- spell words with digraphs (p.T145)

Materials:
SourceBook p. 75
Literacy-at-Work Book p. 28

Suggested Grouping:
Whole class, cooperative groups and individuals

Literacy-at-Work Book, p. 28

Name WRITING

Get Ready to Write

Fill in the chart with feelings people can write about in a poem. Then finish the sentence to tell about each feeling.

Kinds of Feelings	
happiness	I *like rainbows*.
	I ____.
	I ____.
	I ____.
	I ____.

To the teacher: This is the prewriting organizer referenced in the lesson on writing a poem

28 Unit 1 • Snapshots • Plan III • *Ruby the Copycat*

THINK ABOUT WRITING

Ask children what they think a poem is. Ask whether all poems use rhyme. Discuss with children how a poem can be a poem without rhyme. Then help them recognize that in a poem the poet:

- often uses repeated words.
- puts feelings into words.
- sometimes uses different-sized print to help the reader understand his or her feelings.

Put It in Context

Invite children to reread the poem with you and to find words in the poem that repeat. What do they think the feelings are that the poet has put into words? How do they know? Why are some words larger?

INTRODUCE THE WRITING EVENT

Invite children to write poems that use repeated words and express something about feelings.

Prewrite

Ask children to think of a phrase like *I can* that they would like to use in their poem, for example: *I smile* or *I laugh*. Suggest that children use the Prewriting Organizer in the Literacy-at-Work Book to list their phrases. Have children choose:

- the feeling they will put into words.
- the phrase they will repeat.

Draft

Children are now ready to write their poems. As they work, the following questions may help them:

- **Will someone reading my poem know how I feel?**
- **Am I repeating my phrase often?**

Revise

As they revise their poems, children might ask:

- **Is there anything I could add to my poem to help the reader understand my feeling?**
- **Is there any print I can change that would help the reader understand my feeling?**

SHARING TIPS Have children read aloud their poems in cooperative groups to get feedback.

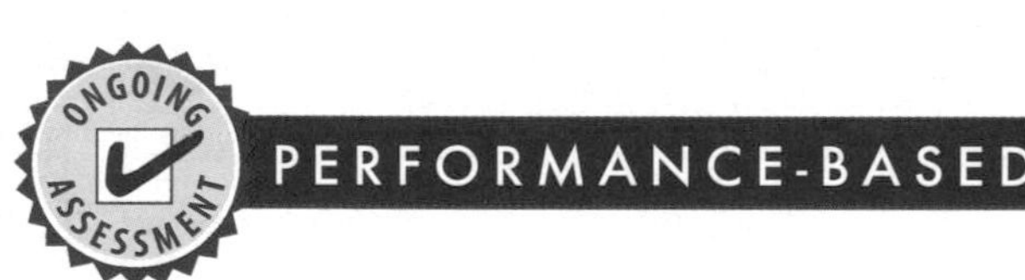

Children's Self Assessment

✔ Did I use repetition?

✔ Did I put my feeling into words?

✔ Did the repetition help me put my feeling into words?

Children may wish to carry this piece through the writing process described in Plan VI, pp. T288–291.

PORTFOLIO Use the Benchmarks to assess children's writing. Suggest that children add their drafts and revisions to their Literacy Portfolios.

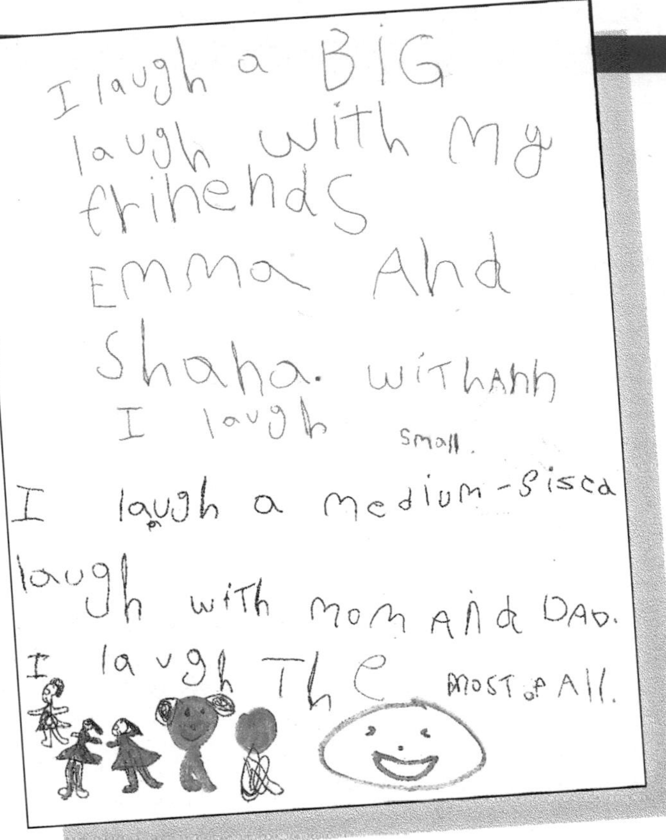

Apprentice sample: phrase repeated; different-sized print used

Technology Options

Children can use the WiggleWorks writing area to create their own poems. Invite them to illustrate their work. Children might wish to print out multiple copies of their poems to give to their family and friends. Encourage children to use the computer writing area for other writing activities. See the WiggleWorks Plus Teaching Plan.

SUPPORTING ALL LEARNERS

Use Sentence Strips

To help children get started in the Writing Event, write on sentence strips the verb phrases that they brainstorm. Children can select a sentence strip and extend the phrase by adding a different ending. Encourage them to write two more sentences in this manner.

CHALLENGE During the Writing Event, children can select a sentence strip and expand upon it by adding different endings. Challenge them to include words whose meanings they can convey visually, such as *w-i-d-e*.

CHILDREN'S WRITING BENCHMARKS		
Novice: The phrase is not repeated often. The phrase does not show a feeling. A feeling is not put into words. Different-sized print is not used to convey feeling.	**Apprentice:** The phrase is repeated often, but the feeling may not be expressed clearly. Different-sized print is sometimes used to convey feelings.	**Proficient:** The phrase is repeated often and the feeling is put into words. The repeated phrase helps show the reader the feeling. Different-sized print is used to convey feelings.

See Daily Language Practice pp. R14-15.

(✔ Unit Test)

ACTION WORDS

GRAMMAR

OBJECTIVE

Children will identify examples of action in *Ruby the Copycat* and in their own writing.

DEFINITION: A verb is a word that shows action.

SYNTACTIC CUEING

❶ Teach and Model

Write the following sentence from *Ruby the Copycat* for children to read aloud: *At lunchtime, Ruby hopped all the way home on one foot.* Have children point to the word that shows action. Remind them that words like *hopped* are verbs. They tell what someone or something does. Ask children to give other examples of action words and write them on the chalkboard. Encourage children to act out the action words.

ACTION WORDS

hop smile
jump read
run take

❷ Put It in Context

Have children locate other action verbs in *Ruby the Copycat*. Write them on a list of chart paper as they are identified. Invite children to ask classmates to confirm whether each word is an action verb. Encourage children to add their own examples of action verbs to the list.

❸ Apply to Writing

Encourage children to share action verbs from their poems and add them to the list. Invite them to use words from the list to change the action in their poems.

CAPITALIZING: PRONOUN I

USAGE

OBJECTIVE

Children will explore capitalization of the pronoun *I*.

GUIDELINE: The pronoun *I* is always written with a capital letter.

❶ Teach and Model

Write the following sentences from *Ruby the Copycat* on the chalkboard.

"I like your bow," whispered Angela.

"I like yours, too," whispered Ruby.

Have volunteers point to the pronoun *I* in each sentence, and ask children what they notice about the letter. Point out that whether or not it begins a sentence, the letter *I* is always capitalized.

❷ Put It in Context

Have children look back at *Ruby the Copycat* to find other places where the pronoun *I* is used. To point out that the word is always capitalized, ask children what they notice about the pronoun *I* each time it appears.

❸ Apply to Writing

Invite children to point out the pronoun *I* if it appears in the poems they wrote. Have them check to see whether they have capitalized it. If not, help them correct it. Have children dictate sentences that contain the word *I* in various positions in the sentence. Write the sentences on the chalkboard without capitalizing the word *I*. Call on volunteers to correct errors in capitalization.

Grammar, Usage, Mechanics Practice, p. 5

Name

Action Words

A word that shows action is a verb.

▶ Underline the verb in each sentence.

1. I play with my rabbits on the lawn.
2. Carla and Roberto feed the rabbits carrots.
3. The rabbits hop everywhere.
4. My cat chases rabbits around the yard.
5. The rabbits run from the cat.

▶ Choose the verb in the box that completes each sentence. Write it on the line.

likes drink watch eat sleep

6. Carla________ rabbits.
7. The rabbits________ the water in the bowl.
8. We________ the rabbits play.
9. My rabbits________ lettuce.
10. At night, the rabbits________ .

GRAMMAR Snapshots • Plan III • *Ruby the Copycat* 5

Grammar, Usage, Mechanics Practice, p. 6

Name

Capitalizing: Pronoun I

The pronoun I is used in the naming part of a sentence. It is always written with a capital letter.

▶ Add the pronoun I to complete each sentence. It is always written with a capital letter.

1. My sister and ____ went to the circus.
2. ____ saw fourteen funny clowns.
3. ____ enjoyed watching the elephants.
4. Jane and ____ fed some of the animals.
5. Before ____ knew it, it was time to go home.
6. ____ didn't know how much ____ would love the circus.
7. ____ hope ____ can go again soon.

▶ What would you do at the circus? Use the pronoun I and your own ideas to finish the sentences.

8. At the circus ____ saw ________ .
9. ____ ate ________ .
10. My friend and ____ liked the ________ best.

6 Snapshots • Plan III • *Ruby the Copycat* MECHANICS

Phonics Connection

You may first wish to do the phonics lesson on digraphs on pp. T152–153.

SPELLING

Words With *ch, th,* and *sh*

chin **much** **both** **thin** **bath** **ship** **shop** **wish**

✷ **Selection Vocabulary**

PRETEST If you would like to pretest using test sentences, see Spelling Practice, p. 38.

OBJECTIVE

Children spell *ch, th* and *sh* words.

❶ Teach

Write the word *chin* on the chalkboard. Have children listen while you say the word. Ask if they hear /k/ or /h/. Say /ch/. The letters *c* and *h* together stand for only one sound. Repeat for *th* and *sh*.

Put It in Context

Have children look through *Ruby the Copycat* to find examples of words that begin or end with *ch, th,* or *sh.* Have volunteers write examples on the chalkboard. Say each word and underline the letters *ch, th,* or *sh.*

❷ Practice

Have children copy and complete the following chart.

Words with		
ch	th	sh

❸ Check

Apply to Writing

Have children proofread their poems, checking the spelling of any word they may have written that contains *ch, th,* or *sh.* Suggest that they jot down any misspelled words and use the spelling strategies they discussed to help themselves remember how to spell these words.

OPTION

Spell Teaser

Ask children to find pairs of words, one beginning with a digraph and the other ending with that digraph, such as *ship* and *wash* or *thin* and *bath.* Then challenge them to use each word pair in a sentence.

TEST Have spelling partners test each other, and then check each other's work. Have them use the words in sentences as they dictate them.

Spelling Practice, p. 3

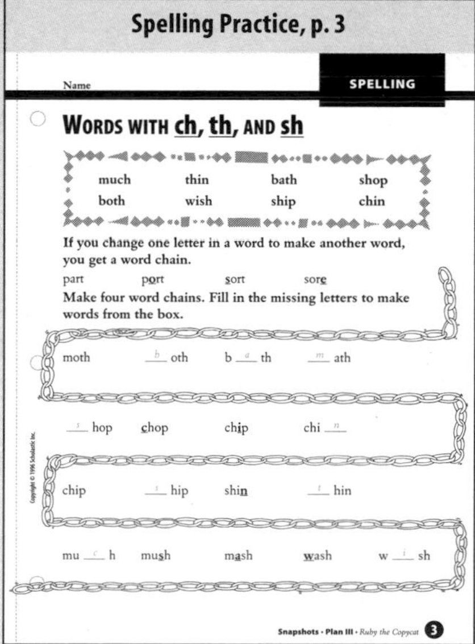

Name SPELLING

WORDS WITH ch, th, AND sh

much thin bath shop
both wish ship chin

If you change one letter in a word to make another word, you get a word chain.

part port sort sore

Make four word chains. Fill in the missing letters to make words from the box.

moth __oth b__th __ath

__hop chop chip chi__

chip __hip shin __hin

mu__h mush mash wash w__sh

Snapshots • Plan III • Ruby the Copycat 3

See Handwriting Practice, p. 3, for practice writing manuscript letters *k, v, w, z, y, x, g, d,* and *q.*

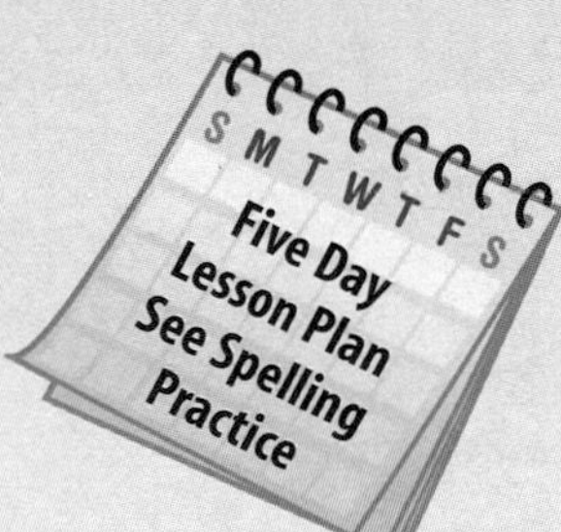

WRITING/VIEWING/VOCABULARY

Draw Describing Words

GOOD FOR HOMEWORK

Materials:
SourceBook p. 75
Drawing paper
Crayons or markers

Time:
About 10 minutes

Suggested Grouping:
Individuals

Ask children to illustrate describing words in ways that match their meaning. As examples, display the unusual type for the words *wide* and *narrow* in the poem "I Can."

Suggest that children choose their own words or write other words from the poem, including *big, tall, high, low, fast,* or *slow*. Provide space on a classroom wall or a bulletin board for children to display the describing words they illustrate. Encourage children to add new describing words to this wacky word wall whenever they wish. VISUAL LITERACY

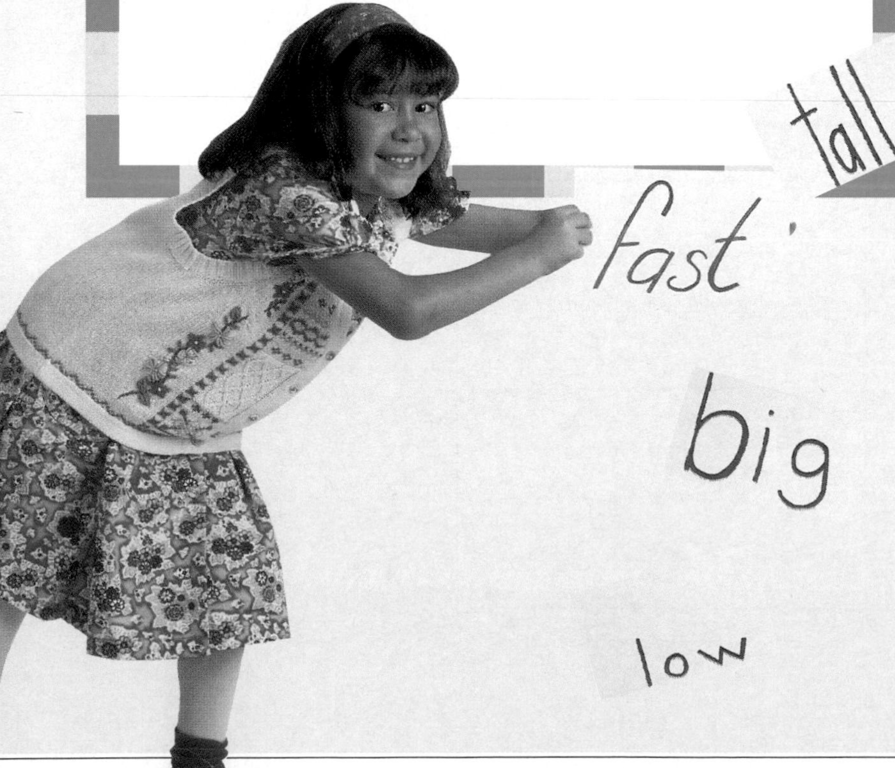

SPEAKING/LISTENING

Contribute to Angela's Journal

GOOD FOR GRADING

Materials:
SourceBook pp. 46–74
Audiocassette player

Time:
About 20 minutes

Suggested Grouping:
Individuals and whole class

Invite children to pretend to be Angela. Encourage them to record a short journal entry describing the day Ruby arrived in class or how Angela felt on the day she and Ruby wore the same dress. They can refer to the story to review Ruby's first day in school or the day of the dress incident.

Children can share their recordings for others to listen to. Then invite them to discuss how Angela's feelings toward Ruby changed.

How to Grade When grading, look for use of first-person pronouns, a description of an event, and a personal reaction to the event.

MINI-LESSON

CHARACTER

TEACH/MODEL Talk with children about character.

THINK ALOUD At the beginning of the story, Angela is flattered that Ruby copies her. But later Angela gets annoyed. Thinking about why Angela's feelings change helps me understand the characters better.

APPLY Invite partners to role-play Angela and Ruby on the day they wear the same dress. How does being someone else help children understand that character?

ACTIVITY FILE

LISTENING/READING/SPEAKING

ESL Perform a Puppet Play

Materials:
SourceBook pp. 46–74
Paper lunch bags
Crayons or markers

Time:
About 30 minutes

Suggested Grouping:
Cooperative groups

Dramatize a scene from the story by having groups of three children use puppets. Suggest to children that they make paper-bag puppets that resemble Ruby, Angela, and Miss Hart. Children can practice reading and improvising their dialogue and then present it to the rest of the class. THE ARTS

MINI-LESSON

WRITE DIRECTIONS

TEACH/MODEL Talk about how to write directions.

- **Directions should be short and easy to read.**
- **It is best to break directions into steps.**
- **The steps should be in the order in which they are to be performed.**
- **As you write, number the steps in the correct order.**

APPLY Have children check the directions that they wrote for their new dance and revise them if needed.

READING/WRITING/LISTENING

Create a Dance

Materials:
Tape of lively music
Audiocassette player
Pencil and paper

Time:
About 20 minutes

Suggested Grouping:
Whole class, individuals, and partners

Recall with children that Ruby had her own unique way of hopping. She hopped so well that all the other children in her class copied her as she moved to the music!

Play some lively music and have children try out new ways to hop or dance to it. Children can write directions for their new movements. Invite children to trade papers with partners. Children will enjoy dancing to the music again, this time following their partner's directions.

Encourage children to write their hopping directions, using the WiggleWorks writing area. Have them illustrate their directions to show the proper way to hop.

BUILDING SKILLS AND STRATEGIES

RUBY THE COPYCAT / I CAN

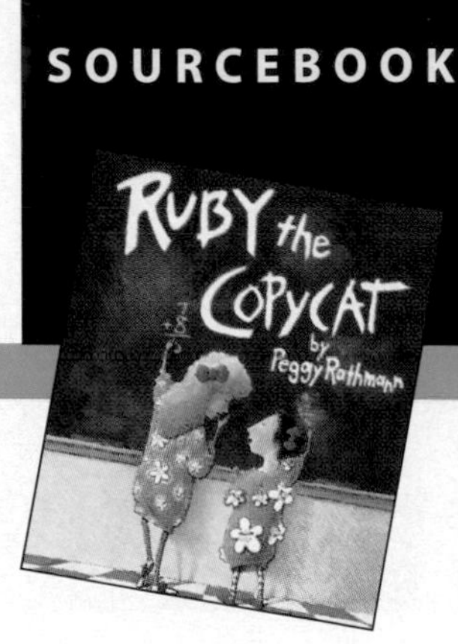

Make Predictions (✔ Unit Test)

Objectives

Children learn to:

- use story clues and personal knowledge and experience to make predictions
- transfer their learning to a new text

Materials:
SourceBook pp. 46–74
Transparency 6
Literacy-at-Work Book pp. 29–31

Time:
About 30 minutes

Suggested Grouping:
Whole class and partners

TESTED	
KEY STRATEGY	
MAKE PREDICTIONS	
Introduce	p. T148
Review	p. R19
Test	p. T311
Reteach	p. R25

Literacy-at-Work Book, p. 29

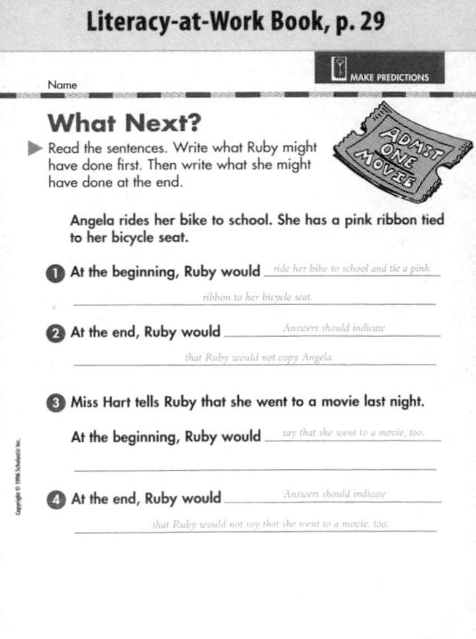

Name

MAKE PREDICTIONS

What Next?

Read the sentences. Write what Ruby might have done first. Then write what she might have done at the end.

Angela rides her bike to school. She has a pink ribbon tied to her bicycle seat.

1. At the beginning, Ruby would *ride her bike to school and tie a pink ribbon to her bicycle seat.*
2. At the end, Ruby would *Answers should indicate that Ruby would not copy Angela.*
3. Miss Hart tells Ruby that she went to a movie last night.
   At the beginning, Ruby would *say that she went to a movie, too.*
4. At the end, Ruby would *Answers should indicate that Ruby would not say that she went to a movie, too.*

Copyright © 1996 Scholastic Inc.

Unit 1 • Snapshots • Plan III • *Ruby the Copycat* 29

✔ Quickcheck

As children worked their way through *Ruby the Copycat*, did they:

✔ make valid predictions about characters and events?

✔ use text clues, picture clues, and their own knowledge and experience to help them make predictions?

YES **If yes, go to ❷ Practice and Apply.**

NO **If no, start at ❶ Teach and Model.**

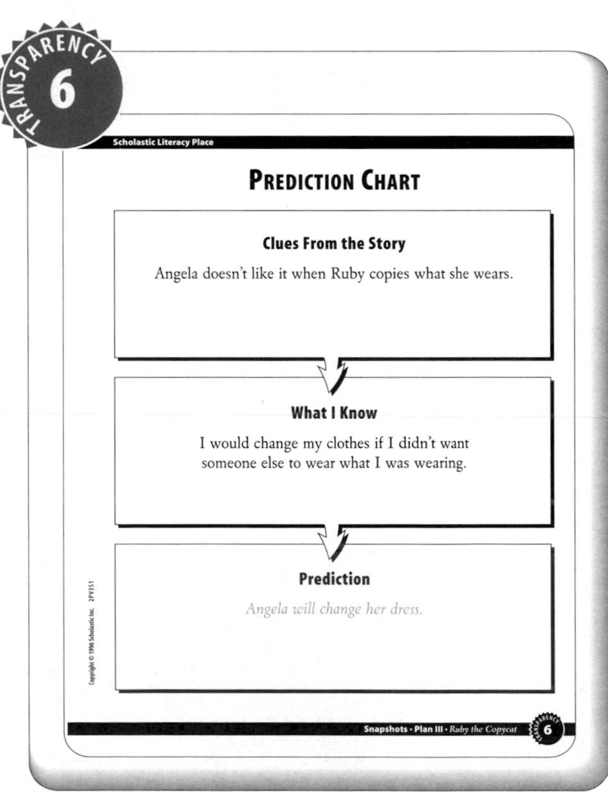

TRANSPARENCY 6

Scholastic Literacy Place

PREDICTION CHART

Clues From the Story
Angela doesn't like it when Ruby copies what she wears.

What I Know
I would change my clothes if I didn't want someone else to wear what I was wearing.

Prediction
Angela will change her dress.

Snapshots • Plan III • *Ruby the Copycat* 6

Annotated transparency for teaching Make Predictions

❶ Teach and Model

Invite children to try their hand at making predictions. Ask them what day of the week it is today. If today is Monday, can they predict what activities they will have? Will they have gym? library? What other predictions can they make? How did they make the predictions?

Lead children to understand that when they make a prediction, they make a logical guess about what might happen. Discuss that they can also make predictions when they read. Using clues from the story and their own knowledge and experience can help them make predictions about what might happen next.

Put It in Context

Have children turn back to *Ruby the Copycat* to review what happened in the story up to and including page 52.

Think Aloud **At the beginning of the story, I learned that Ruby copied Angela by saying that she had also been a flower girl. The story also told me that when Ruby returned from lunch, she copied Angela again by wearing a red bow. Now when I read page 52 and look at the picture, I notice Angela is wearing a sweater with daisies. From what I know about Ruby and from my own experience with copycats, I predict that Ruby will return from lunch wearing a sweater with daisies.**

Ask children to read the next page to confirm the prediction. Have the children continue reading through page 56. Ask what they think will happen next. Why do they think this will happen? Display Transparency 6 and show children how to complete it.

Supporting All Learners

Model

EXTRA HELP Guide children through a daily activity to provide them with extra help making predictions. Before beginning the Practice and Apply activity, take a glass to the sink and turn on the water. Then have children predict what you will do next.

ESL Vocabulary comprehension is necessary for children to make predictions. During the Practice and Apply activity, have second-language learners choose a section from the story. Explain any difficult vocabulary to them, and then model how to make predictions about what will happen.

❷ Practice and Apply

Make a Prediction Chart

PARTNERS Ask pairs of children to find more predictions about Ruby and someone she copies. Encourage children to complete a prediction chart like that on Transparency 6. Lead children to understand that:

- **Ruby copies people she likes.**
- **There are other ways Ruby can copy Angela.**
- **There are other people Ruby might copy.**

OPTION

Make a Prediction

Invite children to make a prediction about what may happen at lunch or recess. Then ask them to write a few sentences to explain their prediction.

❸ Assess

Were children able to make predictions about Ruby?

✔ **Can children make valid predictions about characters and events?**

✔ **Can children justify their examples of predictions, using clues from the story?**

If not, try this:
Use the Review lesson on Make Predictions with Plan VI. Have children continue to make predictions in their Journals.

Children's Self-Assessment

✔ **How did clues in the story help me make predictions?**

Transfer to New Text

Literacy-at-Work Book, p. 30

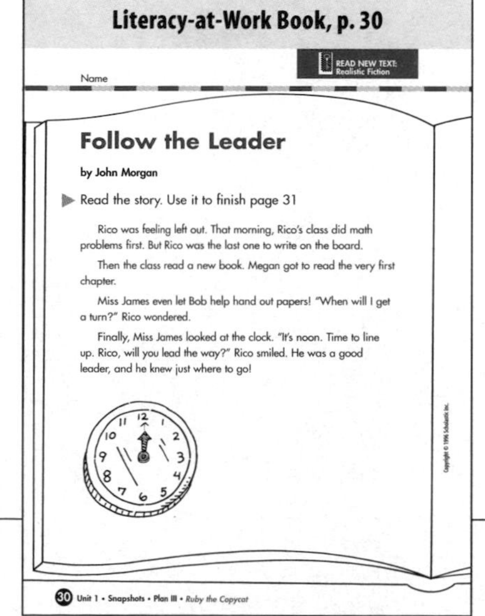
Name

READ NEW TEXT: Realistic Fiction

Follow the Leader

by John Morgan

▶ Read the story. Use it to finish page 31

Rico was feeling left out. That morning, Rico's class did math problems first. But Rico was the last one to write on the board.

Then the class read a new book. Megan got to read the very first chapter.

Miss James even let Bob help hand out papers! "When will I get a turn?" Rico wondered.

Finally, Miss James looked at the clock. "It's noon. Time to line up. Rico, will you lead the way?" Rico smiled. He was a good leader, and he knew just where to go!

30 Unit 1 • Snapshots • Plan III • *Ruby the Copycat*

Literacy-at-Work Book, p. 31

Name

MAKE PREDICTIONS

Which Way?

▶ Draw a picture that shows where Rico and the class from "Follow the Leader" are going. Write a sentence telling about the picture.

Unit 1 • Snapshots • Plan III • *Ruby the Copycat* 31

C

RUBY THE COPYCAT

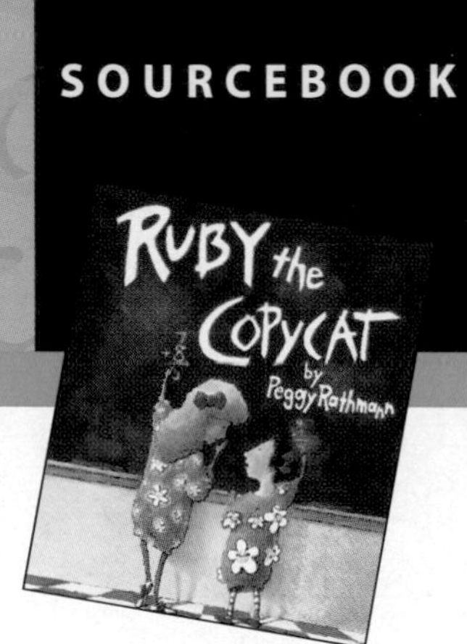

Vowels /o/*o*, /u/*u*

Objectives

Children learn to:

- identify the sound of the short vowels *o* and *u*
- build words that contain /o/ and /u/
- write /o/*o* and /u/*u* words

PHONICS AT A GLANCE

Materials:
Sourcebook pp.46-74
Big Book of Rhymes and Rhythms 2A, p. 8
Magnet Board
Literacy-at-Work Book p. 32-33

Time:
About 15–30 minutes

Suggested Grouping:
Whole class or cooperative groups

✔ Quickcheck

As children worked their way through *Ruby the Copycat,* did they:

✔ recognize the letters *o* and *u* in print?

✔ identify the sounds of the letters *o* as in *hop* and *u* as in *cut.*

YES **If yes, go to the Blending section of ❷ Connect Sound/Symbol.**

NO **If no, start at ❶ Develop Oral Language.**

❶ Develop Oral Language

Phonemic Awareness

Read aloud "My Father Has a Butcher Shop" from the Big Book of Rhymes and Rhythms. As you read, emphasize the words *shop, cuts, hot,* and *runs.* Invite children to join in on repeated readings of the poem.

Have children say the words *shop* and *hot.* Ask what sound they hear in the middle of each word. Then have them say the words *cuts* and *runs.* Ask what sound they hear in the middle of these words.

Encourage children to name other words with /o/. Then ask them to name words with /u/. Children might mention words such as *stop, not, fox, rock, hop; umbrella, fun, cup, bus, but.*

Big Book of Rhymes and Rhythms

My Father Has a Butcher Shop

My father has a butcher shop,
My mother cuts the meat,
And I'm the little hot dog,
That runs around the street.

shop
runs

8

Literacy-at-Work Book, p. 32

Name PHONICS: Vowels /o/o, /u/u

Pick a Sentence

▶ Look at each picture. Pick the sentence that tells about the picture. Write the sentence on the blank line.

Literacy-at-Work Book, p. 33

Name PHONICS: Vowels /o/o, /u/u

Pick a Word

▶ Read each sentence. Underline the word that makes sense in the sentence. Write the word on the line. Then circle other words in the sentence that have the same vowel sound.

1. The gum is (stock, stuck) to the rug.
   stuck
2. The frog (hunts, hops) to the rock.
   hops
3. I got (hut, hot) in the summer sun.
   hot
4. The bus must (stop, stump) for us.
   stop
5. The bugs did not follow the (duck, dock) into the pond.
   duck
6. He had a (cot, cup) of milk and a hot bun for lunch.
   cup

Unit 1 • Snapshots • Plan III • *Ruby the Copycat* 33

❷ Connect Sound/Symbol

Put It in Context

On the chalkboard, write sentences from *Ruby the Copycat:*

> *"But I did! I hopped around the picnic table ten times!"*

Invite children to read the sentences with you. Underline the letter o in *hopped*. Ask children to listen to /o/ as you blend the sounds while running your hand under each letter. Repeat with /u/*u* in the word *but*.

Blending

On the chalkboard or chart paper, write the word list as shown below and the letters *o* and *u* as headings for columns. Read the word list with children, running your hand under the letters and blending the sounds. Invite children to make new words by substituting *o* and *u* for the vowel.

Think Aloud **I can change the word *rib* to *rob* by changing the vowel letter to *o*. Now, who can change the vowel in *rob* to *u* to make a new word?**

Follow the same procedure for another list of *words, such as cab, net, cat,* and *click*.

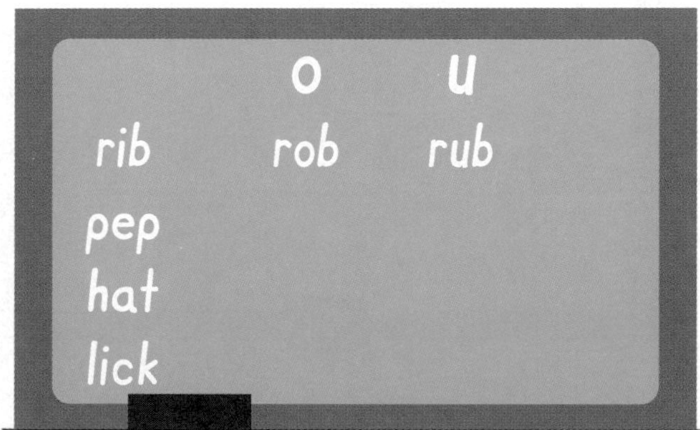

❸ Assess

Write

COOPERTIVE GROUPS Have groups of children come up to the chalkboard to write the word *hop*. Ask them to change one letter to write a new word. Then have them share what they wrote. They may want to continue and make another word.

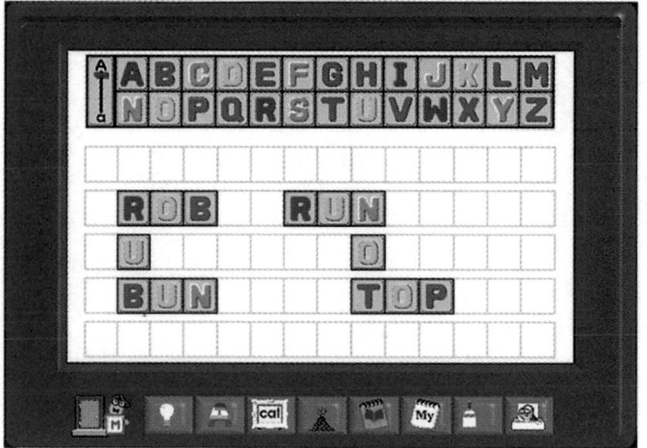

PICTURE CARDS

Write some of the short vowel words that children suggested earlier. Have volunteers underline the short vowel *o* or *u* in each word. Then ask children to make picture cards by writing one of the words and drawing a picture.

See Phonics and Word Building Kit for additional suggestions.

The Magnet Board activity pictured above provides additional practice with short vowels. See the WiggleWorks Plus Teaching Plan for information on this and other Magnet Board activities.

SUPPORTING ALL LEARNERS

Graphic Device

ESL Second-language learners may need additional practice pronouncing the short *o* and *u* words. As children change the vowel in the Blending activity, encourage them to pronounce the three words aloud. Guide them in their pronunciation of the new words.

CHALLENGE After the Blending activity, invite children to make extended word ladders. They can begin by writing in their Journals the first three words from one row. Then challenge them to add as many words as they can by changing one consonant or vowel at a time.

C

RUBY THE COPYCAT/I CAN

SOURCEBOOK

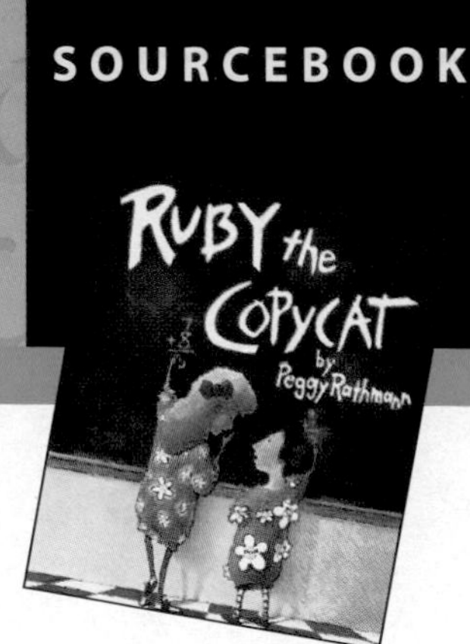

Digraphs *ch, sh, th, wh*

Objectives

Children learn to:

- identify the sounds of the letters *ch, sh, th,* and *wh*
- build words that contain /ch/, /sh/, /th/, and /wh/
- write words with consonant digraphs *ch, sh, th,* and *th*

PHONICS AT A GLANCE

Materials:
Sourcebook pp.46-74
Big Book of Rhymes and Rhythm 2A, p. 9
Magnet Board
Spelling Lesson p. T145
Literacy-At-Work Book p. 34-35

Time:
15–30 minutes

Suggested Grouping:
Whole class and Individuals

Literacy-at-Work Book, p. 34

Literacy-at-Work Book, p. 35

Name PHONICS: ch, sh, th, wh

Solve the Riddles

▶ Use the words in the box to answer the riddles.

whale	thumb
shut	wheel
third	chair
teeth	dish

1. I'm a very big animal. whale
2. I'm something you sit on. chair
3. I'm another word for *plate*. dish
4. I'm on your hand. thumb
5. I'm another word for *close*. shut
6. I'm after second. third
7. I'm something that helps a car move. wheel
8. I'm used to bite food. teeth

Unit 1 • Snapshots • Plan III • Ruby the Copycat 35

✔ Quickcheck

As children worked their way through *Ruby the Copycat* did they:

✔ recognize the letters of the consonant digraphs in print?

✔ identify the sounds of the consonant digraphs in words such as *chair, thin, ship,* and *white*?

YES **If yes, go to the Blending section of ❷ Connect Sound/Symbol.**

NO **If no, start at ❶ Develop Oral Language.**

❶ Develop Oral Language

Phonemic Awareness

Read aloud the poem "She Sells Seashells" from the Big Book of Rhymes and Rhythms. As you read, emphasize the words *she, seashells, seashore,* and *shells*. Read the tongue twister for enjoyment. Encourage children to join in.

Ask what sound they hear at the beginning of *she* and *shells* and in the middle of *seashells and seashore*. Have children repeat those words, emphasizing /sh/.

Big Book of Rhymes and Rhythms

She Sells Seashells

She sells seashells on the seashore.
The shells she sells are seashells I'm sure.
For if she sells shells on the seashore,
Then I'm sure she sells seashore shells.

shells

9

❷ Connect Sound/Symbol

Put It in Context

On the chalkboard, write the following sentences:

The children whispered,
"Ruby is a copycat!"

"Does anyone have something
to share?"

The children cheered and
clapped their hands.

Have children read the sentences with you. Ask volunteers to underline the words with *th, ch, wh,* and *sh*. Blend the sounds in *the, children, whispered, something, share,* and *cheered* as you read the words while running your hand under the letters.

Blending

Demonstrate how to make a Word Builder card. On a 5" x 7" index card, write *lip* in large letters. On smaller self-sticking note sheets, write *ch, wh,* and *sh*. Make a new word by sticking the letters *ch* over the *l* in *lip* to make *chip*. Say the word with children, slowly blending the sounds together.

Have volunteers make other words with the Word Builder card by sticking *wh* and *sh* over the *l* in *lip* to make *whip* and *ship*. Have children read each new word with you.

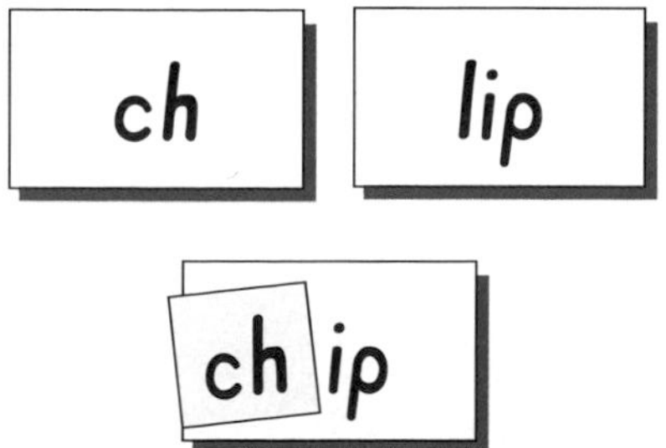

❸ Assess

Write

Invite children to look through the poems they've read in the Big Book of Rhymes and Rhythms to look for any words that contain the consonant digraphs *ch, sh, th,* or *wh*. Have children write the words they find and read them aloud.

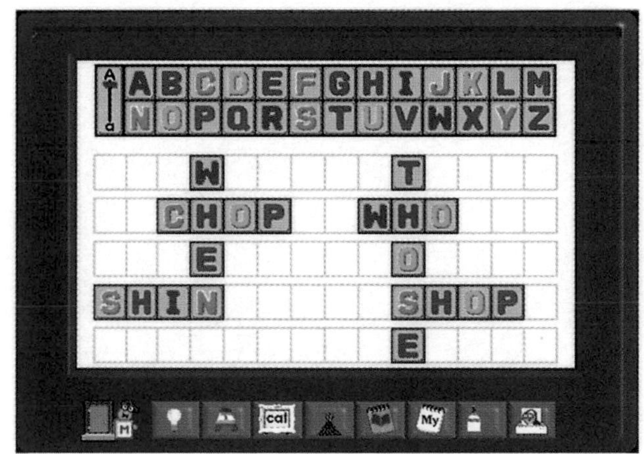

PICTURE THIS
Invite children to draw a picture of items whose names begin with the four digraphs. Ask children to write a silly sentence about what is happening in the picture. For example, "A whale sitting in his chair is thinking about his shoes."

See Phonics and Word Building Kit for additional suggestions.

The Magnet Board activity pictured above provides additional practice with consonant digraphs. See the WiggleWorks Plus Plan for information on this and other Magnet Board activities.

SUPPORTING ALL LEARNERS

Peer Partners

ESL This rhyme is very difficult for native speakers and will be especially challenging for second-language learners. Pair them with native speakers who can support them as they read *She Sells Seashells* aloud.

ACCESS To facilitate the participation of children with motor disabilities in the Blending activity, pair them with children who can help them use the manipulatives to form new words.

BUILDING FLUENCY

Objectives

Children read *The Bunny Hop* for fluency.

Technology Options

Encourage children to listen to the audiocassette recording of *The Bunny Hop.*

The Bunny Hop

Written by Teddy Slater

Illustrated by Larry Di Fiori

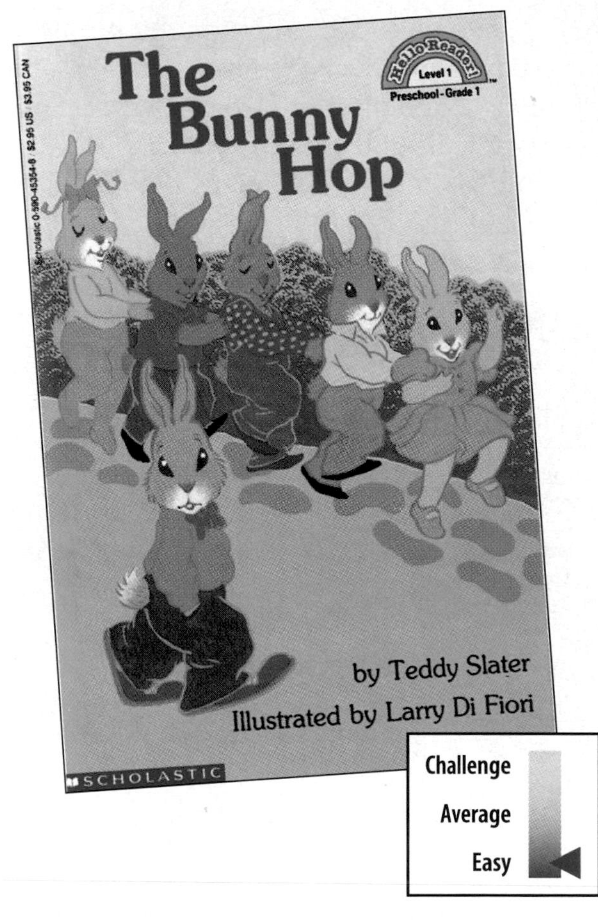

Challenge
Average
Easy

PREVIEW AND READ

Have children read the title and help them read the author's and illustrator's names. As they flip through the book, call attention to the words *waltz, jitterbug, fox-trot,* and *cha-cha-cha*. Help them realize that these words are the names of some dances.

RESPONSE IDEAS

After children have read the book, they can meet with you or with a partner to talk about the story. Questions such as these will help the discussion:

- **How did you feel when you read that no one wanted to dance with Buddy Rabbit?**
- **What did you think was going to happen when Buddy Rabbit heard the "thumpity-thump, thump" and "bumpity-bump" sounds?**

Read Across Texts

- **Think about Ruby the copycat and Buddy Rabbit. What made them feel better at the end of the stories? What did they discover about themselves?**

Shoebox Library For more independent reading opportunities choose books from the Shoebox Library.

Using the Trade Books

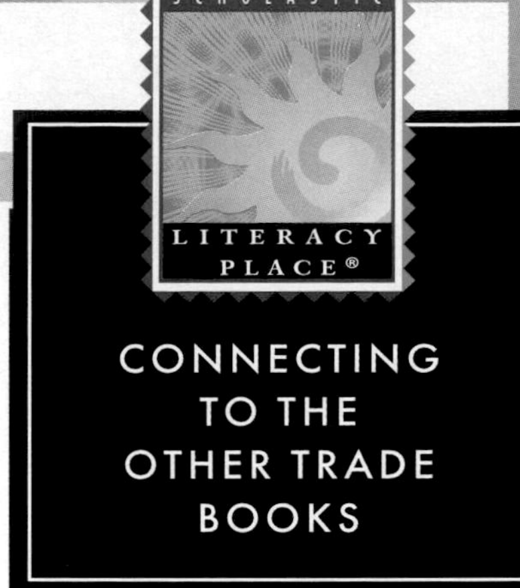

Chester's Way

by Kevin Henkes

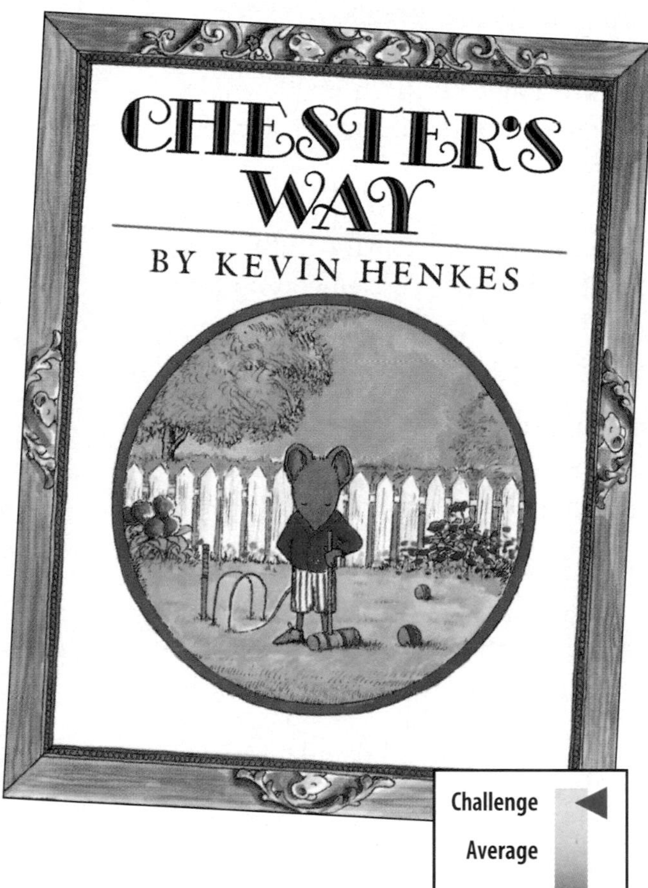

Challenge
Average
Easy

Using the Trade Book Guide

For in-depth teaching ideas, refer to the individual Trade Book Guide for *Chester's Way* by Kevin Henkes.

MAKE UNIT CONNECTIONS:

Personal Voice

Talk About It

Chester and his best friend Wilson like the same things and do everything the same way in *Chester's Way*. But not Lilly! Soon all three discover that they can be best friends and appreciate each other.

Unlike Lilly, at the beginning of *Ruby the Copycat*, Ruby copies the people she admires. But when she displays her own special talent, she realizes that she doesn't have to copy others. After reading *Chester's Way*, children can make connections to answer questions such as these:

- **What makes Lilly special? What did Lilly do so that Chester and Wilson accepted her?**
- **What did Chester and Wilson learn from Lilly? What did Lilly learn from Chester and Wilson?**

Write About It

JOURNAL After reading *Chester's Way*, invite children to write about something else that Lilly might do that would make her special.

Read Across Texts

Have children compare *Chester's Way* to *Ruby the Copycat* by asking questions such as:

- **What do you think Ruby might do if she moved into Chester's neighborhood? What makes you think this?**
- **How might Chester and Wilson get along with Ruby at the beginning of the book? at the end?**

CONNECTING TO THE OTHER TRADE BOOKS

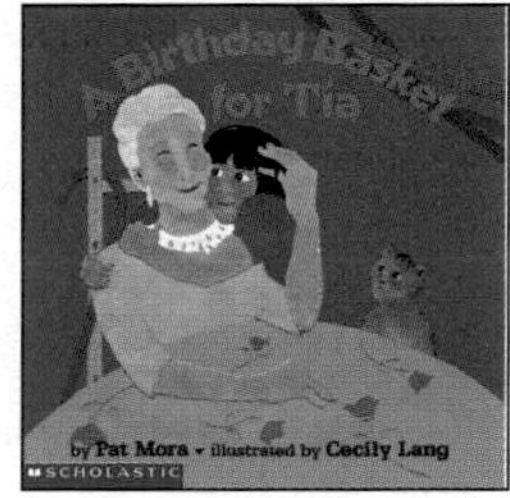

Ask children how they were able to predict what Cecilia would put in Tía's basket and that Ruby would copy Miss Hart.

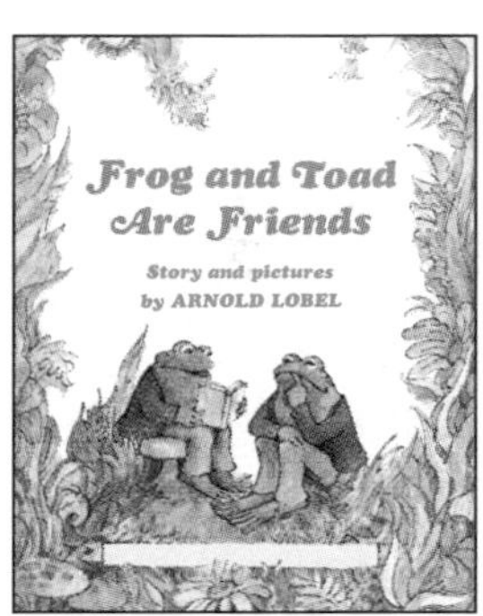

Ask children to compare Frog and Toad's friendship to Ruby and Angela's.

Also for use with this plan

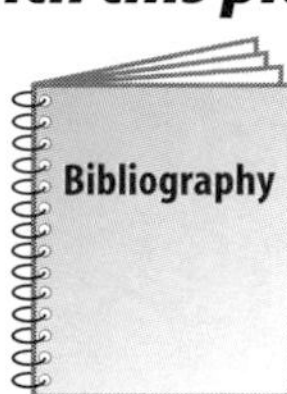

INTEGRATING LEARNING

Curriculum Areas

Math

Children use different pairs of addends to make the same total as Ruby in *Ruby the Copycat*.
See page R6.

Science

Children find out about animal mimicry and decide how it helps certain animals.
See page R6.

Social Studies

Children choose a person they admire and write about one feature they'd like to copy.
See page R7.

The Arts

Children plan methods to reproduce a painting.
See page R7.

Use Your Sports Arena

Copy This!

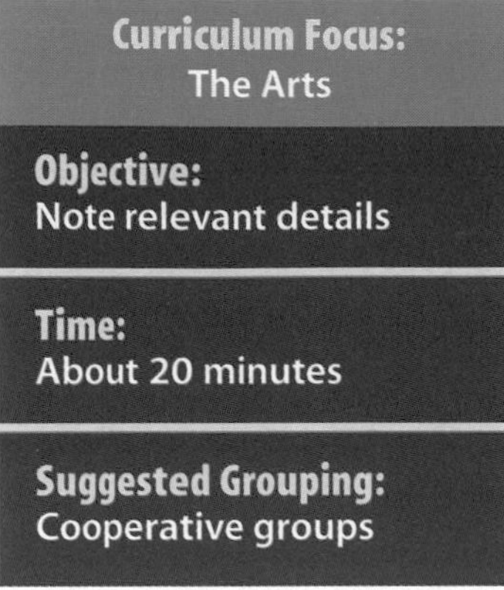

Curriculum Focus: The Arts
Objective: Note relevant details
Time: About 20 minutes
Suggested Grouping: Cooperative groups

ACTIVITY Children copy an illustration or photograph of a sports scene, paying close attention to details. VISUAL LITERACY

Connect to the SourceBook Have children review *Ruby the Copycat,* paying special attention to the illustrator's style.

Make New Discoveries

- Tell children that copying an illustration isn't always easy to do. A true copy is very hard to make because every individual has his or her own style and strengths. Ask children how copying a photograph is different from copying an illustration.
- Choose several illustrations and/or photographs of sports scenes for students to copy. Set it up in the Sports Arena, along with paper and, preferably, colored pencils. Crayons are acceptable, of course, but children will produce greater clarity with the pencils.
- Tell children to copy the illustration or photograph as closely as they can, watching for small details that might easily be left out. You might want to point out details specific to sports illustrations and photographs, such as the number or team name on a uniform, the type of shoes an athlete is wearing, the logo on a baseball bat, etc.

✔ **How to Assess** Did children notice and attempt to copy small details in the illustration they chose?

• Louanne Pig in •

MAKING THE TEAM

Nancy Carlson

PERSONAL VOICE

Plan IV

WHAT CHILDREN WILL DO

play the Talent Scavenger Hunt game

read the selections

- ***Louanne Pig in Making the Team***
  FANTASY
- ***Bruce Thorson: Photographer***
  MENTOR PROFILE

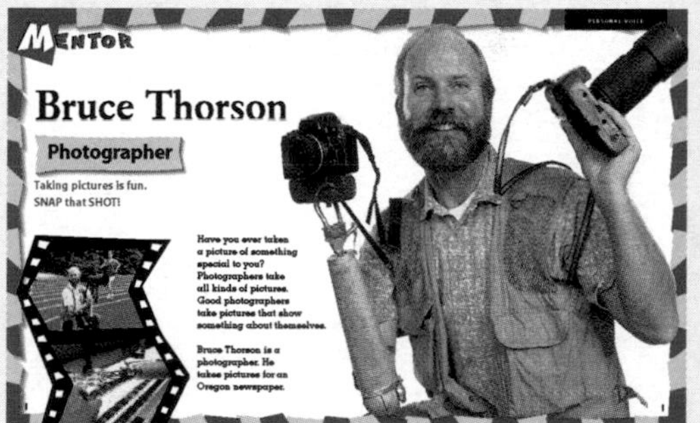

use the key strategy of Plot

blend words with final *e* and 3-letter blends

write directions for others to follow

apply what they learn about themselves and their strengths to their own lives

Assessing Your Students

ASSESSMENT	TEACHER'S SOURCEBOOK	ASSESSMENT KIT
Vocabulary Test	T163	Assessment Handbook
Observation	T164	Assessment Handbook
Assess Reading	T188	Classroom Management Forms
Conference	T188	Assessment Handbook
Performance-Based	T191	Assessment Handbook
Writing Benchmarks	T191	Assessment Handbook
Spelling Tests	T163, T193	Assessment Handbook
Quickcheck	T196, T198, T200	Assessment Handbook
Formal Tests	T311	Unit/Year Tests

Creating a Community of Learners

Talent Hunt Game pp. T160–161

- Work collaboratively
- Recognize own and teammates' strengths
- Listen Critically MINI-LESSON

Demonstrating Independence

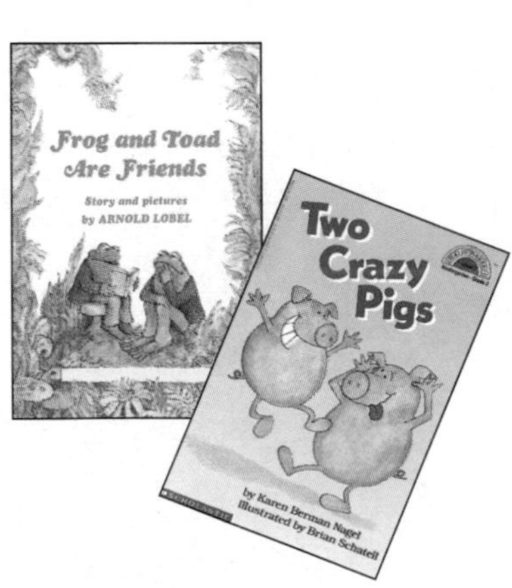

Using the Trade Books: pp. T202–203

- *Two Crazy Pigs* by Karen Berman Nagel
- *Frog and Toad are Friends* by Arnold Lobel

Integrating Learning: p. T104

- Activity: I'd like to be a...

Focus on Phonics

Phonics Lessons

- 3-Letter Blends
- Final *e*

Phonics Kit

Literacy-at-Work Book

- 3-Letter Blends, pp. 44–45
- Final *e*, pp. 46–47

PLAN IV ORGANIZER

Louanne Pig in Making the Team / Photographer: Bruce Thorson

	Instructional Path	Supporting All Learners	Resources and Technology
a **READING THE SOURCES** pp. T218–239	**Build Background** ✔ **Develop Vocabulary** *• squad • tryouts • improve • confidence • victory* **Reading Selections** *Louanne Pig in Making the Team* Photographer: Bruce Thorson  Launch the Key Strategy: Plot ✔ **Assess Reading**	 EXTRA HELP p. T181 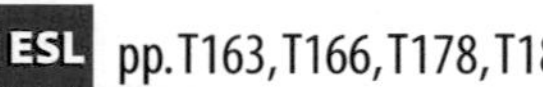 ESL pp. T163, T166, T178, T184 CHALLENGE pp. T163, T176  ACCESS p. T170 MINI-LESSON Compare/Contrast, p. T173 Fantasy, p. T182 Article, p. T185 **Idea File:** p. T189 **Cultural Connections:** pp. T174, T189	**Transparency** Build Background, 7 **Literacy-at-Work Book** Vocabulary, p. 36 Comprehension Check, p. 37  **WiggleWorks™ Plus,** T162, T168, T172, T176, T178 **Additional Technology:** pp. T176, T189
b **INTEGRATING LANGUAGE ARTS** pp. T240–245	✔ **Writing:** Write a Real-Life Story Daily Language Practice **Grammar:** Simple Sentences **Mechanics:** Capitalizing First Words ✔ **Spelling:** Words With Long *a*, *i* *• game • make • chance • same • line • mine • bike • time*	ESL pp. T191, T194  ACCESS p. T191 **Activity File:** pp. T194–195 Role-Playing Good Friends Write a Friendly Letter Create Cheers Ask the Pros MINI-LESSON Friendly Letter, p. T194 Rhythm and Rhyme, p. T195	**Literacy-at-Work Book** Writing, p. 39 **Grammar, Usage, and Mechanics Practice:** pp. 7–8 **Spelling Practice:** p. 4 **Handwriting Practice:** p. 4  **WiggleWorks™ Plus,** pp. T191, T195
 **BUILDING SKILLS AND STRATEGIES** pp. T246–251	✔ Quickcheck ✔ 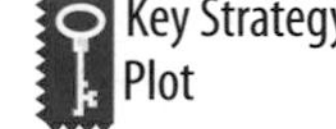 Key Strategy: Plot ✔ Quickcheck Phonics: 3-Letter Blends ✔ Quickcheck Phonics: Final *e*	 EXTRA HELP p. T201 ESL pp. T179, T199  CHALLENGE pp. T197, T201  ACCESS p. T199 **Review:** Character, p. R16	**Transparency** Key Strategy, 8 **Literacy-at-Work Book** Plot, pp. 40–42 Phonics, pp. 44-47  **WiggleWorks™ Plus,** pp. T199, T201

 ✔ = **Assessed**

CREATING A COMMUNITY OF LEARNERS

PLAY THE GAME

Objectives

Children learn to:

- work collaboratively
- recognize their own and teammates' strengths
- talk about what they are good at doing
- listen critically

Materials: None
Time: About 30 minutes
Suggested Grouping: Cooperative groups

Technology Options

Children might enjoy watching a video version of the selection *Louanne Pig in the Talent Show*, available from Live Oaks Media.

Talent Scavenger Hunt

Children use their classmates' **talents** to play a **game** before they read *Louanne Pig in Making the Team,* a story about two animal characters who **discover** what they do well.

INTRODUCE THE GAME

Talk with children about a time the class worked together to make something happen, such as a school play, parents' night, or a party. Ask them to describe how everything got done. If possible, guide the discussion around how different people do different things they are good at doing.

Then invite children to play a game called Talent Scavenger Hunt that will require the different talents of their group members.

PLAY THE GAME

COOPERATIVE GROUPS Divide the class into three or four groups. Tell children they will go on a Talent Scavenger Hunt, where they find things they create. Make up your own list, which might include things such as: a picture of a dinosaur, a paper airplane, or a paragraph entitled, "Why Today Is Special."

Write the list on the chalkboard and before children start the game, make or create each item on the scavenger hunt list. (For example:
Who is good at writing a paragraph?
Who is good at drawing dinosaurs?
Who can make things?)

The point of the game is not to finish first, but to assemble items. After deciding who will do what job, start the game.

THINK ABOUT THE GAME

When all the items are assembled, have each team member take turns sharing what he or she created.

Then, talk about how they worked together to gather all the items on the scavenger hunt.

- **What was fun about this game?**
- **What did you learn about yourself that you did not know before?**
- **What did you learn about a classmate that you didn't realize he or she could do?**
- **Who decided who would do each thing—the person who volunteered or your teammates?** MINI-LESSON

Activity: Make a "The Things We Do Best" Big Book

COOPERATIVE GROUPS Invite children to make a book about what they do best. Working in cooperative groups, have children list three things that each group member does well. Then on oversized construction paper have each child write a sentence for each of the three things he or she does well. Children can draw a self-portrait to illustrate one or more of their sentences. Gather each group's pages together and bind them into a class Big Book entitled "The Things We Do Best" and read the book aloud to children. THE ARTS

MAKE CONNECTIONS

To Children's Lives

DISCUSSION Ask children when being part of a group can help you learn what you are good at doing. Mention activities such as kickball, putting on plays, and other group activities they participate in regularly. Then you might also discuss:

- **What might you do if you want to get better at something you can't do well?**
- **Do you think you might not always know what you're good at doing? Why or why not?**
- **How can you find out what you are good at doing?**

MINI-LESSON

LISTEN CRITICALLY

TEACH/MODEL Model for children how to listen critically when working in a group.

> **THINK ALOUD When I work in a group and it needs volunteers, I think about what I do well. I listen for what jobs need to be done, and I think about what I am good at and like to do. If I hear about a job that someone else is good at, I remind that person that he or she would be good at doing that job. It's part of being a good group member.**

APPLY Ask partners to talk to each other about one thing they do well. Then have them tell what they think their partner does well.

a

READING THE SOURCES

LOUANNE PIG IN MAKING THE TEAM / BRUCE THORSON: PHOTOGRAPHER

Build Background

In the book *Louanne Pig in Making the Team,* two characters **help** each other **practice** for team tryouts—with some surprising **results!**

Objectives

Children learn to:

- pantomime scenes
- expand oral language
- use vocabulary in context

Materials:
Transparency 7
Literacy-at-Work Book p. 36
Word Cards 18–22
Pocket Chart

Time:
About 20 minutes

Suggested Grouping:
Whole class and partners

Literacy-at-Work Book, p. 36

Name VOCABULARY

Making the Team

Write a word from the box on each line.

confidence
tryouts
victory
squad
improve

1. John believes he can dive well. He has confidence.
2. Erin practices skating every day. She will improve.
3. The swim team won the contest. They had a victory.
4. The team needed new players. They held tryouts.
5. The cheerleaders are on a team. They form a squad.

36 Unit 1 • Snapshots • Plan IV • Louanne Pig in Making the Team

ACTIVATE PRIOR KNOWLEDGE

Illustrate a Helping Scene

Ask children to recall how teammates helped each other in the Talent Scavenger Hunt. Invite children to draw a scene showing a circumstance when someone helped them learn to do something new. As an option, children may illustrate themselves helping a younger brother, sister, or friend.

Pantomime a Scene

PARTNERS Invite children to work in pairs to pantomime their helping scenes. Classmates can guess what they are pantomiming. THE ARTS

Make a Help Chart

Use Transparency 7 to list occasions when children have needed help and the people who helped them. After the chart is complete, discuss it with them. Talk about the different ways people can help each other.

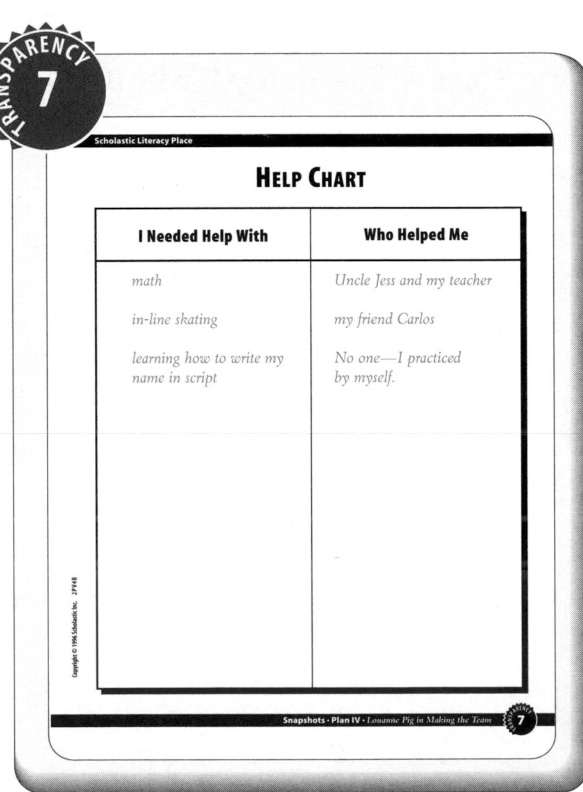

TRANSPARENCY 7

Scholastic Literacy Place

HELP CHART

I Needed Help With	Who Helped Me
math	Uncle Jess and my teacher
in-line skating	my friend Carlos
learning how to write my name in script	No one—I practiced by myself.

Snapshots • Plan IV • Louanne Pig in Making the Team 7

Annotated transparency for building background

Develop Vocabulary

Teach the Concept Words

Strategy: Contextual Redefinition
Provide a cloze sentence for each concept word, and have children supply the missing word. Then encourage them to come to a consensus about each word's meaning.

1. *A small group of us formed a cheering ____ to encourage the baseball team.*
2. *We held ____ to see who could perform the cheers well.*
3. *Most of us ____ when we practice often.*
4. *Believing in ourselves shows the squad has ____.*
5. *Winning their first game was a big ____ for the baseball team.*

Support Words As children are reading *Louanne Pig in Making the Team,* you may want to point out other interesting words in the story.

cartwheel: a jump that's done sideways from one's feet to one's hands and back again

consoled: made to feel better

tackling: stopping and bringing to the ground, especially in football

Personal Word List Children can generate in their Journals their own lists of new and unusual vocabulary they encounter during reading, including words related to football and cheerleading.

VOCABULARY

ORGANIZING CONCEPT: TEAM WORDS

Concept Words

	Word	Definition
✔	tryouts:	tests to see if someone can do something well (p. 77)
✔	squad:	a small group of people who work together (p. 77)
✔	improve:	to make better (p. 86)
	confidence:	a strong belief in someone or something (p. 87)
	victory:	the act of winning (p. 92)

✔ = assessed

See p. T193 for words to pretest and spelling instruction

Technology Options

Invite children to illustrate their helping scenes in the SourceBook Activities writing area.

Supporting All Learners

Peer Partners

ESL Pair children acquiring English with native speakers who can help them identify and define the cheerleading and football vocabulary. After introducing the concept and support words, pairs of children can work together to discuss the new words and to search the story for other related words. Encourage them to write the new words in their Journals under the heading "Football and Cheerleading Words."

CHALLENGE Challenge children to use their verbal skills to enrich the Activate Prior Knowledge activities. Children can take turns verbally expressing the scenes their classmates have drawn or are pantomiming.

a

READING THE SOURCES

LOUANNE PIG IN MAKING THE TEAM/BRUCE THORSON: PHOTOGRAPHER

Prepare to Teach

OBSERVATION

As children read the selections, notice how they:

- ✔ make connections with the *theme* that each person has his or her own special talents.
- ✔ use the *key strategy* of Plot to follow the events in the story.
- ✔ understand the *literary element* of Dialogue.

Use the Individual and Class Plan Checklists in the Classroom Management Forms, pp. 7 and 13.

KEY STRATEGY:

PLOT

Louanne Pig in Making the Team will help children understand that the events in a story make up the plot. The narrative progresses smoothly with a clear beginning, middle, and end. Learning to recognize events as they occur will help readers understand what's happening in each part of the story.

Customize Instruction

FLEXIBLE GROUPING

Teacher Support

Construct meaning by using the key strategy of Plot as children read the selections. Revisit the selections to build understanding of the literary element of Dialogue.

Collaborative

If children are experienced working with partners, have them sit together and read alternate pages of *Louanne Pig in Making the Team*. Encourage them as they read to record questions for discussion later.

Extra Support

Read the story aloud to children without interruption. Then use the Read questions to help them reread the text themselves. Ask children to retell the story in their own words, using clues they find in the pictures and text.

Independent

For children who are ready to read independently, encourage them to finish the story in one sitting. Then have them respond to the questions on page T188.

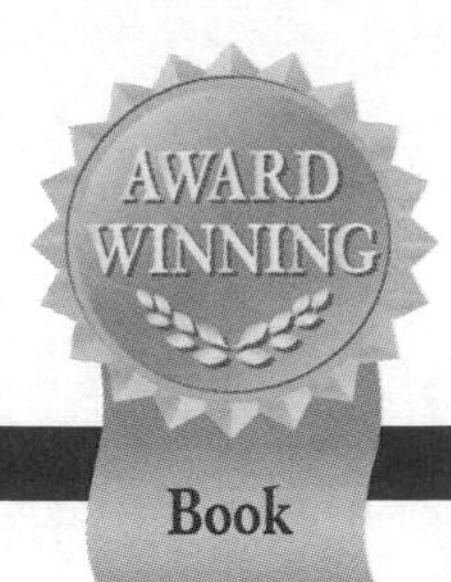

Meet the Author

Nancy Carlson

Nancy Carlson is an award-winning author and artist who likes to write stories that teach children a little lesson. Many of these lessons are inspired by events in her own life. Other stories come from her friends' experiences. She also illustrates her own books, and when she's not working on a book, she creates art for shows and galleries. Children may read about Nancy Carlson on page 142 of the SourceBook.

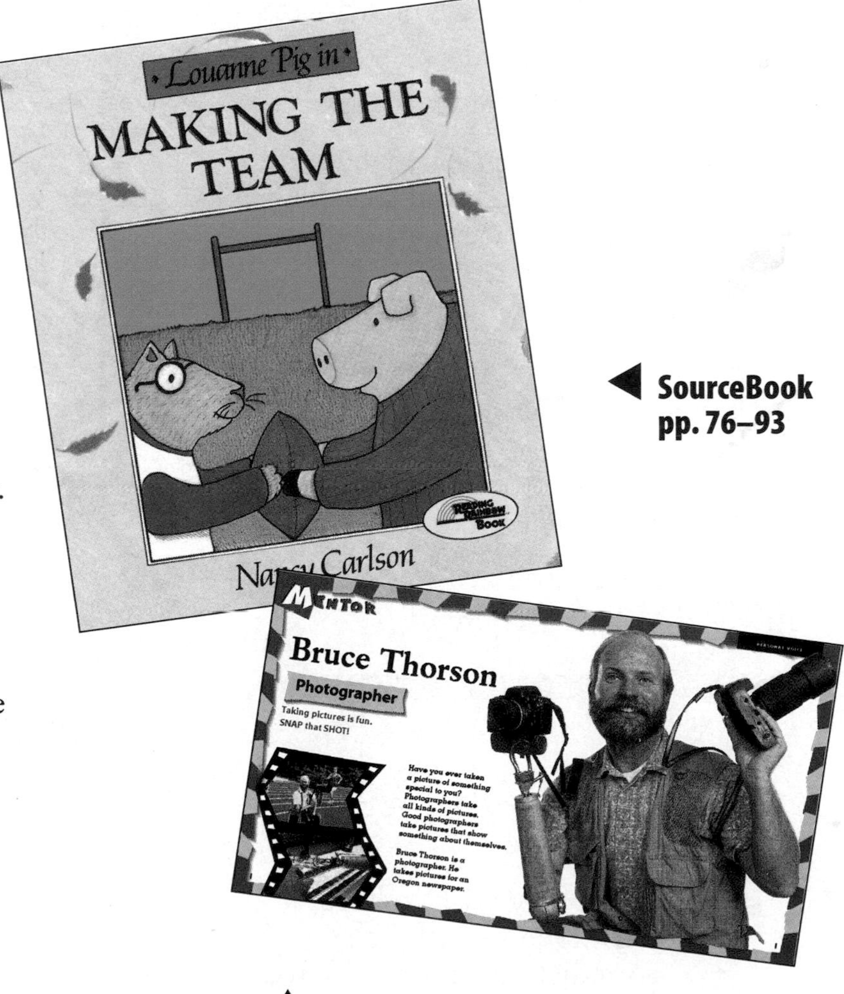

◀ SourceBook pp. 76–93

SourceBook ▲ pp. 94–97

More by Nancy Carlson

- ***Arnie and the New Kid***
  Arnie gains understanding for Philip.
- ***Harriet and the Roller Coaster***
  Harriet shows George she is not intimidated by his taunting.
- ***Louanne Pig in the Perfect Family***
  Louanne appreciates that both her friend George and she are lucky to have the families that they have.

Books for Word Study

- ***One of Three***
  by Angela Johnson
  The youngest of three sisters reflects on her place in the family. **(3-letter blend: *thr*)**
- ***Osa's Pride***
  by Ann Grifalconi
  Osa, a young African girl, learns an important lesson from the wise woman in her village. **(final *e*)**
- ***Squirrels***
  by Brian Wildsmith
  A factual book, it uses art and simple text to offer scientific information. **(3-letter blend: *squ*)**

a

Reading the Sources

Preview and Predict

Reader to Reader

Did you ever want to do something but couldn't do it well? When I read *Louanne Pig in Making the Team,* I couldn't wait to find out what would happen to Louanne and Arnie.

Look at the cover of *Louanne Pig in Making the Team* with children. Read the title and the author's name with them. Discuss the illustration.

- **What do you think it means to "make the team"?**
- **What are the two characters doing?**

Invite the children to flip through the next few pages. Ask children what they think will happen. Will the characters make the team? Record their ideas on chart paper.

What will happen in the story?
The pig will make the team.
The cat will make the team.
Both characters will make the team.

You may wish to have children record their predictions in their Journals.

SOURCE
Fantasy

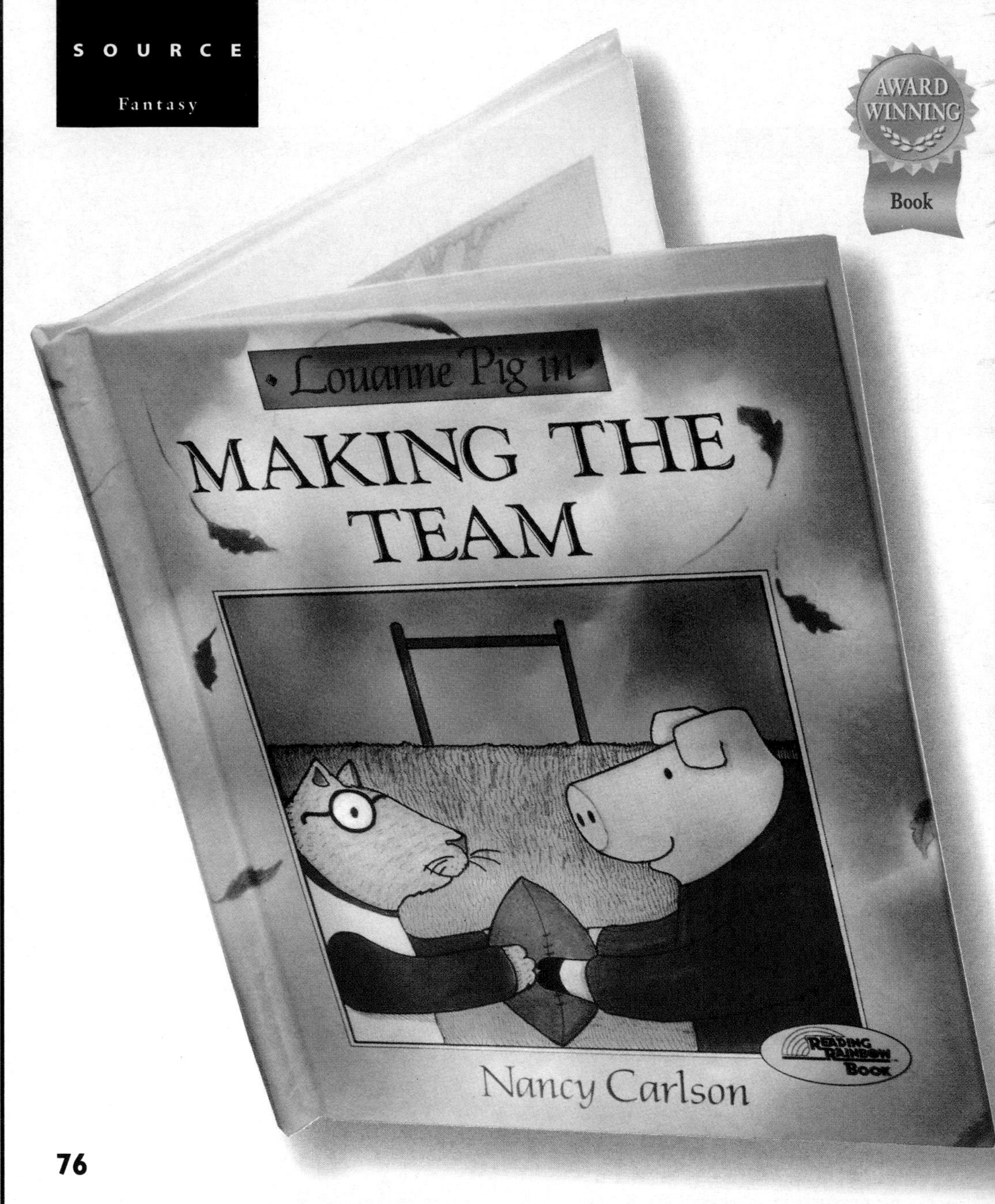

76

PAGE 76 SNAPSHOTS

Supporting All Learners

Preview ESL Pictures offer an effective way of previewing the story with children acquiring English. Prior to reading, guide children through the book, pausing on each page as you select a volunteer to describe to his or her classmates what is happening. **(Use Visuals)** VISUAL LITERACY

One day Louanne and Arnie found something exciting on the school bulletin board. Tryouts for the cheerleading squad and the football team were coming up.

"I'm going to try out for cheerleading," said Louanne.

"And I'm going to try out for the football team," said Arnie.

77

LOUANNE PIG IN MAKING THE TEAM PAGE 77

Guided Reading ▶

LAUNCH THE KEY STRATEGY:

PLOT

THINK ALOUD When I read a story, I pay close attention to what is happening. In the beginning of a story, I try to learn who the main characters are. Then I think about what the characters do in the story. If I try to understand the story events as they happen, I'll have a better understanding of the whole story.

Sometimes what the writer says doesn't tell me everything I need to know. Then I look at the pictures for clues to what is happening. I know from the pictures on the cover and on the first page that Louanne is a pig and Arnie is a cat.

▶ INTEGRATED CURRICULUM **SOCIAL STUDIES** *(See p. R9.)*
Children list the ways that various players contribute to their teams.

a

Guided Reading ▶

❶ **KEY STRATEGY: Plot As I read *Louanne Pig in Making the Team,* I'll keep in mind the story events as they happen. What happens at the beginning of the story?**

Children can use the computer writing area to keep track of important plot events.

That afternoon they hurried over to Arnie's to practice together. ❶

78

PAGE 78 SNAPSHOTS

▶ INTEGRATED CURRICULUM **THE ARTS** *(See p. R9.)*

Children make a pennant for a school team.

Louanne was doing pretty well...

...until she came to the split jump. She couldn't get off the ground.

"Like this, Louanne," said Arnie.

79

LOUANNE PIG IN MAKING THE TEAM PAGE 79

▶ INTEGRATING LANGUAGE ARTS READING/WRITING/SPEAKING *(See p. T195.)*

Guided Reading ▶

INTERVENTION STRATEGY

Text Structure

As children read this page, help them note that the text is in two places. Stop at the end of the first block of text and have children locate the picture that goes with it to the right.

After reading the second block of text, help children note that the corresponding picture is to the left of the text.

Tell the children to watch for other pages in the story where the text is split in this way.

Revisit ◀

Conventions of Print: Ellipses

Point out the ellipses on page 79. Explain that these three dots show that there is a long pause in the middle of the sentence. Read the sentence aloud again.

- **Why do you think the author split up this sentence into two parts rather than putting it all together on the page?**

Help children see that splitting up the sentence creates suspense. The first part of the sentence lets the readers think that Louanne is doing well, and then the second part of the sentence surprises them.

a

Guided Reading ▶

❷ **Word Attack Follow along while I read—"I'm better at shouting," said Louanne—let's stop. That doesn't make sense. Let's read it again. What do you think the word after *at* is? Let's try to figure it out. The word is made up of two shorter words and the picture shows Louanne turning upside down. I think she is doing a cartwheel. What do you think the word is?**

"I'm better at cartwheels," said Louanne. 

80

PAGE 80 SNAPSHOTS

Revisit ◀

Picture Clues

Louanne Pig in Making the Team relies heavily on art and illustration. Help children realize that in order to understand what is happening, they have to look at the pictures carefully. For example, point out that on page 80, Louanne says that she is better at cartwheels. But to learn whether she can do a cartwheel it is necessary to look at the picture. Have children look carefully at other pictures to learn more information than what the text gives.

Supporting All Learners

Revisit

ACCESS Facilitate the participation of children with visual impairments in the Picture Details activity by pairing them with sighted buddies who can explain what is happening in each picture. **(Peer Partners)**

"Let me show you how to do it," said Arnie. ❹

81

LOUANNE PIG IN MAKING THE TEAM PAGE 81

Guided Reading ►

❸ **Compare/Contrast** Who is better at doing cartwheels, Louanne or Arnie? How can you tell?

❹ **Problem/Solution** I know that Louanne wants to try out for the cheerleading squad. What problem does she have? What do you think she can do to solve this problem?

THINK!

Mentor Connection

Who do you think helped module mentor Bruce Thorson learn how to be a sports photographer?

a

Guided Reading ▶

5 **CRITICAL THINKING: Analyze How has Arnie been helping Louanne? How is Louanne helping Arnie now? What does this tell you about them?**

"You ought to be practicing football," said Louanne, and she picked up the football and threw it to Arnie. 5

82

PAGE 82 SNAPSHOTS

PHONICS 3-Letter Blends

Direct attention to the word *threw*. Read the word aloud slowly, and point out the first three letters. Explain that the sounds these letters stand for are blended together when you say the word.

- **What other words do you know that start with the letters *thr*?**

(See Phonics: 3-Letter Blends on pp. T198–199.)

See the WiggleWorks Plus Teaching Plan for more phonics activities.

Arnie missed the catch.

Read On ► ► ►

MINI-LESSON

COMPARE/ CONTRAST

TEACH/MODEL As children read the story, have them compare Louanne and Arnie to each other.

THINK ALOUD When I read a story, I think about how the characters are alike and how they are different. At the beginning of the story I learned that both Louanne and Arnie wanted to try out for a team. Then I found out that Louanne, who wanted to be on the cheerleading squad, could not do a split.

APPLY Ask children to look at pages 82 and 83.

- **What do you learn about Louanne on these pages? What can you tell about Arnie?**

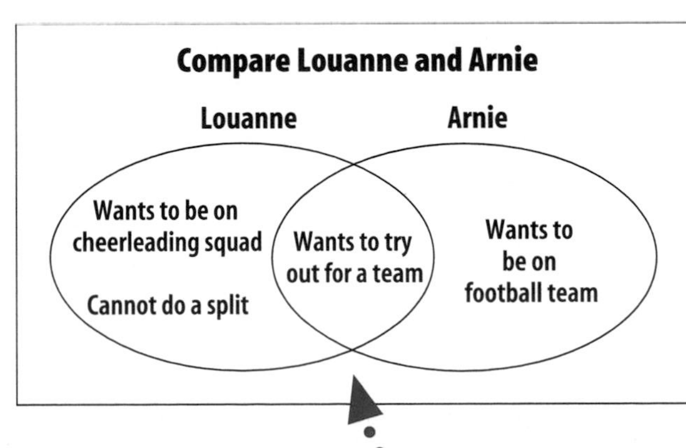

a

Guided Reading ►

❻ **Picture Details The pictures on this page tell me a lot about Arnie and Louanne. In the first picture I see Louanne is catching the football. What can you tell about Arnie from the illustrations?**
VISUAL LITERACY

CULTURAL CONNECTIONS

Louanne throws the football to Arnie. There is another game with the name football, and it is popular all over the world. In the United States this game is called soccer. How is soccer different from football in the United States?
SOCIAL STUDIES

"You have to keep your eye on the ball, Arnie," Louanne told him. "Like this."

❻

"I'm probably better at tackling," said Arnie.

84

PAGE 84 SNAPSHOTS

"Let me show you how to do it," said Louanne.

"Let's try some kicking," said Arnie.

7 8

85

LOUANNE PIG IN MAKING THE TEAM PAGE 85

▶ INTEGRATED CURRICULUM **SCIENCE** *(See p. R8.)*
Children find out how physical activity affects their heartbeat.

▶ INTEGRATING LANGUAGE ARTS **WRITING** *(See p. T194.)*

Guided Reading ▶

7 **Picture Details** **What can you say about Arnie's ability to play football? What clues did you use?**
VISUAL LITERACY

8 **Make Predictions** **What do you think will happen when Arnie tries out for the football team?**

Revisit ◀

Literary Element: Dialogue

Point out the dialogue on this page.

- **Dialogue is the actual words a character says.**
- **In written dialogue, quotation marks come before and after the speaker's words.**

Have children look for dialogue as they read the story.

a

Guided Reading ▶

❾ **Character** **Arnie tries to keep Louanne's spirits up, and Louanne keeps encouraging Arnie. What does this tell you about the two friends?**

All week long Louanne and Arnie met after school to practice for their tryouts. Louanne's jumps didn't improve much, but Arnie kept her spirits up.

"You really look great!" he told her.

Arnie only rarely caught the ball, but Louanne encouraged him.

"I know you're going to make the team!" she said. ❾

86

PAGE 86 SNAPSHOTS

Revisit ◀

Oral Reading: Read Expressively

Reread aloud several pages of the story. Ask children to imitate, or echo. Point out how you use the punctuation marks to help you read expressively.

- **Quotation marks enclose a speaker's exact words and help readers change their tone of voice to show that a different person is speaking.**
- **End punctuation marks, such as exclamation marks, help readers read with expression. Exclamation marks tell us to read the sentence with more emphasis, or stress.**

Technology Options Invite children to tape their rereadings on audiocassettes. They can listen to their recordings for parts to read more expressively. THE ARTS

SUPPORTING ALL LEARNERS

Read

CHALLENGE Invite children to reread page 86 and discuss how Arnie keeps Louanne's spirits up. Help them recall how Ronald Morgan kept his team's spirits up. Challenge children to compare and contrast how Arnie and Ronald Morgan lift their friends' spirits. **(Compare and Contrast)**

- Invite children to create a PlaceMaker greeting card to send to Louanne to keep her spirits up.

When the big day arrived, their confidence was high.

Cheerleading tryouts were first. 

Guided Reading ▶

10 KEY STRATEGY: Plot In the beginning of the story, Louanne decided to try out for the cheerleading squad, and Arnie decided to try out for the football team. What happened after that? What do you think will happen next?

PHONICS **Digraphs *ch, th, wh***

Ask children to find the word *Cheerleading* on page 87, point to the letters *ch*, and read the word aloud.

- **What other words do you know that begin with the same sound?**

Follow a similar procedure with the words *the* and *their*. Repeat with the word *when*.

a

Guided Reading ▸

⓫ KEY STRATEGY: Plot **What happened when Louanne tried out for the cheerleading squad?**

⓬ Word Attack **Let's read page 88 again. How can you figure out the meaning of the word *consoled,* which comes after *Arnie*? In the line above, Arnie tells Louanne not to feel bad. You can see from the picture on the page that Louanne is sad. Arnie also tells Louanne that she can try again next year. The clues in the text and the picture help readers figure out that when you console someone, you try to make that person feel better. You comfort someone.**

Revisit ◂

Word Study: Idiom

To talk about expressions that have special meanings, use the term *top-notch* as an example.

- **You know what the word *top* means. Can anyone tell me what the word *notch* means? Yes, a notch is a nick or a cut on the edge of something. When you put the meanings of those two words together, does it make sense to say that Louanne will be top-notch? No, but *top-notch* also has a special meaning. It means "first rate" or "the best possible."**
- **Let's look in *Louanne Pig in Making the Team* to find other expressions with special meanings.**

Invite children to make posters on the computer that illustrate the idiomatic expressions they find.

Louanne didn't make the squad. ⓫

"Don't feel bad," Arnie
⓬ consoled her. "There's always next year. By then you'll be top-notch."

"Right," said Louanne. "Come on. There's still a little time before your tryout. I'll show you a few last tricks."

"Hey, pig," said Coach Ed. "You're pretty good. Why don't you try out for the team."

89

LOUANNE PIG IN MAKING THE TEAM PAGE 89

Guided Reading ►

13 Picture Clues Coach Ed is asking Louanne to try out for the team. Who is Coach Ed? How can you tell? VISUAL LITERACY

a

Read On ► ► ►

So Louanne and Arnie tried out together. Louanne made the team.

90

PAGE 90 SNAPSHOTS

Revisit ◄

Phonics: Final *e*

Direct children's attention to the word *made* as you read aloud the last sentence on the page. Explain that the silent *e* at the end of the word means that the vowel *a* will be long. Have children find other words in the story with the pattern consonant-vowel-consonant-*e*. *(See Phonics: Final* e *on pp. T200–201.)*

Arnie didn't. ⓮

Suddenly Louanne had an idea.

"Come on, Arnie!" she said. "Cheerleading tryouts are still going on."

Guided Reading ►

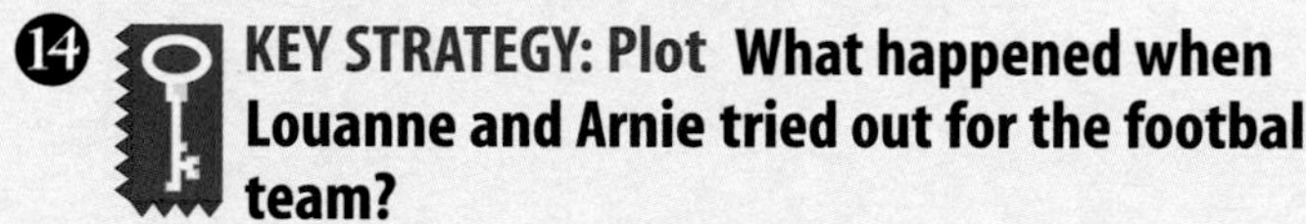

⓮ **KEY STRATEGY: Plot What happened when Louanne and Arnie tried out for the football team?**

⓯ Make Predictions **What did you predict would happen? Were you right?**

Supporting All Learners

Read

EXTRA HELP Before asking Read 14, reinforce children's comprehension of the story by reviewing what has happened so far. Help children identify the turning points and demonstrate how to use them to retell the story. **(Summarize)**

a

Read On ► ► ►

That fall Roosevelt School won every game. Louanne led the team to victory,

MINI-LESSON

and Arnie led the cheers.

92

PAGE 92 SNAPSHOTS

MINI-LESSON

Fantasy

TEACH/MODEL Remind children that stories about imaginary people and happenings are called fiction. Explain that one type of fiction is fantasy. In a fantasy, the events are not the same as those in real life.

THINK ALOUD When I look at the cover, I see a pig and a cat wearing clothes, just as real people do. This tells me that it is a fantasy.

APPLY As children reread the book, ask questions to help them determine that it is a fantasy:

- **Could a real cat do cartwheels?**
- **Would a real pig throw a football?**

Have children page through the SourceBook to identify other examples of fantasy. VISUAL LITERACY

16

17

93

LOUANNE PIG IN MAKING THE TEAM PAGE 93

Guided Reading ▶

16 KEY STRATEGY: Plot **How does the story end?**

17 Make Predictions **Was this what you thought would happen? How did you predict the story would end?**

▶ INTEGRATED CURRICULUM **MATH** *(See p. R8.)*

Children compare ratios by keeping score in a classroom game.

READING THE SOURCES

a

Preview and Predict

READER TO READER

"We learned about Mentor Bruce Thorson by viewing the video. We'll learn more about him in this article by looking at what is written about him and the questions he answers."

Before they read, have children look through the selection to note the different sections. What information do they expect to find that they didn't learn in the video?

MENTOR

Bruce Thorson

Photographer

Taking pictures is fun.
SNAP that SHOT!

Have you ever taken a picture of something special to you? Photographers take all kinds of pictures. Good photographers take pictures that show something about themselv

Bruce Thorson is a photographer. He takes pictures for an Oregon newspaper.

94

PAGE 94 SNAPSHOTS

SUPPORTING ALL LEARNERS

Preview **ESL** Remind children that Bruce Thorson is a photographer and guide them in a discussion about what a photographer does. Invite children to talk about their personal experiences or the experiences of friends and family who take pictures. **(Make Connections)** SOCIAL STUDIES

Read On ▶ ▶ ▶

MINI-LESSON

Article

TEACH/MODEL Explain to children that an article is a piece of writing that gives true information about someone or something. Headings might be used in an article to divide the information into different sections.

THINK ALOUD When I read this article about photographer Bruce Thorson, I noticed that it is divided into three sections. The first section made me think about what a photographer does. The "Questions" section gives answers to questions about Bruce Thorson's job. The last section has tips he gives. The sections made the article easier to understand.

APPLY After they finish reading, list other questions children would like to have Bruce Thorson answer.

a

Guided Reading ▶

1 **Make Inferences** Why does Bruce Thorson drive to a lot of places for his job?

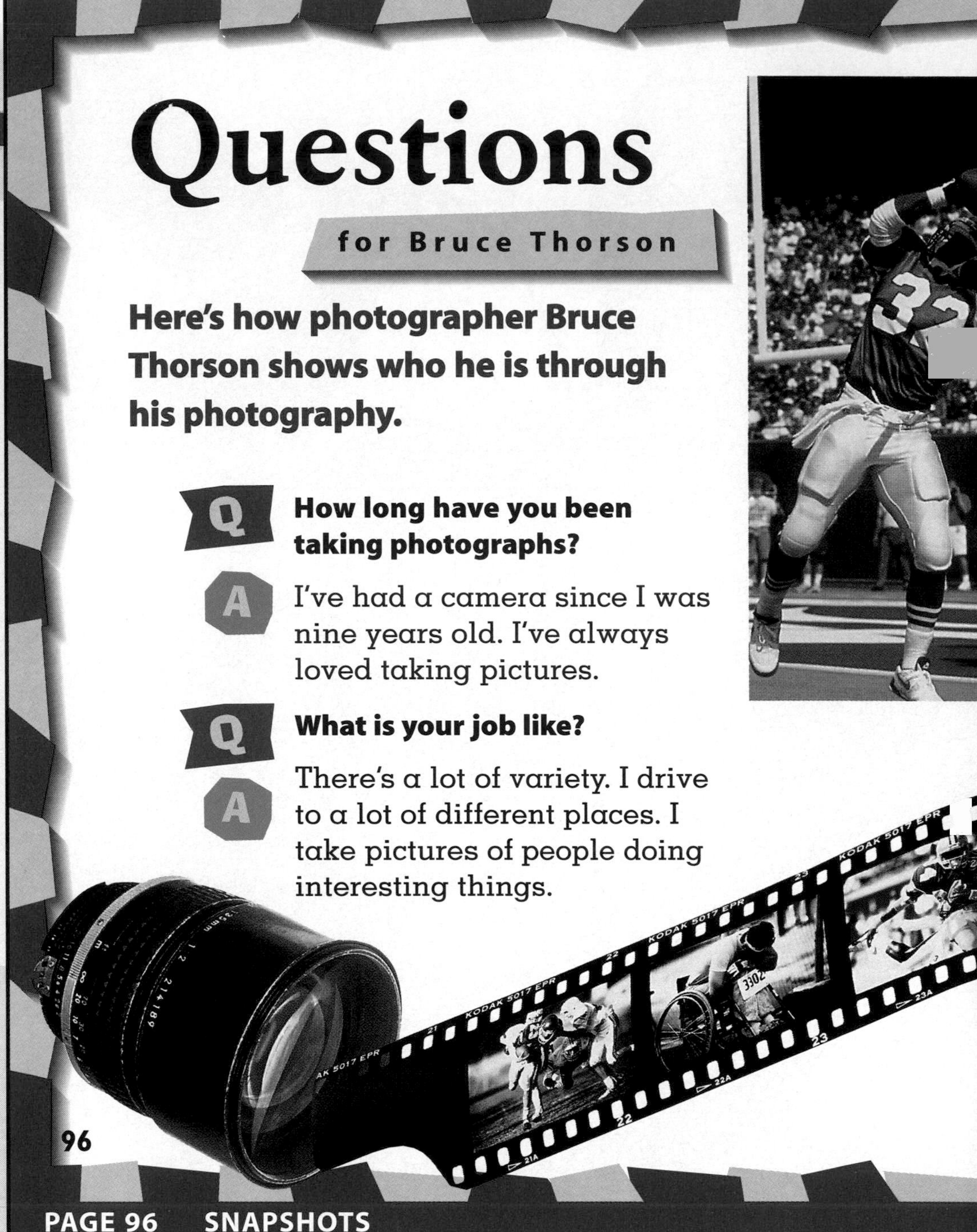

Questions

for Bruce Thorson

Here's how photographer Bruce Thorson shows who he is through his photography.

Q How long have you been taking photographs?

A I've had a camera since I was nine years old. I've always loved taking pictures.

Q What is your job like?

A There's a lot of variety. I drive to a lot of different places. I take pictures of people doing interesting things.

96

PAGE 96 SNAPSHOTS

PHONICS Vowel /o/ *o*

Have children find the words *job* and *lot* on page 96. Ask how the words are alike. You may wish to have children generate a list of familiar words that have the same vowel sound as *job* and *lot.*

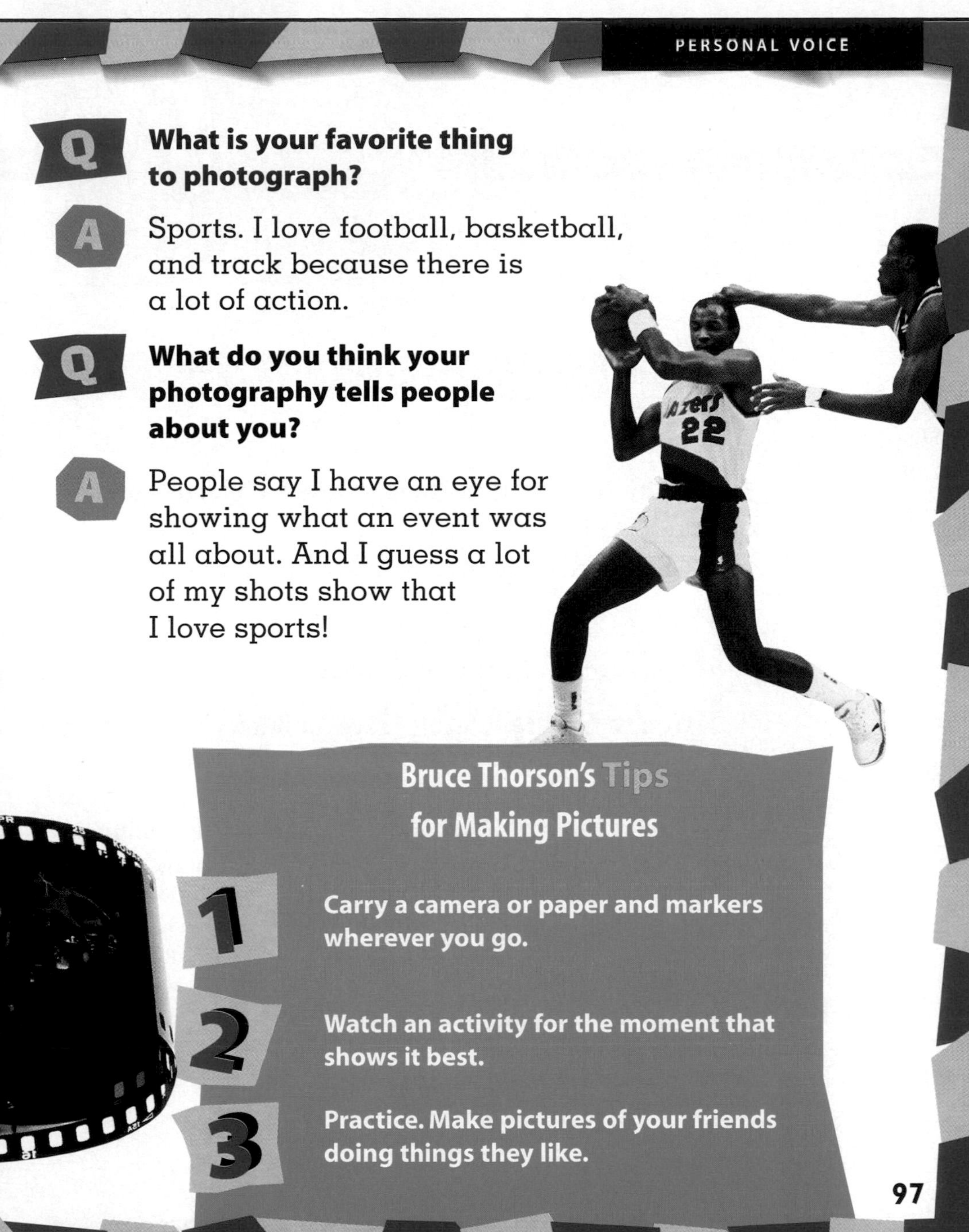

Q What is your favorite thing to photograph?

A Sports. I love football, basketball, and track because there is a lot of action.

Q What do you think your photography tells people about you?

A People say I have an eye for showing what an event was all about. And I guess a lot of my shots show that I love sports!

Bruce Thorson's Tips for Making Pictures

1. Carry a camera or paper and markers wherever you go.
2. Watch an activity for the moment that shows it best.
3. Practice. Make pictures of your friends doing things they like.

Guided Reading ►

2 Make Inferences **Why might Bruce Thorson not enjoy photographing baseball as much as basketball?**

3 Relate to Personal Experience **Bruce Thorson suggests taking a camera or paper and markers with you wherever you go because you never know when something interesting will happen. What might you make pictures of your friends doing?**

4 Main Idea/Details **What is the main idea of this article? What are some details you learned about Bruce Thorson in this profile?**

a

READING THE SOURCES

LOUANNE PIG IN MAKING THE TEAM/BRUCE THORSON: PHOTOGRAPHER

Assess Reading

REFLECT AND RESPOND

Encourage children to share their thoughts, opinions, and questions about *Louanne Pig in Making the Team* and "Photographer Bruce Thorson." You may wish to prompt discussion with the following questions:

- **What did you like most about *Louanne Pig in Making the Team*? What did you like least?**
- **What did Louanne and Arnie do to get better at cheerleading and playing football? *(✔Theme)***
- **What happened at the beginning, middle, and end of this story? *(✔Key Strategy)***
- **How would you describe the conversations between Louanne and Arnie? *(✔Literary Element)***

CHECK PREDICTIONS

Have children return to the predictions they made before reading *Louanne Pig in Making the Team* to check if those predictions were confirmed.

READ CRITICALLY ACROSS TEXTS

- **How did the characters Louanne and Arnie and Mentor Bruce Thorson discover what they were really good at?**

Louanne and Arnie found out what they were good at by accident when they were helping each other. Bruce Thorson found out he was good at photography because he enjoyed taking pictures.

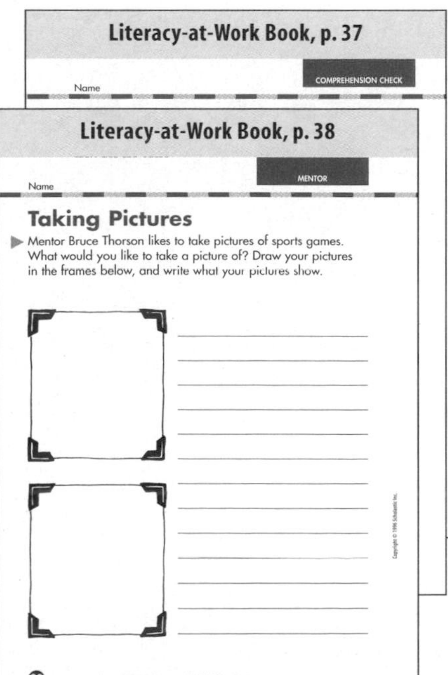
Literacy-at-Work Book, p. 37

COMPREHENSION CHECK

Literacy-at-Work Book, p. 38

MENTOR

Name

Taking Pictures

Mentor Bruce Thorson likes to take pictures of sports games. What would you like to take a picture of? Draw your pictures in the frames below, and write what your pictures show.

38 Unit 1 • Snapshots • Plan IV • Louanne Pig in Making the Team

CONFERENCE

Use the checked questions to assess children's understanding of:

✔ the *theme* of discovering our special talents.

✔ the *key strategy* of Plot.

✔ the *literary element* of Dialogue.

Listen to Children Retell Have children use the illustrations to retell the story. Ask them to use transitional words and phrases to help them—such as *And then* or *The next thing that happened was ....* Assess retelling, using pp. 22–23 in the Assessment Handbook.

Children may wish to add their recordings to their Literacy Portfolios.

Based on your evaluation of your children's responses,

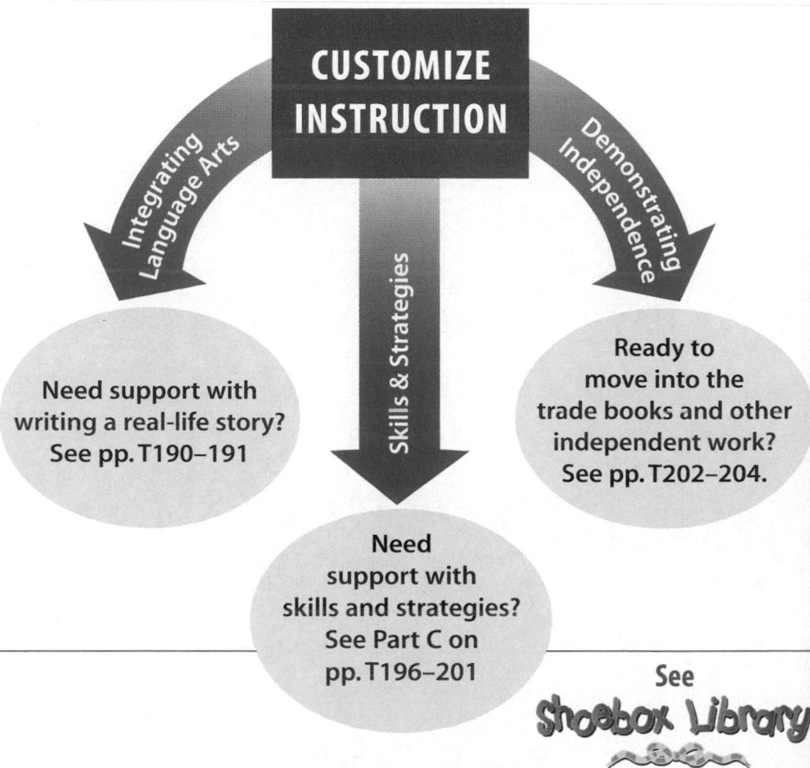

See Shoebox Library

Idea File

REPEATED READING

Technology Options **PARTNER READING** Invite partners to tape-record a reading of the story, with each child taking a turn reading a page. Encourage children to read with expression, especially the dialogue between Louanne and Arnie.

STORY EXTENSION

JOURNAL

Invite children to think of other activities and interests that Louanne and Arnie might have. What else might Arnie be good at? What other activities would Louanne enjoy?

REPEATED READING

READERS THEATER Have children work in groups to stage a Readers Theater presentation of *Louanne Pig in Making the Team*. Children can take the roles of Narrator, Louanne, Arnie, and Coach Ed. Encourage children to expand on the roles presented in the story.

VOCABULARY

HOMEWORK

What would children like to ask Nancy Carlson about *Louanne Pig in Making the Team*? Have children think of questions they would like to ask the author. For example, "Is *Louanne Pig in Making the Team* based on a real experience that you had as a child?" Some children might prefer to share with the author their responses to the story.

CULTURAL CONNECTIONS

THE WORLD OF FOOTBALL

In *Louanne Pig in Making the Team*, Louanne joins the school football team. American football is popular in the United States, but did you know that Gaelic football is played in Ireland, and that there are also Australian and Canadian versions of football, as well as the granddaddy of football games—rugby—first played in England about 150 years ago.

ACTIVITY

Have groups find out about one kind of football played around the world. Encourage them to find facts such as: How many players are on a team? What is the size of the field? How are points scored? Where is the sport played?

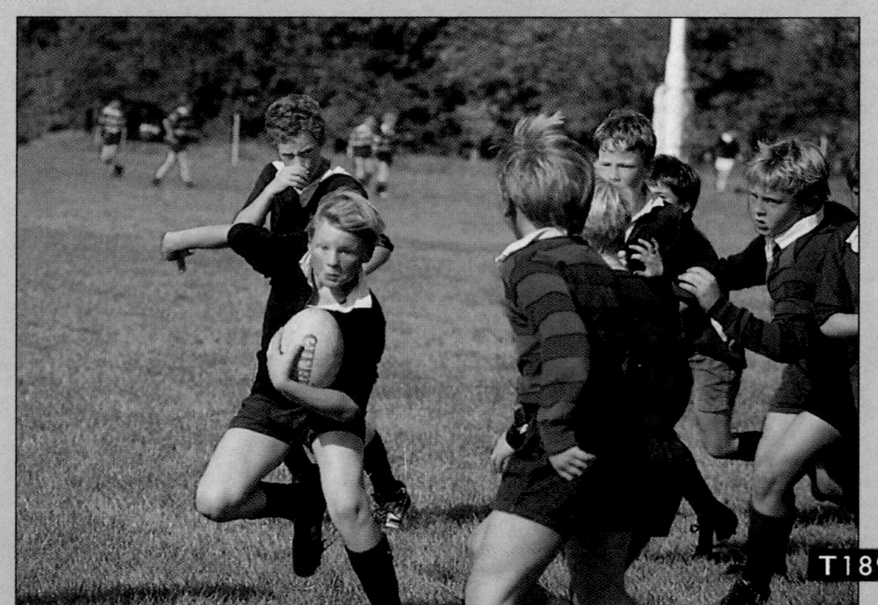

b

INTEGRATING LANGUAGE ARTS

LOUANNE PIG IN MAKING THE TEAM

SOURCEBOOK MODEL

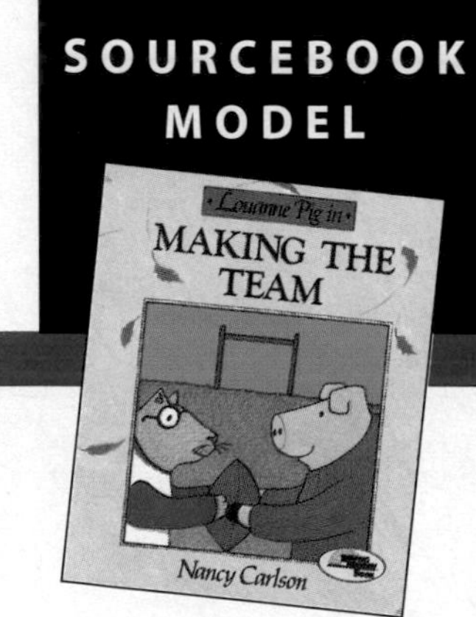

Objectives

Children learn to:

- write a narrative with a theme (pp. T190–191)
- write simple sentences (p. T192)
- capitalize the first word in a sentence (p. T192)
- spell words with *a-e, i-e* (p. T193)

Materials:
SourceBook pp. 76–93
Literacy-at- Work Book p. 39

Suggested Grouping:
Whole class, cooperative groups, and individuals

Literacy-at-Work Book, p. 39

Name — WRITING

Get Ready to Write

Think of someone you would like to help. What would you help this person do? How would you help? Write your answers.

1. Who I would help:
2. What I would help him or her with:
3. How I would help:

To the Teacher: This is the prewriting organizer referenced in the lesson on writing a real-life story.

Unit 1 • Snapshots • Plan IV • *Louanne Pig in Making the Team* 39

WRITE A REAL-LIFE STORY

WRITING

In *Louanne Pig in Making the Team,* the **theme** of friends helping friends provides a model for children to use in **writing** their own **theme story.**

THINK ABOUT WRITING

Ask children for their ideas about what the theme, or main idea, of a story is. If it is hard for them to put into words, encourage them to give examples based on well-known stories. For example, the main idea of *The Three Little Pigs* is that it is important to work hard. Help them see that in a story with a theme:

- The theme is the main idea of the story.
- The characters' actions help readers understand the theme.

Put It in Context

Ask children to look back at *Louanne Pig in Making the Team* and think about the theme of the story. What can Louanne do well that Arnie helps her to realize? What can Arnie do well that Louanne helps him to realize?

- Help children understand that the theme of the story is that friends can help each other discover something they each do well.

Ask children to find parts of the story that show the theme, for example: "Come on Arnie! . . . Cheerleading tryouts are still going on."

INTRODUCE THE WRITING EVENT

Invite children to write a story with a theme. They may want to use the theme that it's good to help someone do something.

Prewrite

Ask children to think of things they might help someone else do, such as learn to ice skate or to solve a problem. Invite them to use the prewriting organizer in the Literacy-at-Work Book as a guide for listing their ideas.

- Have children decide what they want to help someone with—and who the someone would be.
- Have children think about what would happen as they help. What would they say? What would they do?

Draft

It may help children to ask the following questions as they write:

- **Is the main idea or theme of my story helping someone do something?**
- **Am I showing this idea through what the characters in my story are doing?**

Revise

Suggest that children ask:

- **Have I put in enough information about helping a friend do something?**
- **Is there anything I should leave out to make my theme clearer?**

SHARING TIPS Invite groups to share their stories by reading them aloud to each other. Encourage them to say what they like best.

Children's Self Assessment

✔ Does someone help a friend do something in my story?

✔ Do I show the theme by what happens in the story?

Children may wish to carry this piece through the writing process described on pp. T288–291.

PORTFOLIO Use the Benchmarks to assess children's writing. Suggest that children add their drafts and revisions to their Literacy Portfolios.

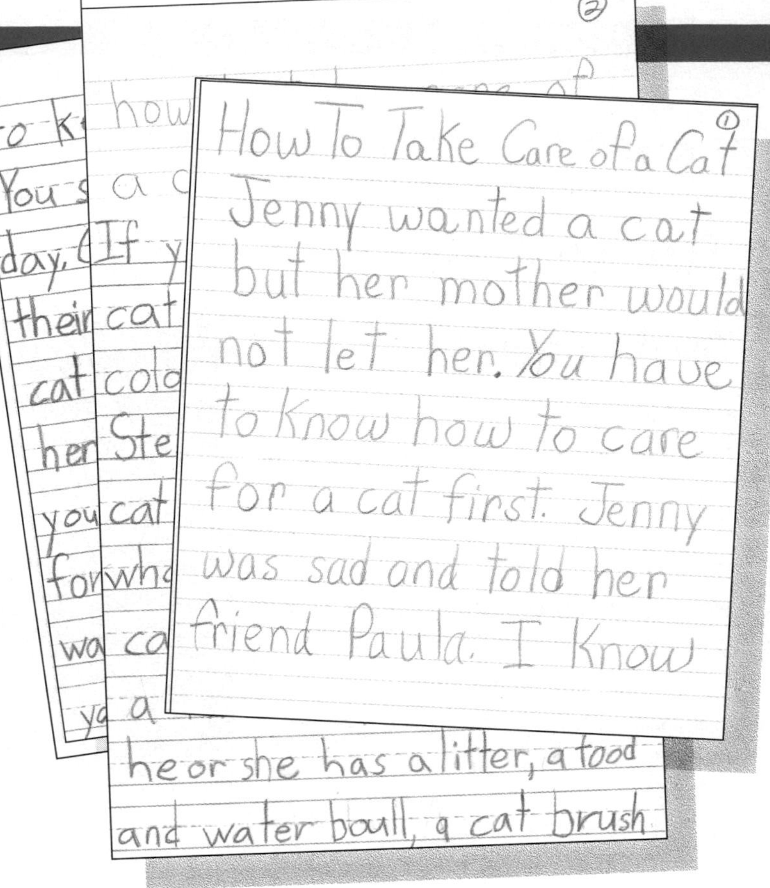

Proficient sample: Theme clearly relates to action.

Technology Options

Invite children to write their fictional pieces in the computer writing area. Suggest that they use the Record Tool during the prewriting stage, to record their ideas for writing. Encourage children to use the Paint Tools to illustrate their stories.

For more writing ideas, see the WiggleWorks Plus Teaching Plan.

SUPPORTING ALL LEARNERS

Step by Step

During Prewrite, divide children into cooperative groups to prepare for the Writing Event. Invite children to choose an idea about helping someone that they would like to write about. Then one child can help another while a third child verbalizes the process. Children can use the new vocabulary and word structures that they learn in this exercise to write their drafts.

ACCESS During Prewrite, after children have chosen their idea about helping someone, work with them to perform the actions involved and help them break these into steps. You may number and write the steps on the chalkboard so children can use them as a guide in the Writing Event.

CHILDREN'S WRITING BENCHMARKS		
Novice: The theme may not be present or may be stated rather than shown. Action in the story may not relate to the theme.	**Apprentice:** The theme is present in the action but is also stated. There is some action in the story that doesn't relate to the theme.	**Proficient:** The theme is clearly present in the action. There is little or no action in the story that doesn't relate to the theme.

b INTEGRATING LANGUAGE ARTS

LOUANNE PIG IN MAKING THE TEAM

SIMPLE SENTENCES

GRAMMAR

OBJECTIVE

Children will identify examples of simple sentences in *Louanne Pig in Making the Team* and in their own writing.

DEFINITION: A simple sentence has a naming part and a telling part that tell a complete thought.

SYNTACTIC CUEING

❶ Teach and Model

Explain that a simple sentence has a naming part (subject) and a telling part (verb) that together tell a complete thought. Write some groups of words on the chalkboard and have children decide which tell a complete thought.

I like animals
My best friend
I have a toy badger
went swimming today

❷ Put It in Context

Have children look through the story *Louanne Pig in Making the Team* to find additional examples of simple sentences. Call on volunteers to read the sentences that they find.

❸ Apply to Writing

Have children look at the stories they wrote checking to make sure that each sentence tells a complete thought.

- **How can you tell whether or not a group of words is a sentence?**

CAPITALIZING FIRST WORD

USAGE

OBJECTIVE

Children will identify the capitalized first word in sentences from the story and in sentences they write.

GUIDELINE: The first word in a sentence begins with a capital letter.

❶ Teach and Model

Have children look back at the first page of *Louanne Pig in Making the Team*. Call on volunteers to read the first word in each sentence and tell what kind of letter it begins with. Point out that the first word in a sentence begins with a capital letter.

❷ Put It in Context

Have children page through *Louanne Pig in Making the Team* to find other sentences. Call on volunteers to read the sentences they find and to confirm that each sentence begins with a capital letter.

❸ Apply to Writing

Have children look over the stories they wrote, focusing on the capitalization of the first word in each sentence. Suggest that children correct any sentences that do not begin with a capital letter.

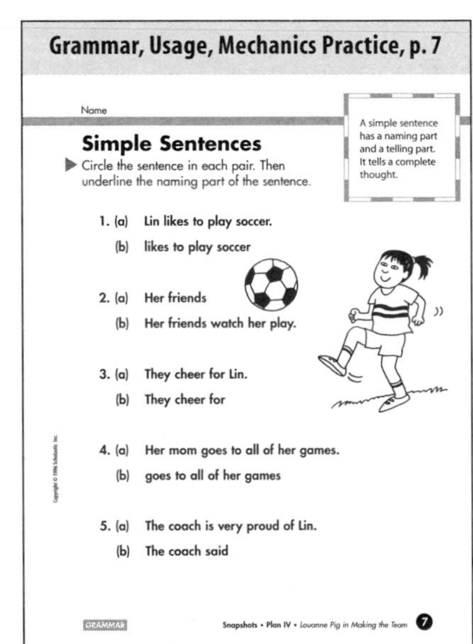

Grammar, Usage, Mechanics Practice, p. 7

Name

Simple Sentences

▶ Circle the sentence in each pair. Then underline the naming part of the sentence.

A simple sentence has a naming part and a telling part. It tells a complete thought.

1. (a) Lin likes to play soccer.
   (b) likes to play soccer
2. (a) Her friends
   (b) Her friends watch her play.
3. (a) They cheer for Lin.
   (b) They cheer for
4. (a) Her mom goes to all of her games.
   (b) goes to all of her games
5. (a) The coach is very proud of Lin.
   (b) The coach said

GRAMMAR — Snapshots • Plan IV • *Louanne Pig in Making the Team* 7

Grammar, Usage, Mechanics Practice, p. 8

Name

Capitalizing First Word

▶ Circle each sentence that is written correctly.

A sentence begins with a capital letter.

1. adam wants to play baseball.
2. The coach told him to show up for practice.
3. Adam and his mom met at the park.
4. they played catch.
5. he was ready.
6. Adam made the team.
7. He felt very proud.

▶ Write the other sentences correctly on the line.

8. ____________________
9. ____________________
10. ____________________

8 Snapshots • Plan IV • *Louanne Pig in Making the Team* — MECHANICS

Phonics Connection

You may first wish to do the phonics lesson on final *e* on pp. T200–201.

SPELLING

Words With Long *a, i*

game **make** **came** **same** **line** **mine** **bike** **time**

✷ Selection Vocabulary

PRETEST If you would like to pretest using test sentences, see Spelling Practice, p. 38.

OBJECTIVE

Children spell long *i* words.

❶ Teach

Write the words *game* and *time* on the chalkboard. Have children read the words and identify the vowel sound in each word. Ask what the two words have in common. *(They have long vowels, they end with* -me.*)* Point out that when a vowel is followed by a consonant and a silent *e*, the vowel sound usually is long.

Put It in Context

Write the following sentences based on *Louanne Pig in Making the Team* on the chalkboard. Have children read the sentences and identify the words with the long *a* and long *i* sounds.

Louanne will make the team.

There is still a little time.

❷ Practice

Have children copy and complete the following chart with list words:

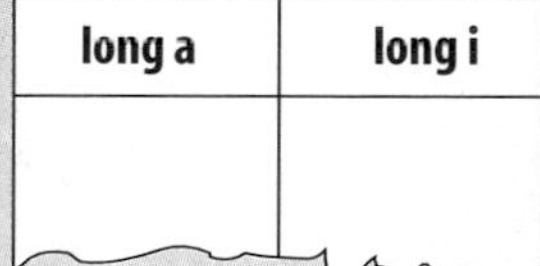

long a	long i

❸ Check

Apply to Writing

Have children use their spelling words to write three sentences about a team they would like to be on.

OPTION

Spell Teaser

The word *game* has more than one meaning. Have children use a dictionary to find both meanings of the word. Have them write sentences for both meanings. Challenge children to write one sentence using both meanings.

TEST To give the spelling test, ask children to write each word after you've spoken it and used it in a sentence. Write the list on the chalkboard and have children check and correct the spelling of the test words.

See Handwriting, p. 4, for practice writing the manuscript letters *L, I, T, E, F,* and *H*.

Spelling Practice, p. 4

SPELLING Name

WORDS WITH LONG a AND LONG i

line same mine came
bike game time make

Fill in the missing letters to make the words from the box. Write the words on the lines. Then connect the dots to make a picture.

GO TEAM!

1. make 4. line 7. same
2. bike 5. game 8. mine
3. time 6. came

4 Snapshots • Plan IV • Making the Team

READING/SPEAKING

ESL Role-Playing Good Friends

Materials:
SourceBook pp. 76–93

Time:
About 20 minutes

Suggested Grouping:
Partners

Ask pairs of children to role-play a few lines of dialogue between Arnie and Louanne after the football game is over. They may congratulate each other on their victory and talents.

Encourage children to reverse roles and role-play again.

WRITING

Write a Friendly Letter

GOOD FOR HOMEWORK

Materials:
Pencil
Paper

Time:
About 20 minutes

Suggested Grouping:
Individuals

Enhance children's self-esteem by inviting them to write friendly letters. Pair them up and have them address their letters to their partners. Children can write one or more sentences that tell something they think their partner does well.

Remind children that letters include the date, a greeting, a body, and a closing with a signature. Encourage them to write letters that are creative and fun. Have children share their friendly letters with their partners.

MINI-LESSON

FRIENDLY LETTER

TEACH/MODEL On the chalkboard, write the sample friendly letter, discuss each part, and label it.

*September 15, 19_*
Dear Arnie,

You are a great cheerleader. I like your cartwheels.

Your friend,
Louanne

APPLY Have children write their own friendly letters.

ACTIVITY FILE

LISTENING/SPEAKING

Create Cheers

GOOD FOR GRADING

Materials: Tape recorder (optional)

Time: About 15–20 minutes

Suggested Grouping: Cooperative groups

Invite children to share cheers they know, or offer some, such as "Two, four, six, eight! Who do we appreciate? Our class!"

Ask children to create original cheers. Mention that cheers are rhythmical and may rhyme. Most importantly, they show team spirit and good sportsmanship. Children might want to plan movements to accompany their cheers.

Encourage volunteers to perform their cheers or tape-record them to share with others.

How to Grade When grading, look for spirit and rhythm or rhyme. If performing, children should speak in appropriate volumes and expressions.

MINI-LESSON

Rhythm and Rhyme

TEACH/MODEL Read a poem, tapping out the rhythm as you read aloud. Have children identify rhyming words in the poem—words that have the same ending sounds.

APPLY Have children read simple rhymes, tapping out the rhythm as they read. Ask volunteers to tell which words rhyme. Write several one-syllable words on the chalkboard, and have children offer rhyming words for each.

READING/WRITING/SPEAKING

Ask the Pros

Materials: Computer, or paper and pencils

Time: About 20 minutes

Suggested Grouping: Cooperative groups

Introduce the activity by asking children, "Is there a knack for helping someone else learn to do something?" Explain that, often, lending a hand is enough. Other times, it's important to give the person clear directions and then to demonstrate.

Encourage children to interview a gym teacher, a music teacher, or an art teacher to find out how they teach games, songs, or art projects.

Invite children to list in the SourceBook Activities writing area several questions they want to ask the teachers and then print the list. Children can then write the responses on the printout.

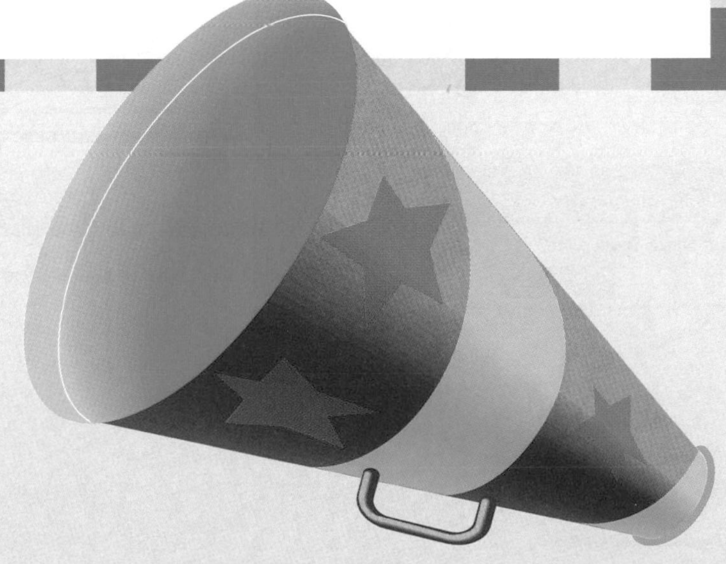

C

BUILDING SKILLS AND STRATEGIES

LOUANNE PIG IN MAKING THE TEAM

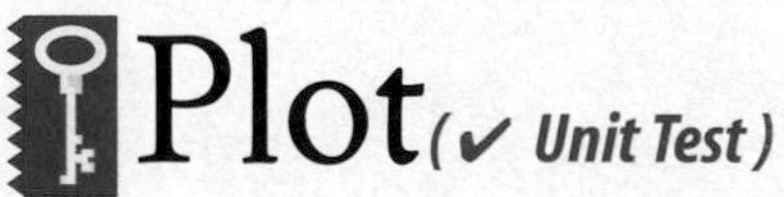

Plot (✔ Unit Test)

Objectives

Children learn to:

- identify the plot of a story
- transfer their learning to a new text

Review:

- see Character (p. R16)

Materials:
SourceBook pp. 76–93
Transparency 8
Literacy-at-Work Book pp. 40–42

Time:
About 30 minutes

Suggested Grouping:
Whole class and partners

TESTED	
KEY STRATEGY	
PLOT	
Introduce	p. T196
Review	p. R18
Test	p. T311
Reteach	p. R25

Literacy-at-Work Book, p. 40

Name PLOT

Teamwork

▶ Number the sentences to show the order in which they happened in the story.

4 Arnie tries out but does not make the football team.

2 Louanne and Arnie help each other practice.

5 Louanne tries out for and makes the football team.

6 Arnie tries out for and makes the cheerleading team.

1 Louanne and Arnie want to try out for teams.

3 Louanne tries out but does not make the cheerleading team.

40 Unit 1 • Snapshots • Plan IV • Louanne Pig in Making the Team

✔ Quickcheck

As children read *Louanne Pig in Making the Team*, did they:

✔ identify the important related events that make up the story?

YES **If yes, go to ❷ Practice and Apply.**

NO **If no, start at ❶ Teach and Model.**

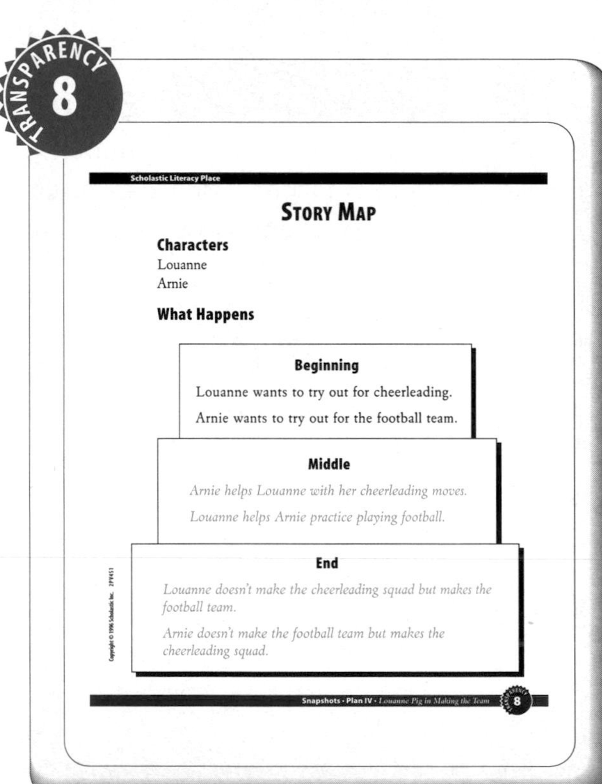

TRANSPARENCY 8

Scholastic Literacy Place

STORY MAP

Characters
Louanne
Arnie

What Happens

Beginning
Louanne wants to try out for cheerleading.
Arnie wants to try out for the football team.

Middle
Arnie helps Louanne with her cheerleading moves.
Louanne helps Arnie practice playing football.

End
Louanne doesn't make the cheerleading squad but makes the football team.
Arnie doesn't make the football team but makes the cheerleading squad.

Snapshots • Plan IV • Louanne Pig in Making the Team 8

Annotated transparency for teaching Plot

❶ Teach and Model

Invite children to tell about a favorite story or movie they have read or seen. Ask them to tell who the characters are and what happens to them at the beginning, middle, and end of the story. Encourage children to tell about the most important events only. When they finish, discuss how telling about the important events helps them enjoy and understand the story better.

Put It in Context

Have children turn back to *Louanne Pig in Making the Team.* Discuss how thinking about who the characters are and what happens to them in each part of the story helps them to enjoy and understand the story more.

Think Aloud **When I think about the story of *Louanne Pig in Making the Team*, I try to remember the most important events in the story. I think about what happens to Louanne and Arnie in the beginning as they both try to make the team. I also think about what good friends they are and what they do to help each other in the middle of the story. And finally, I think about how they encourage each other to the very end.**

Have children identify the important events that took place at the beginning of the story. Display Transparency 8 and explain how the story map can be used to help keep track of the events in the story.

❷ Practice and Apply

Complete a Story Map

PARTNERS Have children work in pairs to find other important events in the middle and end of the story. Distribute a story map like the one on the transparency for children to complete. Then ask questions such as the following to prompt children about events in the middle of the story:

- **What do Louanne and Arnie do to prepare for the tryouts?**
- **What do we learn about Louanne's and Arnie's ability to play football?**
- **What do we learn about their ability as cheerleaders?**

The following questions can help children identify the events at the end of the story:

- **How well does Louanne do at the cheerleading tryouts?**
- **How about Arnie? How well does he do?**
- **What do Louanne and Arnie learn about themselves at the end of the story?**

❸ Assess

Can children identify the plot of the story?

✔ **Can children identify the events in the beginning, the middle, and the end of the story?**

If not, try this:
Use the Review lesson on Plot with Plan VI. Have children continue to identify plots in their Journals.

Children's Self-Assessment

✔ **How did I determine the events in each part of the story?**

SUPPORTING ALL LEARNERS

Graphic Device

ESL The story map is a useful tool that can help second-language learners organize information. During Practice and Apply, help children break the story into beginning, middle, and end and enter each event on the story map. Then have children use the map to retell the plot.

CHALLENGE Children can use their imaginations to create a variation of the story. Following Practice and Apply, encourage them to select one of the three story events and substitute it for an imaginary story event. Challenge them to use these three events to create a new story they can share with their classmates.

Transfer to New Text

Literacy-at-Work Book, p. 41

READ NEW TEXT: Fiction

Name

That's What Friends Are For

by Lisa Chu

Read the story. Use it to finish page 42.

Vera the Butterfly and Morgan the Spider were best friends.

They did everything together. They often wore the same clothes and read the same books. They both played in the same band at school. They even had the same birthday. Vera always had her party in the morning. Morgan always had his party in the afternoon.

Their birthday was one week away. Vera wanted to give Morgan a nice gift. But she had no money.

Vera said, "Let's start our own band. We can play for money."

Morgan liked the idea.

Morgan and Vera put up posters. They passed them around to friends. But no one gave them a job.

Morgan had an idea. Morgan played and sang at Vera's party in the morning.

Vera had an idea, too. She played and sang at Morgan's party in the afternoon.

Both friends thought it was the best gift.

Unit 1 • Snapshots • Plan IV • *Louanne Pig in Making the Team* 41

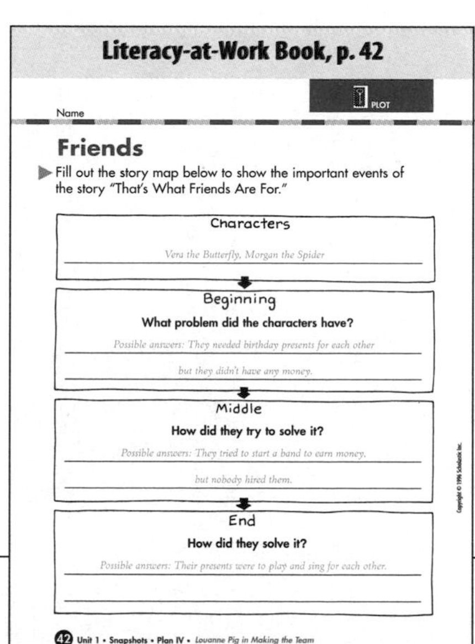

Literacy-at-Work Book, p. 42

PLOT

Name

Friends

Fill out the story map below to show the important events of the story "That's What Friends Are For."

Characters

Vera the Butterfly, Morgan the Spider

Beginning

What problem did the characters have?

Possible answers: They needed birthday presents for each other but they didn't have any money.

Middle

How did they try to solve it?

Possible answers: They tried to start a band to earn money, but nobody hired them.

End

How did they solve it?

Possible answers: Their presents were to play and sing for each other.

42 Unit 1 • Snapshots • Plan IV • *Louanne Pig in Making the Team*

C

LOUANNE PIG IN MAKING THE TEAM

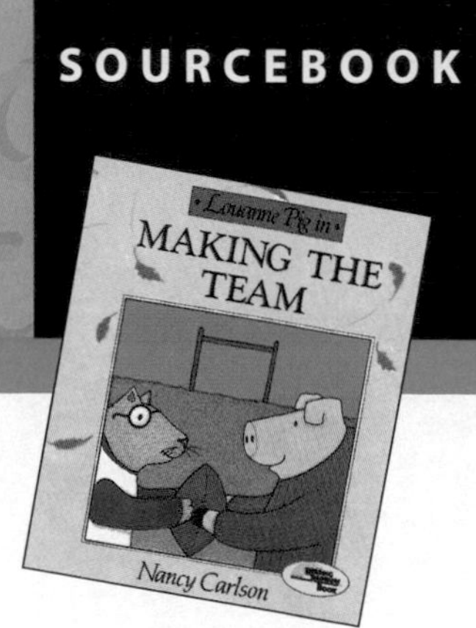

3-Letter Blends

Objectives

Children learn to:

- identify the sounds of three-letter blends: *sch, spl, squ,* and *thr*
- build words that contain *sch, spl, squ,* and *thr*
- write words with three-letter blends

PHONICS AT A GLANCE

Materials:
SourceBook pp. 76–93
Big Book of Rhymes and Rhythms 2A, pp. 10–11
Tracking Device (optional)
Word Building Cards *sch, spl, squ, thr*
Magnet Board
Literacy-at-Work Book pp. 44–45

Time:
About 15–30 minutes

Suggested Grouping:
Whole class or cooperative groups

Literacy-at-Work Book, p. 44

Literacy-at-Work Book, p. 45

Name

PHONICS: 3-Letter Blends

Book Titles

Use the words in the box to finish the title of each book.

Splash
School
Three
Squeeze

The Best School in the Land

The Three Frogs Hop Home

The Biggest Splash of the Summer

How to Squeeze an Orange

Use at least two words in the box to write your own book titles.

squeal split threw

1 ______

2 ______

Unit 1 • Snapshots • Plan IV • Louanne Pig in Making the Team 45

✔ Quickcheck

As children worked their way through *Louanne Pig in Making the Team,* did they:

✔ recognize the letters/sounds in print?

✔ think of a word that begins with a three-letter blend?

YES **If yes, go to the Blending section of 2 Connect Sound/Symbol.**

NO **If no, start at 1 Develop Oral Language.**

1 Develop Oral Language

Phonemic Awareness

Read aloud the poem "My Shoes" from the Big Book of Rhymes and Rhythms. On second and third readings, ask children to join in and read the poem chorally or to echo you. Let volunteers track the print with a pointer. After a few readings, children should be able to recite the rhyme themselves.

Focus on the sounds of the three-letter blend words. Have children say the words *squeaky, splashy, threw,* and *school* after you. These words said together are a bit of a tongue twister. Give children a chance to practice aloud among themselves.

Big Book of Rhymes and Rhythms

My Shoes

My shoes are new and squeaky shoes,
They're very shiny, creaky shoes,
I wish I had my splashy, leaky shoes
That my mother threw away.

I liked my splashy, leaky shoes,
Much better than these creaky shoes,
These shiny, creaky, squeaky shoes
Will be no fun at school today.

squeaky
splashy
threw
school

10–11

❷ Connect Sound/Symbol

Put It in Context

On the chalkboard, write these sentences;

One day Louanne and Arnie found something exciting on the school bulletin board.

Tryouts for the cheerleading squad and the football team were coming up.

Louanne was doing pretty well . . . until she came to the split jump.

She picked up the football and threw it to Arnie.

Underline the letters *spl* in *split,* and ask children to listen for the beginning sounds as you blend and point to each letter. Repeat for the blends in *school, squad,* and *threw.*

Blending

On the chalkboard, write the three-letter blends *spl, squ,* and *thr*. Tell children that by adding letters to these blends, you can create many different words. For example, add the letters *ash* to *spl* to make the word *splash.* Encourage children to make other words beginning with these blends.

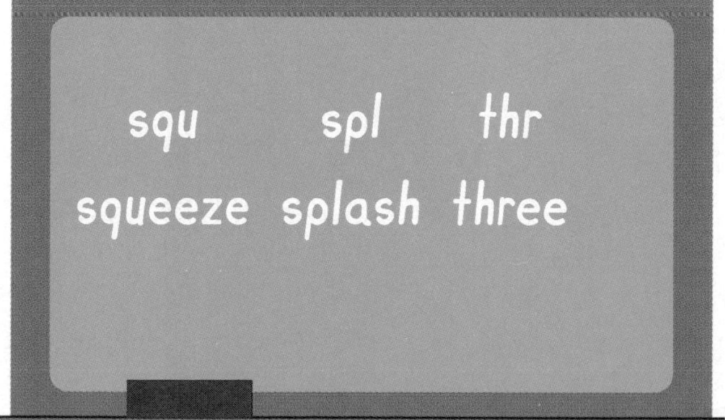

❸ Assess

Write

As a way of assessing children's understanding of these three-letter blends, ask them to write *splish* on a piece of paper. Encourage them to change the three-letter blend to make a new word. They may be able to make other words.

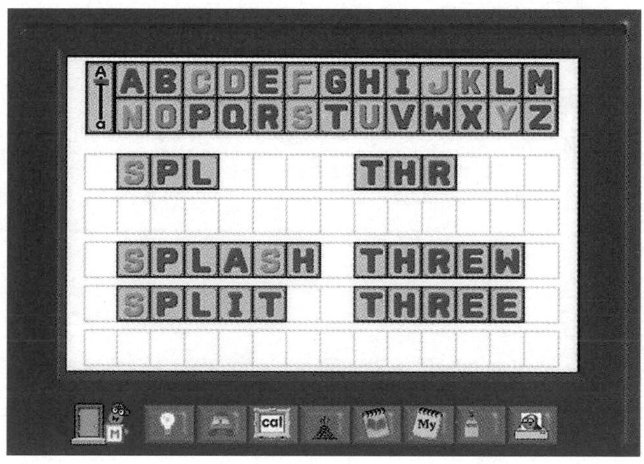

SPLISH SPLASH CARDS

Using some of the words that children suggested earlier and others, encourage children to make three-letter-blend word cards. Play on the idea of flash cards and have children use their "Splish-Splash Cards."

See Phonics and Word Building Kit for additional suggestions.

The Magnet Board activity pictured above provides additional phonics practice. For information on this and other Magnet Board activities, see the WiggleWorks Plus Teaching Plan.

SUPPORTING ALL LEARNERS

Hands-On Learning

ESL Three-letter blends can be very challenging for second-language learners to pronounce. During the Connect Sound/Symbol activity, encourage children to write the blend words on the Magnet Board. Then they can click on each word and listen to its pronounciation until they feel comfortable reading it aloud.

ACCESS During the Blending activity, activate the scanning function on the Magnet Board to facilitate participation of children with physical disabilities. Children can write their own word list on the computer and then share it with classmates.

C

LOUANNE PIG IN MAKING THE TEAM

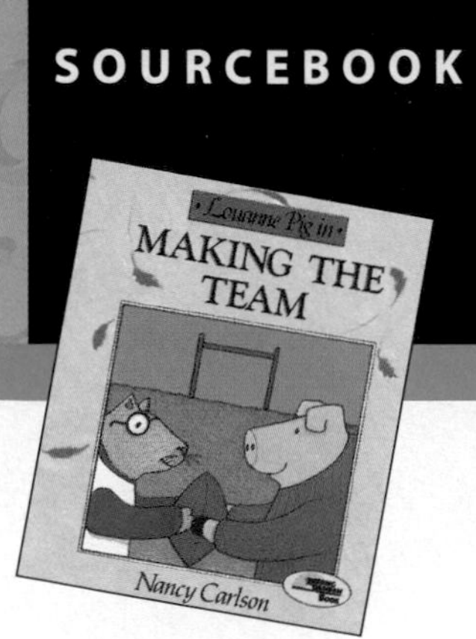

Final *e*

Objectives

Children learn to:

- identify words with the long sound in the CVC*e* pattern
- build words that contain CVC*e*
- write CVC*e* words

PHONICS AT A GLANCE

Materials:
SourceBook pp.76–93
Big Book of Rhymes and Rhythms 2A, pp. 12–13
Word Building Card Ee
Magnet Board
Literacy-at-Work Book pp. 46–47
Spelling Lesson p.T193

Time:
About 15–30 minutes

Suggested Grouping:
Whole class or cooperative groups

✔ Quickcheck

As children worked their way through *Louanne Pig in Making the Team,* did they:

✔ recognize words with the CVC*e* pattern in print?

✔ think of a word with a long vowel sound that ends in *e*?

YES **If yes, go to the Blending section of 2 Connect Sound/Symbol.**

NO **If no, start at 1 Develop Oral Language.**

1 Develop Oral Language

Phonemic Awareness

Read aloud "Five in the Hive" from the Big Book of Rhymes and Rhythms. Read the poem for enjoyment. On repeated readings, ask children to join in and read the poem chorally.

Focus on the sounds of the CVC*e* words. Have children say the words *five* and *hive* after you. Ask whether the vowel sound they hear in each word is long or short. Direct attention to the final *e* in each word. Explain that when children see a word with the pattern consonant-vowel-consonant–final *e*, the first vowel letter is usually pronounced with a long vowel sound and the *e* is silent.

Big Book of Rhymes and Rhythms

Five in the Hive

Over in the meadow,
In a snug little hive,
Lived an old mother bee,
And her baby bees five.
"Buzz," said the mother.
"We buzz," said the five.
So they buzzed all day,
In a snug little hive.

hive

12–13

Literacy-at-Work Book, p. 46

Name PHONICS: Final *e*

Literacy-at-Work Book, p. 47

Name PHONICS: Final *e*

Pick a Word

▶ Read each sentence. Circle the word that makes sense in the sentence. Write the word on the line.

1. He wrote a (not, note) to his wife. note
2. The whole class made a (mat, mate) for the doorway. mat
3. We rode a mile to school on the (hug, huge) bus. huge
4. It was too late to (hid, hide) the gift. hide
5. She (cut, cute) the apple and ate a big bite. cut
6. He went down the (slid, slide) five times. slide
7. I (hop, hope) to win a football at the game. hope
8. He (can, cane) drive the white car. can

▶ Underline all the words in the sentences with final *e*.

Unit 1 • Snapshots • Plan IV • *Louanne Pig in Making the Team* 47

❷ Connect Sound/Symbol

Put It in Context

On the chalkboard, write "That fall Roosevelt School won every game." Underline the final *e* in the word *game*. Read that word aloud, emphasizing the long vowel sound. Then invite children to page through *Louanne Pig in Making the Team* to find other words with the CVC*e* pattern. Write words as they are offered.

Blending

Explain to children how to change the vowel sound in a word from short to long by adding final *e*:

THINK ALOUD I can use *bit* to make another word. If I add *e* to the end of the word, the word becomes *bite*. Listen to the difference in the vowel sounds: *bit, bite*. Now who would like to add *e* to the end of *can* to make *cane?*

Provide a variety of words to which final *e* can be added. Encourage volunteers to come up to the chalkboard and make different words by adding final *e*.

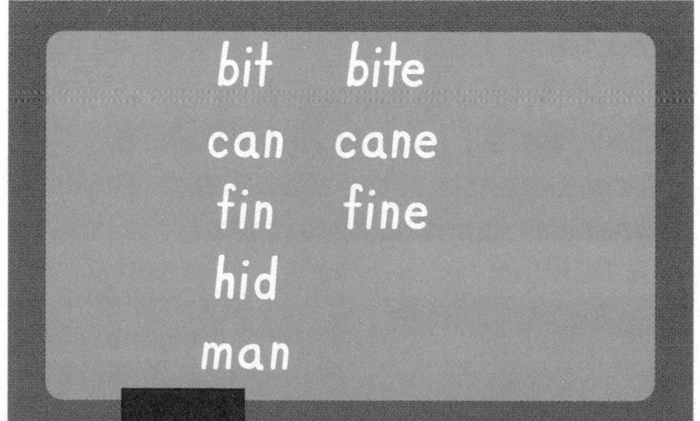

❸ Assess

Write

As a way of assessing children's understanding of the vowel sound in CVC*e* pattern words, write "_*a*_*e*" on the chalkboard and invite groups of children to make words. Groups can share their words with the class by writing them on chart paper.

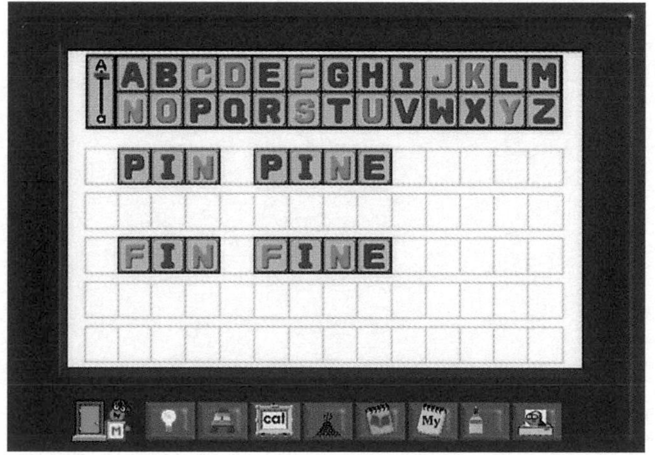

ADD AN *E* WORD MATCH
Invite pairs of children to make cards for CVC and CVCe words. For example, *pan* and *pane*. Have them illustrate each card on the reverse side. Invite children to play a matching game with the completed set of cards.

See Phonics and Word Building Kit for additional suggestions.

The Magnet Board activity pictured above provides additional practice with phonics. For information on this and other Magnet Board activities, see the WiggleWorks Plus Teaching Plan.

SUPPORTING ALL LEARNERS

Use Word Cards

EXTRA HELP Letter cards will provide children with hands-on practice making words that end in *e*. During the Develop Oral Language activity, write a list of three-letter CVC words on the chalkboard. Encourage children to take turns saying each word aloud. Then they can place the *e* card at the end of the word and say the new word aloud.

CHALLENGE Following the Phonics lesson, encourage children to write a list of two-syllable words that end in CVC on the chalkboard. Challenge them to hold up the *e* card at the end of each word and determine which new words are real words.

BUILDING FLUENCY

Objectives

Children read *Two Crazy Pigs* for fluency.

Technology Options

Encourage children to isten to the audiocassette recording of *Two Crazy Pigs*.

Two Crazy Pigs

Written by Karen Berman Nagel
Illustrated by Brian Schatell

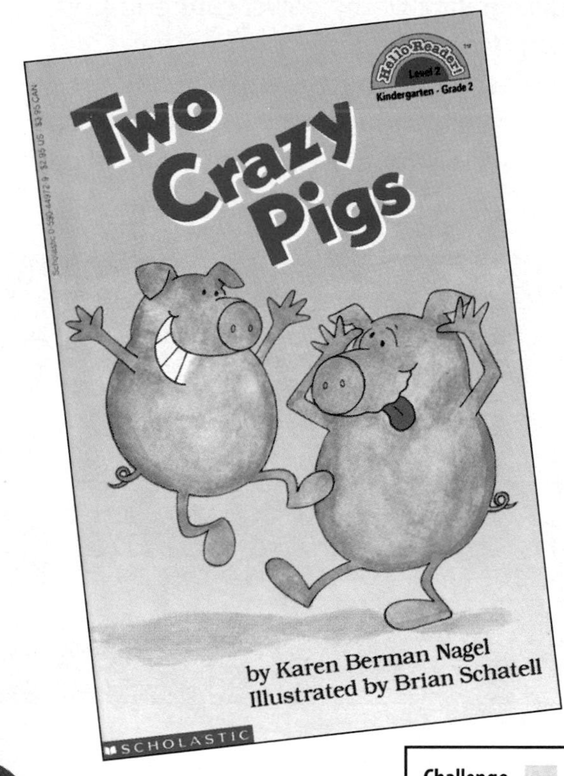

Challenge
Average
Easy

PREVIEW AND READ

Help children read the title and the names of the author and the illustrator. As they flip through the book, ask them to take note of the pictures.

- **Do you think this looks like a fun book to read? What makes you think that?**
- **Look at the expressions on the pigs' faces. What do you think the pigs are thinking about?** VISUAL LITERACY

RESPONSE IDEAS

After children have read the book, they can meet with you or a partner to discuss the story. Questions such as these will help:

- **Why did Mr. and Mrs. Fenster ask the two pigs to leave?**
- **Why were the other animals sorry that the two pigs left?**

Read Across Texts

- **Think about what happened at the end of *Two Crazy Pigs* and *Louanne Pig in Making the Team.* Did either of the endings surprise you? What was surprising about them?**

Shoebox Library For more independent reading opportunities choose books from the Shoebox Library.

CONNECTING TO THE OTHER TRADE BOOKS

Frog and Toad Are Friends

by Arnold Lobel

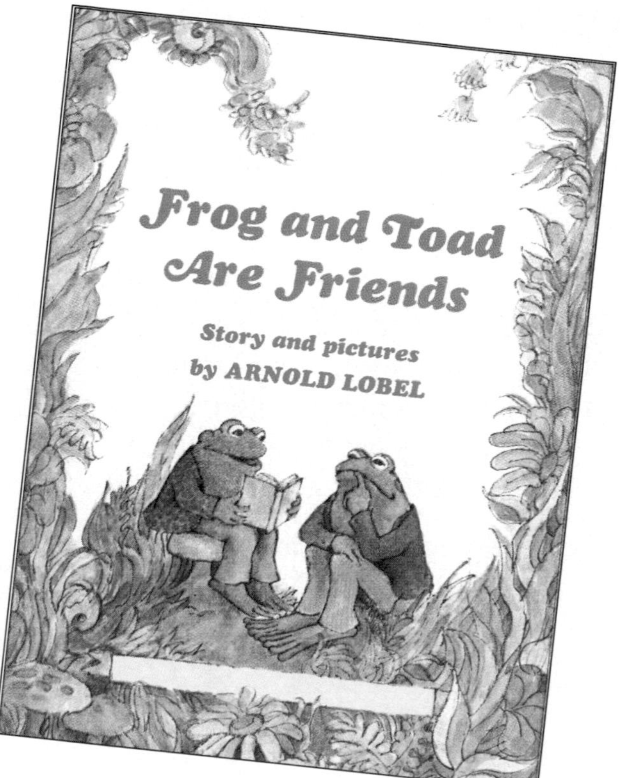

Challenge
Average
Easy

MAKE THEME CONNECTIONS:

FRIENDS HELPING FRIENDS

Talk About It

Good friends help each other in many ways. In *Louanne Pig in Making the Team,* children discover that good friends help each other be successful, even if the results are not what's expected. In *Frog and Toad Are Friends,* children discover that friends help each other in many other ways, too.

- **How do Frog and Toad help each other?**
- **Do you think Frog and Toad make a good team? Why?**

Write About It

After reading *Frog and Toad Are Friends,* invite children to write about a good friend. They can write about what they do together and tell why this friend is so special.

Read Across Texts

After children have finished *Frog and Toad Are Friends,* encourage them to compare this book with *Louanne Pig in Making the Team.* Have them explore such questions as:

- **Frog and Toad cheer each other up when one of them is sad. What other things do they do for each other? What do Louanne and Arnie do for each other?**
- **How are these pairs of friends alike? How are they different?**

USING THE TRADE BOOK GUIDE

For in-depth teaching ideas, refer to the individual Trade Book Guide for *Frog and Toad Are Friends* by Arnold Lobel.

Ask children to compare the friendships between Chester and Wilson and Louanne and Arnie.

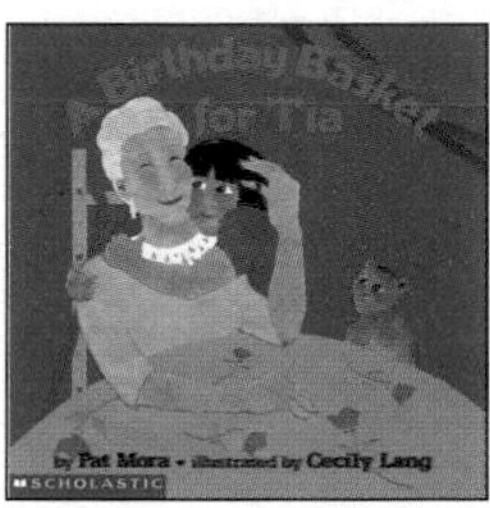

Ask children to think about what Cecilia put into the basket for her great-aunt. What might Louanne put into a birthday basket for Arnie?

Also for use with this plan

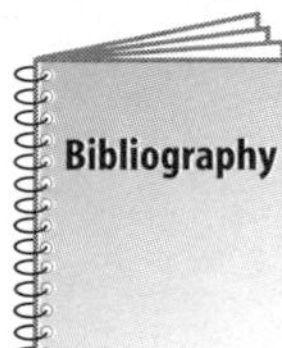

INTEGRATING LEARNING

Curriculum Areas

Math

Children compare ratios by keeping score in a classroom game.
See page R8.

Science

Children find out how physical activity affects their heartbeat.
See page R8.

Social Studies

Children list the ways that various players contribute to their teams.
See page R9.

The Arts

Children make a pennant for a school team.
See page R9

Use Your Sports Arena

I'd Like to Be a . . .

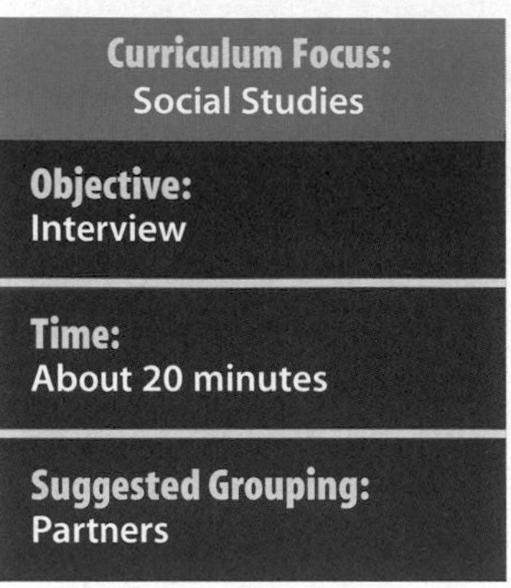
Curriculum Focus: Social Studies

Objective: Interview

Time: About 20 minutes

Suggested Grouping: Partners

ACTIVITY Children choose sports-related jobs and interview one another in character.

Connect to the SourceBook Discuss with children what the characters in *Louanne Pig in Making the Team* thought they wanted to do and what they found they liked to do.

Make New Discoveries

- Explain that not everybody in sports is an athlete or a cheerleader. There are coaches, team managers, team owners, referees and umpires, sports equipment designers, sports-equipment store owners, stadium designers, sports announcers, sports physicians, physical therapists, sports artists, sports photographers, sports reporters, and the list goes on and on.
- Ask children to choose a sports-related job that sounds interesting to them from the list above, or from any others that you or they are aware of.
- Partners can interview one another in the Sports Arena. For starters, children can ask each other why they want to be a ____ and what they would do as a ____.

✔ **How to Assess** Were children able to interview one another?

WORKSHOP 2

Objectives

- Children note consistencies.
- Children make a pictograph about a topic of their choice.

Materials:
Crayons or markers
Posterboard
Scissors
Tape or paste
Magazines (optional)
Ruler
Literacy-at-Work Book p. 48
Index cards

Time:
About 40 minutes

Suggested Grouping:
Whole class

Curriculum Connections:
Math
The Arts

Invite children to find symbols for their graphs in their computer Stamp Art collection.

How to Make a Graph

WHY DO THIS WORKSHOP?

Leaf through any newspaper or magazine and you're likely to find an assortment of graphs. You'll see graphs that show the latest trends, from the top occupations of the future to public-opinion polls on every topic imaginable. The images and graphics used for graphs can be simple or complex. You may see graph information presented in lines, pies, bars, pictures, or with computer generated symbols. To communicate numerical comparisons quickly and clearly, graphs are an obvious tool.

This Workshop will help children understand the advantages of presenting abstract data in concrete visual form. In making pictographs, children learn to manipulate and arrange picture symbols to present an easy-to-grasp image of class opinions on a chosen topic.

Getting Started

UNIT SKILL:

NOTE CONSISTENCIES

JOURNAL Review the pictograph on side 1 of the Workshop Card. Point out that you have to count the pictures to get a total number. Explain how the graph allows you to compare information about different pets. Ask these questions to focus children on the Workshop.

- **How many kinds of pets does the graph show?**

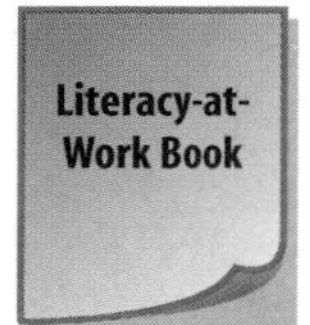

Use page 48 of the Literacy-at-Work Book as support for the Workshop or as a separate activity to develop the Workshop skills.

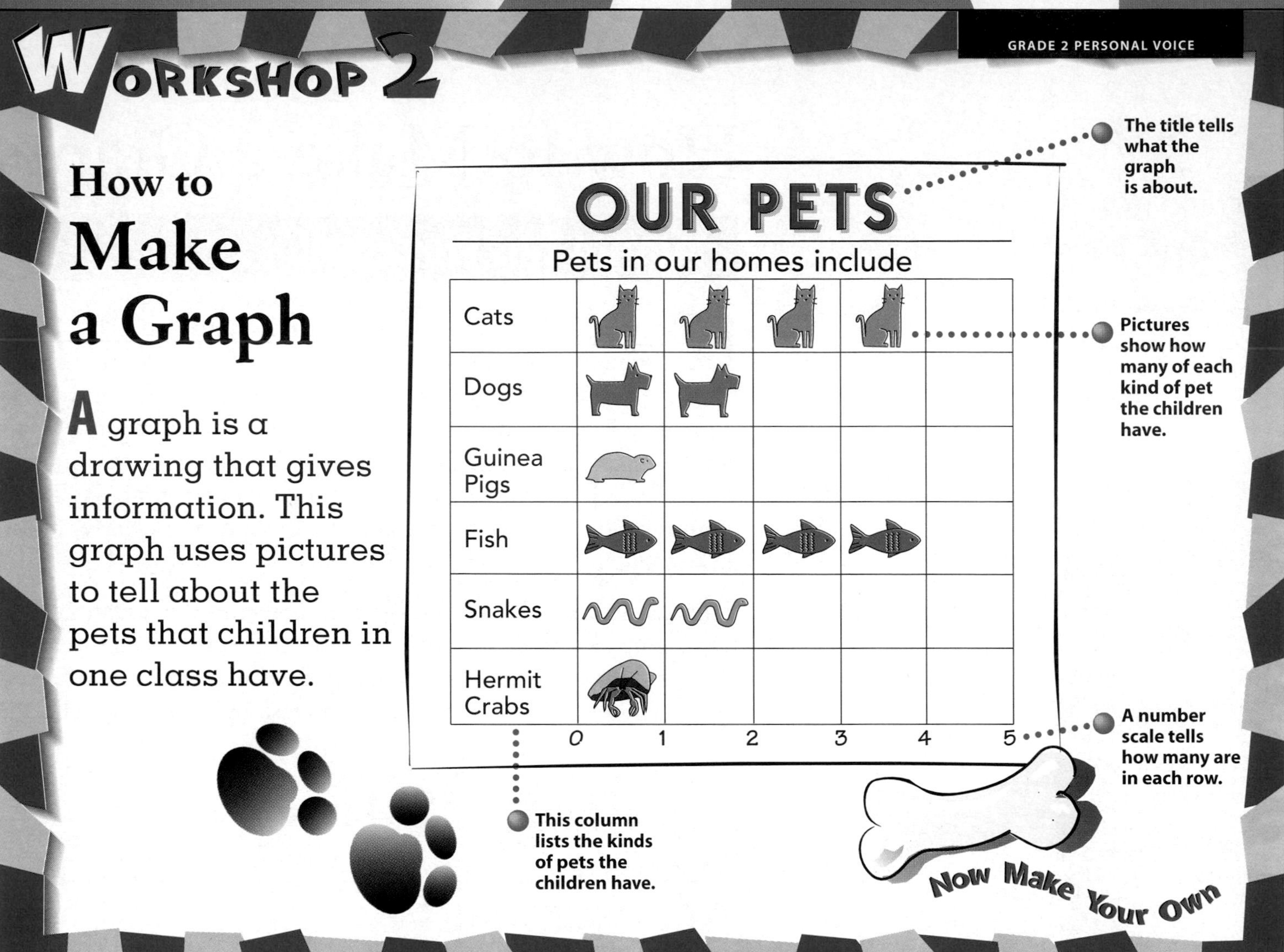

❶ Choose a Topic

Discuss a variety of topics children might like to make a class graph about, such as favorite television programs, songs, or toys. Write the topics on the chalkboard. Have children take a vote to pick the topic they want to graph. If children have difficulty using a graph, you might want to use the Study Skill lesson plan on pages T208 and T209 of your Teacher's SourceBook.

WHOLE CLASS Hang a large piece of posterboard in the front of the classroom so that volunteers can draw lines for the graph.

❷ Make a Class Graph

Make sure children think of at least four categories for the topic. If the topic is favorite fruits, you may suggest a choice between apples, bananas, oranges, or grapes. On the posterboard, ask for volunteers to draw a graph outline like the one on the Workshop Card. Have volunteers write the graph title at the top and list the categories along the left side. Make sure children understand that each picture will stand for the vote of one classmate.

CONNECT TO HOME AND COMMUNITY

Have children ask an older friend or relative to leaf through newspapers and magazines with them to find graphs. Have children list the different types of graphs they find.

SHOP

1 Choose a Topic

What would you like your graph to show about your class? Think about favorite:

- colors
- foods
- games
- books

List other ideas. With your class, choose what you want to make a graph about.

2 Make a Class Graph

- Write a title at the top.
- Write all the words that name favorite things on the left.
- Draw or cut out a picture to show which is your favorite.
- Put your picture in the correct row.
- Find out how many there are in each row.

THINK!
Encourage children to think of topics that haven't been mentioned, such as video games, sports, music, and so on.

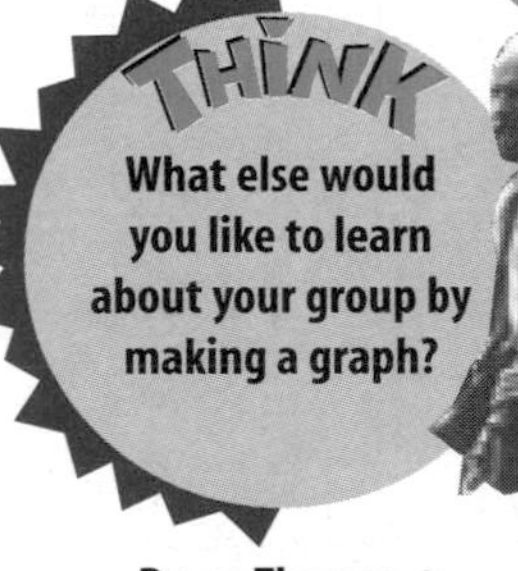

Bruce Thorson ▸ Photographer

ONGOING ASSESSMENT — PERFORMANCE-BASED

Review children's class graph. Ask yourself:

✔ How did children select their symbols or pictures?
✔ Did children graph all the votes?
✔ Did children select an appropriate graph title?

If not, try this:

In upcoming selections, have children vote for their favorite story and make a pictograph of the class survey.

Children's Self-Assessment

✔ Do I know what a pictograph is?

PORTFOLIO

Portfolio Opportunity
Children may want to draw a copy of the class pictograph or take the drawing of the category they voted for and put it in their Portfolios.

CHILDREN'S WORKSHOP BENCHMARKS		
Novice: Children understand how symbols are used on graphs but may not be able to interpret all the information on graphs.	**Apprentice:** Children understand how a graph shows a group's ideas; children can draw pictures for a pictograph. Children may have trouble explaining a graph mathematically.	**Proficient:** Children understand what symbols on a graph mean and can explain what different numbers of symbols indicate. Children also can describe how a graph shows a group's ideas.

WORK

STUDY SKILL

Objective

Children learn how to use graphs to acquire information.

Materials:
Examples of pictographs from encyclopedias, newspapers, and magazines
Workshop Card 1:
Literacy-at-Work Book pp.49-50

Time:
About 30 minutes

Suggested Grouping:
Individuals and cooperative groups

TESTED	
KEY STRATEGY	
GRAPHS	
Introduce	p. T208
Review	p. R23
Test	p. T311
Reteach	p. R27

Use Graphs to Acquire Information

✔ QUICKCHECK

As children completed their Workshops, did they:

- ✔ realize that a graph organizes and presents information?
- ✔ recognize that their pictograph showed the class's ideas about a topic?

YES **If yes, go to ❷ Practice and Apply.**

NO **If no, start at ❶ Teach and Model.**

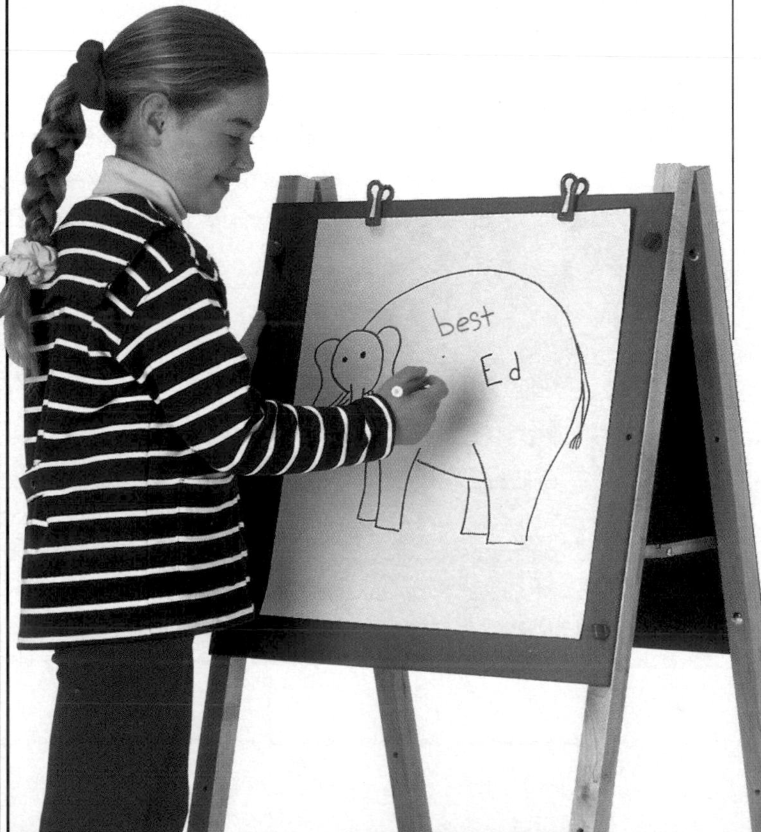

❶ Teach and Model

Put It in Context

Ask children to review their Workshops for a moment. Then discuss the kind of information they can get from graphs. Remind them to think about the pictograph shown on side 1 of the Workshop Card, as well as the one they made. Have children explain what the titles of both graphs tell them (what the surveys are about). Point out that the class graph shows the number of children who chose a specific category. Which category is the most popular? Explain that the graph is called a pictograph because it uses pictures to describe the categories, or items.

Point out that many books and magazines use graphs to compare figures because graphs are clear and easy to read. You may want to display for children some simple graphs, and have them describe what each one shows. Ask children to recall graphs they've seen. Where did they see them? What did the graphs look like? What type of information did the graphs show?

❷ Practice and Apply

Use Graphs

Children can practice using graphs by filling in the graph on pages 49–50 of the Literacy-at-Work Book. After children complete the activity, ask these questions:

- **Why is a graph a good way to keep track of the amount of money you spend?**
- **Can you think of another way to keep track of how much you spend?**
- **Do you think it is easier to read a picture graph or a list? Explain.**
- **What other things can you keep track of with a picture graph?**

Cooperative Groups Have children find the answers to the above questions. Ask a volunteer to report each group's answers.

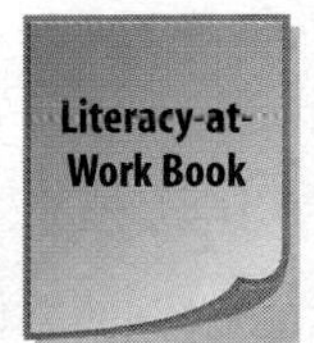

The Study Skill worksheet on pp. 49-50 of the Literacy-at-Work Book gives children practice in using pictographs.

OPTION

Transfer to New Media

Review the pictographs you brought in for the Workshop. Ask children to describe the type of information that each pictograph gives. Have children tell what the picture symbols stand for. You might want to ask specific questions about each graph.

❸ Assess

After children have finished the Study Skill activity, review their work. Ask yourself:

✔ How did children fill in the graph?

✔ Did children know how many items to color in?

✔ Do children know how to read the completed graphs?

If not,try this:

Look for upcoming selections that might be interesting to children. List the titles on the chalkboard, with a short description of each. Ask each child to vote for a title. Write the number of votes next to each title and have children make a pictograph.

Children's Self-Assessment

✔ Can I use a pictograph to count things?

✔ Can I use the pictograph to compare things?

Supporting All Learners

Use Rhythm

EXTRA HELP Children have a natural knack of tying together information with song. During the lesson, direct children's song-making abilities to reinforce their understanding of the pictograph in the Workshop Card. For each symbol, work with children in choosing simple chants that relate to the information. Culminate this playful activity by leading children in a rhyme.

ESL For children acquiring English, using rhythm may be a good strategy to learn how a symbol can represent a group of things in a chart. Work with children in cooperative groups to develop some simple, repetitive, chants. The number of repetitions will depend on the number of items in each category on the pictograph.

3

SECTION

When we try our best, we find out how much we can do.

Make Your Mark

Read all about George Ancona, a photographer.
He makes books for children.

•

Find out what happens when Grace tries her best.
Then meet Larry Malvern, who did his best as Peter Pan!

WHAT'S IN THIS SECTION?

Plan V

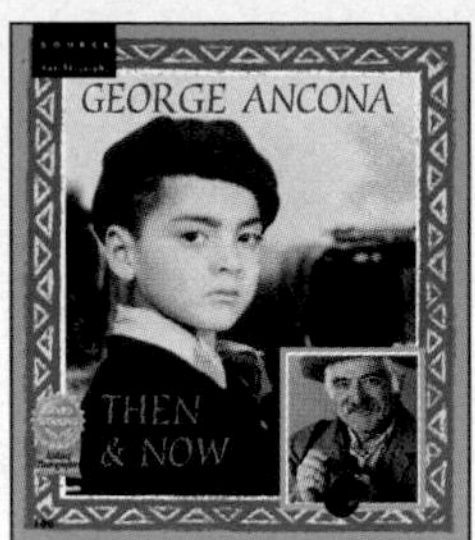

▲ *George Ancona: Then & Now*
by George Ancona
Autobiography

Plan VI

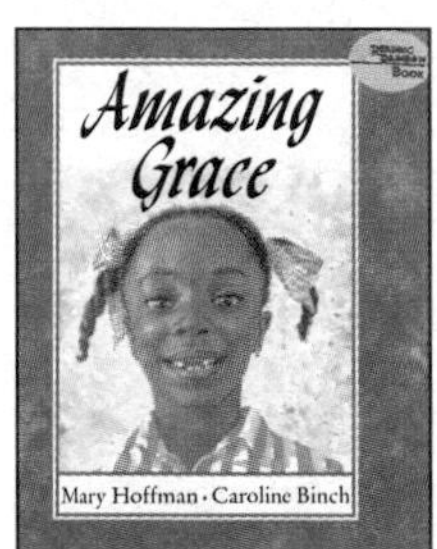

▲ *Amazing Grace*
by Mary Hoffman
Realistic Fiction

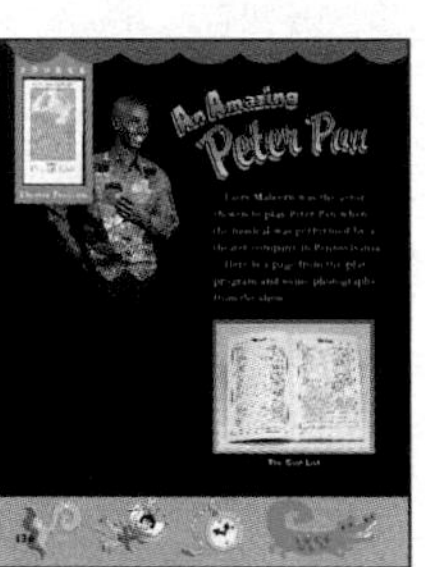

▲ "An Amazing Peter Pan"
Theater Program

PROJECT

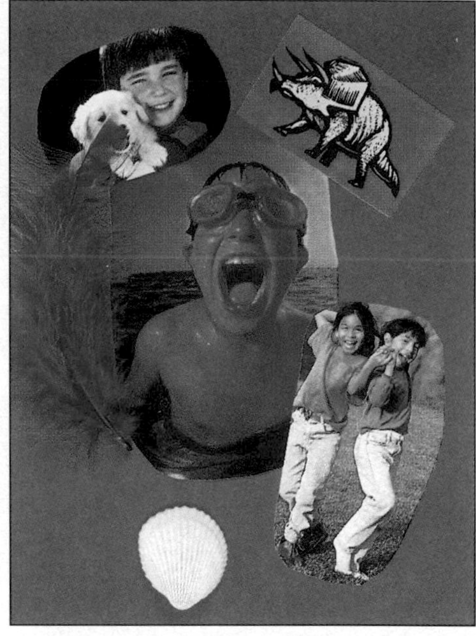

How to Make an Exhibit
Children will put together an exhibit of drawings and photographs of themselves doing things they like and do well.

Connect to Home and Community

Ask children if they have ever done something that they thought was too hard to do. Encourage them to tell you what made them brave enough to try it and how they felt when they discovered they could do this difficult thing.

Invite children to ask family members or friends to tell them about the hardest thing they ever did. Questions children might ask are: Did you worry that you wouldn't be able to do it? How did you succeed in the end? How did the experience make you feel?

Have children choose the most interesting experience they heard about and give an oral report. Remind them to tell how the person felt before and after doing the hardest thing she or he ever did.

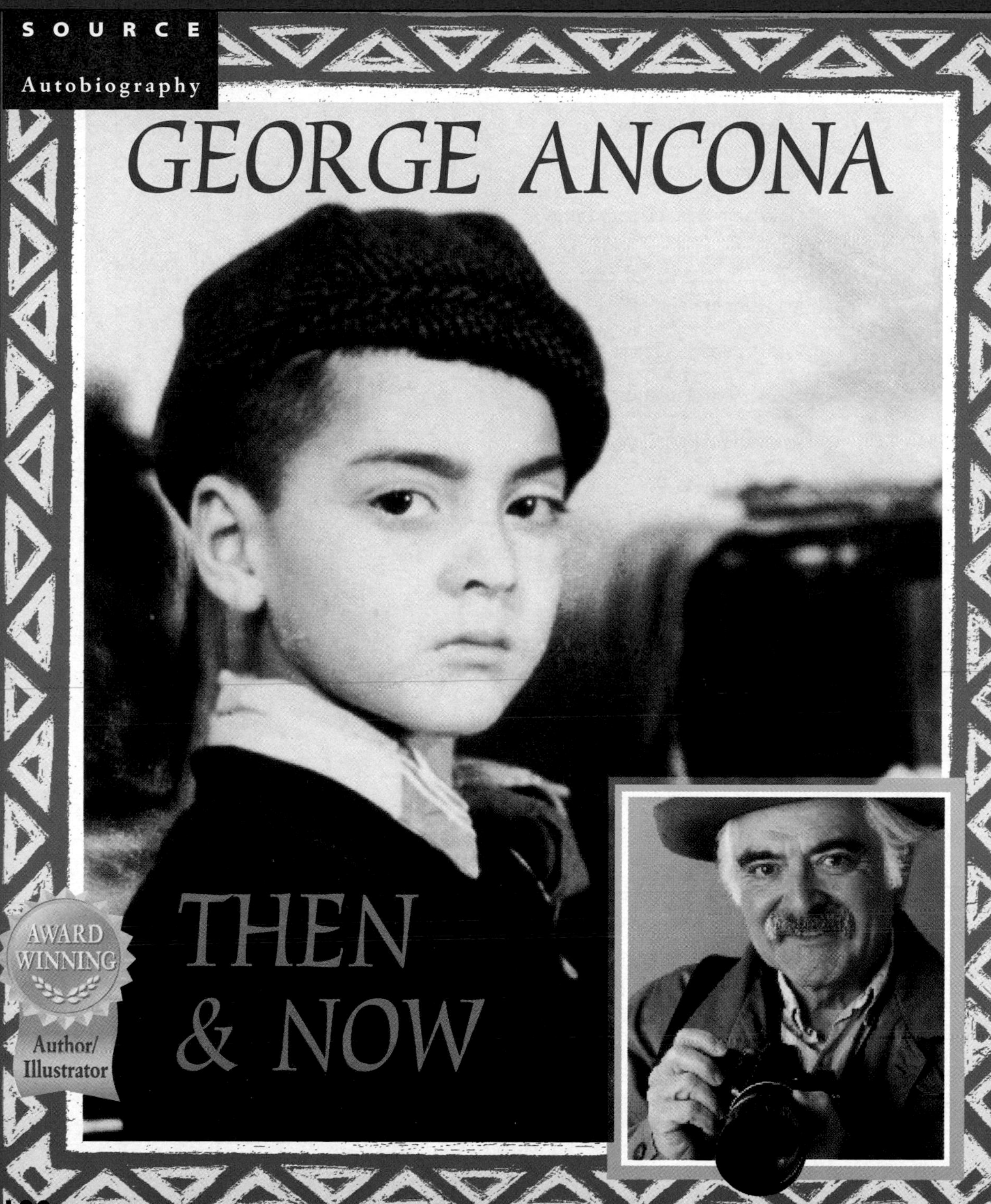

PERSONAL VOICE

Plan V

WHAT CHILDREN WILL DO

share the Big Book *Max Found Two Sticks*

read the selection

- *George Ancona: Then & Now* AUTOBIOGRAPHY

use the key strategy of Main Idea/Details

blend words with /s/*c* and /j/*g*

write captions for a photo essay

apply what they discover about how current interests influence future efforts

Assessing Your Students

ASSESSMENT	TEACHER'S SOURCEBOOK	ASSESSMENT KIT
Vocabulary Test	T219	Assessment Handbook
Observation	T220	Assessment Handbook
Assess Reading	T238	Classroom Management Forms
Conference	T238	Assessment Handbook
Performance-Based	T241	Assessment Handbook
Writing Benchmarks	T241	Assessment Handbook
Spelling Tests	T219, T243	Assessment Handbook
Quickcheck	T246, T248, T250	Assessment Handbook
Formal Tests	T311	Unit/Year Tests

Creating a Community of Learners

Max Found Two Sticks: pp. T216–217

- Explore sound
- Act out a story
- Understand character
- Use onomatopoeia

Demonstrating Independence

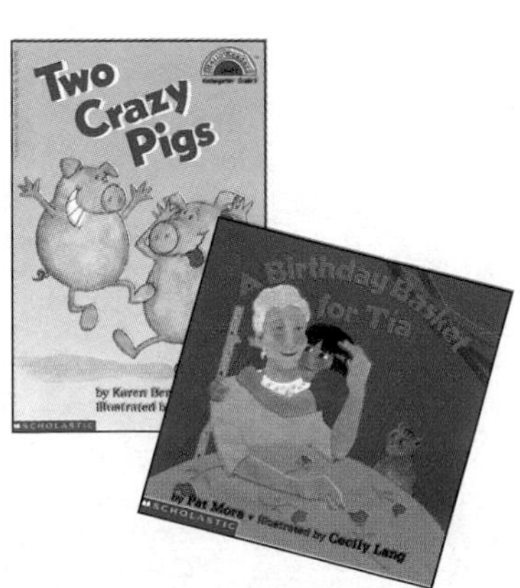

Using the Trade Books: pp. T252–253

- *Two Crazy Pigs* by Karen Berman Nagel
- *A Birthday Basket for Tía* by Pat Mora

Integrating Learning: p. T254

- Prepare for the Project: Thinking About Making an Exhibit

Focus on Phonics

Phonics Lesson

- Soft /s/c, /j/g

Phonics Kit

Literacy-at-Work Book

- Soft /s/c, /j/g, pp. 60–61

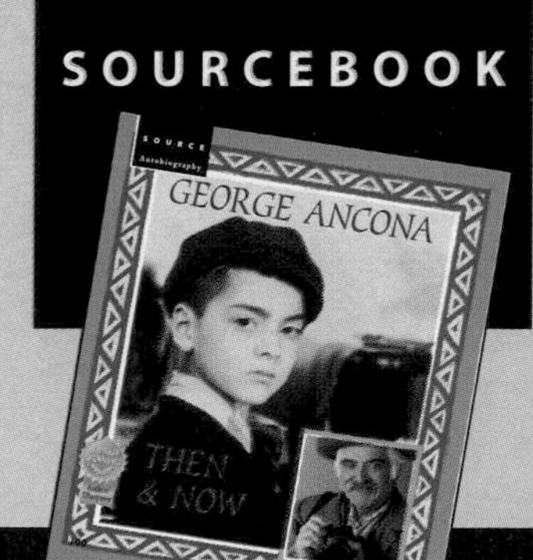

PLAN V ORGANIZER

George Ancona: Then & Now

	Instructional Path	Supporting All Learners	Resources and Technology
a **READING THE SOURCES** pp. T218–239	**Build Background** ✔ **Develop Vocabulary** *• artist • photographer • camera • imagination • hobby* **Reading Selection** *George Ancona: Then & Now* Launch the Key Strategy: Main Idea/Details ✔ **Assess Reading**	ESL pp. T219, T222, T227, T237 CHALLENGE p. T230 ACCESS p. T230 MINI-LESSON Captions, p. T226 Autobiography, p. T 236 **Idea File:** p. T239 **Cultural Connections:** pp. T231, T239	**Transparency** Build Background, 9 **Literacy-at-Work Book** Vocabulary, p. 51 Comprehension Check, p. 52  **WiggleWorks™ Plus,** pp. T218, T220, T222, T223, T226, T227, T232
 **b** **INTEGRATING LANGUAGE ARTS** pp. T240–245	✔ **Writing:** Write a Photo Essay Daily Language Practice ✔ **Grammar:** Action Words: Past Time **Mechanics:** Capitalizing Place Names ✔ **Spelling:** Words With Soft *c* and Soft *g* *• city • fence • cent • place • space • page • cage • age*	ESL pp. T241, T245 ACCESS p. T241 **Activity File:** pp. T244–245 Be a Photographer Talk About Good Times Picture This! Life Stories Game MINI-LESSON Recognize Feelings, p. T245	**Literacy-at-Work Book** Writing, p. 53 **Grammar, Usage, and Mechanics Practice:** pp. 9–10 **Spelling Practice:** p. 5 **Handwriting Practice:** p. 5  **WiggleWorks™ Plus,** pp. T241, T244
c **BUILDING SKILLS AND STRATEGIES** pp. T246–251	✔ Quickcheck Key Strategy: Main Idea/Details ✔ Quickcheck ✔ Context Clues: Specialized Vocabulary ✔ Quickcheck Phonics: Soft /s/*c*, /j/*g*	EXTRA HELP p. T247, T249 ESL p. T251 CHALLENGE pp. T247, T251 ACCESS p. T249 **Review** Summarize, p. R17	**Transparency** Key Strategy, 10 Context Clues, 11 **Literacy-at-Work Book** Main Idea/Details, pp. 54–56 Context Clues, pp. 57–58 Phonics, pp. 60–61  **WiggleWorks™ Plus,** p. T251

✔ = **Assessed**

Share the Big Book

Objectives

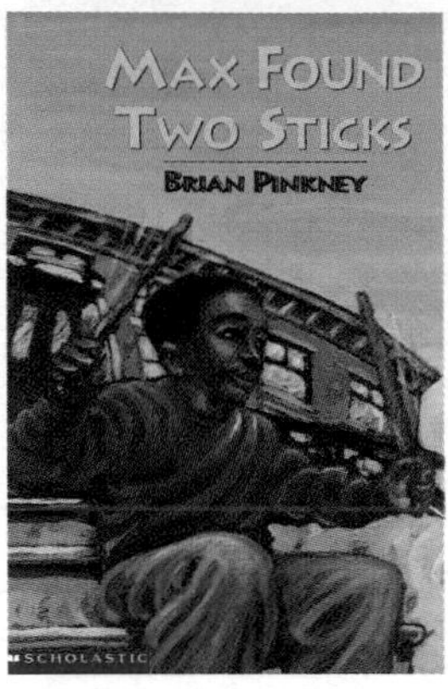

Children learn to:

- explore sound
- act out a story
- understand character
- onomatopoeia

Materials:
Big Book: *Max Found Two Sticks*
Props
Paper and pencil

Time:
About 20–40 minutes

Suggested Grouping:
Whole class, cooperative groups, and individuals

Technology Options

Children may enjoy listening to *Max Found Two Sticks* on audiocassette.

Max Found Two Sticks

Children will reread the Big Book about a boy who uses his **imagination** to make **music** before they read about a photographer who uses his imagination to take **pictures** in *George Ancona: Then & Now*.

Reread the Big Book

Reread *Max Found Two Sticks* aloud, inviting children to join in. You might read the narrative aloud and suggest that children say the words for sounds as a group. Then ask questions to stimulate discussion:

- **What objects did Max play his sticks on? Where did he get those objects?**
- **What instrument do you think Max would like to play? What instrument would you like to play? Why?**
- **Have you ever had a day like Max, when you didn't feel like talking to anybody? Why didn't you feel like talking?**

Children might enjoy writing their response on a copy of the two sticks found on page R42.

Speaking

Act It Out

COOPERATIVE GROUPS Encourage the class or groups to act out the story.

- **Gather props for objects in the book. You might use two pencils, a pail or bucket, a cardboard box, three plastic bottles, and a waste basket.**
- **Have volunteers take the parts of story characters: Max, Grandpa, Max's mother, Cindy, Shaun, Jamal, Max's dad, the twins, and members of a marching band.**
- **Invite one child to be the narrator to read the story aloud as the other children act out their parts. You may wish to alternate narrators.**

Comprehension

Character

Encourage children to discuss Max's character by using a character web like the one found on R41. Write Max's name in a circle on chart paper. Then have children offer words that describe him as you write the words on spokes around the circle. To help children get started, you might ask:

- **Where does Max live?**
- **Does Max need toys in order to have fun? Does he need friends to have fun? What does this tell you about him?**
- **Look closely at the illustrations. What do you learn about how Max feels and thinks from the pictures?**

You may wish to have children draw portraits of Max and write a sentence describing him.

Word Study

Onomatopoeia

Point out the words the author used to describe sounds in the story. Ask children questions such as:

- **What do you notice about these words?**
- **How do the words imitate sounds?**
- **How do these words add to the story?**

Tell children that the occurrence of a word sounding like what it means is called onomatopoeia. Pass out newspaper comics and let children look for onomatopoetic words in the dialogue and art. Write the words children find on a chart, then invite children to add other onomatopoetic words to the list. Display the words for children to use in their writing.

Writing

Write a Storyboard With Onomatopoeia

Discuss places where it is noisy. Have children think about the sounds they might hear there and how they could write words for them. Add to the list of onomatopoetic words on the chart as needed.
Then invite children to write and illustrate one or two storyboard frames for a scene that involves sound, using onomatopoetic words in their writing. Allow children to read their finished storyboards to the class as they dramatize the sounds.

a

Reading the Sources

GEORGE ANCONA: THEN & NOW

Build Background

The Big Book is about a boy who uses his **imagination** and the world around him to make **music.** *George Ancona: Then & Now* tells about a man who uses his imagination to **photograph** the world around him.

Objectives

Children learn to:

- compare photography to drawing
- generate a semantic map
- expand oral language

Materials:
Transparency 9
Literacy-at-Work Book p. 51
Word Cards 23–27
Pocket Chart (optional)

Time:
About 30 minutes

Suggested Grouping:
Whole class

Literacy-at-Work Book, p. 51

Name VOCABULARY

What's Missing?

Use a word from the box to finish each sentence.

artist
hobby
camera
imagination
photographer

1. Eric used his *imagination* to make pictures in his mind.
2. He had a *hobby* he did for fun. He wanted to draw and be an *artist*.
3. Now he uses a camera and is a *photographer*.
4. He takes pictures with his *camera*.

Use one word from the box in a sentence of your own.

Unit 1 • Snapshots • Plan V • George Ancona: Then & Now 51

Activate Prior Knowledge

Share Some Snapshots

Bring to class a few snapshots you've taken. Reveal what about the subject interested you to take a picture. Invite children to bring in their favorite snapshots. Encourage discussion with questions such as:

- **What would you like to take a picture of? Why?**
- **What photographs of yourself do you like best?**

During the first week or so of school, you may want to use this opportunity to take snapshots of your class for a bulletin board display.

Make a Comparison Chart

Show children a photograph and a drawing of the same subject. Use the visuals to discuss how photographs and drawings are alike and different. Keep a chart of children's ideas.

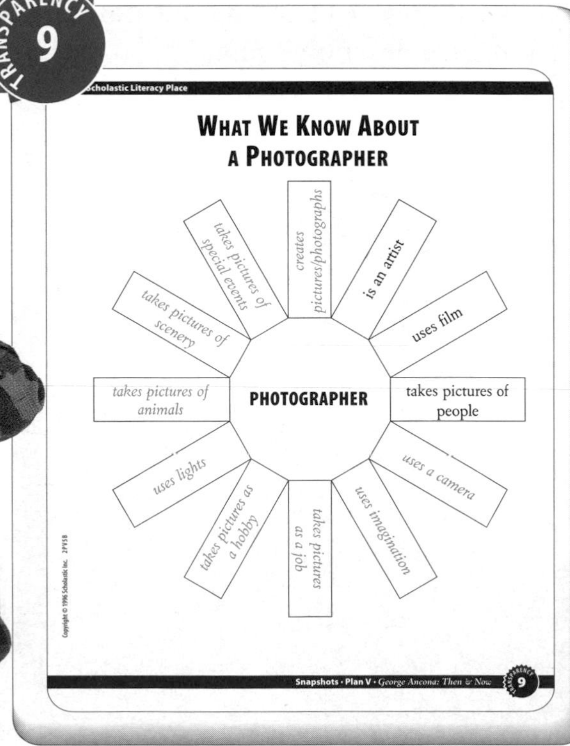

Annotated transparency for teaching concept words

▶ Photographer

Develop Vocabulary

Teach the Concept Words

Strategy: Semantic Map Use Transparency 9 to create a semantic map with children, showing how the word *photographer* is related to other words. Direct children's attention to the center with the word *photographer*. Invite children to brainstorm other words they think of when they hear the word *photographer*. Fill in the Semantic Map with their ideas. Use questions such as the following to encourage children's responses:

- **What tools might a photographer use?**
- **What does a photographer create? In what ways are photographers and artists alike? In what ways are they different?**
- **Why do people become photographers?**
- **What do photographers take pictures of?**

Support Words As children read *George Ancona: Then & Now,* you may want to point out other interesting words in the selection:

cargo: goods carried by ship, airplane, truck, or other vehicle

Coney Island: an amusement park and beach in New York City

dock: a place where ships are loaded and unloaded

Honduras: a country in Central America

Personal Word List As children read *George Ancona: Then & Now,* they can generate their own lists of place words in their Journals.

VOCABULARY

ORGANIZING CONCEPT: PHOTOGRAPHY WORDS

Concept Words

✔	**artist:**	**a person who draws or paints (p. 102)**
✔	**photographer:**	**a person who takes pictures with a camera (p. 103)**
✔	**camera:**	**a kind of box used to take pictures or movies (p. 103)**
	imagination:	**the act of creating pictures or ideas in your mind (p. 107)**
	hobby:	**something that a person does just for fun (p. 110)**

✔ = assessed

S M T W T F S See p. T243 for words to pretest and spelling instruction

Technology Options

Children can use the Wiggle Works tools to help them develop vocabulary. They can use the concept words in their writing, copy concept words onto the Magnet Board, and have the computer read aloud difficult vocabulary. Encourage children to collect other interesting words into their My Words lists as they read. For more ideas, see the WiggleWorks Plus Teaching Plan.

Supporting All Learners

Use Visuals

ESL Visuals will provide second-language learners with ideas they can use to participate in the Semantic Map activity. Bring photographs or pictures of photography-related activities and equipment to share with the class. Display the visuals and encourage children to use them to brainstorm new ideas.

ACCESS Use visuals to help focus children's attention during the Semantic Map activity. While the class is brainstorming, encourage children to search the visuals for words they can use in the Web.

a

READING THE SOURCES

GEORGE ANCONA: THEN & NOW

Prepare to Teach

OBSERVATION

As children read the selection, notice how they:

- ✔ appreciate the *theme* that photography is an imaginative form of self-expression. VISUAL LITERACY
- ✔ use the *key strategy* of Main Idea/Details.
- ✔ recognize the *literary elements* of Autobiography.

Use the Individual and Class Plan Checklists in the Classroom Management Forms, pp. 8 and 14.

KEY STRATEGY:

MAIN IDEA/DETAILS

George Ancona: Then & Now offers children the opportunity to practice the skill of identifying a main idea and its supporting details. The autobiography genre provides life themes as main ideas, which are supported by many details.

Children can use the computer writing area to list main ideas and details as they read.

Customize Instruction

FLEXIBLE GROUPING

Teacher Support

Construct meaning by using the key strategy of Main Idea/Details as children read the selection. Revisit the selection to build understanding of the literary elements of Autobiography.

Collaborative

Children can read with partners to support decoding, pronunciation, and comprehension. Partners can alternate reading using the Record Tool.

Extra Support

Children who need extra support can listen to the selection on audiocassette as they follow along in their texts.

Independent

Let children read silently without interruption, guided by the photographs. Then have them answer the questions on page T238.

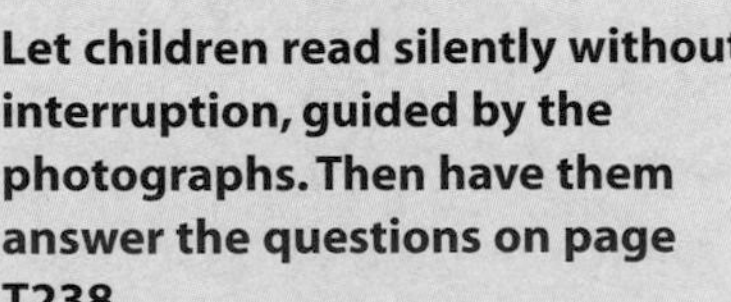

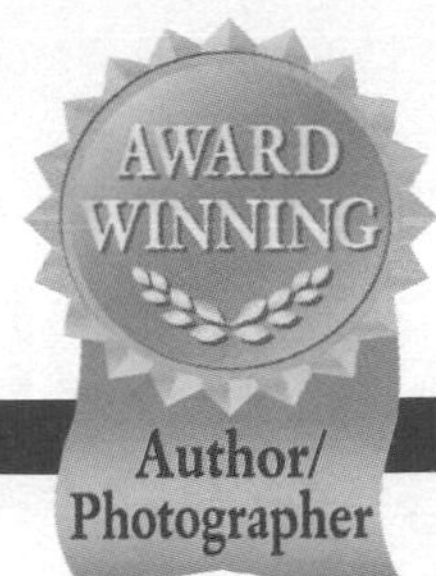

Meet the Author

George Ancona

George Ancona was born in New York City and grew up there, but his parents came from Yucatán in Mexico. George learned Spanish before he learned English. When he was in junior high school, he began to take an active interest in art. He began working in art studios after graduating from high school. Soon he had his own studio where he began doing photography, as well as art, for advertising agencies. When his friend Barbara Brenner asked him to take the photographs for her book *Faces,* his career in children's books began. Since then Ancona has photographed and written many award-winning books.

Books Illustrated by George Ancona

- ***Faces***
  by Barbara Brenner
  These photos show how beautiful and expressive faces can be.
- ***Handtalk Zoo***
  by George Ancona and Mary Beth Miller
  In this lively photo essay, a group of children enthusiastically use signing and finger-spelling to communicate at the zoo.
- ***Helping Out***
  This photo collection portrays people of all ages working together in various settings.

Books for Word Study

- ***Cecily G. and the Nine Monkeys***
  by H. A. Rey
  Nine monkeys befriend a lonely giraffe and team up for adventures. (/j/g, /s/c)
- ***City Storm***
  by Mary Jessica Parker
  The drama of a sudden storm in the city unfolds. (/s/c)
- ***Ginger Jumps***
  by Lisa Campbell Ernst
  A circus dog dreams of a family that will cherish her. (/s/c, /j/g)

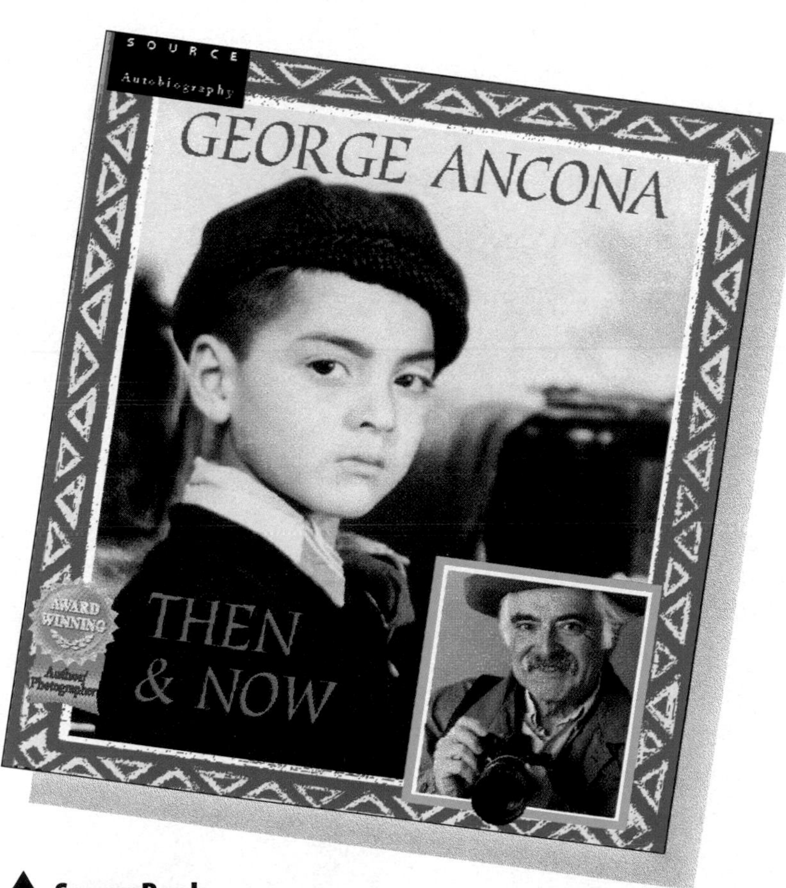

▲ **SourceBook pp. 100–115**

a READING THE SOURCES

Preview and Predict

READER TO READER

"I liked reading about a famous photographer who started out as a regular kid."

Show children the title page, and read the title to them. You can ask:

- **Do you think this story is make-believe—a fiction book? What makes you think so?**
- **If it's not fiction, what kind of selection could this be?**

Invite children to browse through the first part of the selection before they read.

- **Who is the selection about?**
- **Who is telling us this man's story?**
- **What is this man's job?**

List children's ideas on chart paper.

JOURNAL You may wish to have children record what they want to find out in their Journals. Once they finish their reading, they can return to see if their expectations were met.

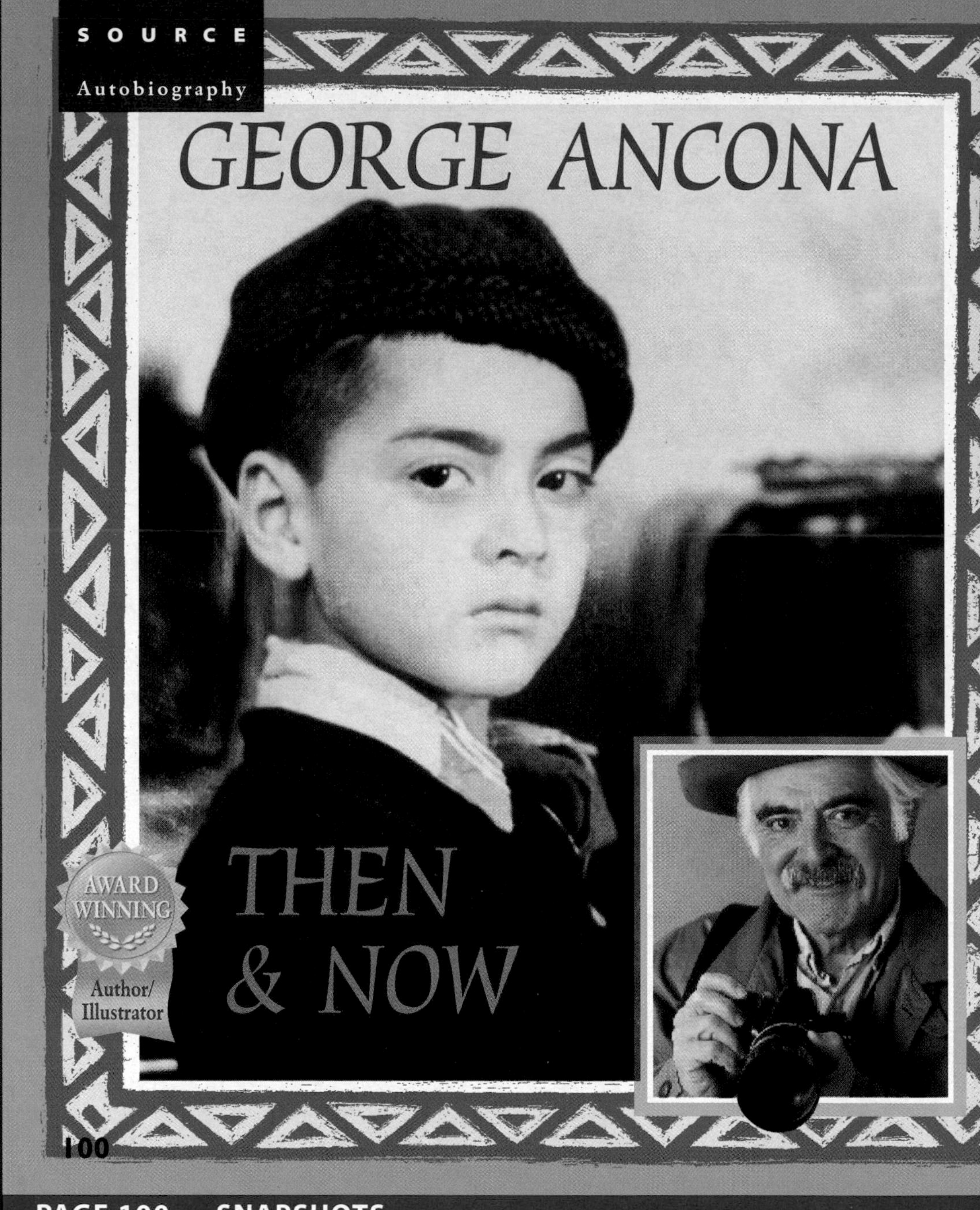

PAGE 100 SNAPSHOTS

SUPPORTING ALL LEARNERS

Preview **ESL** Explain to children that they will be reading a biography about a photographer. Preview the selection by working with children to prepare a list of interview questions they might like to ask him. **(Interview)**

- Invite children to record their interview questions on the computer.

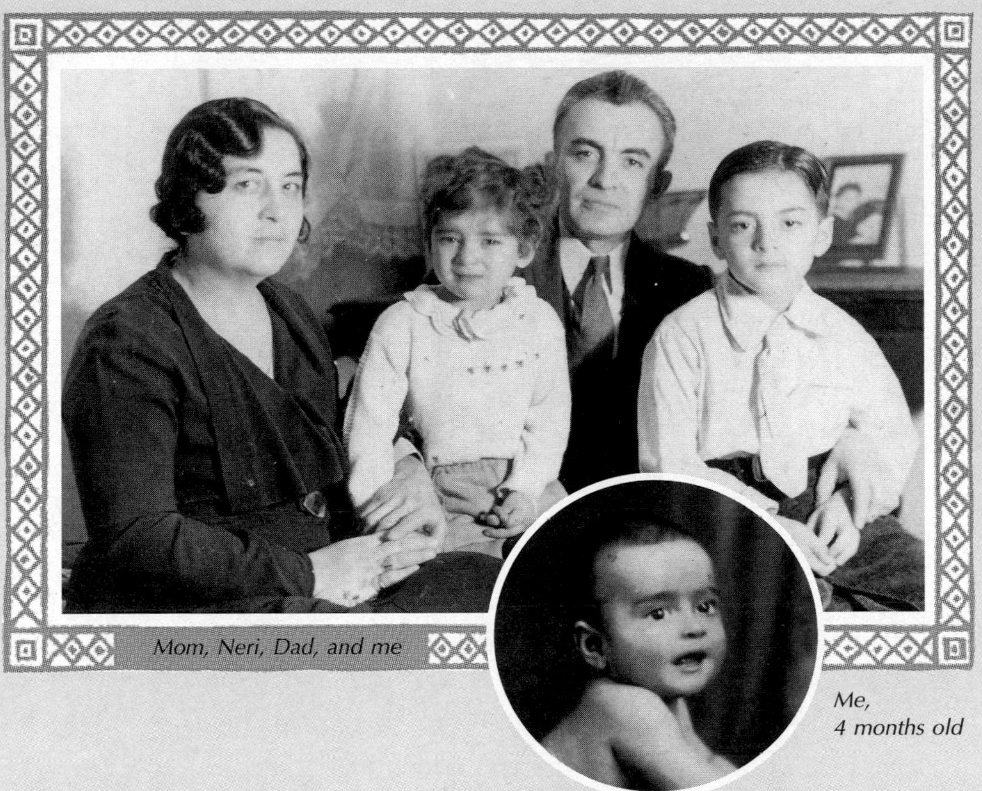

Mom, Neri, Dad, and me

Me,
4 months old

My parents came to the United States from Mexico before I was born. They spoke only Spanish at home. **1** They named me Jorge (**hor** hay), but they called me Jorgito (hor **hee** to). My friends in school called me Georgie.

Now I am known as George Ancona.

Guided Reading ►

LAUNCH THE KEY STRATEGY:

MAIN IDEA/DETAILS

THINK ALOUD I try to look for and figure out the main idea when I read because if I know this important idea, I can understand and enjoy what I'm reading. I know the title is *George Ancona: Then & Now.* From this I can guess that the book is about a man named George Ancona. The pictures on the cover are probably George as a boy and as a man.

1 Autobiography Who is writing George Ancona's story? Is it George Ancona himself or is it someone else? How can you tell?

PHONICS Soft /j/g

Have children find the word *George*, point to the letter g, and read the word aloud.

- **What other words do you know that start with the same sound?**

(*See Phonics: Soft /s/c,/j/g on pp.T250–251.*)

See the Wiggleworks Plus Teaching Plan for more phonics activities.

Guided Reading ▶

❷ **Setting On this page there's a line that begins "When I was little...," and on the next page there's a line that begins "Now I am...." What does this tell us about when the story takes place?**

INTERVENTION STRATEGY

Text Structure

Have children recall that the title of this selection is *George Ancona: Then & Now*. Tell children that the author uses the words *then* and *now* to tell his story about himself. The author uses words in the past tense to tell about his life when he was a boy. He uses words in the present tense to tell about his life now as a grown up.

Curiosity Place

Mr. Ancona's first name in Spanish is Jorge. In English it's George. In Italian it's Giorgio. In German it's Georg. There are probably many versions of children's names throughout the world. Do they know any of them?

Mommy and me at Coney Island

My family lived in Coney Island near the beach
❷ and the amusement park. When I was little I rode the painted ponies on the merry-go-round. Later, I painted pictures of them. My family would look at my pictures and say, "Jorgito is going to be an artist when he grows up!"

Painted ponies, age 20

102

PAGE 102 SNAPSHOTS

Wild mustang, New Mexico

Now I am a photographer.
I look at the world through my camera.

103

GEORGE ANCONA: THEN & NOW PAGE 103

Read On ► ► ►

PHONICS **3-Letter Blends**

Ask children to find the word *through* on page 103, point to the letters *thr,* and read the word aloud. Remind them that the sounds the first three letters stand for are blended together when they say the word.

- **What other words can you think of that start with the letters *thr*?**

a

Guided Reading ►

3 **KEY STRATEGY: Main Idea/Details George Ancona includes many details about his early life. For instance, he lived on Coney Island and loved to look at the ocean. Look at the pictures and captions on this page. What other details can you tell about his early life?**

VISUAL LITERACY

As they read, invite children to record important details, using the computer Record Tools.

MINI-LESSON

CAPTIONS

TEACH/MODEL Point out the photographs and read the captions. Ask children who wrote the captions and how they can tell. See what else they notice about the captions.

THINK ALOUD When I read the captions, I notice that they are brief, that they are not written in complete sentences, and that they tell what the pictures are about.

APPLY As children read the selection, have them note each photograph and the caption that accompanies it. Can they think of alternate captions for some of the photographs?

3

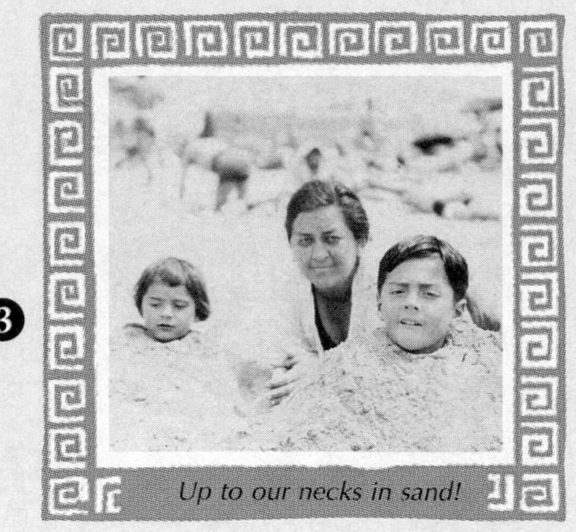

Up to our necks in sand!

A sailor on wheels

Coney Island summer

104

MINI-LESSON

PAGE 104 SNAPSHOTS

► INTEGRATING LANGUAGE ARTS **READING/WRITING/SPEAKING** *(See p. T244.)*

► INTEGRATED CURRICULUM **THE ARTS** *(See p. R11.)*

Children use colored pencils to make a print from a textured surface.

Growing up in Coney Island was exciting. There was always so much to do and see there. I loved the sight of the ocean by day and the bright lights on the rides at night.

I still love to look at the world all around me.

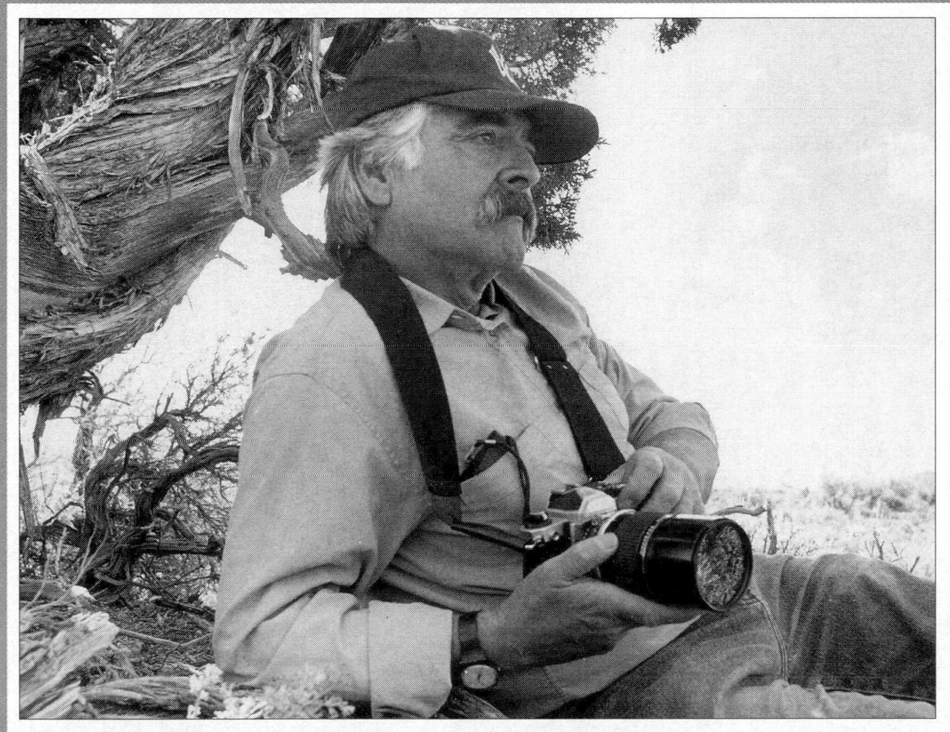

Watching and waiting to take a picture

105

GEORGE ANCONA: THEN & NOW PAGE 105

Read On ► ► ►

SUPPORTING ALL LEARNERS

Read

ESL Guide children acquiring English through a reading of pages 104 and 105 to familiarize them with how to read stories with captioned pictures. Model how you look at the illustrations, read the captions, and then read the rest of the story. During free time, have children draw pictures of themselves and write captions. **(Model)**

You may wish to leave teacher messages about reading stories with captioned pictures.

a

Read On ► ► ►

Dressed for make-believe

106

PAGE 106 SNAPSHOTS

As a child, I was always using my imagination. I had an older cousin who gave me the clothes that he outgrew. My favorite things were an aviator helmet and a pair of knee-high boots. Wearing these, I flew make-believe airplanes around my living room. ❺

Now I use my imagination when I take my photographs and write my books. ❻

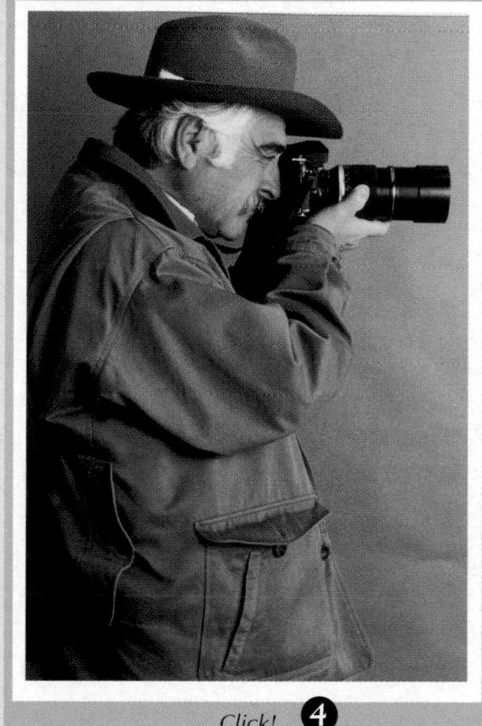

Click! ❹

107

GEORGE ANCONA: THEN & NOW PAGE 107

Guided Reading ►

❹ **Onomatopoeia** **Let's look at the word *click*. Who knows what this word refers to? It reminds me of the sound a camera makes when a photographer takes a picture. What other words sound like the noise they name?**

❺ **KEY STRATEGY: Main Idea/Details** **What is the main idea of the first paragraph on this page? Let's read it together and see if we can make up a sentence that tells the main idea.**

❻ **Compare/Contrast** **Did you notice that George Ancona first tells something about his life as a child and then tells something about his life today? For example, when he was young, he used his imagination when he dressed up in his cousin's clothes. How does he use his imagination as an adult?**

► INTEGRATED CURRICULUM **SCIENCE** *(See p. R10)*

Children make sun prints by taping construction paper forms to a sunny window.

PHONICS Final *e(a-e)*

Ask children to find the word *take* as you read aloud the last sentence on page 107. Remind them that the silent *e* at the end of the word means that the vowel *a* will probably be long. Invite children to find another word on the same page with the pattern consonant–vowel *a*–consonant–*e*.

a

Guided Reading ▶

7 Cause/Effect **When George Ancona's uncle added blue paint to yellow paint, it turned green. Mixing two colors together causes a new color to be created. What happens when you mix yellow and red paint?**

8 Summarize **Let's stop reading at the end of this page and think about what we have learned so far. I'll write down your ideas on the chalkboard. Then let's use the list to summarize what we've read.**

Tio Mario, Neri, and me

My uncle, Tio Mario, worked in a sign shop, which I often visited. I loved watching him mix colors in big buckets of paint. He would take a can of yellow, pour in some blue, and mix it. I was amazed when the paint turned green
7 right before my eyes.

Now I'm still amazed when I look through the
8 camera and see something wonderful.

108

PAGE 108 SNAPSHOTS

Supporting All Learners

CHALLENGE Children will learn something about mixing colors from George Ancona's childhood experience with his Tío Mario. Challenge them to brainstorm what two colors they can mix to get purple. Then encourage them to predict about other color mixes. Have them use paints to mix colors and confirm the outcomes. **(Brainstorm)**

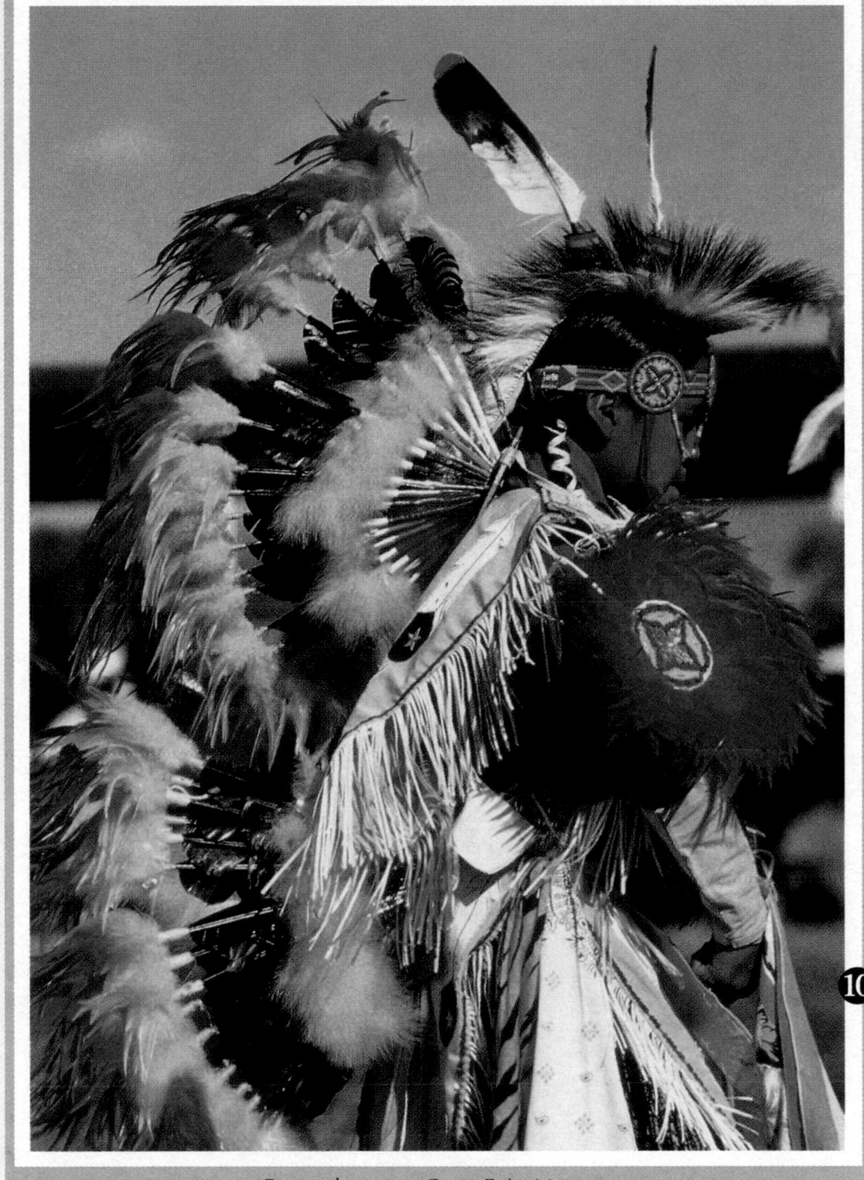

Fancy dancer at Crow Fair, Montana

109

GEORGE ANCONA: THEN & NOW PAGE 109

Read On ► ► ►

CULTURAL CONNECTIONS

The photograph with the caption "Fancy dancer at Crow Fair, Montana" shows a young Native-American man dressed in a costume for a Fancy Dance. This is a fast circular dance that is accompanied by a drum beat. Dances like these are done at social gatherings called powwows.

a

Guided Reading ▶

9 Word Attack **Find a word in the first sentence that is made up of two smaller words. Read the word. Can you figure out the meaning of the word from the two words *week* and *ends*? A word that is made up of two smaller words is a compound word. What other compound words can you find on this page?**

10 CRITICAL THINKING: Synthesize **George Ancona says he never thought he would become a photographer. Why might he have thought this?**

Encourage children to add the compound words to their My Words lists.

Dad, me (circled), and the neighbors

My father's hobby was photography.
I explored the city with him on weekends. 9
We walked along the docks and watched big ships bringing cargo into the port. While my father took pictures, I daydreamed about faraway places.
10 I never thought I would become a photographer, too.

Now I travel all over the world taking photographs of exciting places.

110

PAGE 110 SNAPSHOTS

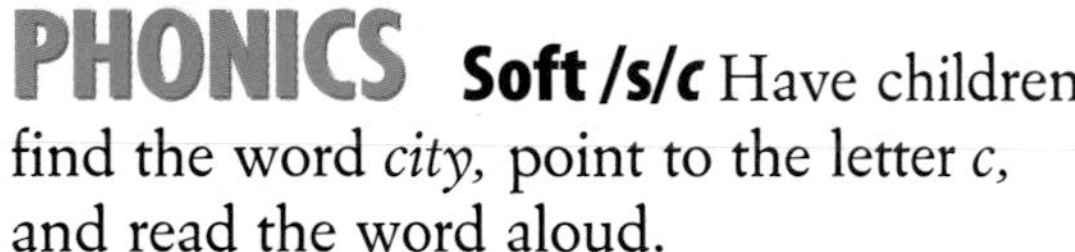

PHONICS **Soft /s/c** Have children find the word *city*, point to the letter *c*, and read the word aloud.

- **What other words do you know that start with the same sound?**

*(See Phonics: Soft /s/*c*, /j/*g *on pp. T250–251.)*

For more phonics activities, see the Wiggleworks Plus Teaching Plan.

▶ INTEGRATED CURRICULUM **MATH** *(See p. R10.)*
Children estimate the distance in a group photo by George Ancona.

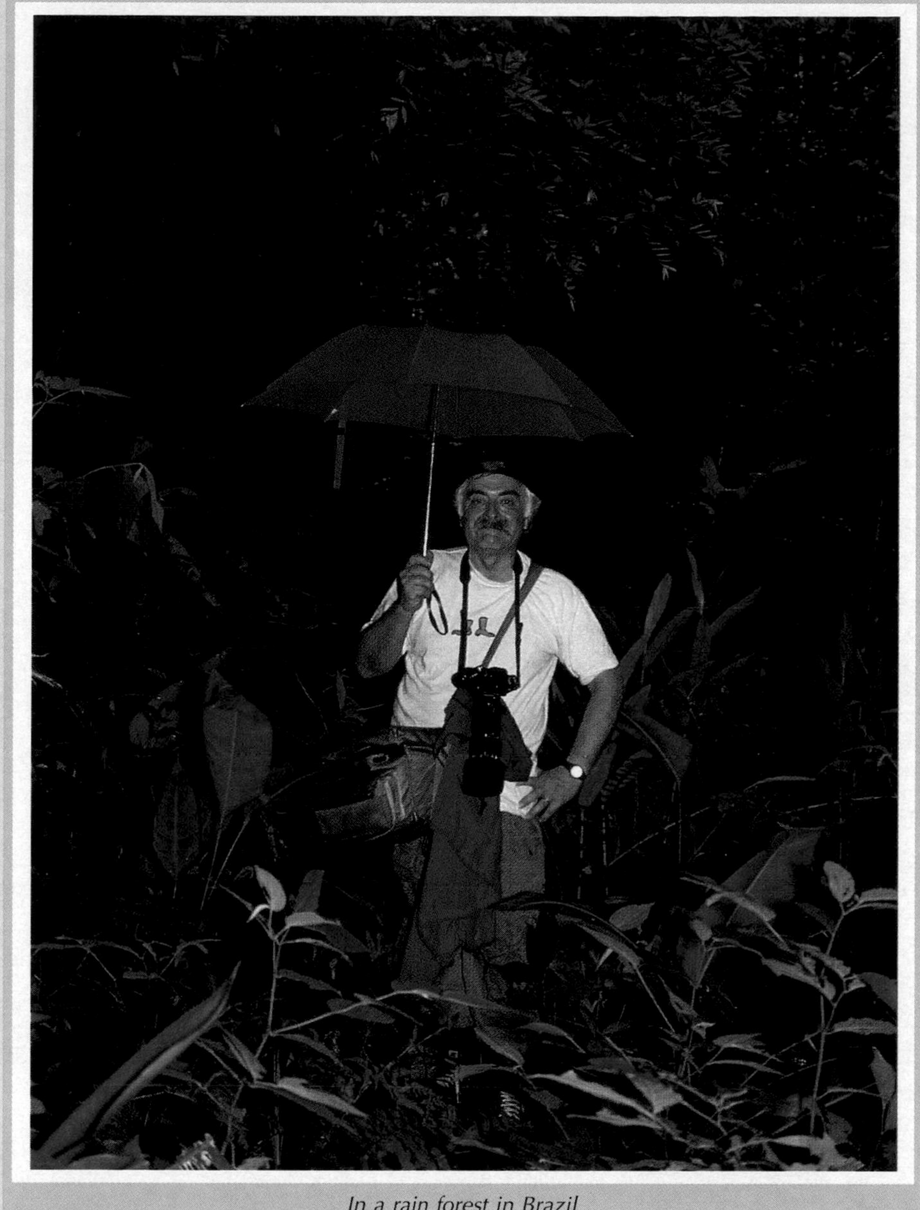

In a rain forest in Brazil

111

GEORGE ANCONA: THEN & NOW PAGE 111

Read On ► ► ►

Read On ► ► ►

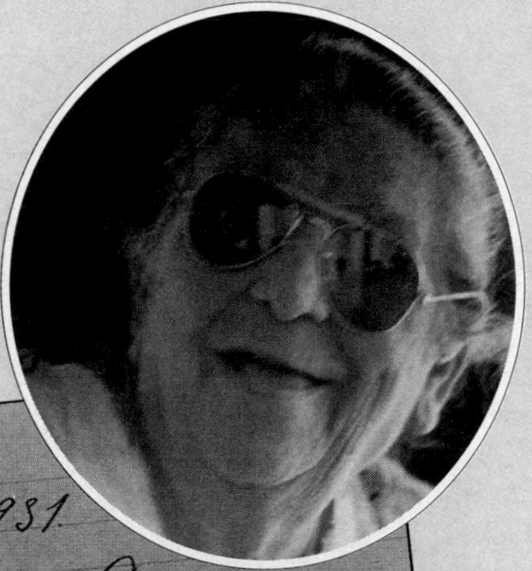

My grandma, Chichi Neri

Mérida, diciembre 1º de 1931.
Niño Jorge Efrain Ancona Diaz
New York
Mi idolatrado hijito:
El día 4 del presente al cumplir
tus dos años de edad hubiese dado gustosa algunos de

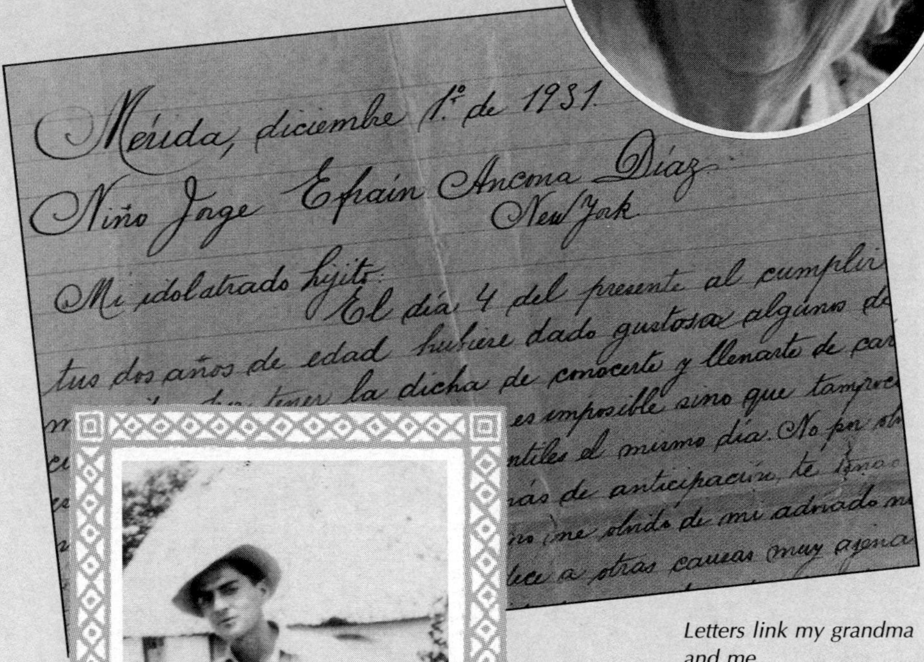

Letters link my grandma and me

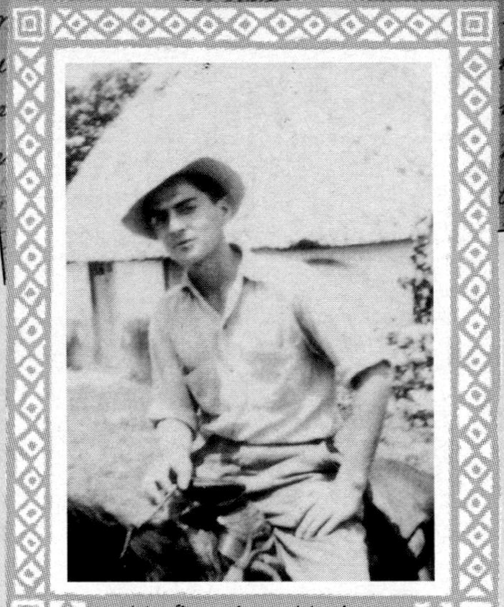

My first trip to Mexico

112

PAGE 112 SNAPSHOTS

When I went to Mexico as a young man, I met my grandmother for the first time. She had been writing to me from the day I was born. Her handwriting was as beautiful as the things she wrote. Through her letters she shared her life story with me. ⓫

Now I share my life stories with my own children, grandchildren . . .

My son Pablo and me ⓬

Guided Reading ►

⓫ **Make Inferences** **How do you think George Ancona felt about his grandmother? Remember to use what you already know and clues from his story to figure out things that he didn't say directly.**

⓬ **Make Inferences** **George Ancona says "Now I share my life stories with my own children, grandchildren. . . ." The picture shows George Ancona with his baby son. From the words, the picture, and the caption, do you think his son is still young or now grown-up? How can you tell?** VISUAL LITERACY

a

Guided Reading ▶

⓭ **CRITICAL THINKING: Evaluate Why do you think George Ancona wrote his autobiography?**

Mexico

Honduras

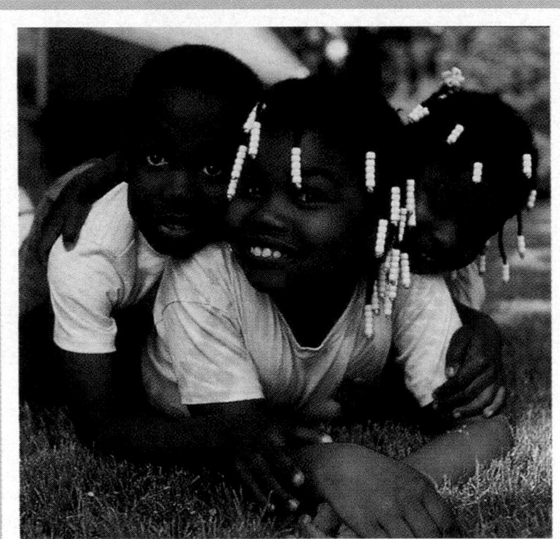

U.S.A.

. . . and children all over the world.

114

PAGE 114 SNAPSHOTS

▶ INTEGRATING LANGUAGE ARTS **VIEWING/WRITING** *(See p. T244.)*

▶ INTEGRATED CURRICULUM **SOCIAL STUDIES** *(See p. R11.)*

Children make a travel brochure using photos of a place they'd like to visit.

MINI-LESSON

AUTOBIOGRAPHY

TEACH/MODEL Explain that an autobiography is the story of a person's life written by that same person. First-person words such as *I, me,* and *my* let readers know that this selection is an autobiography. Read these two sentences aloud and have children decide which sentence would appear in an autobiography.

- **My parents came from Mexico to the United States before I was born.**
- **George Ancona's parents came from Mexico to the United States before he was born.**

APPLY As children reread the selection, ask them to point out first-person words that tell them it is an autobiography.

U.S.A.

Honduras

Brazil

115

GEORGE ANCONA: THEN & NOW PAGE 115

Guided Reading ►

14 **KEY STRATEGY: Main Idea/Details Now that we've read *George Ancona: Then & Now*, what would you say is the main idea of the selection? Who can give some details that tell more about the main idea?**

Supporting All Learners

ESL The pictures of faraway places on pages 114 and 115 may be familiar to some children and will give them an opportunity to share their personal experiences. Motivate children acquiring English to identify the places in these pictures and talk about them with their classmates. **(Make Connections)**

VISUAL LITERACY

Revisit

a READING THE SOURCES

GEORGE ANCONA: THEN & NOW

Assess Reading

REFLECT AND RESPOND

Encourage children to share their thoughts, opinions, and questions about *George Ancona: Then & Now*. You may wish to prompt discussion with these questions:

- **What are some things you learned about photographer George Ancona? *(✔ Key Strategy)***
- **What are some ways in which George Ancona used photography as an imaginative form of self-expression? *(✔ Theme)***
- **If you were writing your autobiography, what would be the most important thing you would want readers to know about you? *(✔ Literary Element)***

CHECK PREDICTIONS

As children read *George Ancona: Then & Now*, were the predictions they set before reading confirmed? Have children return to the chart they made before reading and revise their predictions as necessary.

READ CRITICALLY ACROSS TEXTS

- **How is Max from *Max Found Two Sticks* an artist like George Ancona?**

Max uses his imagination like George Ancona does. Max makes music; George Ancona creates photographs.

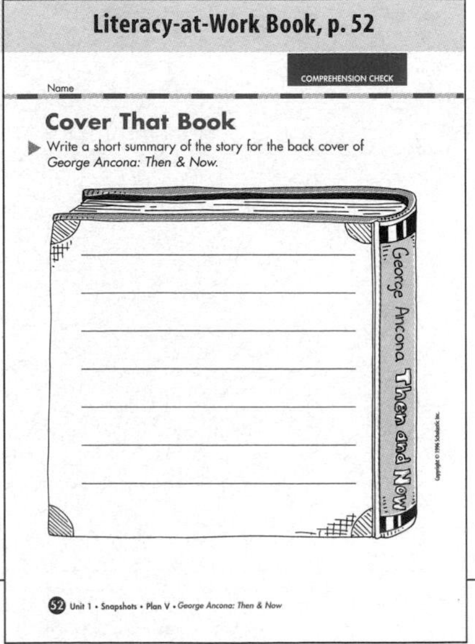

Literacy-at-Work Book, p. 52

Name

COMPREHENSION CHECK

Cover That Book

▶ Write a short summary of the story for the back cover of *George Ancona: Then & Now.*

George Ancona Then and Now

52 Unit 1 • Snapshots • Plan V • *George Ancona: Then & Now*

CONFERENCE

Use the checked questions on this page to assess children's understanding of:

✔ the *key strategy* of Main Idea/Details.

✔ the *theme* of imaginative self-expression.

✔ the *literary elements* of Autobiography.

Listen to Children Read Ask selected children to find the part of the story where George Ancona tells about using his imagination as a child. You may wish to record children as they read the section aloud. Assess oral reading, using pages 22–23 in Assessment Handbook.

Children may wish to add their recordings to their Literacy Portfolios.

Based on your evaluation of your children's responses,

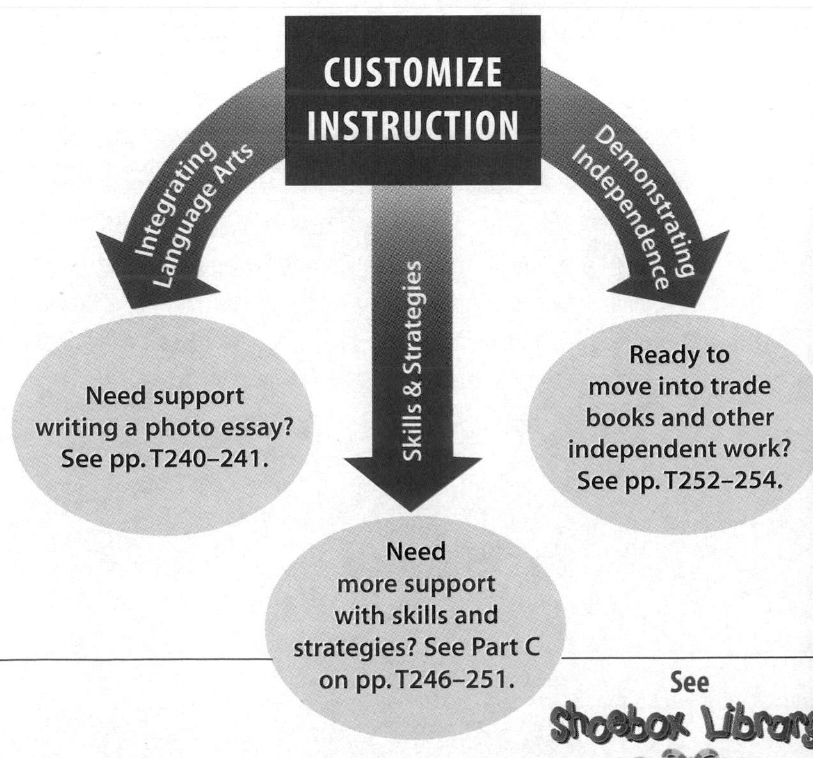

See Shoebox Library

Idea File

VOCABULARY

Invite children to think of questions to ask George Ancona about his life. Suggest that they use photography or place words from the selection. Some children may prefer to share parts of their own life stories with the author.

REPEATED READING

LISTENING Have children listen to the audiocassette selection, *George Ancona: Then & Now,* for factual information about his life. After listening, have them record one fact from his childhood and one from his adulthood. Children may compare their facts with others who have done this activity.

REPEATED READING

PARTNER READING Have pairs of children read *George Ancona: Then & Now* aloud. One partner can read the parts that refer to George Ancona's past and the other can read the sentences that refer to his present life.

BIOGRAPHY

You can have children write three or four sentences about someone whose life—then and now—they would like to know more about. You may be able to use this idea to steer children toward biographies or autobiographies they would like to read.

CULTURAL CONNECTIONS

LOOK AT THE WORLD THROUGH A CAMERA

George Ancona has traveled all over the world, taking photographs of people and places, providing his readers with a chance to see a little bit of what life is like in other cultures and parts of the world.

ACTIVITY

Encourage children to use pictures from old magazines to make their own photo album or collage of people and places around the world. Have them include captions telling where in the world the picture was taken.

SOURCEBOOK MODEL

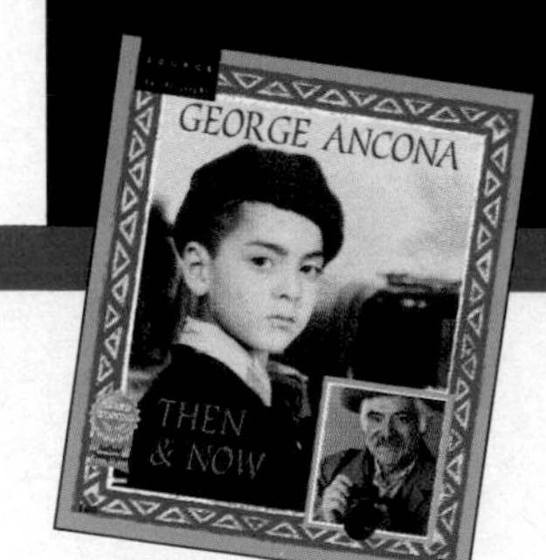

INTEGRATING LANGUAGE ARTS

GEORGE ANCONA: THEN & NOW

Objectives

Children learn to:

- write an informative picture essay about an important experience, using George Ancona's style (pp. T240–241)
- use action verbs in the past time (p. T242)
- capitalize proper nouns (p. T242)
- spell words with soft *c* and *g* (p. T243)

Materials:
SourceBook pp. 100–115
Literacy-at-Work Book p.53

Suggested Grouping:
Whole class and individuals

Literacy-at-Work Book, p. 53

Name | WRITING

Get Ready to Write

Draw pictures about something that is important to you. Put them in the order you like best. Then write about each one.

To the Teacher: This is the prewriting organizer referenced in the lesson on writing a photo essay.

Unit 1 • Snapshots • Plan V • *George Ancona: Then & Now* 53

WRITE A PHOTO ESSAY

WRITING

Using George Ancona's style in *George Ancona: Then & Now,* children write a **picture essay** about an important **experience.**

THINK ABOUT WRITING

Ask children what they think George Ancona's style is. How does the author use words and pictures to give information? Help children see that George Ancona uses photo essays to:

- record an important time or experience and show why it was important.
- give information through photos and the words that go with them.

Put It in Context

Have children look back at the first page of *George Ancona: Then & Now*. Work with them to find the important experience or time in each photo and the words that go with it. Ask why the writer chose to include the photo of himself with his mother at Coney Island.

INTRODUCE THE WRITING EVENT

Let children know that they will write their own photo or picture essay about an important time or experience in George Ancona's style. Suggest that children bring in several photos of themselves at a memorable time, such as a holiday, family gathering, or vacation; or you may set aside a period to draw pictures of the time.

Prewrite

Invite children to use the prewriting organizer in the Literacy-at-Work Book for ideas about how to organize their pictures and what to write to go with them.

Draft

Suggest that children ask the following:

- **Am I giving information about the experience?**
- **Am I saying why the experience was important to me?**

Revise

Children may wish to revise their work by asking:

- **How is my picture essay like George Ancona's?**
- **Are there words I can add to tell more about my experience?**

SHARING TIPS Children can share their picture essays with a partner or in groups. Suggest that they tell which parts they liked best.

Apprentice sample: Picture story doesn't say why the experience was important.

PERFORMANCE-BASED

Children's Self-Assessment

✔ Did I write in the style of George Ancona, using both pictures and words to go with them?

✔ Do the pictures and words say why the experience was important to me?

✔ Did I write words to go with each picture?

Children may wish to carry this piece through the writing process described in Plan VI on pp. T288–291.

Use the Benchmarks to assess children's writing. Suggest that children add their drafts and revisions to their Literacy Portfolios.

Technology Options

Invite children to create their autobiography on the computer in the WiggleWorks writing area. Have children use the Record Tool to record their ideas before they begin writing. They can also make computer-illustration versions of their photographs.

For more writing activities, see the Wiggle Works Plus Teaching Plan.

SUPPORTING ALL LEARNERS

Record

ESL After children acquiring English have written captions under their photographs, encourage them to record a narrative about their own lives. Then they can use the recording to guide them in writing their autobiographies.

ACCESS During the Prewrite and Draft activities, children with physical disabilities can use the computer recorder to "write" their captions and record their personal experiences to create their autobiographies.

CHILDREN'S WRITING BENCHMARKS

Novice:	Apprentice:	Proficient:
There are few pictures. The writing is not informative and does not say why the experience was important. There are not words for each picture.	There are enough pictures. The writing may be informative but not say why the experience was important. There are not words for each picture.	There are enough pictures. The writing is informative and says why the experience was important. There are words to go with each picture.

INTEGRATING LANGUAGE ARTS

GEORGE ANCONA: THEN & NOW

(✔ Unit Test)

S M T W T F S
See Daily Language Practice pp. R14–R15.

ACTION WORDS: PAST TIME

GRAMMAR

OBJECTIVE
Children will identify past-time action words in the selection and in their writing.

DEFINITION: Action words ending in -ed tell about actions in the past.

SYNTACTIC CUEING

❶ Teach and Model

Explain to children that action words, or verbs, can tell about things that happen now or things that happened in the past. Point out that many action words that tell about the past end in *-ed.* Write the sentences below on the chalkboard and use them to model how past-time verbs are formed.

verb + -ed = past time
walk He walked home.
wait I waited for you.
burn She burned the toast.

❷ Put It in Context

Have children return to *George Ancona: Then & Now* and find examples of verbs with *-ed* endings. Then ask children to talk about how each verb refers to action that has already happened.

❸ Apply to Writing

Have children find the verbs with *-ed* endings in their writing. Encourage children to add *-ed* endings to verbs that are in the present time but are expressing actions that have already taken place.

CAPITALIZING PLACE NAMES

MECHANICS

OBJECTIVE
Children will identify capital letters in names of specific places in the story and in their writing.

GUIDELINE: Proper nouns always start with a capital letter.

❶ Teach and Model

Explain to children that when they write the name of a specific place, each word in the name begins with a capital letter. Compare the sentences "I live in a city" and "I live in San Francisco." Explain that names of a particular place, city, state, or country, are proper nouns just as a person's name is. Point out that proper nouns always begin with a capital letter. Write the following place-names on the chalkboard and have volunteers point out the capital letters.

Paris, Texas
San Diego Zoo
Boston Public Library

❷ Put It in Context

Invite children to go back to *George Ancona: Then & Now* and find several examples of proper nouns. Be sure children notice that each begins with a capital letter.

❸ Apply to Writing

Encourage children to look back at their autobiographical writing and identify the proper nouns. Have them correct any mistakes.

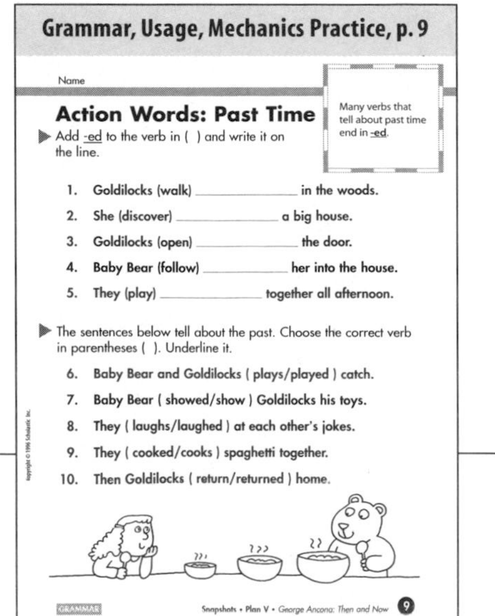

Grammar, Usage, Mechanics Practice, p. 9

Name

Action Words: Past Time

Many verbs that tell about past time end in -ed.

▶ Add -ed to the verb in ( ) and write it on the line.

1. Goldilocks (walk) ________ in the woods.
2. She (discover) ________ a big house.
3. Goldilocks (open) ________ the door.
4. Baby Bear (follow) ________ her into the house.
5. They (play) ________ together all afternoon.

▶ The sentences below tell about the past. Choose the correct verb in parentheses ( ). Underline it.

6. Baby Bear and Goldilocks (plays/played) catch.
7. Baby Bear (showed/show) Goldilocks his toys.
8. They (laughs/laughed) at each other's jokes.
9. They (cooked/cooks) spaghetti together.
10. Then Goldilocks (return/returned) home.

Copyright © 1996 Scholastic Inc.

GRAMMAR Snapshots • Plan V • *George Ancona: Then and Now* 9

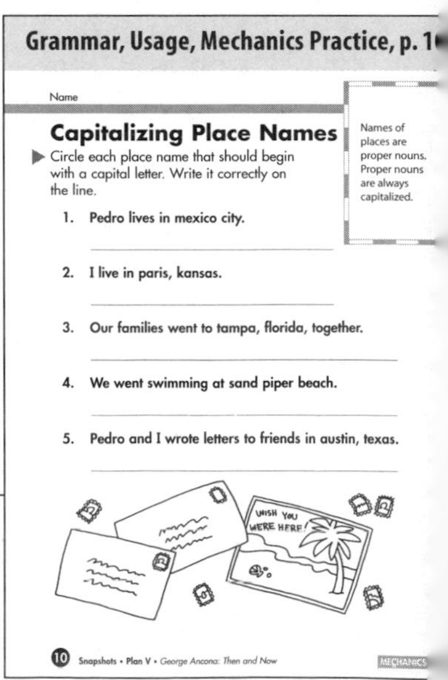

Grammar, Usage, Mechanics Practice, p. 1

Name

Capitalizing Place Names

Names of places are proper nouns. Proper nouns are always capitalized.

▶ Circle each place name that should begin with a capital letter. Write it correctly on the line.

1. Pedro lives in mexico city.
2. I live in paris, kansas.
3. Our families went to tampa, florida, together.
4. We went swimming at sand piper beach.
5. Pedro and I wrote letters to friends in austin, texas.

10 Snapshots • Plan V • *George Ancona: Then and Now* MECHANICS

Phonics Connection

You may first wish to do the phonics lesson on soft /s/c /j/g on pp. 250–251.

SPELLING

Words With Soft *c* and Soft *g*

city **fence** **cent** **place** **space** **page** **cage** **age**

✷ **Selection Vocabulary**

PRETEST If you would like to pretest using test sentences, see Spelling Practice, p. 39.

OBJECTIVE

Children spell soft *c* and soft *g* words.

❶ Teach

Remind children that the letters *c* and *g* can stand for more than one sound. Write this sentence on the chalkboard.

The cool gym is a great place.

Have children read the sentence and identify the words that contain the soft *c* and soft *g* sounds. (*place, gym*)

Put It in Context

Write the following sentences from *George Ancona: Then & Now* on the chalkboard. Have children identify the words with soft g and soft *c* sounds.

I explored the city with him on weekends.

Now I am known as George Ancona.

❷ Practice

Have children copy and complete the following word map.

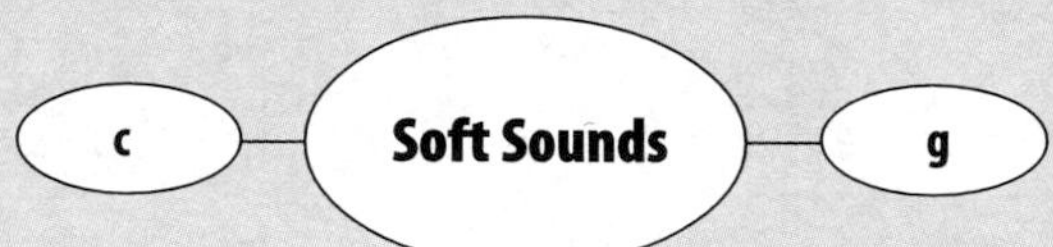

❸ Check

Apply to Writing

Have children proofread their autobiographical writings, checking the spelling of any word they may have written with the soft *c* or *g* sounds. Suggest that they jot down any misspelled words to help themselves remember how to spell these words.

TEST To administer the spelling test, say each word aloud and ask children to write a sentence using the word. Then have children work in pairs and check each other's work.

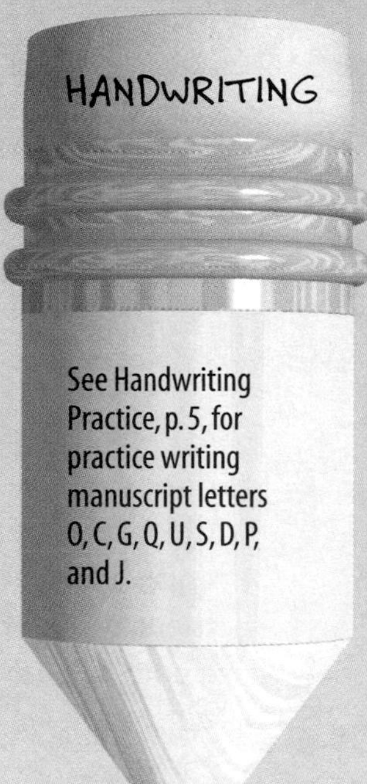

Spelling Practice, p. 5

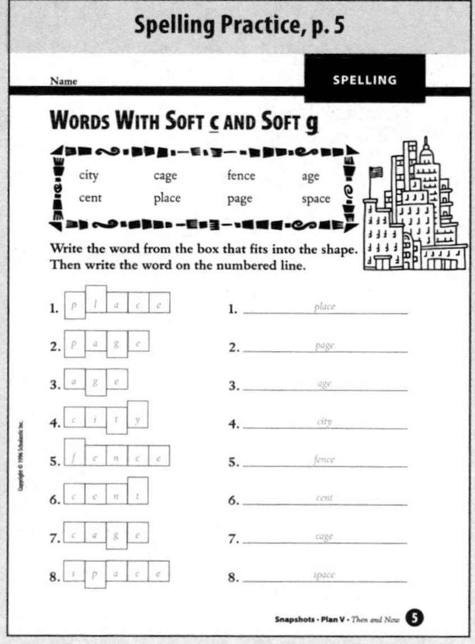
Name SPELLING

WORDS WITH SOFT C AND SOFT G

city cage fence age
cent place page space

Write the word from the box that fits into the shape. Then write the word on the numbered line.

1. place
2. page
3. age
4. city
5. fence
6. cent
7. cage
8. space

Snapshots • Plan V • Then and Now 5

INTEGRATING LANGUAGE ARTS

VIEWING/WRITING

Be a Photographer

GOOD FOR HOMEWORK

Materials:
Paper
Crayons
Yarn
Collage materials

Time
About 20 minutes

Suggested Grouping:
Individuals

Ask children to list five places they would like to photograph and tell why these sites interest them. The places can be in their neighborhood or farther afield. Next to each place name, children can write a brief description of what they would like to photograph there—for example, "Oak Park: children on the playground."

Challenge children to "take pictures" of one of the places on their list by using either drawing or collage materials. When the pictures and captions are finished, children can bring them to class and put them in a collaborative photo album made of construction paper bound with yarn.

READING/WRITING/SPEAKING

Talk About Good Times

Materials:
Chart paper
Markers
Computer

Time
About 15 minutes

Suggested Grouping:
Cooperative groups

Remind children that George Ancona remembered going to Coney Island with his family when he was young. Encourage children to bring in souvenirs, pictures, or other mementos of fun times. Have them jot down ideas to complete the story starter: "When I was little, I..." or "I had fun when...."

Ask children to take turns telling about the fun times they had. Write their ideas on a chart. Children can read the completed chart aloud.

Children can write on the computer about fun times they have had, using a Story Starter to help them begin.

WRITING/VIEWING

ESL Picture This!

Materials: SourceBook pp. 100–115 Photographs

Time About 30 minutes

Suggested Grouping: Whole group and individuals

Talk with children about how people have certain feelings when they look at George Ancona's photographs. Invite children to look at some of the photographs, and talk with them about how each photograph makes them feel. Does it make them feel happy, sad, excited? Does the photograph remind them of things they have done or experiences they have had?

Select an interesting photograph and guide children to write about how it makes them feel and why. Encourage them to share their writing with each other and to talk about the things in the photograph that made them feel the way they did. VISUAL LITERACY

MINI-LESSON

Recognize Feelings

TEACH/MODEL Display a photograph with a happy feeling. Encourage children to look at it and discuss how it makes them feel. Draw attention to expressions on people's faces, colors, and other things in the photograph that make it a happy one.

APPLY Invite children to make a collaborative Happy Collage, using cut-out pictures from old magazines.

SPEAKING/LISTENING

Life Stories Game

GOOD FOR GRADING

Materials: None

Time About 20 minutes

Suggested Grouping: Whole class and partners

Invite children to listen to a partner's oral autobiography. Encourage them to ask questions.

Challenge children to play a guessing game. Each partner can tell two or three things about his or her partner, based on autobiographical information. Have classmates try to guess who is being described. Additional information may need to be given.

How to Grade Look for use of relevant information, descriptive language, and attention to detail.

BUILDING SKILLS AND STRATEGIES

GEORGE ANCONA: THEN & NOW

Main Idea/Details

Objectives

Children learn to:

- recognize the main idea of a selection
- identify details that support the main idea
- transfer their learning to a new text

Review:

- Summarize (p. R17)

Materials:
SourceBook pp. 100–115
Transparency 10
Literacy-at-Work Book pp. 54–56

Time:
About 30 minutes

Suggested Grouping:
Whole class and partners

Literacy-at-Work Book, p. 54

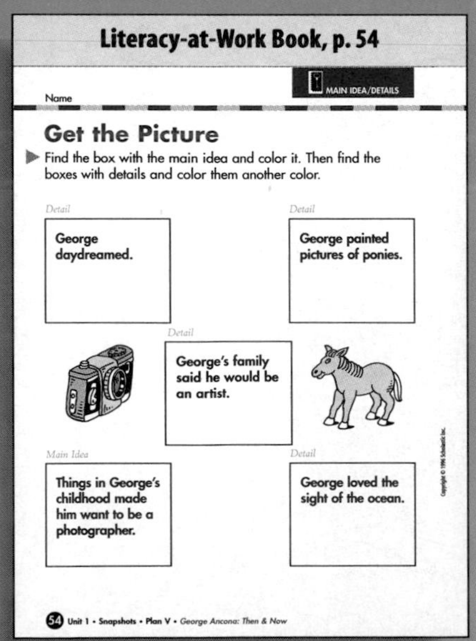

Name

MAIN IDEA/DETAILS

Get the Picture

Find the box with the main idea and color it. Then find the boxes with details and color them another color.

Detail: George daydreamed.

Detail: George painted pictures of ponies.

Detail: George's family said he would be an artist.

Main Idea: Things in George's childhood made him want to be a photographer.

Detail: George loved the sight of the ocean.

54 Unit 1 • Snapshots • Plan V • *George Ancona: Then & Now*

✔ Quickcheck

As students read *George Ancona: Then & Now*, did they:

✔ understand the main idea of the selection?

✔ use details from the selection to build their understanding of the main idea?

YES **If yes, go to ❷ Practice and Apply.**

NO **If no, start at ❶ Teach and Model.**

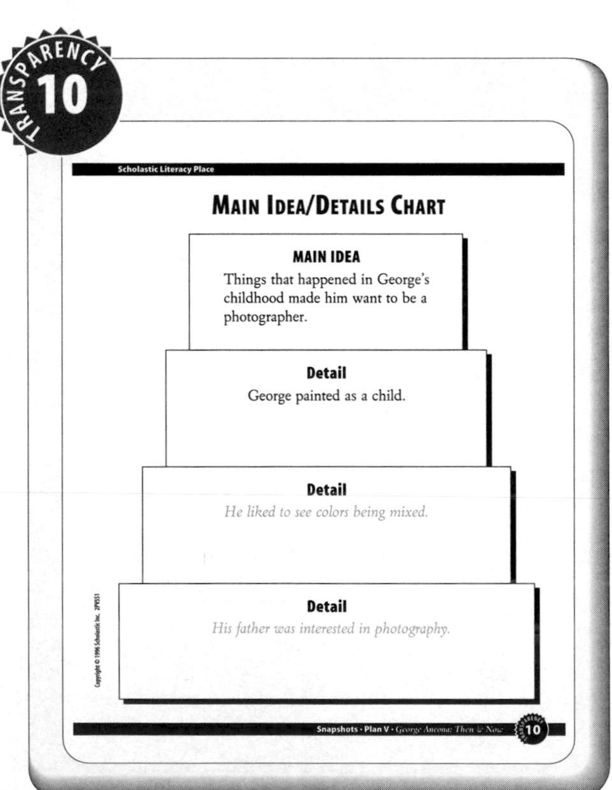

Annotated transparency for teaching Main Idea/Details

❶ Teach and Model

Read or make up a very simple story or folk tale to tell to the class. When you finish, encourage children to tell in one sentence what they think the most important idea in the story was. Ask them for story details to support what they say.

Discuss that when children read stories, sometimes the main idea of the story is very easy to find. The main idea is the most important idea in the story. When it is not easy to figure out, they have to find story clues that will help them determine the main idea.

Put It in Context

Discuss that in *George Ancona: Then & Now,* the main idea is not clearly stated. However, there are a number of clues that point to the main idea—that George Ancona's decision to become a photographer was influenced by his childhood experiences.

Think Aloud **When I started reading, I wondered why George Ancona included so many details about his childhood. When I finished reading, I realized that the details helped explain why he became a photographer.**

Ask children to turn to page 107 of *George Ancona: Then & Now.* Read the paragraph at the top of the page aloud. In it, George Ancona explains that as a child, he was always using his imagination. Discuss how George Ancona uses his imagination as a photographer. Display Transparency 10 and discuss the main idea of the selection. Ask children to find two details in the selection that support the main idea. Record the responses on the transparency.

❷ Practice and Apply

Make a Main Idea/Details Chart

PARTNERS Distribute a Main Idea/Details chart like the one on the transparency. Have pairs of children work together to find more details that tell how George Ancona's childhood influenced his decision to become a photographer. You may want to guide children in their search with questions such as the following:

- **How did growing up on Coney Island influence George Ancona's decision to become a photographer?**
- **What was Tío Mario's influence on George?**
- **What about George Ancona's father? What was his influence?**

Have children give the details they found, and encourage them to tell how these details support the main idea.

❸ Assess

Can children recognize the main idea and identify the details that support the main idea in *George Ancona: Then & Now?*

✔ **Can children understand the main idea?**

✔ **Can children identify details that support the main idea?**

If not, try this:
Look for opportunities for children to identify main ideas and supporting details in upcoming selections and trade books.

Children's Self-Assessment

✔ **How did I know that the details support the main idea?**

Supporting All Learners

Model

EXTRA HELP Some children may need extra help using the selected details to determine the main idea. During the Create a Main Idea/Details Chart Activity, use the transparency as a model and guide children through a reading of the details written there. Then model how to use these details to draw a conclusion about the main idea of the story.

CHALLENGE After the Practice and Apply activity, divide children into pairs and have them exchange their written autobiographical pieces. Encourage them to read their partners' autobiography. Then challenge them to select three details from it and use them to determine the main idea.

Transfer to New Text

Literacy-at-Work Book, p. 55

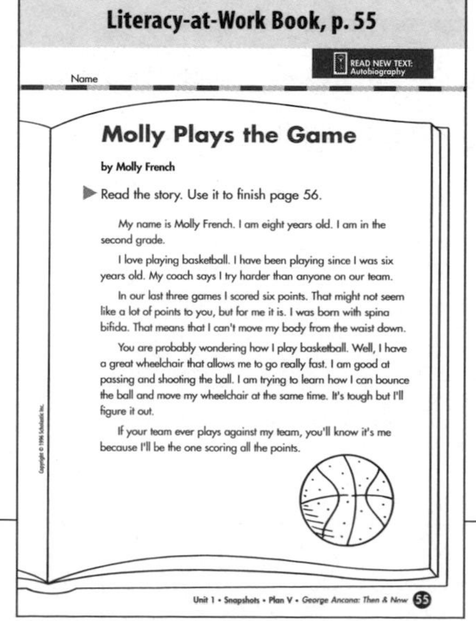

Name

READ NEW TEXT: Autobiography

Molly Plays the Game

by Molly French

▶ Read the story. Use it to finish page 56.

My name is Molly French. I am eight years old. I am in the second grade.

I love playing basketball. I have been playing since I was six years old. My coach says I try harder than anyone on our team.

In our last three games I scored six points. That might not seem like a lot of points to you, but for me it is. I was born with spina bifida. That means that I can't move my body from the waist down.

You are probably wondering how I play basketball. Well, I have a great wheelchair that allows me to go really fast. I am good at passing and shooting the ball. I am trying to learn how I can bounce the ball and move my wheelchair at the same time. It's tough but I'll figure it out.

If your team ever plays against my team, you'll know it's me because I'll be the one scoring all the points.

Unit 1 • Snapshots • Plan V • *George Ancona: Then & Now* 55

Literacy-at-Work Book, p. 56

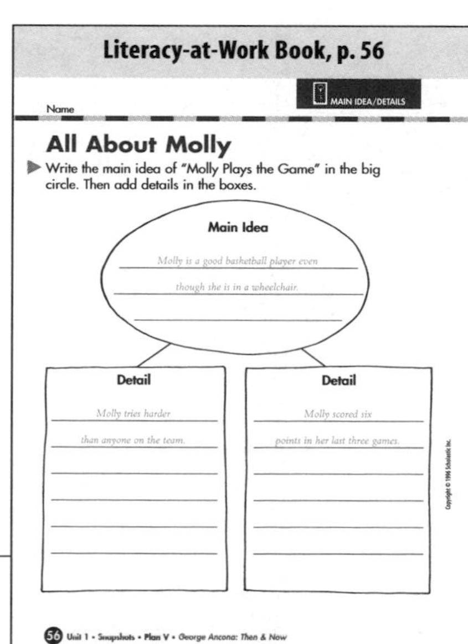

Name

MAIN IDEA/DETAILS

All About Molly

▶ Write the main idea of "Molly Plays the Game" in the big circle. Then add details in the boxes.

Main Idea

Molly is a good basketball player even though she is in a wheelchair.

Detail

Molly tries harder than anyone on the team.

Detail

Molly scored six points in her last three games.

56 Unit 1 • Snapshots • Plan V • *George Ancona: Then & Now*

C

BUILDING SKILLS AND STRATEGIES

GEORGE ANCONA: THEN & NOW

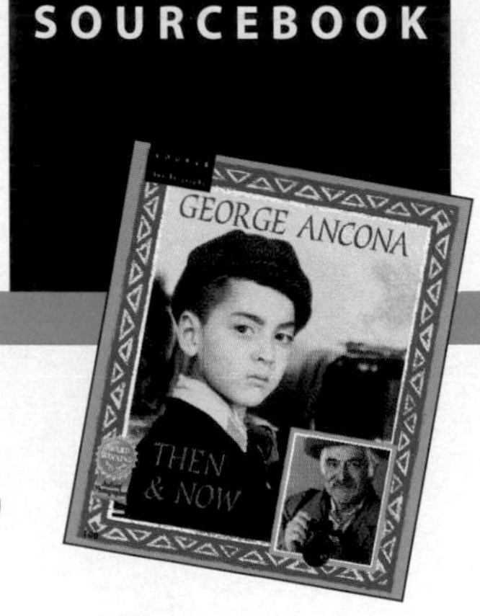

Specialized Vocabulary (✔ Unit Test)

Objectives

Children learn to:

- identify and use context clues to understand the meaning of difficult words
- transfer their learning to a new text

Materials:
SourceBook pp. 100–115
Literacy-at-Work Book pp. 55, 57–58
Transparency 11

Time:
About 20–30 minutes

Suggested Grouping:
Whole class and partners

TESTED	
CONTEXT CLUES	
Introduce	p. T248
Review	p. R20
Test	p. T311
Reteach	p. R26
SEMANTIC CUEING	

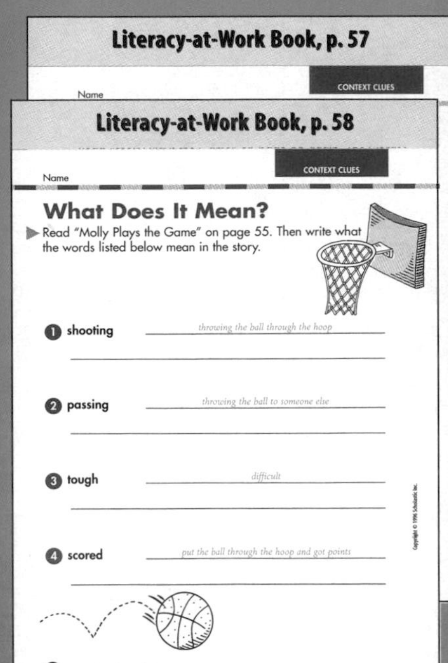

Literacy-at-Work Book, p. 57

Literacy-at-Work Book, p. 58

Name CONTEXT CLUES

What Does It Mean?

Read "Molly Plays the Game" on page 55. Then write what the words listed below mean in the story.

1. shooting — throwing the ball through the hoop
2. passing — throwing the ball to someone else
3. tough — difficult
4. scored — put the ball through the hoop and got points

58 Unit 1 • Snapshots • Plan V • George Ancona: Then & Now

✔ Quickcheck

As children read *George Ancona: Then & Now*, did they:

✔ use context clues to figure out the meaning of new words?

YES If yes, go to ❷ Practice and Apply.

NO If no, start at ❶ Teach and Model.

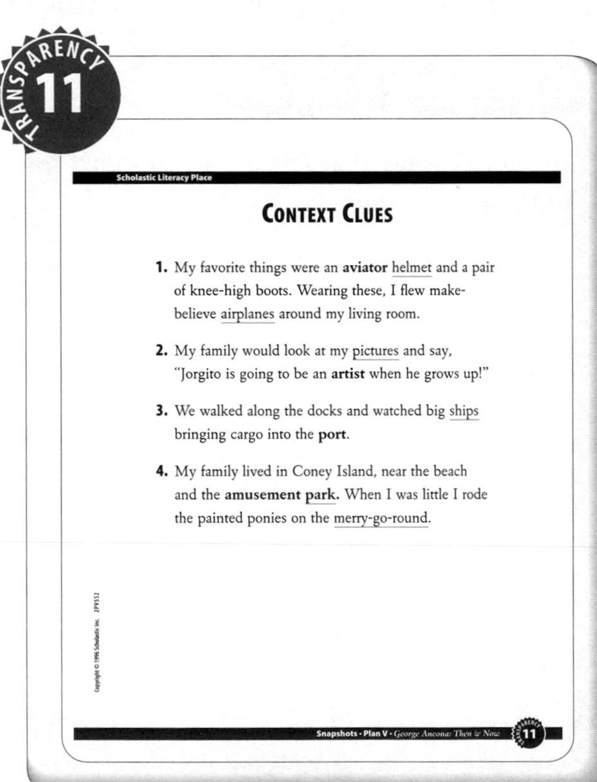

TRANSPARENCY 11

Scholastic Literacy Place

CONTEXT CLUES

1. My favorite things were an **aviator** helmet and a pair of knee-high boots. Wearing these, I flew make-believe airplanes around my living room.
2. My family would look at my pictures and say, "Jorgito is going to be an **artist** when he grows up!"
3. We walked along the docks and watched big ships bringing cargo into the **port**.
4. My family lived in Coney Island, near the beach and the **amusement park**. When I was little I rode the painted ponies on the merry-go-round.

Snapshots • Plan V • George Ancona: Then & Now 11

Annotated transparency for teaching context clues

❶ Teach and Model

Read the following to children:

The bus fare was $1.50.

Ask children what they think the word *fare* means. Encourage them to use what they already know and other words in the sentence to figure out the meaning of the word. Have them check if the meaning they chose makes sense by substituting for *fare*. Explain that children can use a similar process to figure out the meanings of unfamiliar words when they read.

Put It in Context

Display Transparency 11 and read the following sentences from *George Ancona: Then & Now*:

My favorite things were an aviator helmet and a pair of knee-high boots. Wearing these, I flew make-believe airplanes around my living room.

Think Aloud **Some of you may not know what the word *aviator* means. Let's see if we can use clues from the sentences around the word to figure out its meaning. One clue is that when George Ancona wore the aviator's helmet, he pretended to fly airplanes. I know that pilots fly airplanes, and I've seen old pictures of pilots wearing helmets. Let's replace the word *aviator* with the word *pilot*. Yes, that makes sense. So an aviator must be a pilot.**

Have children use a similar process to figure out the meaning of the words in dark print on the transparency. Ask them to tell what clues in the sentences helped them to figure out the meanings.

❷ Practice and Apply

Discover Word Meanings

Have volunteers use the process to figure out the meaning of the words *artist, cargo,* and *port*. Help children identify the following clues for each word:

- someone who paints pictures (artist)
- something a big boat carries (cargo)
- a place where boats come (port)

PARTNERS Have pairs of children work together to use the words in sentences.

OPTION

Using the Dictionary

Point out that another way to learn what a word means is to look it up in a dictionary. Partners who made up sentences can locate each word in the dictionary.

❸ Assess

Were children able to use the text and pictures to figure out new words?

✔ **Can children explain why words make sense in the context of sentences?**

If not, try this:
Look for opportunities in upcoming readings for children to use context clues when reading specialized and unfamiliar vocabulary.

Children's Self-Assessment

✔ **What do you look for when you are reading and come across a word you don't know?**

✔ **In your own words, what's one thing you can do when you come across a new word?**

SUPPORTING ALL LEARNERS

Hands-On Learning

EXTRA HELP Visually highlighting the text where the clues are found will help children identify the context clues. Before you begin the Discover Word Meanings activity, select a paragraph with a difficult word, highlight the context clues, and support children as they determine the word meaning.

ACCESS Prior to the Practice and Apply activity, help children focus on the contextual clues by guiding them through the area of text where the clues are found and helping them highlight the information they need. Then show children how to use the clues to determine meaning of an unknown word or phrase.

C

GEORGE ANCONA: THEN & NOW

SOURCEBOOK

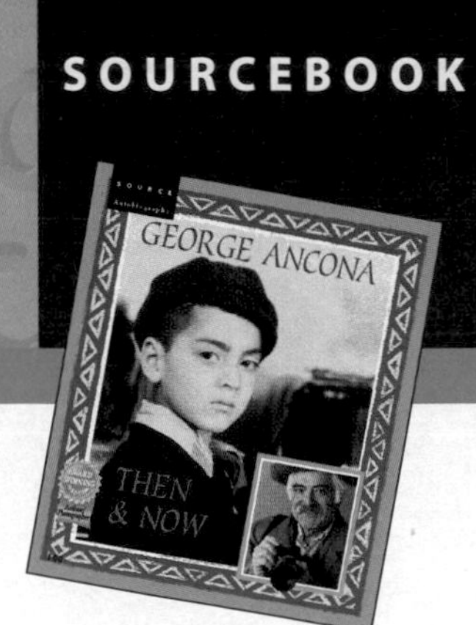

Soft /s/c, /j/g

Objectives

Children learn to:

- identify the sound of soft consonants *c* and *g*
- build words that contain /s/*c* and /j/*g*
- write /s/*c* and /j/*g* words

PHONICS AT A GLANCE

Materials:
SourceBook pp.100–115
Big Book of Rhymes and Rhythms 2A, p. 14
Magnet Board
Literacy-at-Work Book pp. 60–61
Spelling Lesson p.T243

Time:
About 15–30 minutes

Suggested Grouping:
Whole class and partners

Literacy-at-Work Book, p. 60

Name PHONICS: /s/c, /j/g

Literacy-at-Work Book, p. 61

Name PHONICS: /s/c, /j/g

Book Titles

▶ Use the words in the box to finish the title of each book.

Circus Gym
Space Gem

The Huge Gem

A Place in Space

Fancy Gym

The Circus Comes to the City

▶ Use at least two words in the box to write your own book titles.

City Giant
Cage Mice

1 ______

2 ______

Unit 1 • Snapshots • Plan V • *George Ancona: Then & Now* 61

✔ Quickcheck

As children read *George Ancona: Then & Now,* did they:

✔ recognize the sound difference between hard and soft *c* and hard and soft *g*?

✔ think of words that have soft *c* or soft *g* at the beginning or in the middle?

YES **If yes, go to the Blending section of ❷ Connect Sound/Symbol.**

NO **If no, start at ❶ Develop Oral Language.**

❶ Develop Oral Language

Phonemic Awareness

As you read aloud "Georgie Gave Me Fifty Cents" from the *Big Book of Rhymes and Rhythms,* emphasize the words *cents* and *Georgie*. Point out that /s/ starts the word *cents,* and that /j/ starts the word *Georgie*.

Children will be able to join in on the second or third reading, and some may be able to recite the poem on their own. You may want to ask children to think of other words that begin with /s/*c*, such as *city, circus,* and *circle,* and words that begin with /j/*g*, such as *gerbil, germ,* and *gentleman*. Ask for volunteers to add some of these words to the word wall.

Big Book of Rhymes and Rhythms

Georgie Asked for Fifty Cents

Georgie asked his mother,
mother, mother
For fifty cents, cents, cents
To see the elephant, elephant, elephant
Jump over the fence, fence, fence.
He jumped so high, high, high
He reached the sky, sky, sky
And he never came back, back, back
Until the Fourth of July.

Georgie
cents

14

❷ Connect Sound/Symbol

Put It In Context

Help children find the words *city* and *George* in *George Ancona: Then & Now.* Write the words on the chalkboard and underline the letters *c* and *g*. Ask children to listen to the sounds of these letters as you blend them in the words while running your hand under the letters. On the chalkboard, write some of the words children suggested earlier. Then have volunteers underline the *c* or *g* as each word is read aloud by the group.

Blending

Make two column headings on the chalkboard—/s/*c* and /j/*g*. In the first column write *cent*. Run your finger under each letter as you blend the letters to help children pronounce the word. Remind children that each word begins with /s/*c*. Write *gem* in column 2 and repeat procedure. Add other words that begin with /s/*c* or /j/*g* to the appropriate column. Then ask children to follow the blending procedure as they read the words aloud.

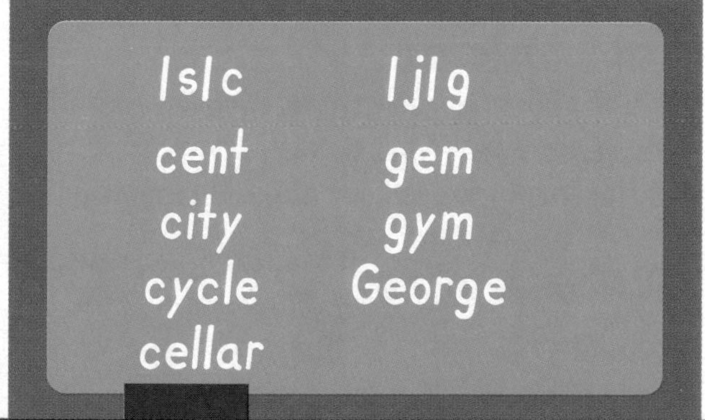

❸ Assess

Write

As a way of assessing children's understanding of /s/*c* and /j/*g*, ask them to write sentences using two words from the list on the chalkboard.

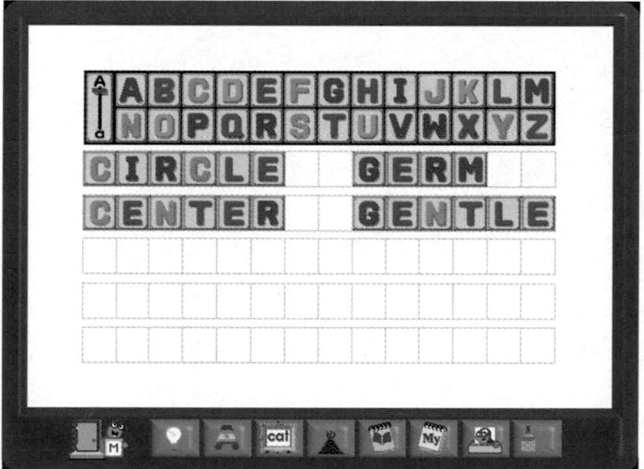

IDENTIFY SOFT *C* AND *G* WORDS

Let every child cut out or draw pictures of words with /s/*c* and /j/*g* and paste them on posterboard to make a collaborative collage. Add labels to identify the soft *c* or *g* words. Display the collage and have children record the words in their Journals.

See Phonics and Word Building Kit for additional suggestions.

The Magnet Board activity pictured above provides additional phonics practice. For information on this and other Magnet Board activities, see the WiggleWorks Plus Teaching Plan.

SUPPORTING ALL LEARNERS

Build on Success

ESL Second-language learners will benefit from additional practice with the /s/*c* and /j/*g* words that are used in the story. Encourage children to look through the story and point out words that begin with these sounds. Guide children in pronouncing the words and write them in two columns on the chalkboard.

CHALLENGE Challenge children to use as many of the /s/*c* words and /j/*g* words that they compiled in the Identify Soft *c* and *g* Words activity as they can in a short story or poem. Encourage them to share their creations with their classmates.

Building Fluency

Objectives

Children read *Two Crazy Pigs* for fluency.

Technology Options

Encourage children to listen to the audiocassette recording of *Two Crazy Pigs*.

Two Crazy Pigs

Written by Karen Berman Nagel
Illustrated by Brian Schatell

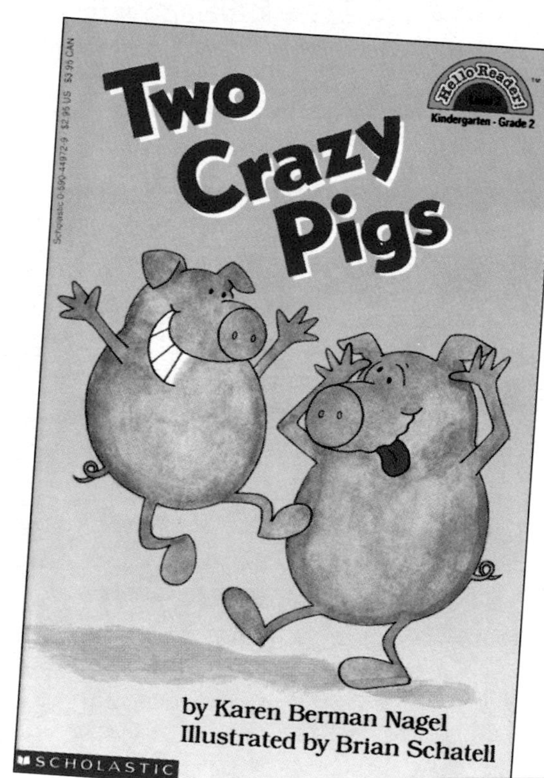

Challenge	
Average	
Easy	◀

Preview and Read

Have children read the title of the book and help them read the author's and the illustrator's names. Ask them to pay attention to the pictures as they flip through the book to find clues that will tell what the book is about.

- **Where does the story take place?**
- **What crazy things do the pigs do?**
- **What do you think will happen to the pigs?**

Response Ideas

After children have read, they can meet with you or a partner to discuss the story. Use questions such as these to discuss:

- **Think about Mr. and Mrs. Fenster and Mr. and Mrs. Henhawk. How are they alike? How are they different?**
- **Why did the Fensters move to the city?**

Read Across Texts

- **Think about *George Ancona: Then & Now* and *Two Crazy Pigs*. What do these two very different stories tell you about imagination?**

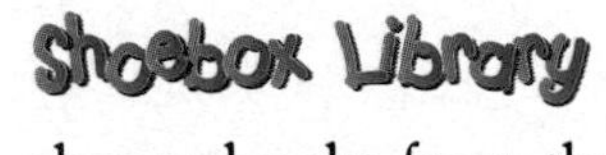

For more independent reading opportunities choose books from the Shoebox Library.

USING THE TRADE BOOKS

A Birthday Basket for Tia

Written by Pat Mora
Illustrated by Cecily Lang

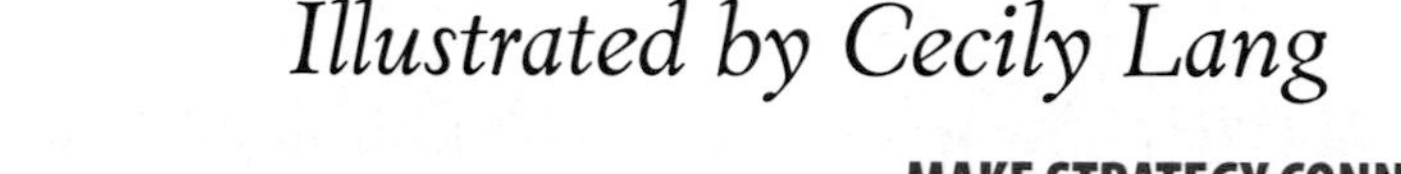

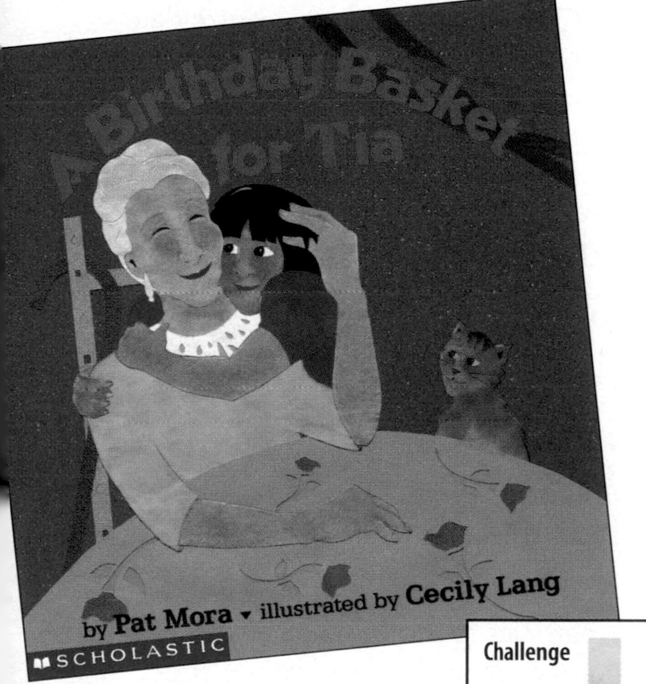

Challenge
Average
Easy

MAKE STRATEGY CONNECTIONS:

MAIN IDEA/DETAILS

Talk About It

The main idea of *George Ancona: Then & Now* is that George uses his imagination and childhood experiences in his work as a photographer. In *A Birthday Basket for Tía,* Cecilia uses her experiences with her great-aunt to plan a birthday present for her. Details show how both George Ancona and Cecilia are close to older family members and proud of their Mexican heritage. After reading *A Birthday Basket for Tía,* have a discussion by asking questions such as these:

- **What are some of the ways that Cecilia and Tía spend time together?**
- **What are some of the things George Ancona enjoyed as a boy?**

Write About It

JOURNAL After reading *A Birthday Basket for Tía,* invite children to write about a special time they spent with a favorite relative. What did they do together? What made the occasion so special?

Read Across Texts

After children have finished reading *A Birthday Basket for Tía,* encourage them to compare it with *George Ancona: Then & Now*. Have them explore this question:

- **If George Ancona took a photograph of Cecilia and Tía, what do you think Cecilia and Tía would be doing?**

USING THE TRADE BOOK GUIDE

For more teaching ideas, refer to the individual Trade Book Guide for *A Birthday Basket for Tía* by Pat Mora.

Encourage children to listen to the audiocassette recording of *A Birthday Basket for Tia.*

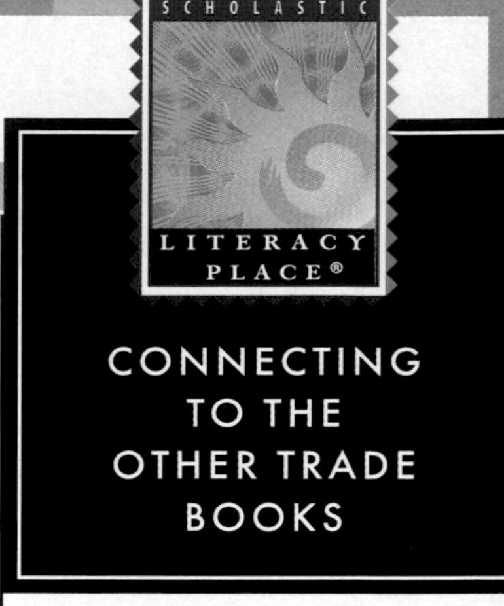

CONNECTING TO THE OTHER TRADE BOOKS

Ask children to compare these illustrations to the photographs in *George Ancona: Then & Now*.

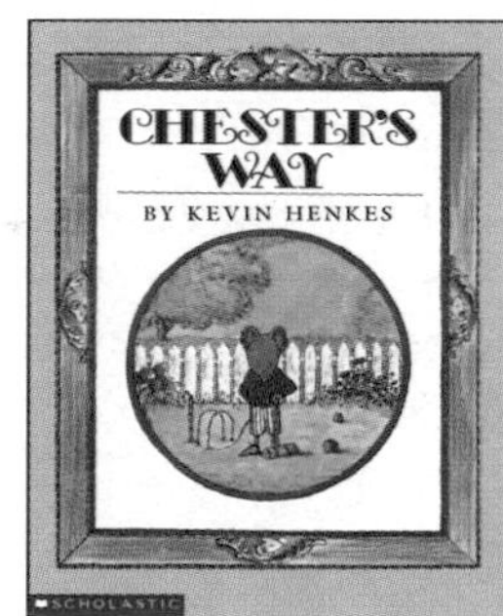

Ask children to compare how Lilly used her imagination with how George uses his. How did imagination make each person special?

Also for use with this plan

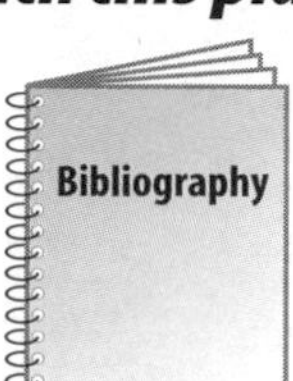

INTEGRATING LEARNING

Curriculum Areas

Math

Children estimate the distance in a group photo by George Ancona.
See page R10.

Science

Children make sun prints by taping construction paper forms to a sunny window.
See page R10.

Social Studies

Children make a travel brochure using photos of a place they'd like to visit.
See page R11.

The Arts

Children use colored pencils to make a print from a textured surface.
See page R11.

Use Your Sports Arena

Where Do They Belong?

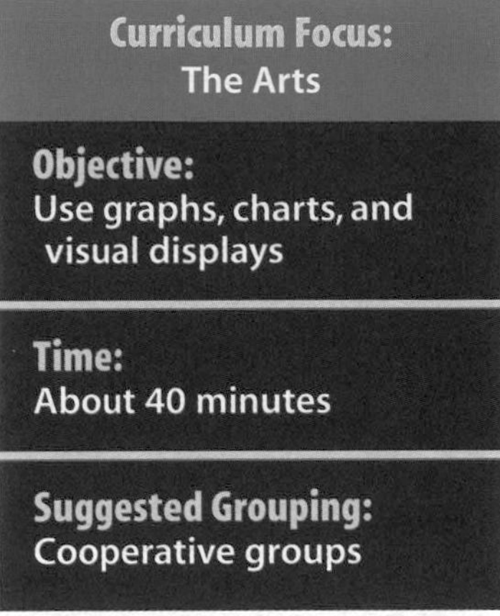

Curriculum Focus: The Arts

Objective: Use graphs, charts, and visual displays

Time: About 40 minutes

Suggested Grouping: Cooperative groups

ACTIVITY Prompt children to think about different things that could be included in an exhibit.

Connect to the SourceBook Children can begin to consolidate their understanding based on the activities in Teaching Plans I–V and in the two Workshops in preparation for the Project included in Teaching Plan VI.

Make New Discoveries

- In the Project (see page T303 of your Teacher's SourceBook), children will demonstrate the literacies and skills they've acquired throughout the unit as they create an exhibit.
- As children develop their exhibits, they'll need to sort through information and clarify their ideas. Revising their trading cards will help them practice incorporating newly acquired information and will demonstrate how work can be improved over time.
- Divide children into three groups: Sports, Art, Hobbies. Challenge them to make a list of objects that belong in their category.
- Suggest that children draw cartoon versions of stories or articles found in the classroom Sports Arena. This is a good way to illustrate how to order and condense a narrative, both visually and verbally.

✔ **How to Assess** Did children's revised trading cards show improvement over their first efforts?

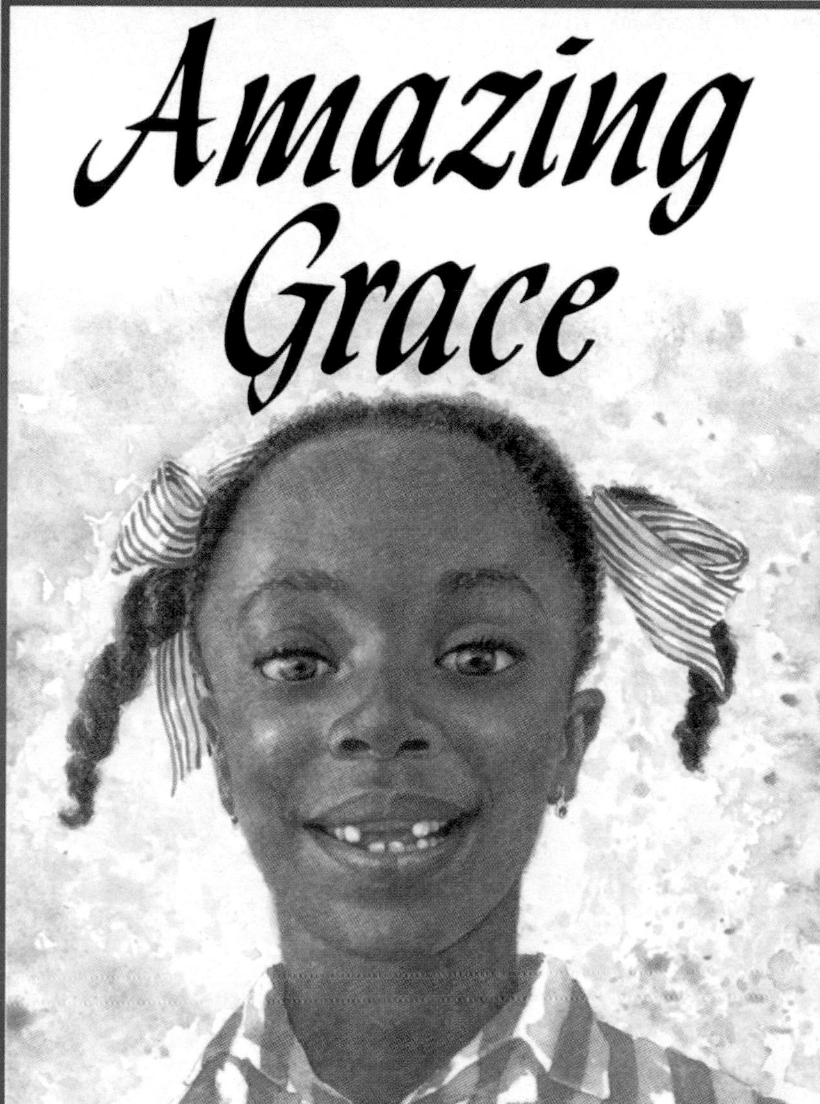

Plan VI

WHAT CHILDREN WILL DO

listen to the Read Aloud *Thunder Cake*

read the selections

- *Amazing Grace* REALISTIC FICTION
- "An Amazing Peter Pan" THEATER PROGRAM

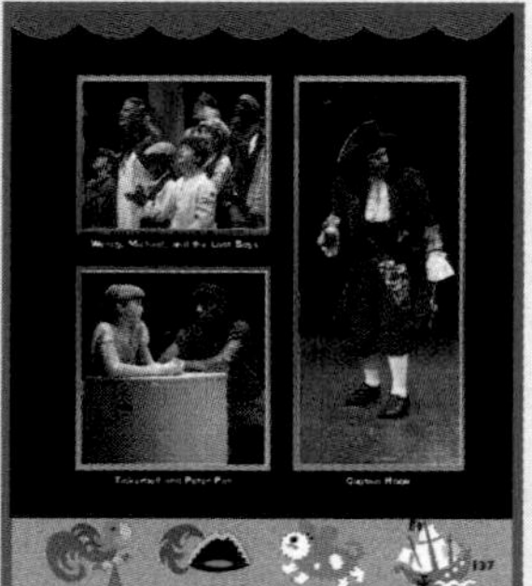

use the key strategy of Theme

blend words with *l*-blends

write about a character in a real-life situation

apply what they learn about overcoming fears and obstacles to their daily lives

Assessing Your Students

ASSESSMENT	TEACHER'S SOURCEBOOK	ASSESSMENT KIT
Vocabulary Test	T261	Assessment Handbook
Observation	T262	Assessment Handbook
Assess Reading	T286	Classroom Management Forms
Conference	T286	Assessment Handbook
Performance-Based	T291	Assessment Handbook
Writing Benchmarks	T291	Assessment Handbook
Spelling Tests	T261, T293	Assessment Handbook
Quickcheck	T296, T298	Assessment Handbook
Formal Tests	T311	Unit/Year Tests

Creating a Community of Learners

Thunder Cake pp. T258–259

- Brainstorm a list of common fears
- Dramatize scenes from the story
- Visualize MINI-LESSON

Demonstrating Independence

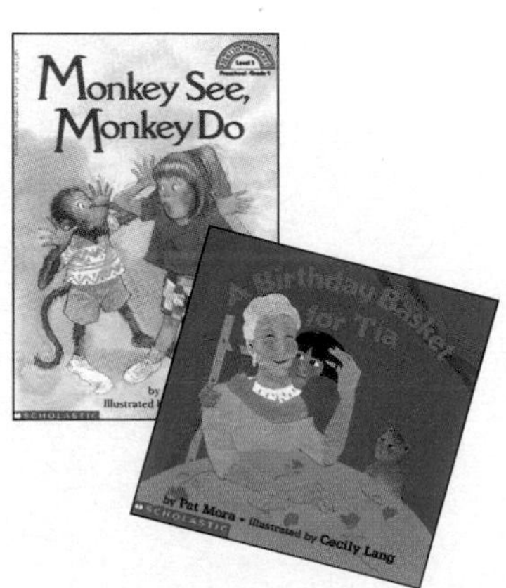

Using the Trade Books: pp. T300–301

- *Monkey See, Monkey Do* by Mark Gave
- *A Birthday Basket for Tía* by Pat Mora

Closing the Unit: p. T302

- Project: Exhibit

Focus on Phonics

Phonics Lesson

- *l* –Blends

Phonics Kit

Literacy-at-Work Book

- *l* –Blends, pp. 71–72
- Review Soft /s/*c*, /j/*g*, p. 73

PLAN VI ORGANIZER

Amazing Grace / "An Amazing Peter Pan"

	Instructional Path	Supporting All Learners	Resources and Technology
a **READING THE SOURCES** pp. T260–287	**Build Background** ✔ **Develop Vocabulary** *• auditions • theater • bullet •stunning • imaginary • amazing* **Reading Selections** *Amazing Grace* "An Amazing Peter Pan"  Launch the Key Strategy: Theme ✔ **Assess Reading**	EXTRA HELP p. T280  ESL pp. T258, T261, T264, T271, T278, T284 CHALLENGE pp. T261, T275 MINI-LESSON Setting, p. T272 Picture Clues, p. T279 Theater Program, p. T 285 **Idea File:** p. T287 **Cultural Connections:** p. T287	**Transparency** Build Background, 12 **Literacy-at-Work Book** Vocabulary, p. 63 Comprehension Check, p. 63  **WiggleWorks™ Plus,** pp. T280, T282 **Additional Technology:** p. T295
b **INTEGRATING LANGUAGE ARTS** pp. T288–295	✔ **Writing:** Write About a Story Character; Daily Language Practice ✔ **Grammar:** Describing Words **Mechanics:** Periods ✔ **Spelling:** Words With Final *e* *• home • vote • stone • stove • grape • shape • snake • shake • hide • spice*	 EXTRA HELP p. T89  ESL pp. T289, T295 **Activity File:** pp. T294–295 Make a Play Poster or Program Write and Perform a Script Write a Book Report Watch a Video of *Peter Pan* MINI-LESSON Oral Expression, p. T294 Book Titles, p. T295	**Literacy-at-Work Book** Writing, p. 64 **Grammar, Usage, and Mechanics Practice:** pp. 11–12 **Spelling Practice:** p. 6 **Handwriting Practice:** p. 6  **WiggleWorks™ Plus,** pp. T291, T294 **Additional Technology:** p. T295
 **BUILDING SKILLS AND STRATEGIES** pp. T296–299	✔ Quickcheck  Launch the Key Strategy: Theme ✔ Quickcheck PHONICS: *l* – Blends	ESL pp. T297, T299 CHALLENGE p. T299 ACCESS p. T297 **Review** Plot, p. R18 Make Predictions, p. R19 Context Clues: Specialized Vocabulary p. R20 PHONICS: /s/*c*, /j/*g*, p. R21	**Transparency** Key Strategy, 13 **Literacy-at-Work Book** Theme, pp. 65–67 Phonics, pp. 71–72 **WiggleWorks™ Plus,** p. T299

✔ = **Assessed**

CREATING A COMMUNITY OF LEARNERS

LISTEN TO THE READ ALOUD

Objectives

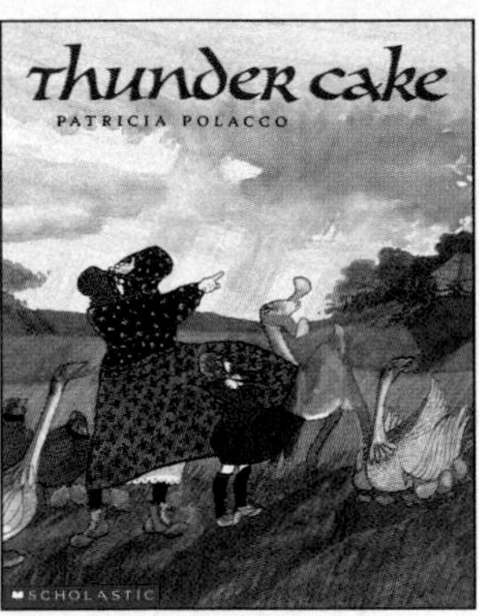

Children learn to:

- **brainstorm a list of common fears**
- **visualize a setting and a storm**
- **dramatize scenes from the story**

Materials: Read Aloud Book: *Thunder Cake*
Time: About 25 minutes
Suggested Grouping: Whole class and cooperative groups

Technology Options

Invite cooperative groups to record their own scary sounds on audiocassettes. Play the recordings and have the rest of the class try to guess what the sounds are.

Thunder Cake

Before reading *Amazing Grace,* introduce children to the **theme** that you can learn to do **anything** you **want,** when they read *Thunder Cake,* the story of a little girl who **overcomes** a fear.

INTRODUCE THE READ ALOUD

COOPERATIVE GROUPS Have children work together to:

- brainstorm and list common sounds people are afraid of.
- share experiences of how they handle the sounds they list.

When children gather as a class again, invite them to compare their lists. Have them identify sounds that are common to all the lists. You may want to point out that talking about a fear is one way to reduce it. Sharing fears often makes people feel safer. Encourage children to mention experiences when older members of their families have shared their wisdom about overcoming fear in ways that were helpful to them.

ESL Pair children acquiring English with native speakers who can support them when they work together to brainstorm sounds people are afraid of. Encourage children to identify the sounds and to imitate unfamiliar sounds for their classmates. (Peer Partner)

LISTEN TO THE READ ALOUD

Display the cover of the book and read the title aloud. Ask children to listen as you read a story about a girl whose grandmother helps her overcome her fear of thunder.

- **Let's listen together to find out how the girl's wise grandmother helps her overcome her fear.**
- **What do you think a Thunder Cake is?**

Think About the Read Aloud

Give children time to share their thoughts and opinions about the story. You may want to encourage the discussion with questions such as:

- **Trade places with the girl. In what ways would you be like her? In what ways would you be different from her?**
- **Trade places with Grandma. How would you help the girl overcome her fear of thunder? What would you do the same way as the grandma in the story? What would you do differently?**
- **Do you think you would like the Thunder Cake? Why or why not?**
- **At the beginning of the story, how do you think the girl feels about herself? Why? How do you think she feels at the end of the story?**
- **As you listened to the story, how did you picture the storm? What did you see? Hear? Feel?** MINI-LESSON

Activity: Dramatization

Have children work in cooperative groups to dramatize a part of the story. Have them choose a favorite scene and role-play characters for a few minutes. Challenge them to improvise further dialogue, scenes, or characters. THE ARTS

Make Connections

To Children's Lives

Encourage children to think about a real-life situation in which they helped someone overcome a fear, or someone helped them do the same. Based on their experience, what advice would they give to the grandmother or to the girl in the story?

MINI-LESSON

Visualize

TEACH/MODEL Read the first two pages of *Thunder Cake* aloud.

> **THINK ALOUD When I listen to these words, I picture in my mind where the story is taking place. I can see fields, and off in the distance I see dark clouds and lightning. I also imagine how the voices of the grandmother and the girl sound.**

APPLY As children listen to you read, have them take turns telling you what pictures they see and what sounds they hear in their minds.

VISUAL LITERACY

a

READING THE SOURCES

AMAZING GRACE / AN AMAZING PETER PAN

Build Background

Like the girl in *Thunder Cake* who **overcame** her fear of thunder, *Amazing Grace* finds out that she can do **anything** she puts her mind to.

Objectives

Children learn to:

- relate personal experiences
- make a "Trying New Things" chart
- develop vocabulary using categories
- expand oral language

Materials:
Transparency 12
Literacy-at-Work Book p. 62
Word Cards 28–33

Time:
About 20 minutes

Suggested Grouping:
Whole class and individuals

Literacy-at-Work Book, p. 62

Name VOCABULARY

Amazing Words

▶ Match each word in the box with its meaning. Write the word on the line.

theater
amazing
auditions
ballet
imaginary
stunning

1. tryouts or tests for parts or roles *auditions*
2. very surprising *amazing*
3. very talented or beautiful *stunning*
4. not real *imaginary*
5. a place to see plays, ballets, or movies *theater*
6. a dance that tells a story *ballet*

▶ Write the word from the box that describes the picture.

ballet

62 Unit 1 • Snapshots • Plan VI • *Amazing Grace*

ACTIVATE PRIOR KNOWLEDGE

Discuss Trying New Things

Encourage children to talk about times when they wanted to do something new but were afraid to try. The following questions will encourage children to share their experiences:

- **What did you want to do? What were you afraid of?**
- **Who helped you overcome your fear? What did that person do or say?**
- **What do you think people can do to help themselves overcome a fear?**
- **How does trying your best help you do what you want to do?**
- **When you try your best to do something, how do you feel about yourself?**

Make a "Trying New Things" Chart

As children respond to the questions, record their answers on Transparency 12 or on a chart modeled on the transparency.

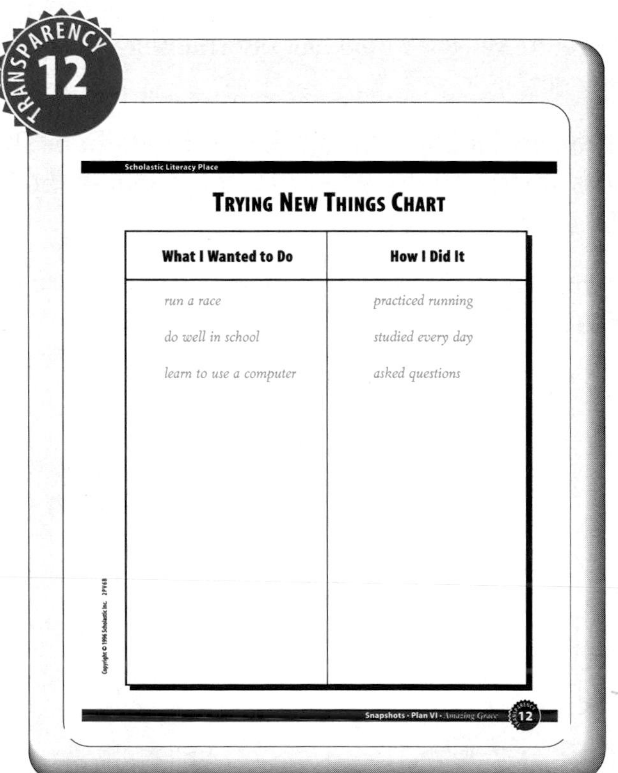
TRANSPARENCY 12

Scholastic Literacy Place

TRYING NEW THINGS CHART

What I Wanted to Do	How I Did It
run a race	*practiced running*
do well in school	*studied every day*
learn to use a computer	*asked questions*

Snapshots • Plan VI • *Amazing Grace* 12

Annotated transparency for building background

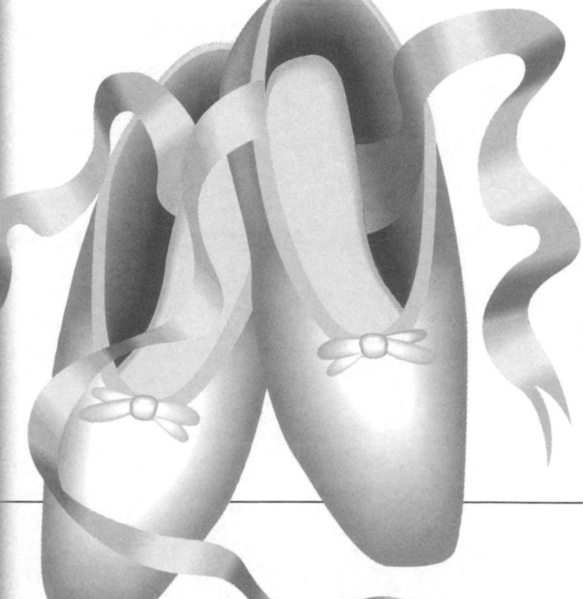

Develop Vocabulary

Strategy: Categories Begin by displaying Word Cards 28–33. Read each concept word aloud, and have children repeat it after you. Discuss the meaning of each word. Then distribute the cards to children. Accept their suggestions for how to group the cards, or suggest two categories: "Words That Name Things" and "Words That Describe Things." As the words are categorized, have each child holding a card move into the appropriate group. After children have categorized all the concept words, encourage them to expand their vocabularies by thinking of additional theater-related words for each category.

OPTION

Create a Word Web

Write *stunning* on the chalkboard or on a chart, and circle it. Children can develop a word web by connecting other circles and writing synonyms for *stunning* in them. Repeat with *amazing*.

Support Words As children read *Amazing Grace*, you may want to point out other unusual words in the story:

fantastic: wonderful; great

play: a story that is acted out, usually on stage

sparkling: shining brightly; glittering

tutu: a short, frilly skirt worn by a ballerina

Personal Word List Children can generate in their Journals their own lists of new and interesting words they encounter during reading, including words related to the theater and performing.

VOCABULARY

ORGANIZING CONCEPT: THEATER WORDS

Concept Words

	auditions:	tryouts for a part in a show (p. 125)
✔	theater:	a place to see movies or plays (p. 128)
✔	ballet:	a kind of dance (p. 129)
	stunning:	very beautiful (p. 129)
	imaginary:	make-believe; not real (p. 131)
✔	amazing:	surprising (p. 135)

✔ = assessed

S M T W T F S

See p. T293 for words to pretest and spelling instruction

Technology Options

Children might enjoy watching the video version of *Amazing Grace*, available from Weston Woods.

Supporting All Learners

Use Visuals

ESL During the Activate Prior Knowledge activity, facilitate participation of children acquiring English by inviting them to express their ideas visually. Children can create storyboards with four pictures that indicate the following: what they wanted to do; what they were afraid of; who helped them overcome the fear; and how that person did it. Then help children use the storyboards to narrate their experiences.

CHALLENGE Following the Develop Vocabulary activities, challenge children to create storyboards with as many pictures as they need to relate a story using the new concept and support words.

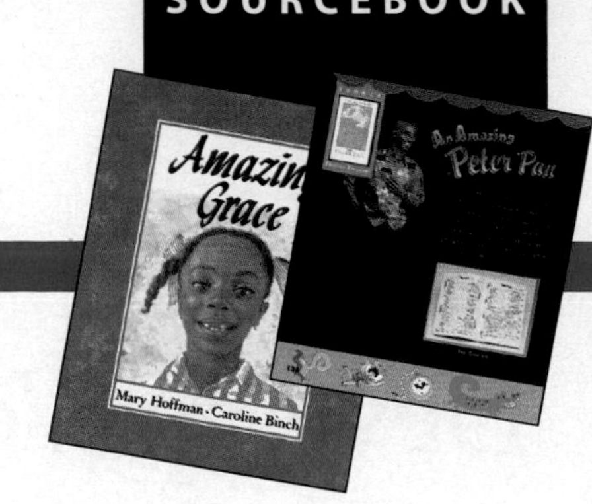

a

Reading The Sources

AMAZING GRACE / AN AMAZING PETER PAN

Prepare to Teach

OBSERVATION

As children read *Amazing Grace*, notice how they:

- ✔ make connections with the *key strategy* of Theme.
- ✔ recognize the *text structure* of Dialogue and distinguish it from Narration.
- ✔ understand the *literary element* of Plot.

Use the Individual and Class Plan Checklists in the Classroom Management Forms, pp. 9 and 15.

KEY STRATEGY:

Theme

Amazing Grace provides an excellent opportunity for children to recognize the theme of the selection as they follow the events and listen to the dialogue. Grace, the main character, demonstrates the theme by doing what she wants to do even though she was initially discouraged by friends. The author also states the theme when the grandmother says, "You can be anything you want, if you put your mind to it."

Customize Instruction

FLEXIBLE GROUPING

Teacher Support

Construct meaning by using the key strategy of Theme as children read the selections. Revisit the selections to build understanding of the text structures of Dialogue and Narration.

Collaborative

Partners can read *Amazing Grace* together. Encourage them to use chunks of dialogue as a structure for reading aloud with a partner.

Extra Support

After reading the story aloud, invite children to read along as you reread it. Use the questions and modeling suggestions to help children understand the relationship between the illustrations and the text.

Independent

Independent readers will want to read the selection without interruption. Use the Assess Reading questions on page T286 to check their understanding of the story.

Meet the Illustrator

Caroline Binch

Caroline Binch lives in England. She loves to travel, and she paints wherever she goes. One of her favorite places to visit is the Caribbean, and several of her children's books are set on the Caribbean Islands. Children can read about Caroline Binch on pp. 142–143 of the SourceBook.

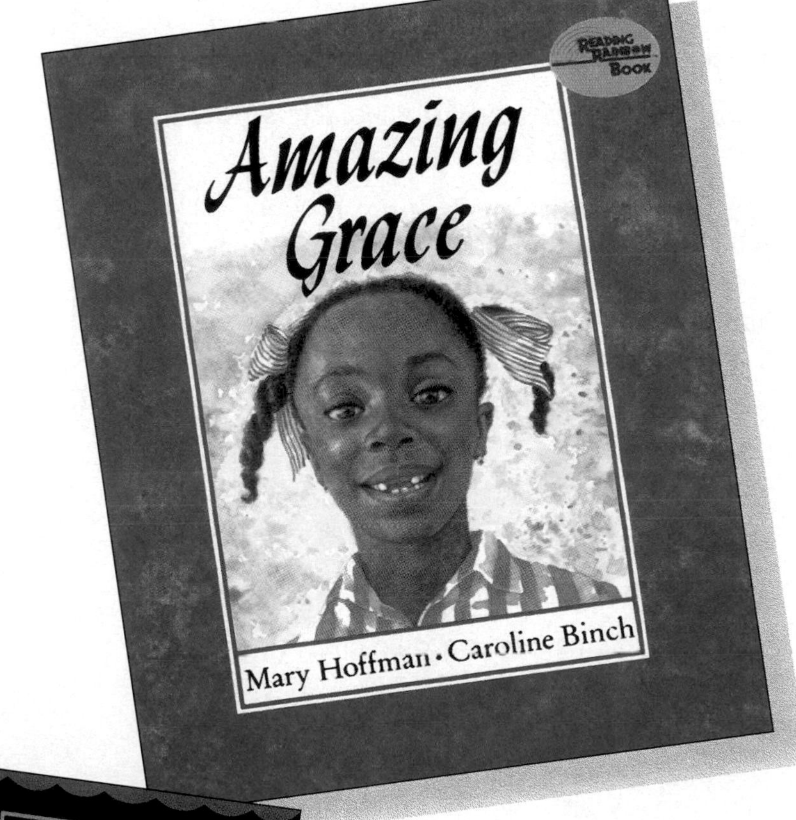

More Illustrations by Caroline Binch

- ***Bountiful Grace***
  by Mary Hoffman
  This sequel to *Amazing Grace* tells more about this spirited girl.
- ***Gregory Cool***
  by Caroline Binch
  Urbanite Gregory visits his island relatives in Tobago and finds some loving surprises.
- ***Hue Boy***
  by Rita P. Mitchell
  This story shows how Hue Boy deals with the well-meaning advice of his neighbors.

Books for Word Study

- ***Aunt Lilly's Laundromat***
  by Melanie Hope Greenberg
  Every day, Aunt Lilly cleans clothes in her laundromat and thinks about her paintings of Haiti, her home.
  (*l*-blends: *cl* and *bl*)
- ***Flap Your Wings***
  by P.D. Eastman
  A mother bird is surprised when one of her hatchlings can't fly.
  (*l*-blend: *fl*)

▲ **SourceBook pp. 116–135**

◀ **SourceBook pp. 136–137**

a

READING THE SOURCES

Preview and Predict

READER TO READER

The girl in this story enjoys hearing tales and acting them out. Some of you might like doing that, too.

Read the title and point out the author's and illustrator's names. VISUAL LITERACY

Invite children to read the first page, then look at the illustrations on the next six.

- **What is Grace doing in the six pictures?**
- **Do you recognize any of the characters Grace is pretending to be?**

Ask children what they want to find out when they read the story. Work with them to create a chart showing what they know about Grace and what they want to find out. They can also predict what they will learn.

We Know: Grace acts out stories.

We Want to Find Out: What makes Grace amazing?

JOURNAL You may wish to have children record in their Journals what they already know, what they want to find out, and what they can predict about *Amazing Grace.*

SUPPORTING ALL LEARNERS

Preview **ESL** Preview the story with children acquiring English by drawing on their personal experiences of performing and seeing others perform. Encourage them to talk about roles they have played and elicit the idea that an actor can portray any character she or he wants. **(Make Connections)**

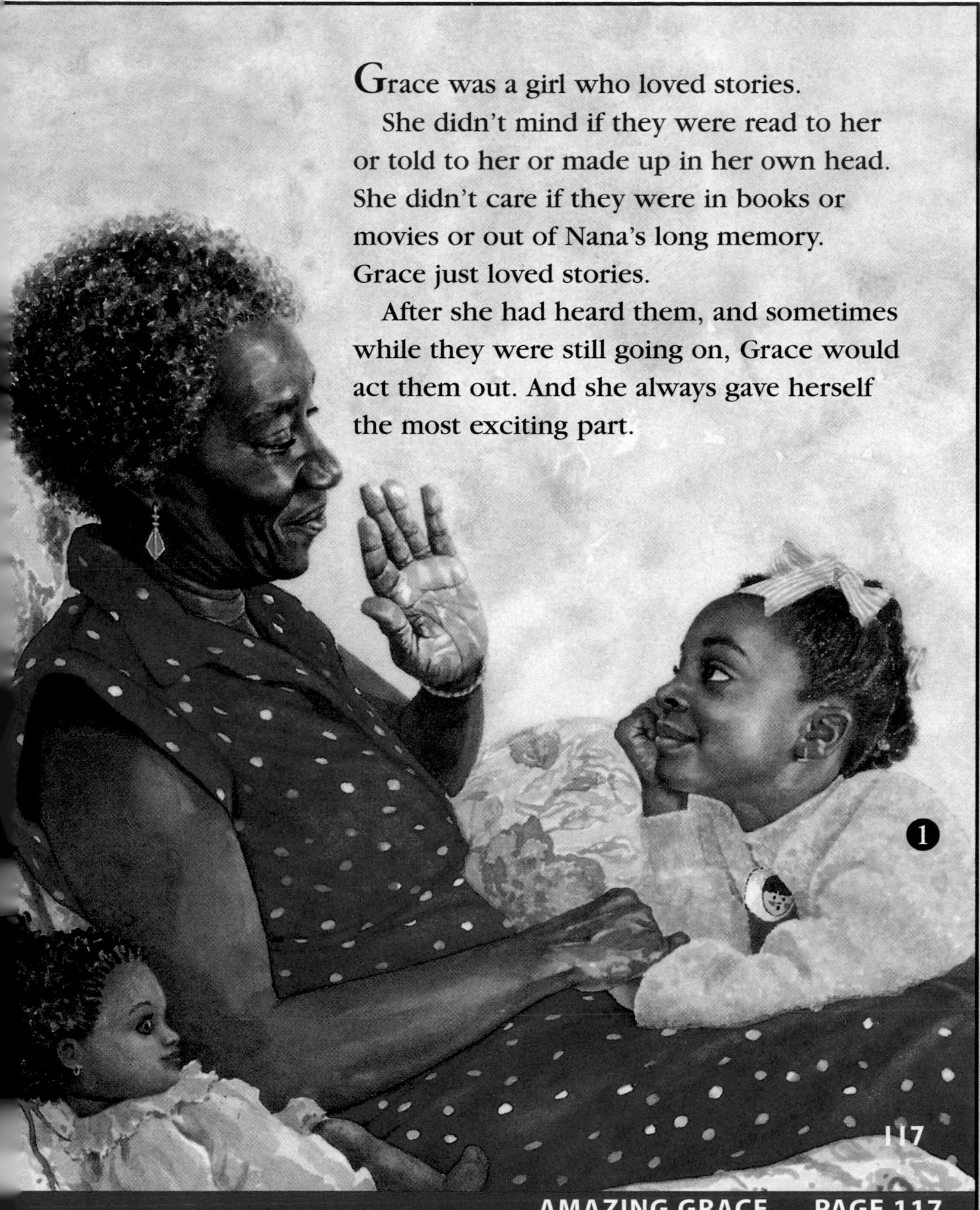

Grace was a girl who loved stories.

She didn't mind if they were read to her or told to her or made up in her own head. She didn't care if they were in books or movies or out of Nana's long memory. Grace just loved stories.

After she had heard them, and sometimes while they were still going on, Grace would act them out. And she always gave herself the most exciting part. ❶

117

AMAZING GRACE PAGE 117

Guided Reading

LAUNCH THE KEY STRATEGY:

THEME

THINK ALOUD Writers usually have an idea to present or a point to make when they write a story, but they don't always tell what that idea or point is. Instead, they show an idea through the events of the story or how the characters behave. After I finish reading, I ask myself what the writer was trying to tell me.

❶ KEY STRATEGY: Theme As I begin to read, I ask myself why the author calls Grace amazing. In the pictures on pages 116 and 117, Grace looks pretty ordinary to me. Why do you think the author considers Grace amazing?

a

Guided Reading ►

❷ Character I know Grace's favorite thing to do. I figured it out from clues in the pictures and words. What do you think is her favorite thing to do? What clues did you find to help you figure it out? VISUAL LITERACY

Revisit ◄

Capitalization: Names

Point out the capital letters in the names Joan of Arc and Anansi. Explain that names of specific people, places, and things are proper nouns. They begin with capital letters. Explain that *Spider* is capitalized because Anansi the Spider is the full name of a character in a book. Point out that in names or titles, little words like *of* and *the* are not capitalized.

► INTEGRATED CURRICULUM **SOCIAL STUDIES** *(See p. R13.)*

Children select costumes and props for a character from a favorite story.

and wove a wicked web as Anansi the Spider.

119

AMAZING GRACE PAGE 119

Read On ► ► ►

PHONICS Final *e* (*o-e*)

Ask children to find the word *wove* on page 119, point to the vowel *o* and final *e*, and read the word aloud. Invite children to generate a list of other words they know with the pattern consonant-vowel-consonant-*e*. Encourage them to look for other words with this pattern as they read the story.

a

Guided Reading ►

3 **Make Inferences** **In the bottom picture on page 120, who is Grace pretending to be? How do you know? What clues in the picture tell you where she pretends to go exploring? What word clue tells you what she is looking for?**

Revisit ◄

Conventions of Print: Ellipses

Point out the ellipses on pages 120 and 121. Explain that the author uses three dots to tell the reader that more information is coming. The list of characters Grace pretends to be is not finished; more characters are coming.

She hid inside the wooden horse at the gates of Troy....

She went exploring for lost kingdoms.... 

120

PAGE 120 SNAPSHOTS

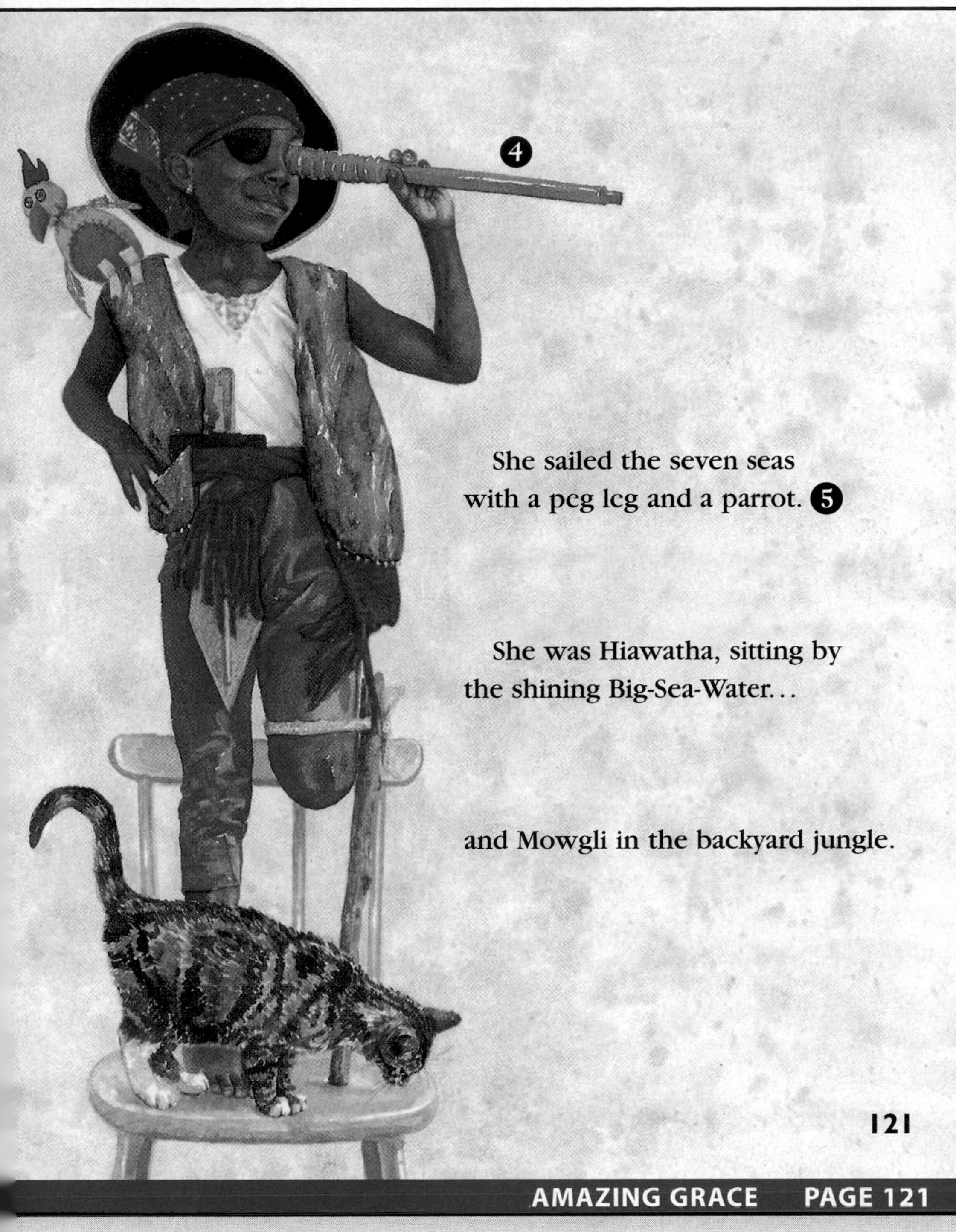

Guided Reading ▶

4 **Picture Clues** **I see some picture clues on page 121 that tell me what Grace pretends next. What clues do you see?** VISUAL LITERACY

5 **Word Attack** **Follow along while I read: "She sailed the seven seas with a peg leg and a . . . ." What do you think the next word is? Let's try to figure it out. The word begins with *p*. In the picture I see a cat, a parrot, and a . . . . Wait, *parrot* begins with *p*. Try the word *parrot* in the sentence to see if it makes sense.**

▶ INTEGRATED CURRICULUM **THE ARTS** *(See p. R13.)*

Children make a set design for one of Grace's characters.

a

Guided Reading ►

6 **Picture Clues** **I've noticed that when Grace acts out adventures from famous stories, she often has a companion. Have you noticed the same thing? Who is Grace's trusty companion for many of her adventures?** VISUAL LITERACY

7 **Prior Knowledge** **What parts do you think Grace plays when she acts out the story of Aladdin? What might she do or say?**

Revisit ◄

Convention of Print: Dashes

Call attention to the dash in the sentence on page 122. Explain that a dash is used to indicate a break in thought. What is the break in thought in this sentence? Have children look for dashes in other sentences and discuss how they are used.

PHONICS *l*-Blends

Have children find the word *played* on page 122, point to the letters *pl,* and read the word aloud. Have children think of other words beginning with the letters *pl*. Ask them to look at page 120, find the word *exploring*, point to the letters *pl*, and read the word aloud. Ask children where they hear the sounds /pl/ in *exploring*.

(See Phonics: l-Blends on pp. T298–299.)

Most of all Grace loved to act out adventure stories and fairy tales. When there was no one else around, Grace played all the parts herself.

She set out to seek her fortune, with no companion but her trusty cat—and found a city with streets paved in gold.

Or she was Aladdin, rubbing his magic lamp to make the
7 genie appear.

6

122

PAGE 122 SNAPSHOTS

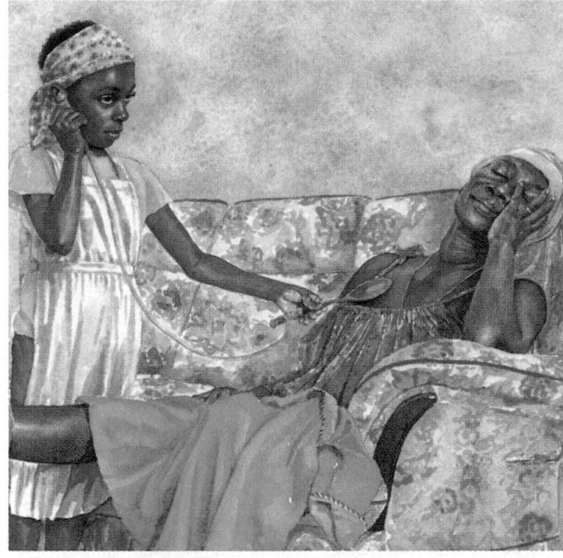

Sometimes she could get Ma and Nana to join in, when they weren't too busy. ❽

Then she was Doctor Grace and their lives were in her hands.

123

AMAZING GRACE PAGE 123

Guided Reading ►

❽ **Distinguish Between Fantasy/Reality In the picture on page 123, I'm not sure whether Grace is still acting or whether this situation is real. What do you think? What clues can you find in the picture and in the words to support your idea?**
VISUAL LITERACY

Supporting All Learners

Read

ESL Many events take place in the first eight pages of the story. Before reading further, reinforce second-language learners' comprehension by rereading these pages aloud. Then pause to give children a turn to summarize what happens on each. **(Summarize)**

a

Guided Reading ▶

❾ **Setting** **Look, Grace isn't outside playing anymore. Where do you think she is? What clues help you to know where she is?** MINI-LESSON

❿ **Make Judgments** **Why does Raj say that Grace can't be Peter Pan? Does he have a good reason? Why or why not?**

MINI-LESSON

SETTING

TEACH/MODEL Explain that where a story takes place is called the setting. Tell children that a story can have one setting or a number of settings.

THINK ALOUD I can tell what the setting of a story is by finding out where the story takes place. As I look through *Amazing Grace*, I see that there are many different locations pictured, so I know that this story has a number of different settings.

APPLY Ask children to look through *Amazing Grace* and identify different settings. Point out that although some of the settings may appear to be in faraway places, they are really in Grace's backyard or neighborhood.

One day Grace's teacher said they would do the play *Peter Pan.* Grace knew who she wanted to be.

When she raised her hand, Raj said, "You can't
❿ be Peter—that's a boy's name."

But Grace kept her hand up.

124

PAGE 124 SNAPSHOTS

"You can't be Peter Pan," whispered Natalie. "He isn't black." But Grace kept her hand up.

"All right," said the teacher. "Lots of you want to be Peter Pan, so we'll have auditions next week to choose parts." She gave them words to learn.

125

Guided Reading ►

INTERVENTION STRATEGY

Recognize Dialogue

When characters speak, their actual words are separated from the rest of the text by quotation marks. If children are confused by quotations, explain that the words appearing inside each pair of marks are the actual words said by the character who is speaking.

PHONICS Vowel /oo/*oo*

Have children find the word *choose* on page 125, point to the letters *oo*, and read the word aloud. Invite them to generate a list of familiar words that contain the same vowel sound, such as *moon* and *room*. Remind them that the letters *oo* stand for two different vowel sounds if they mention a word like *book*.

a

Guided Reading ►

11 **Character** **I can use clues from the pictures on pages 126 and 127 to tell me how Grace feels. I think she looks sad. I'll bet she is disappointed that her friends don't want her to audition for the part of Peter Pan. What do you think? What do the same pictures tell you about how Ma and Nana feel about Grace?** VISUAL LITERACY

12 **Plot** **What is Grace's problem?**

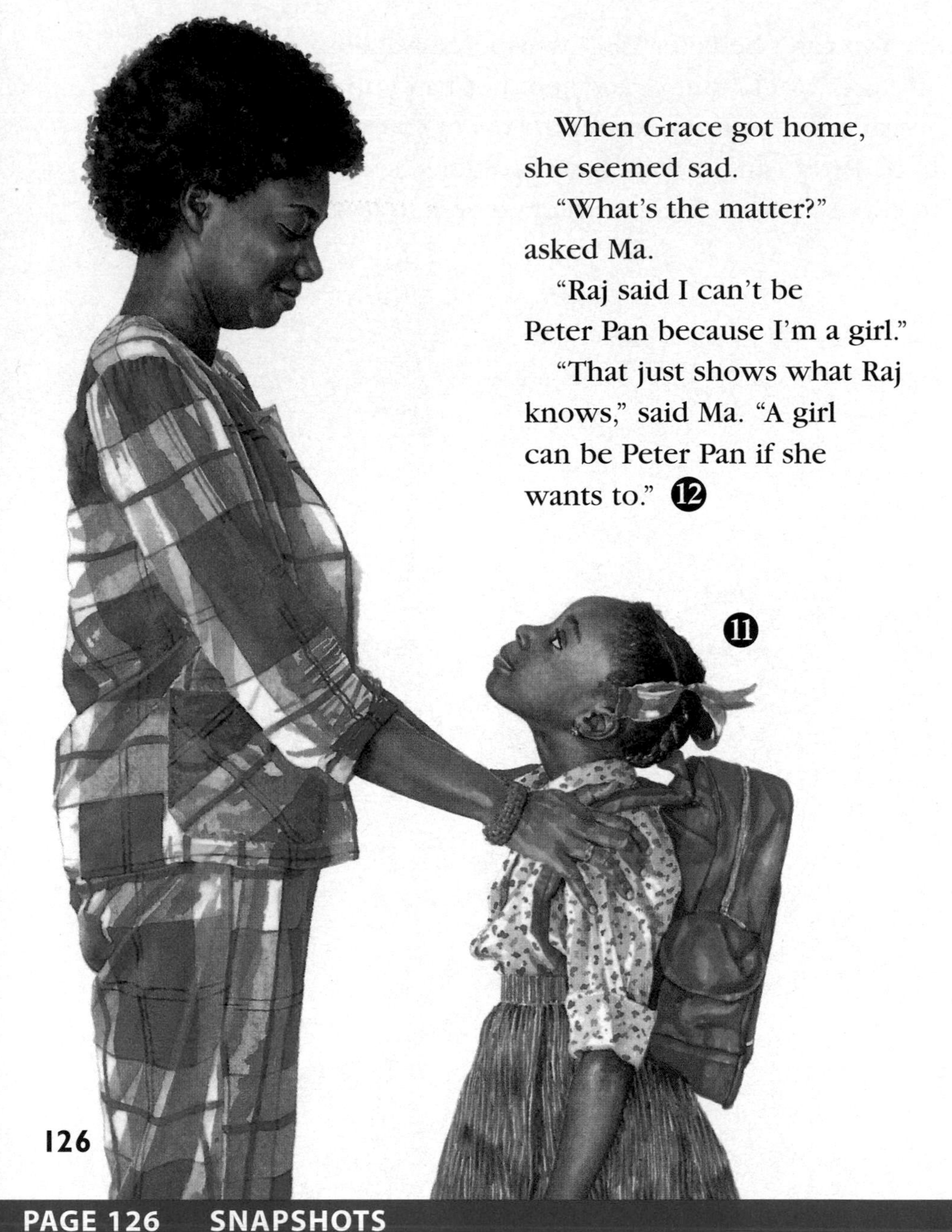

When Grace got home, she seemed sad.

"What's the matter?" asked Ma.

"Raj said I can't be Peter Pan because I'm a girl."

"That just shows what Raj knows," said Ma. "A girl can be Peter Pan if she wants to." **12**

11

126

PAGE 126 SNAPSHOTS

Grace cheered up, then later she remembered something else. "Natalie says I can't be Peter Pan because I'm black," she said.

Ma looked angry. But before she could speak, Nana said, "It seems that Natalie is another one who don't know nothing. You can be anything you want, Grace, if you put your mind to it." ⓭

Guided Reading ►

⓭  **KEY STRATEGY: Theme What do Grace's mother and grandmother say about her problem? What do you think about what they say?**

Revisit ◄

Literary Devices: Dialogue and Narrative

Point out that the text on pages 126 and 127 combines both dialogue and narration. Ask children how they know the difference between the part of the story the narrator tells and the part in which the characters speak.

THINK ALOUD When I see quotation marks in the text, I think about dialogue because I know that quotation marks often show where dialogue begins and ends. I know that the text between the quotation marks tells the actual words that a character speaks.

Have children read aloud only the dialogue on pages 126 and 127. Encourage them to read the speakers' words with the appropriate tone, volume, and expression. Then reread the pages modeling how to combine both dialogue and narration, and have volunteers read after you.

SUPPORTING ALL LEARNERS

Read

CHALLENGE Invite children to reread the last paragraph on page 127 and think about what Nana means when she says Grace can be anything she wants to be. Help children recall what Miss Hart says to Ruby in *Ruby the Copycat*. Challenge children to compare and contrast what Nana says to Grace with what Miss Hart says to Ruby. **(Compare and Contrast)**

a

Guided Reading ▶

⓮ **Plot** **What did Nana and Grace do on Saturday?**

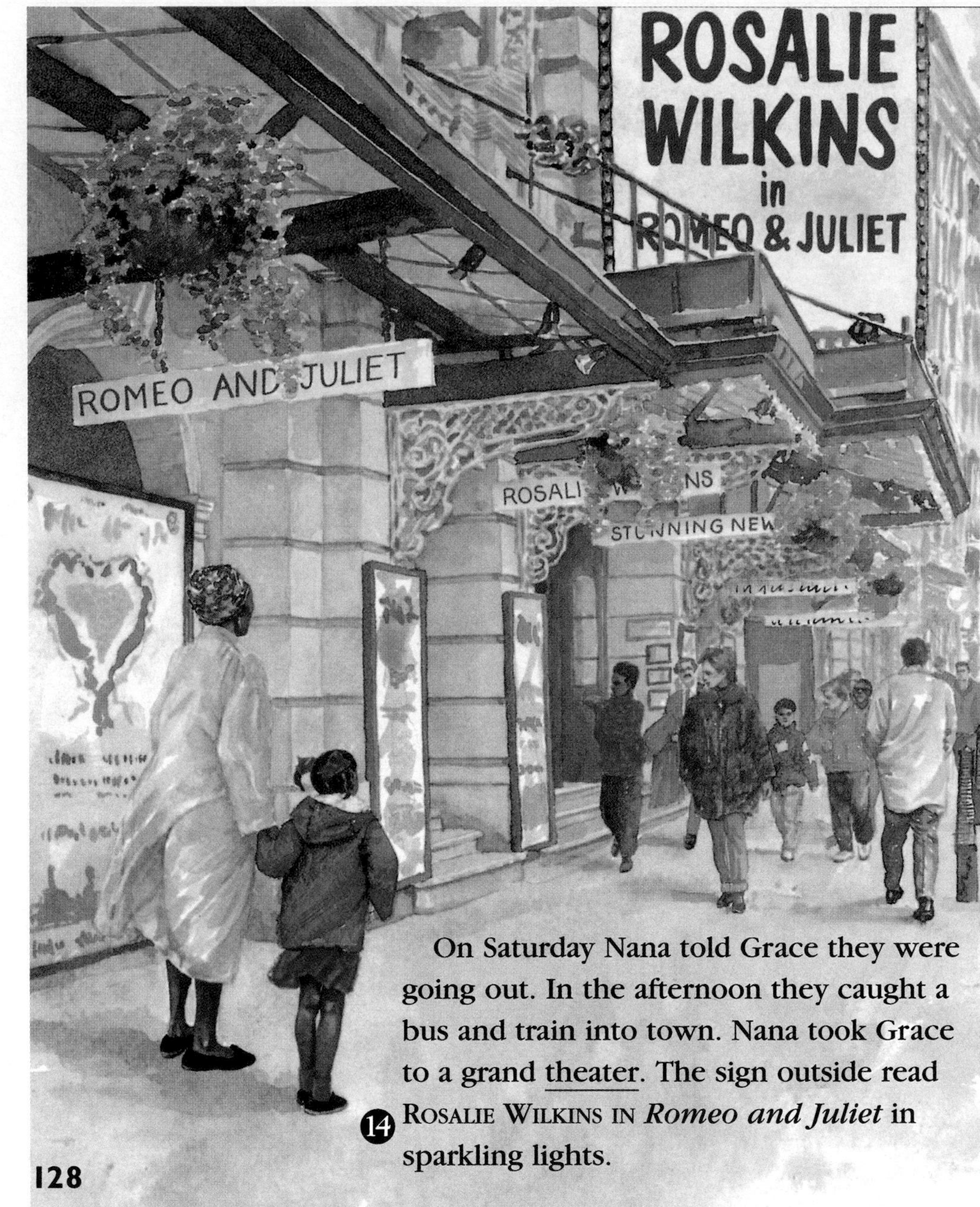

On Saturday Nana told Grace they were going out. In the afternoon they caught a bus and train into town. Nana took Grace to a grand theater. The sign outside read
⓮ ROSALIE WILKINS IN *Romeo and Juliet* in sparkling lights.

128

PAGE 128 SNAPSHOTS

"Are we going to the ballet, Nana?" asked Grace.

"We are, honey, but first I want you to look at this picture."

Grace looked up and saw a beautiful young ballerina in a tutu. Above the dancer it said STUNNING NEW JULIET. ⓯

129

AMAZING GRACE PAGE 129

Guided Reading ▶

⓯ **Make Inferences I think Nana has her reasons for taking Grace to the ballet. I wonder what they are. Why do you think Nana took Grace to the ballet?**

Revisit ◀

Context Clues: Specialized Vocabulary

Remind children that when they read they will often come across words they do not know. Direct their attention to the sign on page 129 that reads "MATINEE 2:00 p.m. TODAY." Read the word *matinee*. Ask children to identify clues that will help them understand the word. Help them see that 2:00 p.m. is a clue that *matinee* means "an afternoon performance."

Follow a similar procedure to help children determine the meaning of *tutu,* referring to the short, fluffy skirt in the picture of the ballerina.

▶ INTEGRATING LANGUAGE ARTS **WRITING/SPEAKING** *(See p. 294.)*

a

Guided Reading ►

⓰ **Make Inferences** **Nana says that she has been offered tickets to see Rosalie dance before. Why do you think Nana picked this particular day to take Grace to see Rosalie dance?**

"That one is little Rosalie from back home in Trinidad," said Nana. "Her granny and me, we grew up together on the island. She's always asking me do I want tickets to see her Rosalie dance—so
⓰ this time I said yes."

130

PAGE 130 SNAPSHOTS

Supporting All Learners

Read

ESL Some children may need help organizing information before they can use it to make predictions. Before asking Read 17, encourage children to retell in their own words what happened when Nana took Grace to the ballet. Then guide them in using this information to make predictions about Grace. **(Retell)**

After the ballet Grace played the part of Juliet, dancing around her room in her imaginary tutu. I can be anything I want, she thought. ⓱

MINI-LESSON

Guided Reading ►

⓱ Make Predictions What does Grace decide after she sees Rosalie dance? Why does she think this? Can you predict what will happen next?

MINI-LESSON

Picture Clues

TEACH/MODEL Tell children that if they look carefully at a story's illustrations, they can often discover information not provided by the words.

THINK ALOUD The words on page 131 tell me that Grace is pretending to dance the part of Juliet from the ballet she saw. The words don't tell me how Grace is feeling, but I can tell from the pictures that Grace is very happy, excited, and confident.

APPLY According to the words, Grace thinks she can be anything she wants. Have children use prior information from the story and information from this picture to predict what they think Grace will choose to be.

VISUAL LITERACY

a

Guided Reading ►

18 **Plot** **It looks to me like Grace is performing for the class. She has her arms stretched out like a ballet dancer or like someone who is trying to fly. Who do you suppose she is pretending to be now? What happened when the class met for auditions on Monday?** VISUAL LITERACY

19 **Make Predictions** **How close were your predictions to what really happened?**

On Monday the class met for auditions to choose who was best for each part.

When it was Grace's turn to be Peter, she knew exactly what to do and all the words to say—she had been Peter Pan all weekend. She took a deep breath and imagined herself flying.

When it was time to vote, the class chose Raj to be Captain Hook and Natalie to be Wendy. There was no doubt who would be Peter Pan. *Everyone*
18 voted for Grace.
19 "You were fantastic!" whispered Natalie.

132

PAGE 132 SNAPSHOTS

Revisit ◄

Conventions of Print: Italics

Ask children to find a word in slanted type on page 132. Explain that this is called italic type, and it gives the word extra emphasis. Read the sentence aloud to children, stressing *everyone.* Have children repeat the sentence after you.

PHONICS /-Blends

Have children find *class* on page 132, point to *cl*, and read the word. Ask children what other words begin with the same sounds. Have them find *flying* (p. 132), point to *fl*, and read the word. Ask what other words begin with the sounds *fl*.

(See Phonics: l-Blends on pp. T298–299.)

For phonics Magnet Board activities, see the Wiggle-Works Plus Teaching Plan.

SUPPORTING ALL LEARNERS

Read EXTRA HELP Draw a graphic comparison between what children predicted and what really happened. Write children's predictions in one column. Then have them guide you in writing what actually happened in a second column. Children can use this chart to respond to Read 19. **(Graphic Device)**

Read On ► ► ►

► INTEGRATED CURRICULUM **SCIENCE** *(See p. R12.)*

Children devise a way for Grace in *Amazing Grace* to fly on stage.

► INTEGRATED CURRICULUM **MATH** *(See p. R12.)*

Children estimate how much space would be needed in their classroom to stage a play.

a

Guided Reading ►

20 Plot Grace, Nana, and Ma all look really happy. What happened at the end of the story?
VISUAL LITERACY

21 CRITICAL THINKING: Evaluate Why do you think Grace is amazing?

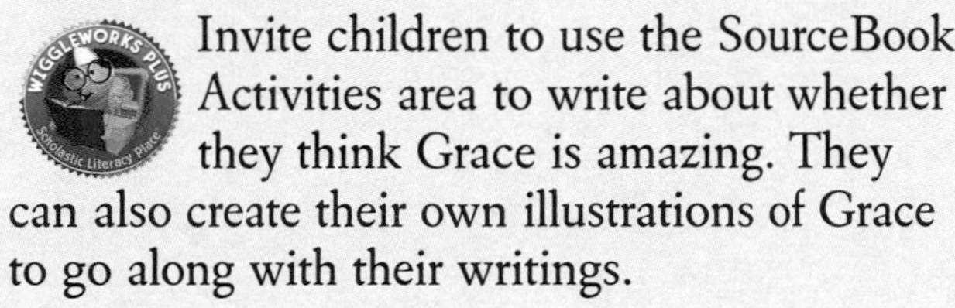

Invite children to use the SourceBook Activities area to write about whether they think Grace is amazing. They can also create their own illustrations of Grace to go along with their writings.

PAGE 134 SNAPSHOTS

► INTEGRATING LANGUAGE ARTS LISTENING/VIEWING *(See p. T295.)*

Revisit ◄

Genre: Realistic Fiction

Discuss the elements of this story that make it realistic fiction. Use the following questions to encourage children's active participation in the discussion:

- **Could the events in this story take place in real life, or is this a story that could never happen?**
- **What clues help you decide?**

Point out the following clues:

- **The art is realistic and the people in the illustrations look like real people.**
- **The characters act in ways real people act.**
- **Everything that happens in the story could take place in real life.**

20

The play was a big success and Grace was an amazing Peter Pan.

After it was all over, she said, "I feel as if I could fly all the way home!" 22

"You probably could," said Ma.

"Yes," said Nana. "If Grace put her mind to it, she can do anything she want." 23

Guided Reading ►

22 **Draw Conclusions** **Why does Grace feel as if she could fly all the way home?**

23 **KEY STRATEGY: Theme** **An author often writes a story to tell readers something he or she has found to be true about life. What do you think the author of *Amazing Grace* is trying to tell you about life? How do you think you'll be able to use this idea in your own life?**

Reading the Sources

Preview and Predict

Reader to Reader

"Plays are different from movies and television. When you go to a play, you see and hear people playing the characters live."

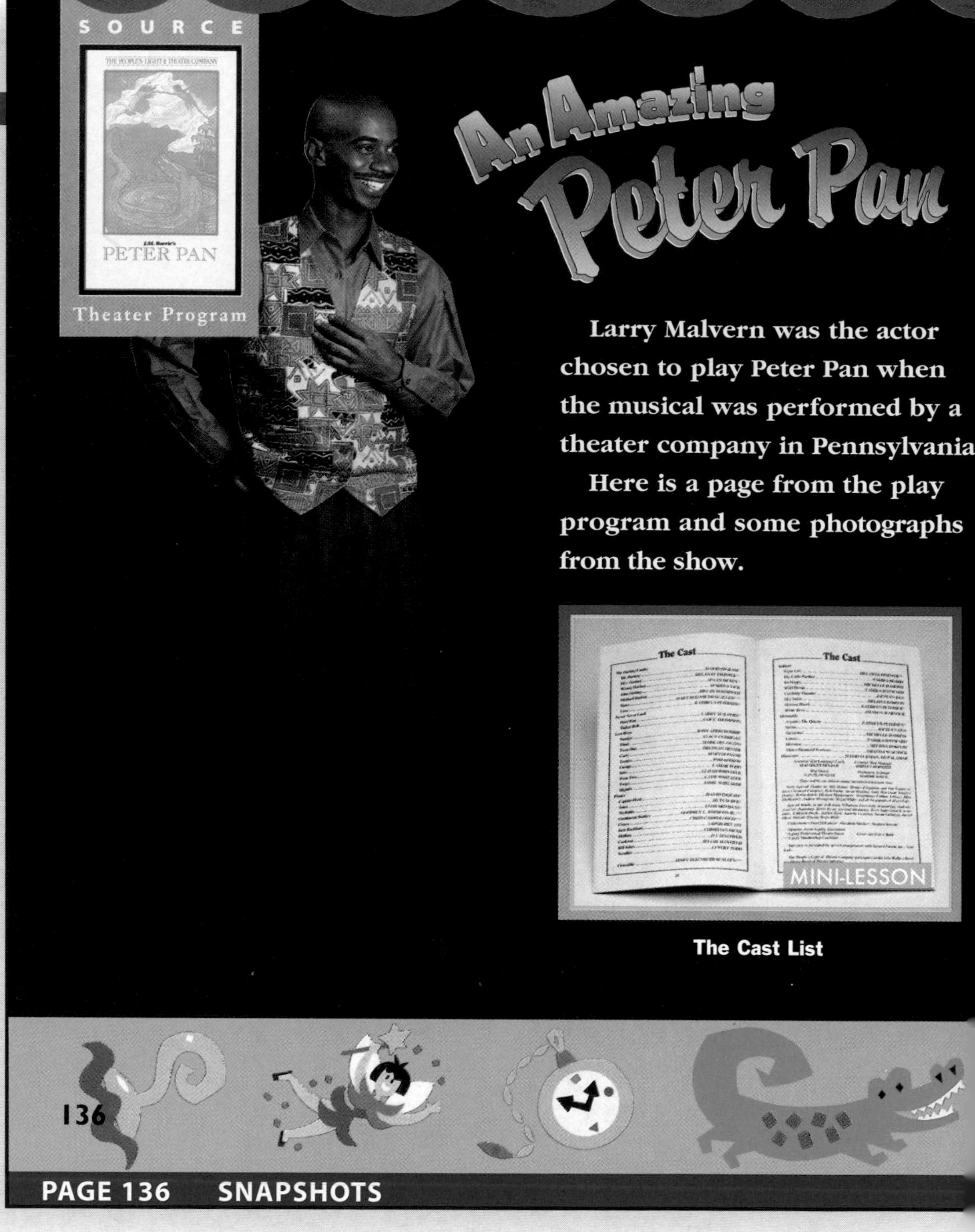

Read the title of the article and invite children to respond to the pictures before they read. You may want to have the story or a recording of *Peter Pan* available to children before they read the article.

- **What do you know about the story of Peter Pan? Who are the characters? What happens in the story?**
- **How are the people in the pictures dressed? Why do you think they are dressed this way?**
- **What would you like to know about these people?**
- **What do you think this article is about?**
- **What would you like to find out by reading the article?**

JOURNAL: Have children use their Journals to record their predictions about the article "An Amazing Peter Pan." They can also record what they want to find out when they read the article.

Supporting All Learners

Preview

ESL Preview the selection with second-language learners by helping them to identify the characters and talk about their costumes. As a class, have those who are familiar with *Peter Pan* retell the story or act out different parts of it to ensure classmates' comprehension. **(Make Connections)**

- Children can tape their retellings on audiocassettes.

Technology Options

Wendy, Michael, and the Lost Boys

Tinkerbell and Peter Pan

Captain Hook

137

AN AMAZING PETER PAN PAGE 137

Guided Reading ►

1 Picture Clues One of these photographs shows an actor without his costume and makeup. The other photographs show actors from a theater company performing a play in their costumes and makeup. What play are they performing? What clues helped you identify the play? VISUAL LITERACY

2 CRITICAL THINKING: Synthesize Why do you think Grace might be especially interested in seeing this play performed by a professional theater company?

► INTEGRATING LANGUAGE ARTS **WRITING** *(See p. T294.)*

MINI-LESSON

Theater Program

TEACH/MODEL Direct children's attention to the photographs and the play program on pages 136 and 137. Point out that the photographs show actors in a professional production of *Peter Pan*. Have children find the cast list in the play program. Explain that the program lists the characters in the play followed by the names of the actors who play each part.

APPLY Ask children about the photographs on pages 136 and 137:

- **Name some characters that would be on the cast list.**
- **Which actor will be listed as playing Peter Pan?**

a

READING THE SOURCES

AMAZING GRACE / AN AMAZING PETER PAN

Assess Reading

REFLECT AND RESPOND

Invite children to share their thoughts, opinions, and questions about *Amazing Grace*. You may wish to prompt discussion with the following questions:

- **Was the title of the story a good one? Why do you think the author chose this title?**
- **How did telling herself "I can be anything" help Grace do her best? *(✔ Key Strategy)***
- **If, like Grace, you were afraid to try something new or different, what would you do?**
- **What about the dialogue makes the story seem real? *(✔ Text Structure)***
- **What clues in the story helped you predict the ending? *(✔ Literary Element)***

CHECK PREDICTIONS

Review with children the chart they created before reading the story. Have them respond to what they wanted to find out. Were their predictions correct?

READ CRITICALLY ACROSS TEXTS

- **If Grace could meet Larry Malvern, what might she ask him about his role as Peter Pan?**

She might ask him how he got the role, what kinds of things helped him prepare to play the part, and if he had any fears about performing in a play.

Literacy-at-Work Book, p. 63

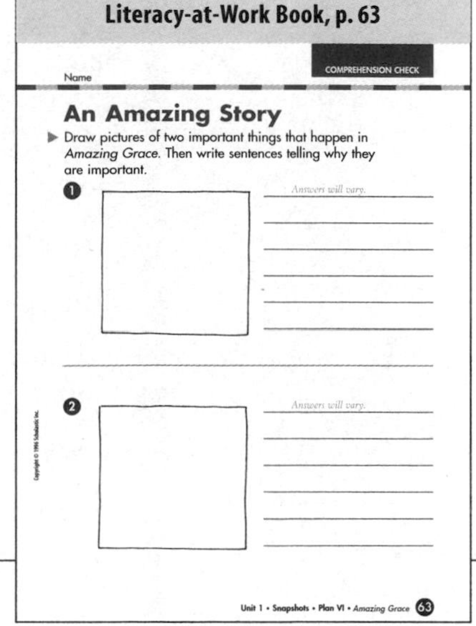
Name

COMPREHENSION CHECK

An Amazing Story

▶ Draw pictures of two important things that happen in *Amazing Grace*. Then write sentences telling why they are important.

1 Answers will vary.

2 Answers will vary.

Unit 1 • Snapshots • Plan VI • Amazing Grace 63

CONFERENCE

Use the checked questions on this page to assess children's understanding of:

✔ the *key strategy* of Theme; here, that you can be anything you want to be if you put your mind to it.

✔ the *text structure* of Dialogue as distinguished from Narration.

✔ the *literary element* of Plot.

Listen to Children Read Ask selected children to find and read the part of the story where Grace's classmates tell her she can't be Peter Pan. Ask them to explain what is going on. You may wish to tape-record children as they read the selection aloud. Assess oral reading, using pages 22–23 in the Assessment Handbook.

Children may wish to add their recordings to their Literacy Portfolios.

Based on your evaluation of your children's responses,

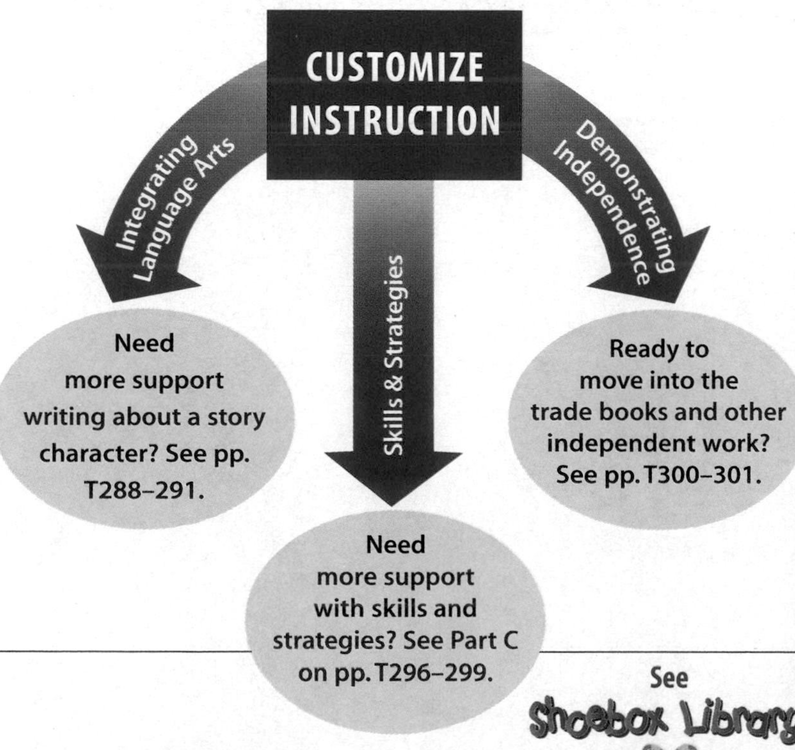

See Shoebox Library

Idea File

VOCABULARY

Ask children to think of questions they would like to ask Grace after her performance of *Peter Pan*. Encourage children to include vocabulary pairs of from the story in questions. Children can interview each other. Or children may wish to write their questions in their Journals.

REPEATED READING

READERS THEATER Assign the roles of the narrator, Grace, Ma, Nana, Raj, Natalie, and the teacher, and have children read the story aloud. Since the narration is extensive, you may want to assign more than one child to this role. Demonstrate expressive reading by reading the first few pages yourself.

REPEATED READING

CHUNKING Practice oral fluency by having children take turns reading aloud a passage, page, or chunk of the story. Stress that children should pay attention to the punctuation that distinguishes the dialogue from the narrative portions of the story.

HOMEWORK

Have children find some information about one of the characters Grace pretended to be: Joan of Arc, Anansi the Spider, the Trojan Horse, Hiawatha, Mowgli, or Aladdin. They can write notes on index cards. Encourage them to share their information.

CULTURAL CONNECTIONS

TABLEAU FROM LITERATURE

Grace pretends to be many characters from stories popular around the world. The story of Joan of Arc is famous all over the world; Anansi is a character in many West African countries; and Aladdin's adventures come to us from the Arab world.

ACTIVITY

Ask children what character they would like to be from one of the stories mentioned in the book or others they may know. Encourage children to make a drawing of themselves dressed as the character to share with the class in a display.

b

SOURCEBOOK

Amazing Grace
Mary Hoffman · Caroline Binch

Writing Process Workshop

AMAZING GRACE

Write About a Story Character

Children will use the **writing process** to help them write about a story **character.** Using *Amazing Grace* as a model, they will develop a realistic character in a **real-life** situation.

Objectives

Children learn to:

Prewrite

- choose a topic
- brainstorm ideas
- make decisions about Role

Draft Write about a story character in a real-life situation

Revise Work with peers and receive teacher feedback

Proofread Check spelling, period at the end of a declarative sentence

Materials:
Sourcebook pp. 116–135
Literacy-at-Work Book p. 64

Suggested Grouping:
Whole class or individuals

Literacy-at-Work Book, p. 64

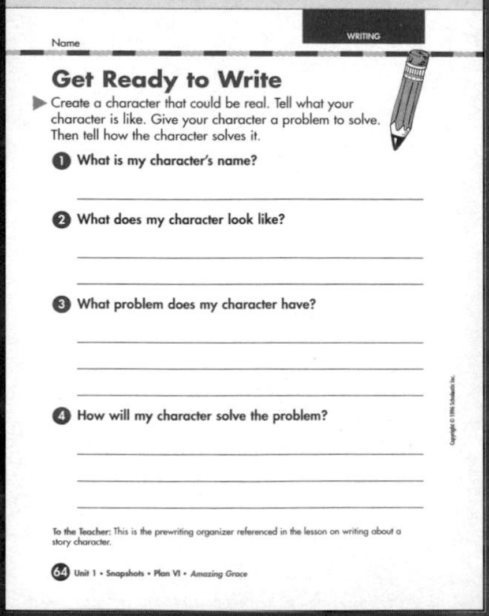

Name ______ WRITING

Get Ready to Write

Create a character that could be real. Tell what your character is like. Give your character a problem to solve. Then tell how the character solves it.

1. What is my character's name?
2. What does my character look like?
3. What problem does my character have?
4. How will my character solve the problem?

To the Teacher: This is the prewriting organizer referenced in the lesson on writing about a story character.

64 Unit 1 • Snapshots • Plan VI • Amazing Grace

Getting Started

Introduce Story Character

To write about a story character:

- describe the character's appearance.
- tell what the character does.
- tell about the thoughts and feelings of the character.

Invite children to think about the characters they read about recently that they liked or found particularly interesting. Children can list and share the names of the memorable characters and talk about how they got to know them through reading. Working together, create a chart of these memorable characters on the chalkboard. Here is a sample that one class might create:

Memorable Characters

Book Title	Character	Description
Ruby the copycat	Ruby	• wears a red bow • copies everyone
Making the Team	Louanne Pig	• looks like a girl • plays football

Introduce the Assignment

What's Your Character Like?

Write about a character. How will the character act? How does the character feel? What thoughts does the character have?

Model What Children Will Do

Have children look back at *Amazing Grace* to see how Mary Hoffman reveals what Grace is like. Lead children to see that the author describes Grace through her actions, thoughts, and feelings.

After the ballet Grace played the part of Juliet, dancing around her room in her imaginary tutu. ❶ *I can be anything I want, she thought.* ❷

❶ The writer describes the character's actions.

❷ The writer describes the character's thoughts or feelings.

Prewrite

Choose Your Topic

Put the following questions on the chalkboard and have children jot down the answers to these questions in their journals.

Who will my character be?

What will my character look like?

What will my character do?

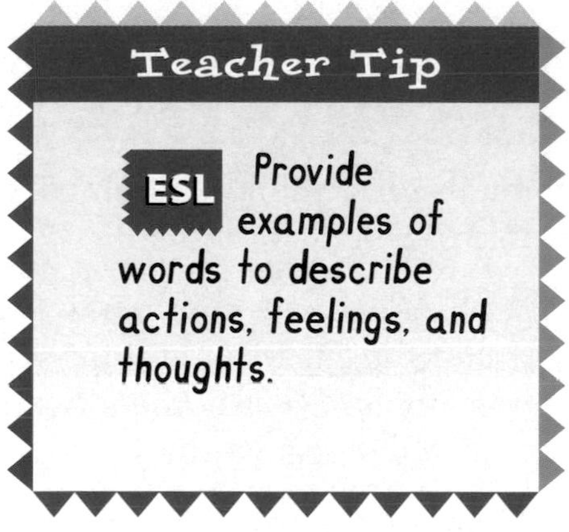

Brainstorm Ideas

Now that children have selected characters, have them brainstorm more information about their characters. Have them add traits to a web of character traits. The following is a sample web one child might make.

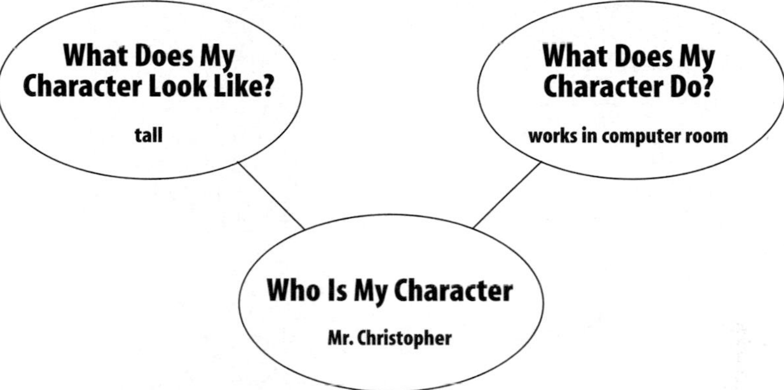

Make Decisions

Now challenge children to make even more decisions.

Will they be telling about the character or will someone else? Who will be reading about their character? Will they plan to use their character in a story later? Will they include an illustration of their character. They have already decided who their characters will be and what their characters are like. After their discussions, children are ready to write.

Here is how one child might answer these questions:

Role: I will be a story writer and tell about my character, just as the author Mary Hoffman does in *Amazing Grace*.

Audience: My audience will be my classmates.

Format: I will write about my character in the form of a description.

Topic: My topic is Mr. Christopher in the computer room.

Move on to the next page ▶ ▶ ▶

b

Writing Process Workshop

Draft

Based on the decisions they made in Prewrite, let children begin writing about their story characters. Here is a sample of a rough draft written by a second grader.

*Mr. Christopher*❶ *He works in comptr rom.*❷ *He is a tall man. He is Hasim*❸ *I like him a lot*

❶ **Tells who the character is.**

❷ **Tells what the character does.**

❸ **Describes the character's appearance.**

Revise

Remind children that revising gives them the opportunity to improve their writing. Now that they have completed a rough draft of their character descriptions, help them polish their work. Encourage children to first read through their character descriptions and ask themselves the following questions. After they have read their character descriptions, they can get feedback from a peer or the teacher by using similar questions.

- **Does my character seem like a real person?**
- **Did I tell what my character does?**
- **Did I describe thoughts and feelings of my character?**
- **Did I describe my character's appearance?**
- **Do I give enough information to help my audience understand my character?**

Teacher Tip

Set aside an area of the chalkboard where children can sign up for a conference.

Proofread

Note: You may want to teach the lesson on p. T292 before children proofread their character descriptions.

Have children proofread their revisions. They may want to start with the following questions:

- **Have you spelled the name of your character correctly?**
- **Do your sentences end with the correct punctuation, especially at the end of declarative sentences?**

After making corrections, children may want to have a peer also edit their story.

Teacher Tip

By editing their own work, children will develop a sense of ownership about their writing.

Publish

CREATE A CLASSROOM BOOK OF CHARACTERS: Children can combine their descriptions into a classroom book, arranging the works in alphabetical order by character names. You might also have children number the pages and prepare a table of contents.

CREATE A CHARACTER COLLAGE: Invite children to create a collage that illustrates the character and the real-life situation they wrote about. Display the artwork accompanied by the children's writing.

TECHNOLOGY: Children might input their descriptions on the computer so they can print out several copies: a copy for the classroom book, a copy for the collage, and a copy to take home.

SPEAKING/LISTENING: Children may enjoy reading their character descriptions aloud to classmates or to younger children. Following the reading, authors can answer questions from the audience.

prentice Sample ▶

Mr. Christopher.
He works in computer room. He is a tall man. He is hasim.
I like him a lot.

◀ Describes what character does.

◀ Describes character's appearance.

◀ Has been proofread but not completely corrected for grammar, usage, mechanics, and spelling.

▲ Does not give thoughts and feelings of the character.

SUPPORTING ALL LEARNERS

Make Connections

ESL Making real-life connections may help children acquiring English get a better understanding of the meaning of the words *audience, format,* and *topic*. During prewrite, help children identify a character, and encourage them to give examples of real situations in which the character has been involved.

EXTRA HELP As writers often do, encourage children to think of a friend or relative they know well and write about that particular person.

Technology Options

Invite children to write about their story characters in the SourceBook Activities writing area. Suggest that they record their ideas, using the Record Tool, before they begin writing.

PERFORMANCE-BASED

Children's Self-Assessment The following questions may help children assess their own work:

- ✔ Would a classmate or a younger child want to read about my story character?
- ✔ Have I described my character in some of the ways Mary Hoffman described Grace?
- ✔ What did I do well in writing about a character?
- ✔ What could I do better the next time I write about a story character?

CHILDREN'S WRITING BENCHMARKS

Novice:	Apprentice:	Proficient:
Writing describes little about what the character does. It does not describe the character's appearance or give thoughts and feelings. It has not been proofread and corrected for errors.	Writing somewhat describes what character does. It describes character's appearance but may not give character's thoughts and feelings. It has been proofread but may not be corrected for errors.	Writing fully describes what the character does. It describes character's appearance and gives character's thoughts and feelings. It has been proofread and corrected for grammar, usage, mechanics, and spelling.

b

INTEGRATING LANGUAGE ARTS

S M T W T F S
See Daily Language Practice pp. R14-15.

(✓ Unit Test)

DESCRIBING WORDS

GRAMMAR

OBJECTIVE
Children identify adjectives in *Amazing Grace* and in their own writing.

DEFINITION: An adjective describes a person, place, or thing.

SYNTACTIC CUEING

❶ Teach and Model

Write the adjective phrases on the chalkboard below on chart paper or on the class chalkboard. Ask children to identify the words that describe a person, a place, or a thing. Ask children why *young ballerina* presents a clearer, more interesting picture than *ballerina.* Repeat the process with the other examples. Explain that words that describe people, places, and things are called adjectives and that writers use them to make their writing clearer and more interesting.

young ballerina
grand theater
magic lamp

❷ Put It in Context

Ask children to find other examples of adjectives in *Amazing Grace.*

❸ Apply to Writing

Ask volunteers to read sentences from their stories that contain adjectives. Have other volunteers identify the adjective in the sentence. Children might want to start collecting colorful adjectives in their Journals for use in their future writing experiences.

PERIODS

MECHANICS

OBJECTIVE
Children identify periods in *Amazing Grace* and in their writing.

GUIDELINE: A telling sentence ends in a period.

❶ Teach and Model

Explain that a sentence that makes a statement or tells something ends with a period. Present the following two sentences from *Amazing Grace* as examples:

Grace was a girl who loved stories.

The play was a big success and Grace was an amazing Peter Pan.

Ask children to identify the punctuation mark at the end of each sentence.

❷ Put It in Context

Have children find and read aloud other sentences from *Amazing Grace* that end with periods. Discuss other forms of end punctuation if children discover them as they read through *Amazing Grace.*

❸ Apply to Writing

Have children check their telling, or statement, sentences in their stories to make sure that each ends in a period.

Grammar, Usage, Mechanics Practice, p. 11

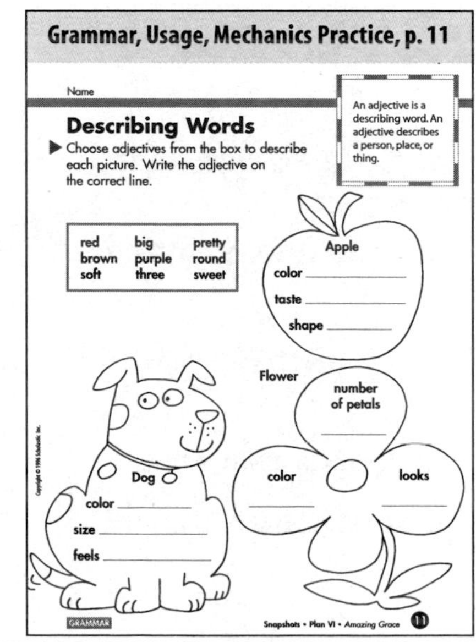
Name

An adjective is a describing word. An adjective describes a person, place, or thing.

Describing Words

▶ Choose adjectives from the box to describe each picture. Write the adjective on the correct line.

red	big	pretty
brown	purple	round
soft	three	sweet

Apple
color ______
taste ______
shape ______

Dog
color ______
size ______
feels ______

Flower
number of petals
color
looks

GRAMMAR Snapshots • Plan VI • Amazing Grace 11

Grammar, Usage, Mechanics Practice, p. 12

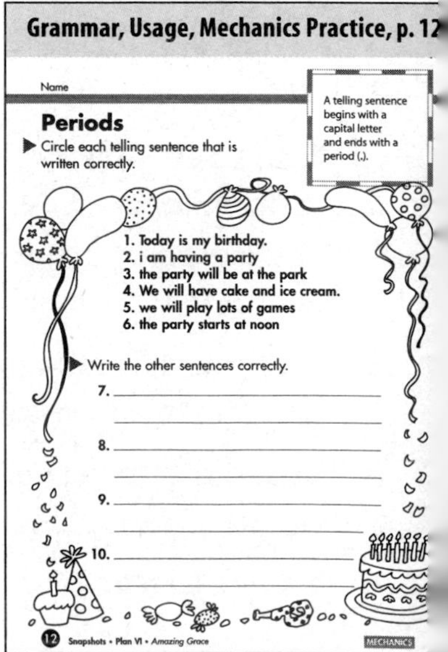
Name

A telling sentence begins with a capital letter and ends with a period (.).

Periods

▶ Circle each telling sentence that is written correctly.

1. Today is my birthday.
2. i am having a party
3. the party will be at the park
4. We will have cake and ice cream.
5. we will play lots of games
6. the party starts at noon

▶ Write the other sentences correctly.

7. ______
8. ______
9. ______
10. ______

12 Snapshots • Plan VI • Amazing Grace MECHANICS

Looking Back at Words

You may first wish to review the phonics lessons on words with final *e* on pp. T200–201.

SPELLING

Words With Final *e*

home **vote** **stone** **stove** **grape** **shape** **snake** **shake** **hide** **spice**

✷ **Selection Vocabulary**

PRETEST If you would like to pretest using test sentences, see Spelling Practice, p. 39.

OBJECTIVE

Children spell final *e* words.

❶ Teach

Write the following words on the chalkboard: *made, bite, note.* Ask children to say each word and identify the vowel sound. Point out that each word has a long vowel sound and follows the same spelling pattern: a vowel followed by a consonant and final *e.*

Put It in Context

Write the following sentences from *Amazing Grace* on the chalkboard. Have children read each sentence and identify the words that follow the vowel-consonant-final *e* spelling pattern.

"I feel as if I could fly all the way home!"

"You can't be Peter—that's a boy's name."

"This time I said yes."

❷ Practice

Have children copy and complete the following chart:

Long Vowel-Consonant-Silent e		
long *o*	long *a*	long *i*

❸ Check

Apply to Writing

Have children proofread their writing about story characters. Encourage them to check the spelling of any word they may have written that contains a long vowel sound followed by a consonant and final *e.*

TEST Dictate each word, use it in a sentence, then repeat it as children write it. Ask children to suggest their own sentences for any five test words. Suggest that they use the word list or a dictionary to check the spelling of each word.

See Handwriting Practice, p. 6 for practice reviewing manuscript letters *A, K, N, M, V, W, X, Y,* and *Z.*

Spelling Practice, p. 6

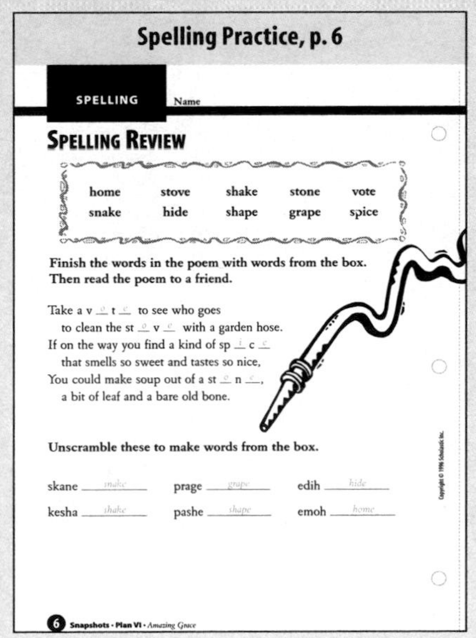
SPELLING Name

SPELLING REVIEW

home stove shake stone vote
snake hide shape grape spice

Finish the words in the poem with words from the box. Then read the poem to a friend.

Take a v _ t _ to see who goes
to clean the st _ v _ with a garden hose.
If on the way you find a kind of sp _ c _
that smells so sweet and tastes so nice,
You could make soup out of a st _ n _,
a bit of leaf and a bare old bone.

Unscramble these to make words from the box.

skane snake prage grape edih hide
kesha shake pashe shape emoh home

6 Snapshots • Plan VI • Amazing Grace

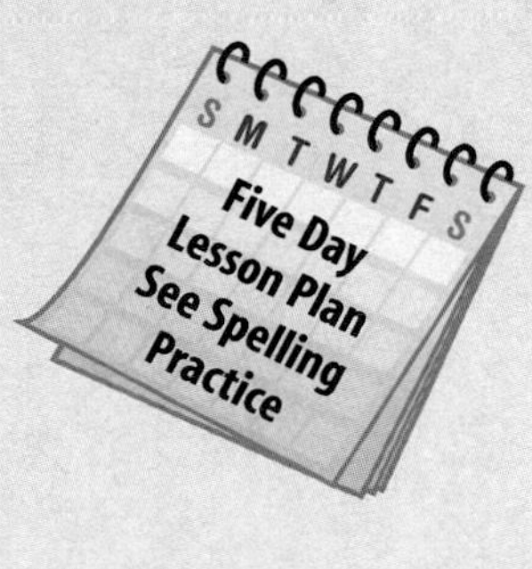

b

INTEGRATING LANGUAGE ARTS

AMAZING GRACE

WRITING

Make a Play Poster or Program

GOOD FOR HOMEWORK

Materials:
SourceBook pp. 116–137
Poster paper
Markers

Time:
About 15 minutes

Suggested Grouping:
Individuals

Ask children to look back to the ballet poster on page 129 or the play program on page 136. Discuss the information found on a play poster (name, date, time, and location of the play, and possibly the names of the leading performers) and the play program (name of the play and a list of characters with the name of the actor who is playing each role).

Invite children to create a poster or play program for Grace's class's performance of *Peter Pan* or for the performance of the script they write in the next activity.

Encourage children to illustrate their posters and programs, if they wish. Display their work in the classroom. VISUAL LITERACY

WRITING/SPEAKING

Write and Perform a Script

Materials:
SourceBook pp. 116–137
Pencil
Paper
Computer (optional)

Time:
About 30 minutes

Suggested Grouping:
Partners or cooperative groups

Introduce this activity by reading some dialogue from *Amazing Grace*. Pages 124, 125, 129, and 130 provide good examples.

Invite children to improvise dialogue for a familiar story or folk tale. Have them record their improvisations on paper. Help children insert characters' names and a narrator if necessary to complete a simple script. Groups can then read their scripts aloud for the class. THE ARTS

Children can write their improvisations on the computer and then insert characters' names. Print copies of the script for group members to read aloud, or have them record the dialogues on the computer.

MINI-LESSON

ORAL EXPRESSION

TEACH/MODEL Help children practice reading chunks of *Amazing Grace* aloud for fluency and expression. Read a few pages aloud yourself to model how to vary intonation, pitch, and speaking rate.

APPLY Have children read aloud with a partner or in cooperative groups. Suggest that children tape-record their reading so they can listen to themselves and note how they are doing.

WRITING/SPEAKING

Write a Book Report

GOOD FOR GRADING

Materials: Classroom library

Time: About 25 minutes

Suggested Grouping: Individuals

Ask children to recall that at the beginning of *Amazing Grace,* the author told about different characters and heroes.

Invite children to choose a favorite character from a story they've read. Have them write a book report with the title and author's name, identifying the character and why they liked the character.

Encourage volunteers to role-play their characters in situations from the stories. Help them find, make, or adapt props and costumes appropriate to the characters and situations.

How to Grade Check to see that children have used capital letters for the title and author's name and complete sentences with correct end punctuation.

MINI-LESSON

Book Titles

TEACH/MODEL Display a variety of books and read some of the titles. Ask children what they notice about the way each title is written. Explain that the important words in a title begin with capital letters. Little words like *and, of,* and *the* are not capitalized unless they are the first or last word of the title.

APPLY Ask children to list the titles of two books they have read and two they would like to read.

LISTENING/VIEWING

ESL Watch a Video of *Peter Pan*

Materials: Video or recording of *Peter Pan*; TV and VCR or audiocassette player

Time: 2–3 sessions of about 30 minutes each

Suggested Grouping: Whole class and individuals

Technology Options **Invite** children to watch a video or listen to a recording of *Peter Pan*. Discuss the story, and encourage children to tell about the parts of *Peter Pan* they liked best. Read aloud parts of the book *Peter Pan* if a video or recording is unavailable.

Ask children to choose their favorite character and think of three adjectives to describe the character. Classmates can compare their adjectives with those of others who have chosen the same character.

Encourage children to draw pictures of their favorite characters and write the adjectives describing them on the paper. Post the pictures in the classroom, and allow children to add new adjectives as they think of them. VISUAL LITERACY

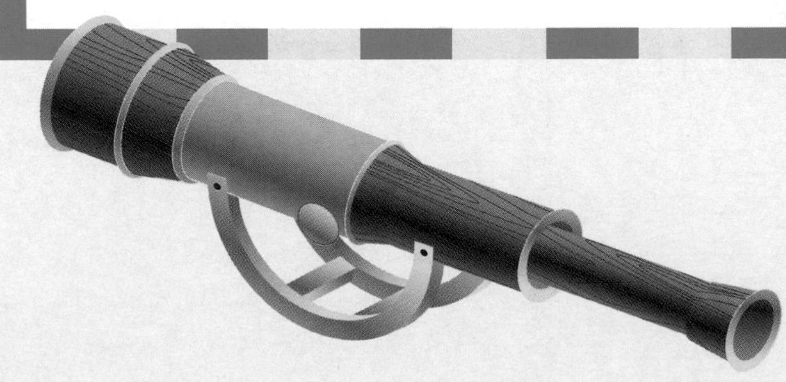

C

BUILDING SKILLS AND STRATEGIES

AMAZING GRACE

Theme

Objectives

Children learn to:

- identify the theme of a story
- transfer their learning to a new text

Review:

- Plot (p. R18)
- Make Predictions (p. R19)
- Context Clues: Specialized Vocabulary (p. R20)
- Phonics: /s/c, /j/g (p. R21)

Materials:
SourceBook pp. 116–135
Transparency 13
Literacy-at-Work Book pp. 65–67

Time:
About 30 minutes

Suggested Grouping:
Whole class and cooperative groups

Literacy-at-Work Book, p. 65

Name

THEME

Get the Message

The message of *Amazing Grace* is that you can be anything you want to be. Write three parts of the story where the author gives you this message.

Part 1

Possible answer: Ma said that a girl can be Peter Pan if she wants.

Part 2

Possible answer: Nana said that Grace can be anything she wants if she puts her mind to it.

Part 3

Possible answer: Grace saw a ballet starring a ballerina from Trinidad.

Unit 1 • Snapshots • Plan VI • *Amazing Grace* 65

✔ Quickcheck

As children read *Amazing Grace*, did they:

✔ identify what the story is about?

✔ see the points the author was trying to make?

 **If yes, go to ❷ Practice and Apply.**

 **If no, start at**  **Teach and Model.**

TRANSPARENCY 13

Scholastic Literacy Place

THEME CHART

Author's Point

You can be anything you want to be.

1. What does Grace want to be?

Peter Pan in the play

2. What events help make the author's point?

- Grace's mother and grandmother tell her that she can do anything she wants if she sets her mind to it.
- *Grace sees a poster of a beautiful ballerina from Trinidad.*
- *Grace sees a ballet starring the ballerina.*

Snapshots • Plan VI • *Amazing Grace* 13

Annotated transparency for teaching Theme

❶ Teach and Model

Have children recall a folk tale that the class has read together and tell what it is about. Then have them explore the possible themes of the story by asking: "Why do you think the author wrote this story? What points do you think the author was trying to make?" Encourage children to come up with different ideas and give reasons for them.

Put It in Context

Have children explore the theme of *Amazing Grace*. Discuss how thinking about what the characters do and say and what happens to them can help children identify a theme.

Think Aloud **Amazing Grace is about a girl named Grace who loves to act out stories. When her teacher announces that the class is going to put on the play *Peter Pan*, Grace knows exactly who she wants to be—Peter Pan. But Raj and Natalie tell her that she can't be Peter Pan. She isn't a boy, and she is black! But at the end of the story, with the encouragement and support of her mother and grandmother, Grace pulls it off and gets the part. I know that sometimes authors make their points through the events in the story. Perhaps one point the author of this story was trying to make was: You can be or do anything you want. For Grace, this meant she could be Peter Pan if she wanted to.**

Display Transparency 13. Discuss the author's point shown and have children answer the first question. Then have them return to the story to identify events that help the author make her point.

❷ Practice and Apply

Make a Theme Chart

COOPERATIVE GROUPS Have children work in groups to identify another theme in the story. Provide guidance by reminding them to think about what the characters say and do and what happens to them. Encourage them to give details to support their ideas. The following thoughts may be used to get them started:

- **Imagination lets you travel to faraway places.**
- **Talking with others can help you learn more about yourself.**

You may want to distribute a chart like the one on the transparency for children to complete to help them organize their thinking.

❸ Assess

Can children identify different themes in *Amazing Grace*?

✔ **Can children tell what the story is about?**

✔ **Can children tell what points the author is trying to make?**

If not, try this:
As children read upcoming selections in the SourceBook and stories in the Shoebox Library, encourage them to identify themes and write them in their Journals.

Children's Self-Assessment

✔ **Did I identify events that helped me understand the author's point?**

SUPPORTING ALL LEARNERS

Key Points

ESL Before you begin the Put It in Context activity, support second-language learners by pointing out the illustrations which depict the events that enable Grace to solve her problem. Encourage them to talk about what they see in the pictures to help them focus on the important events.

ACCESS Before you begin the Practice and Apply activity, help children identify the events that enable Grace to solve her problem by paging through the selection and guiding them in pointing out the different passages where these events are described. Then children can focus on these smaller passages when identifying the important events.

Transfer to New Text

Literacy-at-Work Book, p. 66

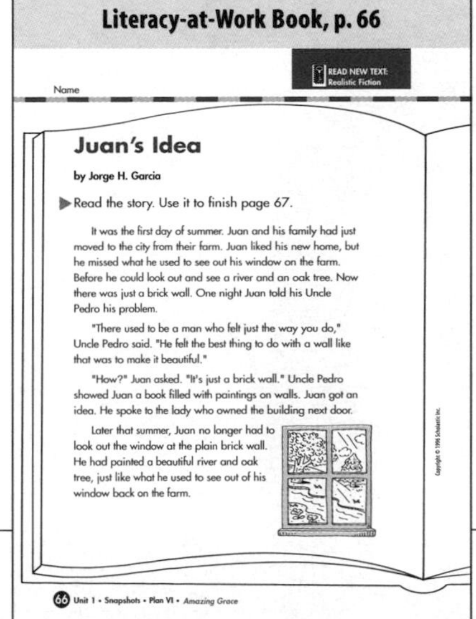

Name

READ NEW TEXT: Realistic Fiction

Juan's Idea

by Jorge H. Garcia

▶ Read the story. Use it to finish page 67.

It was the first day of summer. Juan and his family had just moved to the city from their farm. Juan liked his new home, but he missed what he used to see out his window on the farm. Before he could look out and see a river and an oak tree. Now there was just a brick wall. One night Juan told his Uncle Pedro his problem.

"There used to be a man who felt just the way you do," Uncle Pedro said. "He felt the best thing to do with a wall like that was to make it beautiful."

"How?" Juan asked. "It's just a brick wall." Uncle Pedro showed Juan a book filled with paintings on walls. Juan got an idea. He spoke to the lady who owned the building next door.

Later that summer, Juan no longer had to look out the window at the plain brick wall. He had painted a beautiful river and oak tree, just like what he used to see out of his window back on the farm.

66 Unit 1 • Snapshots • Plan VI • *Amazing Grace*

Literacy-at-Work Book, p. 67

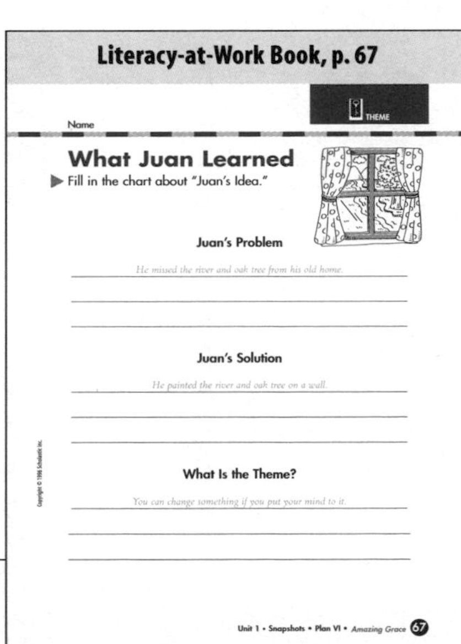

Name

THEME

What Juan Learned

▶ Fill in the chart about "Juan's Idea."

Juan's Problem

He missed the river and oak tree from his old home.

Juan's Solution

He painted the river and oak tree on a wall.

What Is the Theme?

You can change something if you put your mind to it.

Unit 1 • Snapshots • Plan VI • *Amazing Grace* 67

C

AMAZING GRACE

SOURCEBOOK

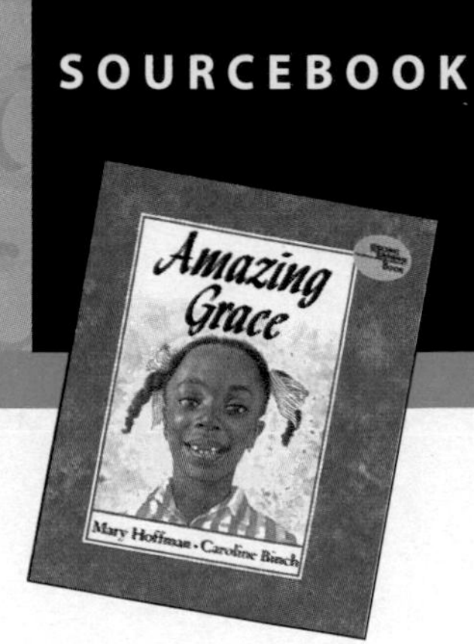

l-Blends

Objectives

Children learn to:

- identify the sounds of of *l*-blends *bl, cl, fl,* and *pl*
- build words that contain *bl, cl, fl,* and *pl*
- write words with *l*-blends

PHONICS AT A GLANCE

Materials:
SourceBook pp. 116–135
Big Book of Rhymes and Rhythms 2A, p. 15
Tracking Device (optional)
Word Building Cards for *l*-blends
Magnet Board
Literacy-at-Work Book pp. 71–72

Time:
About 15–30 minutes

Suggested Grouping:
Whole class and cooperative groups

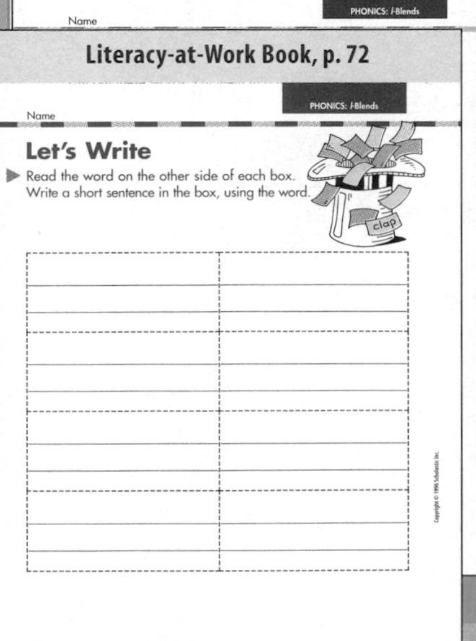
Literacy-at-Work Book, p. 71

Literacy-at-Work Book, p. 72

Let's Write

Read the word on the other side of each box. Write a short sentence in the box, using the word.

✔ Quickcheck

As children worked their way through *Amazing Grace,* did they:

✔ recognize *l*-blends in print in lowercase form? in uppercase form?

✔ think of words that begin with *l*-blends?

YES **If yes, go to the Blending section of ❷ Connect Sound/Symbol.**

NO **If no, start at ❶ Develop Oral Language.**

❶ Develop Oral Language

Phonemic Awareness

Read aloud "A Flea and a Fly in a Flue" from the *Big Book of Rhymes and Rhythms*. Be sure children understand the meaning of *flue* and *flaw*. Also point out that *flee* and *flea* sound the same but have different meanings. Invite them to join in on the second or third reading. You may want to track the print as you read.

Focus on the sounds of the *l*-blends. Say the words *flea, fly, flaw,* and *flue.* Have children repeat the words after you. Ask what sounds the children hear at the beginning of these words. Encourage them to look at the word wall to see if they can find other words that begin with *l*-blends.

Big Book of Rhymes and Rhythms

A Flea and a Fly in a Flue

A flea and a fly in a flue
Were caught, so what could they do?
Said the fly, "Let us flee."
Said the flea, "Let us fly."
So they flew through a flaw in the flue.

flea

15

❷ Connect Sound/Symbol

Put It in Context

Write the following sentences from *Amazing Grace* on the chalkboard:

Grace played all the parts herself.

"He isn't black."

On Monday the class met for auditions.

She took a deep breath and imagined herself flying.

Underline the *l*-blends. Ask children to listen to the sounds as you point to the letters and blend the sounds in the word.

Blending

Place *l*-blend cards on the chalk rail. Write *tank* on the chalkboard and hold the *bl* card over the *t*.

Think Aloud **If I change the *t* in tank to *bl,* I make *blank.* Say it as I run my finger under it.**

Use the *pl* and *cl* cards to make *plank* and *clank*. Continue with *came* (*blame, flame*), *got* (*blot, clot, plot*), and *tow* (*blow, flow*).

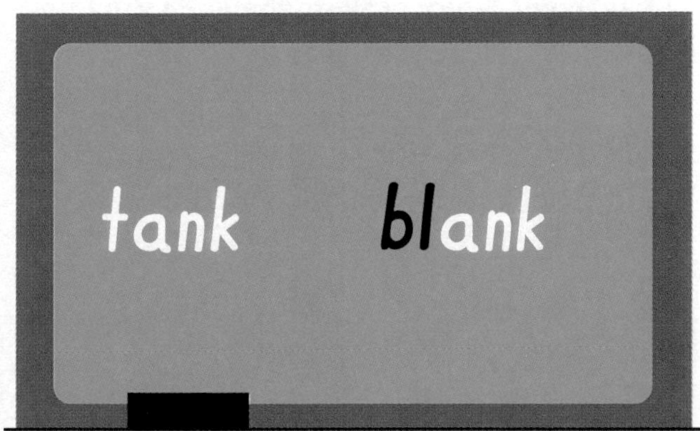

❸ Assess

Write

Have children dictate sentences with *l*-blend words. Write the sentences and have volunteers underline words with *l*-blends.

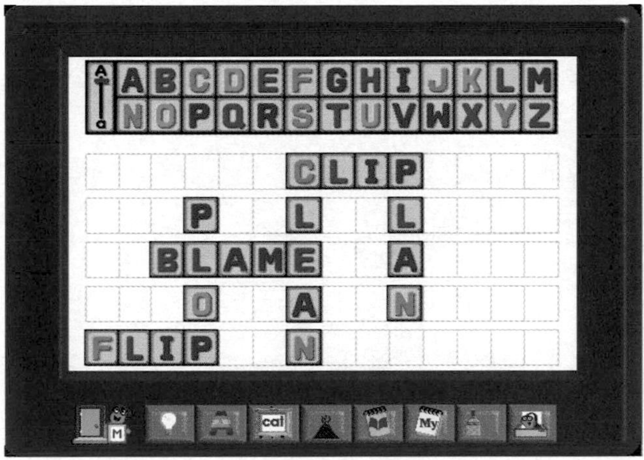

IDENTIFY L-BLEND WORDS

Encourage children to offer other words that begin with *bl, cl, fl,* and *pl.* Write them on the chalkboard. Call on volunteers to underline the first two letters in each word. Have children say the words along with you.

See Phonics and Word Building Kit for additional suggestions.

The Magnet Board activity pictured above provides additional phonics practice. For information on this and other Magnet Board activities, see the WiggleWorks Plus Teaching Plan.

SUPPORTING ALL LEARNERS

Multisensory Techniques

ESL During the Develop Oral Language activity, support second-language learners' phonemic awareness of the *l*-blend by encouraging them to clap each time they hear the sound. After reading "A Flea and A Fly in a Flue" several times, pause when you come to an *l*-blend word and invite children to pronounce it aloud for you.

CHALLENGE Have one child select a passage from a trade book and read it aloud to a partner. Challenge the partner to clap each time an *l*-blend word is read. Then partners can change roles.

BUILDING FLUENCY

Objective

Children read *Monkey See, Monkey Do* for fluency.

Technology Options

Encourage children to listen to the audiocassette recording of *Monkey See, Monkey Do*.

Monkey See, Monkey Do

Written by Marc Gave

Illustrated by Jacqueline Rogers

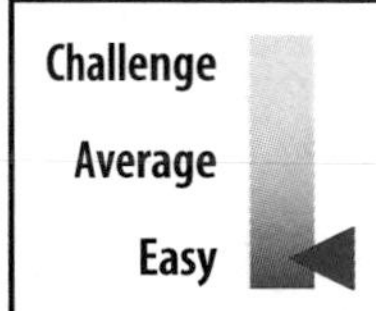

PREVIEW AND READ

Help children read the title of the book and the author's and illustrator's names. As they flip through the book, ask them to take note of what the monkeys do.

- **What are the monkey and the girl doing on the cover? Why do they look surprised?**
- **What do you think the monkeys might do in this book? What makes you think this?**

RESPONSE IDEAS

After children have read the book, they can meet with you or a partner to discuss it. Questions such as these will help the discussion:

- **What things do the monkeys do that you like to do?**
- **Read your favorite rhyming part of the book. What do you like about it? Try acting it out.**

Read Across Texts

- **Think about *Amazing Grace*. What does Grace like to do? Which of those things do you think monkeys would also like to do?**

Shoebox Library For more independent reading opportunities choose books from the Shoebox Library.

USING THE TRADE BOOKS

A Birthday Basket for Tía

Written by Pat Mora
Illustrated by Cecily Lang

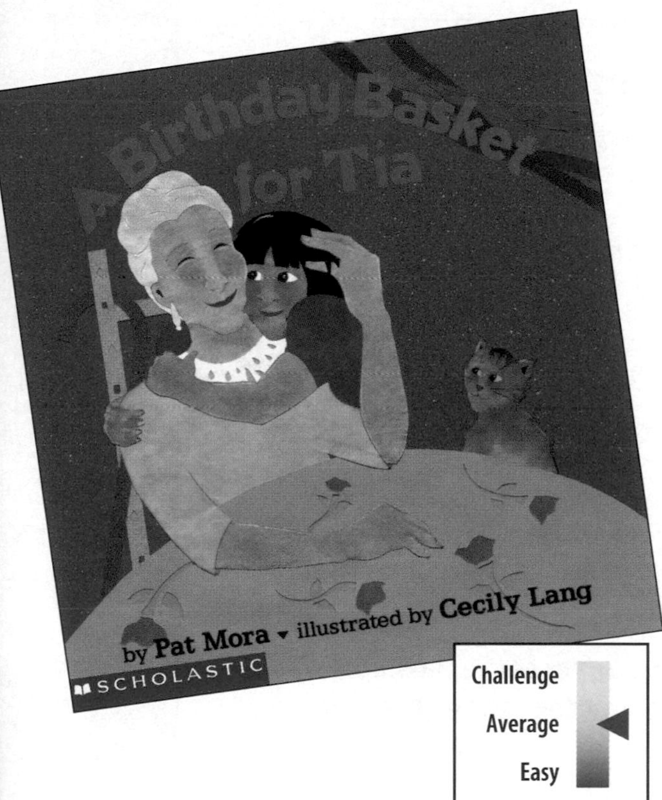

Challenge
Average
Easy

MAKE LITERARY ELEMENT CONNECTIONS:

PLOT

Talk About It

In *Amazing Grace,* Grace wants to be Peter Pan in the school play. The problem is that she may not get the part because she is a girl and she is African American. In *A Birthday Basket for Tía,* Cecilia has a different problem—she has to think of a birthday present to give her great-aunt. Discuss that in both stories, a very special person plays a part in helping each girl solve her problem.

- **Think about why Tía is special to Cecilia and why Nana is special to Grace. How are the relationships alike? How are they different?**
- **How is Grandma's relationship with the girl in *Thunder Cake* like the other two relationships?**

Write About It

After reading *A Birthday Basket for Tía,* invite the children to write about their favorite part of the story.

Read Across Texts

After reading *A Birthday Basket for Tía,* encourage children to relate it to *Amazing Grace.*

- **If Nana were Cecilia's great-aunt, what might Nana get for her birthday? Why?**
- **If Tía were Grace's great-aunt, what might she say or do to help Grace feel better?**

USING THE TRADE BOOK GUIDE

For more teaching ideas, refer to the individual Trade Book Guide for *A Birthday Basket for Tía* by Pat Mora.

Encourage children to listen to the audiocassette recording of *A Birthday Basket for Tía.*

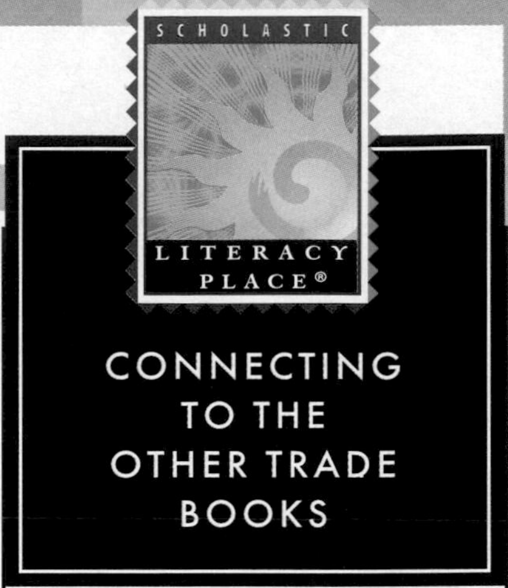

CONNECTING TO THE OTHER TRADE BOOKS

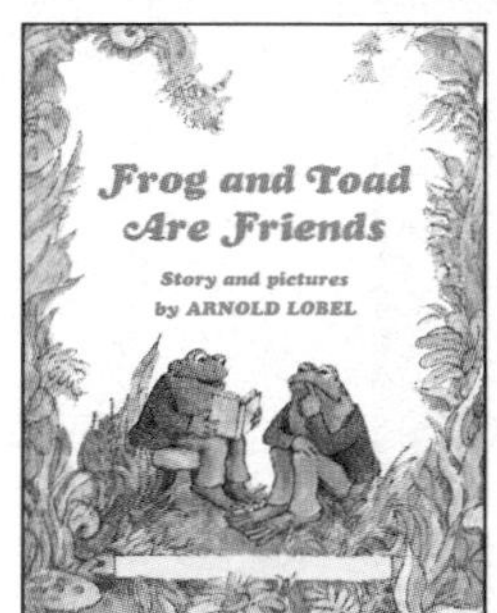

Ask children who have read *Frog and Toad Are Friends* to tell how the two friends are alike and how they are different from the characters in *Amazing Grace*.

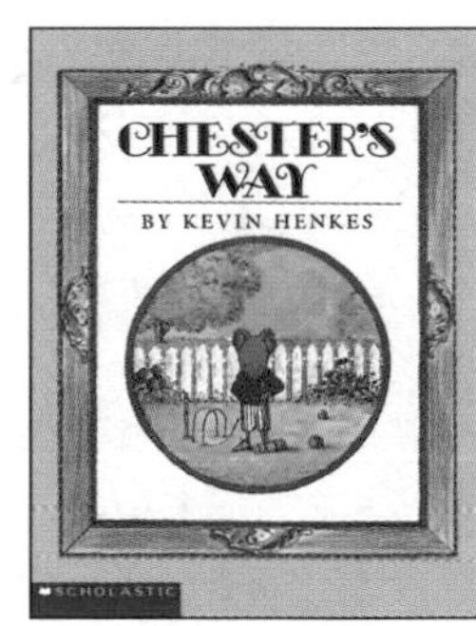

Ask children who have read *Chester's Way* how Lilly and Grace from *Amazing Grace* are alike and how they are different.

Also for use with this plan

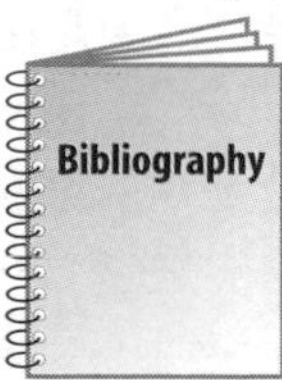

Closing the Unit

This section of *Snapshots* will help children **use what they've learned.** The **demonstration project** gives children the chance to **look back** at what they've learned and to **present their understandings.** They can **share their knowledge** with family members during a family literacy night and with community mentors who use the unit's literacies and skills in their daily lives.

Demonstration Project

Children have worked with many kinds of problems throughout the unit. They've experienced making a trading card and a graph in the workshops. They're now ready to make an exhibit in the project that begins on the next page.

Visit Our Place

Family Literacy Night Your classroom Sports Arena can become the centerpiece for an event to which children can invite family members. In addition to a student-planned presentation, a family literacy night is the perfect opportunity to involve families in learning. You and your students could set up stations around the classroom to let family members participate in the active learning that's going on in your classroom.

- **A reading corner with SourceBooks and Trade Books can allow families to try a shared reading experience.**
- **Include a writing center with great ideas for group writing.**
- **Families might enjoy doing some of the Integrated Language Arts and Integrated Curriculum activities.**
- **If possible, set up a corner of the classroom where the Meet the Mentor video can be observed.**

Inviting Community Mentors Invite a community member who can present real-life applications of the *Snapshots* literacies and skills to your class or at family literacy night. For example, you might invite:

- **a coach.**
- **a photographer.**
- **a cheerleader.**

Work with your class to develop a list of questions and send them to the speaker ahead of time. For example, you might ask a photographer about the most common problem he or she has with shooting photographs of people.

PROJECT

Objectives

Children learn to:

- express themselves through the things they enjoy doing.
- choose relevant materials to make an exhibit about themselves.
- use the presentation skill of show-and-tell.

Materials:
Literacy-at-Work Book pp. 76-77
Paper and pencils
Markers or crayons
Photos and drawings of children
Tape
Posterboard
Children's favorite things

Time:
About 40 minutes

Suggested Grouping:
Individuals

Curriculum Connections:
Social Studies
The Arts

How to Make an Exhibit

WHY DO THIS PROJECT?

When a museum presents an exhibit about someone such as Benjamin Franklin or Rosa Parks, the curators try to select a variety of things—objects, pictures, audio and visual recordings—that will make the person come alive for us. The chosen materials must be relevant to the subject's life and personality. They must tell us not only what the subject accomplished but also what kind of person he or she was. When such an exhibit is successful, we come away from it with a sense of who the person was.

In making an exhibit about themselves, children will have an opportunity to do something not usually afforded historical figures: they'll get to choose which items best represent them. As they consider what to communicate to others about themselves, children will broaden the thinking they did during the Workshops, in which they made autobiographical trading cards and a class graph.

Getting Started

UNIT SKILL:

CHOOSE FOR RELEVANCE

To prepare children for the Project, devote some time to a general discussion about the picture on the Project Card showing objects exhibited in the Baseball Hall of Fame. You could ask any of the following questions:

- **What does each object in the picture tell about the player it represents?**
- **Why do you think the people who created the Baseball Hall of Fame chose each object and picture shown in the illustration?**

CONNECT TO HOME AND COMMUNITY

Have children ask an older relative or friend to take them to a local exhibition at a museum for natural history, art, or sports. This will allow children to see firsthand the things displayed for a specific theme.

Troubleshooting

If children lack objects or pictures or a way of transporting them, suggest alternative ways of including them in their exhibits (making drawings or writing descriptions). Make sure you know what favorite things children intend to exhibit. Pets and valuable or dangerous objects are probably best represented by pictures.

1 Gather Good Ideas

With the class, discuss the kinds of things that might be good to show in an exhibit. Encourage children to think about their accomplishments, and emphasize that other things, such as their families, their interests and hobbies, and their personalities, are also important in giving a complete picture. Emphasize that children should choose objects that tell something interesting about themselves and their accomplishments, not what great possessions they have.

INDIVIDUALS Have individuals list accomplishments, activities, and traits to be highlighted in the exhibit.

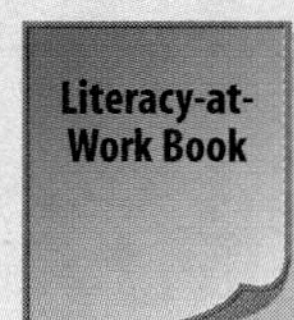

Children can use page 76 of the Literacy-at-Work Book to plan their exhibit.

JECT

GRADE 2 PERSONAL VOICE

PROJECT

How to Make an Exhibit

An exhibit is a collection of pictures, writings, or objects that give information about something or someone. Here is part of an exhibit about baseball players at the Baseball Hall of Fame. Together, all these objects help show who these players were.

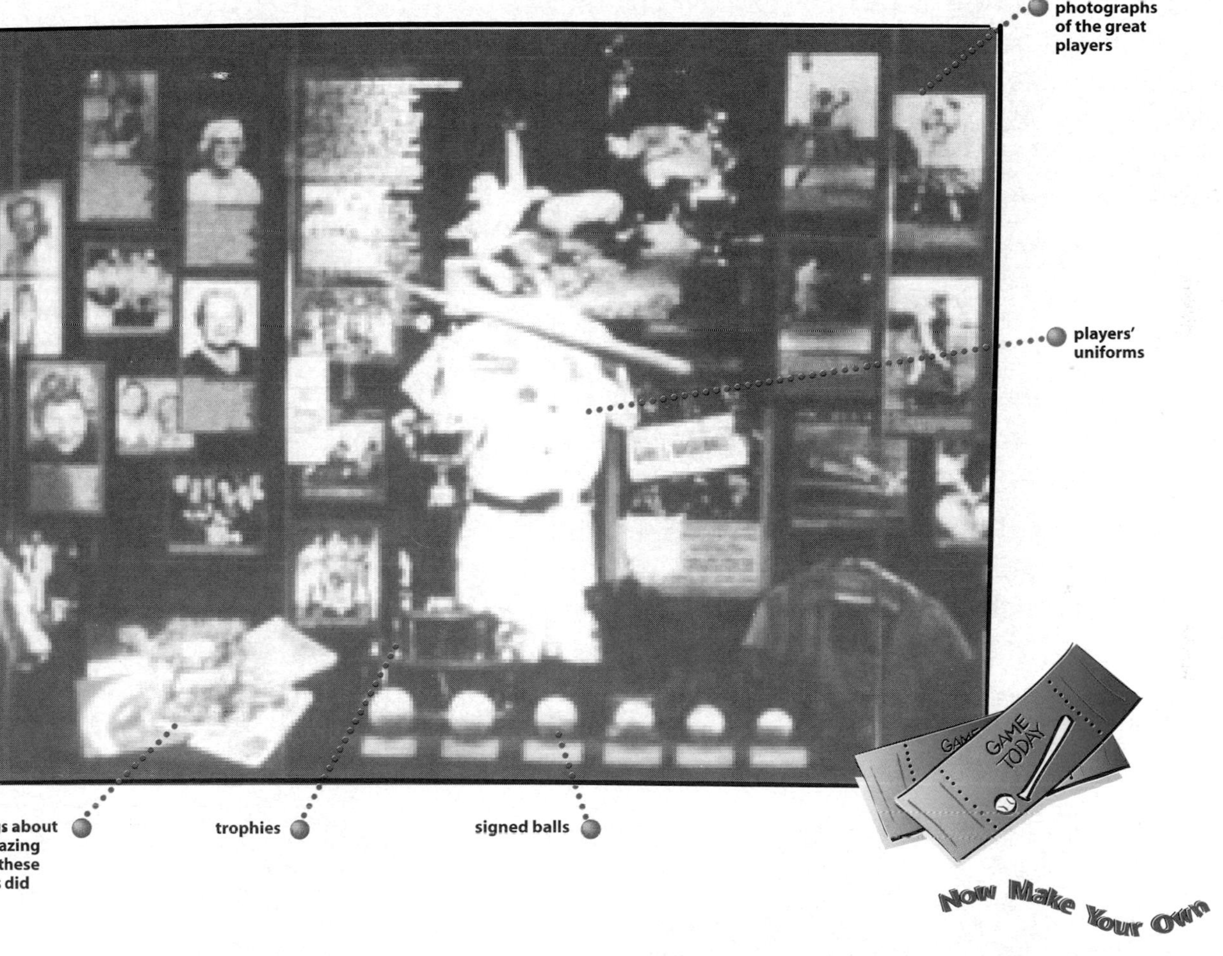

Children can use a unit Story Starter to help them write descriptions of labels for their exhibitions. Encourage children to create their labels using computer writing and drawing tools.

SUPPORTING ALL LEARNERS

ESL Stimulate language practice by guiding the class in a tour around all the exhibits, as one would do in a real museum. As children comment on the objects, suggest to second-language learners that they teach their classmates the names of objects in their first language. **(Hands-on Learning)**

❷ Make Your Exhibit

Point out to children that their exhibits should include written descriptions or labels, as well as pictures, of their favorite things. Explain to children that all objects in their exhibits need to be clearly visible. Several items related to a single topic should be grouped together. Children may want to experiment by using blocks or boxes to hold up and display some of their favorite things.

COOPERATIVE GROUPS Children can help one another arrange their exhibits.

Plan Your Exhibit

Children can also use the questions on page 77 of the Literacy-at-Work Book for assessing progress up to this point and for adjusting their work as needed.

Use the Presentation Skill lesson plan on pages T308 and T309 of the Teacher's SourceBook to support children in giving their show-and-tell presentations of their exhibits.

Literacy-at-Work Book

Children can use page 77 of the Literacy-at-Work Book in their exhibits.

ONGOING ASSESSMENT — PERFORMANCE-BASED

After children have finished their exhibits, review their work. Ask yourself:

- ✔ Did children display things that showed their strong points?
- ✔ Were children's arrangements organized?
- ✔ How did children coordinate their visuals with their written texts?

If children have trouble selecting things for their exhibit, try this:

Ask children to think of objects that would be suitable for exhibits about different topics, such as football, dance, music, or toys.

Children's Self-Assessment

- ✔ Did I include all the important things about myself in my exhibit?

PORTFOLIO

Portfolio Opportunity **After children have completed this Project, you may want to take photographs of their exhibits so they can put the photos in their Portfolios as examples of work well done. They may also include the drawings and writings they did especially for the exhibits.**

JECT

1 Gather Good Ideas

Think about things you've done well or that interest you. Draw pictures or bring in photos of yourself doing these things. Gather some objects that show these interests.

2 Make Your Exhibit

Decide which pictures or objects to show. Write about yourself and these interests. Hang your pictures and writing. Place some of your favorite things nearby.

Exhibit Checklist

Does your exhibit include:

- pictures of you?
- your favorite things?
- writing about your interests?

Tools

- paper and pencil
- markers or crayons
- photographs or drawings of you
- tape or paste
- posterboard
- favorite things

CONGRATULATIONS You have shown who you are in several interesting ways!

Bruce Thorson Photographer

CHILDREN'S PROJECT BENCHMARKS		
Novice: Children may select only a single interesting accomplishment or feature; children are able to select appropriate favorite things but may have difficulty doing relevant drawings and writings for the exhibit.	**Apprentice:** Children select some interesting accomplishments and features for exhibit; some materials, especially those children draw or write, may not be relevant to the desired image.	**Proficient:** Children select interesting accomplishments and features about themselves for exhibit; children write, draw and choose materials that are relevant to the desired image.

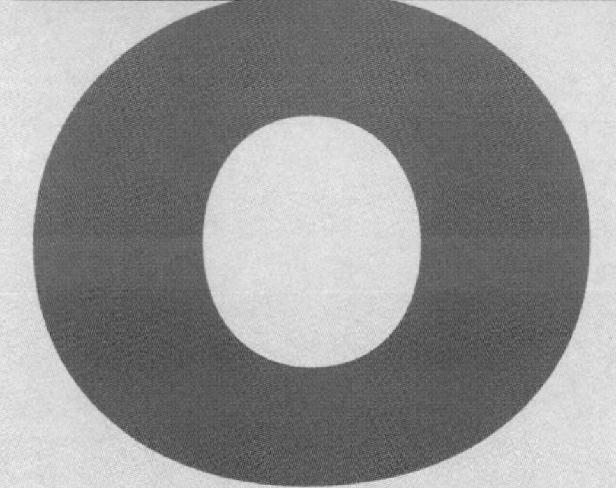

Presentation Skill

Objective

Children make an oral presentation of their exhibit.

Materials:
Children's exhibits
Audiocassette recorder (optional)
Blank audiotapes (optional)

Time:
About 40 minutes

Suggested Grouping:
Cooperative groups

Show and Tell

❶ Teach and Model

Put It in Context

With the class, review the Projects for a moment. How did children display their exhibit items? What things do they like most about the displays? What did they learn about their fellow classmates that they didn't know before? Could you suggest ways to improve the exhibit?

Cooperative Groups Have children work in cooperative groups to critique their exhibits.

❷ Practice and Apply

Show and Tell

Now help children actually tell about their exhibits. Explain that in some museums, guides walk groups of visitors through the museum and explain works of art to them. Have children pretend they are guides in a museum in which their exhibits are displayed. What would they say about their exhibits to a group of visitors? Have them think about these questions:

- **What parts of your exhibits would need the most explanation?**
- **Where would you stand and indicate objects as you talked about your exhibits?**

OPTION

Transfer to New Media

Children can make an audiotape of their show-and-tell presentations. What will they have to tell in a taped presentation that they wouldn't need to in a live one? Children might want to invite other classes to listen to the tapes as they view the exhibits.

JECT

❸ Assess

After children have finished their show-and-tell presentations, review their work. Ask yourself:

- ✔ Did children clearly explain why they selected certain things for their exhibits?
- ✔ Were children organized in their presentations?

If not, try this:
Look through the upcoming selections and Trade Books for real and fictional characters that would interest children. List them on the chalkboard with a short description of each. Ask children to choose one character and make a list of things that might be in an exhibit about that person. Then have them sketch an arrangement of these things. What would children say about the person based upon the items chosen?

Children's Self-Assessment

- ✔ Did I include some of my favorite things? What were they?

Supporting All Learners

Working in Groups

EXTRA HELP To help prepare children for their show and tell, have them share feedback. Working in groups, encourage group members to ask lots of questions to each other about the exhibits. This practice of providing information for the group will prepare each child for a class presentation.

ACCESS Some children may stay more focused if they could prepare with a partner for the exhibit. During the show and tell their partner can stand beside them, asking questions that they went over together.

CHALLENGE For budding young critics, choose volunteers to give a review of the show at its conclusion. They can offer feedback to small groups of their classmates in the form of praise and constructive criticism.

End of Unit Assessment

Student Assessment

✓ Follow-Up on Baseline Assessment

The Baseline Assessment established the conceptual level at which each child began the unit. By repeating this task, children demonstrate the growth they have accomplished over the course of the unit.

Have children repeat the exercise they did for the Baseline Assessment for this unit, bringing photos of themselves to class and explaining what they are doing in the pictures. Compare children's oral and written explanations of what they are doing in the photographs with those they gave before the unit began. Refer to the unit concepts for *Snapshots* and ask yourself whether the child's present work reflects a greater understanding of them.

As a check on your evaluation, ask children questions which will reveal whether the unit concepts have become part of their thinking. For example: If I wanted to learn all about you from a picture of you, what would you be doing in it?

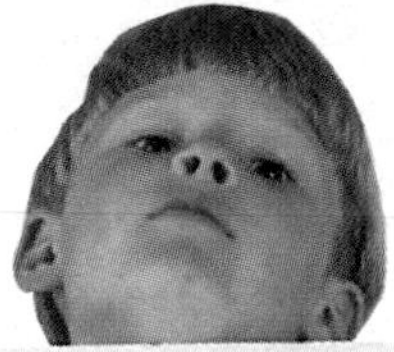

See the Assessment Handbook for:

- Guidelines for Assessment Planning
- Methods of Assessment including Observation and Portfolio
- Tools for Assessment including Literacy Record and Literacy Log
- Oral Reading Assessment
- Rubrics for Evaluation
- Grading Guidelines

✓ K-W-L

Refer to the K-W-L chart you have been working on throughout the unit. Finish filling in the "What Did We Learn" section. Have children write briefly about what they still want to learn about expressing themselves through the activities they choose.

✓ Student Self-Assessment

Children should complete the What Did I Learn page. They can assess whether they have learned what they stated they wanted to learn. In either case you can confer with each child in order to suggest means for fulfilling their learning interest.

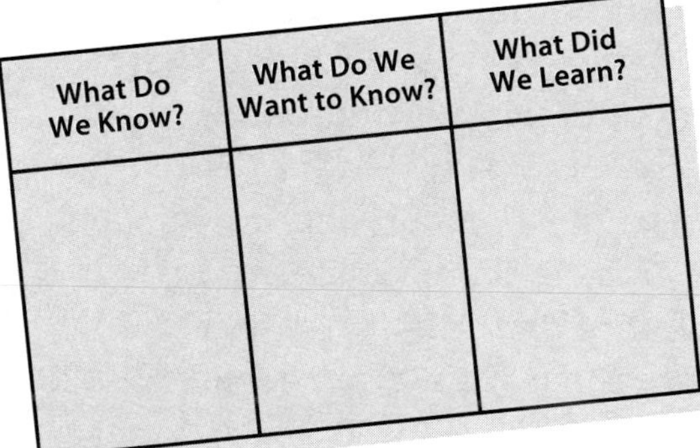

✓ Observational Checklist

Use the Individual and Class Unit Checklists for *Snapshots*, pp. 16 and 17 of the Classroom Management Forms, to record your end-of-unit evaluations and observations of each child.

✓ Performance-Based Assessment

Workshops, projects, and writing activities are good opportunities for performance assessment. The benchmarks mentioned in the teacher's edition, and child self-assessment pieces are good assessment tools.

✓ Portfolio

Allow children time to sort through the material they've saved for their Portfolios. Distribute the Portfolio Checklist on page 96 of the Assessment Handbook to help children decide what to keep in their *Snapshots* Portfolio.

✓ Testing

See the Unit Vocabulary Test in the Assessment Kit.

To help prepare children for the *Snapshots* unit test, see the Teacher's Test Manual.

Forms A and B of the test and directions for administering, scoring, and using the tests are in the Teacher's Test Manual.

Teacher Notes

Teacher Portfolio

Begin or add to your *Snapshots* Portfolio by collecting material that worked for you in teaching this unit. Some items you might include are:

- articles from language arts and reading journals, newspapers, and other sources that document community and professional interaction on the topic of personality development in children.
- videotapes of the children as they work on the projects.
- audiocassettes of teacher-child conferences and of children reading or discussing *Ronald Morgan Goes to Bat* or "Top Ten."

Journal Writing

You can organize and record your thoughts about teaching this unit in your Journal. The following questions may help to focus your thinking.

- What activities appealed most to children?
- Which parts of the unit did not interest children? How can I teach these parts differently?
- Which parts of the unit were omitted because of a lack of time? How can I make time for them next year?

Teacher Self-Assessment

Spend a few minutes critiquing your own teaching.

- **Did I help children discover their own talents?**
- **Did I motivate children to think about what they like to do best?**
- **Did I provide opportunities for children to do new and different activities?**

Glossary

activities
things that you do
Art and swimming the **activities** I like best.

amazing
surprising
The huge amount of snow in our yard is **amazing**.

announced
said or told
The teacher happily **announced** the date of the play.

artist
a person who draws or paints
The **artist** painted a picture of our school.

auditions
tests for a part in a show
He watched the **auditions** for the roles of Jack and Sam in the play.

ballet
a kind of dance
People dance on their toes when they do **ballet**.

ballet

baseball
a game played by two teams with a bat and a ball
In **baseball**, players try to hit the ball with a bat and run around the bases.

basketball
a game played by two teams trying to throw a large ball through a high hoop
He runs fast and jumps high when he plays **basketball**.

camera
a kind of box used to take pictures or movies
My **camera** takes very good pictures.

camera

clutched
held tightly
She **clutched** the ball when she caught it.

computer
a machine that does many kinds of work very quickly
I wrote a story on a **computer**.

computer

confidence
a strong belief in someone's actions
The teacher had **confidence** that I would pass the test.

crafts
things that are handmade
We saw many beautiful baskets at the **crafts** fair.

helmet
a hard hat that protects the head
His **helmet** protected his head when he fell off the bike.

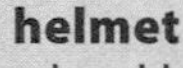

helmet

hobby
something that a person does just for fun
Collecting stamps is a **hobby** many people like.

imaginary
make-believe, not real
The talking animals in the story are **imaginary**.

imagination
the act of creating pictures or ideas in your mind
He used a lot of **imagination** to help him paint pictures.

improve
to make better
If she studies, she can **improve** her grades.

modeled
showed
My friend **modeled** the way to make an airplane.

murmured
spoke in a low, soft voice
I couldn't hear what he said because he **murmured**.

photographer
a person who takes pictures with a camera.
A **photographer** took a picture of my class.

practice
to do something again and again
We **practice** for the class play every day.

recited
said out loud in front of a group
He **recited** his poem in front of the class.

scribbled
wrote quickly or without care
She messily **scrib-bled** a note as she rushed out of the house.

sneaker
a soft shoe with a flat rubber bottom
The laces on one **sneaker** came untied.

sneaker

soccer
a game played by two teams with a ball that can be moved with every part of the body except the hands
She kicks the ball far when she plays **soccer**.

soccer

squad
a small group of people who work together
The police **squad** was getting ready for the parade.

stunning
very beautiful
The queen's costume was **stunning**.

theater
a place to see movies or plays
The **theater** was showing a good movie.

squad

tiptoed
walked on the toes
She **tiptoed** quietly down the hall.

tryouts
tests to see if a person can do something well
Tryouts for the band are this afternoon.

victory
the act of winning
The captain led our team to **victory**.

whispered
spoke very softly
She **whispered** his name in my ear.

Authors and Illustrators

Caroline Binch pages 116-135

Caroline Binch loves to travel. One of her favorite places is Trinidad, the Caribbean island where Grace's family comes from. Binch has worked with author Mary Hoffman on another book about Grace, called *Bountiful Grace.* She also illustrated *Hue Boy* by Rita Mitchell. She wrote and illustrated *Gregory Cool.* Both books are about boys in the Caribbean!

Nancy Carlson pages 76-93

Nancy Carlson likes all kinds of sports—just like her character, Lou Ann. She hopes that her stories will help kids discover that they can do all kinds of things! Her book, *Harriet and the Roller Coaster,* shows why it can be good to try new things. *Arnie and the New Kid* is about two boys who each learn what it means to be a good friend.

Mari Evans page 75

When Mari Evans was in the fourth grade, a story she wrote was published in the school's newspaper. Her father was so proud he told everyone in the family! Knowing that her father believed she had talent made Evans want to keep on writing. Today she is best known for her poems, but she also writes articles, stories, and TV shows.

Patricia Reilly Giff pages 18-41

Patricia Reilly Giff was a teacher for many years. She began to write stories to make her students laugh. She wanted to tell them they were special. Now she is the author of many books, such as *The Beast in Ms. Rooney's Room.* She wrote another story about Ronald Morgan called *Today Was a Terrible Day.*

WHAT'S BEHIND THE TAB?

Options for Integrating Your Curriculum

	MATH	SCIENCE	SOCIAL STUDIES	THE ARTS
Plan I	**Class Favorites** Conduct a class survey about favorite fruits and make a graph like the one shown in "Top Ten." *(page R2)*	**Have a Ball** Test various balls and discover their different properties. *(page R2)*	**Choose Your Favorite Place** List the top three places you'd like to visit and make a graph. *(page R3)*	**Illustrate Numbers** Illustrate the numerals for the favorite activities in the "Top Ten" graph. *(page R3)*
Plan II	**Chart a Relay Race** Chart the results of a fast-walking relay race to see how practice helped Ronald in *Ronald Morgan Goes to Bat. (page R4)*	**Explore Motion** Diagram the movement of a ball rebounding against a wall. *(page R4)*	**Make a Sports Scrapbook** Make a scrapbook of a team sport showing players encouraging each other. *(page R5)*	**Show the Path of a Ball** Make a simple flipbook to show the path of a moving ball. *(page R5)*
Plan III	**Copy Ruby the Copycat** Use different pairs of addends to make the same total as Ruby in *Ruby the Copycat. (page R6)*	**Copycats in Nature** Find out about animal mimicry, and decide how it helps certain animals. *(page R6)*	**Choose a Role Model** Choose a person you admire and write about one feature you'd like to copy. *(page R7)*	**Copycat Art** Make a plan to reproduce a painting. *(page R7)*
Plan IV	**Keep Score** Compare ratios by keeping score in a classroom game. *(page R8)*	**Measure Your Heartbeat** Find out how physical activity, such as the ones in *Louanne Pig in Making the Team,* affects your heartbeat. *(page R8)*	**Teamwork** List the ways that various players contribute to their teams. *(page R9)*	**Create a Pennant** Make a pennant for a school team. *(page R9)*
Plan V	**Measure a Group Photo** Estimate the distance in a group photo by George Ancona in *George Ancona: Then & Now. (page R10)*	**Make Sun Prints** Make sun prints by taping construction paper forms to a sunny window. *(page R10)*	**Create a Travel Brochure** Make a travel brochure using photos of a place you'd like to visit. *(page R11)*	**Make Prints From Rubbings** Use colored pencils to make a print from a textured surface. *(page R11)*
Plan VI	**Estimate Space for a Play** Estimate how much space would be needed in your classroom to stage a play. *(page R12)*	**How Does Peter Pan Fly?** Devise a way for Grace in *Amazing Grace* to fly on stage. *(page R12)*	**Outfit a Character** Select costumes and props for a character from a favorite story. *(page R13)*	**Create a Set Design** Make a set design for one of Grace's characters. *(page R13)*

INTEGRATED CURRICULUM: "Top Ten"

MATH

Class Favorites

Objective:
Use Charts, Graphs, and Visual Displays

Materials:
Grid paper
Pencils

Time:
About 30 minutes

Suggested Grouping:
Whole class

Teacher Guidance:
Moderate

Outside Research:
None

Advance Preparation:
Gather materials

Activity

Children conduct a class survey about favorite fruits and graph their results. VISUAL LITERACY

Connect to the SourceBook

Review the Favorite Activity graph on page 15 of the SourceBook.

Make New Discoveries

- Have children give the names of various kinds of fruit. Write each name on the chalkboard.
- Ask children to write each fruit on the grid paper in the same way the activities were written in the SourceBook graph.
- Ask each child to choose his or her favorite fruit and to raise a hand when you call out the name.
- Children count the hands for each fruit, and create a graph showing the information.

✔ How to Assess

Were children able to make accurate graphs using the data they collected in the survey?

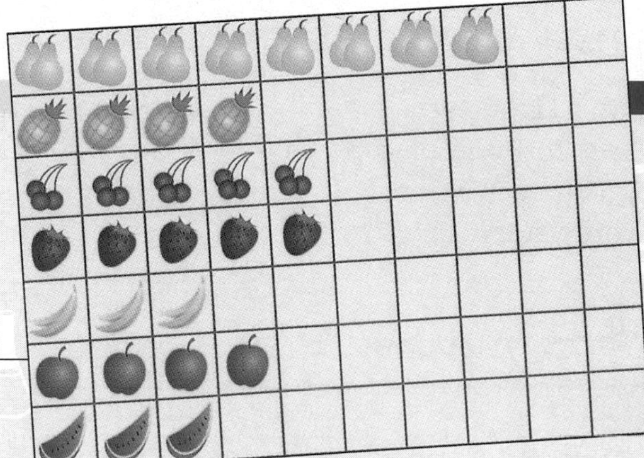

SCIENCE

Have a Ball

Objective:
Note Relevant Details

Materials:
An assortment of balls, such as basketballs, softballs, table tennis balls

Time:
About 30 minutes

Suggested Grouping:
Cooperative groups

Teacher Guidance:
Moderate

Outside Research:
None

Advance Preparation:
Gather materials. Ask children to bring in balls from home.

Activity

Children test various balls and discover their different properties.

Connect to the SourceBook

The graph on page 15 shows that playing ball is the favorite activity of the second graders in the survey. Ask children why different balls are used for different games.

Make New Discoveries

- Help children to name some of the different properties of a ball, such as weight, hardness, size, and bounce.
- Have children test the properties of the balls gathered.
- Ask children to classify the properties needed for a ball used in a game of their choice.

✔ How to Assess

Were children able to find and discuss differences in the properties of various balls?

SOCIAL STUDIES

Choose Your Favorite Place

Objective: Collect Data

Materials: U.S. map (optional)

Time: About 30 minutes

Suggested Grouping: Individuals

Teacher Guidance: Moderate

Outside Research: None

Advance Preparation: Gather materials

Activity

Children list the top three locations they'd like to visit, take a survey, and make a graph. VISUAL LITERACY

Connect to the SourceBook

Discuss some of the favorite things mentioned in "Top Ten." Ask children what U.S. locations they think would be popular with second graders.

Make New Discoveries

- Ask children to name a place, area, or landmark they'd most like to visit. Write the locations on the chalkboard. Children should keep a running tally of votes.
- Have children make a graph showing their favorite locations. They can use checkmarks to represent each vote.

✔ How to Assess

Did children's graphs show the data they collected?

THE ARTS

Illustrate Numbers

Objective: Brainstorm Multiple Approaches

Materials: Paper and pencils; Crayons or markers

Time: About 30 minutes

Suggested Grouping: Individuals or cooperative groups

Teacher Guidance: Low

Outside Research: None

Advance Preparation: Gather materials

Activity

Children illustrate the numerals for the favorite activities in the graph. VISUAL LITERACY

Connect to the SourceBook

Have children refer to the graph on page 15 of "Top Ten." Ask them each to pick one of the activities.

Make New Discoveries

- Have children who picked the same activity group together.
- Ask children to think of ways that they can decorate the number of the activity in such a way that it shows what the activity is. For example, the number one might be made to look like a person catching a ball.
- Children make illustrated numerals and exchange them to guess the activity. They can check their interpretations by using the graph.

✔ How to Assess

Did children's illustrations reflect the activities?

INTEGRATED CURRICULUM: *Ronald Morgan Goes to Bat*

MATH

Chart a Relay Race

Objective: Analyze Information

Materials: Rulers, Watch

Time: About 30 minutes

Suggested Grouping: Cooperative groups

Teacher Guidance: Low

Outside Research: None

Advance Preparation: Gather materials. You may want to do this activity in the gym or in the play area outside.

Activity

Children chart the results of a fast-walking relay race.

Connect to the SourceBook

Review pages 37 to 40 in the SourceBook. Ask children how practice helped Ronald.

Make New Discoveries

- Divide the class into relay groups. Each group races on its own. Children pass the ruler to each other in the relay.
- A member of each group counts the number of passes completed in two minutes.
- Have children do two or three races. Have each group compare their results for each race and decide what accounted for any change.

✔ How to Assess

Were children able to draw reasonable conclusions about any change in the results of the races?

SCIENCE

Explore Motion

Objective: Use Diagrams and Illustrations

Materials: Paper and pencil, Balls that bounce well

Time: About 30 minutes

Suggested Grouping: Partners

Teacher Guidance: Low

Outside Research: None

Advance Preparation: Gather materials.

Activity

Children diagram the movement of a ball rebounding against a wall. VISUAL LITERACY

Connect to the SourceBook

Review the illustrations in the SourceBook that show the ball in motion.

Make New Discoveries

- Partners experiment rolling a ball at various angles against a wall.
- One child rolls the ball slowly and the partner observes and makes a simple diagram to show the motion. Partners change roles.
- Partners diagram several different rebounds and draw conclusions about their results.

✔ How to Assess

Were children able to draw reasonable conclusions about the direction of a rebounding ball from their diagrams?

SOCIAL STUDIES

Make a Sports Scrapbook

Objective: Sort Information

Materials: Newspapers or sports magazines; Construction paper; Glue; Scissors

Time: About 40 minutes

Suggested Grouping: Partners

Teacher Guidance: Moderate

Outside Research: Low

Advance Preparation: Ask children to bring in sports magazines and newspapers.

Activity

Children make a scrapbook of a team sport showing players encouraging each other.

VISUAL LITERACY

Connect to the SourceBook

Even though Ronald isn't a great player, his team appreciates his spirit. Ask children how team spirit can help a team's performance.

Make New Discoveries

- Children work with partners who share the same favorite sport.
- Partners cut out photos and glue them to construction paper or create their own sports drawings.
- Children write captions or labels for each picture or drawing. They can also create dialogue balloons.

✔ How to Assess

Did children write captions or dialogue that matched their visual material?

THE ARTS

Show the Path of a Ball

Objective: Use Diagrams and Illustrations

Materials: Paper squares (3" x 3") or self-adhesive notepads; markers or crayons; stapler

Time: About 40 minutes

Suggested Grouping: Cooperative groups

Teacher Guidance: Moderate

Outside Research: None

Advance Preparation: Staple together 15–20 paper squares for each child or distribute notepads.

Activity

Children make a simple flipbook to show the path of a moving ball.

VISUAL LITERACY

Connect to the SourceBook

Ronald finally hits the baseball when he opens his eyes and watches the path it follows.

Make New Discoveries

- Have children think of a bouncing ball or a ball being tossed in the air. Have them draw the path of a moving ball.
- Have children draw a ball (a large dot will work well) on one corner of the bottom sheet of their flipbooks. On successive pages they gradually change the position of the ball according to the path they planned.

✔ How to Assess

Did children's flipbooks show the path of a moving ball?

INTEGRATED CURRICULUM: *Ruby the Copycat*

MATH

Copy Ruby the Copycat

Objective:
Understand Part-Whole Relationships

Materials:
Paper clips
Paper and pencil

Time:
About 30 minutes

Suggested Grouping:
Partners

Teacher Guidance:
Low

Outside Research:
None

Advance Preparation:
Gather materials.

Activity

Children use different pairs of addends to make the same total.

Connect to the SourceBook

Display the illustration of Ruby and Angela on page 46 [the title page showing Angela and Ruby doing addition problems on the chalkboard]. Write "7 + 8 = 15" on the chalkboard.

Make New Discoveries

- Give each pair of children 15 paper clips. Challenge them to use the paper clips to figure out other number pairs that add up to the sum of 15.
- Ask them to write down their number pairs. If children increase one of the numbers by 1, what happens to the other number in the pair? Have the whole class review and compare the different combinations.

✔ How to Assess

Did children notice the relationship between the pairs of addends?

SCIENCE

Copycats in Nature

Objective:
Interpret Information

Materials:
Reference books with photos of animals (optional)

Time:
About 20 minutes

Suggested Grouping:
Whole class

Teacher Guidance:
Moderate

Outside Research:
Low

Advance Preparation:
Gather materials.

Activity

Children find out about animal mimicry, and decide how it helps certain animals survive.

Connect to the SourceBook

Ruby copies her friend because she wants to be like that person. Ask children if they know about any copycats in nature.

Make New Discoveries

Tell children about each animal below, and ask them how mimicry helps the animal.

- The viceroy butterfly looks like the monarch, which is poisonous to birds that eat it.
- The treehopper is an insect that looks like a thorn.
- The frogfish looks like seaweed.
- The robber fly looks like a bumblebee.

✔ How to Assess

Did children understand how each animal's appearance helps it survive?

SOCIAL STUDIES

Choose a Role Model

Objective: Make Judgments

Materials: Paper and pencil

Time: About 20 minutes

Suggested Grouping: Individuals

Teacher Guidance: Low

Outside Research: None

Advance Preparation: Gather materials.

Activity

Children choose a person they admire and write about a feature of that person that they like to copy.

Connect to the SourceBook

Ruby copies people she admires, but she doesn't necessarily copy the qualities that make these people special. Ask children if the things that Ruby copies really change her.

Make New Discoveries

• Discuss the difference between a person's talents and character.

• Ask children to think of someone in their community, a historical figure, or a celebrity whom they admire for his or her character.

• Ask children to decide which of the person's qualities they would like to copy and to write a few sentences explaining why.

✔ How to Assess

Did children choose qualities that could be emulated?

THE ARTS

Copycat Art

Objective: Make a Plan

Materials: Paper and pencil, Tracing paper, Illustrated art books, Crayons or markers, Rulers, Grid paper

Time: About 30 minutes

Suggested Grouping: Individuals

Teacher Guidance: Low

Outside Research: Low

Advance Preparation: Gather materials.

Activity

Children plan methods to reproduce a painting.

VISUAL LITERACY

Connect to the SourceBook

Review with children the passages that show the things that Ruby copied. Can you think of ways to copy things you like?

Make New Discoveries

• Children look through some art books and select a fairly simple picture that they like.

• Have children plan how they might copy the picture. Suggest they use things such as tracing paper, grid paper, and rulers.

• Children make their copies and compare them with the book reproductions.

✔ How to Assess

Did children use their plans to make recognizable copies of pictures?

INTEGRATED CURRICULUM: *Louanne Pig in Making the Team*

MATH

Keep Score

Objective: Interpret Information

Materials: Crumpled paper, Wastebaskets, Paper and pencil

Time: About 30 minutes

Suggested Grouping: Cooperative groups

Teacher Guidance: Low

Outside Research: None

Advance Preparation: Gather materials

Activity

Children compare ratios by keeping score in a classroom game.

Connect to the SourceBook

Review page 93 in the Literacy SourceBook which shows the scoreboard. Ask volunteers to tell what they know about keeping score for ball games.

Make New Discoveries

- Divide the class into teams. Have teams shoot their crumpled paper balls into a wastebasket. Each child takes five shots and records his or her score.
- Teams calculate the total number of baskets and the total number of attempts. Then they compare their results and determine which team was most successful.

✔ How to Assess

Did children compare scores to find the most successful team?

SCIENCE

Measure Your Heartbeat

Objective: Collect Data

Materials: Stopwatch or clock with second hand, Paper and pencil

Time: About 30 minutes

Suggested Grouping: Individuals

Teacher Guidance: Moderate

Outside Research: None

Advance Preparation: Gather materials.

Activity

Children find out how physical activity affects their heartbeat.

Connect to the SourceBook

Discuss the activities that Louanne and Arnie had to do to be selected for the teams. Ask children how physical exercise affects people.

Make New Discoveries

- Show children how to find their heartbeat or pulse on the side of their neck by pressing with their middle two fingers just under their jawbone.
- Children count their pulses for a fifteen-second period that you call out. They record the number of pulses when they are at rest, after walking for about three minutes, and after running in place for about three minutes.
- Children compare and explain their results.

✔ How to Assess

Did children draw reasonable conclusions about the data they collected?

SCORE					
TEAM A					
TEAM B					

SOCIAL STUDIES

Teamwork

Objective: Understand Part-Whole Relationships

Materials: Paper and pencil

Time: About 40 minutes

Suggested Grouping: Cooperative groups

Teacher Guidance: Low

Outside Research: None

Advance Preparation: Gather materials.

Activity

Children list the ways that various players contribute to their teams.

Connect to the SourceBook

Louanne and Arnie both wanted to join teams, but they picked the wrong ones. Ask children what it takes to be on a particular team.

Make New Discoveries

- Ask children to choose their favorite team activity. They needn't pick sports; activities such as music and drama are also considered team efforts.
- Groups brainstorm to list the roles that different people on the team play.

✔ How to Assess

Did children's lists reflect the idea that a team depends on each of its players?

THE ARTS

Create a Pennant

Objective: Select Information

Materials: Pieces of felt or construction paper, Pencils, Scissors, Glue

Time: About 30 minutes

Suggested Grouping: Individuals

Teacher Guidance: Low

Outside Research: None

Advance Preparation: Gather materials. You might want to make cardboard pennant shapes for children to trace.

Activity

Children make a pennant for a school team. VISUAL LITERACY

Connect to the SourceBook

Have children look at the illustrations where the cheerleaders use pom–poms. Ask them to think of other ways that a team is cheered on.

Make New Discoveries

- Have children cut out a pennant shape from felt or construction paper.
- Have them pick a favorite sport.
- Have children cut designs from the felt or construction paper and glue them to the pennant. Encourage children to use both images and words.

✔ How to Assess

Did children's pennants support teams playing the sports they chose?

INTEGRATED CURRICULUM: *George Ancona: Then & Now*

MATH

Measure a Group Photo

Objective:
Use Diagrams and Illustrations

Materials:
Paper and pencil
Rulers

Time:
About 30 minutes

Suggested Grouping:
Cooperative groups

Teacher Guidance:
Low

Outside Research:
None

Advance Preparation:
Gather materials.

Activity

Children estimate the distance in a group photo.

Connect to the SourceBook

Review with children all the group photographs in *George Ancona: Then & Now.*

Make New Discoveries

- Have children look at the large group photo on page 110.
- Tell groups to brainstorm a way to estimate the distance from the person on the far right to the person on the far left.
- If children have difficulty, suggest that they guess the average height of a child in the photo and use that as a guide for measuring.

✔ How to Assess

Did children use reasonable criteria to find the distance in the group photo?

SCIENCE

Make Sun Prints

Objective:
Make a Plan

Materials:
Construction paper
Index cards
Pencils
Scissors
Tape

Time:
About 30 minutes

Suggested Grouping:
Individuals

Teacher Guidance:
Moderate

Outside Research:
None

Advance Preparation:
Gather materials. The prints will need to be taped to sunlit windows for about a week.

Activity

Children make sun prints by taping construction paper forms to a sunny window. VISUAL LITERACY

Connect to the SourceBook

Discuss the lit and shadow areas of each photo in the SourceBook.

Make New Discoveries

- Have children make a stencil from an index card. Ask them to draw a simple form and cut it out. Either the positive or negative shape can be used as the stencil.
- Have children tape the stencil over a sheet of medium-colored construction paper. (Blue or green works well.)
- Tape the stencil and construction paper to a window that gets a lot of sunlight (cutout side facing the sun.) Remove the stencils after a week.

✔ How to Assess

Did children plan their stencils properly?

SOCIAL STUDIES

Create a Travel Brochure

Objective: Document Information

Materials: Travel magazines, Paper and pencils, Glue or tape

Time: About 40 minutes

Suggested Grouping: Partners

Teacher Guidance: Low

Outside Research: Moderate

Advance Preparation: Gather materials. Ask children to bring in unwanted travel or geographic magazines.

Activity

Children make a travel brochure using photos of a place they like to visit. VISUAL LITERACY

Connect to the SourceBook

Have children look at the photos of the different places around the world in *George Ancona: Then & Now.*

Make New Discoveries

- Have partners look through the magazines and pick a place that interests them. Then they can cut out pictures of the place they selected.
- Have them fold a piece of paper in half for the brochure and glue or tape the photos in an arrangement on the front cover. Inside the brochure, they should write about the place they've chosen.

✔ How to Assess

Did children select and arrange photos so that their travel brochures were appealing?

THE ARTS

Make Prints From Rubbings

Objective: Use Charts, Graphs, and Visual Displays

Materials: Paper, Colored pencils, Textured items such as coins, leaves, fabric

Time: About 40 minutes

Suggested Grouping: Individuals

Teacher Guidance: Moderate

Outside Research: None

Advance Preparation: Gather materials.

Activity

Children use colored pencils to make a print from a textured surface. VISUAL LITERACY

Connect to the SourceBook

Discuss how George Ancona's photos record the things he sees with his camera. Ask children what other ways there might be to record images.

Make New Discoveries

- Have children place a sheet of white paper over one of the items. (Coins are good to start with.) Tell them to use colored pencils to rub color over the paper. They'll see the shape and texture of the item on the paper.
- Children can experiment by arranging different items and using different colors to make a design.

✔ How to Assess

Did children's designs take advantage of the shapes and textures of the items they chose?

INTEGRATED CURRICULUM: *Amazing Grace*

MATH

Estimate Space for a Play

Objective: Make a Plan

Materials: Grid paper Pencils

Time: About 40 minutes

Suggested Grouping: Cooperative groups

Teacher Guidance: Low

Outside Research: None

Advance Preparation: Gather materials.

Activity

Children estimate how much space would be needed in their classroom to stage a play.

Connect to the SourceBook

Explain to children that part of putting on a play, as Grace and her class did in the story, is considering the space needed for the stage and the audience.

Make New Discoveries

- Groups think of ways to estimate how much of the classroom would be needed to stage the play *Peter Pan.*
- Have them draw diagrams on grid paper to show the stage. Groups compare diagrams and discuss their methods.
- As an extension, children might estimate how many people the rest of the classroom would hold as the audience.

✔ How to Assess

Did children's diagrams illustrate reasonable estimates of the space needed for the play?

THE MOVIE STAR THEATER SAT., AUG 21, 9 PM

THE MOVIE STAR THEATER SAT., AUG 21, 9 PM

THE MOVIE STAR THEATER SAT., AUG 2

SCIENCE

How Does Peter Pan Fly?

Objective: Use Diagrams and Illustrations

Materials: Paper and pencil

Time: About 30 minutes

Suggested Grouping: Partners

Teacher Guidance: Low

Outside Research: None

Advance Preparation: Gather materials.

Activity

Children devise a way for Grace in *Amazing Grace* to fly on stage.
VISUAL LITERACY

Connect to the SourceBook

Have children look at the illustrations in *Amazing Grace* where Grace is pretending to be Peter Pan. Ask children who know the story of Peter Pan to describe the character.

Make New Discoveries

- Explain to children that in many stage productions, the character of Peter Pan flies across the stage.
- Have partners devise ways that they could make Grace, who is playing Peter Pan, fly on stage.
- Ask partners to make diagrams of their ideas and label them.

✔ How to Assess

Did children's diagrams explain how they would make Peter Pan fly on stage?

SOCIAL STUDIES

Outfit a Character

Objective:
Note Relevant Details

Materials:
Paper and pencil

Time:
About 40 minutes

Suggested Grouping:
Partners

Teacher Guidance:
Low

Outside Research:
None

Advance Preparation:
Gather materials.

Activity

Children select costumes and props for a character from a favorite story.

Connect to the SourceBook

Discuss with children how Grace used appropriate props and costumes for the different characters that she acted out.

Make New Discoveries

- Have partners select a character they both know and enjoy.
- Ask children to think about where and when the story took place. What kinds of clothing would the character wear? What tools or objects would the character use? Have them write down their ideas.
- Partners describe the props and costumes to the rest of the class, who try to guess the identity of the character.

✔ How to Assess

Did children include appropriate details in their descriptions of the costumes and props?

THE ARTS

Create a Set Design

Objective:
Use Charts, Graphs, and Visual Displays

Materials:
Shoeboxes
Modeling clay
Construction paper
Pencils
Crayons or markers
Scissors
Glue

Time:
About 40 minutes

Suggested Grouping:
Cooperative groups

Teacher Guidance:
Low

Outside Research:
None

Advance Preparation:
Gather materials.

Activity

Children make a set design for one of Grace's characters.

Connect to the SourceBook

Review the passages and illustrations in the story that show Grace using props and costumes as she performs some of her favorite characters. Ask children what they think the background scenery might look like.

Make New Discoveries

- Children pick one of Grace's characters.
- They use the art materials to create how they think the rest of the scene might look. Encourage them to use three-dimensional objects in their set design.

✔ How to Assess

Did children design sets that would enhance Grace's characters?

Daily Language Practice

Week 1

	MONDAY	TUESDAY	WEDNESDAY	THURSDAY	FRIDAY
SKILLS	**Grammar:** Question Sentences **Spelling:** *r*-blends	**Mechanics:** Question Mark **Spelling:** *r*-blends	**Grammar:** Question Sentences **Spelling:** *r*-blends	**Mechanics:** Question Mark **Spelling:** *r*-blends	**Skills Review**
PRACTICE	who colored the grass red in this dawing	can your dog do ticks	where did you go on your tip	is this school made of bicks	did the ice cream tuck tip over
ANSWERS	Who colored the grass red in this drawing?	Can your dog do tricks?	Where did you go on your trip?	Is this school made of bricks?	Did the ice cream truck tip over?

Week 2

	MONDAY	TUESDAY	WEDNESDAY	THURSDAY	FRIDAY
SKILLS	**Grammar:** Naming Places **Spelling:** *s*-blends	**Mechanics:** Commas **Spelling:** *s*-blends	**Grammar:** Naming Places **Spelling:** *s*-blends	**Mechanics:** Commas **Spelling:** *s*-blends	**Skills Review**
PRACTICE	in our park in detroit we sim and play on the sings	do you own a sed in fairbanks alaska	he wrote the word "texas" in the sand with a sick	we had a morning sack in gary indiana	my grandparents sim in the lake in chicago illinois
ANSWERS	In our park in **Detroit,** we swim and play on the swings.	Do you own a sled in Fairbanks**,** Alaska?	He wrote the word **"Texas"** in the sand with a stick.	We had a morning snack in Gary**,** Indiana.	My grandparents swim in the lake in **Chicago, Illinois.**

Week 3

	MONDAY	TUESDAY	WEDNESDAY	THURSDAY	FRIDAY
SKILLS	**Grammar:** Action Words **Spelling:** Digraphs	**Mechanics:** Capitalizing Pronoun *I* **Spelling:** Digraphs	**Grammar:** Action Words **Spelling:** Digraphs	**Mechanics:** Capitalizing Pronoun *I* **Spelling:** Digraphs	**Skills Review**
PRACTICE	she threw a chin stick for her dog to fetch	i wich i were rich	they ate too mush candy, and it made them sick	i think it's fun to chop for clothes	when i fell down, i knocked a ship off my tooth.
ANSWERS	She **threw** a thin stick for her dog to fetch.	**I** wish **I** were rich.	They **ate** too much candy, and it **made** them sick.	**I** think it's fun to shop for clothes.	When **I fell** down, **I knocked** a chip off my tooth.

Week 4

	MONDAY	TUESDAY	WEDNESDAY	THURSDAY	FRIDAY
SKILLS	**Grammar:** Simple Sentences **Spelling:** Long *a*, Long *i (a-e, i-e)*	**Mechanics:** Capitalizing First Word **Spelling:** Long *a*, Long *i (a-e, i-e)*	**Grammar:** Simple Sentences **Spelling:** Long *a*, Long *i (a-e, i-e)*	**Mechanics:** Capitalizing First Word **Spelling:** Long *a*, Long *i (a-e, i-e)*	**Skills Review**
PRACTICE	we cam to school early today	the class stood in a lin	his grandma will mak him lunch	they had tim to play one more gam	your bik is the sam as min
ANSWERS	We came to school early today.	**The** class stood in a line.	His grandma will make him lunch.	**They** had time to play one more game.	**Your** bike is the same as mine.

Week 5

	MONDAY	TUESDAY	WEDNESDAY	THURSDAY	FRIDAY
SKILLS	**Grammar:** Action Words: Past Time **Spelling:** soft *c* and *g*	**Mechanics:** Capitalizing Place Names **Spelling:** soft *c* and *g*	**Grammar:** Action Words: Past Time **Spelling:** soft *c* and *g*	**Mechanics:** Capitalizing Place Names **Spelling:** soft *c* and *g*	**Skills Review**
PRACTICE	yesterday we walk to the new fense	is this the road to new york sity	draw in the empty spase on the paig	are the animals kept in cajes in the boston zoo	last year Tom hike through the wide open spases of wyoming
ANSWERS	Yesterday we **walked** to the new fence.	Is this the road to **New York City?**	**Draw** in the empty space on the page.	Are the animals kept in cages in the **Boston Zoo?**	Last year Tom **hiked** through the wide open spaces of **Wyoming.**

Week 6

	MONDAY	TUESDAY	WEDNESDAY	THURSDAY	FRIDAY
SKILLS	**Grammar:** Describing Words **Spelling:** Review	**Mechanics:** Period **Spelling:** Review	**Grammar:** Describing Words **Spelling:** Review	**Mechanics:** Period **Spelling:** Review	**Skills Review**
PRACTICE	the hungry fox wanted to eat the juicy graps	i will vot for Ann for president	on our way hom we saw a pretty green snak	the dog buried the bone under a ston	we had big bowls of hot, spisey chili
ANSWERS	The **hungry** fox wanted to eat the **juicy** grapes.	I will vote for Ann for president**.**	On our way home we saw a **pretty green** snake.	The dog buried the bone under a stone**.**	We had **big** bowls of **hot, spicy** chili.

REVIEW

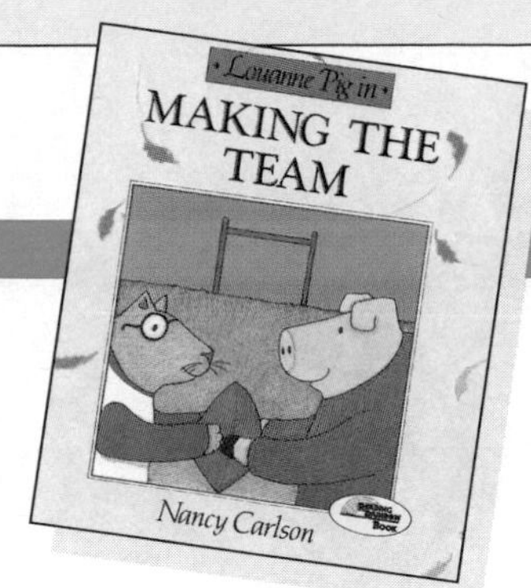

Character

Objective:
Children review the use of words and pictures to identify character traits.

Materials:
SourceBook pp. 76–93
Literacy-at-Work Book p. 43

Time:
About 15 minutes

Suggested Grouping:
Cooperative groups

TESTED	
KEY STRATEGY	
CHARACTER	
Introduce	p. T84
Review	p. R16
Test	p. T311
Reteach	p. R24

1 Review

Remind children that when they read *Ronald Morgan Goes to Bat,* they described Ronald's character. Ask them what clues they used to understand how and why Ronald acted and felt as he did. Did they think about what he said and did? Did they look at the pictures? Talk about how understanding Ronald's character can add to their enjoyment of the story.

2 Practice and Apply

Put It in Context

COOPERATIVE GROUPS Ask children to read page 86 of *Louanne Pig in Making the Team* in the SourceBook. Have cooperative groups create a list of at least two words or phrases that describe each character. Remind them to begin by reading the page and looking at the pictures for clues.

Then suggest they use these clues and what they already know about people to describe Louanne and Arnie. Have children compare their group's results with those of the other groups.

Have children record their descriptive words on character maps. They may complete the maps with descriptions of the characters from other pages.

3 Assess

Were children able to accurately describe the characters in this story?

- ✔ Could they use the words and pictures for clues to character?
- ✔ Could they use prior knowledge to make further inferences or confirm their observations of character?

If not, try this:

See Reteach Lesson on p. R24.

Children's Self-Assessment

- ✔ Did I use word and picture clues to describe the characters?
- ✔ Did I use what I already know about people to help me describe the characters?

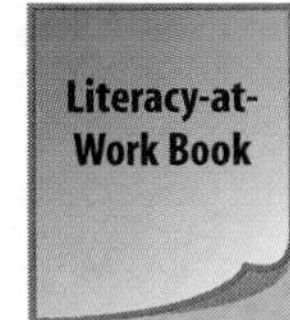

See p. 43 in the Literacy-at-Work Book for more support.

Summarize

Objective:
Children review how to identify and summarize the main points of a story.

Materials:
SourceBook pp. 100–115
Literacy-at-Work Book p. 59

Time:
About 15 minutes

Suggested Grouping:
Whole class, partners

TESTED	
KEY STRATEGY	
SUMMARIZE	
Introduced	p. T32
Review	p. R17
Test	p. T311
Reteach	p. R24

1 Review

Remind children that after they read "Top Ten" they summarized the survey. Ask them to explain what they did in order to summarize. How did they find the main points of "Top Ten"? How did they use those points in their summaries?

2 Practice and Apply

Put It in Context

Have children look at the first page of *George Ancona: Then & Now,* read the title, and talk about the pictures. Then help children summarize that information, retelling in one sentence what the first page is about.

Partners Have children work with partners to use a summary chart to find the main points in the rest of the selection. They may head the chart "Then" and "Now." Encourage children to complete the chart by looking at the pictures and by reading captions and introductory sentences to paragraphs. Then ask each group to retell in two or three sentences what this selection is about.

3 Assess

Were children able to summarize the selection?

- ✔ Did they use titles, pictures, captions, and introductory sentences to find the main points?
- ✔ Did they retell the main points in two or three summary sentences?

If not, try this:

See Reteach Lesson on p. R24.

Children's Self-Assessment

- ✔ Did I use the title and beginning sentences to find the main points?
- ✔ Did I use pictures and captions to find the main points?
- ✔ Was I able to use the main points in retelling the story?

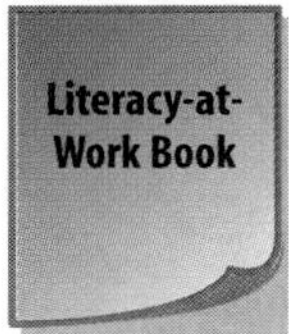

See p. 59 in the Literacy-at-Work Book for more support.

REVIEW

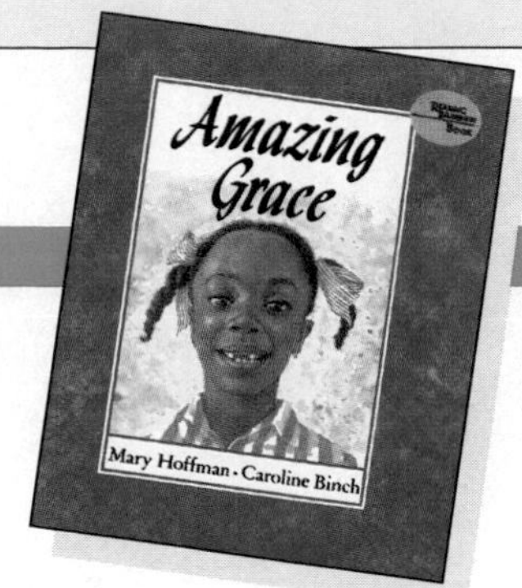

Plot

Objective:
Children will review plot and use that knowledge to retell the plot of a selection.

Materials:
SourceBook pp. 116–135
Literacy-at-Work Book p. 68

Time:
About 15 minutes

Suggested Grouping:
Whole class and cooperative groups

TESTED	
KEY STRATEGY	
PLOT	
Introduce	p. T196
Review	p. R16
Test	p. 311
Reteach	p. R25

1 Review

Discuss with children that the plot of a story includes events from the beginning, middle, and end. Ask them to explain the steps they followed to retell the plot of *Louanne Pig in Making the Team*. How did they decide where each part of the story started and ended? How did they pick out important story events?

2 Practice and Apply

Put It in Context

Working with the whole class, decide which pages of *Amazing Grace* form the beginning, middle, and end. Help the class create a graphic organizer for plot by listing these pages in three columns on the chalkboard. Have children suggest at least one event from each part of the story and list it in the correct column. What did they learn from each section of the story?

COOPERATIVE GROUPS Divide the class into cooperative groups to complete the graphic organizer. Have each group use the organizer to retell the plot of the story, using the important events from the beginning, middle, and end. Remind children to keep the events in order.

3 Assess

Were children able to retell the plot of the story?

- ✔ Could they identify the beginning, middle, and end of the story?
- ✔ Could they pick out important events from each section?
- ✔ Could they retell those events in order?

If not, try this:

See Reteach Lesson on p. R25.

Children's Self-Assessment

- ✔ Did I find the beginning, middle, and end of the story?
- ✔ Did I list the important events in each section?
- ✔ Did I retell those events in order?

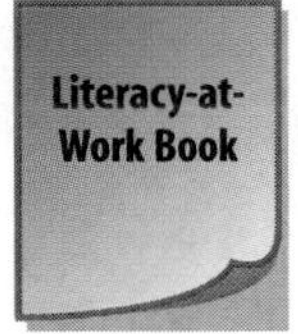

See p. 68 in the Literacy-at-Work Book for more support.

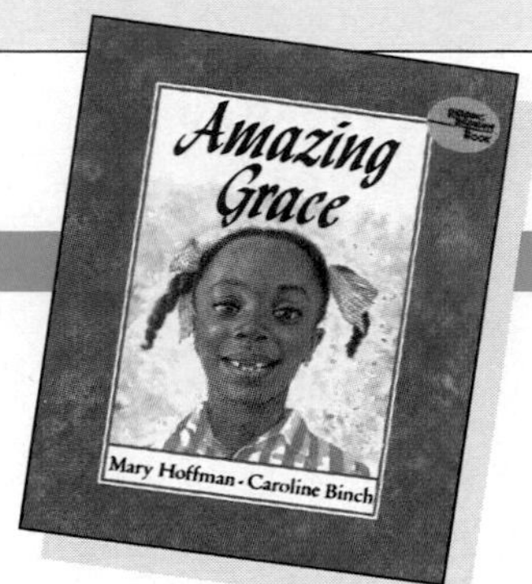

Make Predictions

Objective:
Children review strategies for making predictions.

Materials:
SourceBook pp. 116–135
Literacy-at-Work Book p. 69

Time:
About 15 minutes

Suggested Grouping:
Whole class and partners

TESTED	
KEY STRATEGY	
MAKE PREDICTIONS	
Introduced	p. T148
Review	p. R19
Test	p. T311
Reteach	p. R25

❶ Review

Remind children that when they read *Ruby the Copycat* they made predictions about story events. Ask if they can recall which clues helped them predict what might come next in the story. Did they look at the pictures and think about what had happened? Did they use what they knew from their own lives?

❷ Practice and Apply

Put It in Context

Discuss with children what they learned about Grace from the first part of *Amazing Grace.* Point out that on page 124 of the SourceBook Grace knew at once what character she wanted to be in the play *Peter Pan*. Ask children how they knew which character Grace would choose. What story clues did they use? Did they use what they know about people to make a prediction? Ask children to choose partners to work with to review other predictions they made about Grace, such as whether she would try out for the part of Peter Pan or what she would do when she got home from the ballet. Encourage them to give reasons for their predictions. Suggest they use a graphic organizer such as "What I Know + Clues From the Story = Prediction" to do this.

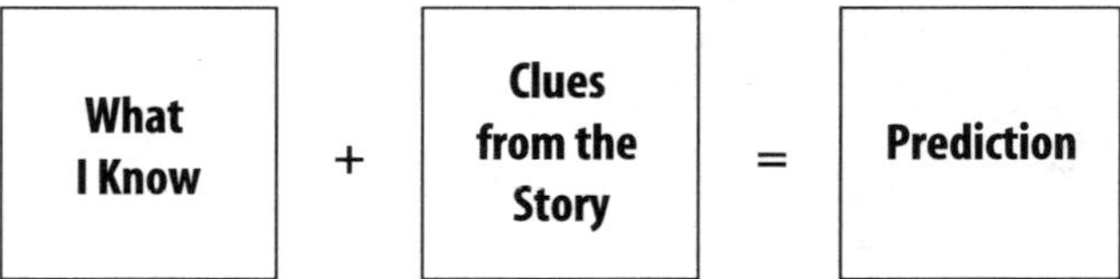

❸ Assess

Were children able to make reasonable predictions?

✔ Did they use clues from the words and pictures to make a logical guess?

✔ Did they refer to their own knowledge and experience in making predictions?

If not, try this:

See Reteach Lesson on p. R25.

Children's Self-Assessment

✔ Did I use story words and pictures to make my predictions?

✔ Did my predictions come true in the story?

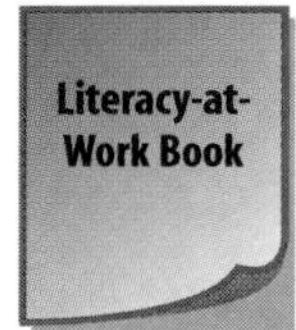

See p. 69 in the Literacy-at-Work Book for more support.

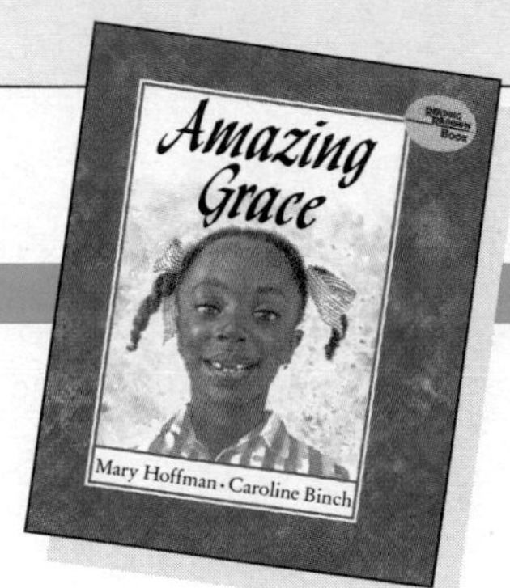

Context Clues

Objective:
Children review context clues to understand specialized vocabulary.

Materials:
SourceBook pp. 116–135
Literacy-at-Work Book p. 70

Time:
About 15 minutes

Suggested Grouping:
Cooperative groups

TESTED	
CONTEXT CLUES	
SPECIALIZED VOCABULARY	
Introduce	p. T248
Review	p. R20
Test	p. T311
Reteach	p. R26

1 Review

Ask children if they remember how they figured out the meaning of the word *aviator* in *George Ancona: Then & Now*. Have children recall that, as a child, George wore an aviator's helmet and pretended to fly an airplane. Ask what clues in the sentence helped them figure out the meaning. What word means the same thing as *aviator*?

2 Practice and Apply

Put It in Context

Have children turn to page 129 of *Amazing Grace* in the SourceBook and read the first sentence in the third paragraph. Point out that *tutu* is a special word used in ballet. Ask children to use the information from the paragraph and the picture on this page to figure out the meaning of *tutu*. Then have them substitute another word for *tutu* in the sentence to check their understanding.

Have children work in cooperative groups to list other unfamiliar words in the story and use context clues to figure out the meanings. Create a graphic organizer to record the words children list and the clues they use.

3 Assess

Were children able to use context clues to understand the meaning of specialized words?

- ✔ Did they use both words and picture clues?
- ✔ Did they replace the word in the sentence with other words to check their understanding?

If not, try this:

See Reteach Lesson on p. R26.

Children's Self-Assessment

- ✔ Did I use context clues to understand new words?
- ✔ Did I use both picture and word clues to help me understand words I didn't know?
- ✔ Did I use other words in the sentence to check my understanding of an unfamiliar word?

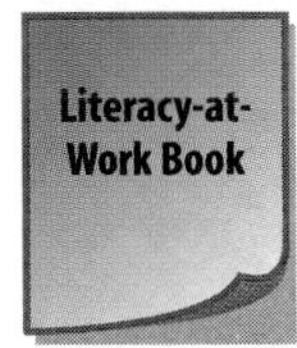

See p. 70 in the Literacy-at-Work Book for more support.

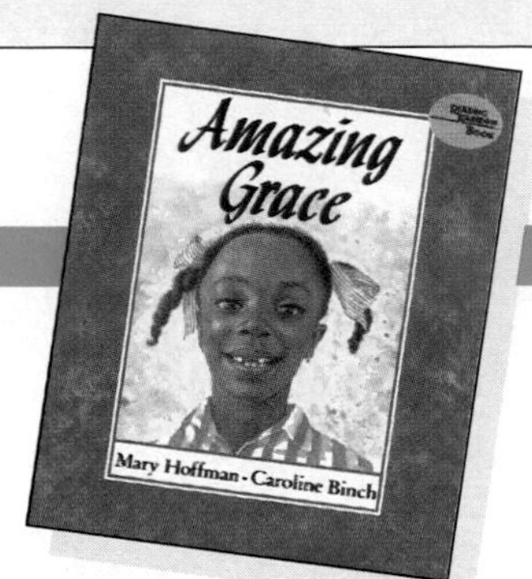

Phonics: Soft /s/*c*, /j/*g*

Objective:
Children will review their understanding of /s/*c* and /j/*g*.

Materials:
Chalkboard, chalk, paper, pencils
Literacy-at-Work Book p. 71

Time:
About 10 minutes

Suggested Grouping:
Whole class

1 Review

Say this sentence—"Cindy drew a giraffe"—and have children repeat it. Ask children which word in the sentence starts with /s/*c*. Then ask them which word starts with /j/*g*. Write the sentence on the chalkboard and ask a child to underline the word that starts with /s/. Then ask another child to circle the word that starts with /j/. Ask children to listen to the sounds of these letters as you blend them in the words. Follow the same procedure with the following sentences:

The giant drank cider.

The gerbil ate the celery.

2 Practice and Apply

Put It in Context

Write *city* and *genie* on the chalkboard and underline the letters *c* and *g*. Ask children to say these words and listen to the sounds made by *c* and *g*.

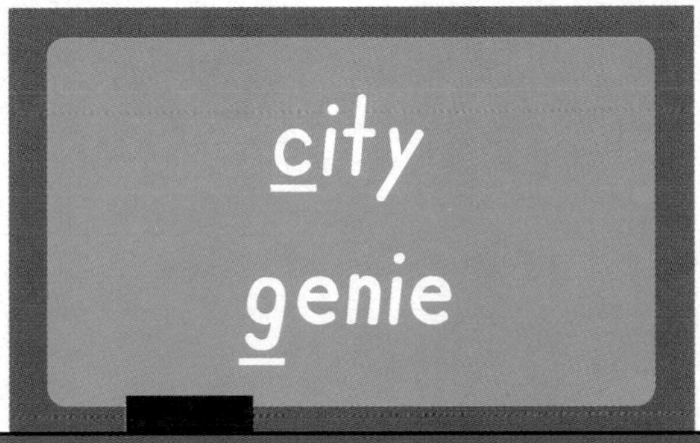

Help children fold a piece of paper in half and write *city* as a heading for one half and *genie* as a heading for the other half. Then ask children to think of other words they know that begin with the soft *c* and *g* sounds. Have them write these words under the heading with the same beginning sound. Suggest these words if more examples are needed: *giant, cell, ceiling, gerbil, cent, gym, gentle.*

3 Assess

- ✔ *Can children recognize the soft c and soft g sounds?*
- ✔ *Can children write words that begin with /s/c and /j/g?*

If not, try this:
See Reteach Lesson on p. R26.

Children's Self-Assessment

- ✔ What sound do I hear at the beginning of *city*?
- ✔ What sound do I hear at the beginning of *gerbil*?
- ✔ What letter stands for the sound in each word?

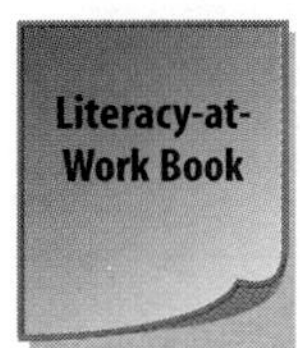

See p. 71 in the Literacy-at-Work Book for more support.

Study Skill: Lists

Objective:
Children review how they can use lists to acquire information.

Materials:
Project card
Literacy-at-Work Book p. 74

Time:
About 15 minutes

Suggested Grouping:
Whole class

TESTED	
STUDY SKILLS	
LISTS	
Introduce	p. T96
Review	p. R22
Test	p. T311
Reteach	p. R27

❶ Review

Ask children to give some examples of lists they have made or read in books or magazines. Have them explain why lists are useful. What kinds of information do you get from lists?

❷ Practice and Apply

Put It in Context

Remind children that they used the Exhibit Checklist before they arranged exhibits about themselves. Discuss how the checklist was helpful. What kind of information was on the checklist? Explain that a checklist is only one kind of list. Explore other lists children may have made as they planned their exhibits.

Together make a list of other exhibits children might like to create. Then have them organize the list. It could be arranged from the least popular to the most popular exhibit ideas. Or, it could be organized by topic. You might use the list to plan future projects. Children can create their own checklists for putting together an exhibit.

❸ Assess

Were children able to use lists?

- ✔ Did they understand why lists are useful?
- ✔ Were they able to get information from lists?
- ✔ Were they able to make their own lists?

If not, try this:

Take the opportunity to discuss lists as children choose the top three places they'd like to visit for a social studies project. See Reteach Lesson on page R27.

Children's Self-Assessment

- ✔ Do I understand why lists may be helpful?
- ✔ Was I able to make my own list?
- ✔ Can I get information from a list?

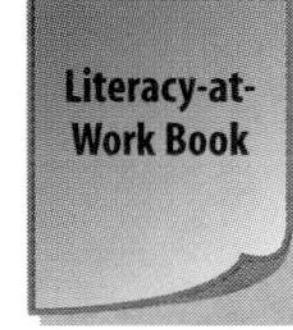

See p. 74 in the Literacy-at-Work Book for more support.

Study Skill: Graphs

Objective:
Children review how to acquire information from graphs.

Materials:
Project card
Literacy-at-Work Book p. 75

Time:
About 20 minutes

Suggested Grouping:
Whole class

TESTED	
STUDY SKILLS	
GRAPHS	
Introduce	p. T205
Review	p. R23
Test	p. T311
Reteach	p. R27

1 Review

Have children recall the different graphs they have read or made. Remind them of the pictograph shown on side 1 of the Workshop Card. In what other books have they seen graphs? Discuss what graphs look like and why they might make one. What kind of information did the graphs show? How was the information on the graph organized?

2 Practice and Apply

Put It in Context

Ask children if any of them used graphs in the exhibits about themselves. If not, how could they show something about themselves on a graph? Have them describe what the graph might look like.

Help children transfer information from their personal exhibits to a class graph. Each child may choose a favorite activity from his or her exhibit. List the activities and tally the results. Then have the class create a pictograph showing what children like to do.

3 Assess

Were children able to acquire information from graphs?

- ✔ Could they give examples of graphs?
- ✔ Did they know what kind of information graphs show?
- ✔ Were they able to create a graph about the class?

If not, try this:

Continue to talk about graphs as you conduct a class survey and graph the results for a math project. See the Reteach Lesson on page R27.

Children's Self-Assessment

- ✔ Was I able to describe some graphs?
- ✔ Can I read graphs to get information?
- ✔ Can I make a graph to show something about myself?

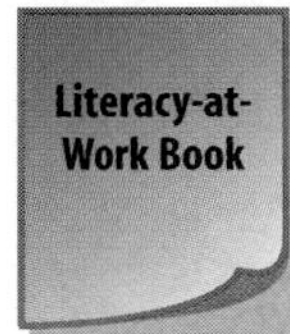

See p. 75 in the Literacy-at-Work Book for more support.

RETEACH

CHARACTER

❶ Construct

Your cousin Tim is your age but lives far away. Tomorrow you'll meet him for the first time. You're excited. "Tim plays baseball," Mom tells you. "He has lots of friends on his team." When Tim arrives, he jumps out of the car, holding a glove in his hand. He has a big grin on his face. Do you think you'll get along?

❷ Connect

If you listen to what Mom said and saw how Tim acted, you probably thought he's a friendly boy who likes sports. That describes his character. You also get to know characters in stories. Listen to what other characters say about them and watch what they say and do.

As you read with children, pick out characters from the trade books and describe their traits. These additional resources can enrich children's understanding of character.

❸ Confirm

How would you explain ways to figure out what a story character is like? If you were going to write a story about a friend, what would your friend say and do? How would someone else describe your story character?

SUMMARIZE

❶ Construct

You were very busy at school yesterday. You did a lot of work in class and then played with friends. When you got home, your grandma asked, "What did you do today?" You told her only the most important events. How did you choose what to talk about?

❷ Connect

By talking about only the most important events, you summarized your day. You can summarize stories or parts of stories in the same way.

Read aloud a selection from a trade book or show a video, and together with children summarize the story. You can use these additional resources to check children's understanding of summarizing.

❸ Confirm

What is summarizing? How would you explain it to someone you know? Summarize a movie or video you just saw for a friend.

PLOT

❶ Construct

You watch the beginning of a video at your friend's house, but it's dinnertime. You have to go home. You eat quickly and go back. Then you watch the end of the video with your friend. You don't quite understand the story, though. Why not? What would you ask your friend to tell you?

❷ Connect

You saw the beginning and end of the video. If you ask your friend what happened in the middle, you'd know the whole plot. When you read, you can understand the plot of a story if you know the beginning, middle, and end.

This would be a good time to read with children and discuss story plot together. The trade books make excellent resources for practicing this skill.

❸ Confirm

How would you explain plot? What should you be sure to include when you tell a friend the plot of a movie you just saw?

MAKE PREDICTIONS

❶ Construct

Your neighbor walks his dog every morning. You see him leave while you eat breakfast. He gets back when you leave for school. Every morning, he waves at you and smiles. This morning at breakfast, you saw him walk out with his dog. You are about to leave for school. What do you think will happen next?

❷ Connect

When you guessed you'll see your neighbor, and he'll wave and smile, you made a prediction. By using clues from a story and what you already know, you can make predictions about what will happen next when you read.

When you read the trade books or library materials to the class, stop occasionally and allow children to make predictions. Observe whether they use story clues and their own experiences to make predictions.

❸ Confirm

How would you explain making a prediction? Look out the window. What prediction can you make about tomorrow's weather?

RETEACH

CONTEXT CLUES

❶ Construct

Your dad tries to start the car and nothing happens. He opens the hood and looks in. "I think the battery is dead," he explains. If you don't know what a battery is, what clues help you figure out the meaning of the word?

❷ Connect

When you think about what your dad said, you use context to figure out that the car won't start unless the battery is working. You can use context to figure out a word you don't know when you read, too. Look for clues in the words and sentences around it.

When you come across words children don't know as you read together, guide them to use context clues.

❸ Confirm

How can you figure out a new word when you read? Where might you look for clues to figure out new words?

PHONICS: SOFT /S/C, /J/G

❶ Construct

Show children the word *giant* and say the word, emphasizing the soft *g* sound. Then ask children to stand up and take a giant step every time they hear a soft *g* sound like the beginning of *giant*. You can use words like these: *giraffe, girl, gym, genie, gentle, glad, goat, gerbil.*

Repeat this activity for the soft *c* sound using the words *city, cent, crayon, cell, calendar, celery, carrot.*

❷ Connect

As you read this poem, ask children to draw a *c* or a *g* in the air when they hear a word that begins with the soft *g* or soft *c*.

**I saw a gentle giant eating cereal and drinking
citrus cider.
He kept a pet giraffe named Cindy
In a gym where he would find her.**

❸ Confirm

Ask a volunteer to draw a giant on the chalkboard and then draw a speech balloon coming from the giant's mouth. Invite children to write words in the balloon that begin with soft *g*. Repeat for words that begin with soft *c*.

STUDY SKILL: LISTS

❶ Construct

It's Saturday morning, and your family has a lot of shopping to do. You need new shoes and some crayons for school. Your mom needs stamps to mail a letter. "I hope we don't forget anything." Mom says. How could you help her remember everything?

❷ Connect

To help Mom remember everything, you could make a list. You could organize your list by writing down the stores you need to go to. Then under each store write the items you need to buy. Making lists as you read can help you remember important ideas or story events.

This would be a good time to use lists as you read with children. They might make a list of unfamiliar words, or story characters and their traits. Use either trade books or other books for making lists.

❸ Confirm

What does a list look like? How might it be helpful? Make a list of things you want to do on Saturday.

STUDY SKILL: GRAPHS

❶ Construct

Look through some books, magazines, and newspapers in your classroom library. See how many graphs you can find. Which ones are pictographs? How can you tell? What information do they give?

❷ Connect

You may have found pictographs in social studies and science books, or in newspapers and magazines. You knew they were pictographs because they used pictures to give information. Other graphs may have used bars, lines, or pie shapes. Look for pictographs as you read. They present information in an easy, clear way.

When you read with students, work with them on understanding graphs. Trade books, newspapers, magazines, and textbooks may all present opportunities to gather information from graphs.

❸ Confirm

Explain what a graph shows. Why do some graphs use pictures? What kinds of pictures might you use on a graph that shows how you spend your allowance?

RETEACH

QUESTION SENTENCES

Reteach

Sentences that ask are asking sentences, or questions. Asking sentences begin with capital letters and end with question marks.

PRACTICE

Circle each question.

1. **Have you been on an airplane?**
2. **Did you meet the pilot?**
3. **You must wear your safety belt.**
4. **Do you think that's a good idea?**
5. **It's time to land.**

COMMAS

Reteach

Use a comma between the name of a city and a state or country in an address.

PRACTICE

Add commas where they belong.

1. **Rosa moved from Taos New Mexico to Los Angeles California.**
2. **Lee visited his uncle in Tokyo Japan.**
3. **We are going to spend our vacation in Chicago Illinois.**
4. **Last year we had a great vacation in Orlando Florida.**
5. **I am going to move from Trenton New Jersey to Phoenix Arizona.**

NAMING PLACES

Reteach

Some nouns name special places. These special nouns begin with capital letters.

PRACTICE

Write each special noun correctly.

1. **george washington park** ________
2. **museum of natural history** ________
3. **elm street** ________
4. **harriet tubman school** ________
5. **university of vermont** ________

ACTION WORDS

Reteach

Most sentences have an action part. One word in the action part names the action. That word is the verb.

PRACTICE

Underline the action verb in each sentence.

1. **I live on a farm.**
2. **All day long the cows eat grass.**
3. **The hens lay big eggs every morning.**
4. **My brother and I collect the eggs.**
5. **We also feed the hogs.**

ACTION WORDS: PAST TIME

Reteach

Some verbs name actions that happened before now, or in the past.

PRACTICE

Add *-ed* to each verb to show what happened in the past. Write the verb.

1. **We (talk) ________ to Grandma on the phone.**
2. **She (want) ________ to come see us yesterday.**
3. **But Muff, her cat, (climb) ________ a tree.**
4. **Grandma (call) ________ the fire department.**
5. **A fire fighter (help) ________ get Muff down.**

DESCRIBING WORDS

Reteach

Adjectives can tell size, shape, color, and how many. They also tell how something tastes or smells, or how something sounds or feels.

PRACTICE

Circle the adjectives in each sentence.

1. **We saw four insects in our backyard.**
2. **A red and black ladybird rested on a leaf.**
3. **A buzzing bee took nectar from a flower.**
4. **A caterpillar crawled up the rough bark of a tree.**
5. **We almost stepped on a tiny ant!**

TEACHER RESOURCES: BIBLIOGRAPHY

Books for Independent Reading

EASY

The Beast in Ms. Rooney's Room
by Patricia Reilly Giff
Dell, 1992 ★ 🌐
A sympathetic teacher gives Richard "The Beast" Best the confidence to enter a reading contest.

The Day Jimmy's Boa Ate the Wash
by Trinka Hakes Noble
illustrated by Steven Kellogg
Scholastic, 1994 🦋 ★
An ordinary class trip becomes a hilarious adventure.

Faces
by Barbara Brenner
illustrated by George Ancona
Dutton, 1970 🦋 🌐
These photos show how beautiful and expressive all kinds of faces can be.

Handtalk Zoo
by George Ancona and Mary Beth Miller
Four Winds, 1989 🎭 🌐 ✹
In this lively photo essay, a group of children use signing and finger-spelling enthusiastically to communicate at the zoo.

Hue Boy
by Rita P. Mitchell
illustrated by Caroline Binch
Dial, 1993 ✹ 🌐 🖩
This contemporary Caribbean story shows how Hue Boy deals with the well-meaning advice of his neighbors.

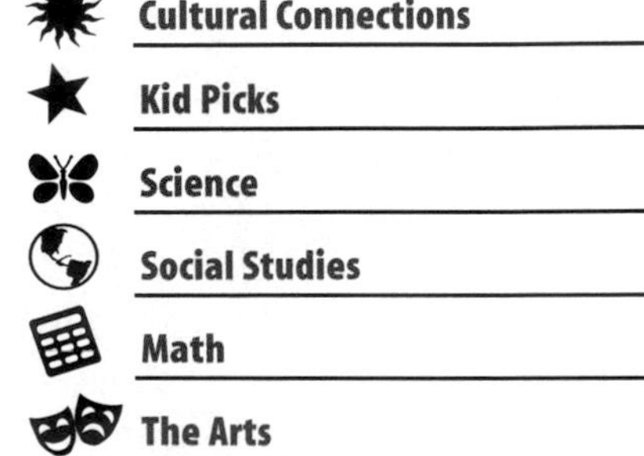

It's About Time
by Lee Bennett Hopkins
Simon & Schuster, 1993 🎭 🖩
Children will easily identify with these poems that talk about common daily activities.

The Princess and the Pea
by Janet Stevens
Scholastic, 1990 ✹ 🎭
In this classic tale, a young woman proves that she is a princess in an unusual way.

This Is the Way We Go to School
by Edith Baer
Scholastic, 1992 ★ 🌐
Lively rhymes and pictures tell about children all over the world.

AVERAGE

Arnie and the New Kid
by Nancy Carlson
Viking, 1990 ✹ ★ 🌐
When he breaks his leg, Arnie gains understanding for Philip, a boy in a wheelchair.

Arthur's Teacher Trouble
by Marc Brown
Joy Street, 1989 ★ 🌐
Arthur participates in the school Spellathon with funny results.

Boundless Grace
by Mary Hoffman
illustrated by Caroline Binch
Dial, 1995 ✹ 🌐
This sequel to *Amazing Grace* tells more about this spirited girl.

Helping Out
by George Ancona
Scholastic, 1993 🌐 ✹
This photo collection depicts people of all ages working together in various settings.

Roxaboxen
by Alice McLerran
illustrated by Barbara Cooney
Scholastic, 1993 🌐 ✹
Enter the fantasy town created from rocks and boxes by children.

Watch Out, Ronald Morgan!
by Patricia Reilly Giff
Viking, 1985 ★ 🦋
Ronald sees the world from a brand new perspective after a teacher advises him to get glasses.

What Kind of Baby-Sitter Is This?
by Delores Johnson
Scholastic, 1993 ✹ 🌐
An African-American boy feels better about his new sitter when he learns she loves baseball.

CHALLENGING

A Boy Called Slow
by Joseph Bruchac
Putnam, 1995 ✹ 🌐
This biography tells of a Dakota boy who grew up to lead his people.

Going to My Gymnastics Class
by Susan Kuklin
Bradbury, 1991 ✹ 🌐
In this photo essay, Gasp tells about his experiences taking gymnastics lessons.

Gregory Cool
by Caroline Binch
Dial, 1994 🌐 ✹
Urbanite Gregory visits his island relatives in Tobago and finds some surprises.

Sara Kate, Superkid
by Susan Beth Pfeiffer
Holt, 1994 ★ 🦋
Sara Kate had always been an ordinary kid—but now she seems to have superpowers that make her a basketball star.

Soccer Sam
by Jean Marzollo
Random House, 1989 ✹ 🌐
A visiting cousin from Mexico starts to feel at home when he joins in a soccer game.

Song Lee in Room 2B
by Suzy Kline
Scholastic, 1995 ★ ✹ 🦋
Song Lee and her classmate Horrible Harry find that second grade continues to be full of funny events.

BOOKS FOR WORD STUDY

Aunt Lilly's Laundromat
by Melanie Hope Greenberg
Dutton, 1994
(*l*-blends: *cl* and *bl*)

City Storm
by Mary Jessica Parker
Scholastic, 1991
(soft *c*)

Ginger Jumps
by Lisa Campbell Ernst
Bradbury, 1990
(soft *j* and soft *g*)

Hot Hippo
by Mwenye Hadithi
Little Brown, 1986
(short *o* and consonant digraphs *sh*, *th*, and *wh*)

One of Three
by Angela Johnson
Scholastic, 1993
(three-letter blend *thr*)

The Princess and the Beggar
by Anne Sibley O'Brien
Scholastic, 1993
(*r*-blends: *gr*, *pr*, and *tr*)

Shy Charles
by Rosemary Wells
Dial, 1988
(consonant digraphs *ch* and *sh*)

Slither, Swoop, Swing
by Alex Ayliffe
Viking, 1993
(*s*-blends)

Books in Other Languages

Spanish

Una canasta para Tía
by Pat Mora
Scholastic, 1994
A little girl prepares a birthday gift for her aunt with great imagination.

Crisantemo
by Kevin Henkes
Everest, 1993 ★
Crisantemo loves her name, but in school her classmates make fun of it. Then something happens that makes her feel proud again.

El cuento de Ferdinando
by Munro Leaf
Lectorum VK, 1988 ★
Ferdinando is a gentle bull who would rather sit and smell the flowers than fight in a bullring.

Jorge Ancona, antes y ahora
by Jorge Ancona
Scholastic, 1995 ★
The famous Mexican-American photographer tells his life story through pictures.

Ruby, mono ve, mono hace
by Peggy Rathmann
Colección Mariposa
Scholastic, 1995 ★
A girl copies her classmates until she finds out that she is also special.

Sapo y Sepo son amigos
by Arnold Lobel
Colección Infantil Alfaguara
Alfaguara/Santillana, 1992 ★
These two well-known animals have a great time being friends.

Turquesita
by Silvia Dobovoy and Raúl Villagómez
Colección Barril Sin Fondo
C.E.L.T.A., 1991
Little fish Turquesita has to go to the mill to grind some seaweed and plankton. But to do that she has to cross a very difficult spot and listen to some advice. What should she do?

Chinese

All in a Day
by Mitsumasa Anno
Shen's, 1970
Brief Chinese text and beautiful art by ten famous illustrators who depict the lives of children from eight different countries.

Frog and Toad Are Friends
by Arnold Lobel
Shen's
A Chinese translation of five short tales about these two friends.

For Reading Aloud

Honey, I Love
by Eloise Greenfield
illustrated by Leo & Diane Dillon
Harper, 1986
This collection of poems centers around the experiences of an imaginative African-American girl.

Pie-Biter
by Ruthanne L. McCunn
illustrated by You-Shah Tang
Design Enterprises of San Francisco, 1993
This legend, in the tradition of John Henry and Paul Bunyan, tells of a boy who comes from China to America to help build the railroad. He is soon known by everyone for his strength, his skill, and his love for eating pie.

Simple Pictures Are Best
by Nancy Willard
illustrated by Tomie dePaola
Scholastic, 1995 ★
A shoemaker and his wife want everything but the kitchen sink in their anniversary picture.

Teacher's Bookshelf

I Never Have It Made
by Jackie Robinson
Ecco Press, 1995
The autobiography of the African American who became one of the country's greatest baseball heroes.

In These Girls Hope is a Muscle
by Madeleine Blais
Grove Press, 1994
This book documents one year in the lives of female high school athletes.

Rain of Gold
by Victor Villasenor
Dell, 1991
This epic novel weaves the parallel stories of two families, one in Mexico and one in the United States.

Songs of My People: African Americans: A Self Portrait
by Eric Easter, D. Michael Cheers and Dudley M. Brooks
Little Brown, 1992
Fifty African American photo journalists contributed to this stunning photo essay on the African American experience.

Technology

Audio

Playing Right Field
Scholastic ★
This wonderful song captures what it feels like to play ball when you're not the starting player.

Shake Sugaree
Music for Little People
Taj Mahal introduces children to music of different cultures and to the roots of today's favorite music.

Software

Arthur's Teacher Trouble
Broderbund ★ (IBM, MAC, CD-ROM) Marc Brown's funny story in interactive form.

The New Kid on the Block
Broderbund ★ (IBM, MAC, CD-ROM)
This interactive poetry collection by Jack Prelutsky includes animation and other features.

Video

Amazing Grace
Weston Woods
Lovely music accompanies the video version of this special story.

The Day Jimmy's Boa Ate the Wash
Weston Woods ★
This class trip is full of surprises.

Louanne Pig in the Talent Show
Live Oaks Media
This is the video version of *Louanne Pig in Making the Team.*

Peachboy
Rabbits Ears
This favorite tale from Japan is much like the English tale of Tom Thumb.

Today Was a Terrible Day
Live Oaks Media ★
Ronald Morgan must cope with a day in which everything seems to go wrong.

baseball

basketball

soccer

computer

crafts

activities

clutched

helmet

practice

sneaker

announced

tiptoed

modeled

murmured

recited

whispered

scribbled

tryouts

squad

confidence

improve

victory

artist

hobby

camera

imagination

photographer

auditions

ballet

stunning

imaginary

amazing

theater

Name

READ ALL ABOUT IT

Story Title ______________________________

Why I like this book: ______________________________

____

____

____

____

This picture shows what I like best about the book.

Name

TEACHER RESOURCES

Make Predictions

Story Title ____________________

INFORMATION FROM THE SELECTION

WHAT I ALREADY KNOW

PREDICTION

WHAT ACTUALLY HAPPENS IN THE SELECTION

Name

STORY STEPS

Story Title ______________________________

Tell the last thing that happened.

Tell what the main character did.

Tell something that happened.

Tell something about the main character.

Tell what the story is about.

Name

Character Web

Story Title ____________________

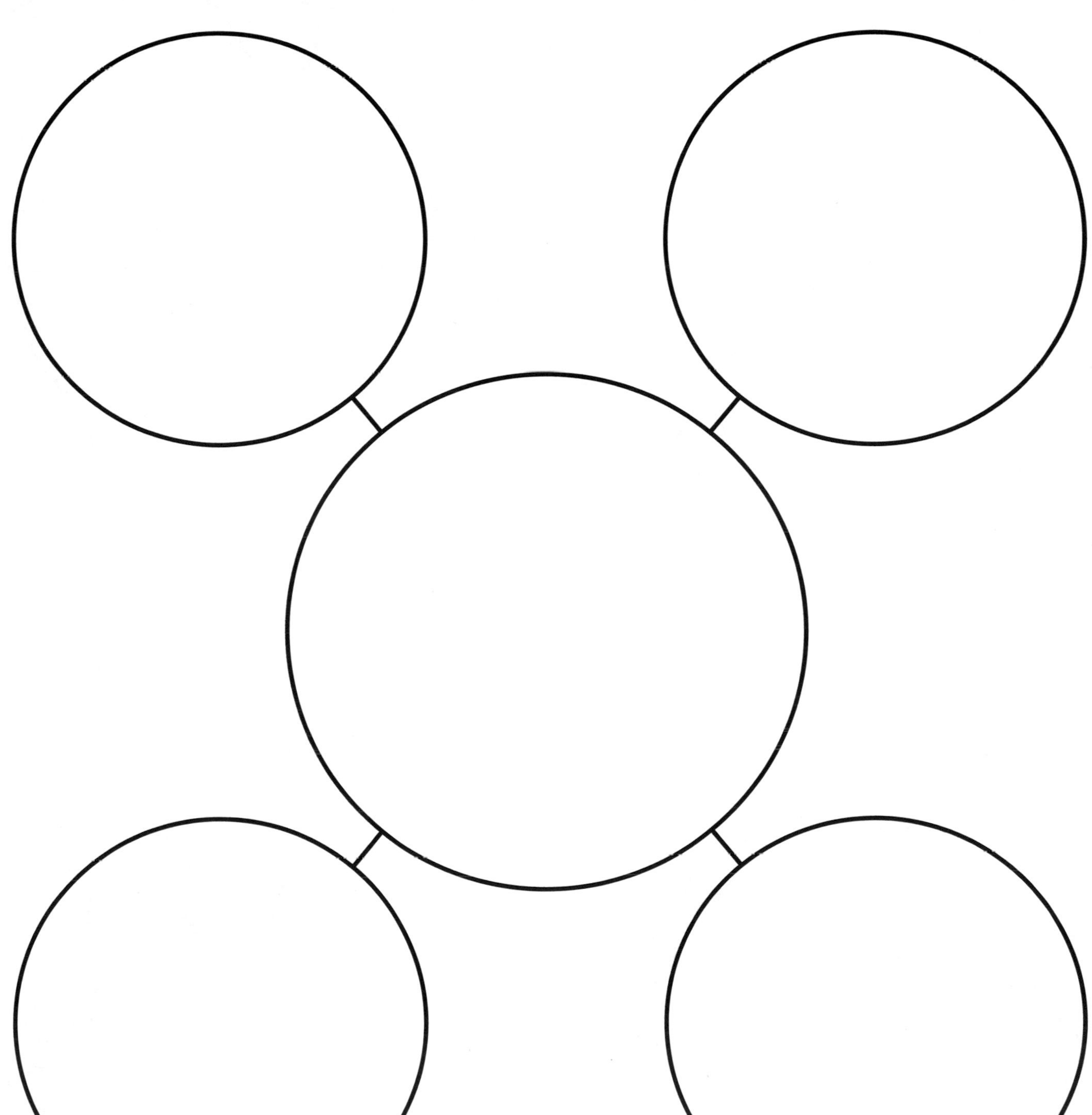

TEACHER RESOURCES

Name

MAX FOUND TWO STICKS

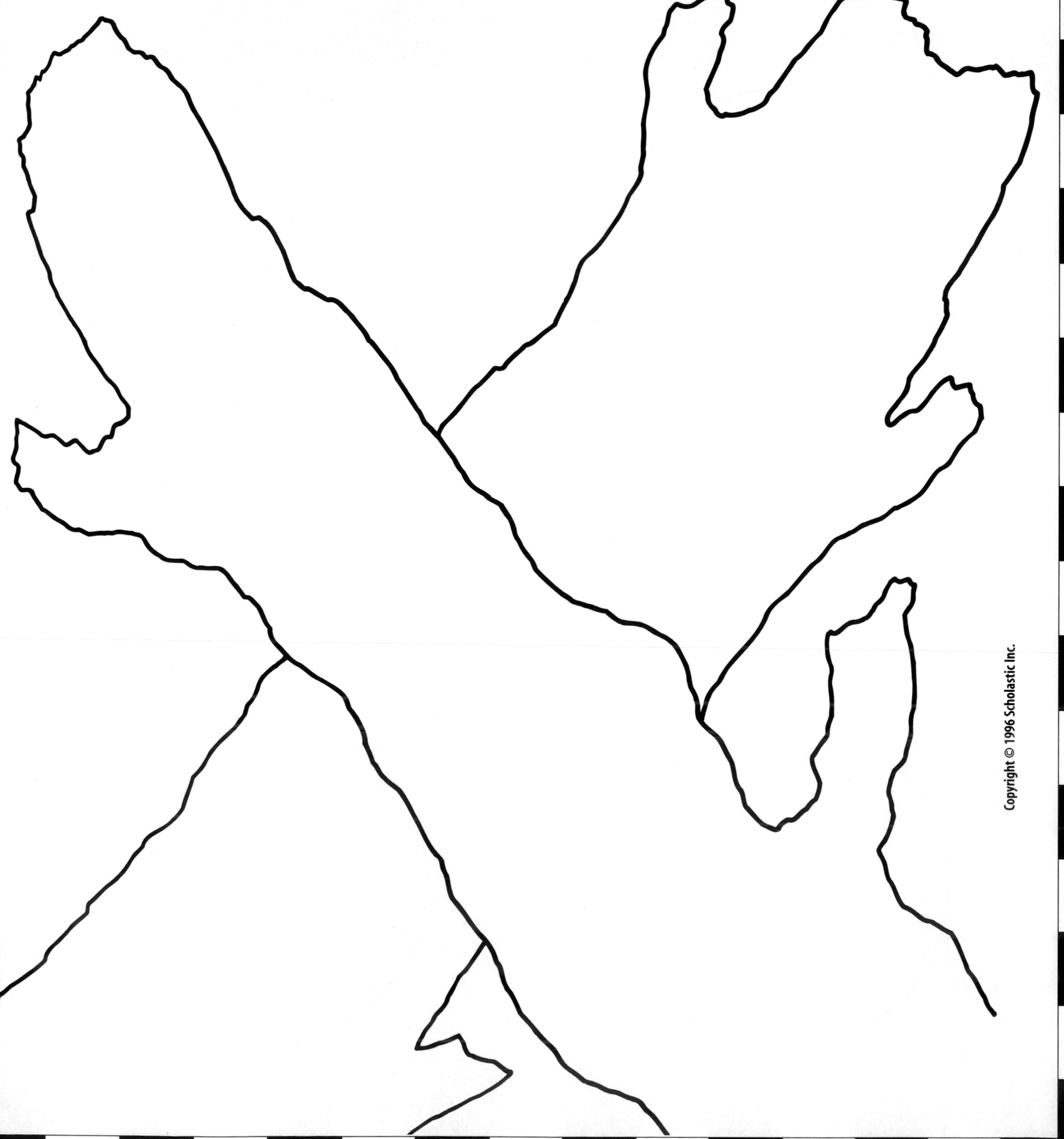

INDEX

INDEX

Oral Reading

Reading Across Texts

Vocabulary Development

WRITING AND LANGUAGE ARTS SKILLS AND STRATEGIES

Conventions of Language

Instruction in Writing

Integrated Language Arts Activity File

INDEX

Listening

INDEX

Research and Study Skills

Viewing

Writing Process

INTEGRATED CURRICULUM ACTIVITIES

The Arts

Math

Science

Social Studies

INDEX

Instructional Issues

ASSESSMENT

References to Assessment Handbook

Teacher Self-Assessment

Tested Skills

Reading Skills and Strategies

Language Arts Skills and Strategies

Tests

Spelling Tests

Vocabulary Tests

Unit Tests

Cultural Connections

INDEX

GROUPING STRATEGIES

Cooperative Groups

Flexible Grouping

Individuals

Interest Groups

Partners

Whole Class

Real-Life Connections

Journal

Mentors

Places

Projects

Strand Connections

Workshops

Supporting All Learners

Access

Challenge

ESL

INDEX

Extra Help

TECHNOLOGY

Listening Center Audiocassettes

Scholastic Network

Wiggleworks Plus

Other Technology

Videos

Literature

Genre

Drama

Fiction

Myths, Legends, Fables, and Tales

Nonfiction

INDEX

Poetry

SOURCES AND TEXT TYPES

TITLES, AUTHORS, AND ILLUSTRATORS

INDEX

CREDITS AND ACKNOWLEDGMENTS

ACKNOWLEDGMENTS

Grateful acknowledgment is made to the following sources for permission to reprint from previously published material. The publisher has made diligent efforts to trace the ownership of all copyrighted material in this volume and believes that all necessary permissions have been secured. If any errors or omissions have inadvertently been made, proper corrections will gladly be made in future editions.

Cover: all photos © David S. Waitz for Scholastic Inc.

Interior: Cover from STELLALUNA by Janell Cannon. Illustration copyright © 1993 by Janell Cannon. Published by Harcourt Brace Publishers. Cover from THUNDER CAKE by Patricia Polacco. Illustration copyright © 1990 by Patricia Polacco. Published by Philomel Books, a division of The Putnam & Grosset Group.

PHOTOGRAPHY AND ILLUSTRATION CREDITS

Photos: Photo Coordination & Styling by Parker/Boon Productions

Cover: © David S. Waitz for Scholastic Inc. p. ii bc: © Scott Campbell for Scholastic Inc. p. iii: © Grant Huntington for Scholastic Inc. p. vi bl, bc: © Stanley Bach for Scholastic Inc.; tr: © Gerry Lewin for Scholastic Inc. p. vii br: © Stanley Bach for Scholastic Inc. p. T5 c: © Stanley Bach for Scholastic Inc. p. T6 br: © Scott Campbell for Scholastic Inc. p. T6 tr: © Ana Esperanza Nance for Scholastic Inc. p. T7 tr: © Gerry Lewin for Scholastic Inc. p. T8 tr: © Gerry Lewin for Scholastic Inc. p. T10 mr: © Gerry Lewin for Scholastic Inc. p. T11 bl: © Gerry Lewin for Scholastic Inc. p. T12 bc: © Scott Campbell for Scholastic Inc. p. T14 tr: © Grant Huntington for Scholastic Inc. p. T15: © Donna F. Aceto for Scholastic Inc. p. T25 mr: © Ana Esperanza Nance for Scholastic Inc.; br: © Larry S. Voight/Photo Researchers, Inc. p. T30 bl: © Scott Campbell for Scholastic Inc. p. T31 bc: © Scott Campbell for Scholatic Inc. p. T34 bl: © Scott Campbell for Scholastic Inc. p. T38 bl: © Scott Campbell for Scholastic Inc. p. T42 tr: © Grant Huntington for Scholastic Inc. pp. T44-T45 bc: © Grant Huntington for Scholastic Inc. p. T48 tr: © Grant Huntington for Scholastic Inc. p. T49 tl: © Tornberg Associates. p. T77 tr: © Focus on Sports; br: © Al Tielemans/Duomo Photography, Inc. p. T82 bl: © Scott Campbell for Scholastic Inc. p. T83 br: © Ana Esperanza Nance for Scholastic Inc. p. T86 bl: © Grant Huntington for Scholastic Inc. p. T88 bc: © Grant Huntington for Scholastic Inc. p. T90 bl: © Grant Huntington for Scholastic Inc. p. T96 bc: © Scott Campbell for Scholastic Inc. p. T99 c: © Stanley Bach for Scholastic Inc. p. T100 tr: © Scott Campbell for Scholastic Inc.; br: © Grant Huntington for Scholastic Inc. p. T102 tr: © John Fortunato for Scholastic Inc. pp. T104-T105 bc: © John Fortunato for Scholastic Inc. p. T106 bc: © Scott Campbell for Scholastic Inc. p. T108 tr: © Scott Campbell for Scholastic Inc. p. T109 tl: Courtesy of Scholastic Trade Department. p. T141 tr: © Ana Esperanza Nance for Scholastic Inc.; br: © The Estate of Ed Lettau/Peter Arnold, Inc. p. T146 bl: © Scott Campbell for Scholastic Inc.; c, bc: © Grant Huntington for Scholastic Inc. p. T147 br: © Grant Huntington for Scholastic Inc. p. T150 bc: © Grant Huntington for Scholastic Inc. p. T152 bc: © Grant Huntington for Scholastic Inc. p. T158 tr: © Grant Huntington for Scholastic Inc. pp. T160-T161 bc: © Ken Karp for Scholastic Inc. p. T162 bc: © Scott Campbell for Scholastic Inc. p. T164 tr: © Scott Campbell for Scholastic Inc. p. T165 tl: © Mark LaFavor. p. T189 br: © K. Gibson/SuperStock, Inc. p. T194 bl: © Scott Campbell for Scholastic Inc. p. T202 bl: © Grant Huntington for Scholastic Inc. p. T205 br: © Grant Huntington for Scholastic Inc. p. T208 bl: © Scott Campbell for Scholastic Inc. p. T211 c: © Jade Albert/FPG International Corp. p. T212 br: © Gerry Lewin for Scholastic Inc. p. T212 tr: © Ana Esperanza Nance for Scholastic Inc. p. T214 tr: © Stanley Bach for Scholastic Inc. pp. T216-T217 c: © Grant Huntington for Scholastic Inc. p. T218 bc: © Stanley Bach for Scholastic Inc. p. T220 tr: © Grant Huntington for Scholastic Inc. p. T221 tl: © Penguin USA. p. T239 tr: © Robert McElroy/Woodfin Camp & Associates, Inc.; mr: © David S. Waitz for Scholastic Inc.; br: © James Blank/The Stock Market. p. T244 bl: © International Stock; bc: © Donovan Reese/Tony Stone Image; br: © Tony Stone Images. p. T245 br: © Ana Esperanza Nance for Scholastic Inc. p. T250 bc: © Grant Huntington for Scholastic Inc. p. T254 br: © Hillench and Bradsby/Scholastic Library; c: © John Lei for Scholastic Inc.; br: © Jeffrey Spielman/Image Bank. p. T257 tr: © John Fortunato for Scholastic Inc. pp. T258-T259 bc: © John Fortunato for Scholastic Inc. p. T262 tr: © Scott Campbell for Scholastic Inc. p. T265: Courtesy of Caroline Binch. p. T287 br: © M. & E. Bernheim/Woodfin Camp & Associates, Inc. p. T294 bl: © Ana Esperanza Nance for Scholastic Inc. p. T298 bc: © Scott Campbell for Scholastic Inc. p. T303 br: © Grant Huntington for Scholastic Inc. p. T308 bc: © Ana Esperanza Nance for Scholastic Inc. p. T309 bl: © Scott Campbell for Scholastic Inc. p. T310 bl: © Grant Huntington for Scholastic Inc. p. R2 basketball: © David S. Waitz for Scholastic Inc.; baseball: © James Levin /FPG International Corp. p. R4 bc: David S. Waitz for Scholastic Inc. p. R5 bl: © Cole Riggs for Scholastic Inc. p. R6 br: © Breck Kent/Animals Animals. p. R7 bl: © Richard Hutchings/Photo Researchers, Inc.; br: © SuperStock, Inc. p. R9 bl: © Ken Karp for Scholastic Inc. p. R10 bl: © Richard Lee for Scholastic Inc. p. R11 bl: © George Ranalli/Photo Researchers, Inc.; br: © Halley Ganges for Scholastic Inc. p. R12 br: © John Lei for Scholastic Inc. p. R13 br: © John Lei for Scholastic Inc. p. R24 bc: © John Fortunato for Scholastic Inc. p. R29 mr: © Scott Campbell for Scholastic Inc. p. R30 bc: © Grant Huntington for Scholastic Inc. p. R31 c: © Focus on Sports.

Upfront pages: All reduced facsimilies of Student Anthologies, Teacher's Editions, ancillary components, and interior pages are credited, if necessary, in their original publication format. p. 2: © David Mager for Scholastic Inc. p. 3 tl: © Stephen Ogilvy for Scholastic Inc.; br: © David S. Waitz for Scholastic Inc.; bl: © Stanley Bach for Scholastic Inc. p. 8: © Todd Joyce for Scholastic Inc. p. 10: © David S. Waitz Photography/Alleycat Design, Inc. for Scholastic Inc. p. 19: © Bie Bostrom for Scholastic Inc. p. 22: © Les Marsillo for Scholastic Inc. p. 23: © Les Marsillo for Scholastic Inc. p. 25 bc: Courtesy of NASA. p. 27: © Bie Bostrom for Scholastic Inc. p. 28: © John Lei for Scholastic Inc. p. 32 bl: © David S. Waitz for Scholastic Inc. p. 33 tr: © David S. Waitz for Scholastic Inc.; br: © Stanley Bach for Scholastic Inc.

Illustrations: Gary Ferster, Steve Stankiewicz, Steve Sullivan.

ACKNOWLEDGMENTS

Grateful acknowledgment is made to the following sources for permission to reprint from previously published material. The publisher has made diligent efforts to trace the ownership of all copyrighted material in this volume and believes that all necessary permissions have been secured. If any errors or omissions have inadvertently been made, proper corrections will gladly be made in future editions.

Cover: all photos © David S. Waitz for Scholastic Inc.

Interior: "Ronald Morgan Goes to Bat" from RONALD MORGAN GOES TO BAT by Patricia Reilly Giff, illustrated by Susanna Natti. Text copyright © 1988 by Patricia Reilly Giff. Illustrations copyright © 1988 by Susanna Natti. Reprinted by permission of Viking Penguin, a division of Penguin Books USA Inc. "Babe Ruth": TM/© 1995 Family of Babe Ruth and the Babe Ruth Baseball League, Inc. Under license authorized by Curtis Management Group, Indianapolis, IN. "Juan Gonzalez:" Upper Deck and the card/hologram combination are trademarks of The

Upper Deck Company, are reproduced with permission of The Upper Deck Company, are the exclusive property of The Upper Deck Company, and may not be reproduced without the express written consent of The Upper Deck Company. The Texas Rangers insignias depicted in this publication are reproduced with the permission of Major League Baseball Properties, are the exclusive property of the Texas Rangers, and may not be reproduced without their written consent. The Juan Gonzalez baseball card is also used by permission of Major League Baseball Players Association. "Ruby the Copycat" from RUBY THE COPYCAT by Peggy Rathmann. Copyright © 1991 by Margaret Rathmann. Reprinted by permission of Scholastic Inc. "I Can" by Mari Evans from SINGING BLACK published by Reed Visuals, 1979. Reprinted by permission of the author. Cover and illustration by Floyd Cooper from PASS IT ON: AFRICAN-AMERICAN POETRY FOR CHILDREN by Wade Hudson and Cheryl Hudson. Illustrations copyright © 1993 by Floyd Cooper. Published by Scholastic Inc. by arrangement with JUST US BOOKS. Reprinted by permission. "Louanne Pig in Making the Team" from LOUANNE PIG IN MAKING THE TEAM by Nancy Carlson. Copyright © 1985 by Nancy Carlson. Reprinted by permission of Carolrhoda Books, Inc. All rights reserved. GEORGE ANCONA: THEN & NOW by George Ancona. Copyright © 1996 by Scholastic Inc. "Amazing Grace" from AMAZING GRACE by Mary Hoffman, illustrated by Caroline Binch. Text copyright © 1991 by Mary Hoffman. Illustrations copyright © 1991 by Caroline Binch. Reprinted by permission of Dial Books for Young Readers, a division of Penguin Books USA Inc. Theatre program and cast list from PETER PAN is used by kind permission of The People's Light & Theatre Company. Cover from A BIRTHDAY BASKET FOR TÍA by Pat Mora, illustrated by Cecily Lang. Illustration copyright © 1992 by Cecily Lang. Published by Simon & Schuster Books for Young Readers, Simon & Schuster Children's Publishing Division. Cover from CHESTER'S WAY by Kevin Henkes. Illustration copyright © 1988 by Kevin Henkes. Published by Viking Penguin, a division of Penguin Books USA Inc. Cover from FROG AND TOAD ARE FRIENDS by Arnold Lobel. Illustration copyright © 1970 by Arnold Lobel. Published by HarperCollins Publishers. Cover from MAX FOUND TWO STICKS by Brian Pinkney. Illustration copyright © 1994 by Brian Pinkney. Published by Simon & Schuster Books for Young Readers, Simon and Schuster Children's Publishing Division.

Photography and Illustration Credits

Selection Opener Photographs by David S. Waitz Photography/Alleycat Design, Inc.

Photos: p. 3 br: © Gerry Lewin for Scholastic Inc. pp. 8-9 c: © Stanley Bach for Scholastic Inc. p. 10 cl: © Stanley Bach for Scholastic Inc.; br: © Dick Clintsman for Scholastic Inc.; tl: © Ken Karp for Scholastic Inc. p. 11 tl: © Nicole Katano for Scholastic Inc.; tc © Stanley Bach for Scholastic Inc.; br: © Tom Raymond for Scholastic Inc. p. 12 tl, bl: © Tom Raymond for Scholastic Inc.; tr: © Dick Clintsman for Scholastic Inc. p. 13 c: © Stanley Bach for Scholastic Inc. p. 14 cr, cl: © Nicole Katano for Scholastic Inc. p. 43 bc: © Bob Lorenz for Scholastic Inc. pp. 44-45 all: © Stanley Bach for Scholastic Inc. pp. 94-95 all: © Gerry Lewin for Scholastic Inc. p. 96 tr: © Mitchell Layton/DUOMO; bl: © Gerry Lewin for Scholastic Inc. pp. 96-97 bc: © John Bessler for Scholastic Inc., © Bruce Thorson film strip of Thorson photos. p. 97 cr: © Bruce Thorson. pp. 98-99 c: © Jade Albert/FPG International Corp. p. 100 c: © Efrain Ancona; br: © Marina Ancona. p. 101 tc, c: Courtesy George Ancona. p. 102 tl: © Efrain Ancona; br: © George Ancona. p. 103 c: © George Ancona from the book man and mustang, Macmillan. p. 104 all: © Efrain Ancona. p. 105 c: © George Ancona. p. 106 c: © Efrain Ancona. p. 107: © Marina Ancona. p. 108 c: © Efrain Ancona. p. 109 c: © George Ancona. p. 110 c: Courtesy George Ancona. p. 111 c: © Nelson Barbosa Dos Santos. p. 112 bl: © Fausto Diaz Triay; tr: © George Ancona; c: Courtesy George Ancona. p. 113 bc: © Beth Cummins. p. 114 tl, bl: © George Ancona; tr: © Thomas Pinot. p. 115 tl, cr: © George Ancona; bl: © Arleia Martins. p. 136 c: © Blanche Mackey for Scholastic Inc.; cr: © Bie Bostrom for Scholastic Inc. p. 137 all: Mark Garvin/Courtesy of People's Light Theater. p. 138 br: © Joseph Nettis/Photo Researchers, Inc. p. 139 tr: © John Lei for Scholastic Inc; br: © Gerry Lewin for Scholastic Inc. p. 140 cl: © Nicole Katano for Scholastic Inc. p. 141 bc: © Tony Freeman/Photo Edit; tr: © Bonnie Rauch/Photo Researchers, Inc.; cl: © David S. Waitz for Scholastic Inc. p. 142 br: © Mark Lafavor. p. 143 br: © Tornberg Associates.

Illustrations: pp. 2-3: Jackie Snider; p.42: Brian Dugan; pp. 136-137: Mary Thelen.

Workshops and Project Card Credits

Photograph on "Rebecca Ushler" trading card by Bassetti Photo, Minotola, NJ. Information about Rebecca Ushler by permission of Mr. and Mrs. Fred Ushler. "Our Pets" graph from *SuperScience® Red*, September 1989. Copyright © 1989 by Scholastic Inc. Reprinted by permission. SuperScience® Red is a registered trademark of Scholastic Inc.

Photos: Workshop 1: Back of card: br: © Gerry Lewin for Scholastic Inc.; bc: © Stanley Bach for Scholastic Inc. Workshop 2: Back of card: br: © Gerry Lewin for Schlastic Inc.; bc: © Stanley Bach for Scholastic Inc. Project: Front of card: c: Courtesy of National Baseball Hall of Fame. Back of card: br: © Gerry Lewin for Scholastic Inc.; bc: © Stanley Bach for Scholastic Inc.

Illustrations: John Holm.

TEACHER NOTES

Teacher Notes

TEACHER NOTES

TEACHER NOTES

Teacher Notes

TEACHER NOTES